GIRL GENIUS

Omnibus Volume One

Agatha Awakens

READ MORE COMICS ONLINE AT:

WWW.GIRLGENIUS.NET

MONDAY • WEDNESDAY • FRIDAY

Girl Genius Novels by Phil & Kaja Foglio:

Agatha H and the Airship City

Agatha H and the Clockwork Princess

Other Graphic Novels by Phil Foglio:

What's New with Phil & Dixie Collection

Robert Asprin's MythAdventures®

Buck Godot, zap gun for hire:
• *Three Short Stories*
• *PSmIth*
• *The Gallimaufry*

Omnibus Volume One
Agatha Awakens

PHIL & KAJA FOGLIO

A Tom Doherty Associates Book   NEW YORK

This is a work of fiction. All of the characters, organizations, and events portrayed in this novel are either products of the author's imagination or are used fictitiously.

GIRL GENIUS OMNIBUS VOLUME ONE: AGATHA AWAKENS

Copyright © 2012 by Studio Foglio, LLC
All rights reserved.

A Tor Book
Published by Tom Doherty Associates, LLC
175 Fifth Avenue
New York, NY 10010

www.tor-forge.com

Tor® is a registered trademark of Tom Doherty Associates, LLC.

Girl Genius® is a registered trademark of Studio Foglio, LLC.

ISBN 978-0-7653-3132-8

CIP DATA—TK

First Edition: January 2012

The story collected in this Omnibus was originally published in the Girl Genius comic book issues 1-10, and later in Volumes 1-3 of the Girl Genius Premium Collection from Studio Foglio, LLC.

Printed in China

0 9 8 7 6 5 4 3 2 1

Girl Genius: Agatha's Awakening

Story by:
Phil & Kaja Foglio

Art by:
Phil Foglio

—with—
Beetleburg Clank Inks by:
Brian Snōddy

—and—
Colors by:
Cheyenne Wright
Mark McNabb
Laurie E. Smith
Kaja Foglio

Cover colors by Cheyenne Wright
Logos, Lettering, & Book Design by Kaja Foglio

:CONTENTS:

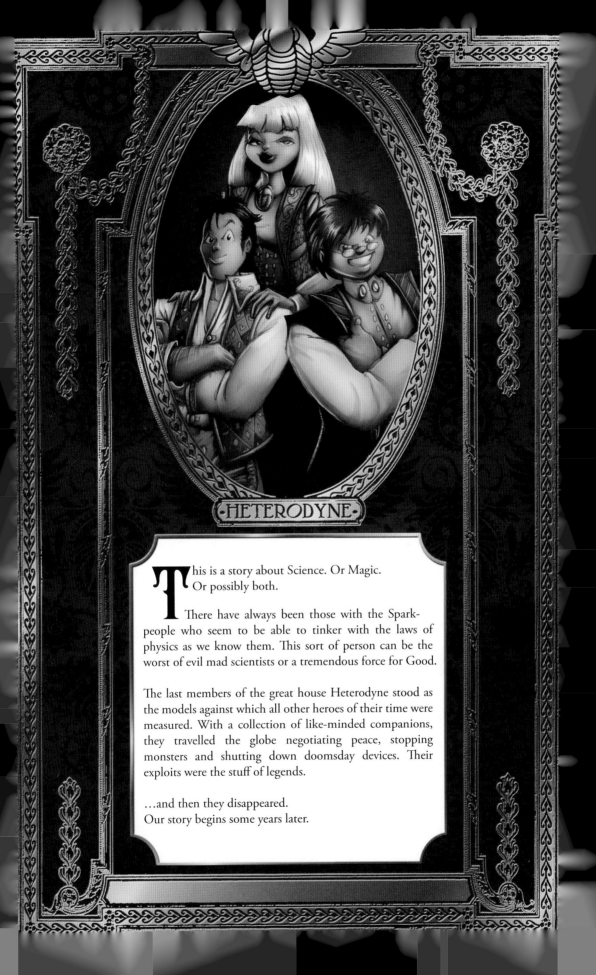

·HETERODYNE·

This is a story about Science. Or Magic.
Or possibly both.

There have always been those with the Spark-
people who seem to be able to tinker with the laws of
physics as we know them. This sort of person can be the
worst of evil mad scientists or a tremendous force for Good.

The last members of the great house Heterodyne stood as
the models against which all other heroes of their time were
measured. With a collection of like-minded companions,
they travelled the globe negotiating peace, stopping
monsters and shutting down doomsday devices. Their
exploits were the stuff of legends.

…and then they disappeared.
Our story begins some years later.

SOME CHARACTERS

AGATHA CLAY

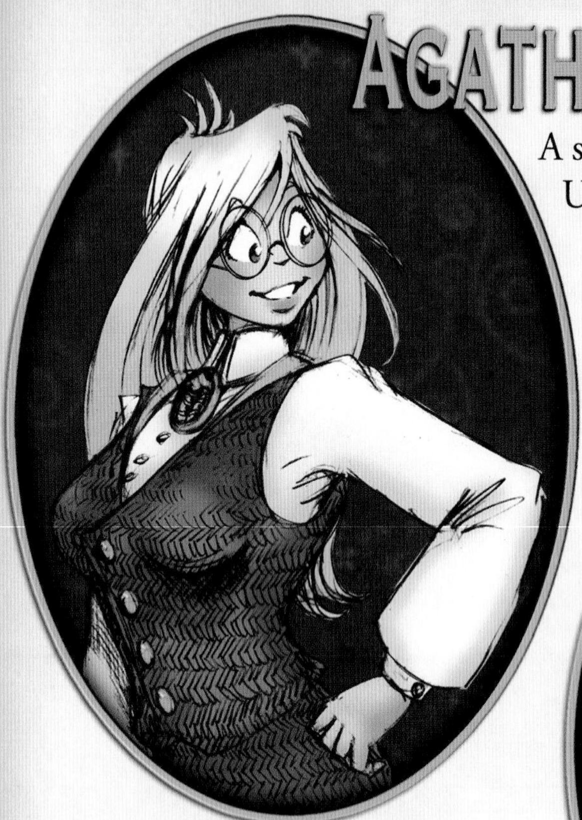

A student at Transylvania Polygnostic University. Agatha studies hard, but she has trouble concentrating and nothing she builds ever *works.* That's all about to change…

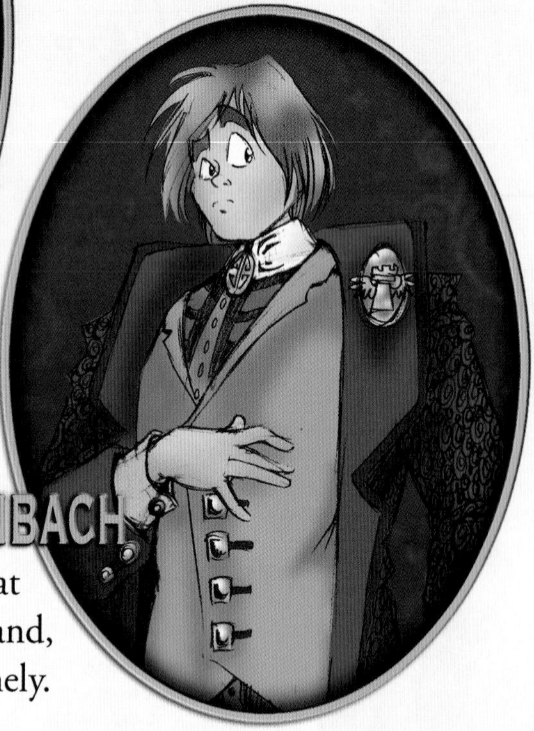

GILGAMESH WULFENBACH

The Baron's son has been away at school for years. He's brilliant, and, now that he's home, kind of lonely.

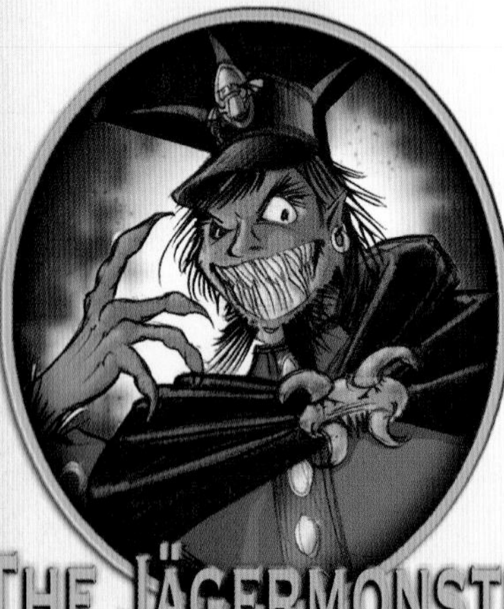

THE JÄGERMONSTERS

These fearsome soldiers once served the Heterodyne family. Now, they work for the Baron.

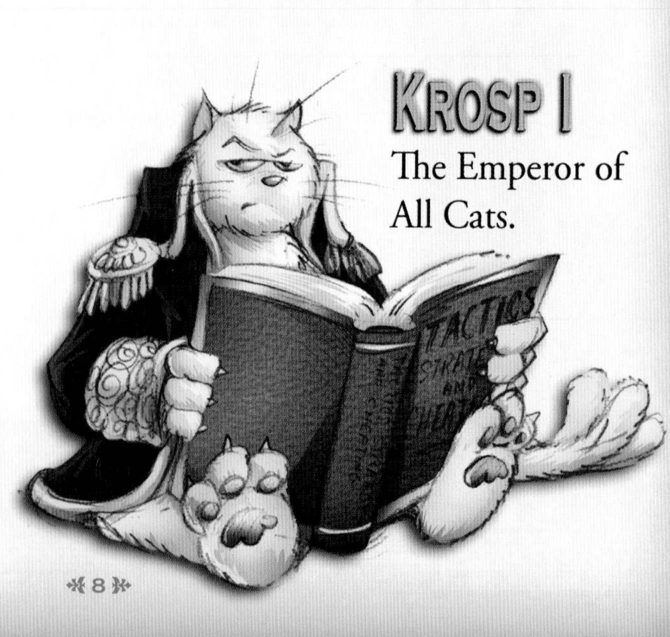
TACTICS

KROSP I

The Emperor of All Cats.

OF NOTE

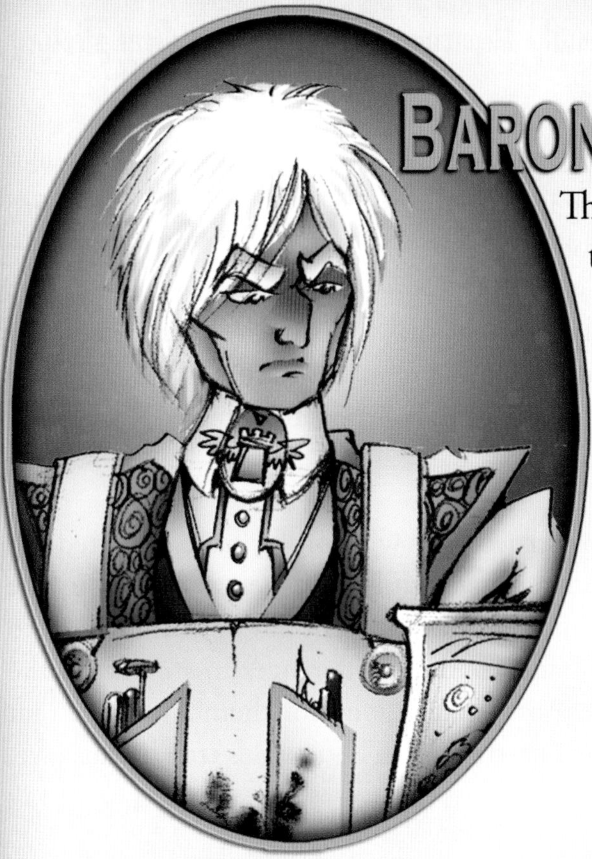

BARON WULFENBACH

The Baron rules the land and keeps the peace–mostly because no one else can. He'd much rather be working in his lab.

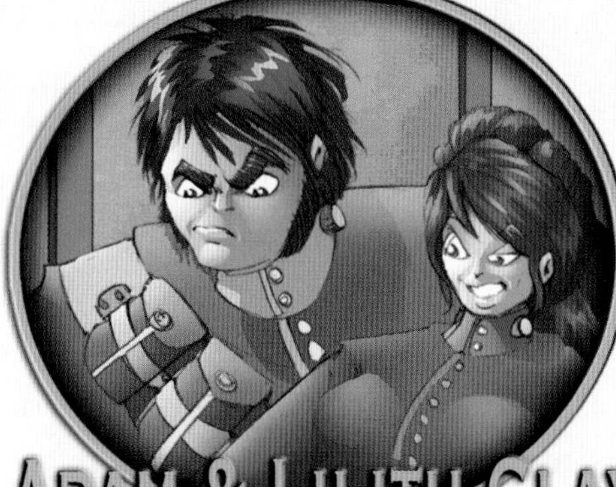

ADAM & LILITH CLAY

The construct couple who raised Agatha. She thinks of them as her parents.

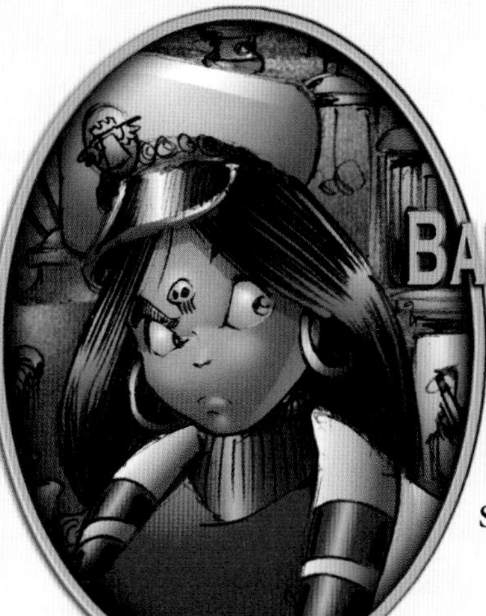

BANGLADESH DUPREE

Bang was a ruthless pirate queen, but then someone wiped out her fortress, and all her pirates. Now she works for the Baron.

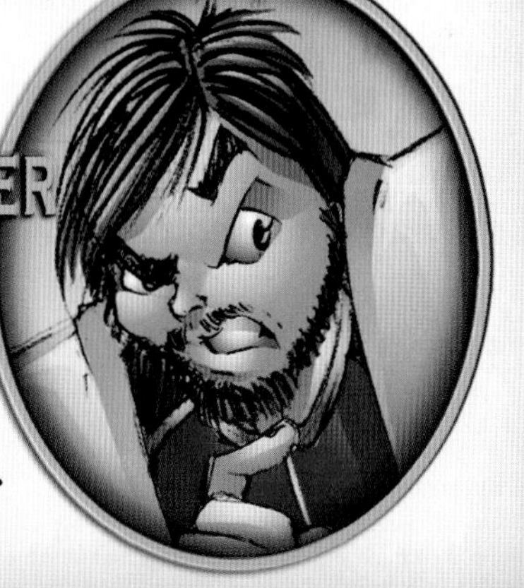

MOLOCH VON ZINZER

A down-on-his-luck soldier and part-time thief. Moloch and his brother Omar have been making their way across the Baron's lands.

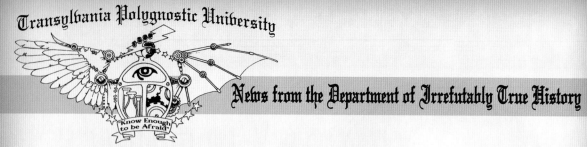

Transylvania Polygnostic University

News from the Department of Irrefutably True History

Transylvania Polygnostic University students[1] who read sensationalistic novels when they should be studying or conducting important research will all be familiar with the exploits of the legendary Agatha Heterodyne.

We, in the Department of Irrefutably True History, have long felt that the life of this exceptional person is worthy of attention of a more scholarly nature. Thus, as an aid to students taking our new series of courses, we are pleased to offer the following textbook in an easy-to-follow pictorial format.

Unscrupulous foreign publishers, concerned only with profit, have distorted the historical facts concerning Agatha Heterodyne, her family, and her associates to the point that the narrative contained within this account will no doubt be entirely new to the majority of readers. We trust you will consider these differences in story with the gravity that befits intelligent students who know what is good for them and agree that we, as experts, are the final authority on these matters.[2] You'll know it's true because we, your instructors, say so.

These courses and their associated textbooks are based upon our meticulous research of the last ten years, in which we gratefully acknowledge the aid of the Department of Alternate Realities and Temporal Uncertainty. Here you will find the actual, factual account of what happened in the early years of Agatha Heterodyne's career, starting from the lowest point in her life–her final day as a student here at Transylvania Polygnostic.

Thanks to the support we receive from the current administration at TPU, our students are hereby authorized to peruse these texts during other, less interesting classes (such as Prof. Strout's Theoretical Potential of Pickled Herring as a Low-Cost Power Source lectures). In exchange you are expected to maintain good grades, curb your monsters and not blow up school property if you can possibly avoid it.

And finally, students, remember—your future arch-nemeses are out there somewhere, studying hard. Don't make it easy for them.

–Professors Foglio & Foglio
Department of Irrefutably True History
Transylvania Polygnostic University

1 and faculty–you know who you are.
2 Occasional guesswork and narrative license have been applied in cases where facts were uncertain or where documented occurrences would have been more amusing if only they had happened in some other way. Other than that, it's all true. We swear.

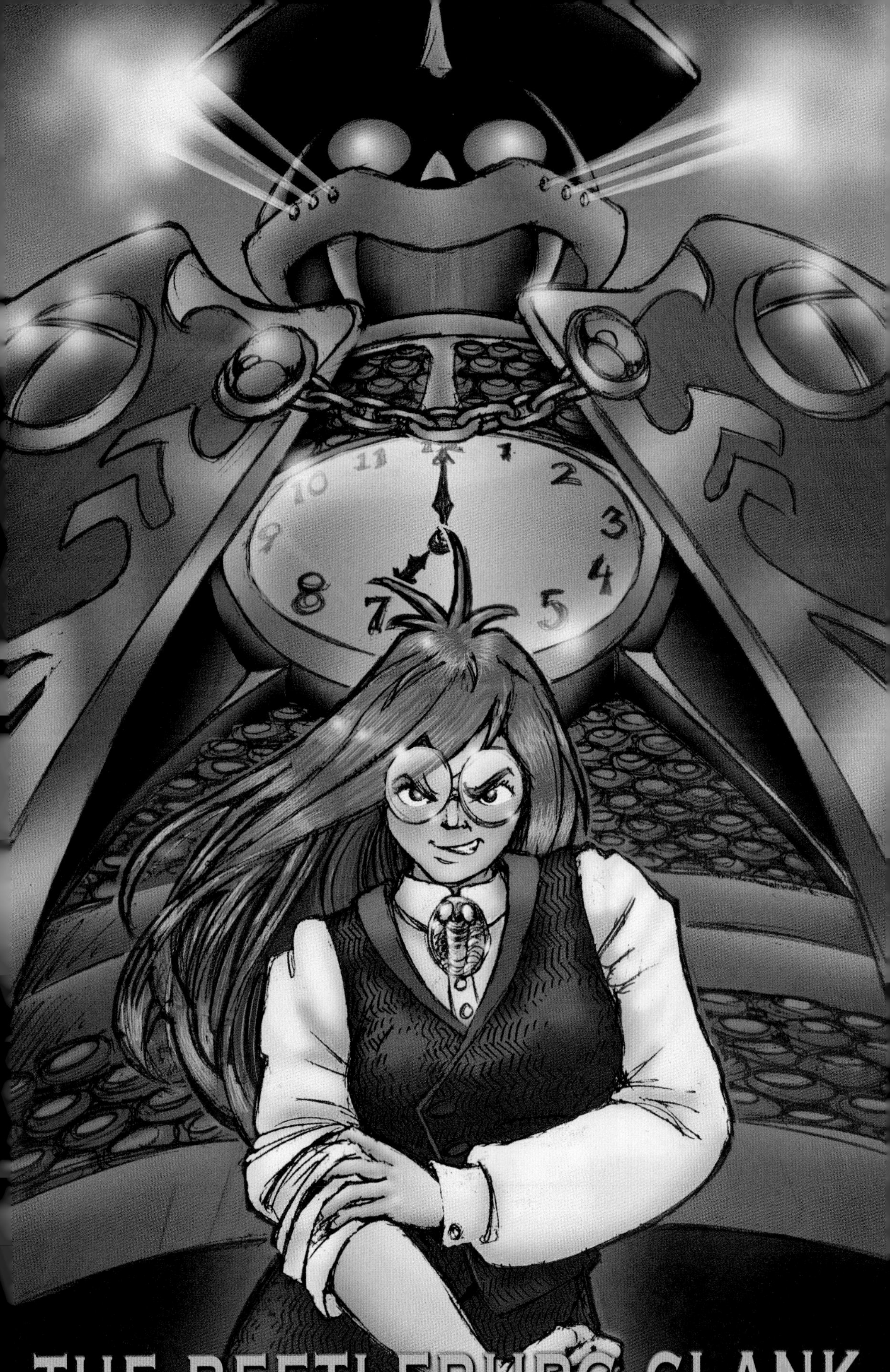
1
2
3
4
5
7
8
9
10
11

THE BEETLEBURG CLANK

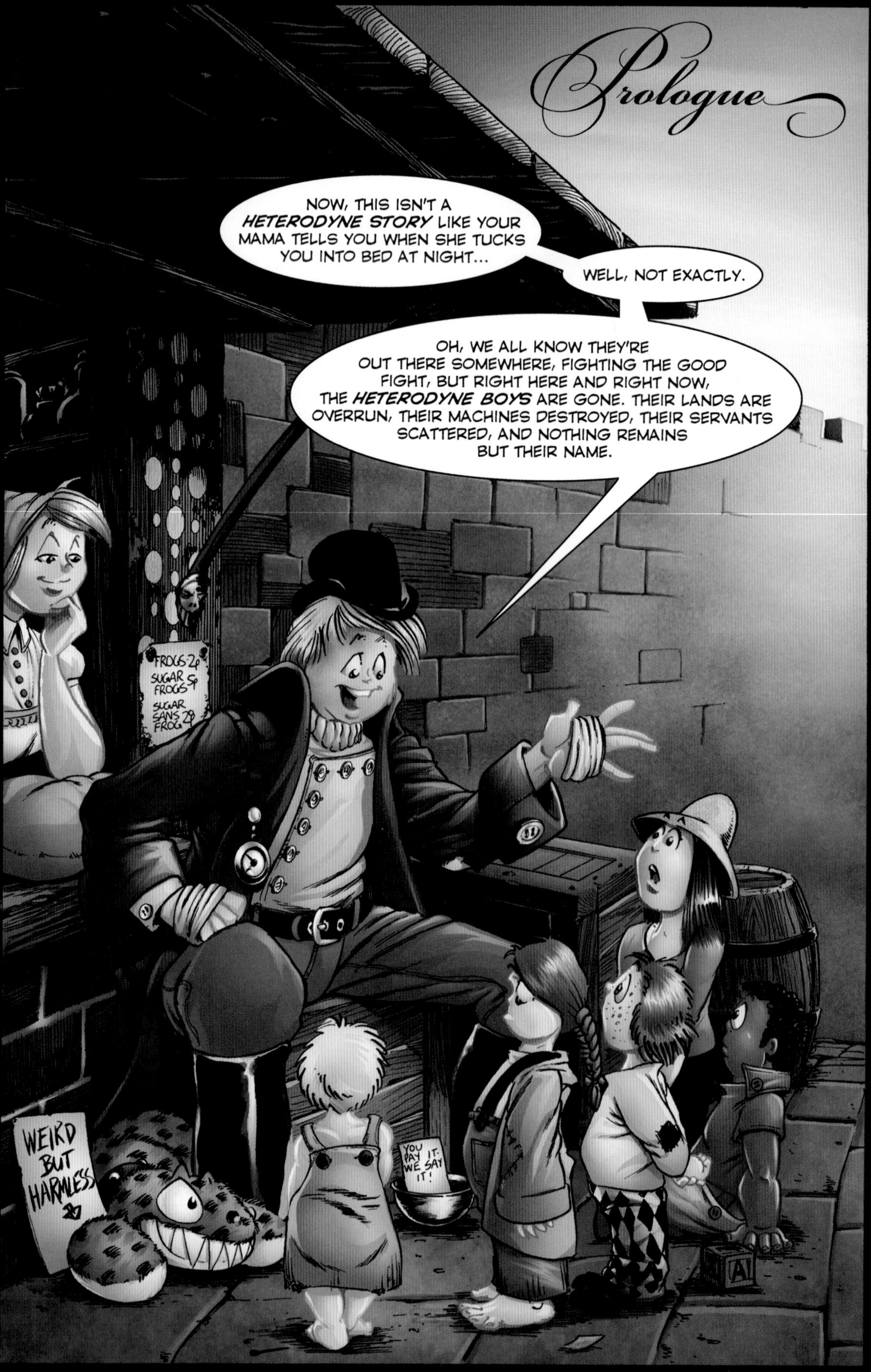
Prologue
NOW, THIS ISN'T A HETERODYNE STORY LIKE YOUR MAMA TELLS YOU WHEN SHE TUCKS YOU INTO BED AT NIGHT...
WELL, NOT EXACTLY.
OH, WE ALL KNOW THEY'RE OUT THERE SOMEWHERE, FIGHTING THE GOOD FIGHT, BUT RIGHT HERE AND RIGHT NOW, THE HETERODYNE BOYS ARE GONE. THEIR LANDS ARE OVERRUN, THEIR MACHINES DESTROYED, THEIR SERVANTS SCATTERED, AND NOTHING REMAINS BUT THEIR NAME.
FROGS 2p
SUGAR FROGS 5p
SUGAR SANS FROG 2p
WEIRD BUT HARMLESS
YOU PAY IT- WE SAY IT!

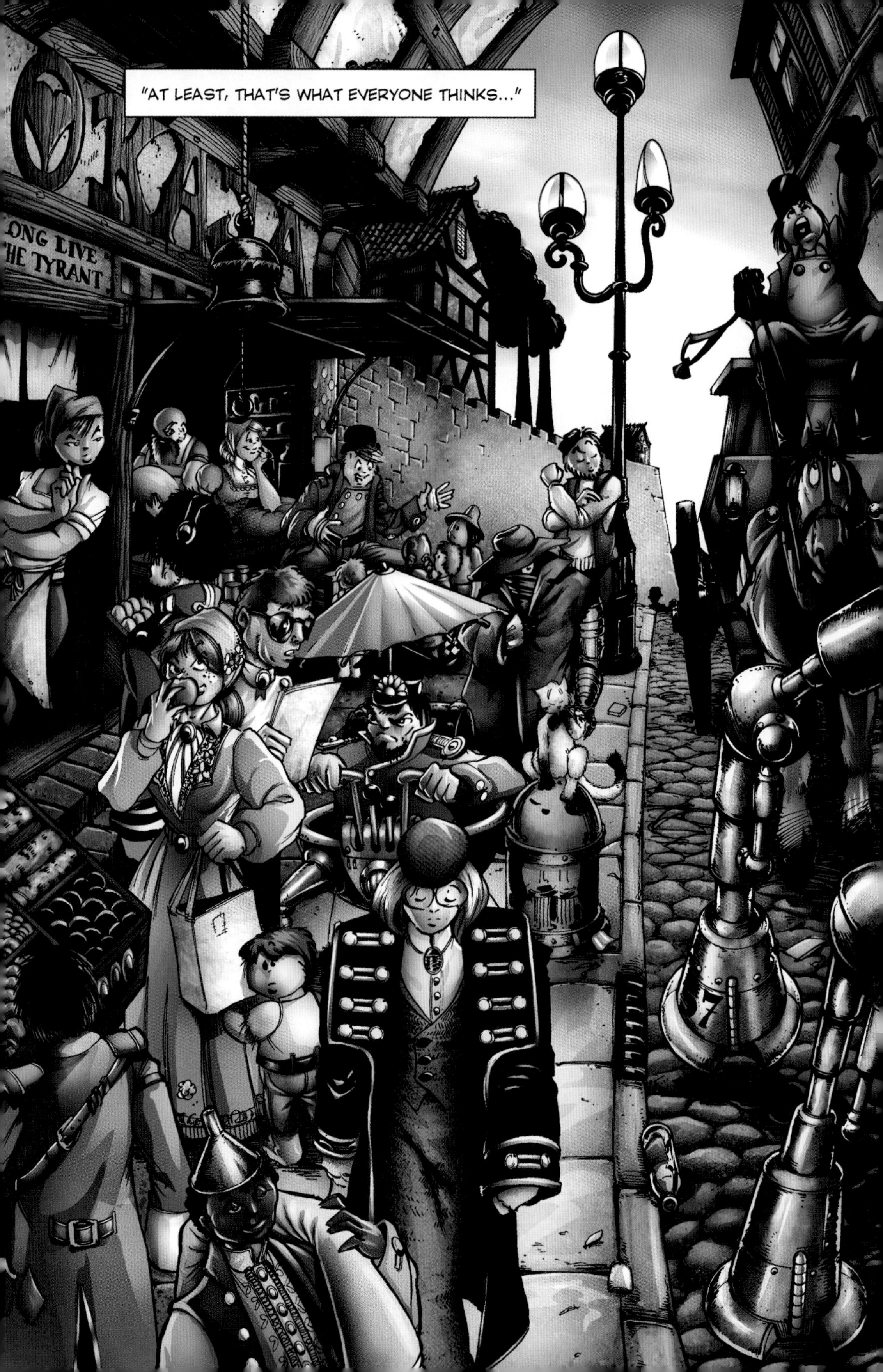
"AT LEAST, THAT'S WHAT EVERYONE THINKS..."
ONG LIVE
HE TYRANT

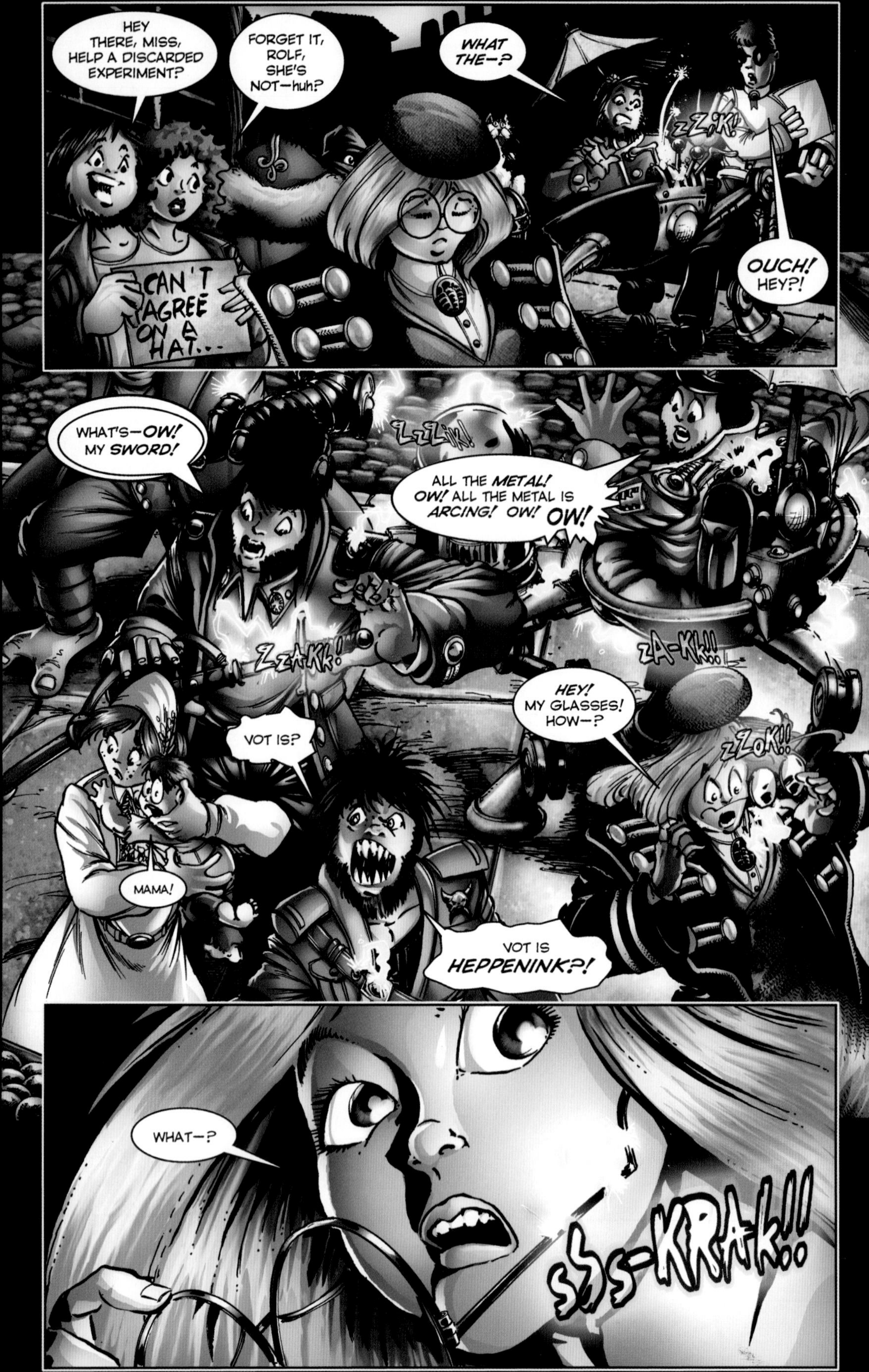
HEY THERE, MISS, HELP A DISCARDED EXPERIMENT?
FORGET IT, ROLF, SHE'S NOT—huh?
WHAT THE—?
CAN'T AGREE ON A HAT...
zZiK!
OUCH! HEY?!
WHAT'S—OW! MY SWORD!
ZzZLik!
ALL THE METAL! OW! ALL THE METAL IS ARCING! OW! OW!
ZzAKk!
zA-KK!!
HEY! MY GLASSES! HOW—?
VOT IS?
zZoK!!
MAMA!
VOT IS HEPPENINK?!
WHAT—?
sSs-KRAK!!

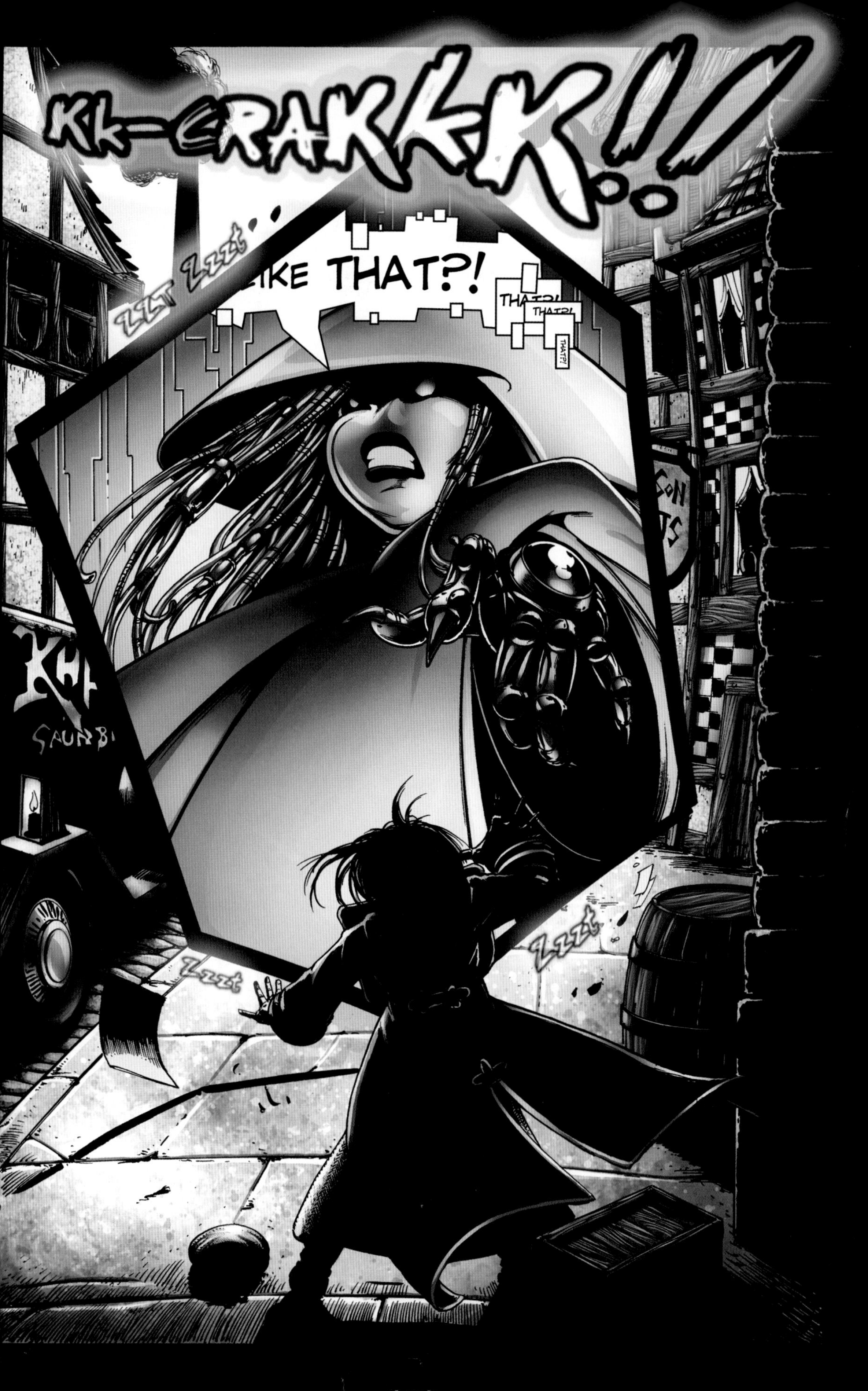
KK-CRAKKK!!
ZZZT Zzzt..
LIKE THAT?!
THAT?!
THAT?!
THAT?!
Zzzt
Zzzt

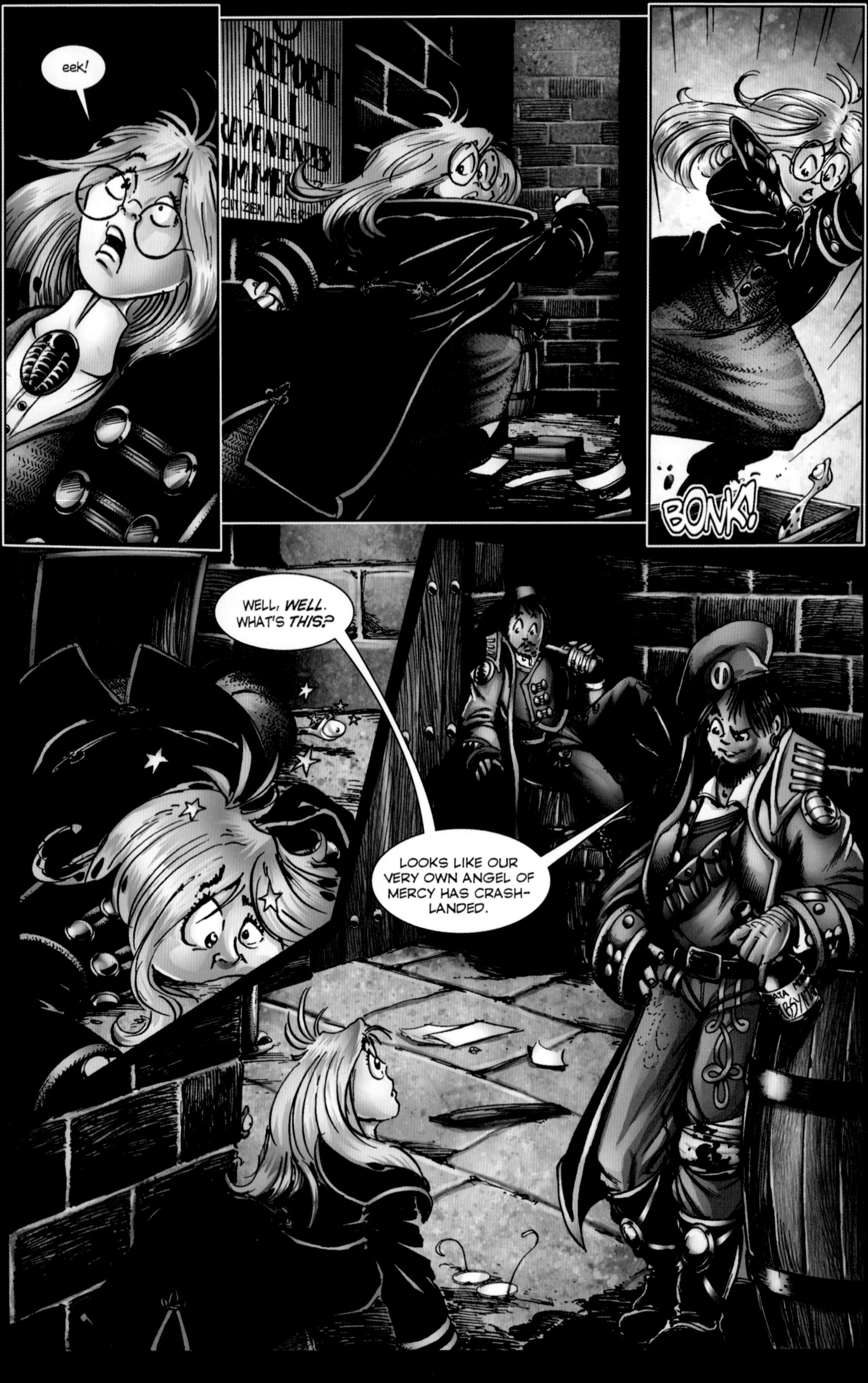
eek!
REPORT
ALL
BONK!
WELL, *WELL*. WHAT'S *THIS?*
LOOKS LIKE OUR VERY OWN ANGEL OF MERCY HAS CRASH-LANDED.

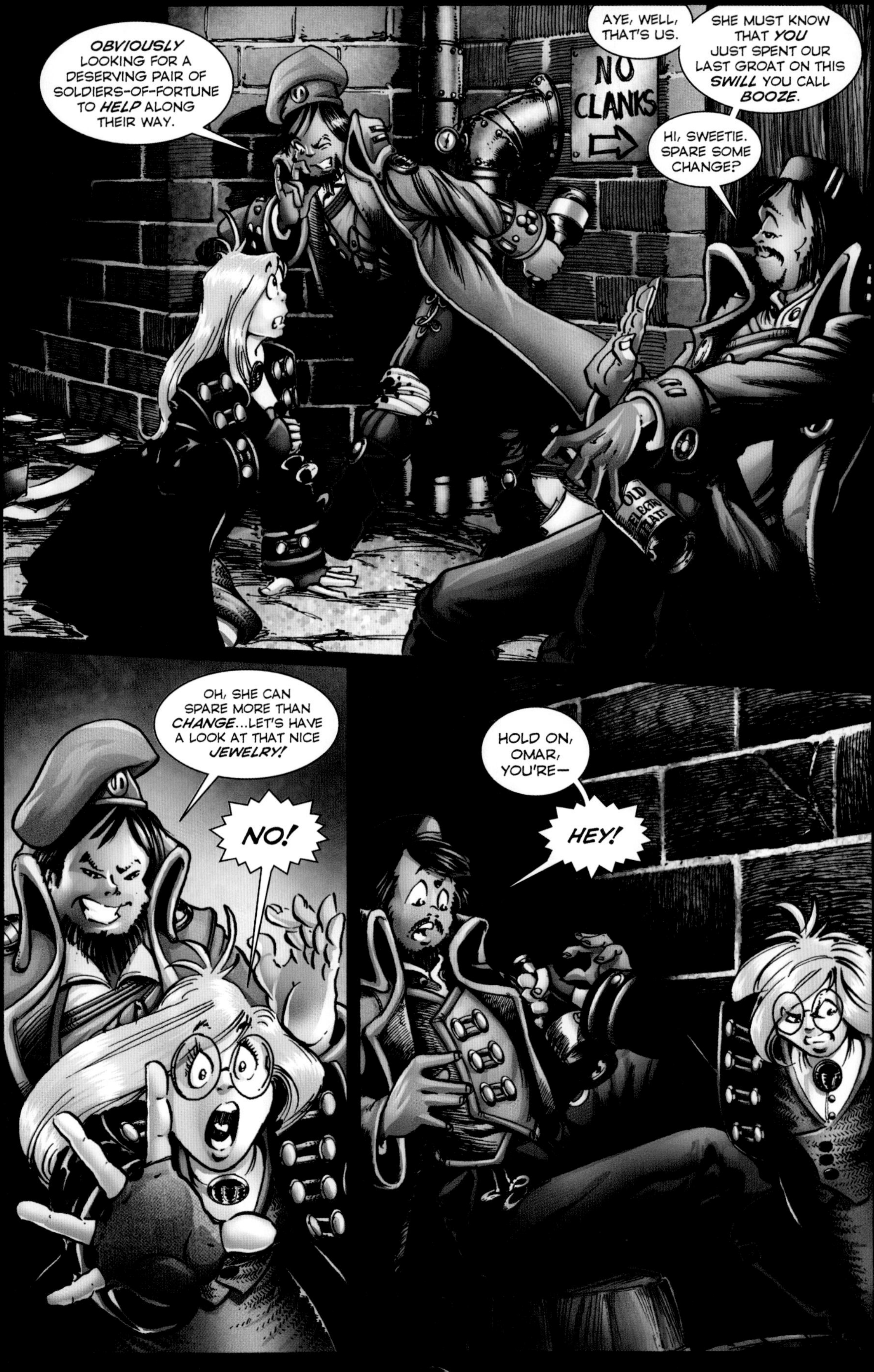
OBVIOUSLY LOOKING FOR A DESERVING PAIR OF SOLDIERS-OF-FORTUNE TO HELP ALONG THEIR WAY.
AYE, WELL, THAT'S US.
SHE MUST KNOW THAT YOU JUST SPENT OUR LAST GROAT ON THIS SWILL YOU CALL BOOZE.
NO CLANKS
HI, SWEETIE. SPARE SOME CHANGE?
OH, SHE CAN SPARE MORE THAN CHANGE...LET'S HAVE A LOOK AT THAT NICE JEWELRY!
NO!
HOLD ON, OMAR, YOU'RE—
HEY!

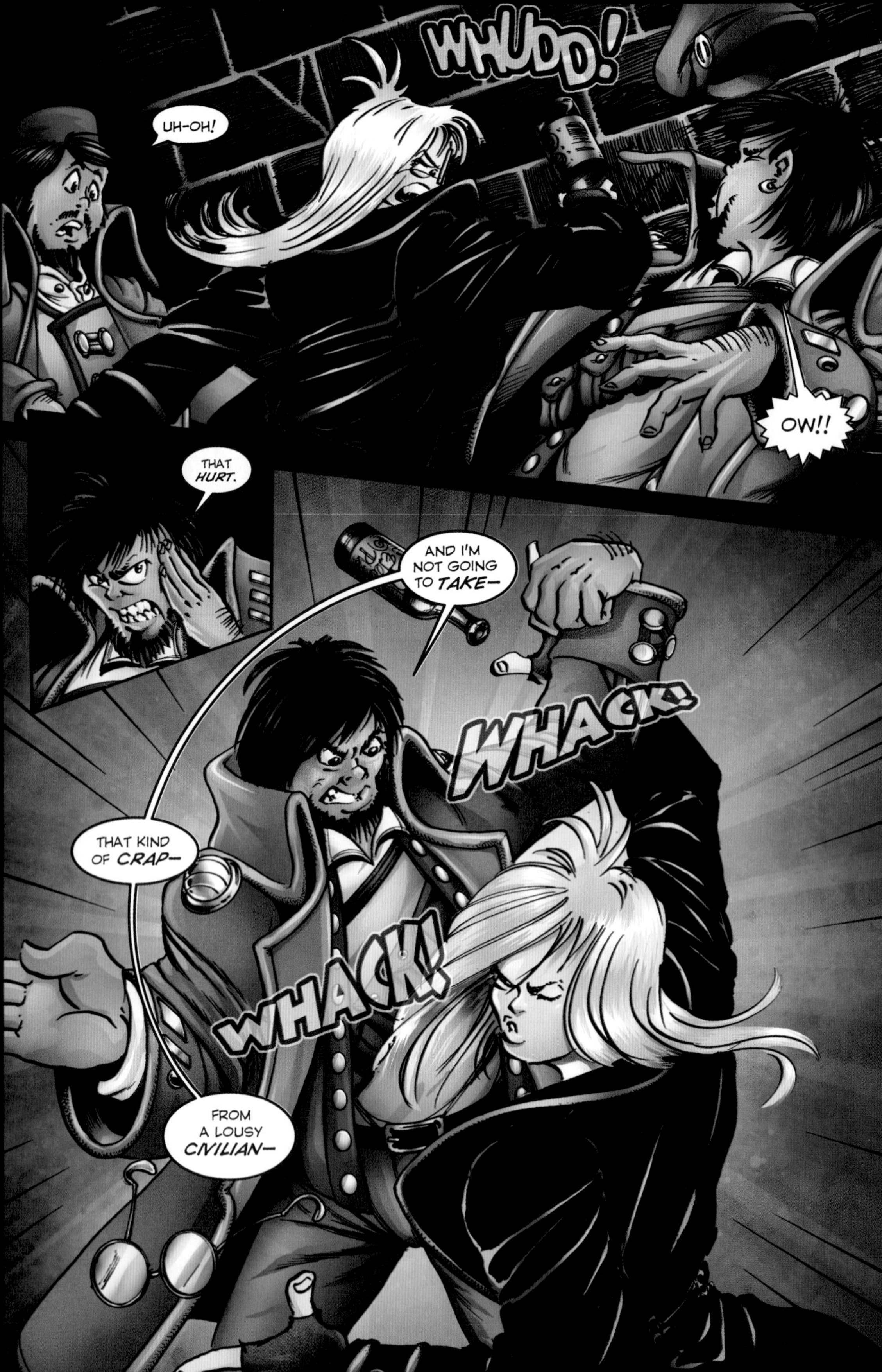
WHUDD!
UH-OH!
OW!!
THAT HURT.
AND I'M NOT GOING TO TAKE—
WHACK!
THAT KIND OF CRAP—
WHACK!
FROM A LOUSY CIVILIAN—

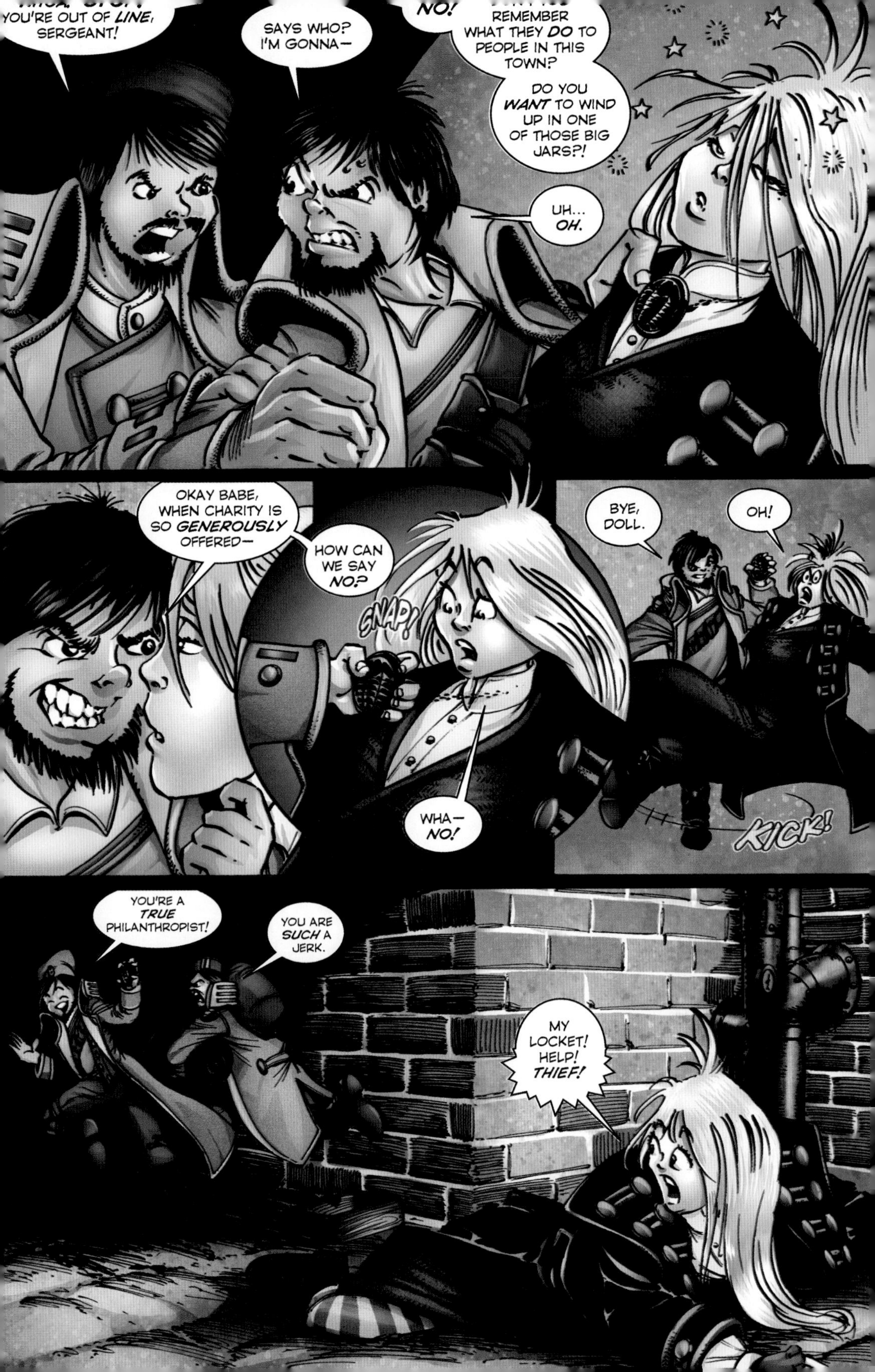
YOU'RE OUT OF *LINE*, SERGEANT!
SAYS WHO? I'M GONNA—
NO!
REMEMBER WHAT THEY ***DO*** TO PEOPLE IN THIS TOWN?
DO YOU ***WANT*** TO WIND UP IN ONE OF THOSE BIG JARS?!
UH... ***OH.***
OKAY BABE, WHEN CHARITY IS SO ***GENEROUSLY*** OFFERED—
HOW CAN WE SAY ***NO?***
SNAP!
WHA— ***NO!***
BYE, DOLL.
OH!
KICK!
YOU'RE A ***TRUE*** PHILANTHROPIST!
YOU ARE ***SUCH*** A JERK.
MY LOCKET! HELP! ***THIEF!***

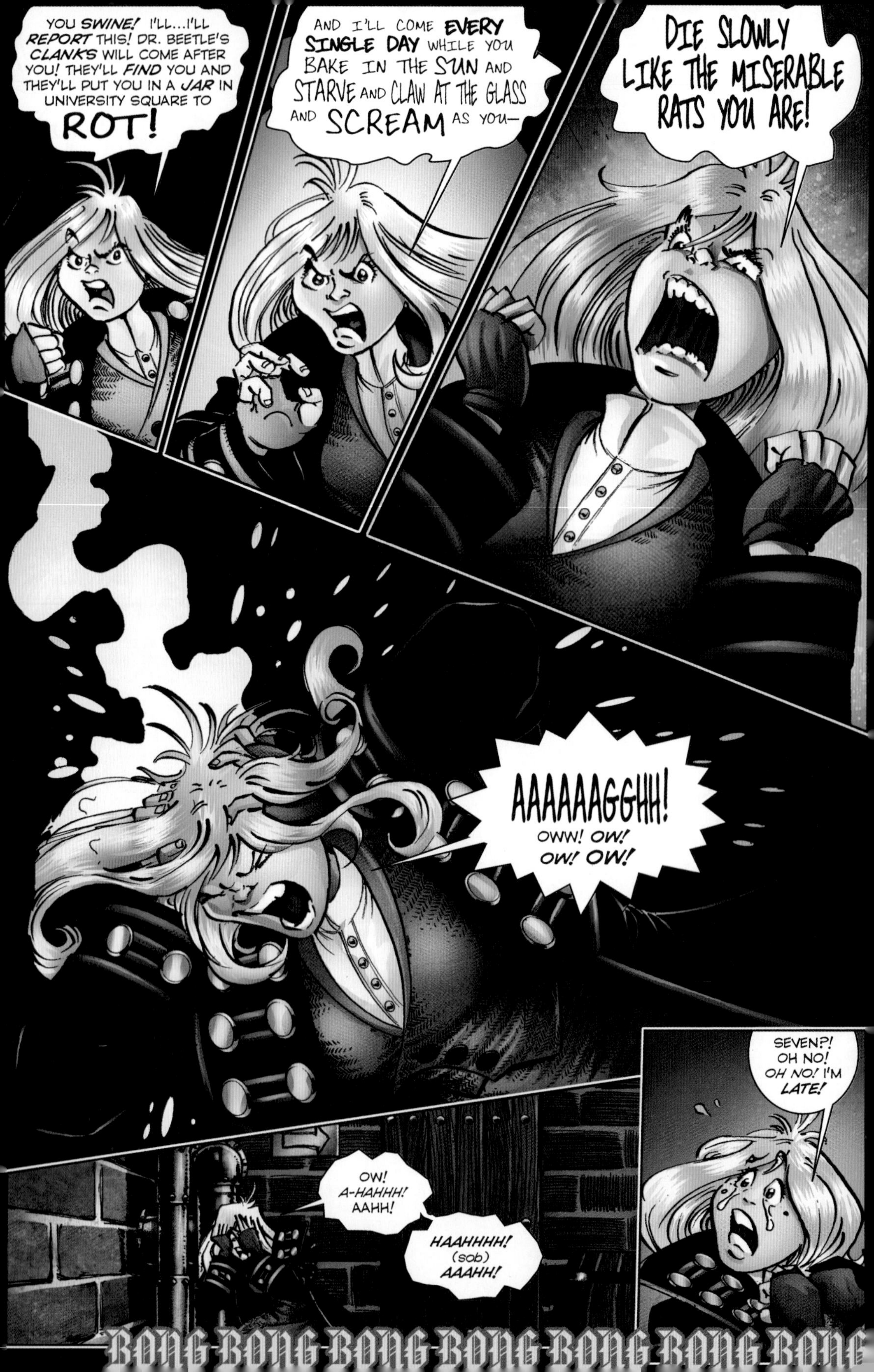
YOU SWINE! I'LL...I'LL REPORT THIS! DR. BEETLE'S CLANKS WILL COME AFTER YOU! THEY'LL FIND YOU AND THEY'LL PUT YOU IN A JAR IN UNIVERSITY SQUARE TO ROT!
AND I'LL COME EVERY SINGLE DAY WHILE YOU BAKE IN THE SUN AND STARVE AND CLAW AT THE GLASS AND SCREAM AS YOU—
DIE SLOWLY LIKE THE MISERABLE RATS YOU ARE!
AAAAAAGGHH! OWW! OW! OW! OW!
OW! A-HAHHH! AAHH!
HAAHHHH! (sob) AAAHH!
SEVEN?! OH NO! OH NO! I'M LATE!
BONG BONG BONG BONG BONG BONG BONG

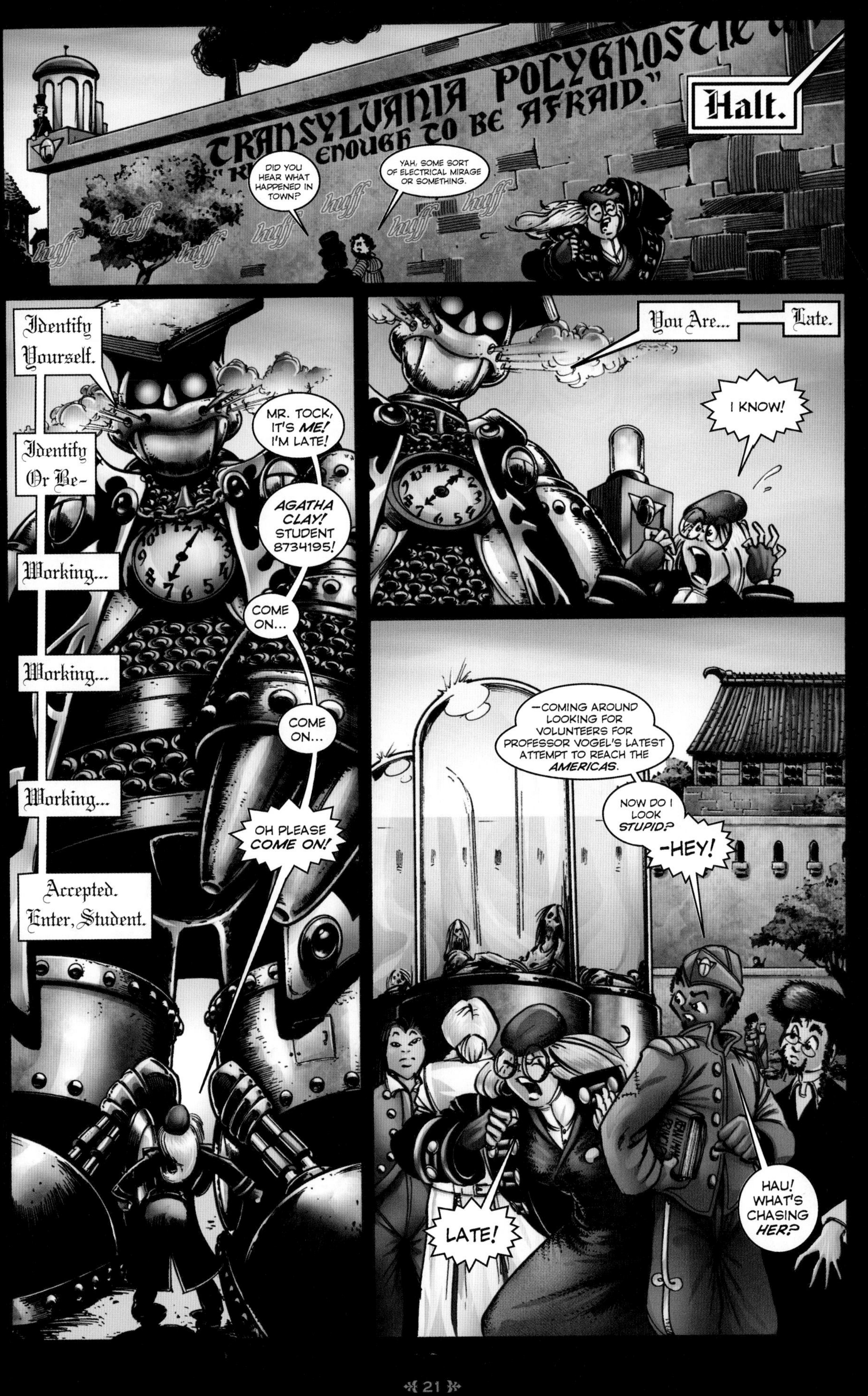
TRANSYLVANIA POLYGNOSTIC
"KN... ENOUGH TO BE AFRAID."
Halt.
DID YOU HEAR WHAT HAPPENED IN TOWN?
YAH, SOME SORT OF ELECTRICAL MIRAGE OR SOMETHING.
huff huff huff huff huff huff
Identify Yourself.
MR. TOCK, IT'S ME! I'M LATE!
Identify Or Be-
AGATHA CLAY! STUDENT 8734195!
Working...
COME ON...
Working...
COME ON...
Working...
OH PLEASE COME ON!
Accepted. Enter, Student.
You Are... Late.
I KNOW!
—COMING AROUND LOOKING FOR VOLUNTEERS FOR PROFESSOR VOGEL'S LATEST ATTEMPT TO REACH THE AMERICAS.
NOW DO I LOOK STUPID?
-HEY!
LATE!
HAU! WHAT'S CHASING HER?

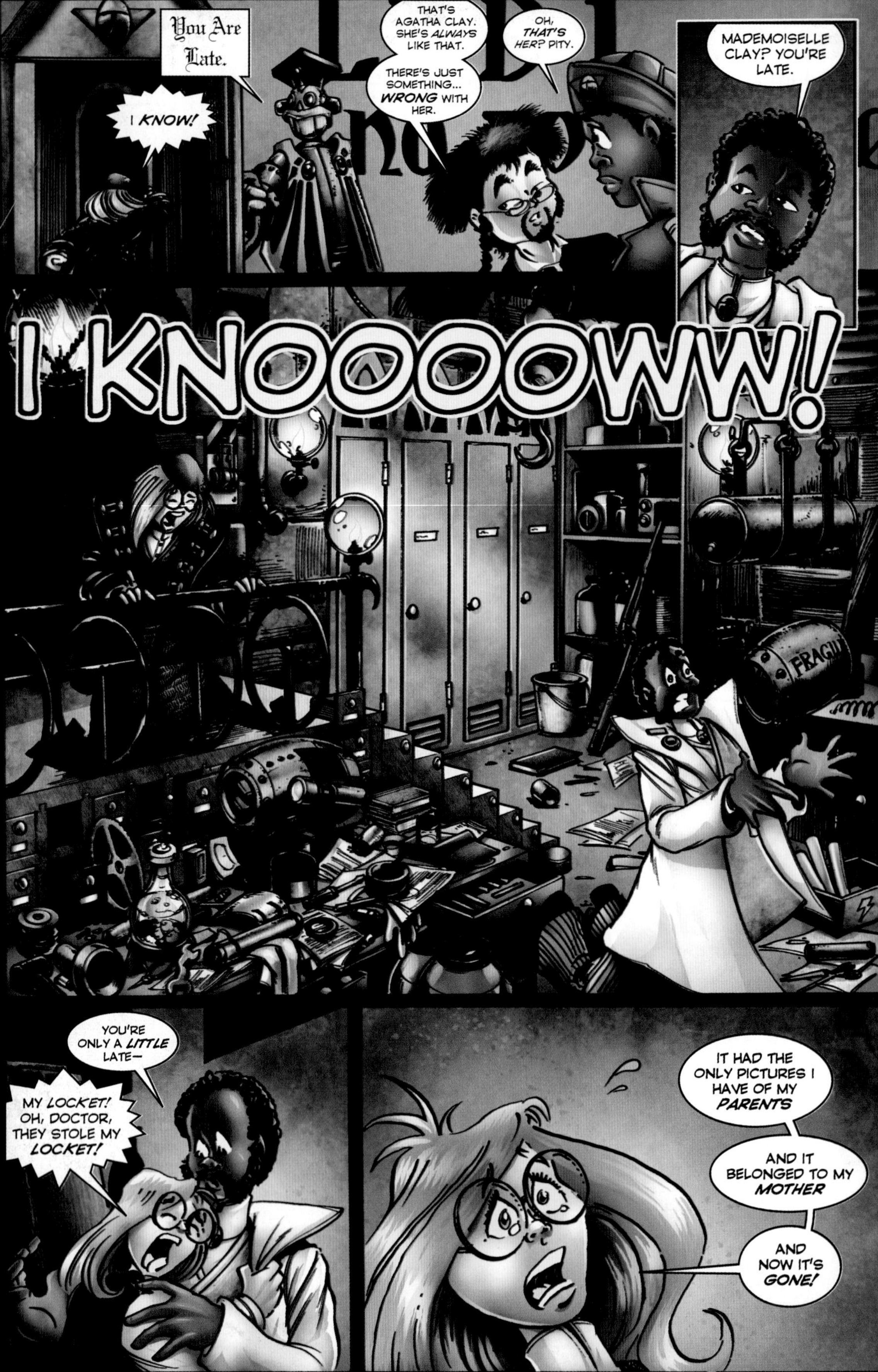
You Are Late.
I KNOW!
THAT'S AGATHA CLAY. SHE'S ALWAYS LIKE THAT.
THERE'S JUST SOMETHING... WRONG WITH HER.
OH, THAT'S HER? PITY.
MADEMOISELLE CLAY? YOU'RE LATE.
I KNOOOOWW!
FRAGIL
YOU'RE ONLY A LITTLE LATE—
MY LOCKET! OH, DOCTOR, THEY STOLE MY LOCKET!
IT HAD THE ONLY PICTURES I HAVE OF MY PARENTS
AND IT BELONGED TO MY MOTHER
AND NOW IT'S GONE!

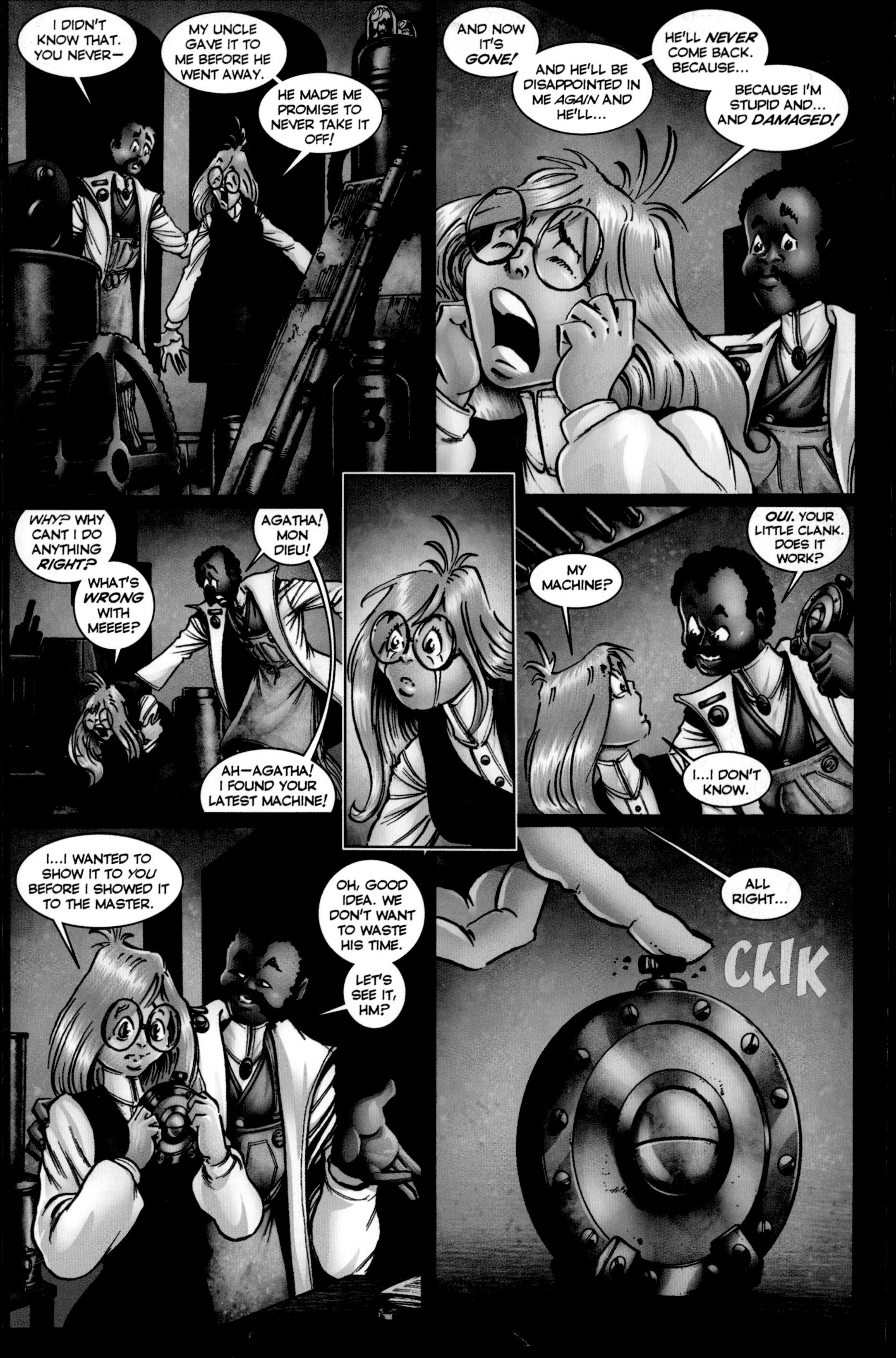

I DIDN'T KNOW THAT. YOU NEVER—
MY UNCLE GAVE IT TO ME BEFORE HE WENT AWAY.
HE MADE ME PROMISE TO NEVER TAKE IT OFF!
AND NOW IT'S *GONE!*
AND HE'LL BE DISAPPOINTED IN ME *AGAIN* AND HE'LL...
HE'LL *NEVER* COME BACK. BECAUSE...
BECAUSE I'M STUPID AND... AND *DAMAGED!*
WHY? WHY CANT I DO ANYTHING *RIGHT?*
WHAT'S *WRONG* WITH MEEEE?
AGATHA! MON DIEU!
AH—AGATHA! I FOUND YOUR LATEST MACHINE!
MY MACHINE?
OUI. YOUR LITTLE CLANK. DOES IT WORK?
I...I DON'T KNOW.
I...I WANTED TO SHOW IT TO *YOU* BEFORE I SHOWED IT TO THE MASTER.
OH, GOOD IDEA. WE DON'T WANT TO WASTE HIS TIME.
LET'S SEE IT, HM?
ALL RIGHT...
CLIK

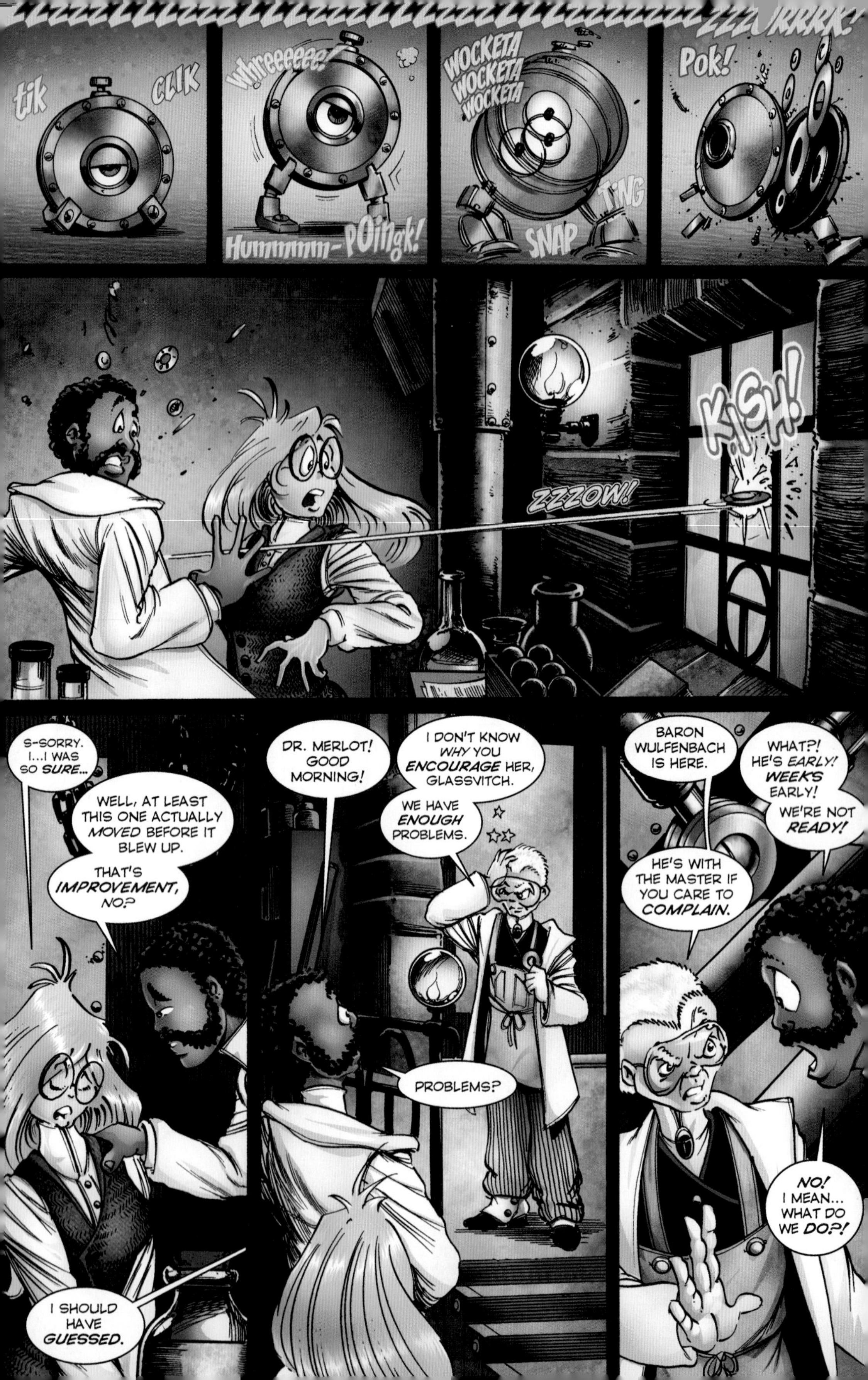
ZZZURRRK!
tik
CLIK
Whreeeeee!
Hummmmm-POingk!
WOCKETA WOCKETA WOCKETA
SNAP
TING
Pok!
KiSH!
ZZZOW!
S-SORRY. I...I WAS SO SURE...
WELL, AT LEAST THIS ONE ACTUALLY MOVED BEFORE IT BLEW UP.
THAT'S IMPROVEMENT, NO?
I SHOULD HAVE GUESSED.
DR. MERLOT! GOOD MORNING!
I DON'T KNOW WHY YOU ENCOURAGE HER, GLASSVITCH.
WE HAVE ENOUGH PROBLEMS.
PROBLEMS?
BARON WULFENBACH IS HERE.
WHAT?! HE'S EARLY! WEEKS EARLY!
WE'RE NOT READY!
HE'S WITH THE MASTER IF YOU CARE TO COMPLAIN.
NO! I MEAN... WHAT DO WE DO?!

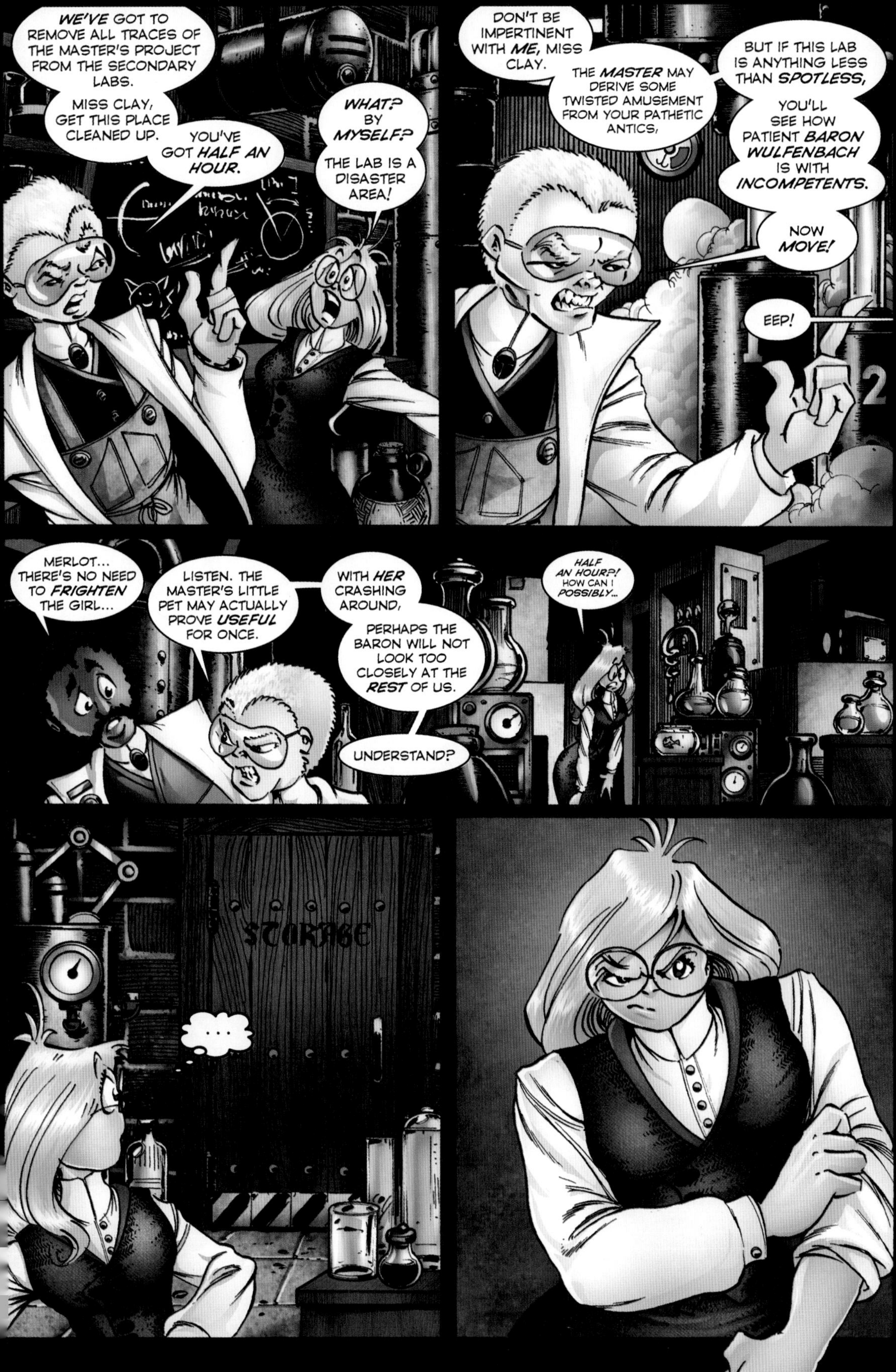
WE'VE GOT TO REMOVE ALL TRACES OF THE MASTER'S PROJECT FROM THE SECONDARY LABS.
MISS CLAY, GET THIS PLACE CLEANED UP.
YOU'VE GOT HALF AN HOUR.
WHAT? BY MYSELF?
THE LAB IS A DISASTER AREA!
DON'T BE IMPERTINENT WITH ME, MISS CLAY.
THE MASTER MAY DERIVE SOME TWISTED AMUSEMENT FROM YOUR PATHETIC ANTICS,
BUT IF THIS LAB IS ANYTHING LESS THAN SPOTLESS,
YOU'LL SEE HOW PATIENT BARON WULFENBACH IS WITH INCOMPETENTS.
NOW MOVE!
EEP!
MERLOT... THERE'S NO NEED TO FRIGHTEN THE GIRL...
LISTEN. THE MASTER'S LITTLE PET MAY ACTUALLY PROVE USEFUL FOR ONCE.
WITH HER CRASHING AROUND,
PERHAPS THE BARON WILL NOT LOOK TOO CLOSELY AT THE REST OF US.
UNDERSTAND?
HALF AN HOUR?! HOW CAN I POSSIBLY...
STORAGE
...

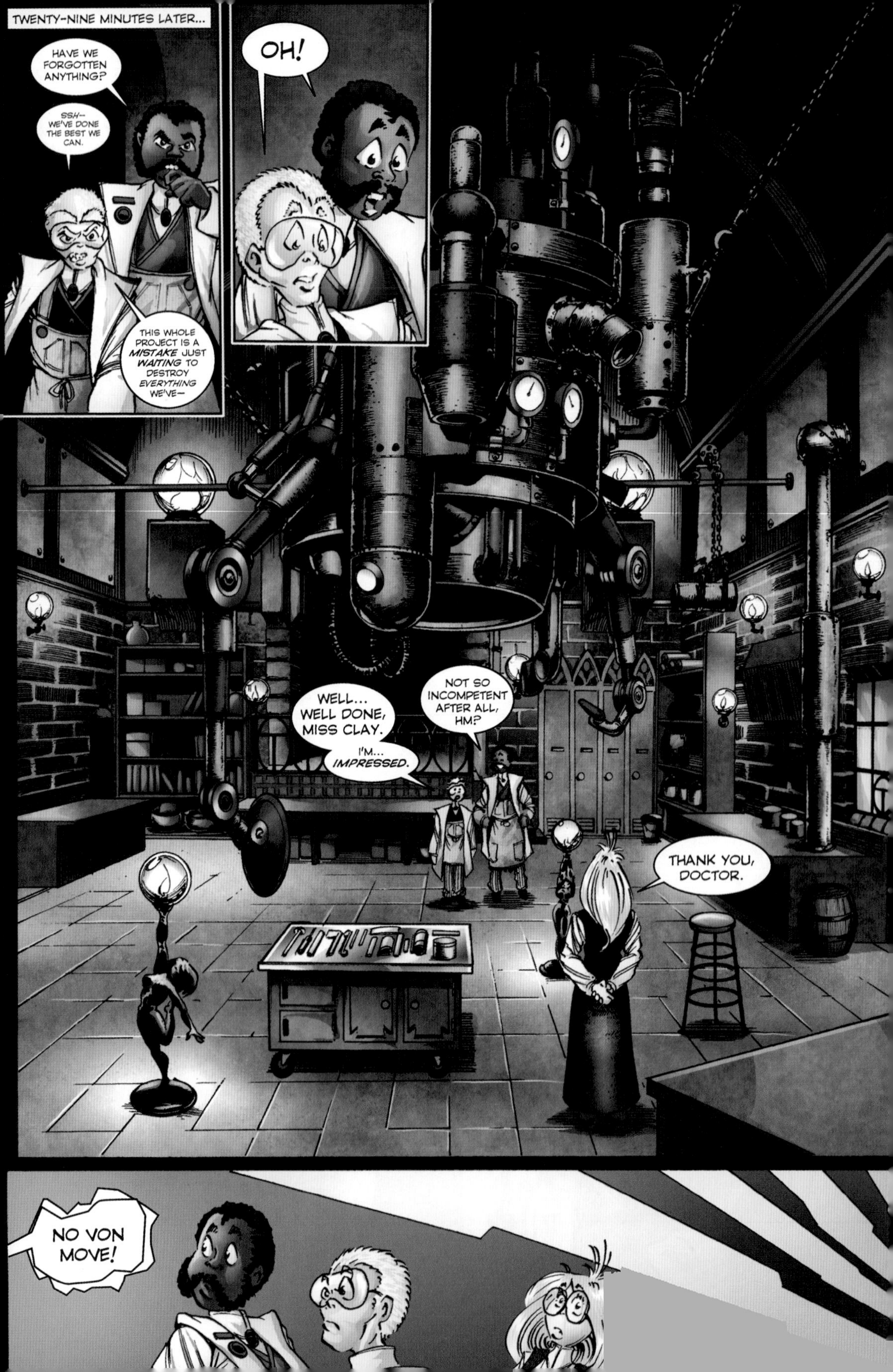

TWENTY-NINE MINUTES LATER...
HAVE WE FORGOTTEN ANYTHING?
SSH-- WE'VE DONE THE BEST WE CAN.
THIS WHOLE PROJECT IS A *MISTAKE* JUST *WAITING* TO DESTROY *EVERYTHING* WE'VE--
OH!
WELL... WELL DONE, MISS CLAY.
I'M... *IMPRESSED.*
NOT SO INCOMPETENT AFTER ALL, HM?
THANK YOU, DOCTOR.
NO VON MOVE!

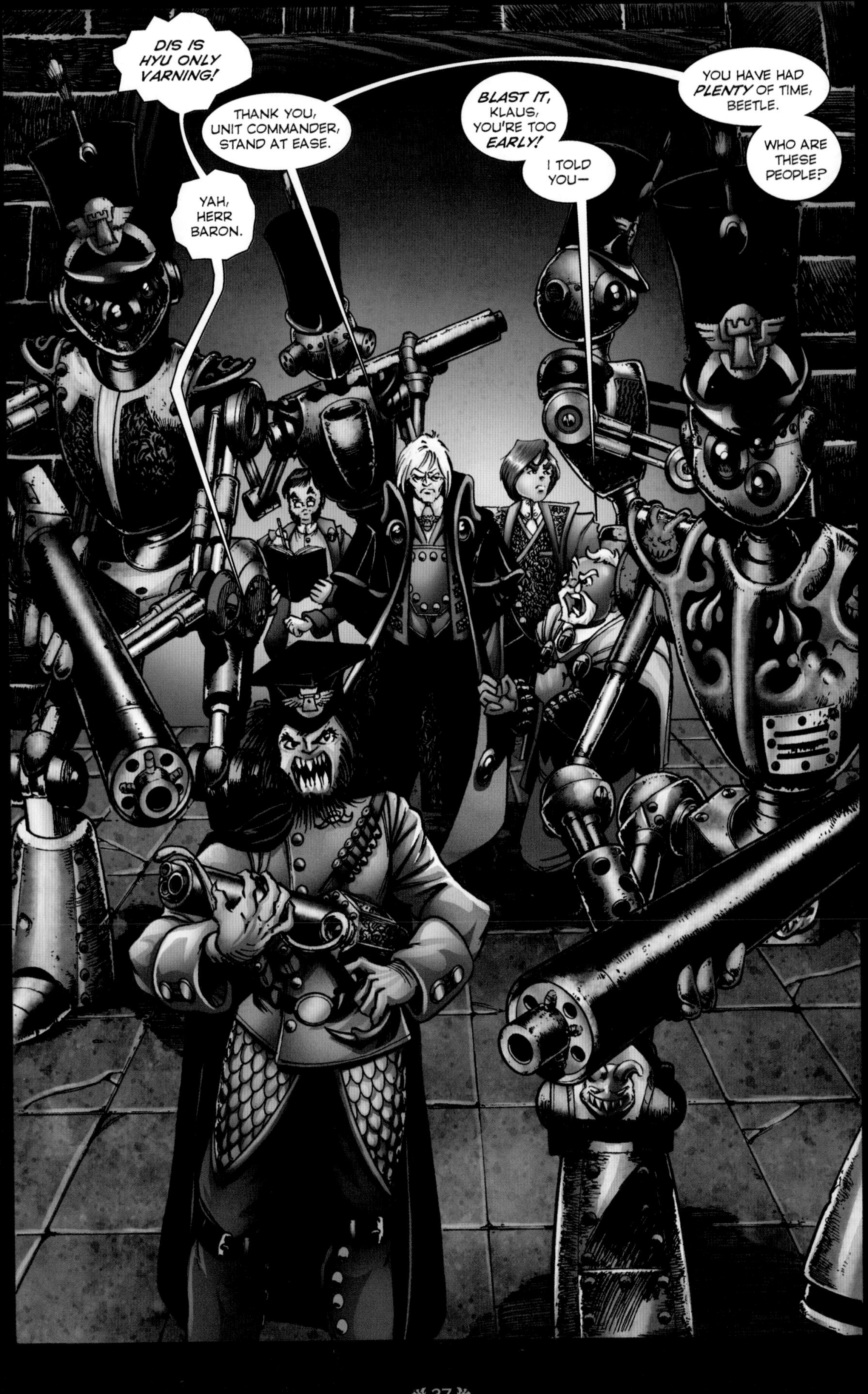
DIS IS HYU ONLY VARNING!
YAH, HERR BARON.
THANK YOU, UNIT COMMANDER, STAND AT EASE.
BLAST IT, KLAUS, YOU'RE TOO EARLY!
I TOLD YOU—
YOU HAVE HAD PLENTY OF TIME, BEETLE.
WHO ARE THESE PEOPLE?

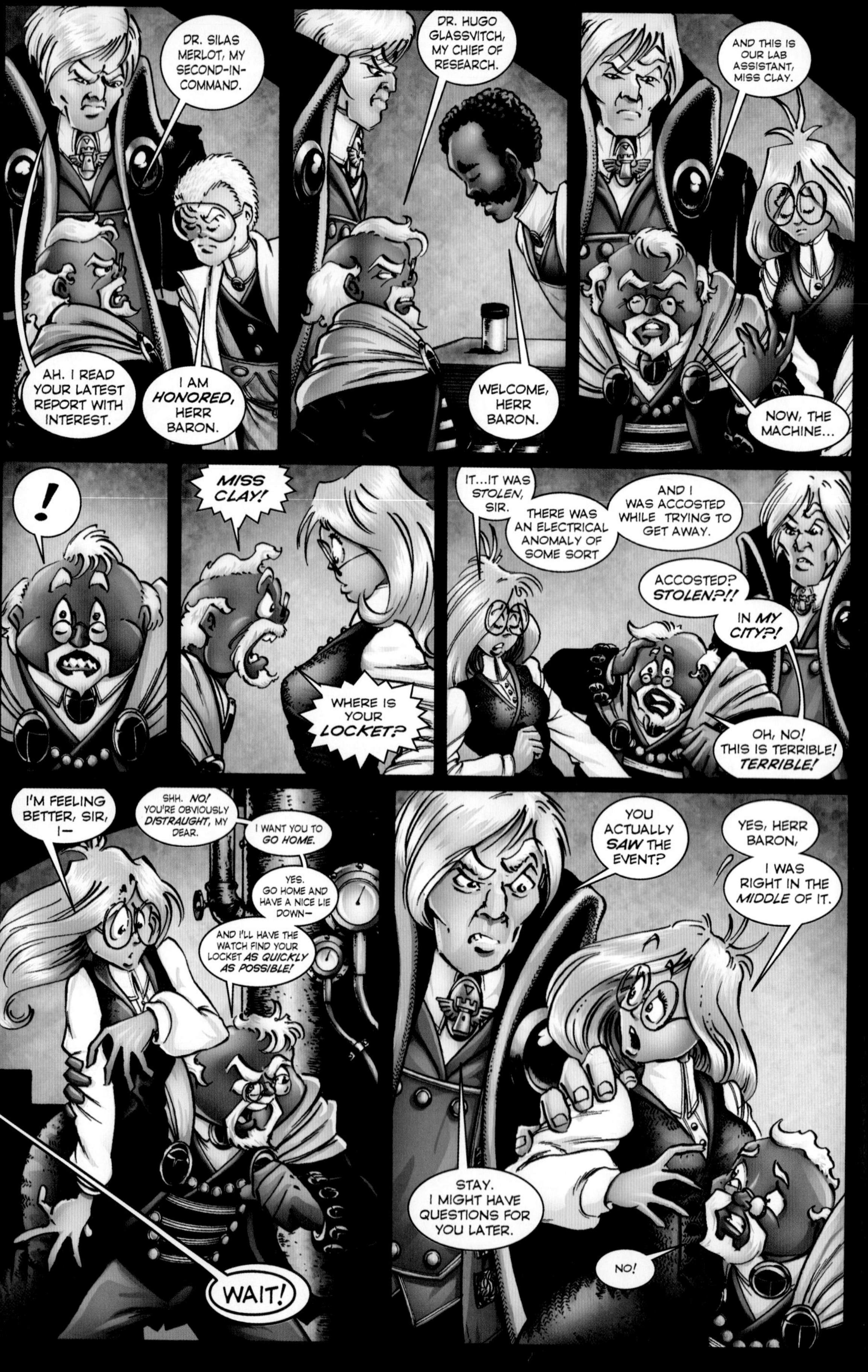
DR. SILAS MERLOT, MY SECOND-IN-COMMAND.
AH. I READ YOUR LATEST REPORT WITH INTEREST.
I AM HONORED, HERR BARON.
DR. HUGO GLASSVITCH, MY CHIEF OF RESEARCH.
WELCOME, HERR BARON.
AND THIS IS OUR LAB ASSISTANT, MISS CLAY.
NOW, THE MACHINE...
!
MISS CLAY!
WHERE IS YOUR LOCKET?
IT...IT WAS STOLEN, SIR.
THERE WAS AN ELECTRICAL ANOMALY OF SOME SORT
AND I WAS ACCOSTED WHILE TRYING TO GET AWAY.
ACCOSTED? STOLEN?!!
IN MY CITY?!
OH, NO! THIS IS TERRIBLE! TERRIBLE!
I'M FEELING BETTER, SIR, I—
SHH. NO! YOU'RE OBVIOUSLY DISTRAUGHT, MY DEAR.
I WANT YOU TO GO HOME.
YES. GO HOME AND HAVE A NICE LIE DOWN—
AND I'LL HAVE THE WATCH FIND YOUR LOCKET AS QUICKLY AS POSSIBLE!
WAIT!
YOU ACTUALLY SAW THE EVENT?
YES, HERR BARON,
I WAS RIGHT IN THE MIDDLE OF IT.
STAY. I MIGHT HAVE QUESTIONS FOR YOU LATER.
NO!

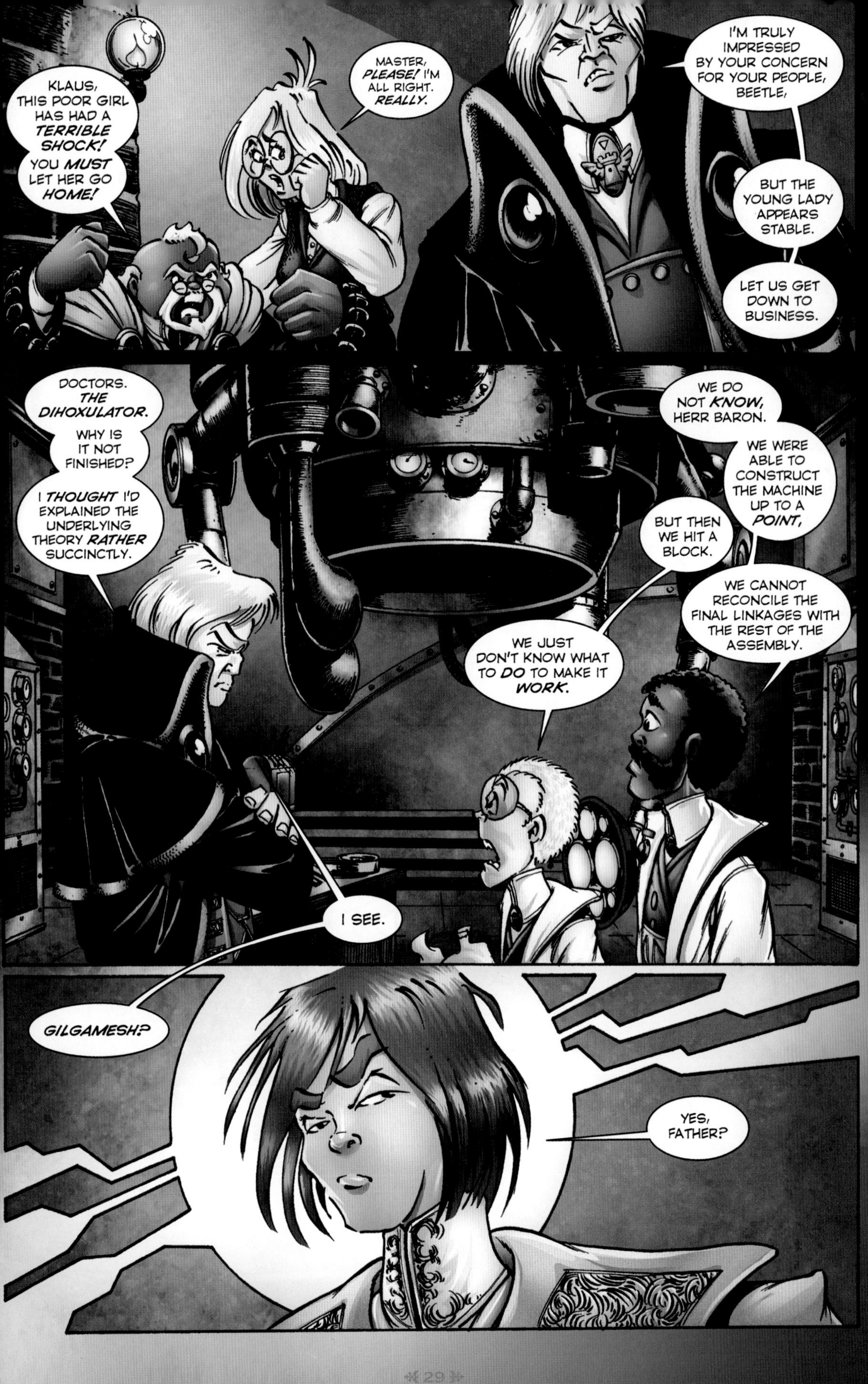
KLAUS, THIS POOR GIRL HAS HAD A *TERRIBLE SHOCK!* YOU *MUST* LET HER GO *HOME!*
MASTER, *PLEASE!* I'M ALL RIGHT. *REALLY.*
I'M TRULY IMPRESSED BY YOUR CONCERN FOR YOUR PEOPLE, BEETLE,
BUT THE YOUNG LADY APPEARS STABLE.
LET US GET DOWN TO BUSINESS.
DOCTORS. *THE DIHOXULATOR.*
WHY IS IT NOT FINISHED?
I *THOUGHT* I'D EXPLAINED THE UNDERLYING THEORY *RATHER* SUCCINCTLY.
WE DO NOT *KNOW,* HERR BARON.
WE WERE ABLE TO CONSTRUCT THE MACHINE UP TO A *POINT,*
BUT THEN WE HIT A BLOCK.
WE CANNOT RECONCILE THE FINAL LINKAGES WITH THE REST OF THE ASSEMBLY.
WE JUST DON'T KNOW WHAT TO *DO* TO MAKE IT *WORK.*
I SEE.
GILGAMESH?
YES, FATHER?

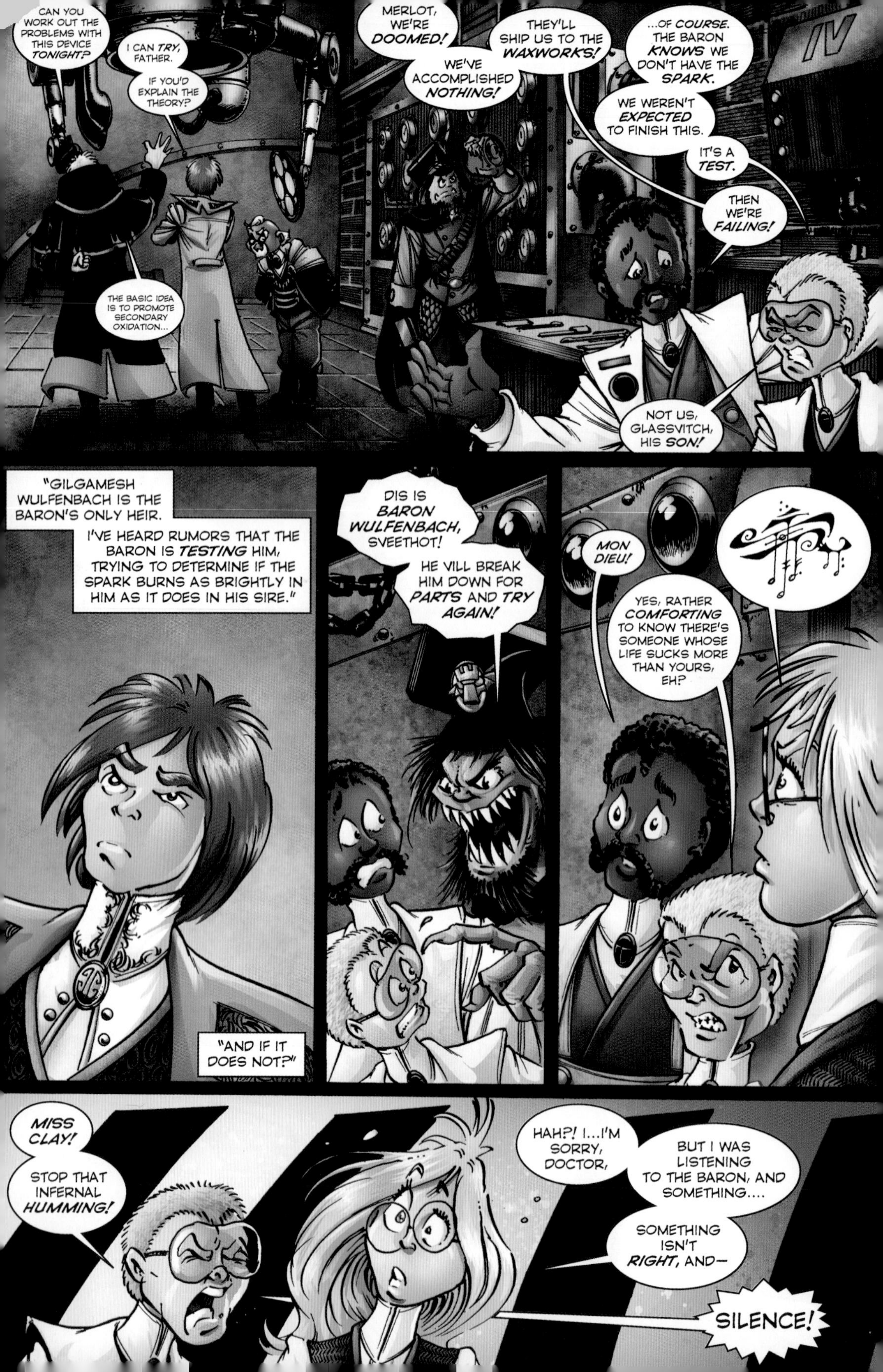
CAN YOU WORK OUT THE PROBLEMS WITH THIS DEVICE TONIGHT?
I CAN TRY, FATHER.
IF YOU'D EXPLAIN THE THEORY?
THE BASIC IDEA IS TO PROMOTE SECONDARY OXIDATION...
MERLOT, WE'RE DOOMED!
WE'VE ACCOMPLISHED NOTHING!
THEY'LL SHIP US TO THE WAXWORKS!
...OF COURSE. THE BARON KNOWS WE DON'T HAVE THE SPARK.
WE WEREN'T EXPECTED TO FINISH THIS.
IT'S A TEST.
THEN WE'RE FAILING!
NOT US, GLASSVITCH, HIS SON!
"GILGAMESH WULFENBACH IS THE BARON'S ONLY HEIR.
I'VE HEARD RUMORS THAT THE BARON IS TESTING HIM, TRYING TO DETERMINE IF THE SPARK BURNS AS BRIGHTLY IN HIM AS IT DOES IN HIS SIRE."
"AND IF IT DOES NOT?"
DIS IS BARON WULFENBACH, SVEETHOT!
HE VILL BREAK HIM DOWN FOR PARTS AND TRY AGAIN!
MON DIEU!
YES, RATHER COMFORTING TO KNOW THERE'S SOMEONE WHOSE LIFE SUCKS MORE THAN YOURS, EH?
MISS CLAY!
STOP THAT INFERNAL HUMMING!
HAH?! I...I'M SORRY, DOCTOR,
BUT I WAS LISTENING TO THE BARON, AND SOMETHING....
SOMETHING ISN'T RIGHT, AND—
SILENCE!

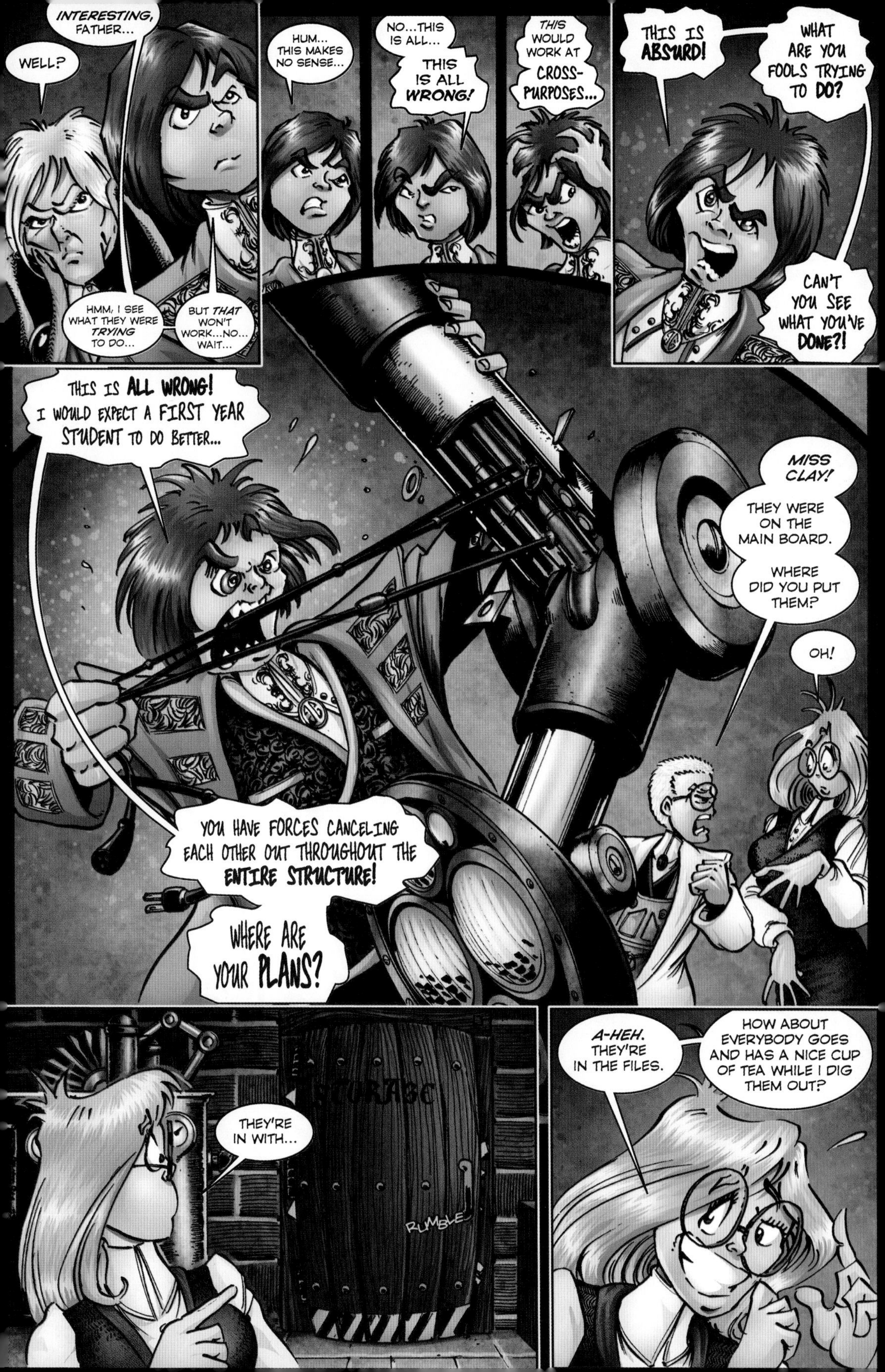
INTERESTING, FATHER...
WELL?
HMM, I SEE WHAT THEY WERE TRYING TO DO...
BUT THAT WON'T WORK...NO... WAIT...
HUM... THIS MAKES NO SENSE...
NO...THIS IS ALL...
THIS IS ALL WRONG!
THIS WOULD WORK AT CROSS-PURPOSES...
THIS IS ABSURD!
WHAT ARE YOU FOOLS TRYING TO DO?
CAN'T YOU SEE WHAT YOU'VE DONE?!
THIS IS ALL WRONG! I WOULD EXPECT A FIRST YEAR STUDENT TO DO BETTER...
YOU HAVE FORCES CANCELING EACH OTHER OUT THROUGHOUT THE ENTIRE STRUCTURE!
WHERE ARE YOUR PLANS?
MISS CLAY!
THEY WERE ON THE MAIN BOARD.
WHERE DID YOU PUT THEM?
OH!
THEY'RE IN WITH...
RUMBLE
A-HEH. THEY'RE IN THE FILES.
HOW ABOUT EVERYBODY GOES AND HAS A NICE CUP OF TEA WHILE I DIG THEM OUT?

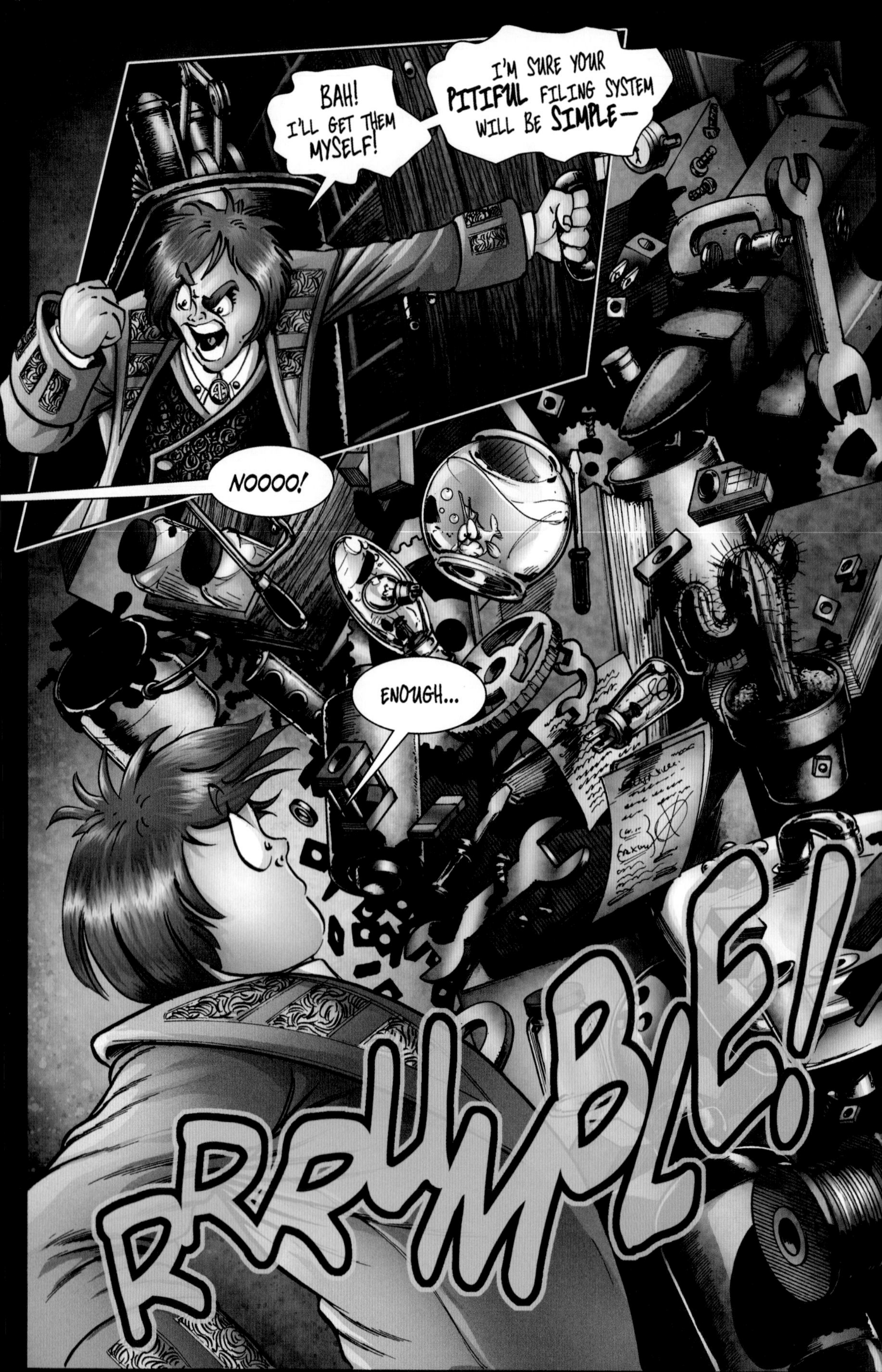
I'M SURE YOUR PITIFUL FILING SYSTEM WILL BE SIMPLE—
BAH! I'LL GET THEM MYSELF!
NOOOO!
ENOUGH...
RRUMBLE!

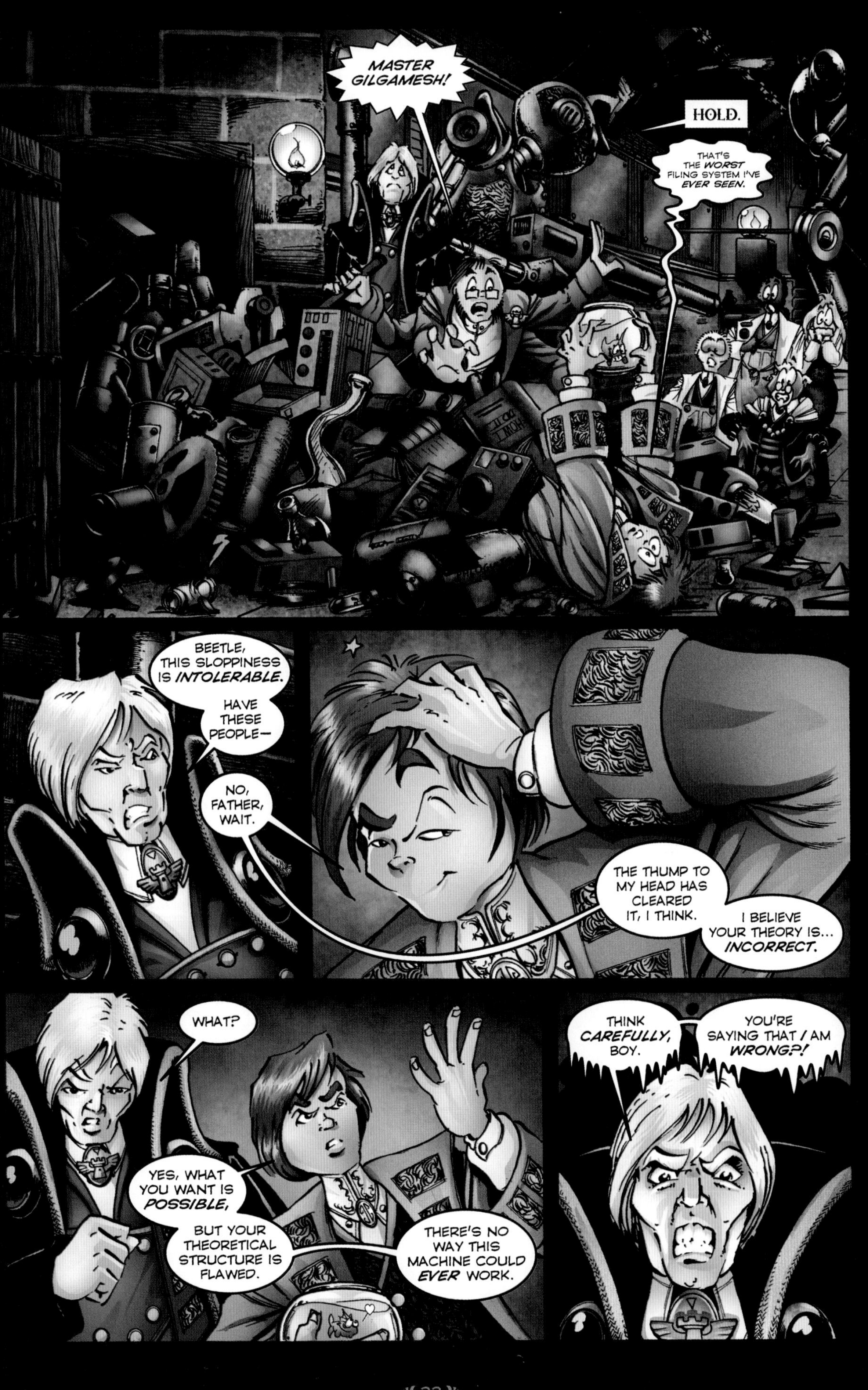
MASTER GILGAMESH!
HOLD.
THAT'S THE WORST FILING SYSTEM I'VE EVER SEEN.
BEETLE, THIS SLOPPINESS IS INTOLERABLE.
HAVE THESE PEOPLE—
NO, FATHER, WAIT.
THE THUMP TO MY HEAD HAS CLEARED IT, I THINK.
I BELIEVE YOUR THEORY IS... INCORRECT.
WHAT?
YES, WHAT YOU WANT IS POSSIBLE,
BUT YOUR THEORETICAL STRUCTURE IS FLAWED.
THERE'S NO WAY THIS MACHINE COULD EVER WORK.
THINK CAREFULLY, BOY.
YOU'RE SAYING THAT I AM WRONG?!

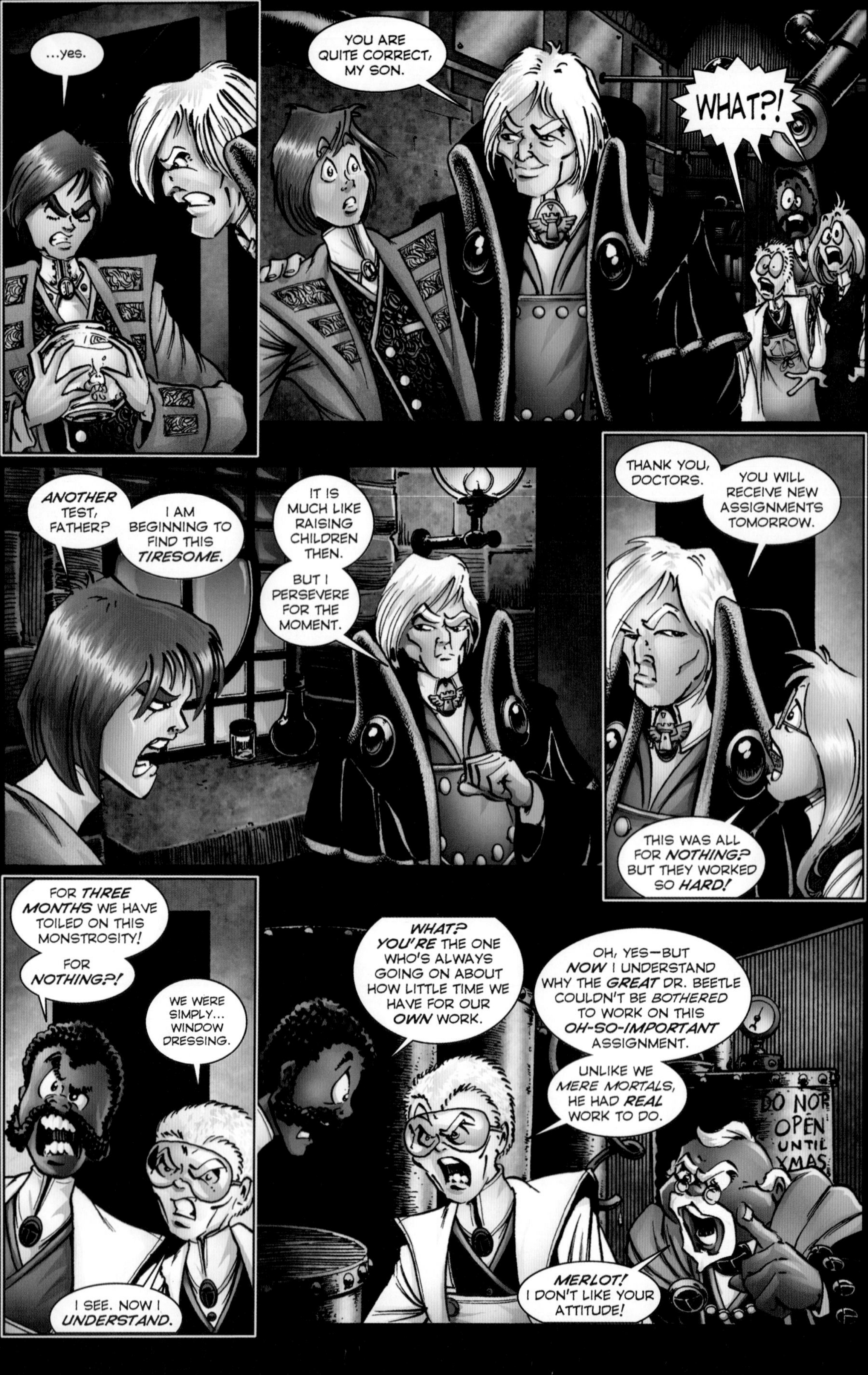
...yes.
YOU ARE QUITE CORRECT, MY SON.
WHAT?!
ANOTHER TEST, FATHER?
I AM BEGINNING TO FIND THIS TIRESOME.
IT IS MUCH LIKE RAISING CHILDREN THEN.
BUT I PERSEVERE FOR THE MOMENT.
THANK YOU, DOCTORS.
YOU WILL RECEIVE NEW ASSIGNMENTS TOMORROW.
THIS WAS ALL FOR NOTHING? BUT THEY WORKED SO HARD!
FOR THREE MONTHS WE HAVE TOILED ON THIS MONSTROSITY!
FOR NOTHING?!
WE WERE SIMPLY... WINDOW DRESSING.
I SEE. NOW I UNDERSTAND.
WHAT? YOU'RE THE ONE WHO'S ALWAYS GOING ON ABOUT HOW LITTLE TIME WE HAVE FOR OUR OWN WORK.
OH, YES—BUT NOW I UNDERSTAND WHY THE GREAT DR. BEETLE COULDN'T BE BOTHERED TO WORK ON THIS OH-SO-IMPORTANT ASSIGNMENT.
UNLIKE WE MERE MORTALS, HE HAD REAL WORK TO DO.
DO NOT OPEN UNTIL XMAS
MERLOT! I DON'T LIKE YOUR ATTITUDE!

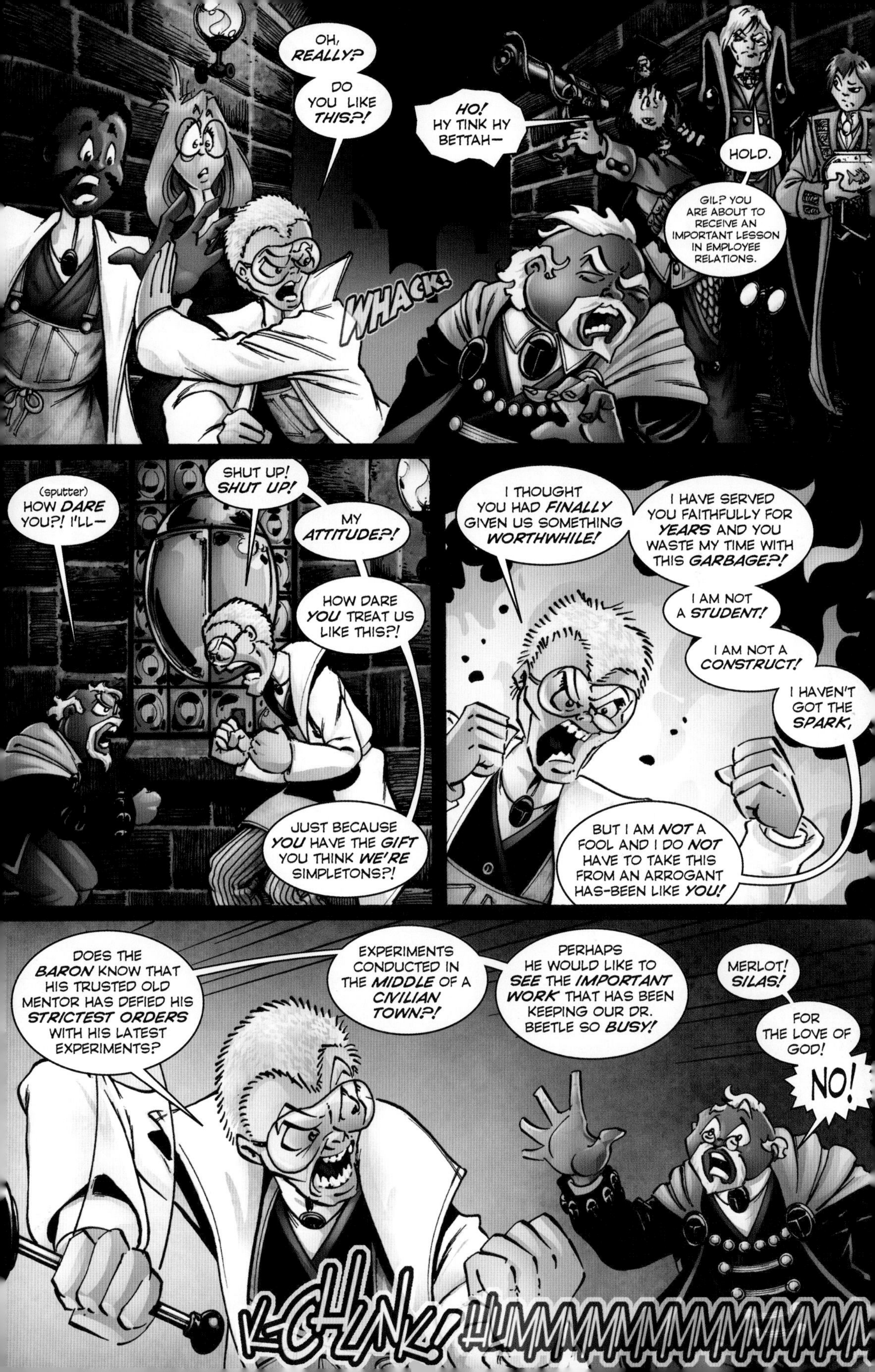
OH, REALLY?
DO YOU LIKE THIS?!
HO! HY TINK HY BETTAH—
HOLD.
GIL? YOU ARE ABOUT TO RECEIVE AN IMPORTANT LESSON IN EMPLOYEE RELATIONS.
WHACK!
(sputter) HOW DARE YOU?! I'LL—
SHUT UP! SHUT UP!
MY ATTITUDE?!
HOW DARE YOU TREAT US LIKE THIS?!
JUST BECAUSE YOU HAVE THE GIFT YOU THINK WE'RE SIMPLETONS?!
I THOUGHT YOU HAD FINALLY GIVEN US SOMETHING WORTHWHILE!
I HAVE SERVED YOU FAITHFULLY FOR YEARS AND YOU WASTE MY TIME WITH THIS GARBAGE?!
I AM NOT A STUDENT!
I AM NOT A CONSTRUCT!
I HAVEN'T GOT THE SPARK,
BUT I AM NOT A FOOL AND I DO NOT HAVE TO TAKE THIS FROM AN ARROGANT HAS-BEEN LIKE YOU!
DOES THE BARON KNOW THAT HIS TRUSTED OLD MENTOR HAS DEFIED HIS STRICTEST ORDERS WITH HIS LATEST EXPERIMENTS?
EXPERIMENTS CONDUCTED IN THE MIDDLE OF A CIVILIAN TOWN?!
PERHAPS HE WOULD LIKE TO SEE THE IMPORTANT WORK THAT HAS BEEN KEEPING OUR DR. BEETLE SO BUSY!
MERLOT! SILAS!
FOR THE LOVE OF GOD!
NO!
K-CHUNK! HUMMMMMMMMMMMMMM

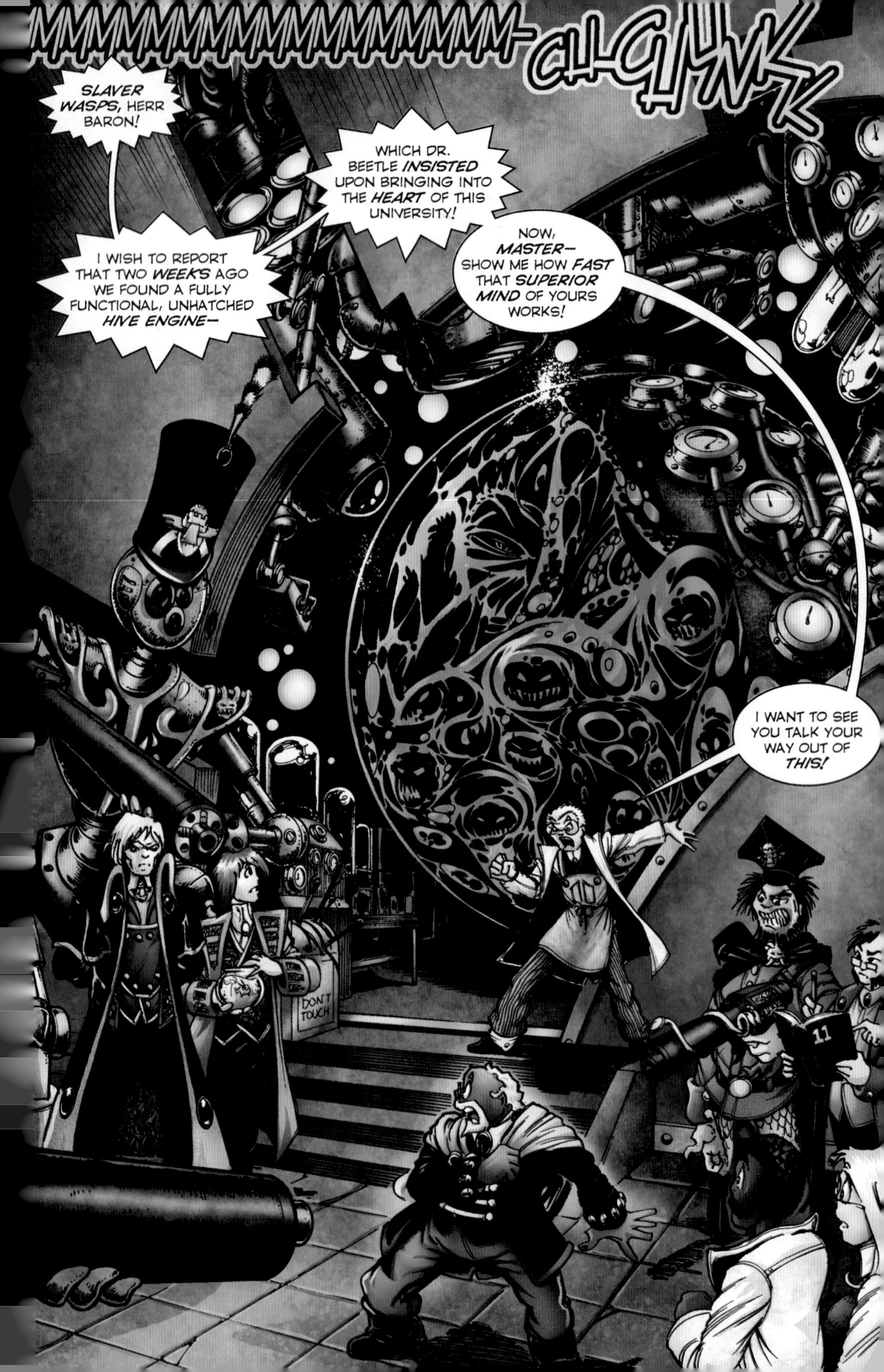
MMMMMMMMMMMMMMMMMM—CLLCLUNK
SLAVER WASPS, HERR BARON!
I WISH TO REPORT THAT TWO WEEKS AGO WE FOUND A FULLY FUNCTIONAL, UNHATCHED HIVE ENGINE—
WHICH DR. BEETLE INSISTED UPON BRINGING INTO THE HEART OF THIS UNIVERSITY!
NOW, MASTER— SHOW ME HOW FAST THAT SUPERIOR MIND OF YOURS WORKS!
I WANT TO SEE YOU TALK YOUR WAY OUT OF THIS!
DON'T TOUCH
11

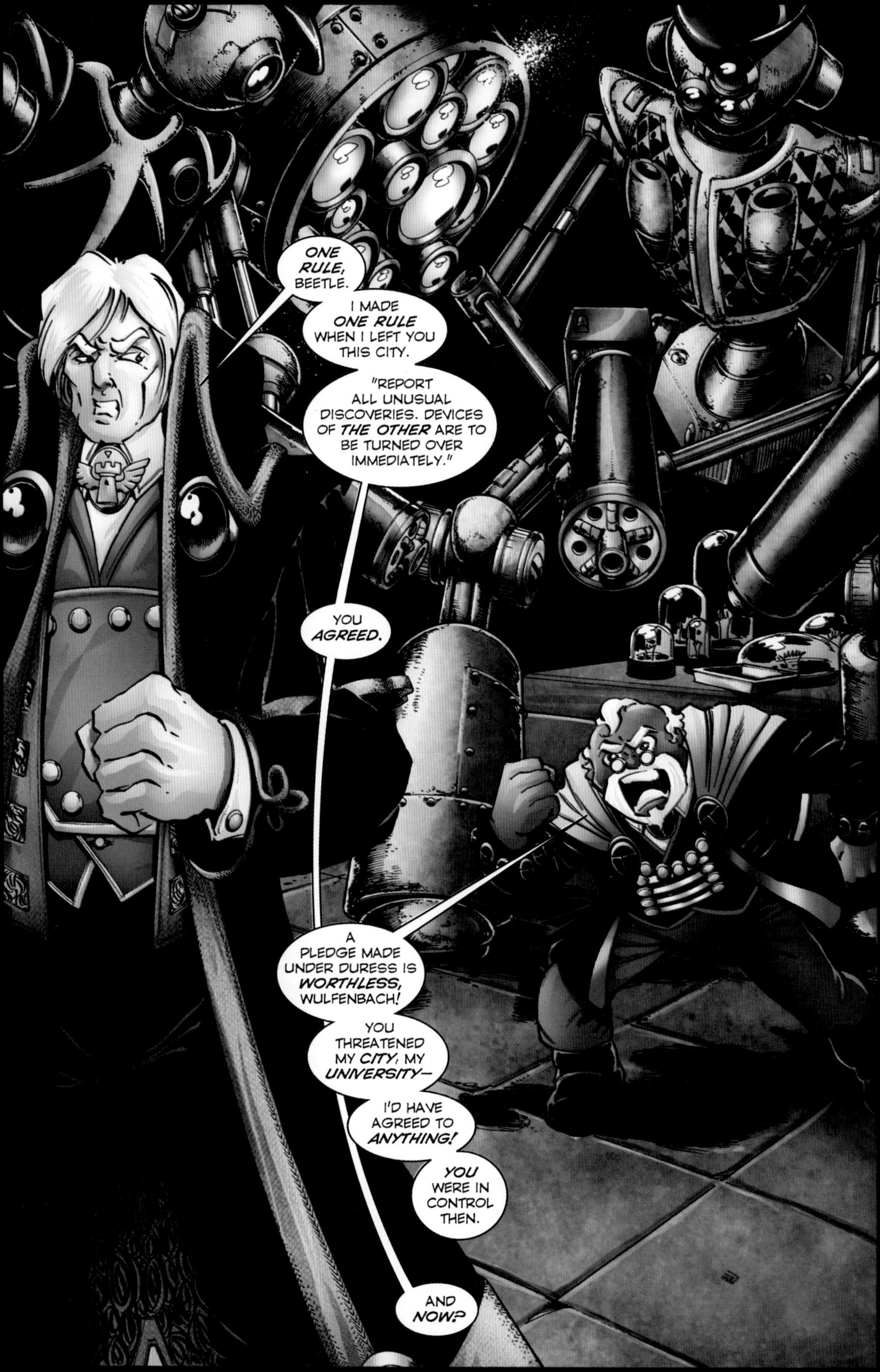
ONE RULE, BEETLE.
I MADE ONE RULE WHEN I LEFT YOU THIS CITY.
"REPORT ALL UNUSUAL DISCOVERIES. DEVICES OF THE OTHER ARE TO BE TURNED OVER IMMEDIATELY."
YOU AGREED.
A PLEDGE MADE UNDER DURESS IS WORTHLESS, WULFENBACH!
YOU THREATENED MY CITY, MY UNIVERSITY—
I'D HAVE AGREED TO ANYTHING!
YOU WERE IN CONTROL THEN.
AND NOW?

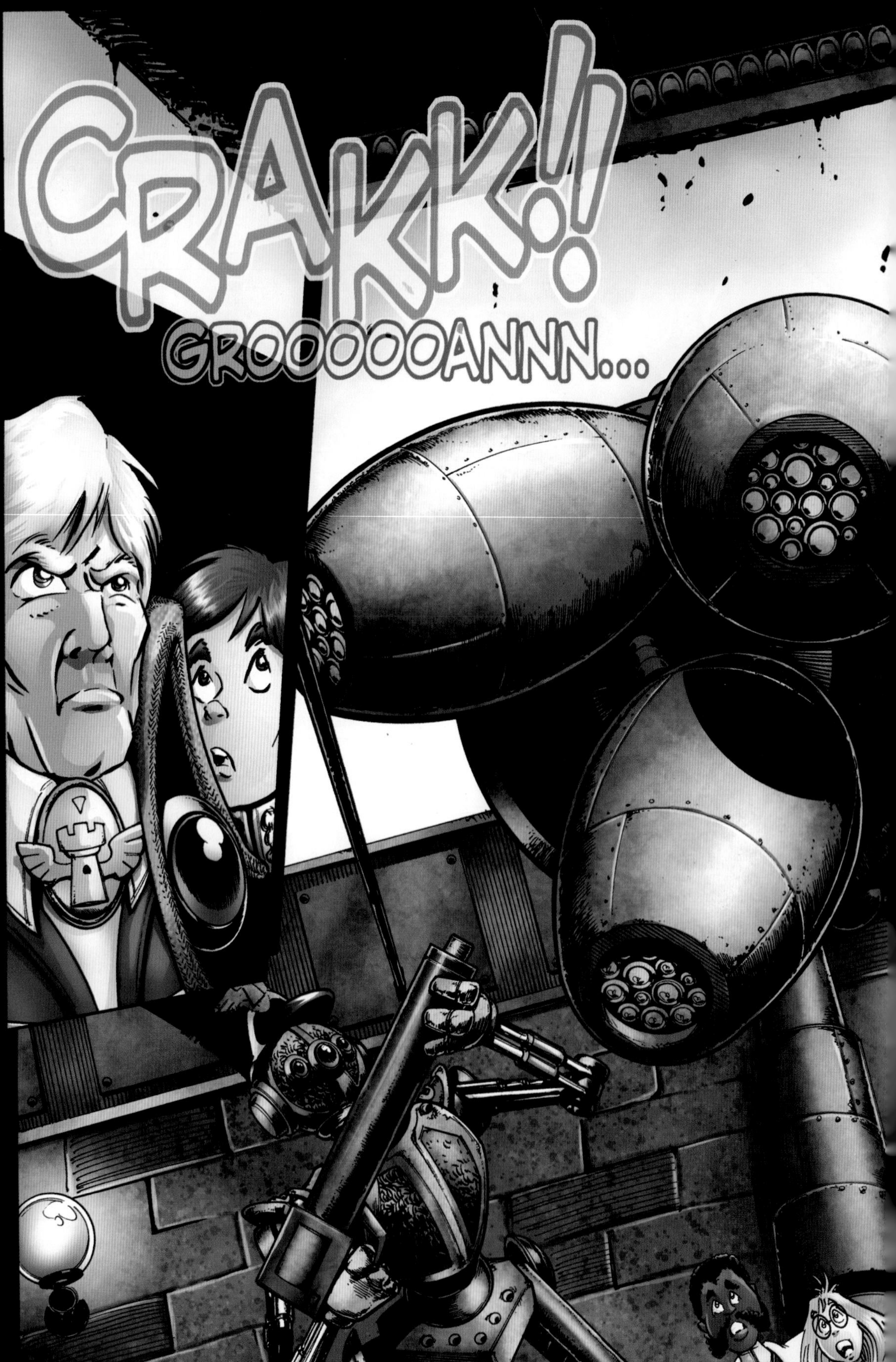
CRAKK!!
GROOOOOOANNN...

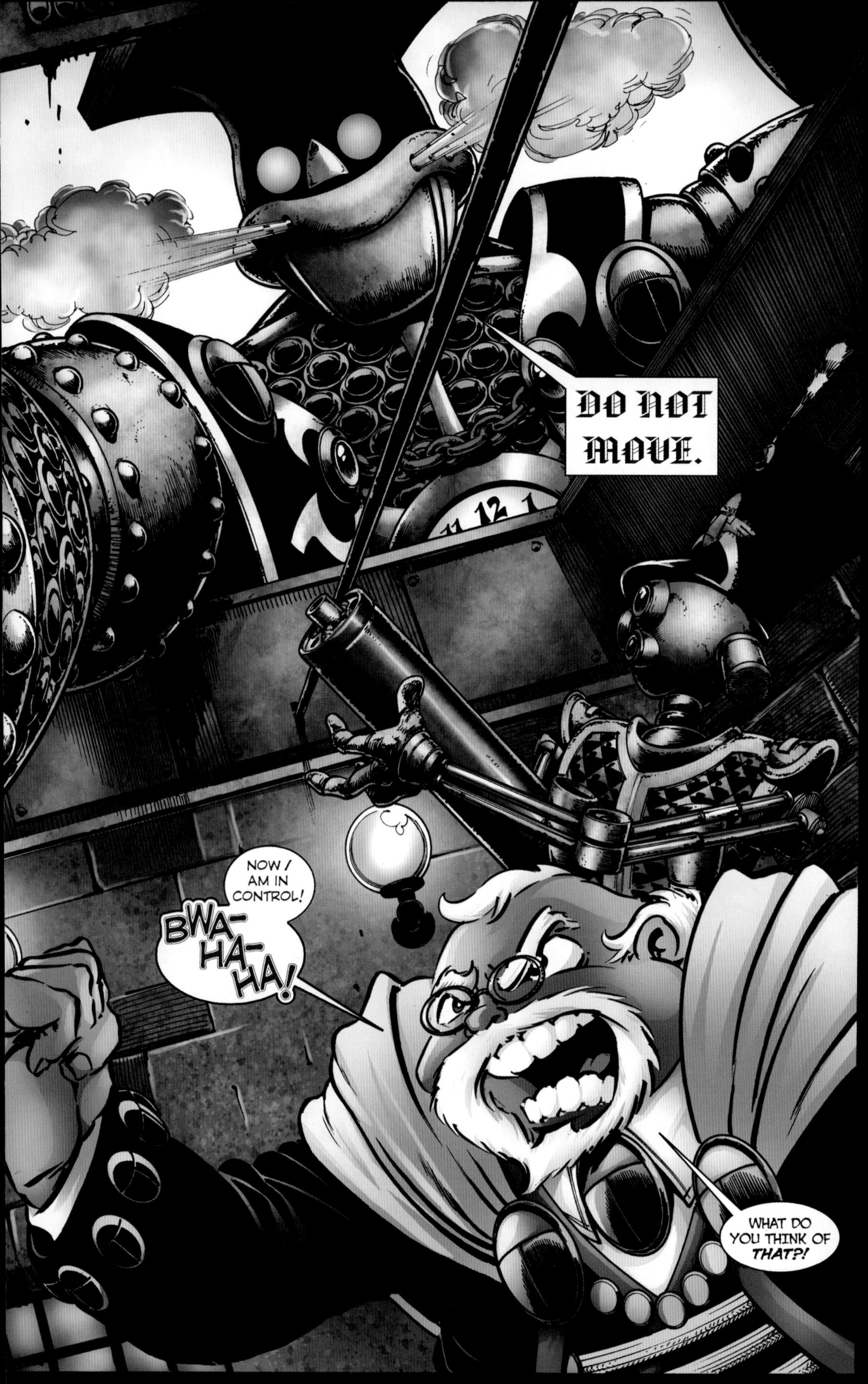
DO NOT MOVE.
NOW I AM IN CONTROL!
BWA-HA-HA!
WHAT DO YOU THINK OF *THAT?!*

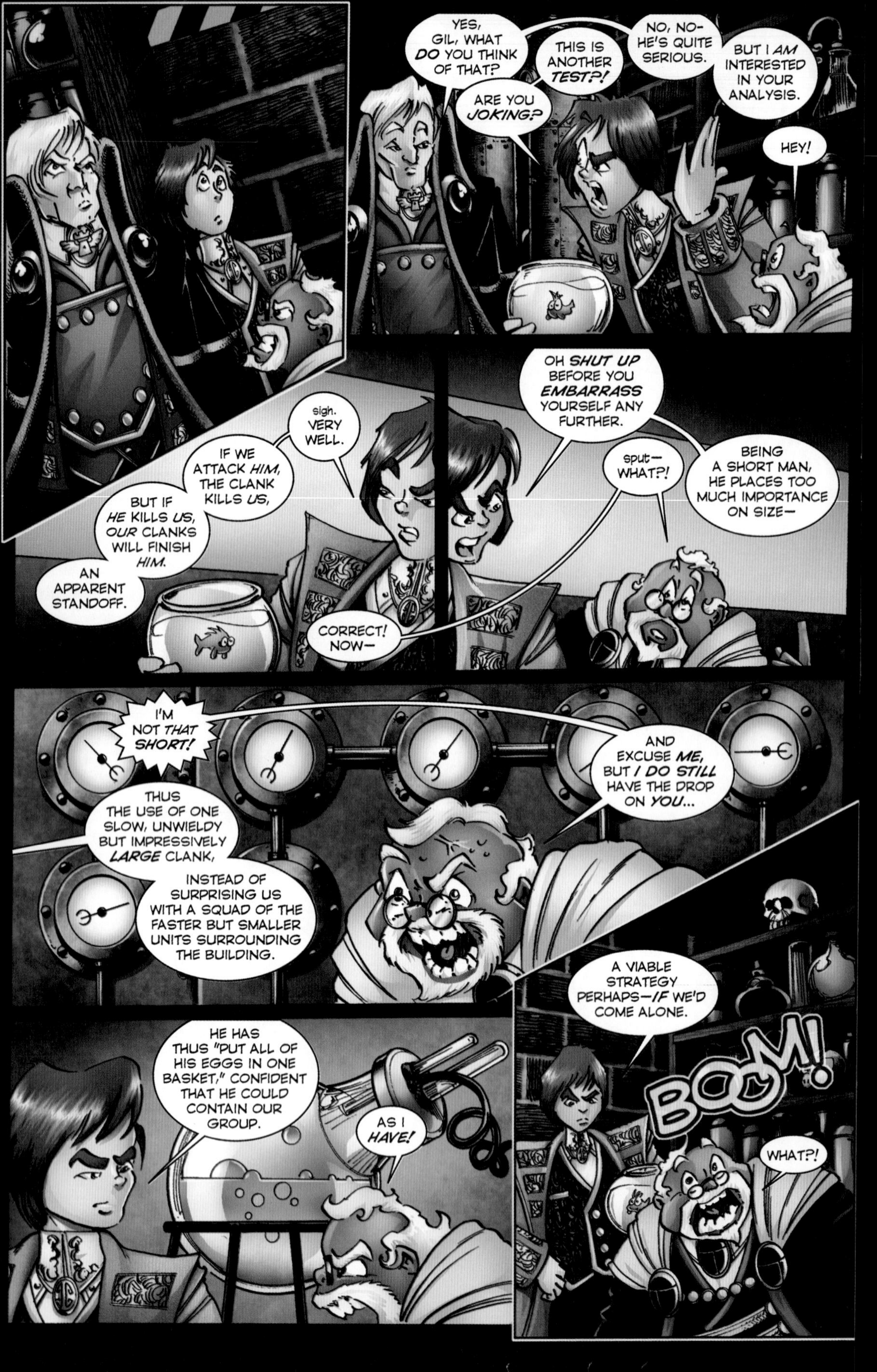
YES, GIL, WHAT DO YOU THINK OF THAT?
ARE YOU JOKING?
THIS IS ANOTHER TEST?!
NO, NO- HE'S QUITE SERIOUS.
BUT I AM INTERESTED IN YOUR ANALYSIS.
HEY!
sigh. VERY WELL.
IF WE ATTACK HIM, THE CLANK KILLS US,
BUT IF HE KILLS US, OUR CLANKS WILL FINISH HIM.
AN APPARENT STANDOFF.
CORRECT! NOW—
OH SHUT UP BEFORE YOU EMBARRASS YOURSELF ANY FURTHER.
sput— WHAT?!
BEING A SHORT MAN, HE PLACES TOO MUCH IMPORTANCE ON SIZE—
I'M NOT THAT SHORT!
THUS THE USE OF ONE SLOW, UNWIELDY BUT IMPRESSIVELY LARGE CLANK,
INSTEAD OF SURPRISING US WITH A SQUAD OF THE FASTER BUT SMALLER UNITS SURROUNDING THE BUILDING.
AND EXCUSE ME, BUT I DO STILL HAVE THE DROP ON YOU...
HE HAS THUS "PUT ALL OF HIS EGGS IN ONE BASKET," CONFIDENT THAT HE COULD CONTAIN OUR GROUP.
AS I HAVE!
A VIABLE STRATEGY PERHAPS—IF WE'D COME ALONE.
BOOM!
WHAT?!

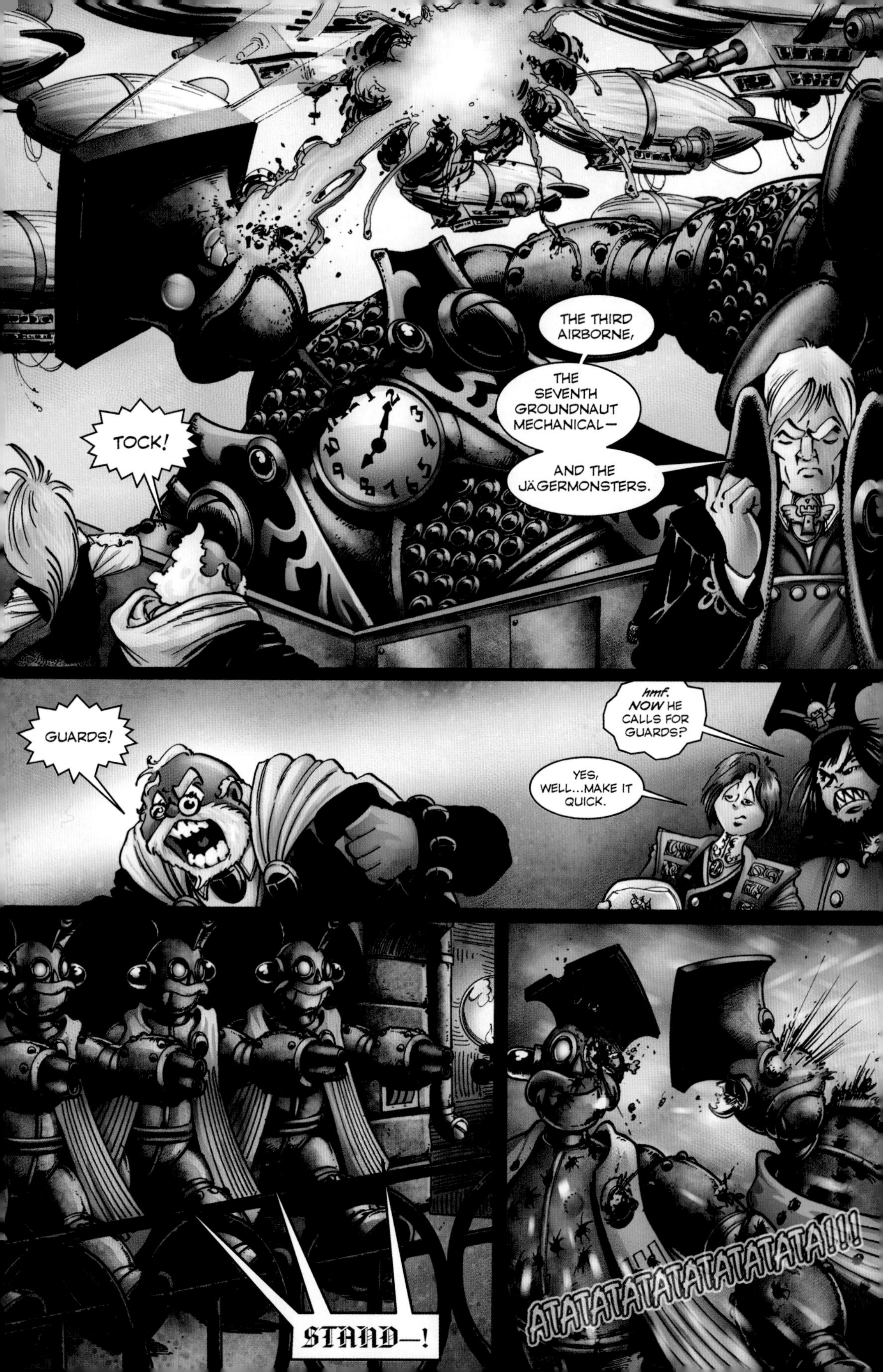
THE THIRD AIRBORNE,
THE SEVENTH GROUNDNAUT MECHANICAL—
AND THE JÄGERMONSTERS.
TOCK!
GUARDS!
hmf. NOW HE CALLS FOR GUARDS?
YES, WELL...MAKE IT QUICK.
STAND—!
ATATATATATATATATATATA!!!

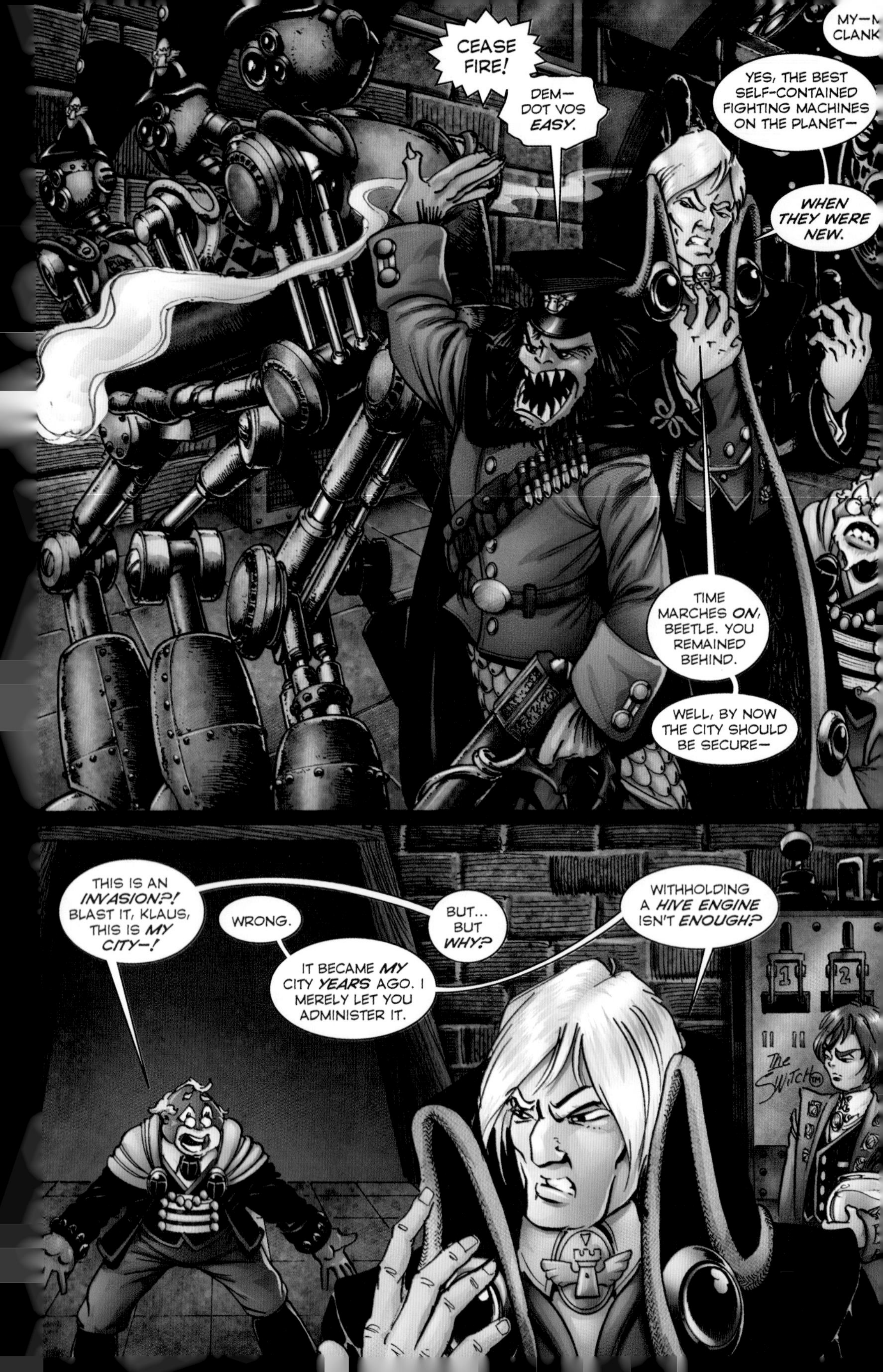
CEASE FIRE!
DEM— DOT VOS EASY.
MY—M CLANK
YES, THE BEST SELF-CONTAINED FIGHTING MACHINES ON THE PLANET—
WHEN THEY WERE NEW.
TIME MARCHES ON, BEETLE. YOU REMAINED BEHIND.
WELL, BY NOW THE CITY SHOULD BE SECURE—
THIS IS AN INVASION?! BLAST IT, KLAUS, THIS IS MY CITY—!
WRONG.
IT BECAME MY CITY YEARS AGO. I MERELY LET YOU ADMINISTER IT.
BUT... BUT WHY?
WITHHOLDING A HIVE ENGINE ISN'T ENOUGH?
1
2
THE SWITCH™

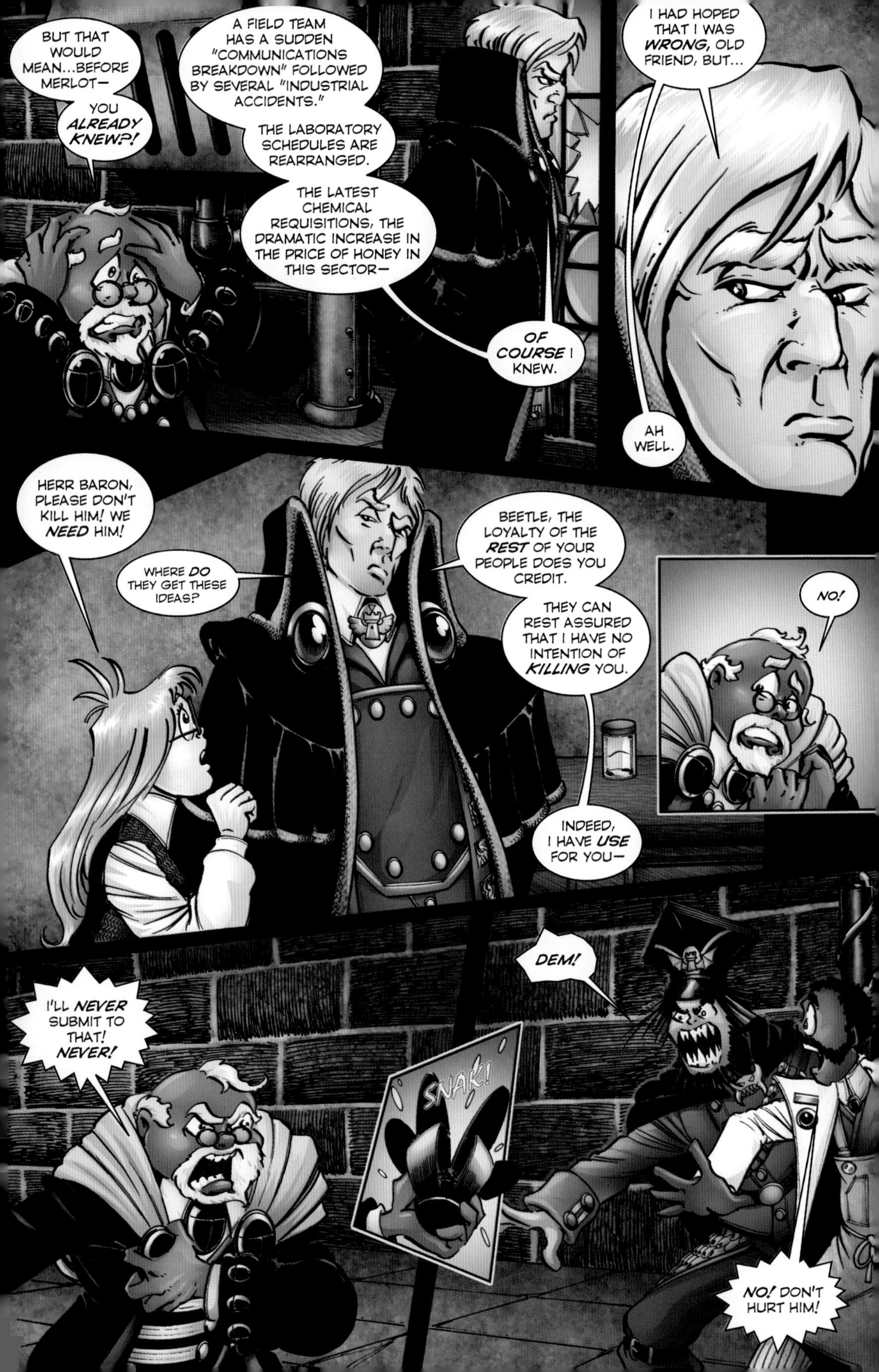

BUT THAT WOULD MEAN...BEFORE MERLOT—
YOU ALREADY KNEW?!
A FIELD TEAM HAS A SUDDEN "COMMUNICATIONS BREAKDOWN" FOLLOWED BY SEVERAL "INDUSTRIAL ACCIDENTS."
THE LABORATORY SCHEDULES ARE REARRANGED.
THE LATEST CHEMICAL REQUISITIONS, THE DRAMATIC INCREASE IN THE PRICE OF HONEY IN THIS SECTOR—
OF COURSE I KNEW.
I HAD HOPED THAT I WAS WRONG, OLD FRIEND, BUT...
AH WELL.
HERR BARON, PLEASE DON'T KILL HIM! WE NEED HIM!
WHERE DO THEY GET THESE IDEAS?
BEETLE, THE LOYALTY OF THE REST OF YOUR PEOPLE DOES YOU CREDIT.
THEY CAN REST ASSURED THAT I HAVE NO INTENTION OF KILLING YOU.
INDEED, I HAVE USE FOR YOU—
NO!
I'LL NEVER SUBMIT TO THAT! NEVER!
DEM!
SNAK!
NO! DON'T HURT HIM!

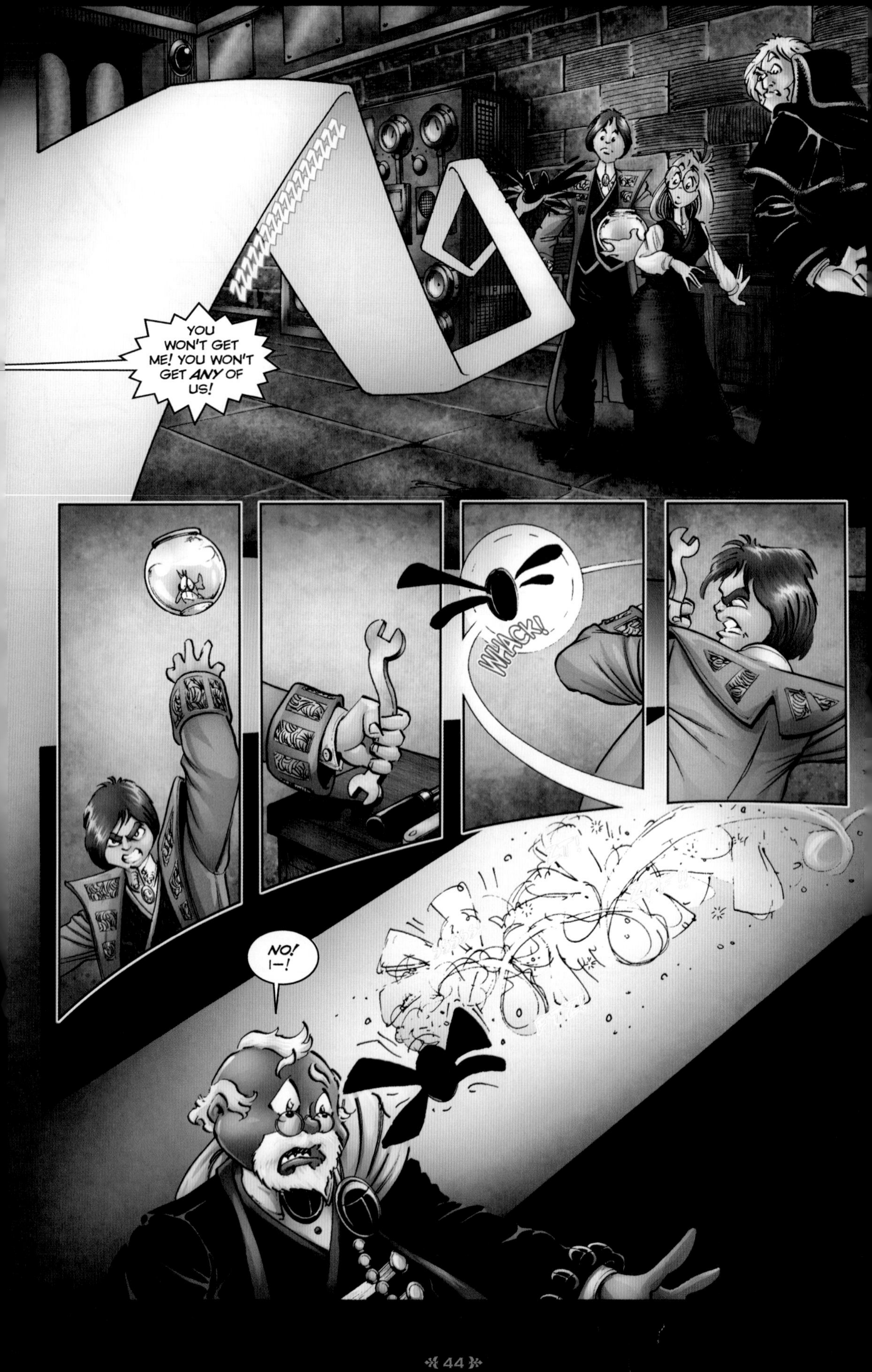
YOU WON'T GET ME! YOU WON'T GET *ANY* OF US!
WHACK!
NO! I—!

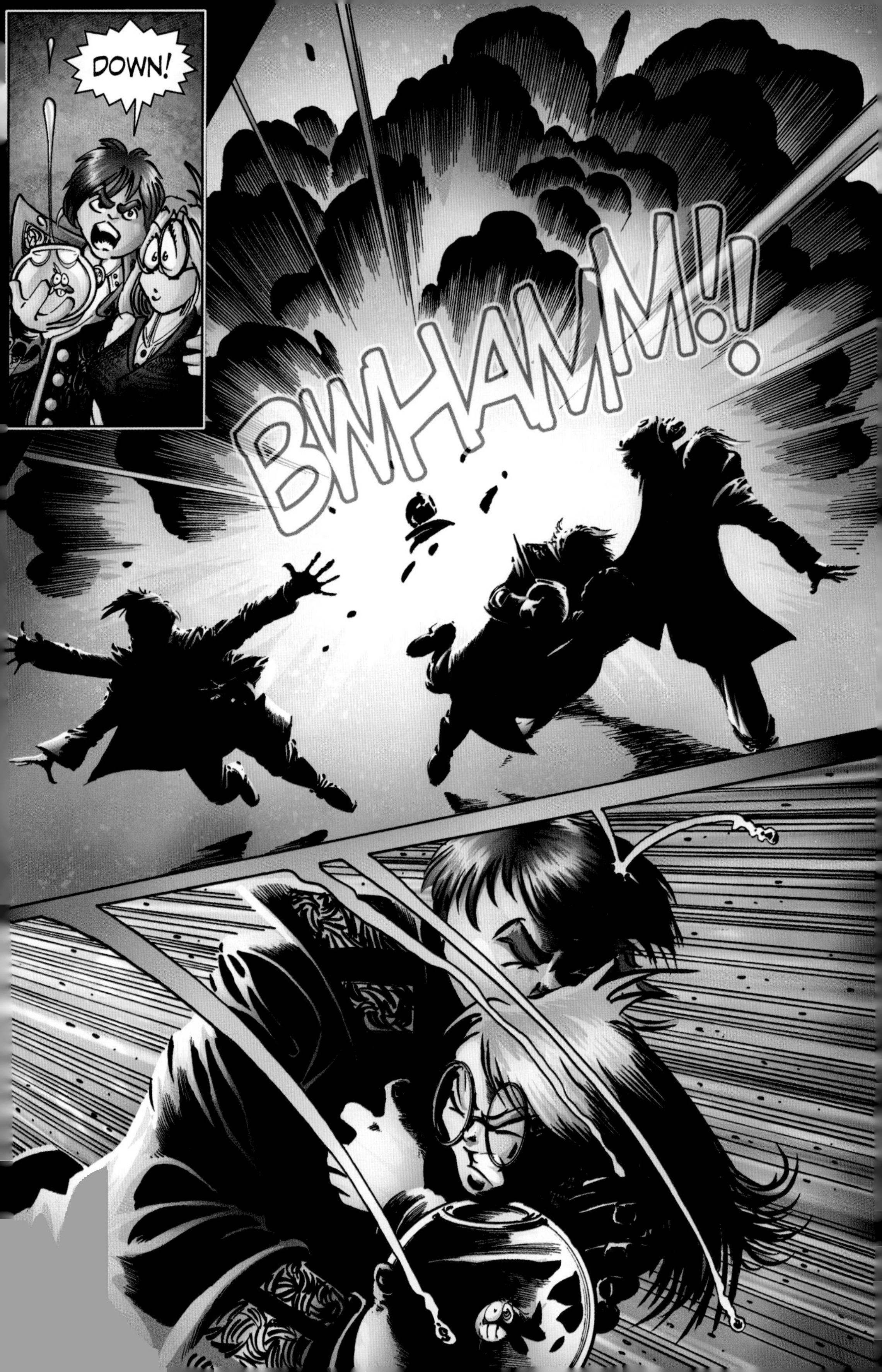
DOWN!
BWHAMM!!

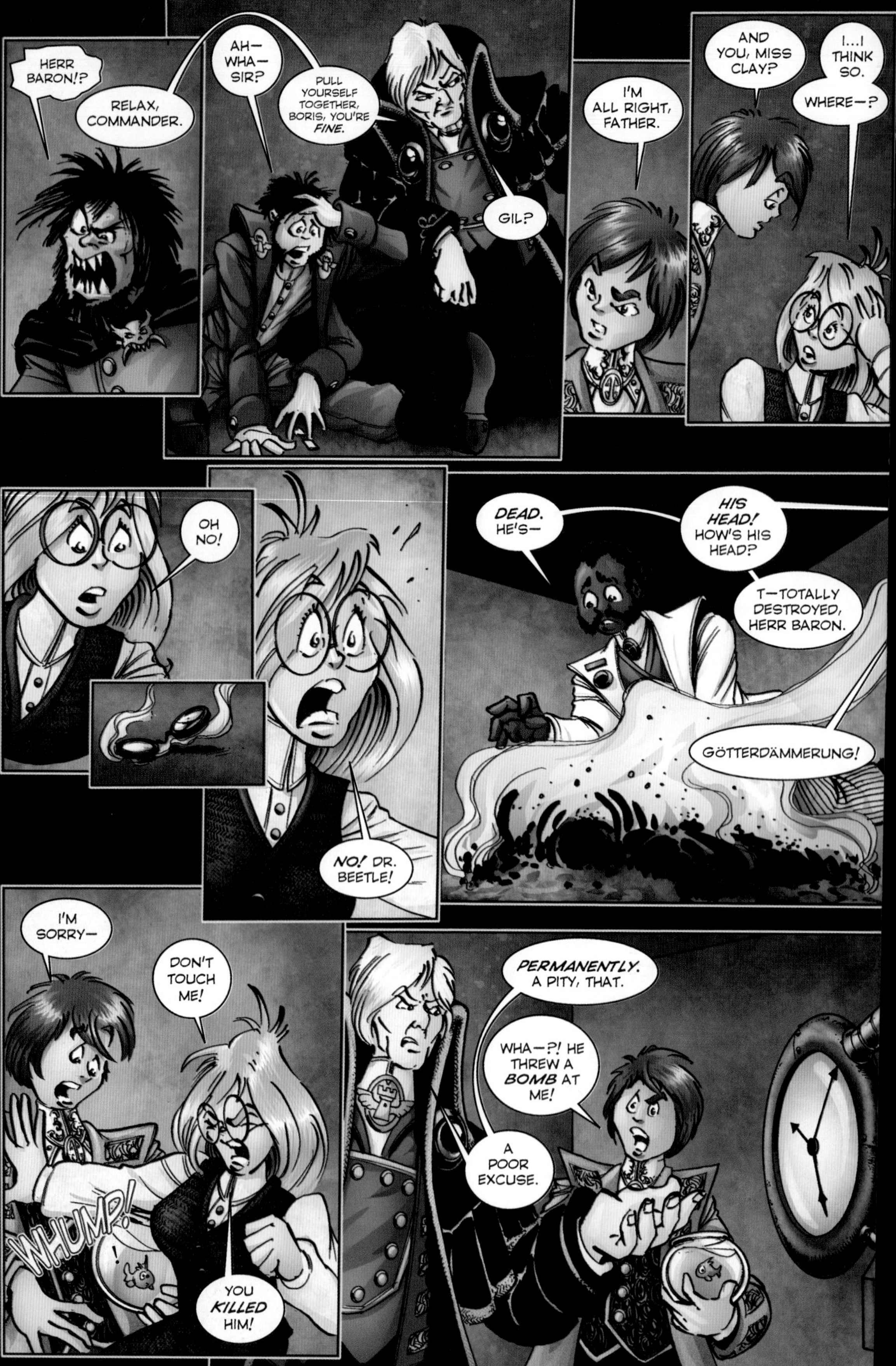

HERR BARON!?
RELAX, COMMANDER.
AH— WHA— SIR?
PULL YOURSELF TOGETHER, BORIS, YOU'RE *FINE.*
GIL?
I'M ALL RIGHT, FATHER.
AND YOU, MISS CLAY?
I...I THINK SO.
WHERE—?
OH NO!
NO! DR. BEETLE!
DEAD. HE'S—
HIS HEAD! HOW'S HIS HEAD?
T—TOTALLY DESTROYED, HERR BARON.
GÖTTERDÄMMERUNG!
I'M SORRY—
DON'T TOUCH ME!
WHUMP!
!
YOU *KILLED* HIM!
PERMANENTLY. A PITY, THAT.
WHA—?! HE THREW A *BOMB* AT ME!
A POOR EXCUSE.

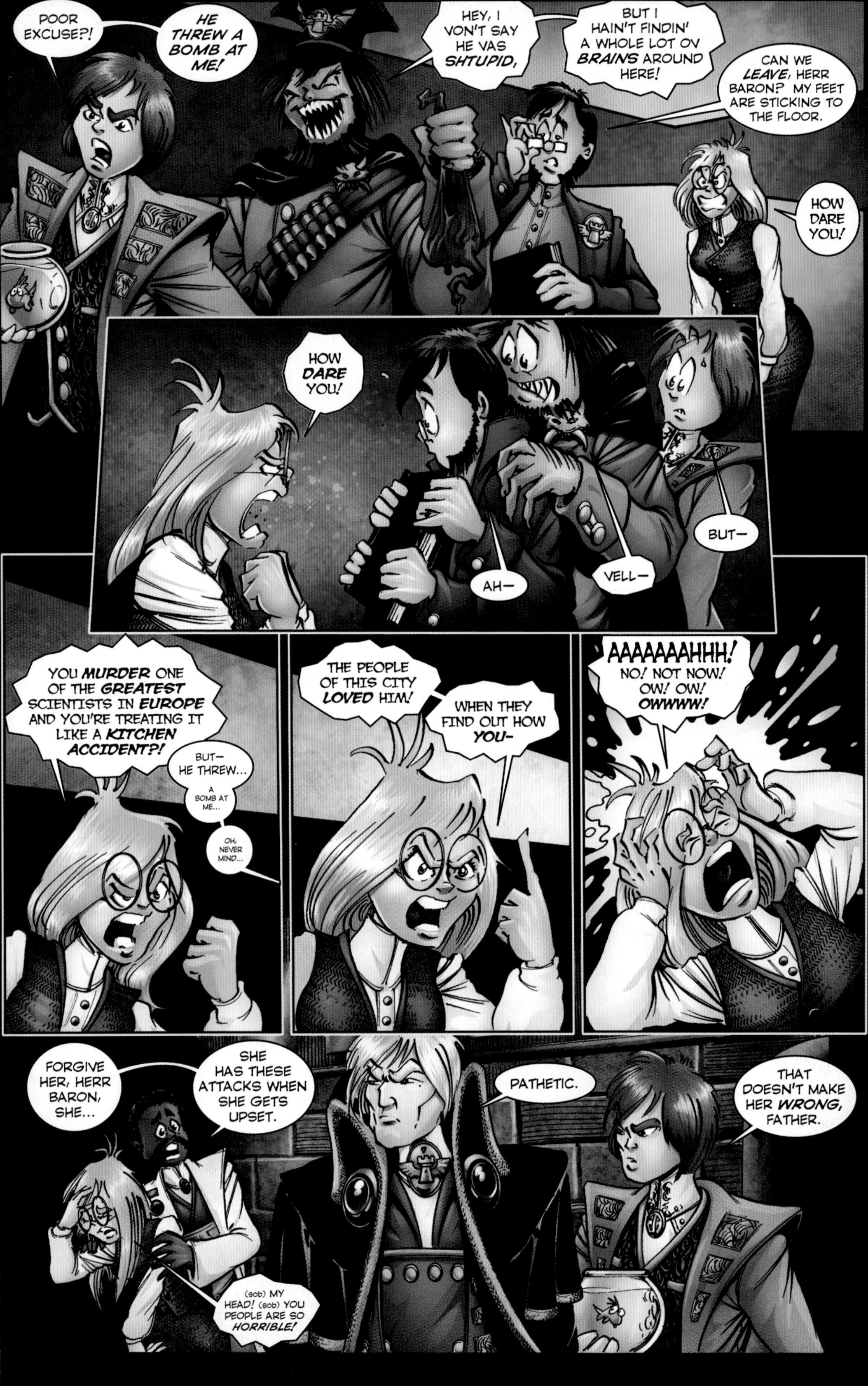
POOR EXCUSE?!
HE THREW A BOMB AT ME!
HEY, I VON'T SAY HE VAS SHTUPID,
BUT I HAIN'T FINDIN' A WHOLE LOT OV BRAINS AROUND HERE!
CAN WE LEAVE, HERR BARON? MY FEET ARE STICKING TO THE FLOOR.
HOW DARE YOU!
HOW DARE YOU!
AH—
VELL—
BUT—
YOU MURDER ONE OF THE GREATEST SCIENTISTS IN EUROPE AND YOU'RE TREATING IT LIKE A KITCHEN ACCIDENT?!
BUT— HE THREW...
A BOMB AT ME...
OH, NEVER MIND...
THE PEOPLE OF THIS CITY LOVED HIM!
WHEN THEY FIND OUT HOW YOU-
AAAAAAAHHH! NO! NOT NOW! OW! OW! OWWWW!
FORGIVE HER, HERR BARON, SHE...
SHE HAS THESE ATTACKS WHEN SHE GETS UPSET.
PATHETIC.
THAT DOESN'T MAKE HER WRONG, FATHER.
(sob) MY HEAD! (sob) YOU PEOPLE ARE SO HORRIBLE!

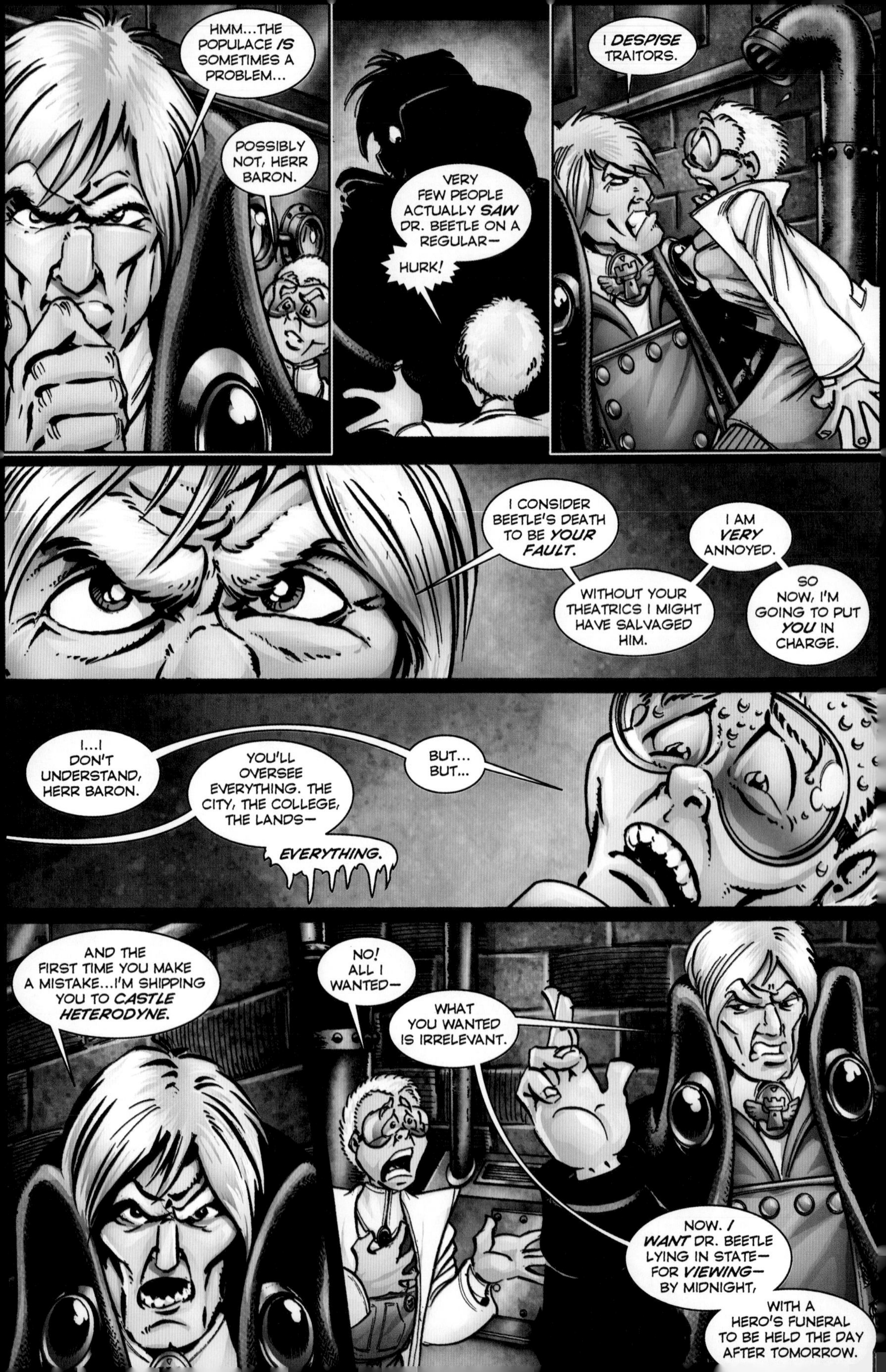
HMM...THE POPULACE *IS* SOMETIMES A PROBLEM...
POSSIBLY NOT, HERR BARON.
VERY FEW PEOPLE ACTUALLY *SAW* DR. BEETLE ON A REGULAR—
HURK!
I *DESPISE* TRAITORS.
I CONSIDER BEETLE'S DEATH TO BE *YOUR FAULT*.
WITHOUT YOUR THEATRICS I MIGHT HAVE SALVAGED HIM.
I AM *VERY* ANNOYED.
SO NOW, I'M GOING TO PUT *YOU* IN CHARGE.
I...I DON'T UNDERSTAND, HERR BARON.
YOU'LL OVERSEE EVERYTHING. THE CITY, THE COLLEGE, THE LANDS—
EVERYTHING.
BUT... BUT...
AND THE FIRST TIME YOU MAKE A MISTAKE...I'M SHIPPING YOU TO *CASTLE HETERODYNE*.
NO! ALL I WANTED—
WHAT YOU WANTED IS IRRELEVANT.
NOW. *I WANT* DR. BEETLE LYING IN STATE— FOR *VIEWING*— BY MIDNIGHT,
WITH A HERO'S FUNERAL TO BE HELD THE DAY AFTER TOMORROW.

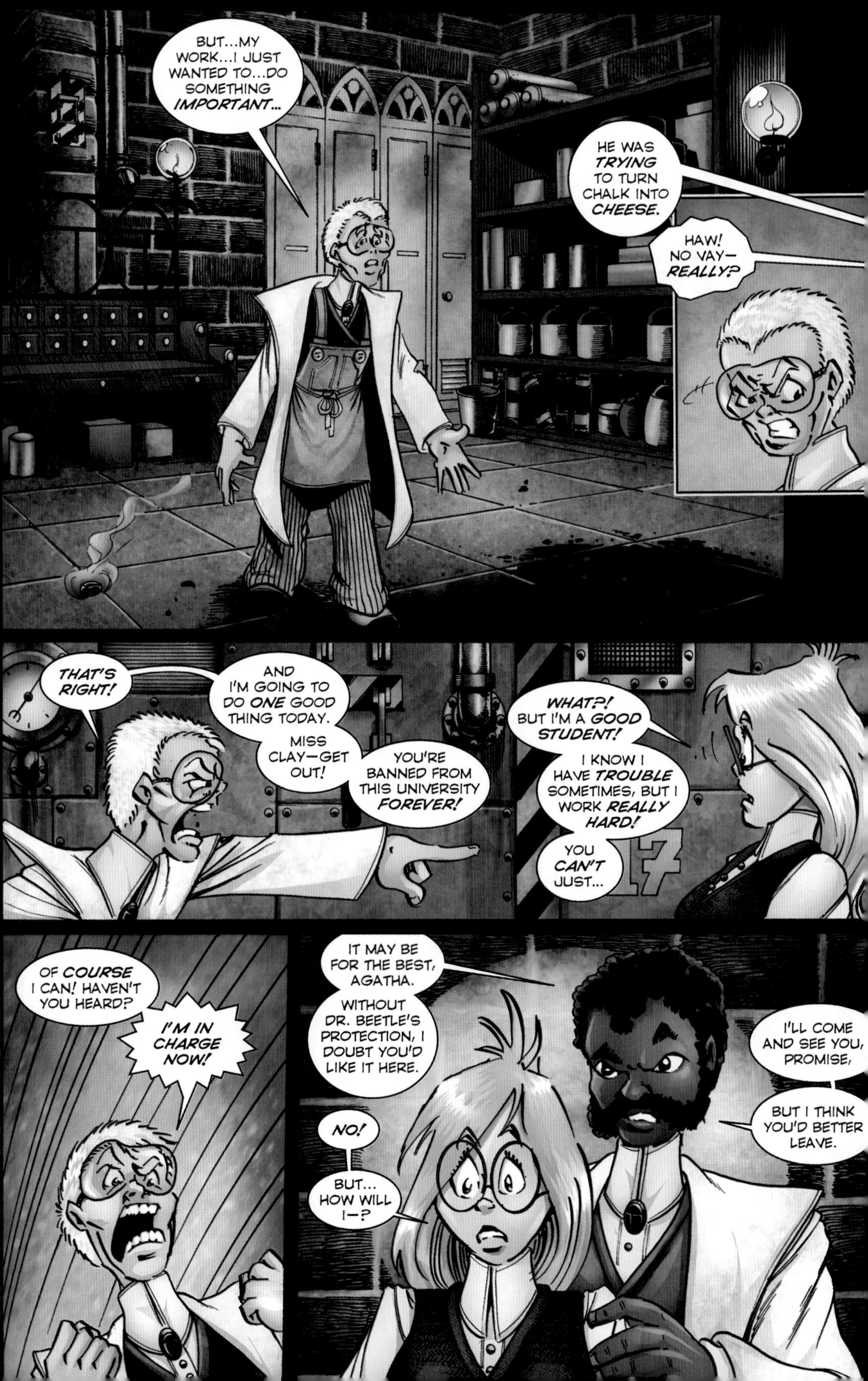

BUT...MY WORK...I JUST WANTED TO...DO SOMETHING *IMPORTANT*...
HE WAS *TRYING* TO TURN CHALK INTO *CHEESE.*
HAW! NO VAY— *REALLY?*
THAT'S RIGHT!
AND I'M GOING TO DO *ONE* GOOD THING TODAY.
MISS CLAY—GET OUT!
YOU'RE BANNED FROM THIS UNIVERSITY *FOREVER!*
WHAT?! BUT I'M A *GOOD STUDENT!*
I KNOW I HAVE *TROUBLE* SOMETIMES, BUT I WORK *REALLY HARD!*
YOU *CAN'T* JUST...
OF *COURSE* I CAN! HAVEN'T YOU HEARD?
I'M IN CHARGE NOW!
IT MAY BE FOR THE BEST, AGATHA.
WITHOUT DR. BEETLE'S PROTECTION, I DOUBT YOU'D LIKE IT HERE.
NO!
BUT... HOW WILL I—?
I'LL COME AND SEE YOU, PROMISE,
BUT I THINK YOU'D BETTER LEAVE.

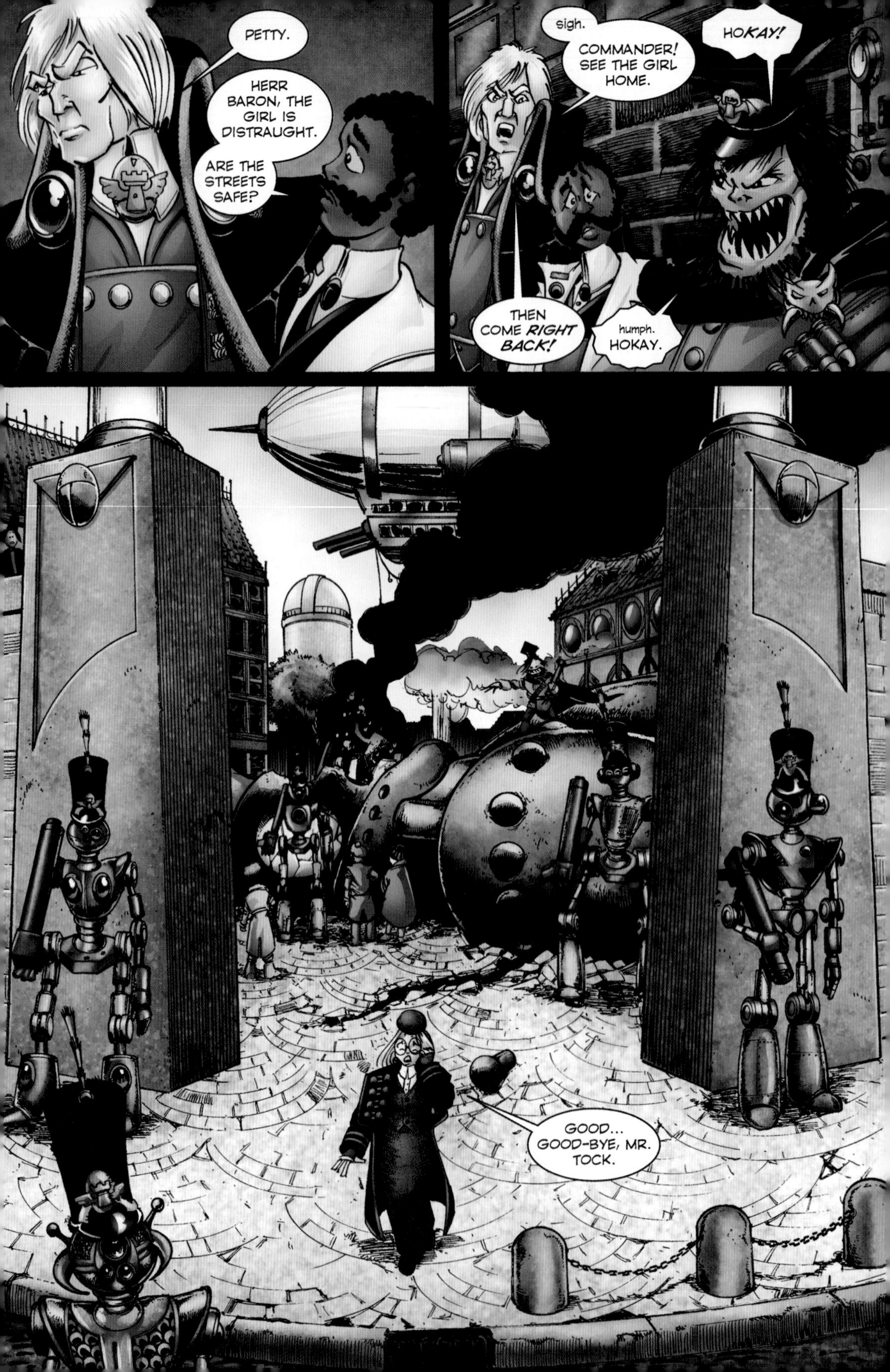
PETTY.
HERR BARON, THE GIRL IS DISTRAUGHT.
ARE THE STREETS SAFE?
sigh.
COMMANDER! SEE THE GIRL HOME.
HOKAY!
THEN COME RIGHT BACK!
humph. HOKAY.
GOOD... GOOD-BYE, MR. TOCK.

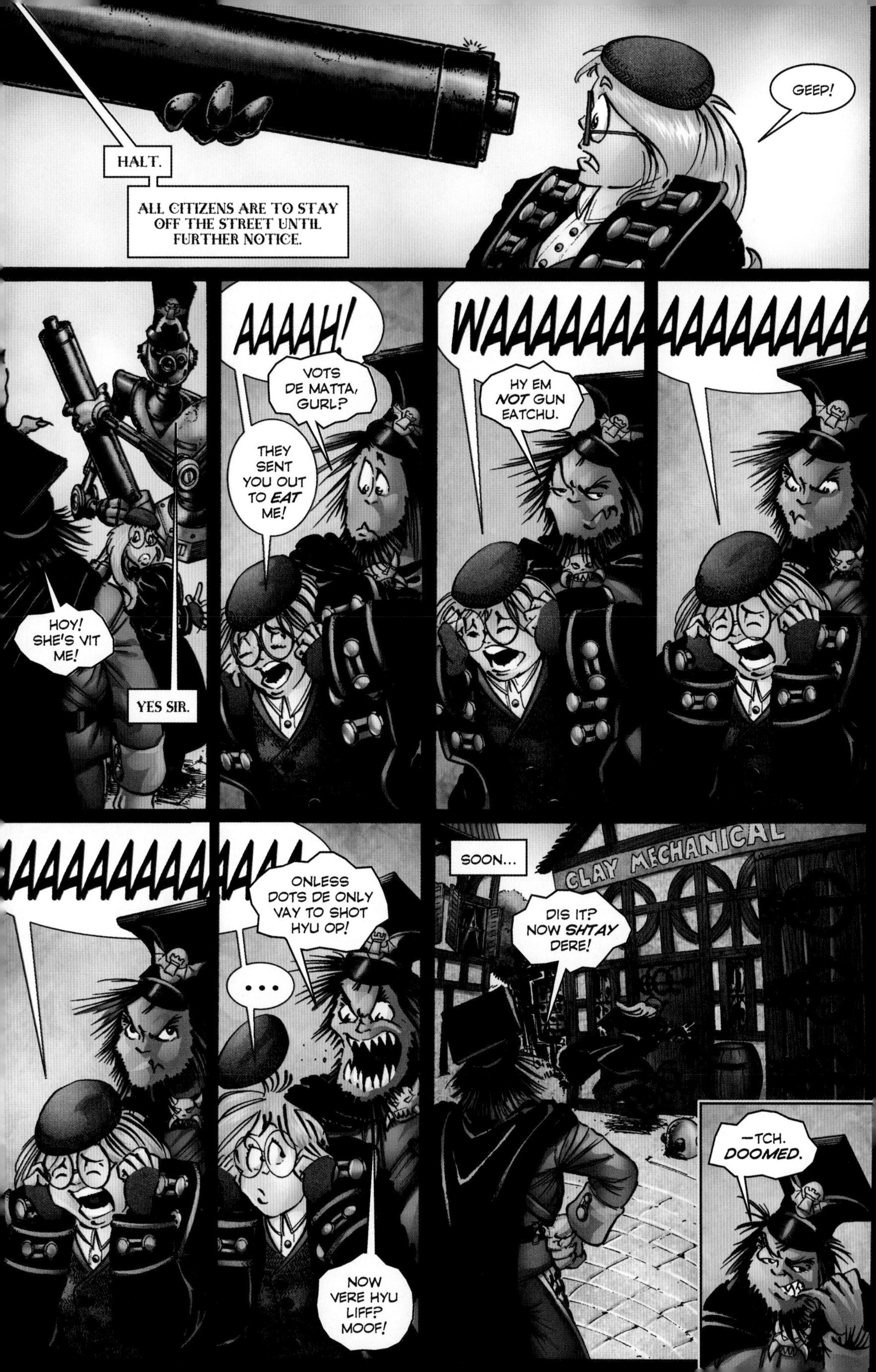
HALT.
ALL CITIZENS ARE TO STAY OFF THE STREET UNTIL FURTHER NOTICE.
GEEP!
HOY! SHE'S VIT ME!
YES SIR.
AAAAH!
THEY SENT YOU OUT TO EAT ME!
VOTS DE MATTA, GURL?
WAAAAAAAAAAAAAAAAAAAAAAAAAAAAAAA
HY EM NOT GUN EATCHU.
...
ONLESS DOTS DE ONLY VAY TO SHOT HYU OP!
NOW VERE HYU LIFF? MOOF!
SOON...
CLAY MECHANICAL
DIS IT? NOW SHTAY DERE!
—TCH. DOOMED.

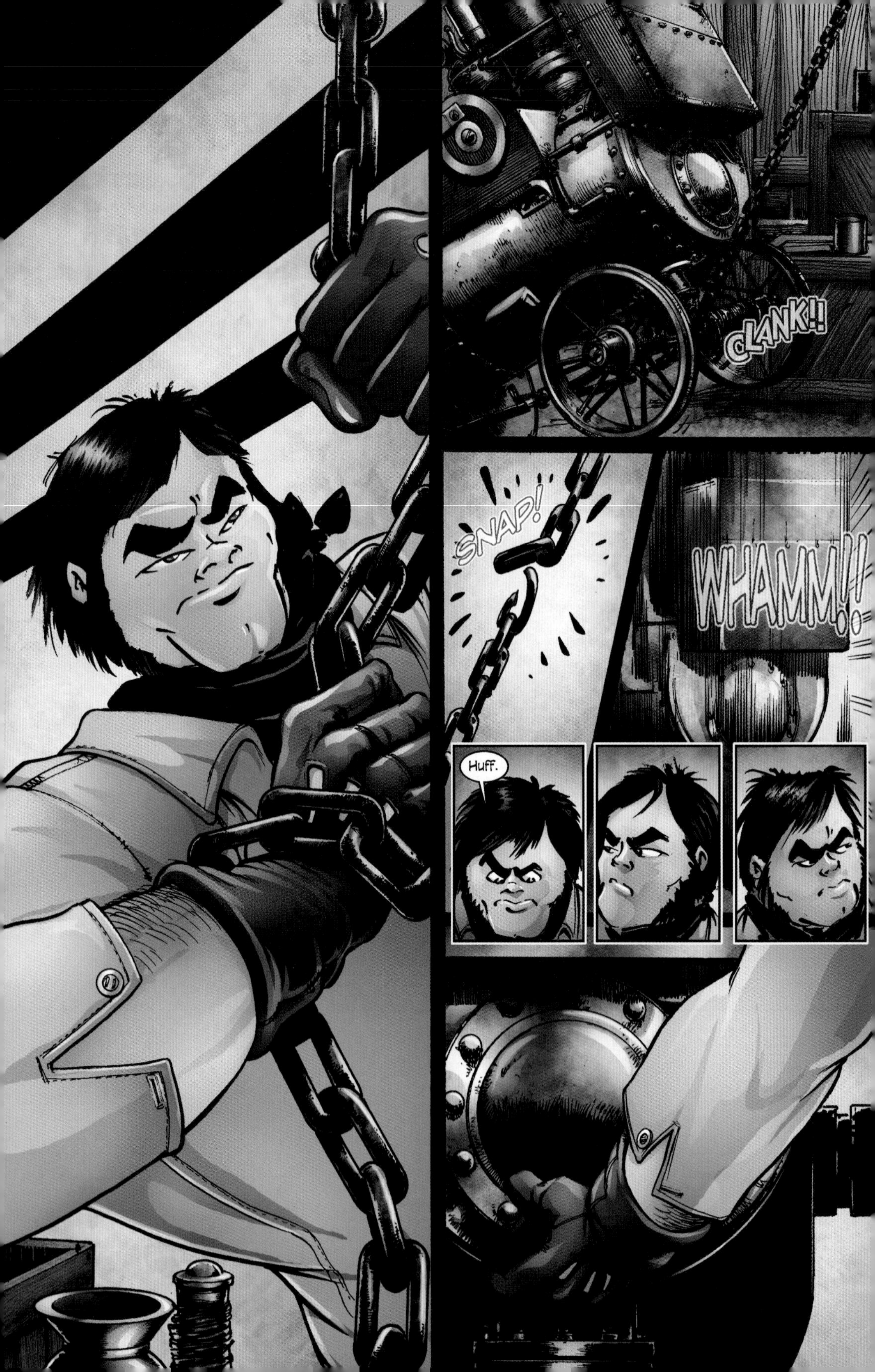
CLANK!!
SNAP!
WHAMM!!
Huff.

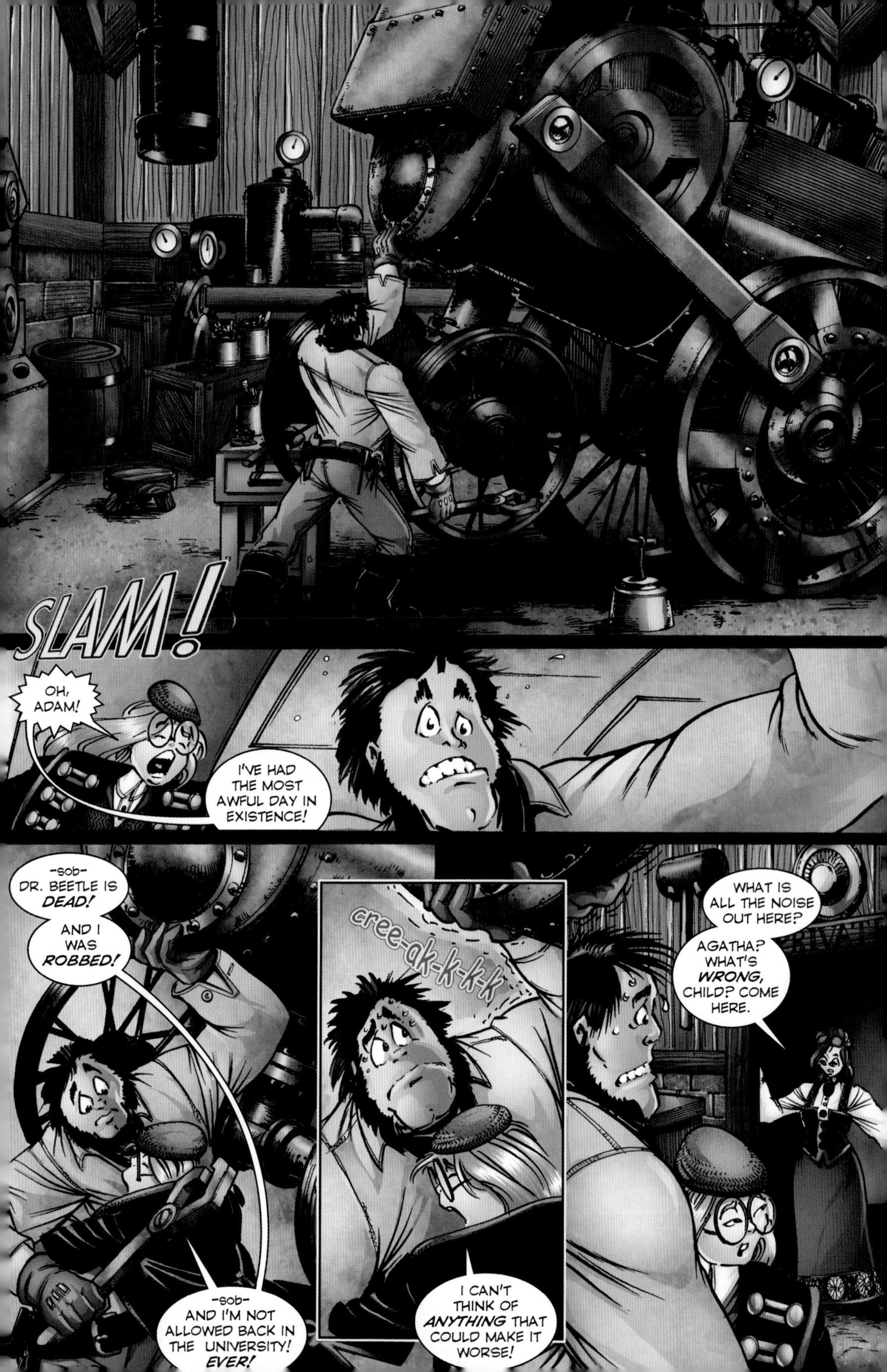
SLAM!
OH, ADAM!
I'VE HAD THE MOST AWFUL DAY IN EXISTENCE!
-sob- DR. BEETLE IS DEAD!
AND I WAS ROBBED!
-sob- AND I'M NOT ALLOWED BACK IN THE UNIVERSITY! EVER!
cree-ak-k-k-k-k
I CAN'T THINK OF ANYTHING THAT COULD MAKE IT WORSE!
WHAT IS ALL THE NOISE OUT HERE?
AGATHA? WHAT'S WRONG, CHILD? COME HERE.

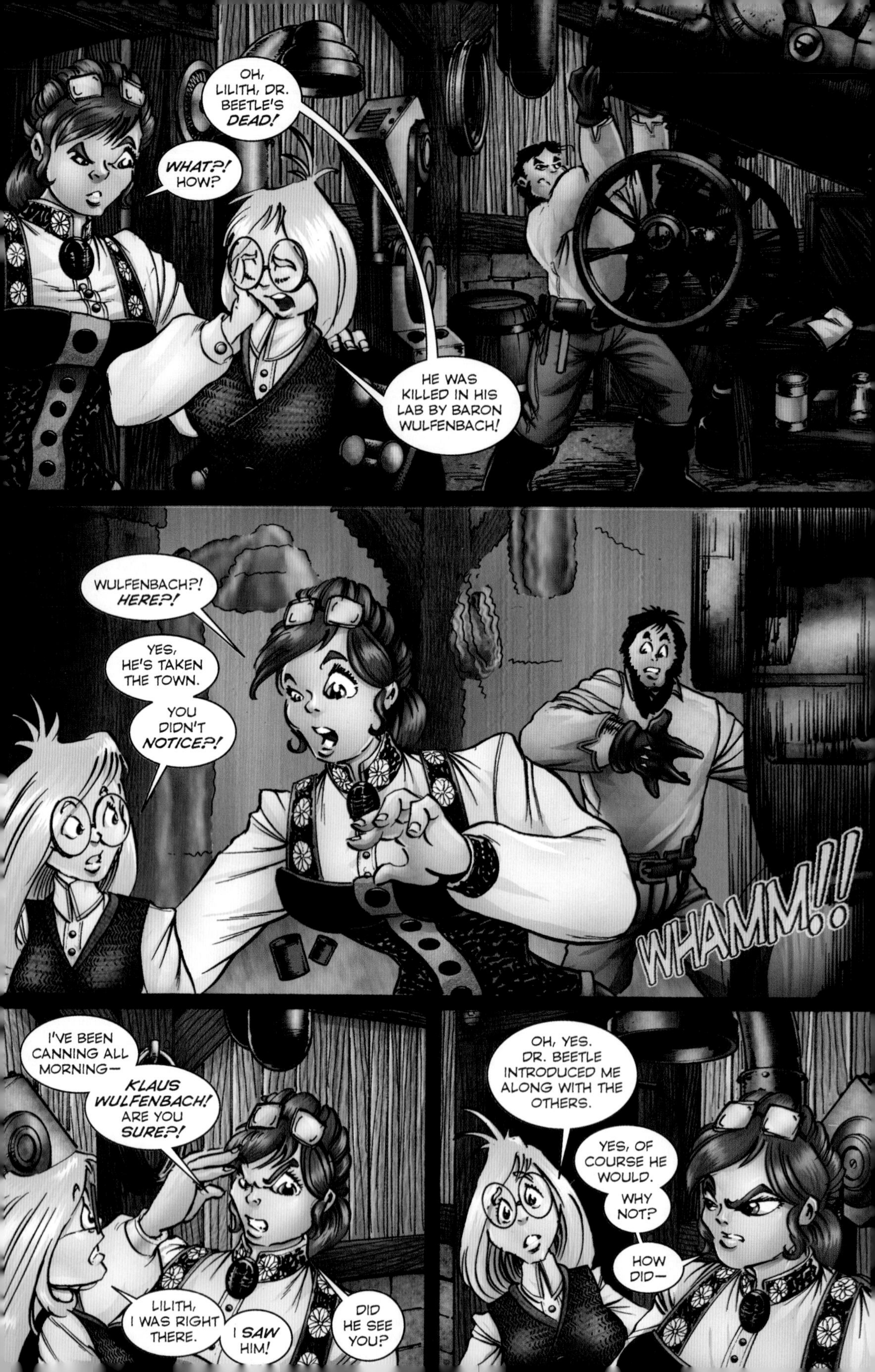
OH, LILITH, DR. BEETLE'S *DEAD!*
WHAT?! HOW?
HE WAS KILLED IN HIS LAB BY BARON WULFENBACH!
WULFENBACH?! *HERE?!*
YES, HE'S TAKEN THE TOWN.
YOU DIDN'T *NOTICE?!*
WHAMM!!
I'VE BEEN CANNING ALL MORNING—
KLAUS WULFENBACH! ARE YOU *SURE?!*
LILITH, I WAS RIGHT THERE.
I *SAW* HIM!
DID HE SEE YOU?
OH, YES. DR. BEETLE INTRODUCED ME ALONG WITH THE OTHERS.
YES, OF COURSE HE WOULD.
WHY NOT?
HOW DID—

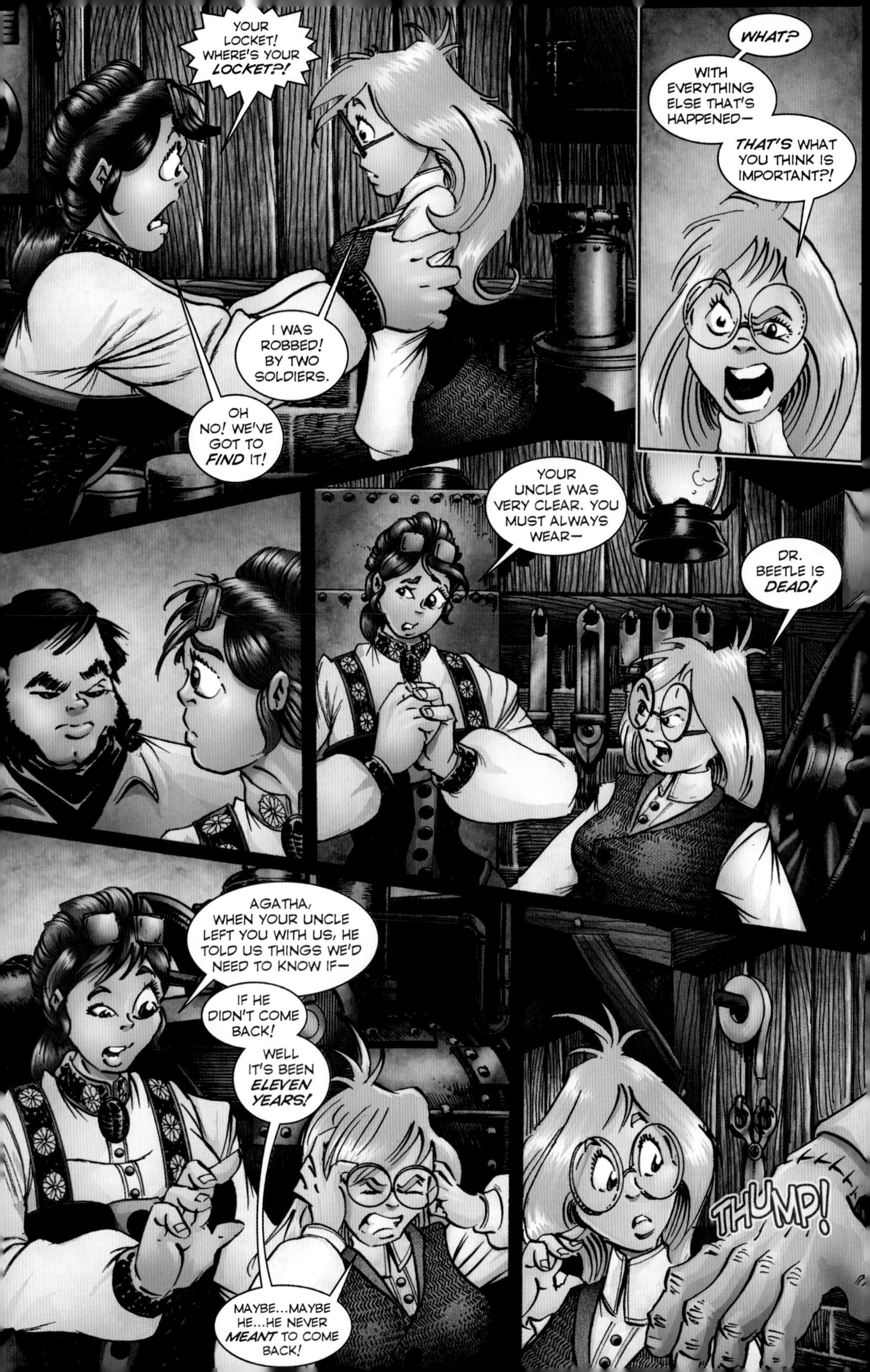

YOUR LOCKET! WHERE'S YOUR LOCKET?!
I WAS ROBBED! BY TWO SOLDIERS.
OH NO! WE'VE GOT TO FIND IT!
WHAT?
WITH EVERYTHING ELSE THAT'S HAPPENED—
THAT'S WHAT YOU THINK IS IMPORTANT?!
YOUR UNCLE WAS VERY CLEAR. YOU MUST ALWAYS WEAR—
DR. BEETLE IS DEAD!
AGATHA, WHEN YOUR UNCLE LEFT YOU WITH US, HE TOLD US THINGS WE'D NEED TO KNOW IF—
IF HE DIDN'T COME BACK!
WELL IT'S BEEN ELEVEN YEARS!
MAYBE...MAYBE HE...HE NEVER MEANT TO COME BACK!
THUMP!

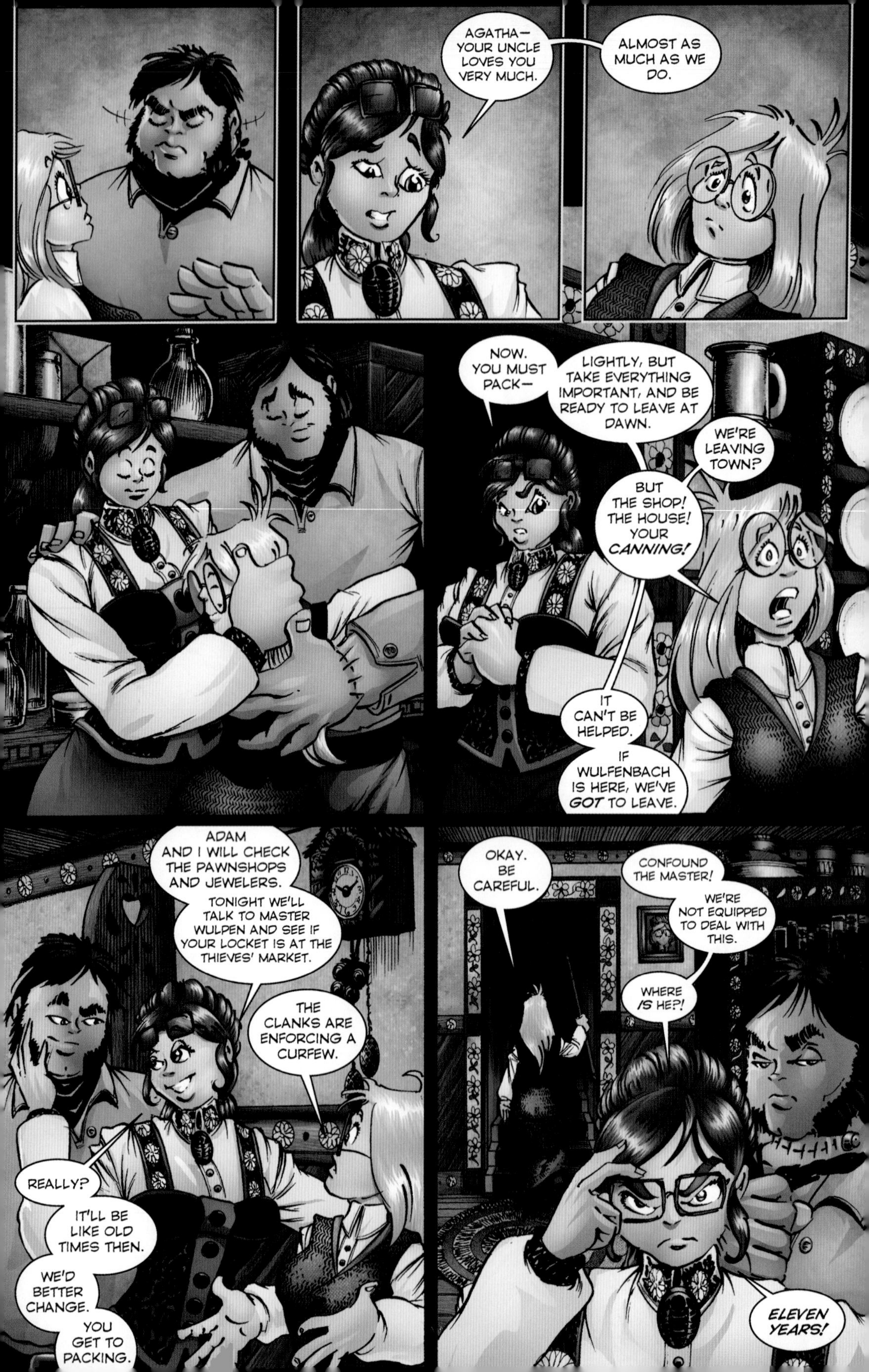
AGATHA—
YOUR UNCLE LOVES YOU VERY MUCH.
ALMOST AS MUCH AS WE DO.
NOW. YOU MUST PACK—
LIGHTLY, BUT TAKE EVERYTHING IMPORTANT, AND BE READY TO LEAVE AT DAWN.
WE'RE LEAVING TOWN?
BUT THE SHOP! THE HOUSE! YOUR *CANNING!*
IT CAN'T BE HELPED.
IF WULFENBACH IS HERE, WE'VE *GOT* TO LEAVE.
ADAM AND I WILL CHECK THE PAWNSHOPS AND JEWELERS.
TONIGHT WE'LL TALK TO MASTER WULPEN AND SEE IF YOUR LOCKET IS AT THE THIEVES' MARKET.
THE CLANKS ARE ENFORCING A CURFEW.
REALLY?
IT'LL BE LIKE OLD TIMES THEN.
WE'D BETTER CHANGE.
YOU GET TO PACKING.
OKAY. BE CAREFUL.
CONFOUND THE MASTER!
WE'RE NOT EQUIPPED TO DEAL WITH THIS.
WHERE *IS* HE?!
ELEVEN YEARS!

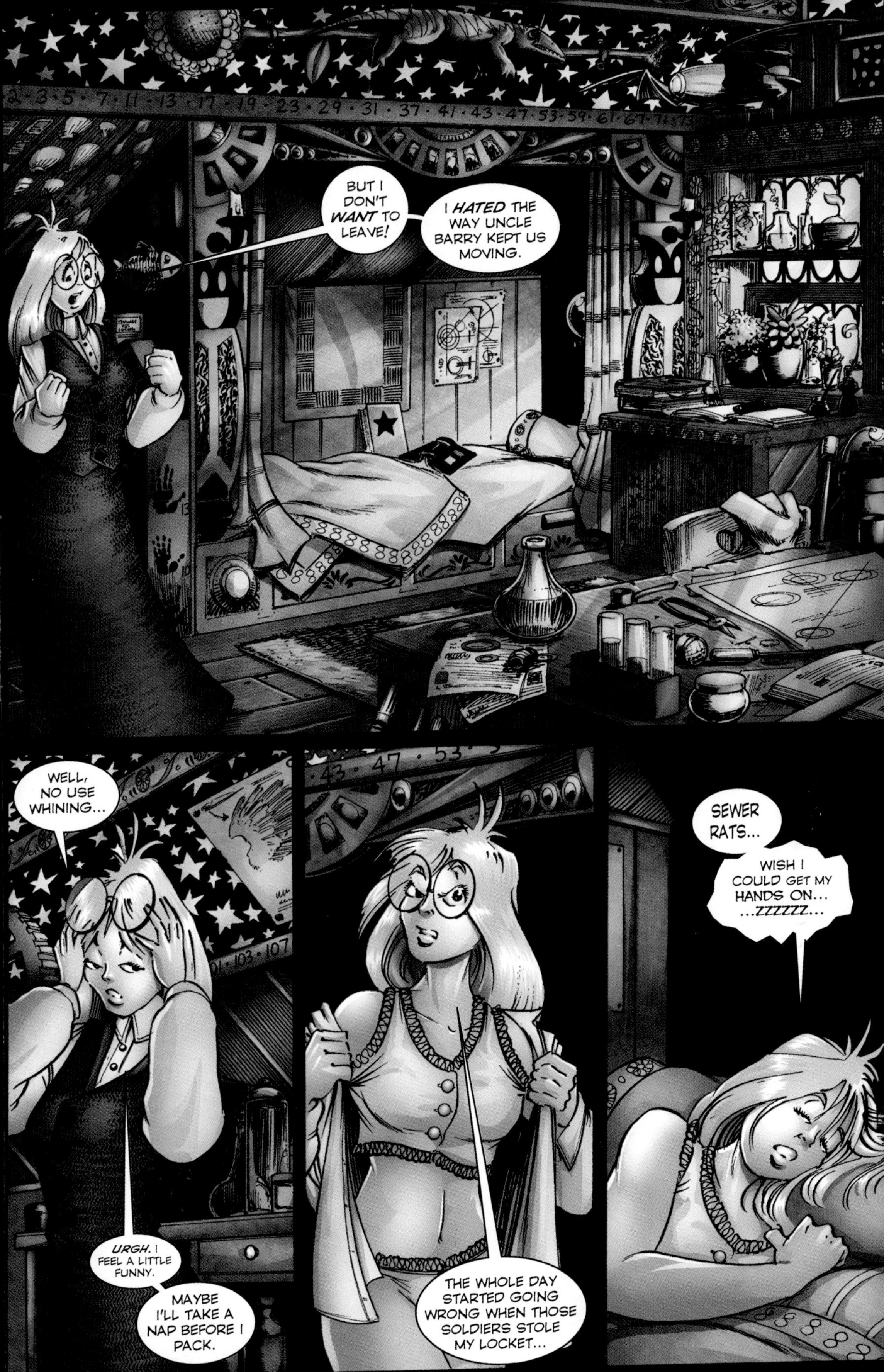
2 · 3 · 5 · 7 · 11 · 13 · 17 · 19 · 23 · 29 · 31 · 37 · 41 · 43 · 47 · 53 · 59 · 61 · 67 · 71 · 73
BUT I DON'T *WANT* TO LEAVE!
I *HATED* THE WAY UNCLE BARRY KEPT US MOVING.
WELL, NO USE WHINING...
URGH. I FEEL A LITTLE FUNNY.
MAYBE I'LL TAKE A NAP BEFORE I PACK.
THE WHOLE DAY STARTED GOING WRONG WHEN THOSE SOLDIERS STOLE MY LOCKET...
SEWER RATS...
WISH I COULD GET MY HANDS ON... ...ZZZZZZ...

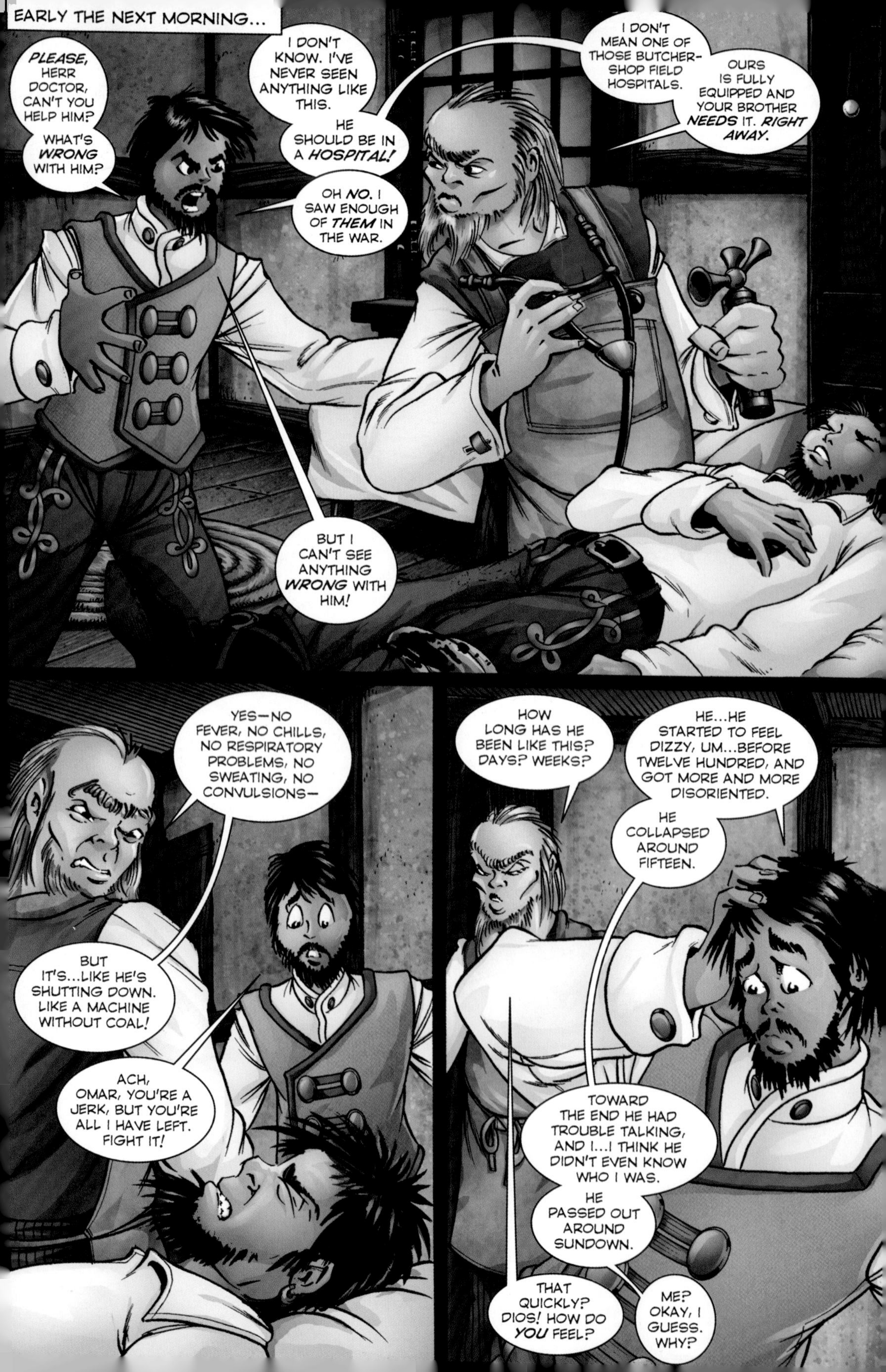
EARLY THE NEXT MORNING...
PLEASE, HERR DOCTOR, CAN'T YOU HELP HIM?
WHAT'S WRONG WITH HIM?
I DON'T KNOW. I'VE NEVER SEEN ANYTHING LIKE THIS.
HE SHOULD BE IN A HOSPITAL!
OH NO. I SAW ENOUGH OF THEM IN THE WAR.
I DON'T MEAN ONE OF THOSE BUTCHER-SHOP FIELD HOSPITALS.
OURS IS FULLY EQUIPPED AND YOUR BROTHER NEEDS IT. RIGHT AWAY.
BUT I CAN'T SEE ANYTHING WRONG WITH HIM!
YES—NO FEVER, NO CHILLS, NO RESPIRATORY PROBLEMS, NO SWEATING, NO CONVULSIONS—
BUT IT'S...LIKE HE'S SHUTTING DOWN. LIKE A MACHINE WITHOUT COAL!
ACH, OMAR, YOU'RE A JERK, BUT YOU'RE ALL I HAVE LEFT. FIGHT IT!
HOW LONG HAS HE BEEN LIKE THIS? DAYS? WEEKS?
HE...HE STARTED TO FEEL DIZZY, UM...BEFORE TWELVE HUNDRED, AND GOT MORE AND MORE DISORIENTED.
HE COLLAPSED AROUND FIFTEEN.
TOWARD THE END HE HAD TROUBLE TALKING, AND I...I THINK HE DIDN'T EVEN KNOW WHO I WAS.
HE PASSED OUT AROUND SUNDOWN.
THAT QUICKLY? DIOS! HOW DO YOU FEEL?
ME? OKAY, I GUESS. WHY?

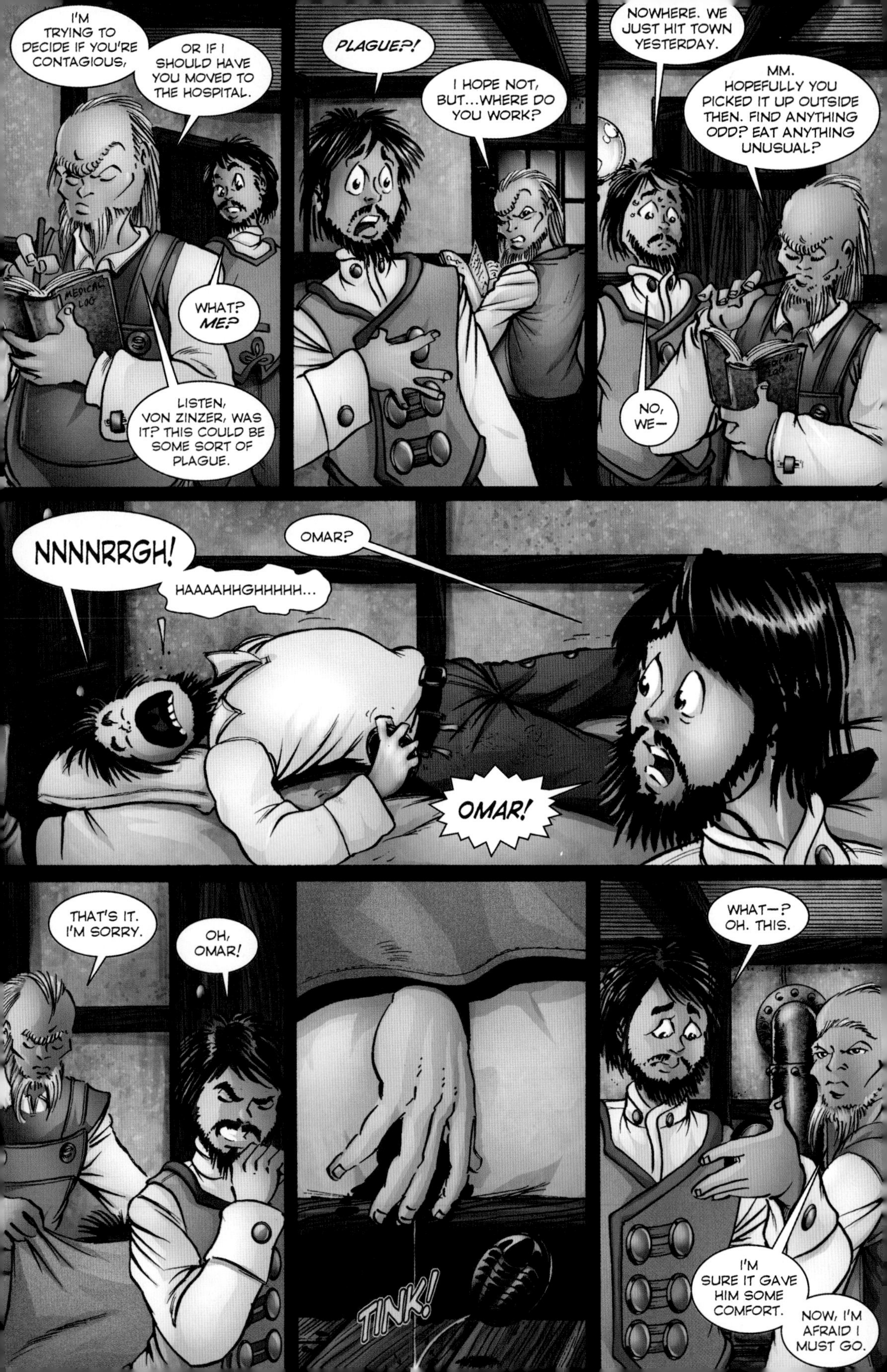
I'M TRYING TO DECIDE IF YOU'RE CONTAGIOUS,
OR IF I SHOULD HAVE YOU MOVED TO THE HOSPITAL.
MEDICAL LOG
WHAT? ME?
LISTEN, VON ZINZER, WAS IT? THIS COULD BE SOME SORT OF PLAGUE.
PLAGUE?!
I HOPE NOT, BUT...WHERE DO YOU WORK?
NOWHERE. WE JUST HIT TOWN YESTERDAY.
MM. HOPEFULLY YOU PICKED IT UP OUTSIDE THEN. FIND ANYTHING ODD? EAT ANYTHING UNUSUAL?
NO, WE—
NNNNRRGH!
HAAAAHHGHHHHH...
OMAR?
!
OMAR!
THAT'S IT. I'M SORRY.
OH, OMAR!
TINK!
WHAT—? OH. THIS.
I'M SURE IT GAVE HIM SOME COMFORT.
NOW, I'M AFRAID I MUST GO.

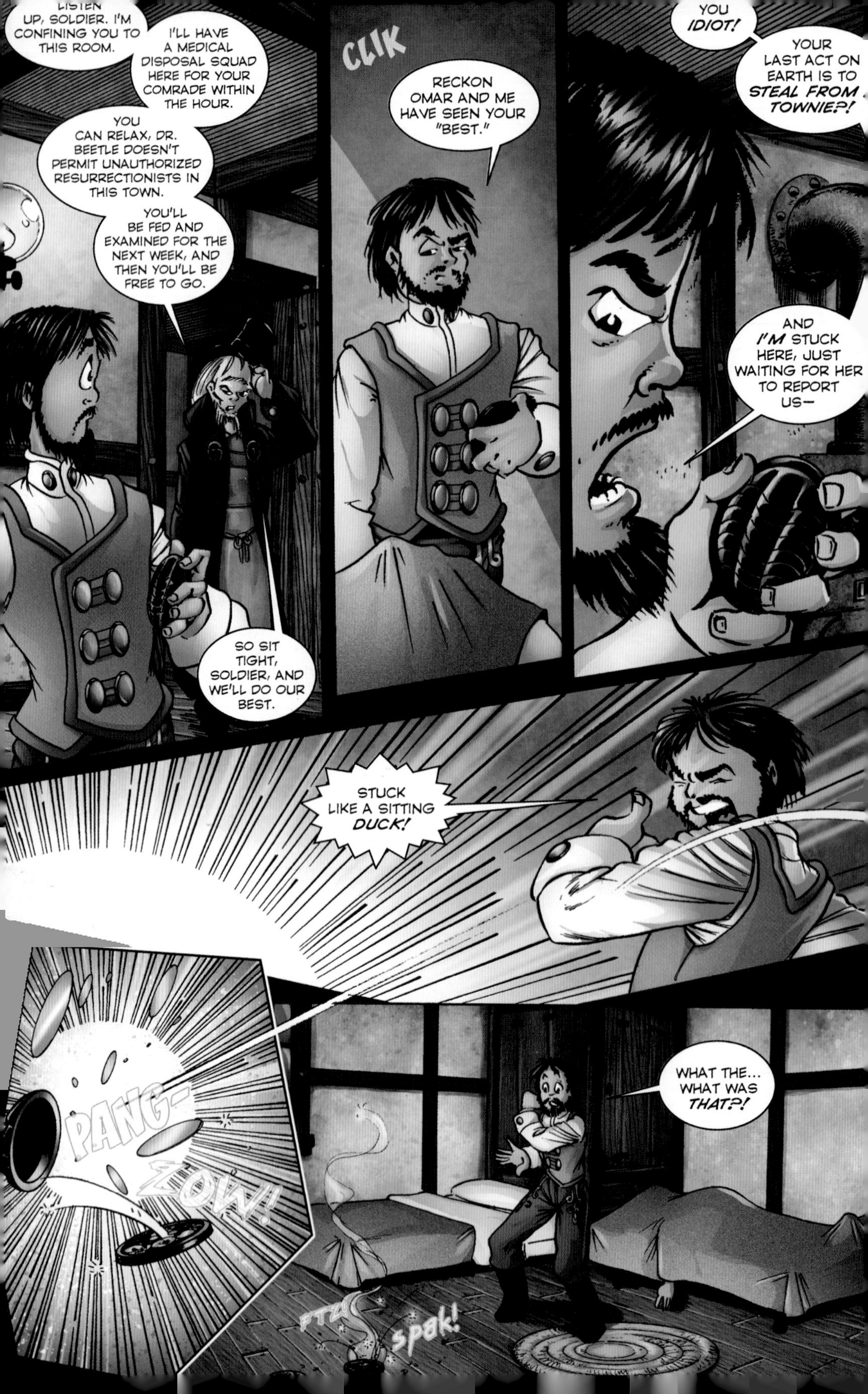
LISTEN UP, SOLDIER. I'M CONFINING YOU TO THIS ROOM.
I'LL HAVE A MEDICAL DISPOSAL SQUAD HERE FOR YOUR COMRADE WITHIN THE HOUR.
YOU CAN RELAX, DR. BEETLE DOESN'T PERMIT UNAUTHORIZED RESURRECTIONISTS IN THIS TOWN.
YOU'LL BE FED AND EXAMINED FOR THE NEXT WEEK, AND THEN YOU'LL BE FREE TO GO.
SO SIT TIGHT, SOLDIER, AND WE'LL DO OUR BEST.
CLIK
RECKON OMAR AND ME HAVE SEEN YOUR "BEST."
YOU *IDIOT!*
YOUR LAST ACT ON EARTH IS TO *STEAL FROM TOWNIE?!*
AND *I'M* STUCK HERE, JUST WAITING FOR HER TO REPORT US—
STUCK LIKE A SITTING *DUCK!*
PANG-
ZOW!
FTZ
spak!
WHAT THE... WHAT WAS *THAT?!*

HUH. THIS LOCKET HAD SOME SORT OF MECHANISM INSIDE IT.

TOO COMPLICATED TO BE A WATCH.

I'VE NEVER SEEN ANYTHING LIKE THIS.

WHAT DID IT DO?!

DAUGHTER OF THUNDER...

THIS THING KILLED OMAR!

THERE'S NO PLAGUE!

YEAH, HE STARTED ACTING STRANGE AFTER THAT GIRL—

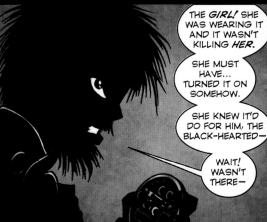

THE GIRL! SHE WAS WEARING IT AND IT WASN'T KILLING HER.

SHE MUST HAVE... TURNED IT ON SOMEHOW.

SHE KNEW IT'D DO FOR HIM, THE BLACK-HEARTED—

WAIT! WASN'T THERE—

A LABEL! YES!

"IF FOUND, RETURN TO AGATHA CLAY, CLAY MECHANICAL, FORGE STREET, BEETLEBURG. REWARD."

A REWARD, HUH? I'LL GIVE HER A REWARD A'RIGHT, AND SHE'LL MAKE NO REPORTS WHEN I'M DONE WITH HER.

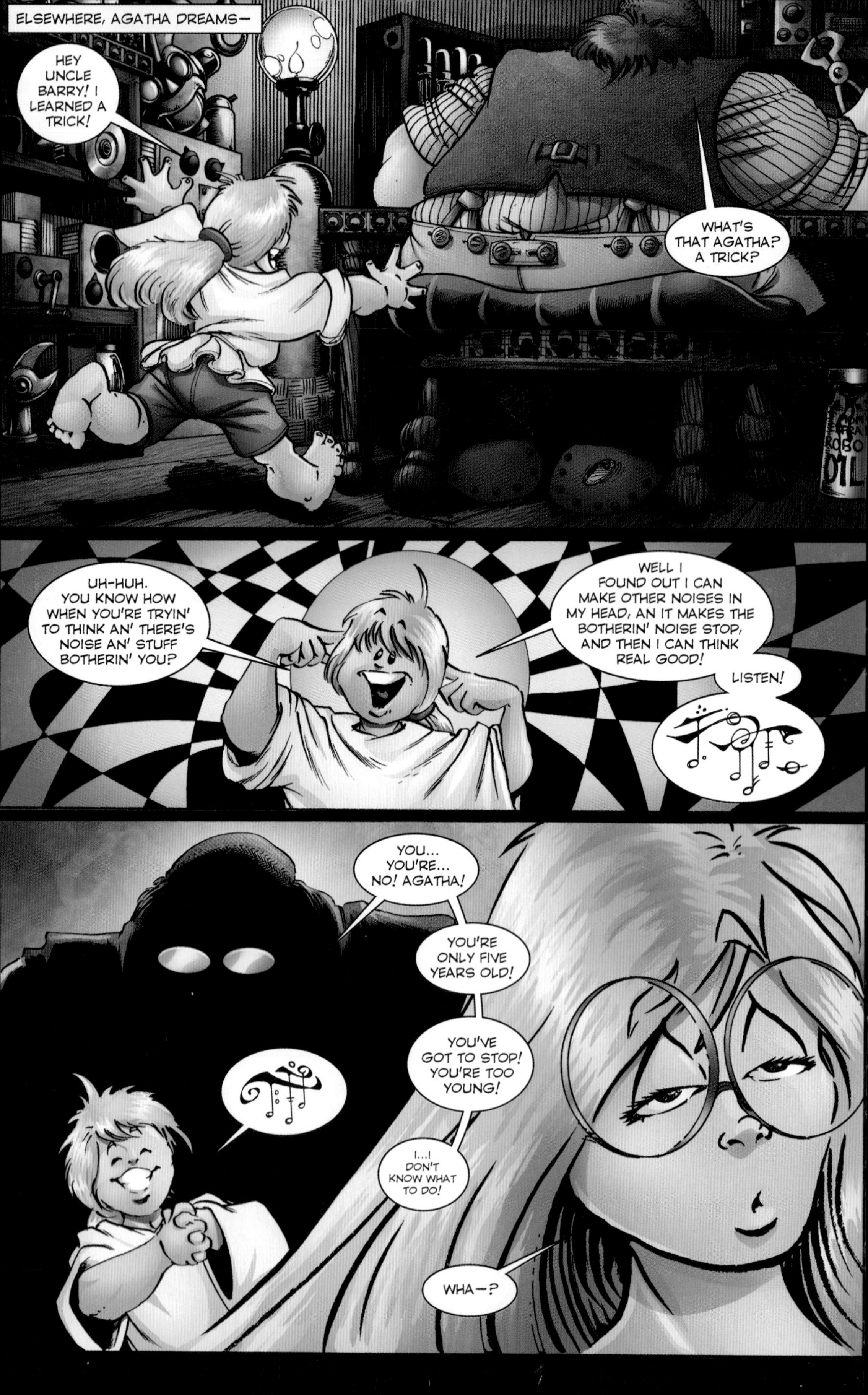
ELSEWHERE, AGATHA DREAMS—
HEY UNCLE BARRY! I LEARNED A TRICK!
WHAT'S THAT AGATHA? A TRICK?
UH-HUH. YOU KNOW HOW WHEN YOU'RE TRYIN' TO THINK AN' THERE'S NOISE AN' STUFF BOTHERIN' YOU?
WELL I FOUND OUT I CAN MAKE OTHER NOISES IN MY HEAD, AN IT MAKES THE BOTHERIN' NOISE STOP, AND THEN I CAN THINK REAL GOOD!
LISTEN!
YOU... YOU'RE... NO! AGATHA!
YOU'RE ONLY FIVE YEARS OLD!
YOU'VE GOT TO STOP! YOU'RE TOO YOUNG!
I...I DON'T KNOW WHAT TO DO!
WHA—?

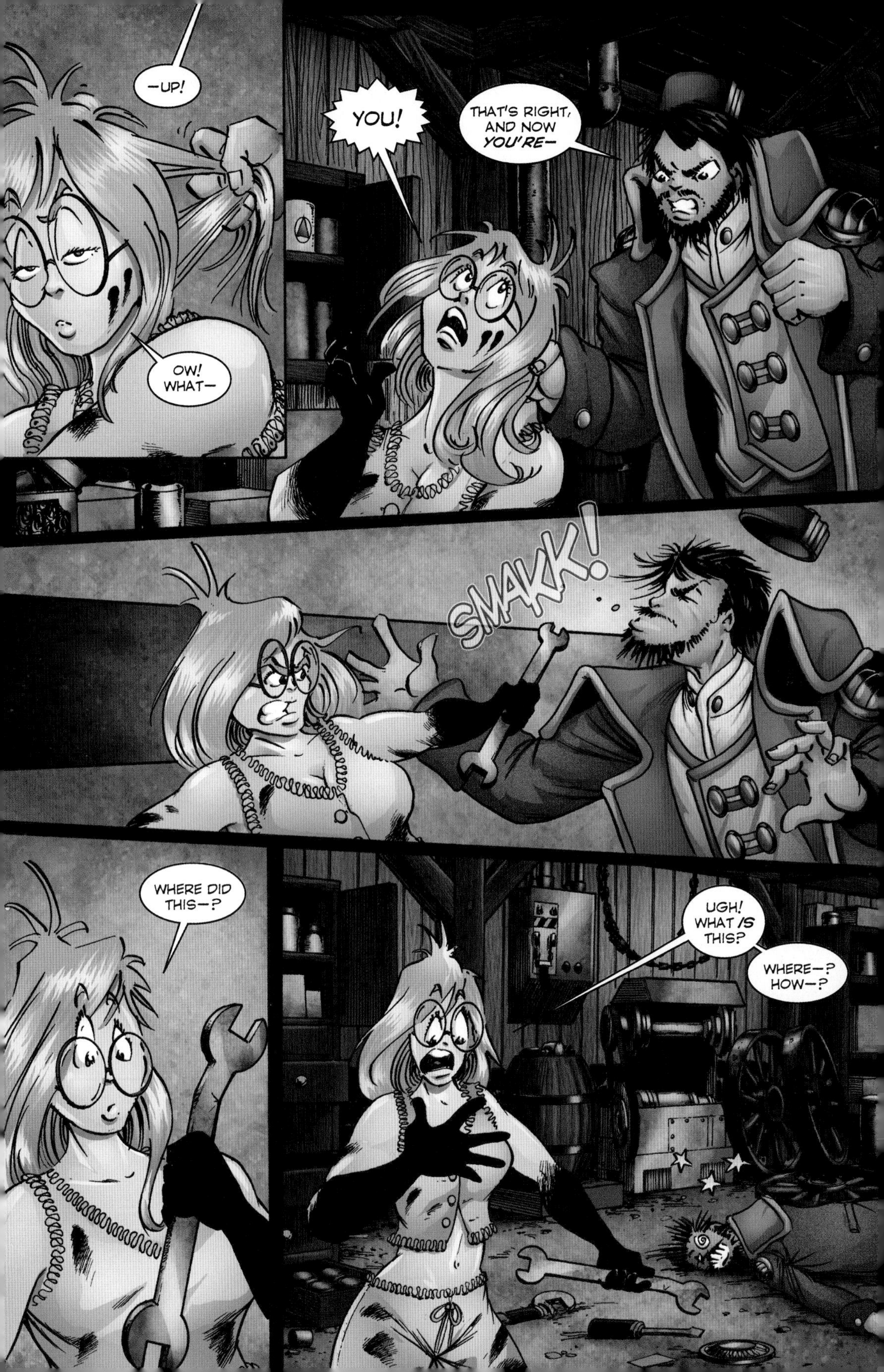
—UP!
OW! WHAT—
YOU!
THAT'S RIGHT, AND NOW *YOU'RE*—
SMAKK!
WHERE DID THIS—?
UGH! WHAT *IS* THIS?
WHERE—? HOW—?

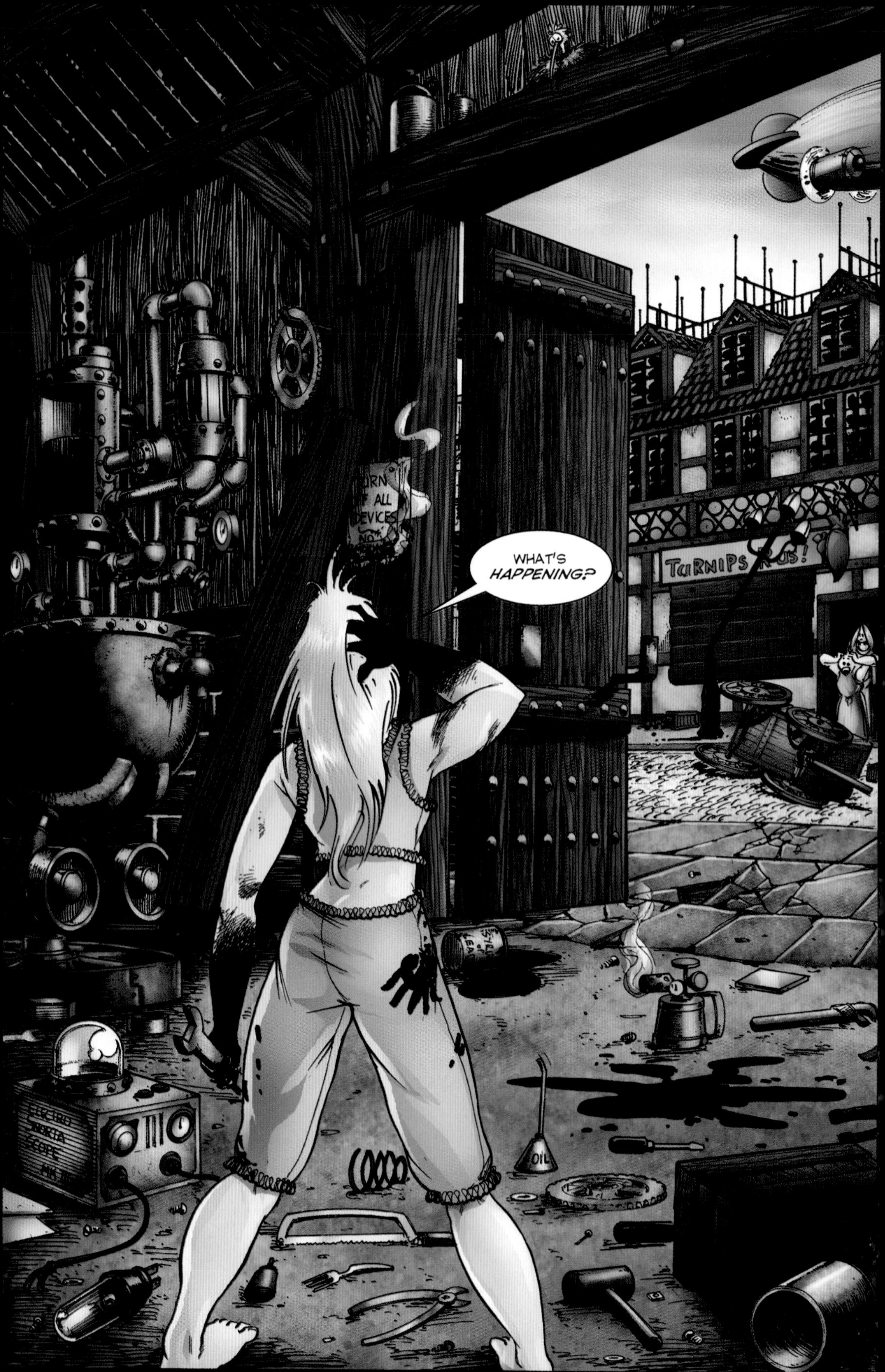
WHAT'S HAPPENING?
TURNIPS
OIL

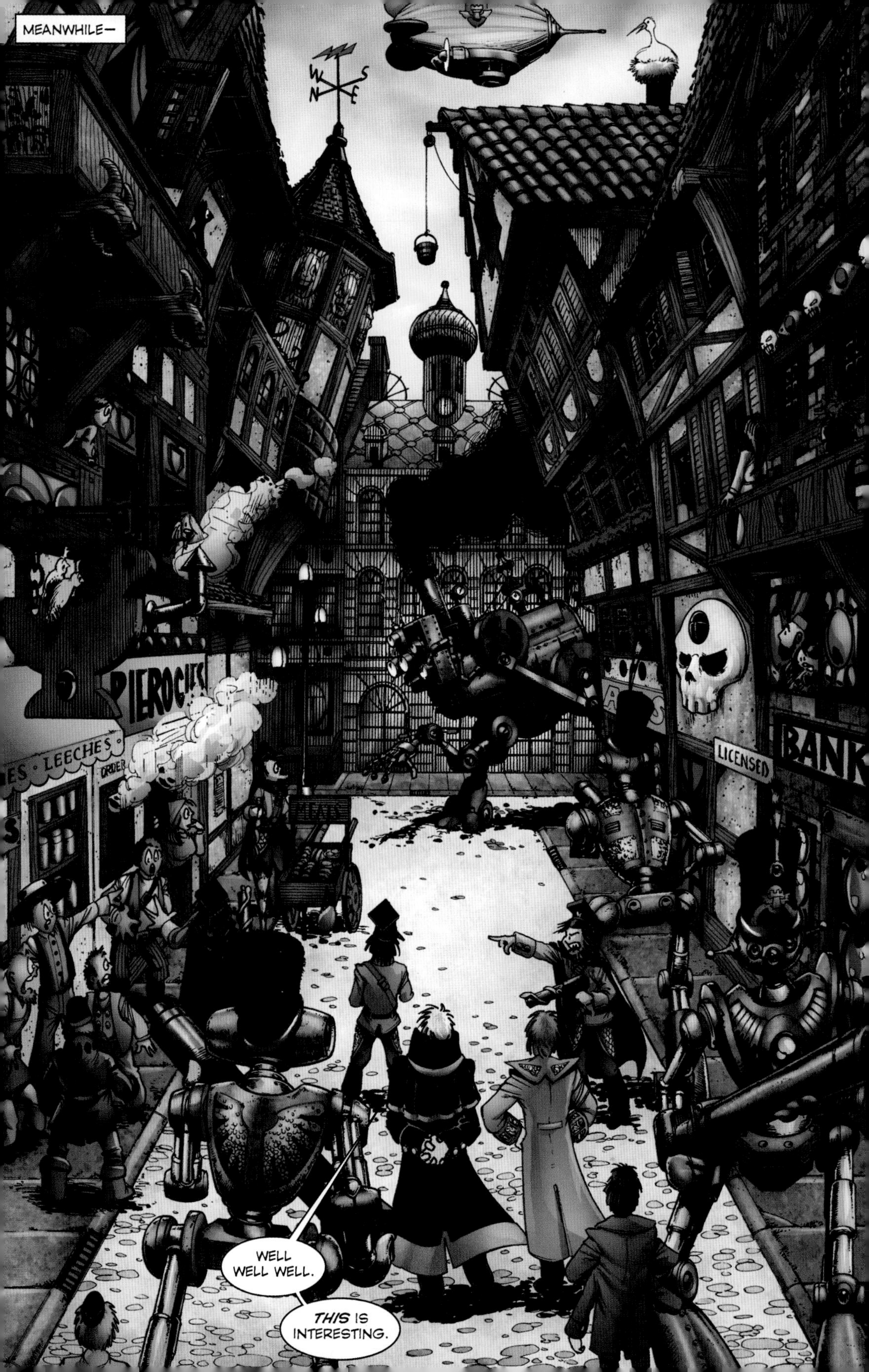
MEANWHILE—
PIEROGIES
LEECHES
LICENSED
BANK
WELL WELL WELL.
THIS IS INTERESTING.

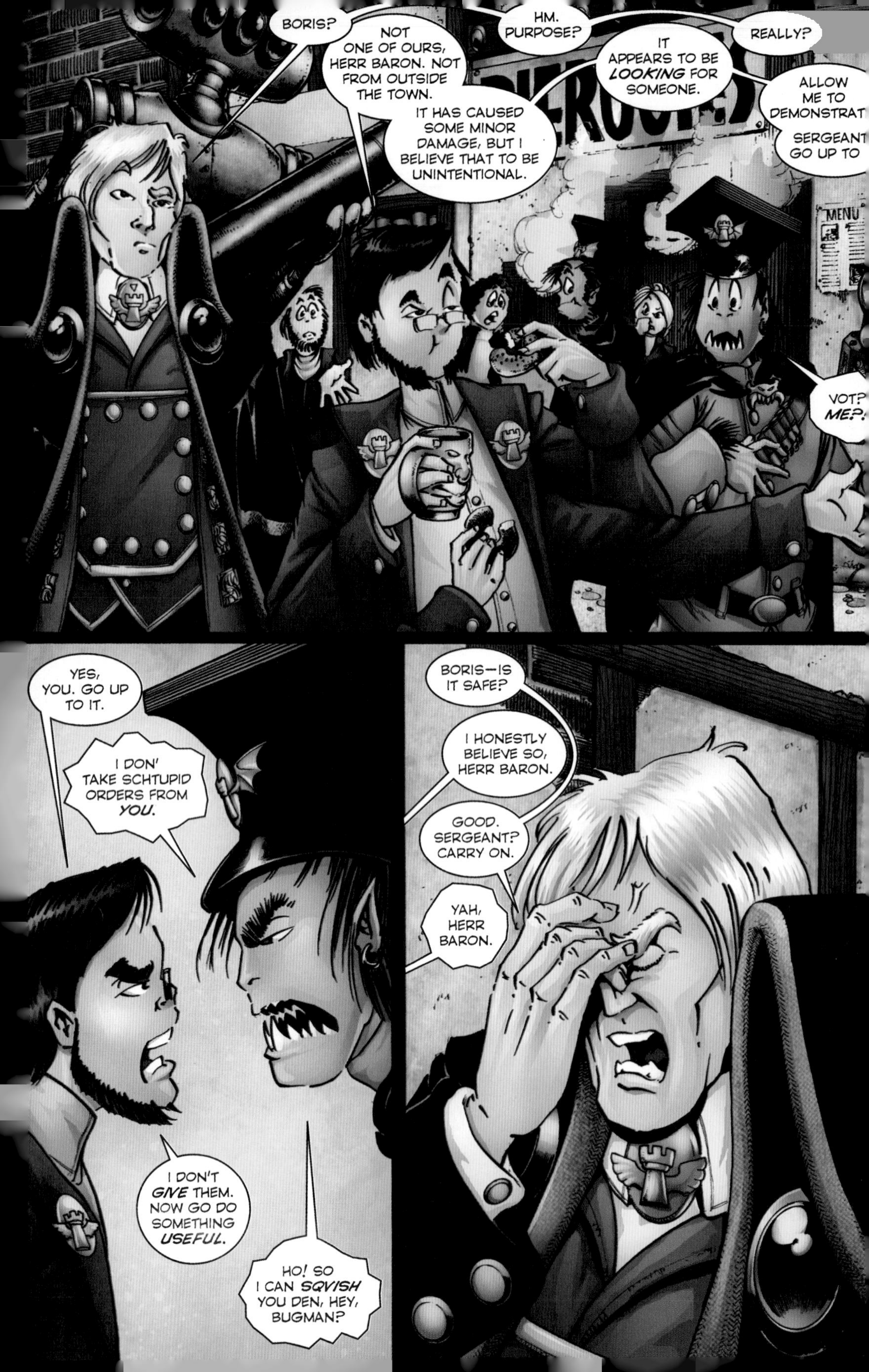
BORIS?
NOT ONE OF OURS, HERR BARON. NOT FROM OUTSIDE THE TOWN.
IT HAS CAUSED SOME MINOR DAMAGE, BUT I BELIEVE THAT TO BE UNINTENTIONAL.
HM. PURPOSE?
IT APPEARS TO BE *LOOKING* FOR SOMEONE.
REALLY?
ALLOW ME TO DEMONSTRAT
SERGEANT GO UP TO
VOT? *ME?!*
YES, YOU. GO UP TO IT.
I DON' TAKE SCHTUPID ORDERS FROM *YOU*.
I DON'T *GIVE* THEM. NOW GO DO SOMETHING *USEFUL*.
HO! SO I CAN *SQVISH* YOU DEN, HEY, BUGMAN?
BORIS—IS IT SAFE?
I HONESTLY BELIEVE SO, HERR BARON.
GOOD. SERGEANT? CARRY ON.
YAH, HERR BARON.
MENU

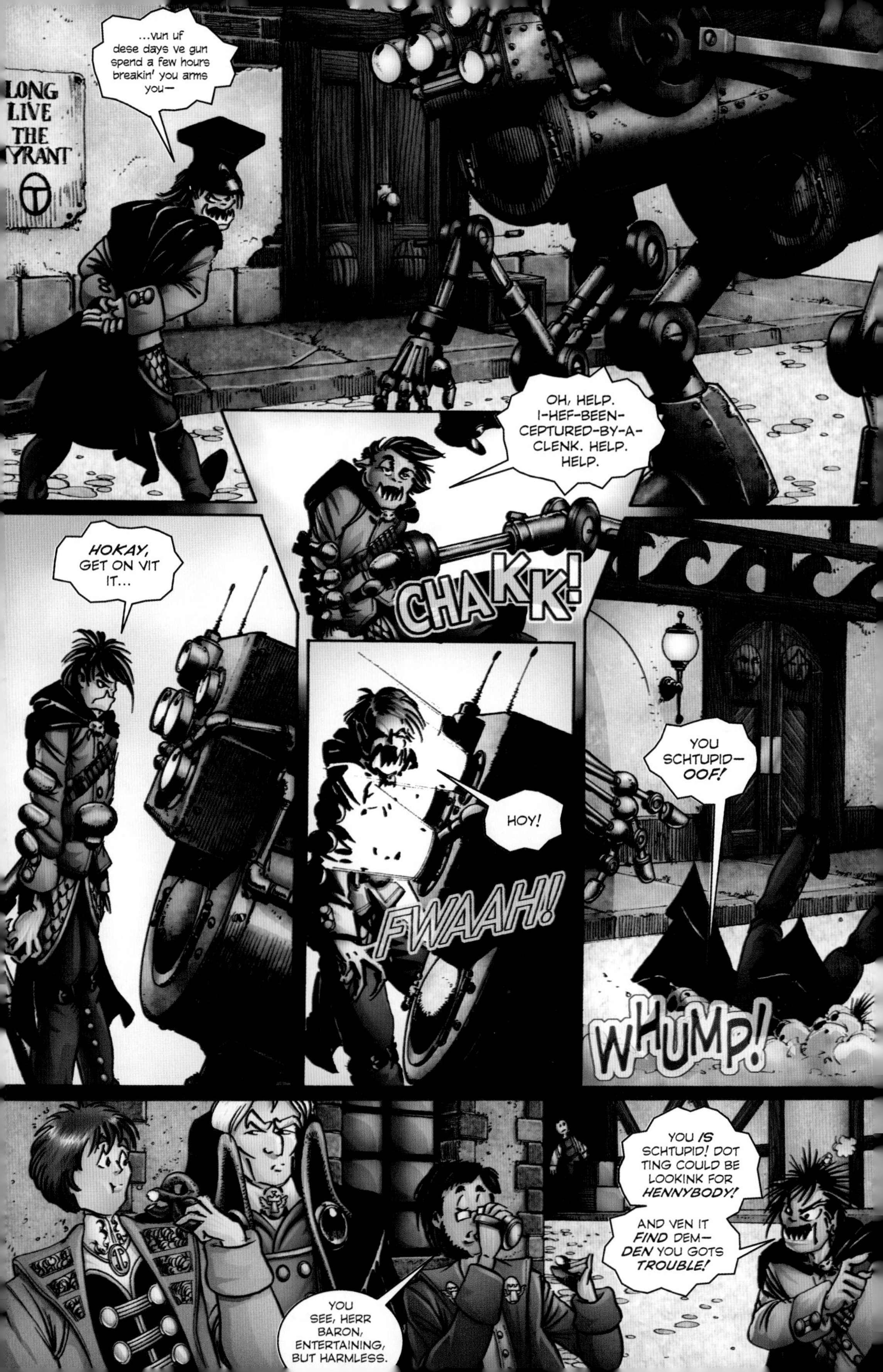
LONG LIVE THE YRANT
…vun uf dese days ve gun spend a few hours breakin' you arms you—
OH, HELP. I-HEF-BEEN-CEPTURED-BY-A-CLENK. HELP. HELP.
CHAKK!
HOKAY, GET ON VIT IT…
HOY!
FWAAAH!
YOU SCHTUPID—OOF!
WHUMP!
YOU IS SCHTUPID! DOT TING COULD BE LOOKINK FOR HENNYBODY!
AND VEN IT FIND DEM—DEN YOU GOTS TROUBLE!
YOU SEE, HERR BARON, ENTERTAINING, BUT HARMLESS.

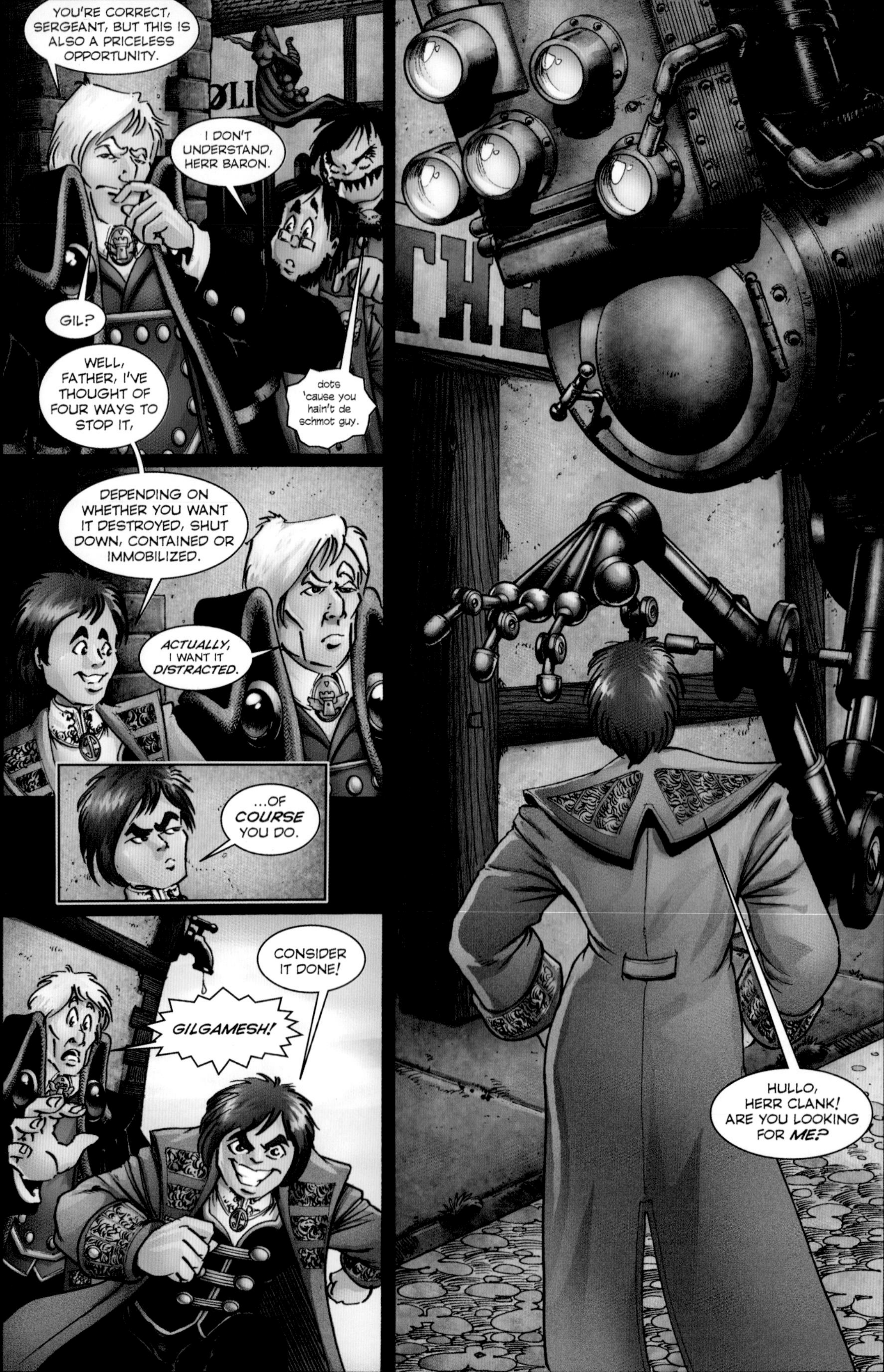
YOU'RE CORRECT, SERGEANT, BUT THIS IS ALSO A PRICELESS OPPORTUNITY.
I DON'T UNDERSTAND, HERR BARON.
GIL?
dots 'cause you hain't de schmot guy.
WELL, FATHER, I'VE THOUGHT OF FOUR WAYS TO STOP IT,
DEPENDING ON WHETHER YOU WANT IT DESTROYED, SHUT DOWN, CONTAINED OR IMMOBILIZED.
ACTUALLY, I WANT IT *DISTRACTED.*
...OF *COURSE* YOU DO.
CONSIDER IT DONE!
GILGAMESH!
HULLO, HERR CLANK! ARE YOU LOOKING FOR *ME?*

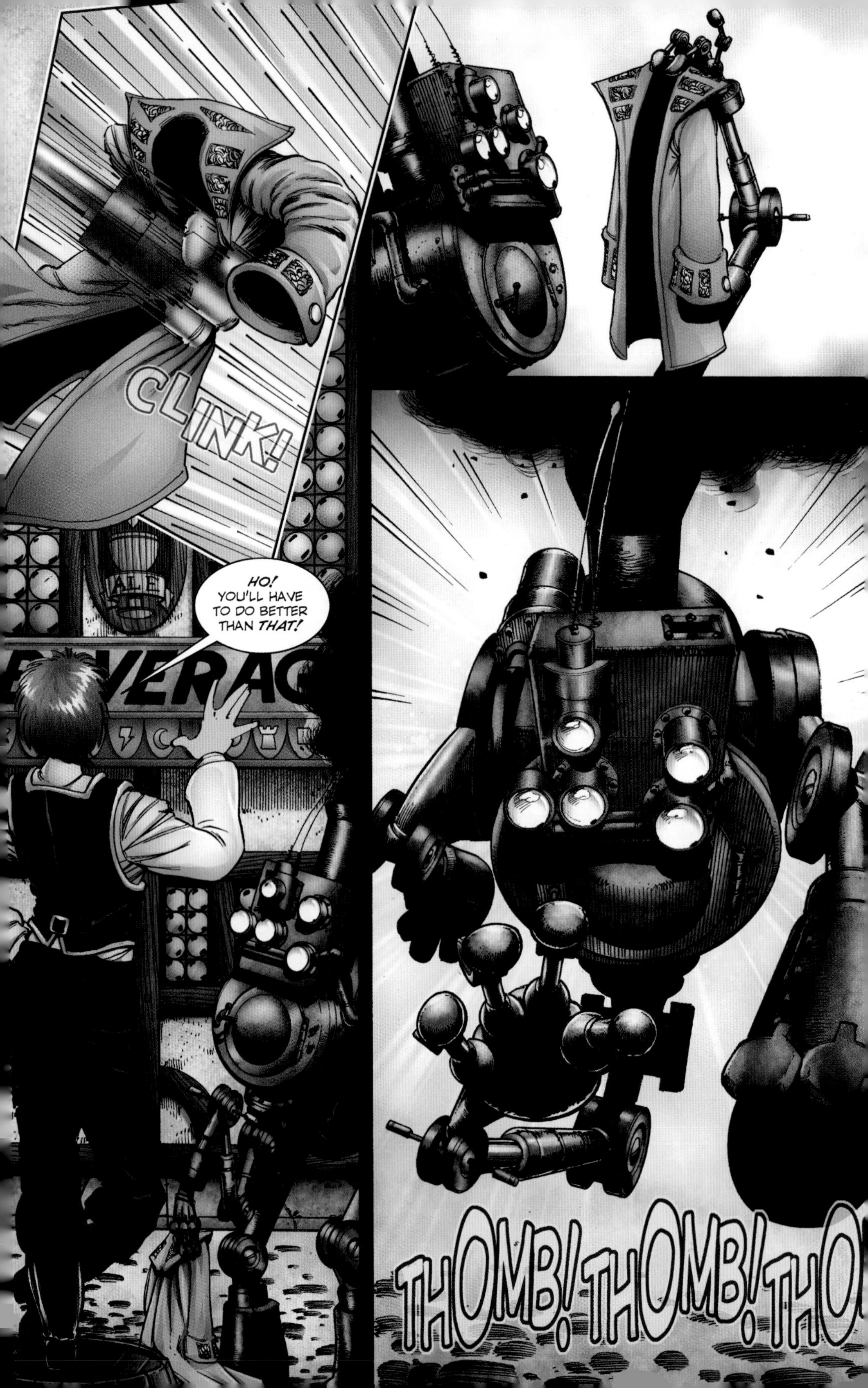
CLINK!
HO! YOU'LL HAVE TO DO BETTER THAN *THAT!*
THOMB! THOMB! THO

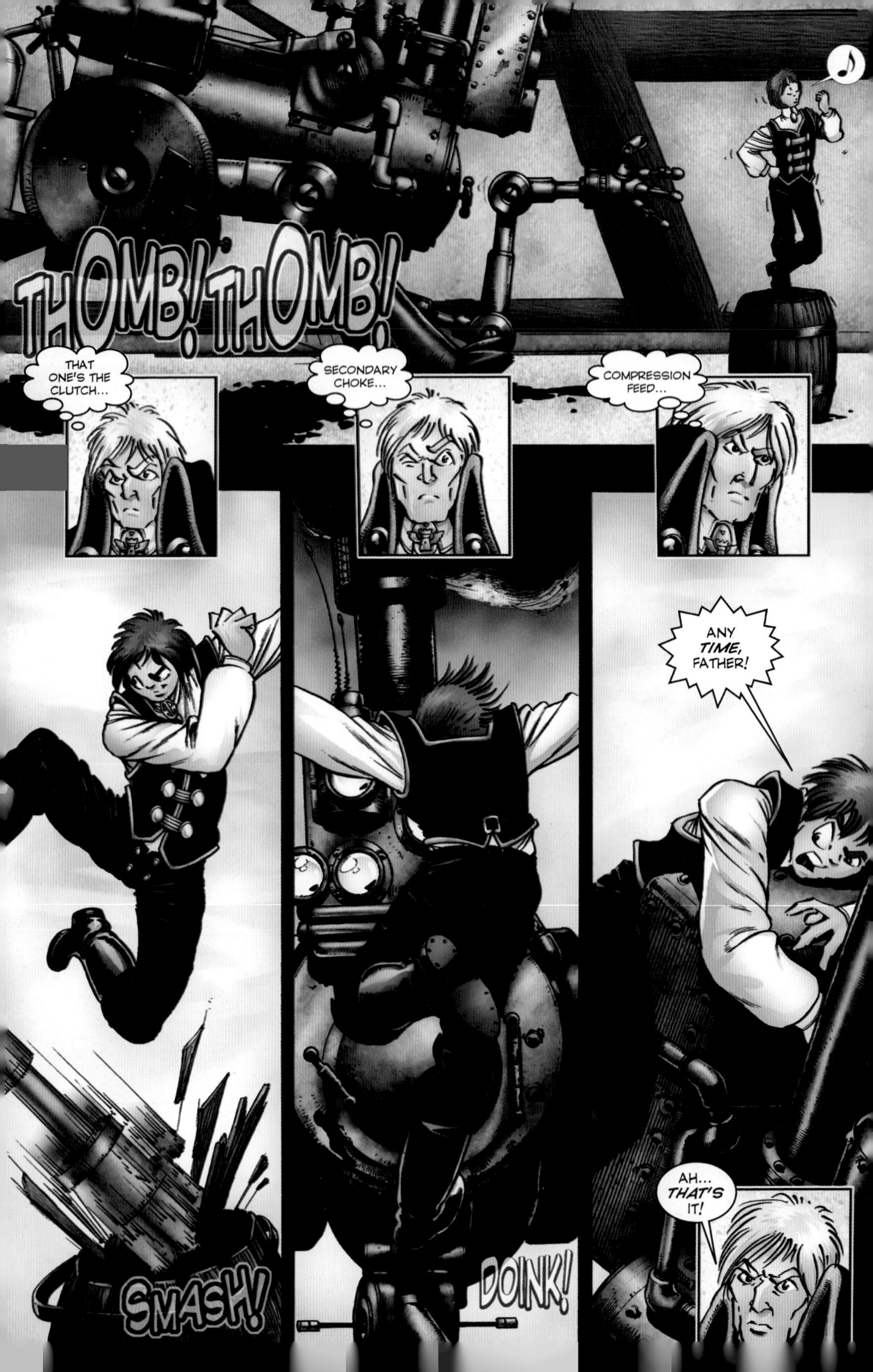

THOMB! THOMB!
THAT ONE'S THE CLUTCH...
SECONDARY CHOKE...
COMPRESSION FEED...
ANY *TIME,* FATHER!
SMASH!
DOINK!
AH... *THAT'S* IT!

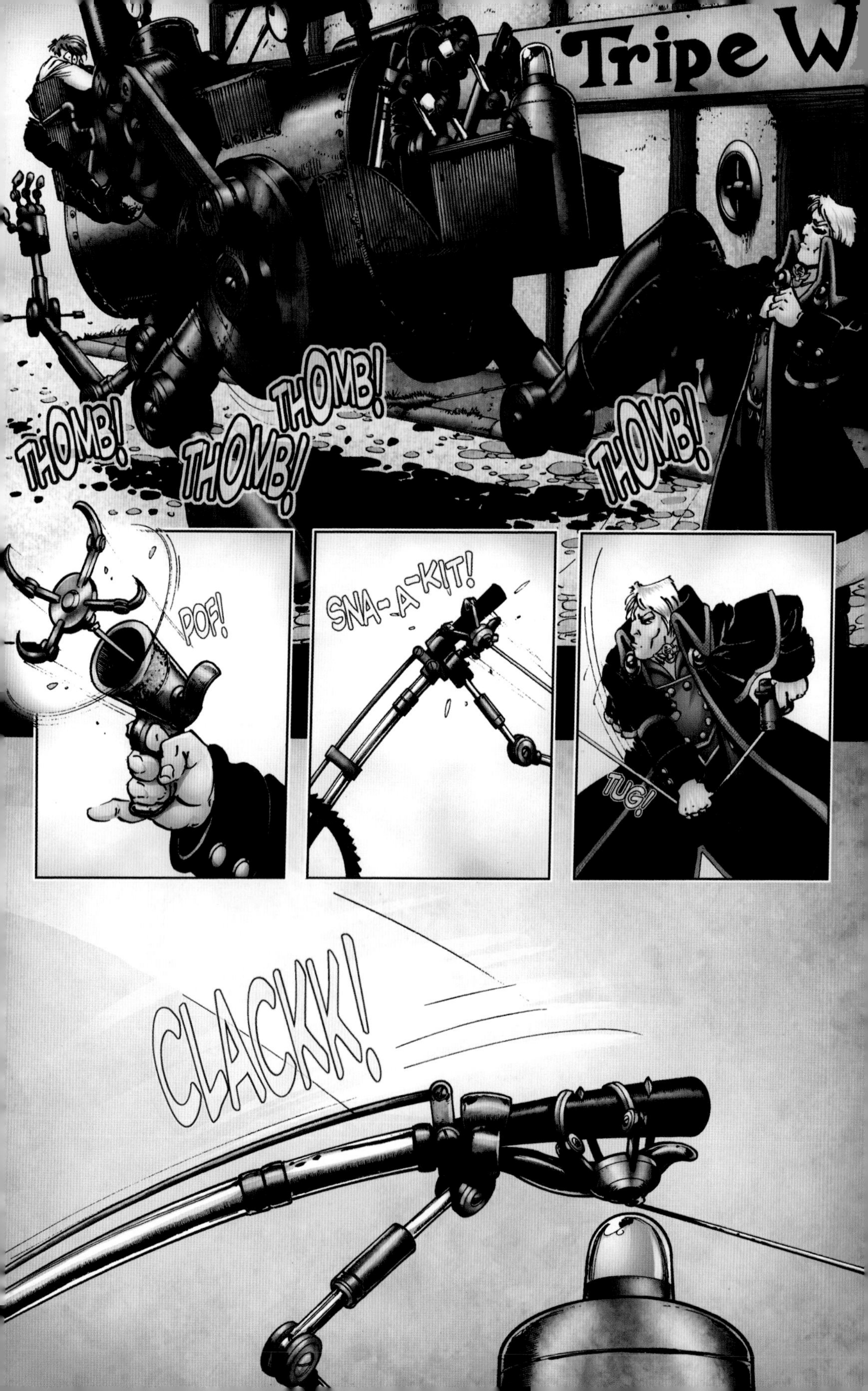
Tripe W
THOMB!
THOMB!
THOMB!
THOMB!
POF!
SNA-A-KIT!
TUG!
CLACKK!

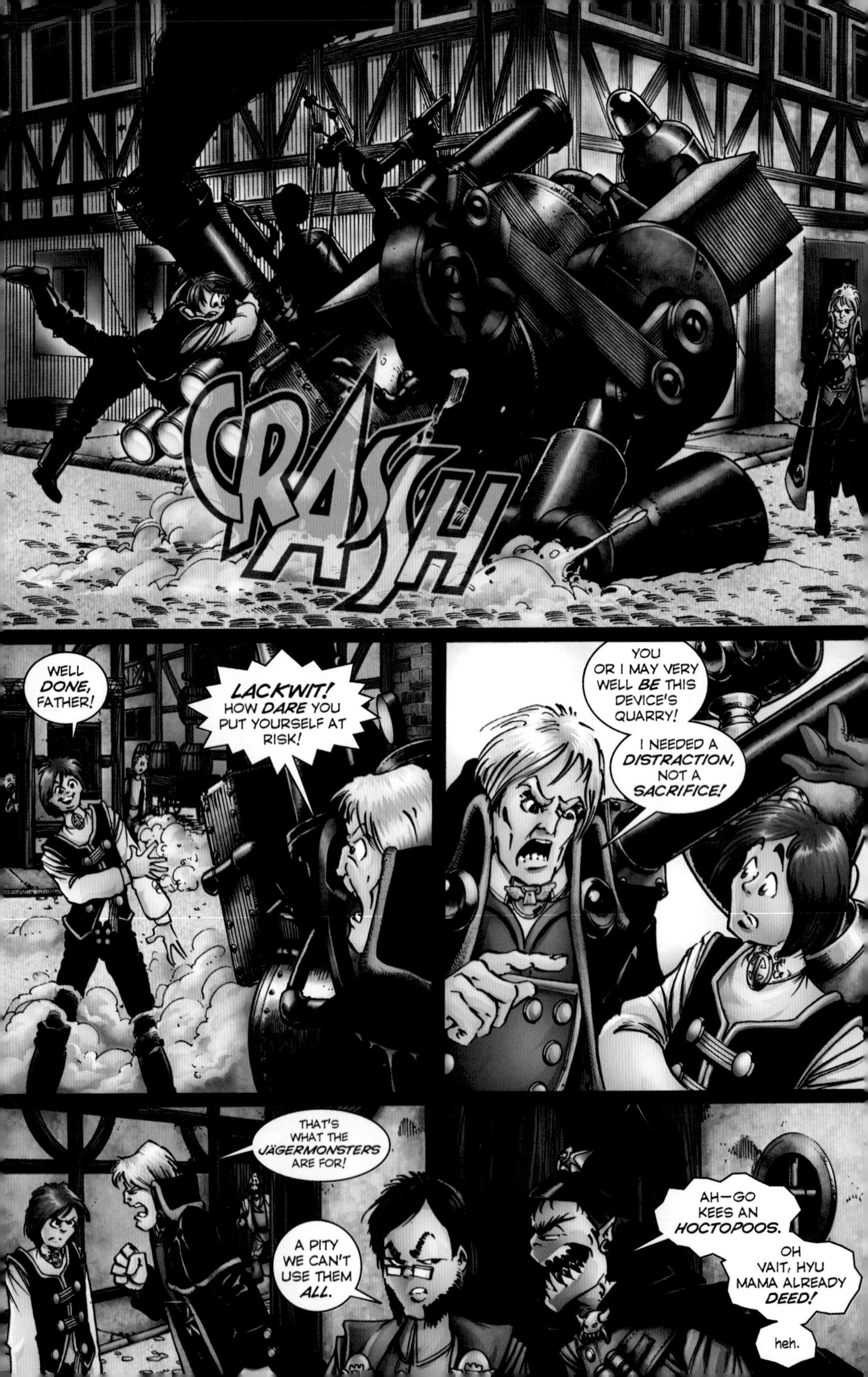
CRASH
WELL DONE, FATHER!
LACKWIT! HOW DARE YOU PUT YOURSELF AT RISK!
YOU OR I MAY VERY WELL BE THIS DEVICE'S QUARRY!
I NEEDED A DISTRACTION, NOT A SACRIFICE!
THAT'S WHAT THE JÄGERMONSTERS ARE FOR!
A PITY WE CAN'T USE THEM ALL.
AH—GO KEES AN HOCTOPOOS.
OH VAIT, HYU MAMA ALREADY DEED!
heh.

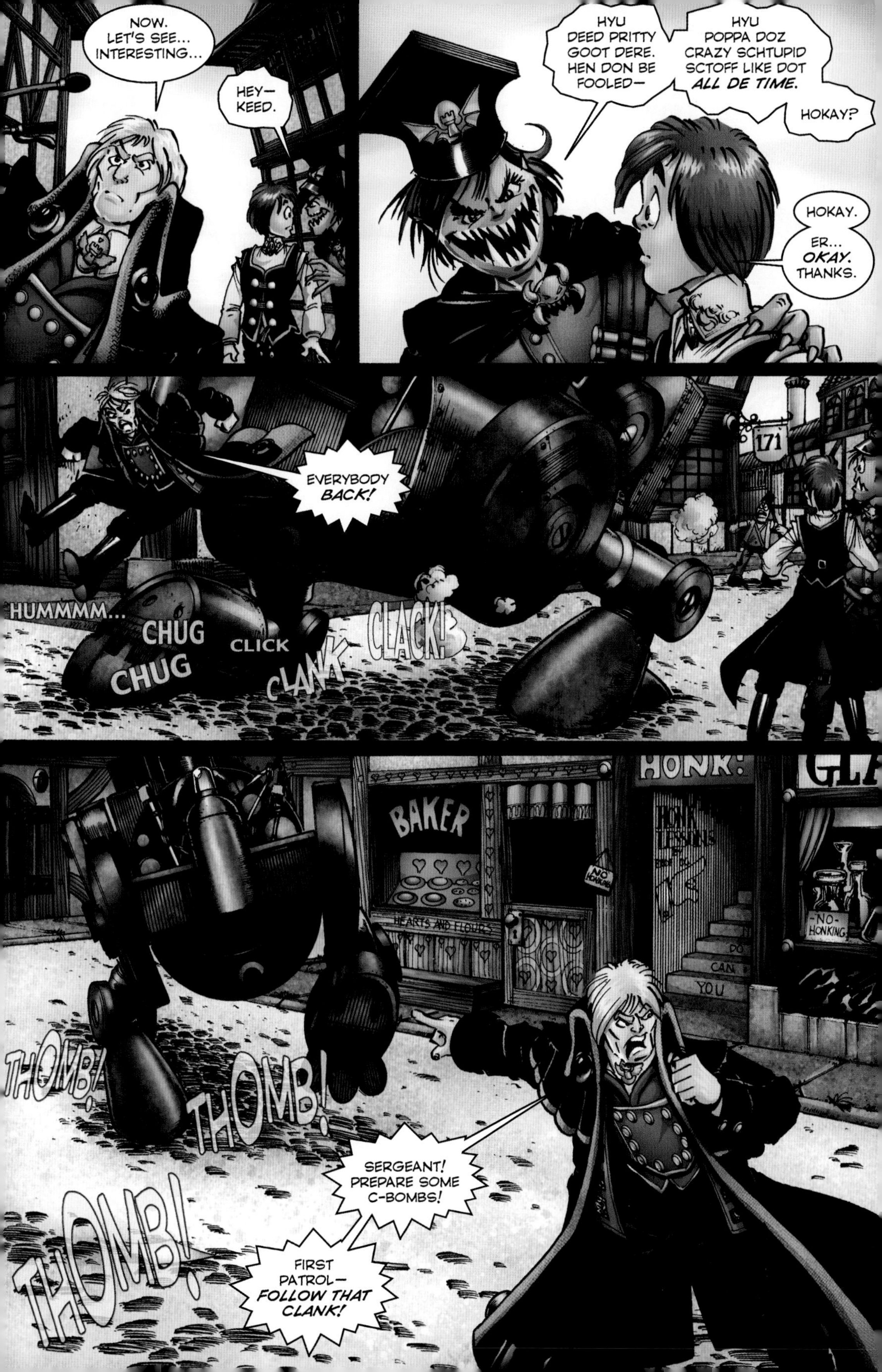
NOW. LET'S SEE... INTERESTING...
HEY— KEED.
HYU DEED PRITTY GOOT DERE. HEN DON BE FOOLED—
HYU POPPA DOZ CRAZY SCHTUPID SCTOFF LIKE DOT ALL DE TIME.
HOKAY?
HOKAY.
ER... OKAY. THANKS.
171
EVERYBODY BACK!
HUMMMM...
CHUG
CHUG
CLICK
CLANK
CLACK!
HONK!
BAKER
HONK LESSONS
NO HONKING
HEARTS AND FLOURS
-NO- HONKING
DO CAN YOU
THOMB!
THOMB!
THOMB!
SERGEANT! PREPARE SOME C-BOMBS!
FIRST PATROL— FOLLOW THAT CLANK!

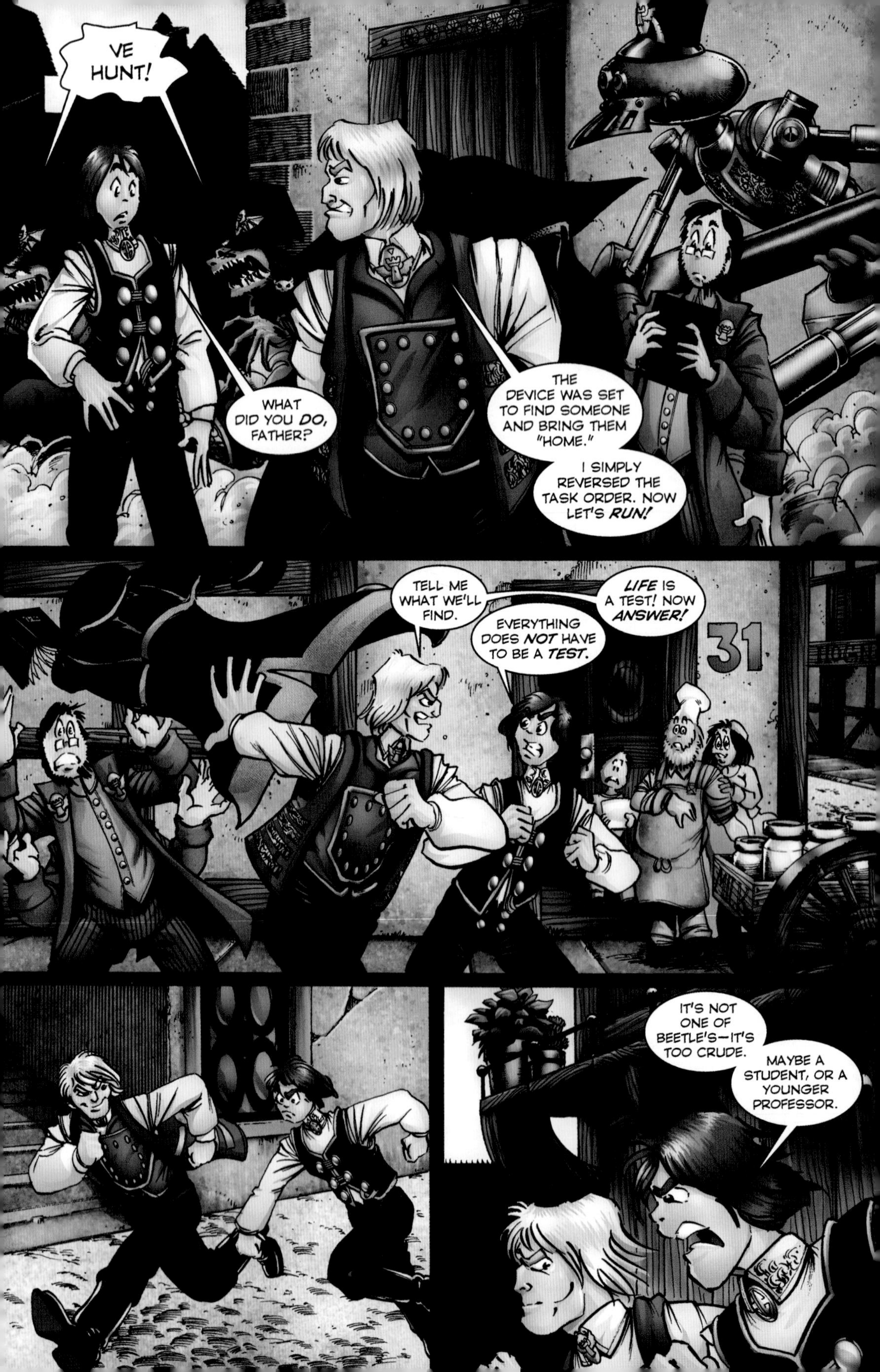
VE HUNT!
WHAT DID YOU *DO,* FATHER?
THE DEVICE WAS SET TO FIND SOMEONE AND BRING THEM "HOME."
I SIMPLY REVERSED THE TASK ORDER. NOW LET'S *RUN!*
TELL ME WHAT WE'LL FIND.
EVERYTHING DOES *NOT* HAVE TO BE A *TEST*.
LIFE IS A TEST! NOW *ANSWER!*
31
IT'S NOT ONE OF BEETLE'S—IT'S TOO CRUDE.
MAYBE A STUDENT, OR A YOUNGER PROFESSOR.

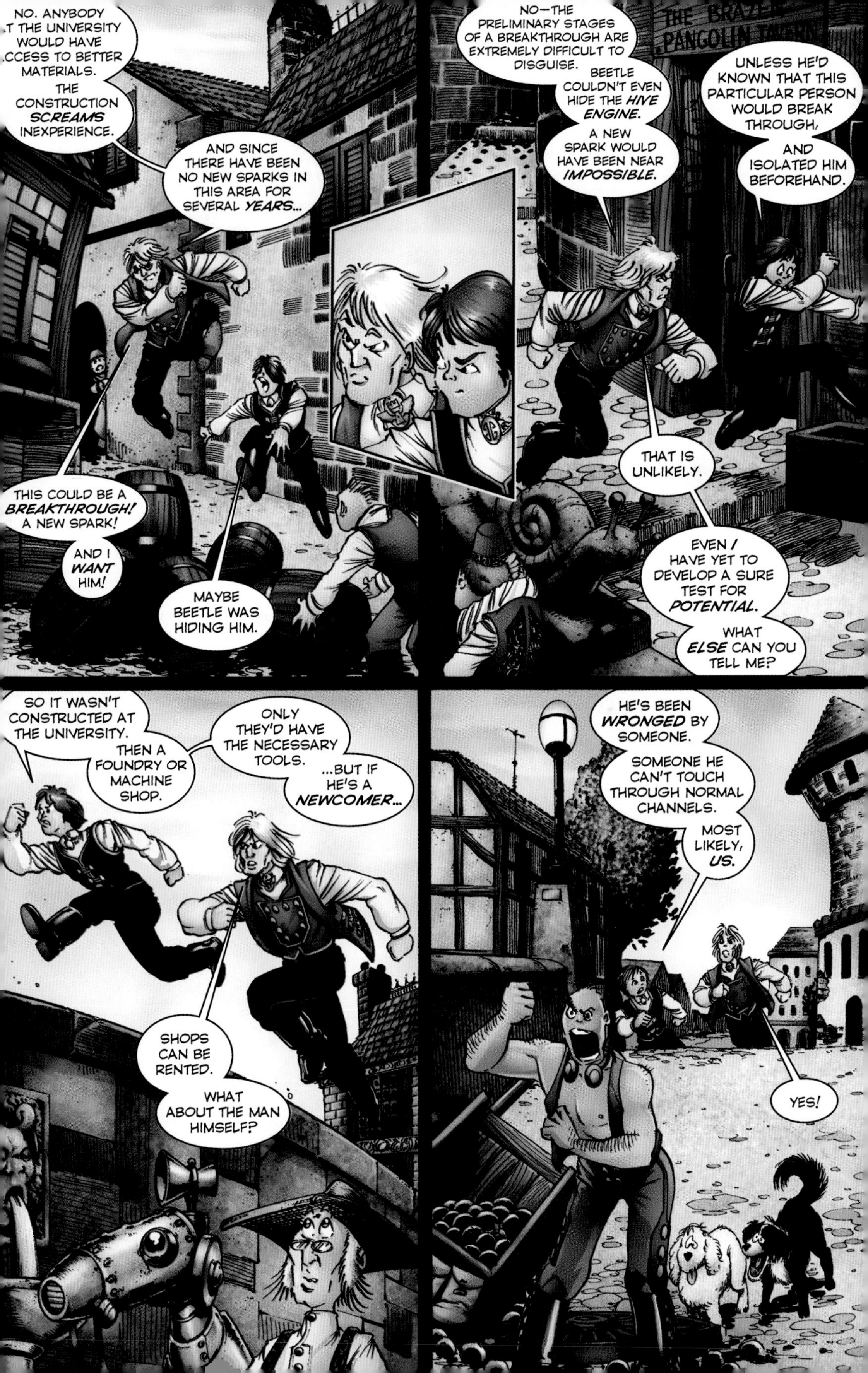

NO. ANYBODY AT THE UNIVERSITY WOULD HAVE ACCESS TO BETTER MATERIALS.
THE CONSTRUCTION SCREAMS INEXPERIENCE.
AND SINCE THERE HAVE BEEN NO NEW SPARKS IN THIS AREA FOR SEVERAL YEARS...
THIS COULD BE A BREAKTHROUGH! A NEW SPARK!
AND I WANT HIM!
MAYBE BEETLE WAS HIDING HIM.
NO—THE PRELIMINARY STAGES OF A BREAKTHROUGH ARE EXTREMELY DIFFICULT TO DISGUISE.
BEETLE COULDN'T EVEN HIDE THE HIVE ENGINE.
A NEW SPARK WOULD HAVE BEEN NEAR IMPOSSIBLE.
THE BRAZEN PANGOLIN TAVERN
UNLESS HE'D KNOWN THAT THIS PARTICULAR PERSON WOULD BREAK THROUGH,
AND ISOLATED HIM BEFOREHAND.
THAT IS UNLIKELY.
EVEN I HAVE YET TO DEVELOP A SURE TEST FOR POTENTIAL.
WHAT ELSE CAN YOU TELL ME?
SO IT WASN'T CONSTRUCTED AT THE UNIVERSITY.
THEN A FOUNDRY OR MACHINE SHOP.
ONLY THEY'D HAVE THE NECESSARY TOOLS.
...BUT IF HE'S A NEWCOMER...
SHOPS CAN BE RENTED.
WHAT ABOUT THE MAN HIMSELF?
HE'S BEEN WRONGED BY SOMEONE.
SOMEONE HE CAN'T TOUCH THROUGH NORMAL CHANNELS.
MOST LIKELY, US.
YES!

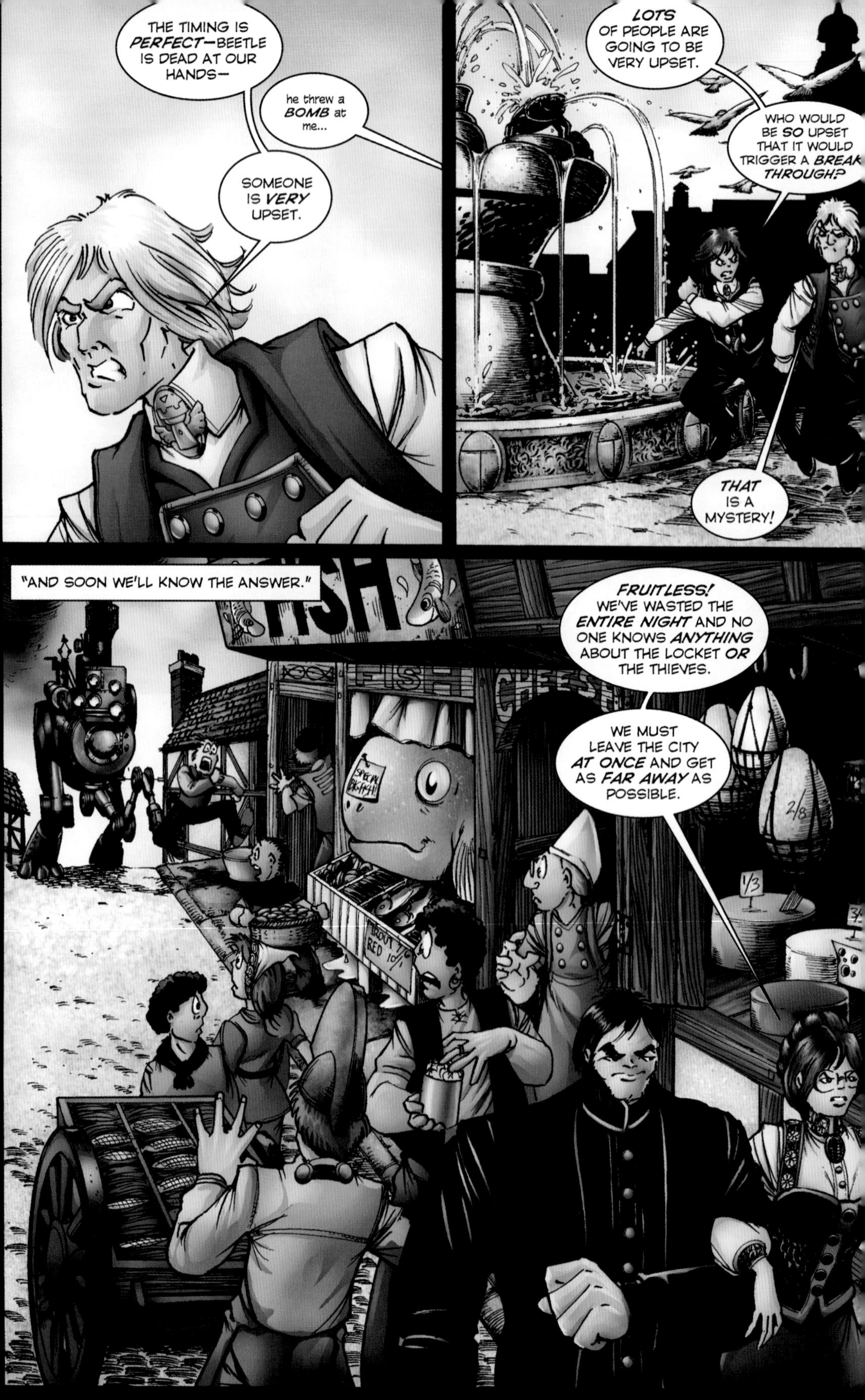
THE TIMING IS *PERFECT*—BEETLE IS DEAD AT OUR HANDS—
he threw a *BOMB* at me...
SOMEONE IS *VERY* UPSET.
LOTS OF PEOPLE ARE GOING TO BE VERY UPSET.
WHO WOULD BE *SO* UPSET THAT IT WOULD TRIGGER A *BREAKTHROUGH?*
THAT IS A MYSTERY!
"AND SOON WE'LL KNOW THE ANSWER."
FISH
FRUITLESS! WE'VE WASTED THE *ENTIRE NIGHT* AND NO ONE KNOWS *ANYTHING* ABOUT THE LOCKET *OR* THE THIEVES.
WE MUST LEAVE THE CITY *AT ONCE* AND GET AS *FAR AWAY* AS POSSIBLE.

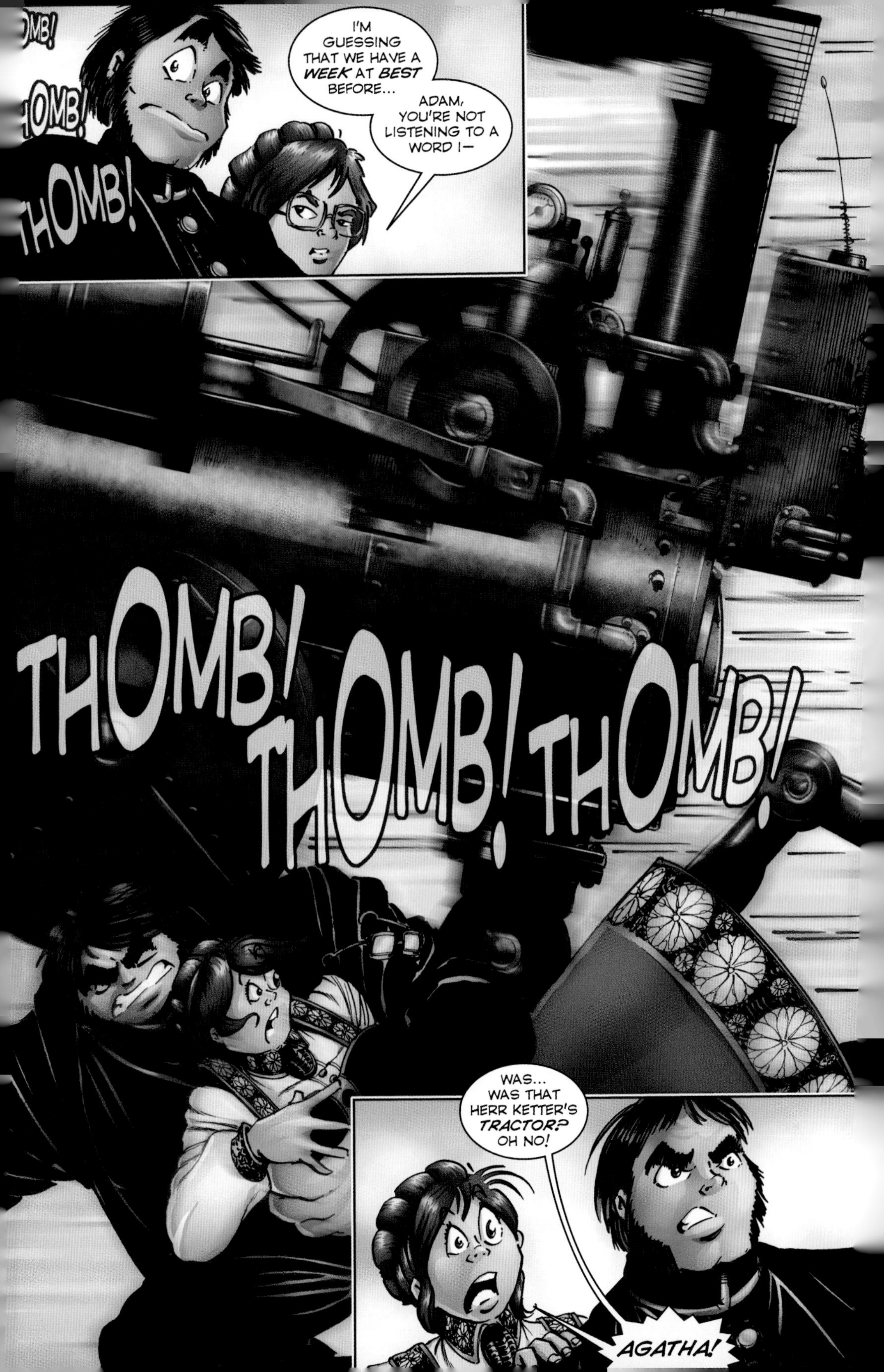
THOMB!
THOMB!
THOMB!
I'M GUESSING THAT WE HAVE A *WEEK* AT *BEST* BEFORE...
ADAM, YOU'RE NOT LISTENING TO A WORD !—
THOMB! THOMB! THOMB!
WAS... WAS THAT HERR KETTER'S *TRACTOR?* OH NO!
AGATHA!

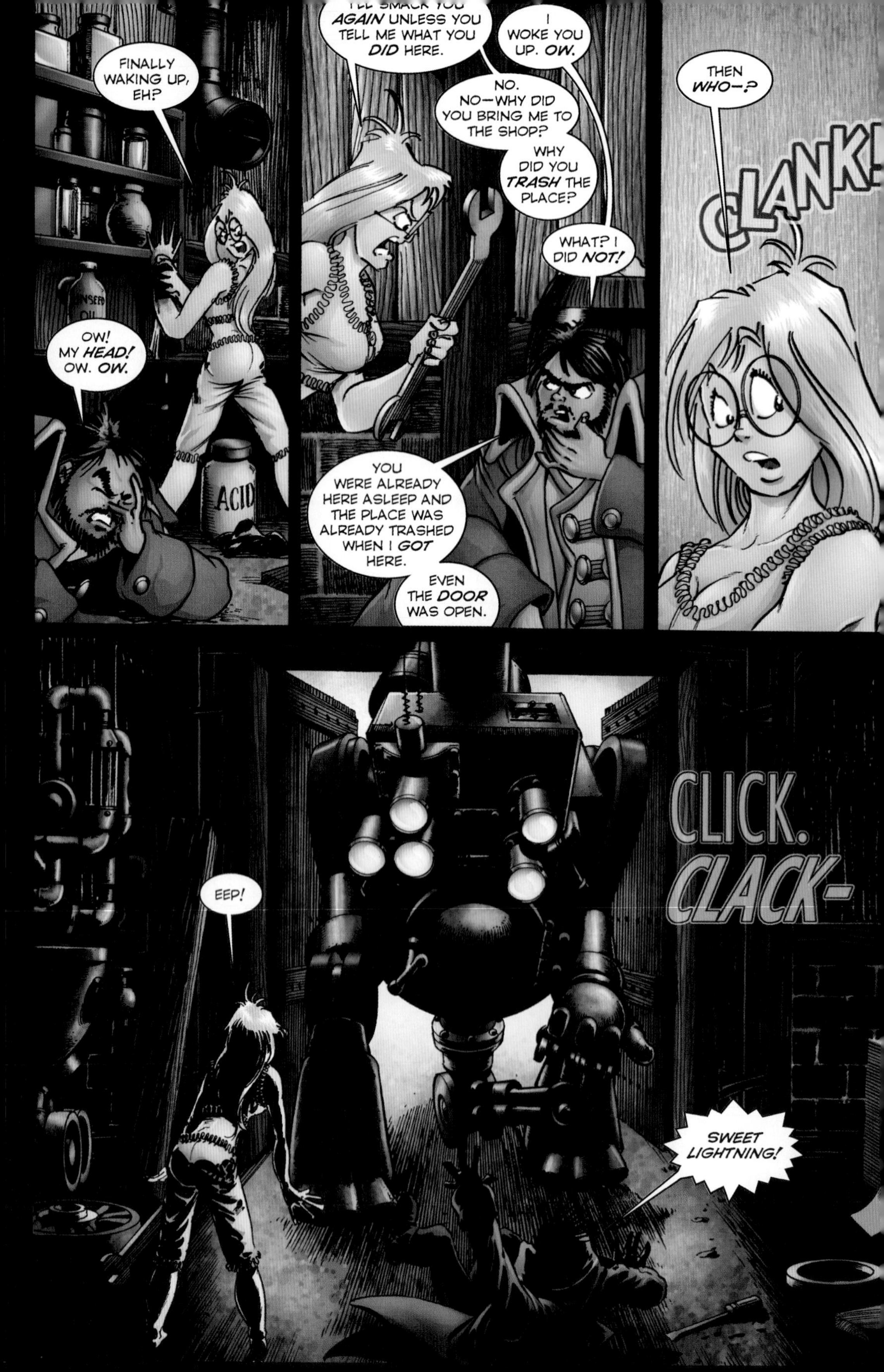
FINALLY WAKING UP, EH?
OW! MY *HEAD!* OW. *OW.*
ACID
AGAIN UNLESS YOU TELL ME WHAT YOU *DID* HERE.
I WOKE YOU UP. *OW.*
NO. NO—WHY DID YOU BRING ME TO THE SHOP?
WHY DID YOU *TRASH* THE PLACE?
WHAT? I DID *NOT!*
YOU WERE ALREADY HERE ASLEEP AND THE PLACE WAS ALREADY TRASHED WHEN I *GOT* HERE.
EVEN THE *DOOR* WAS OPEN.
THEN *WHO—?*
CLICK.
CLACK-
EEP!
SWEET LIGHTNING!

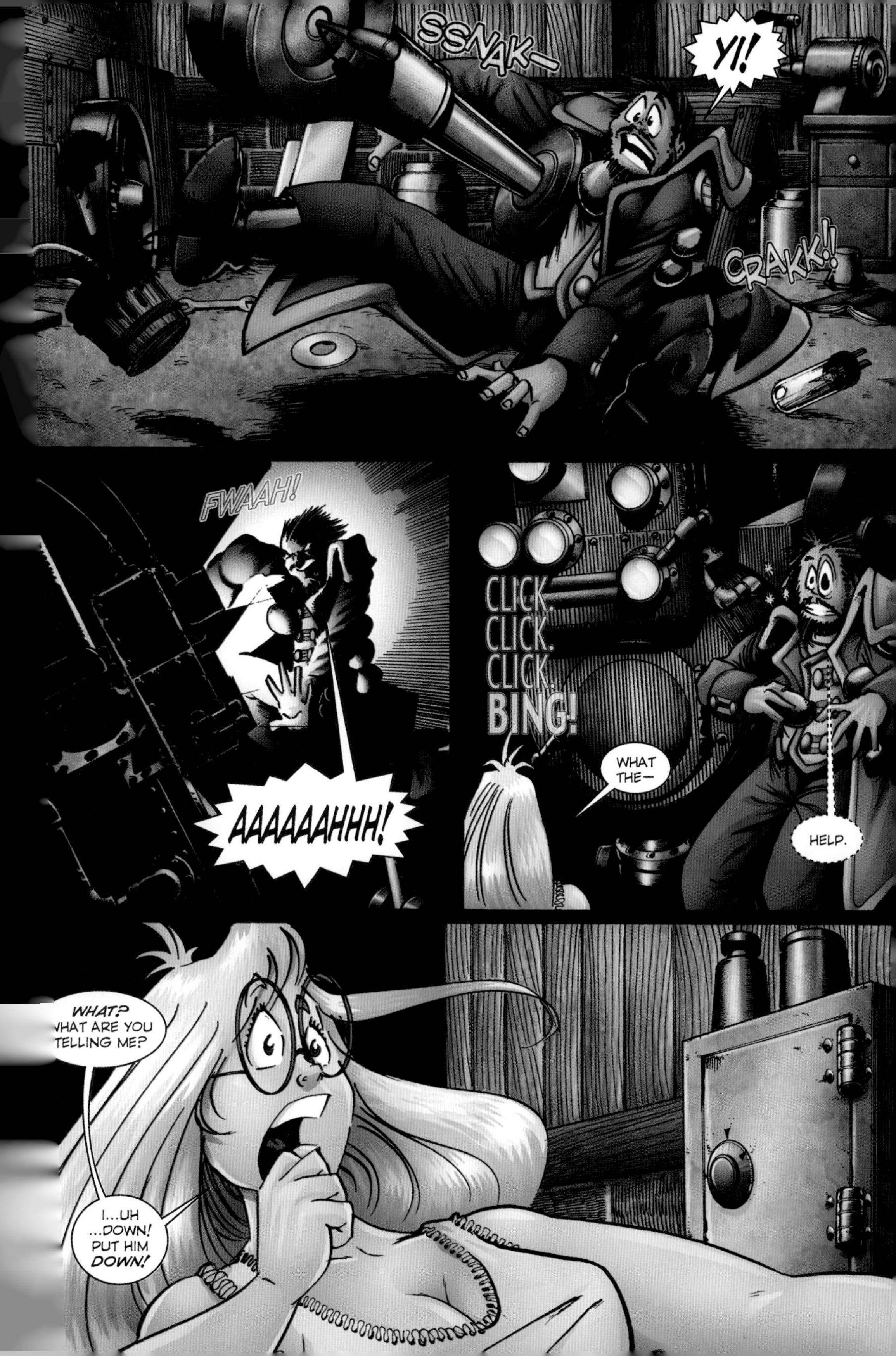
SSNAK—
YI!
CRAKK!!
FWAAH!
AAAAAAHHH!
CLICK.
CLICK.
CLICK.
BING!
WHAT THE—
HELP.
WHAT? WHAT ARE YOU TELLING ME?
I...UH ...DOWN! PUT HIM DOWN!

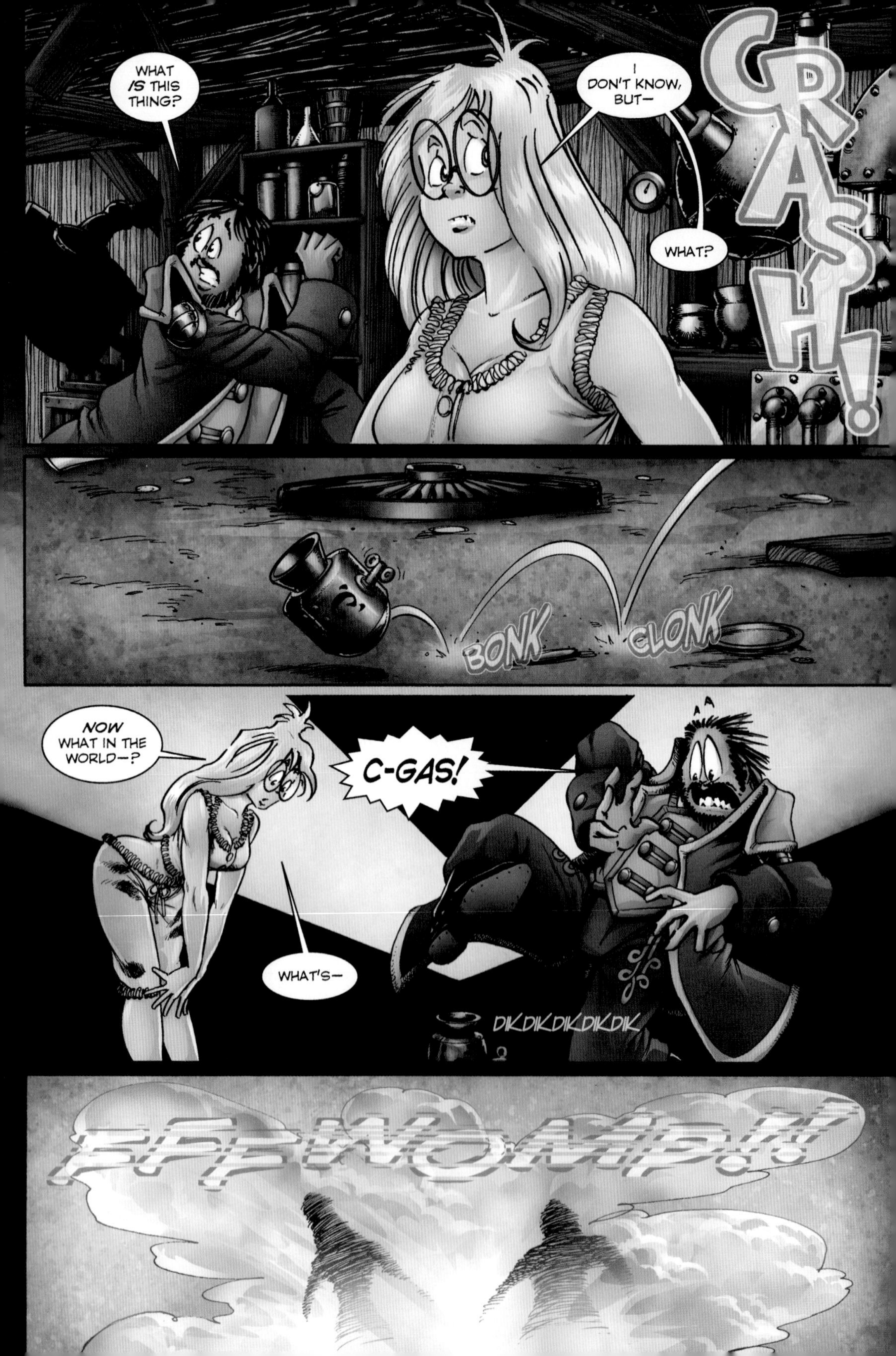
WHAT *IS* THIS THING?
I DON'T KNOW, BUT—
WHAT?
CRASH!
BONK
CLONK
NOW WHAT IN THE WORLD—?
C-GAS!
WHAT'S—
DIKDIKDIKDIKDIK
FFFSWOOMP!!!

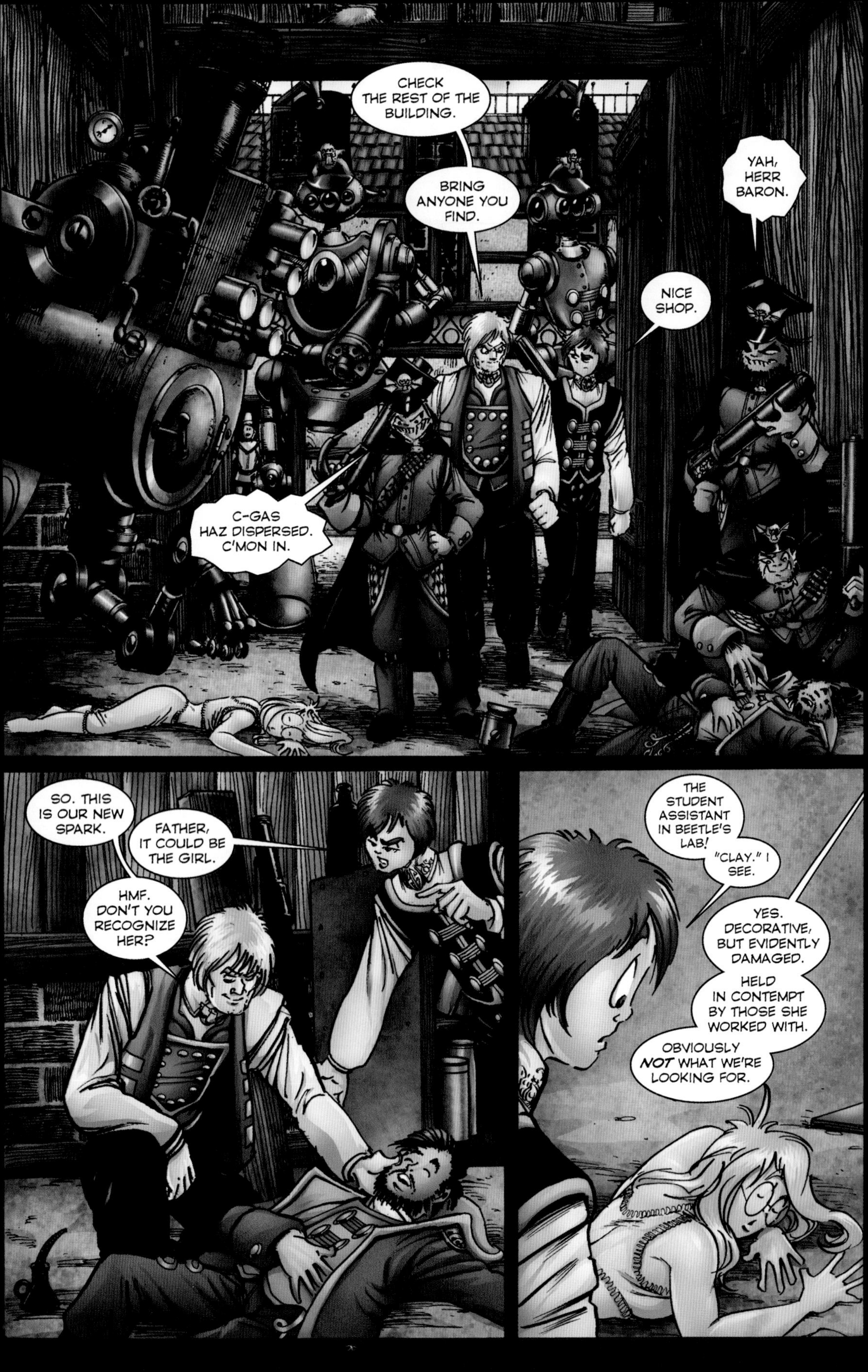
CHECK THE REST OF THE BUILDING.
BRING ANYONE YOU FIND.
YAH, HERR BARON.
NICE SHOP.
C-GAS HAZ DISPERSED. C'MON IN.
SO. THIS IS OUR NEW SPARK.
FATHER, IT COULD BE THE GIRL.
HMF. DON'T YOU RECOGNIZE HER?
THE STUDENT ASSISTANT IN BEETLE'S LAB!
"CLAY." I SEE.
YES. DECORATIVE, BUT EVIDENTLY DAMAGED.
HELD IN CONTEMPT BY THOSE SHE WORKED WITH.
OBVIOUSLY *NOT* WHAT WE'RE LOOKING FOR.

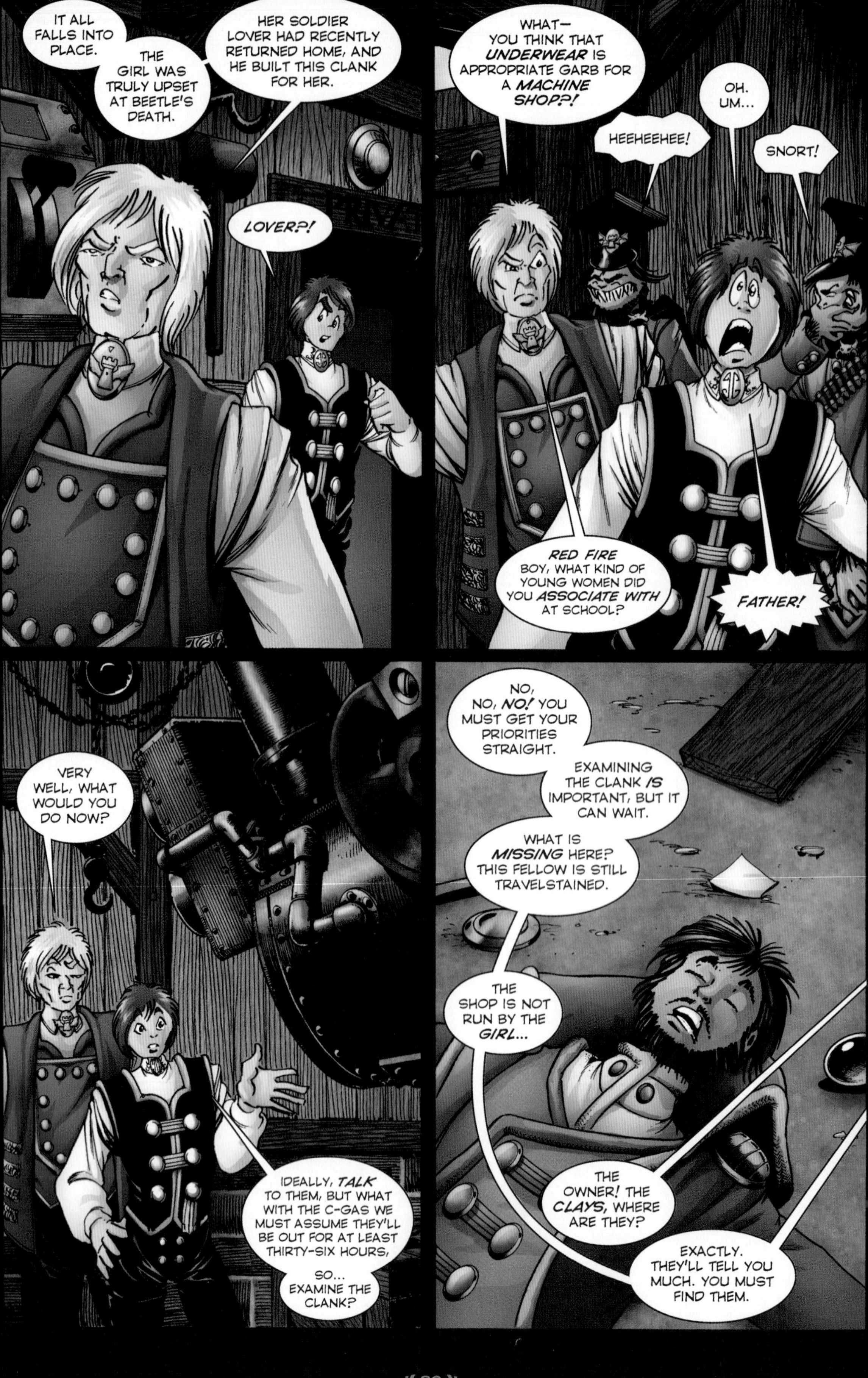
IT ALL FALLS INTO PLACE.
THE GIRL WAS TRULY UPSET AT BEETLE'S DEATH.
HER SOLDIER LOVER HAD RECENTLY RETURNED HOME, AND HE BUILT THIS CLANK FOR HER.
LOVER?!
WHAT—YOU THINK THAT UNDERWEAR IS APPROPRIATE GARB FOR A MACHINE SHOP?!
HEEHEEHEE!
OH. UM...
SNORT!
RED FIRE BOY, WHAT KIND OF YOUNG WOMEN DID YOU ASSOCIATE WITH AT SCHOOL?
FATHER!
VERY WELL, WHAT WOULD YOU DO NOW?
IDEALLY, TALK TO THEM, BUT WHAT WITH THE C-GAS WE MUST ASSUME THEY'LL BE OUT FOR AT LEAST THIRTY-SIX HOURS,
SO... EXAMINE THE CLANK?
NO, NO, NO! YOU MUST GET YOUR PRIORITIES STRAIGHT.
EXAMINING THE CLANK IS IMPORTANT, BUT IT CAN WAIT.
WHAT IS MISSING HERE? THIS FELLOW IS STILL TRAVELSTAINED.
THE SHOP IS NOT RUN BY THE GIRL...
THE OWNER! THE CLAYS, WHERE ARE THEY?
EXACTLY. THEY'LL TELL YOU MUCH. YOU MUST FIND THEM.

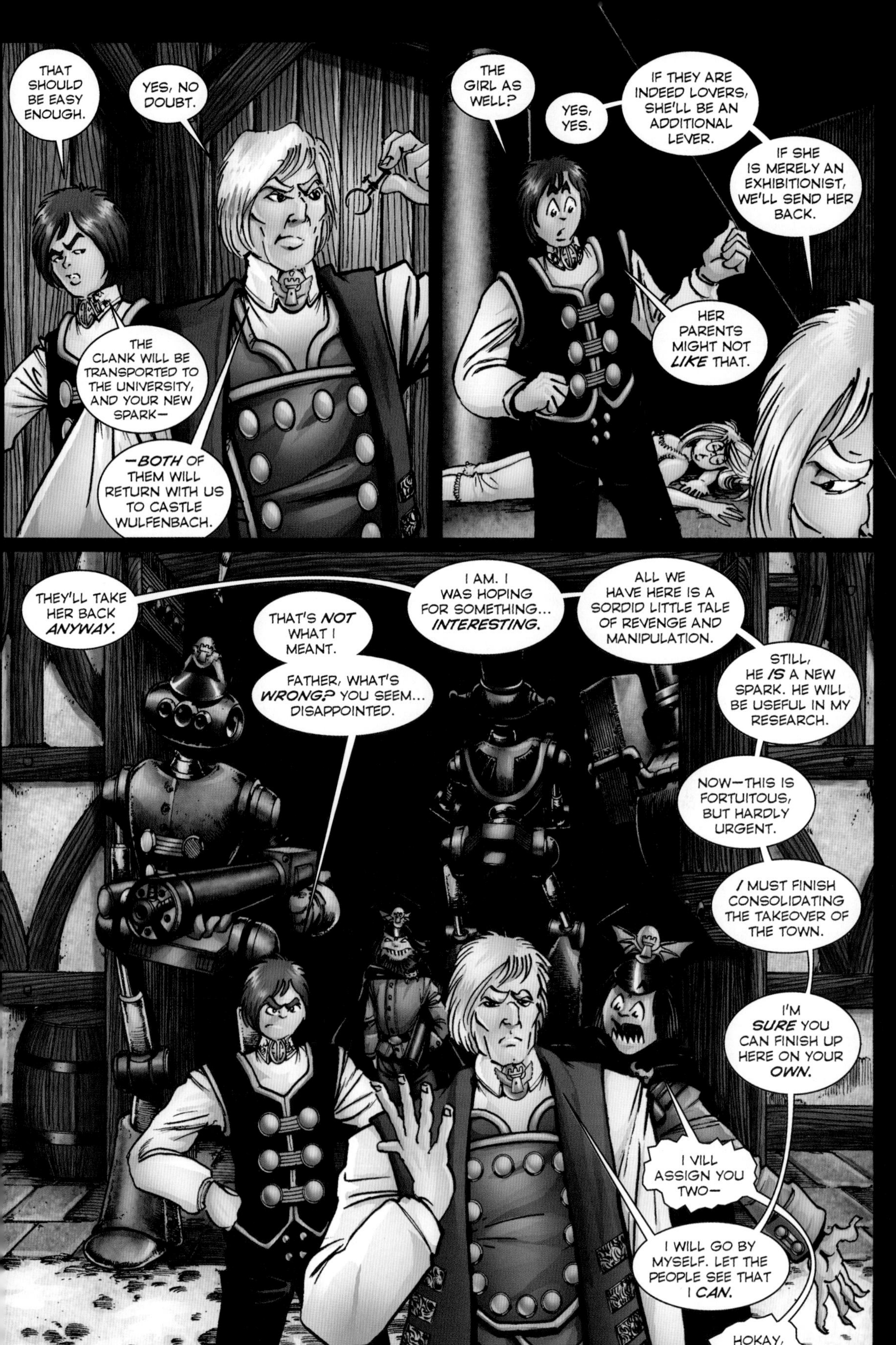
THAT SHOULD BE EASY ENOUGH.
YES, NO DOUBT.
THE CLANK WILL BE TRANSPORTED TO THE UNIVERSITY, AND YOUR NEW SPARK—
—BOTH OF THEM WILL RETURN WITH US TO CASTLE WULFENBACH.
THE GIRL AS WELL?
YES, YES.
IF THEY ARE INDEED LOVERS, SHE'LL BE AN ADDITIONAL LEVER.
IF SHE IS MERELY AN EXHIBITIONIST, WE'LL SEND HER BACK.
HER PARENTS MIGHT NOT LIKE THAT.
THEY'LL TAKE HER BACK ANYWAY.
THAT'S NOT WHAT I MEANT.
FATHER, WHAT'S WRONG? YOU SEEM... DISAPPOINTED.
I AM. I WAS HOPING FOR SOMETHING... INTERESTING.
ALL WE HAVE HERE IS A SORDID LITTLE TALE OF REVENGE AND MANIPULATION.
STILL, HE IS A NEW SPARK. HE WILL BE USEFUL IN MY RESEARCH.
NOW—THIS IS FORTUITOUS, BUT HARDLY URGENT.
I MUST FINISH CONSOLIDATING THE TAKEOVER OF THE TOWN.
I'M SURE YOU CAN FINISH UP HERE ON YOUR OWN.
I VILL ASSIGN YOU TWO—
I WILL GO BY MYSELF. LET THE PEOPLE SEE THAT I CAN.
HOKAY, HERR BARON.

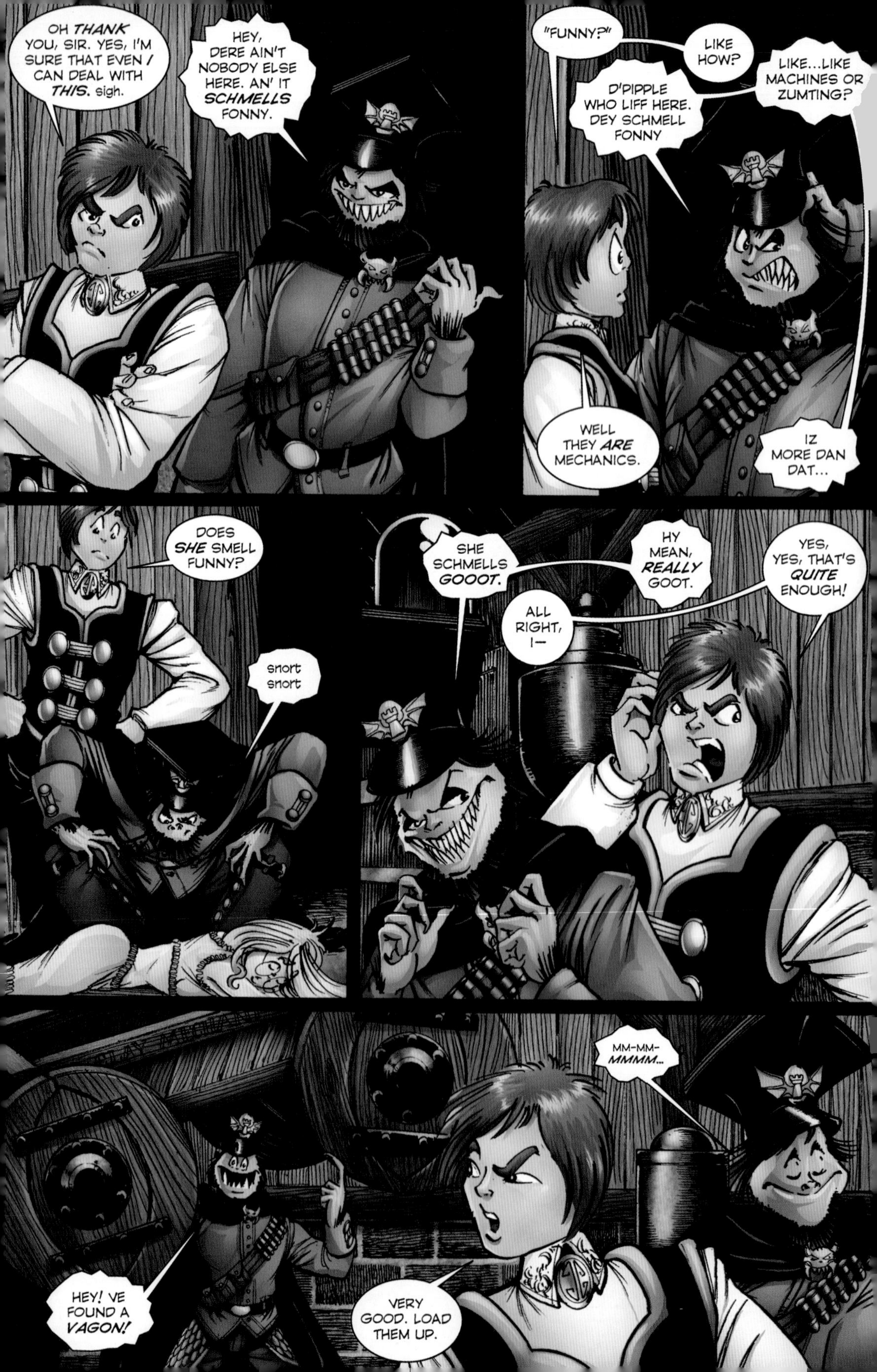
OH THANK YOU, SIR. YES, I'M SURE THAT EVEN I CAN DEAL WITH THIS. sigh.
HEY, DERE AIN'T NOBODY ELSE HERE. AN' IT SCHMELLS FONNY.
"FUNNY?"
LIKE HOW?
D'PIPPLE WHO LIFF HERE. DEY SCHMELL FONNY
LIKE...LIKE MACHINES OR ZUMTING?
WELL THEY ARE MECHANICS.
IZ MORE DAN DAT...
DOES SHE SMELL FUNNY?
snort snort
SHE SCHMELLS GOOOT.
HY MEAN, REALLY GOOT.
ALL RIGHT, I—
YES, YES, THAT'S QUITE ENOUGH!
MM-MM-MMMM...
HEY! VE FOUND A VAGON!
VERY GOOD. LOAD THEM UP.

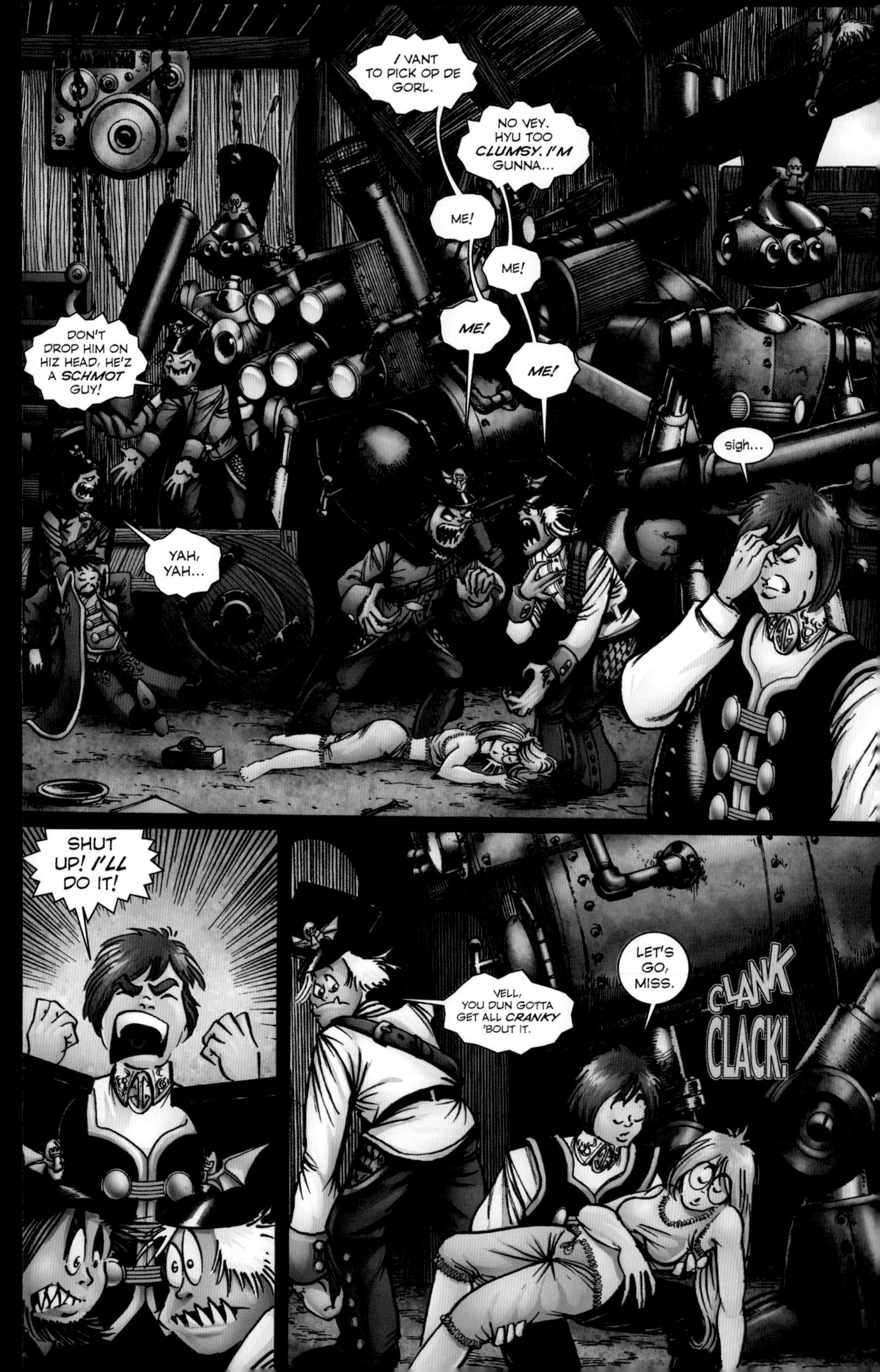
I VANT TO PICK OP DE GORL.
NO VEY. HYU TOO CLUMSY. I'M GUNNA...
ME!
ME!
ME!
ME!
DON'T DROP HIM ON HIZ HEAD, HE'Z A SCHMOT GUY!
YAH, YAH...
sigh...
SHUT UP! I'LL DO IT!
VELL, YOU DUN GOTTA GET ALL CRANKY 'BOUT IT.
LET'S GO, MISS.
CLANK
CLACK!

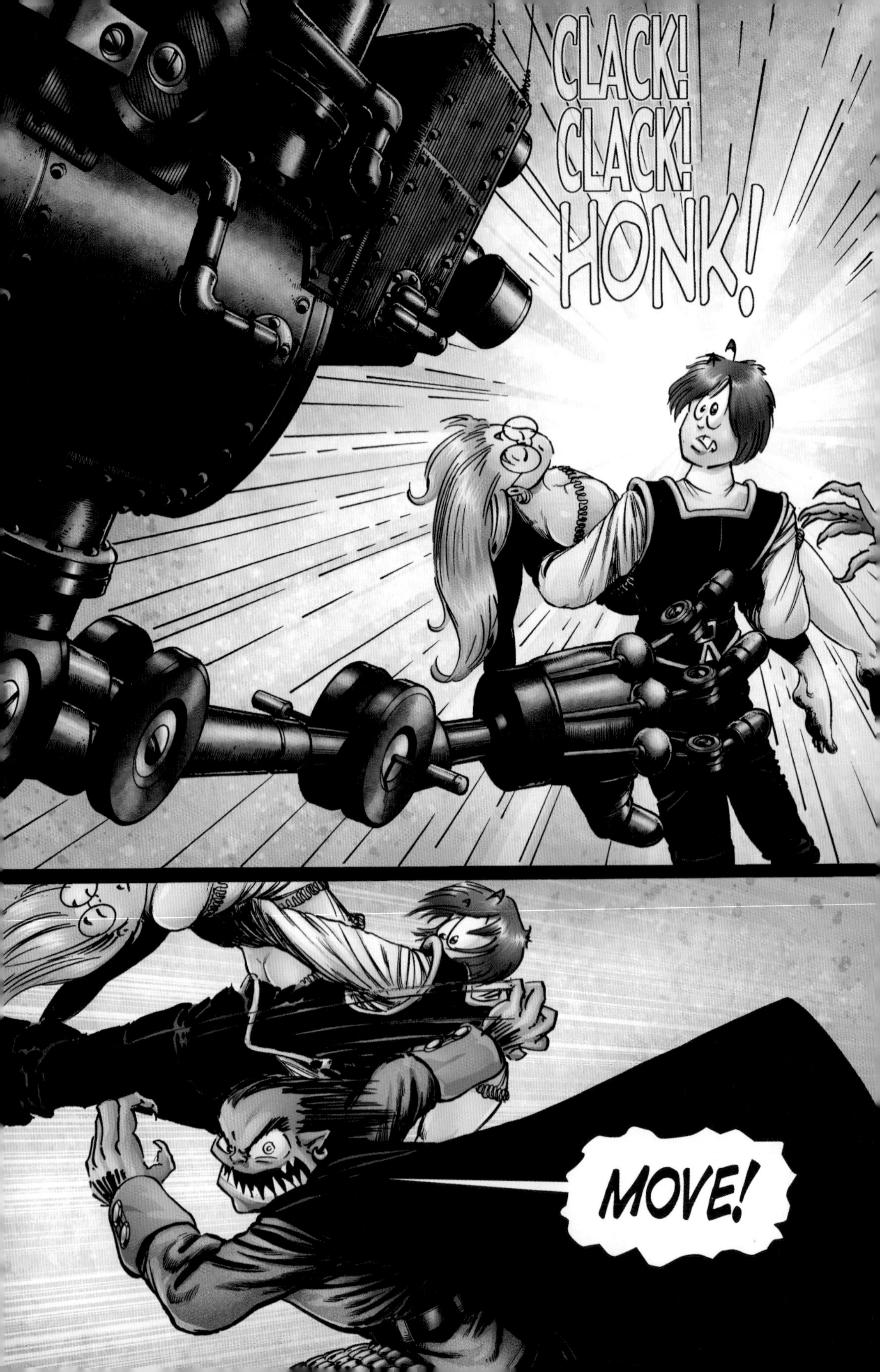
CLACK!
CLACK!
HONK!
MOVE!

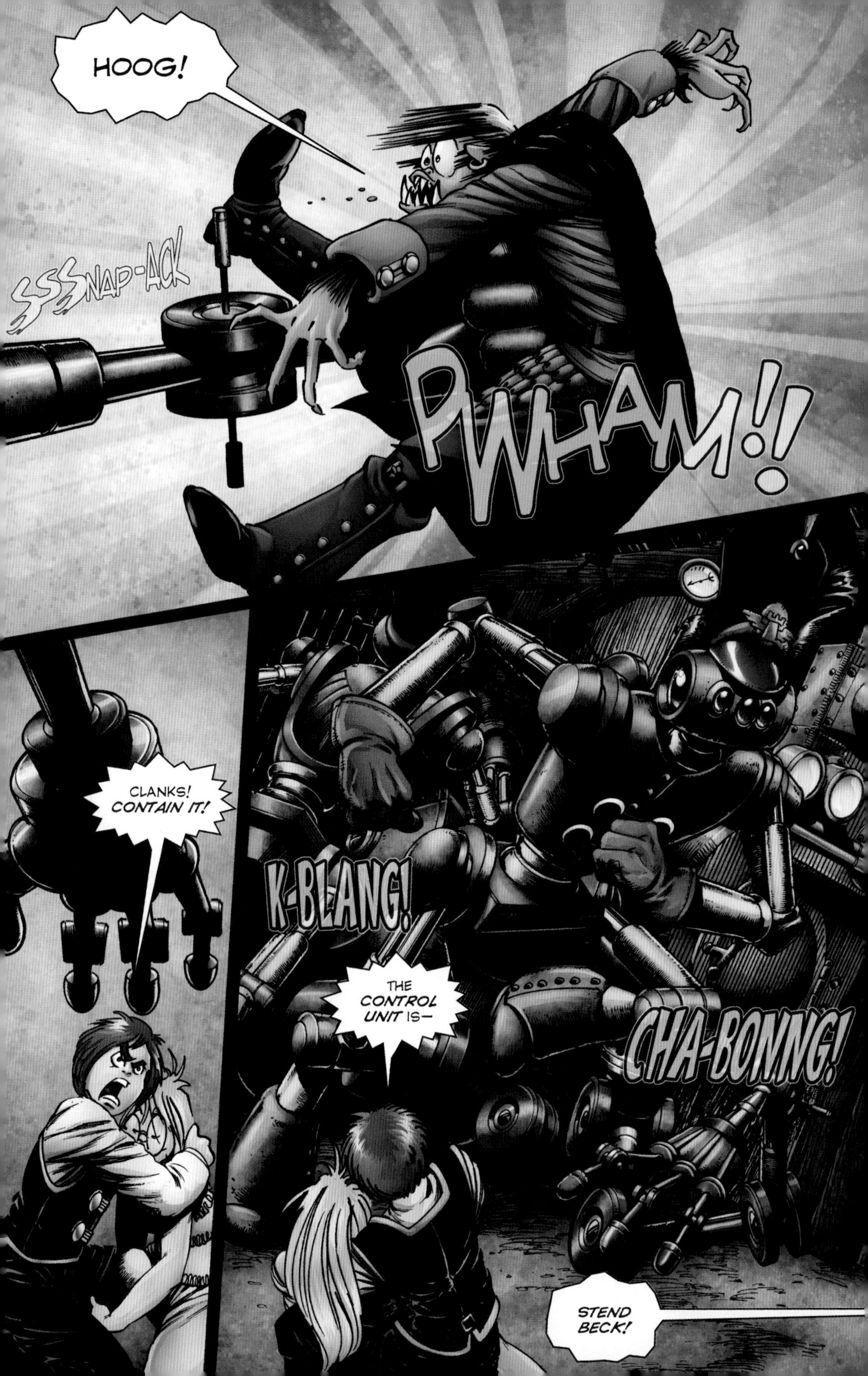
HOOG!
SSSNAP-ACK
PWHAM!!
CLANKS! CONTAIN IT!
K-BLANG!
THE CONTROL UNIT IS—
CHA-BONNG!
STEND BECK!

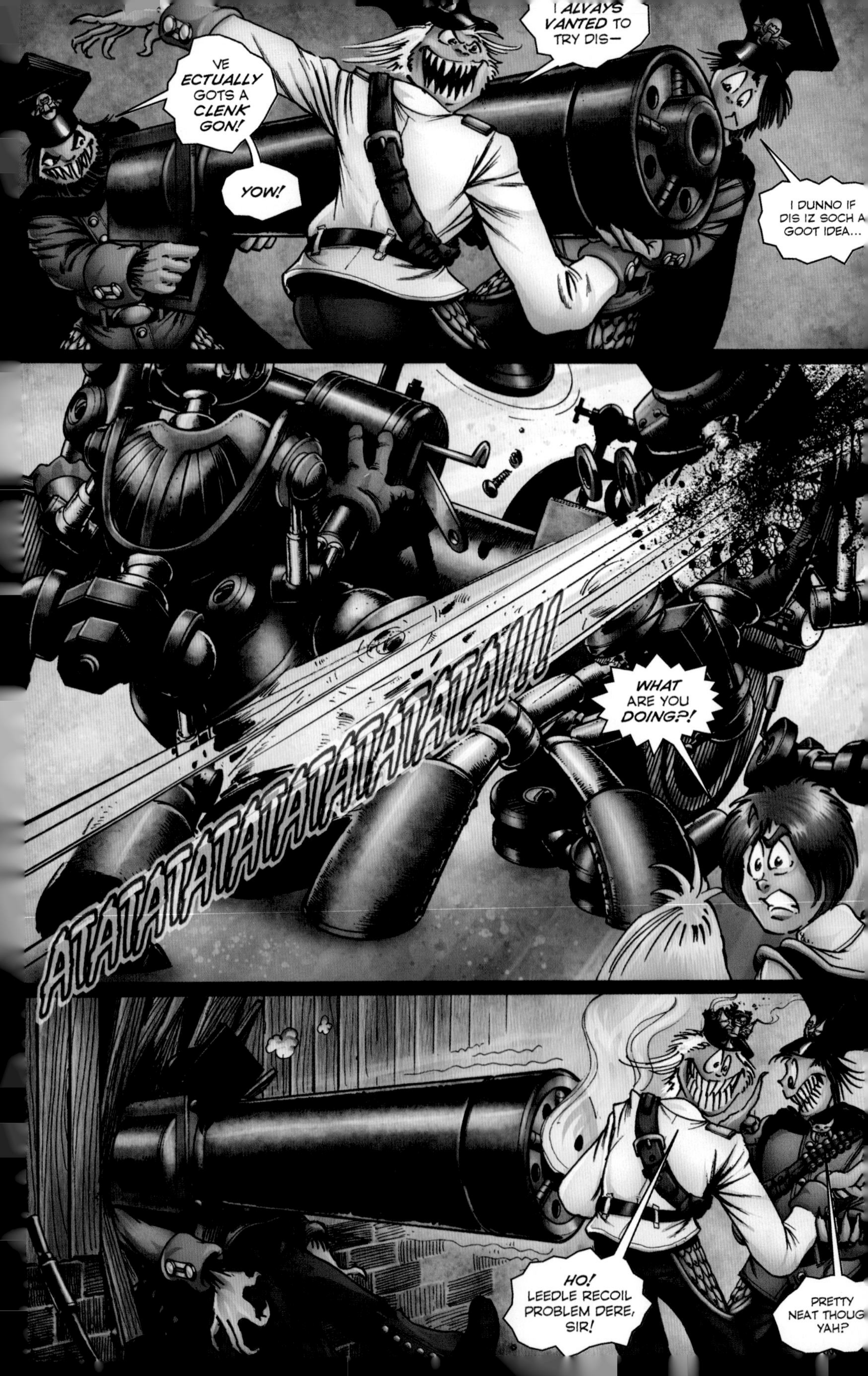
VE ECTUALLY GOTS A CLENK GON!
I ALWAYS VANTED TO TRY DIS—
YOW!
I DUNNO IF DIS IZ SOCH A GOOT IDEA...
ATATATATATATATATATATAT!!!!
WHAT ARE YOU DOING?!
HO! LEEDLE RECOIL PROBLEM DERE, SIR!
PRETTY NEAT THOUG YAH?

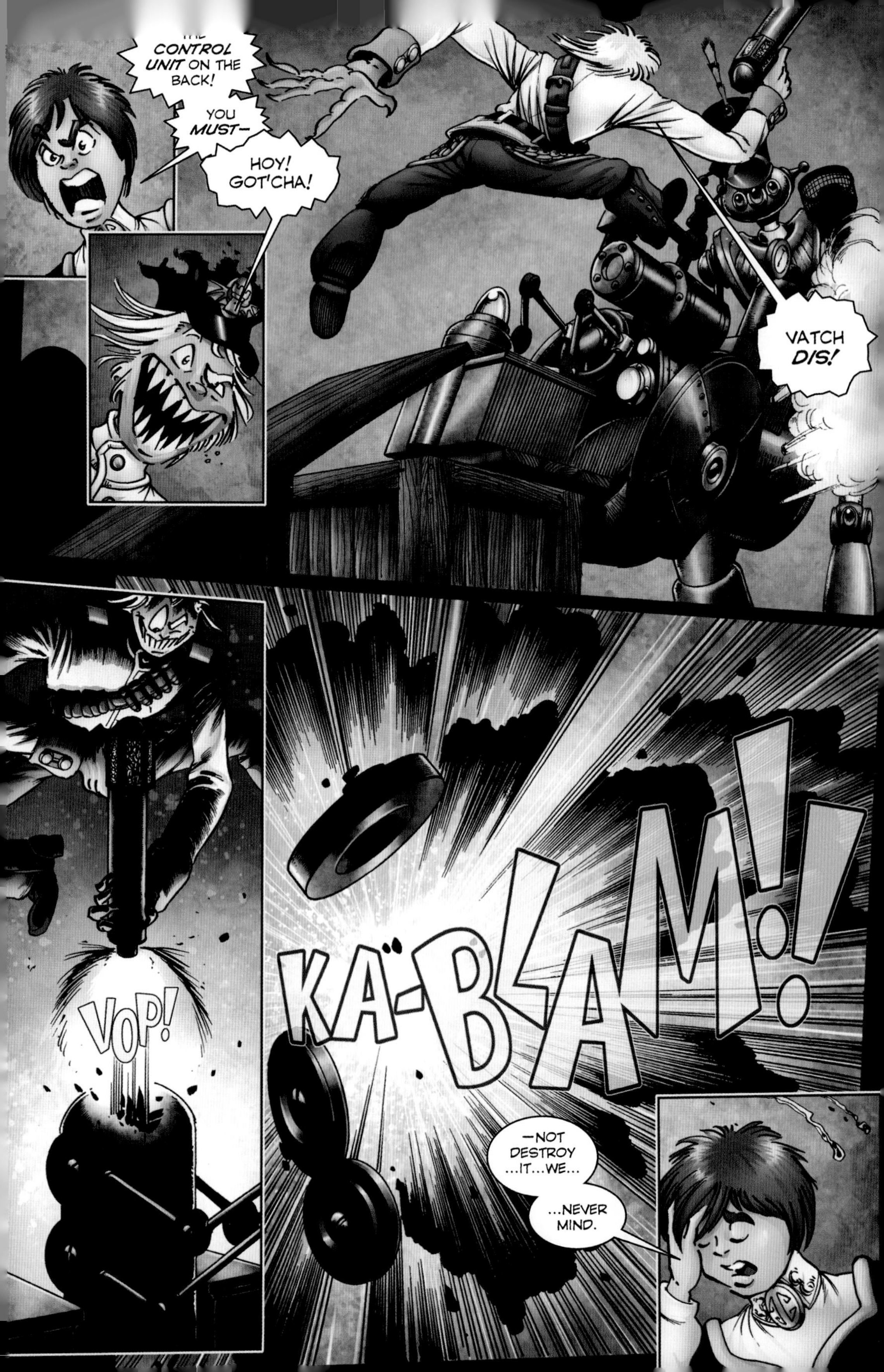
CONTROL UNIT ON THE BACK!
YOU MUST—
HOY! GOT'CHA!
VATCH DIS!
VOP!
KA-BLAM!!
—NOT DESTROY ...IT...WE...
...NEVER MIND.

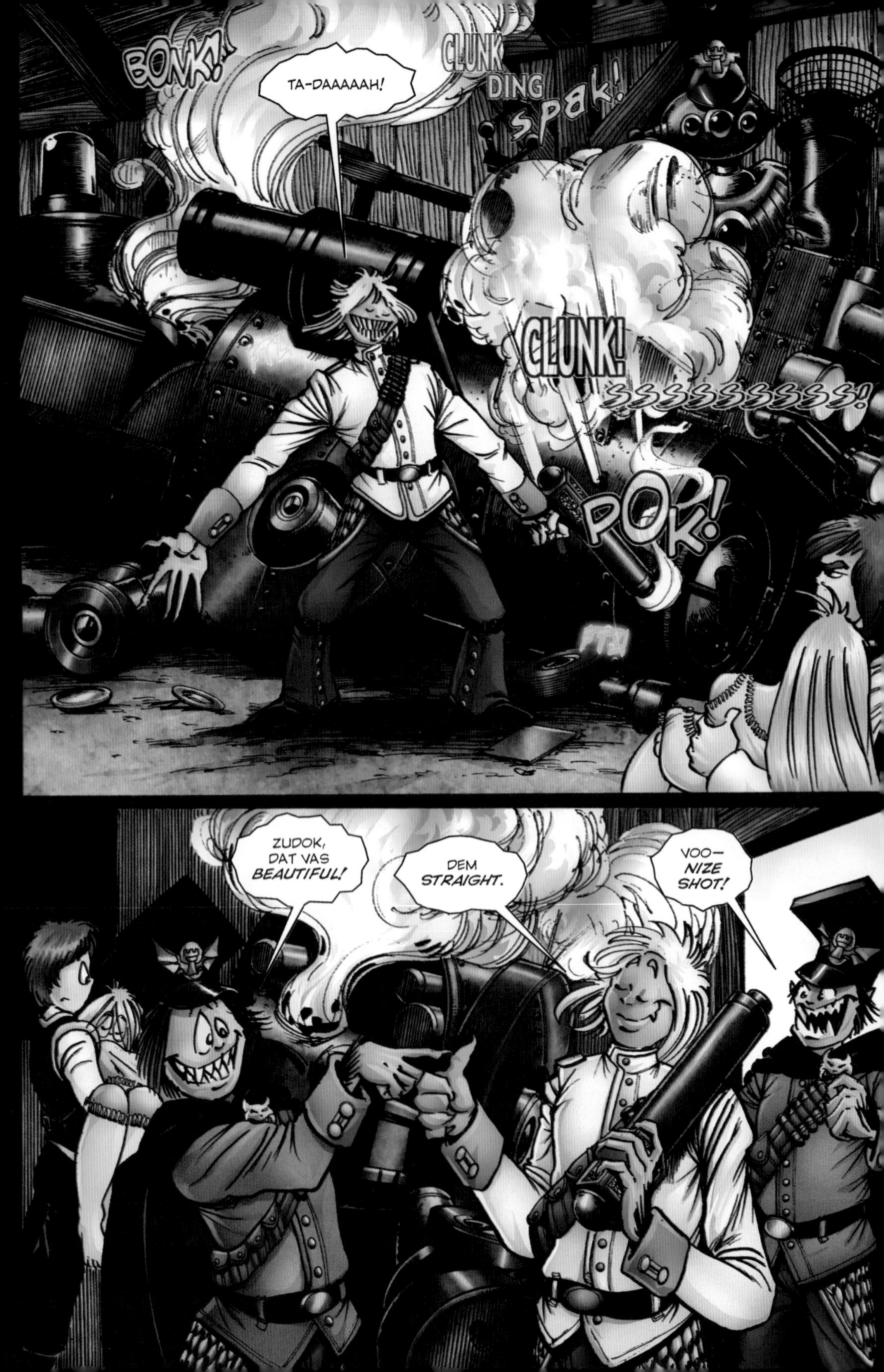
BONK!
TA-DAAAAAH!
CLUNK
DING
SPAK!
CLUNK!
SSSSSSSSSSS!
POK!
ZUDOK, DAT VAS *BEAUTIFUL!*
DEM *STRAIGHT.*
VOO-*NIZE SHOT!*

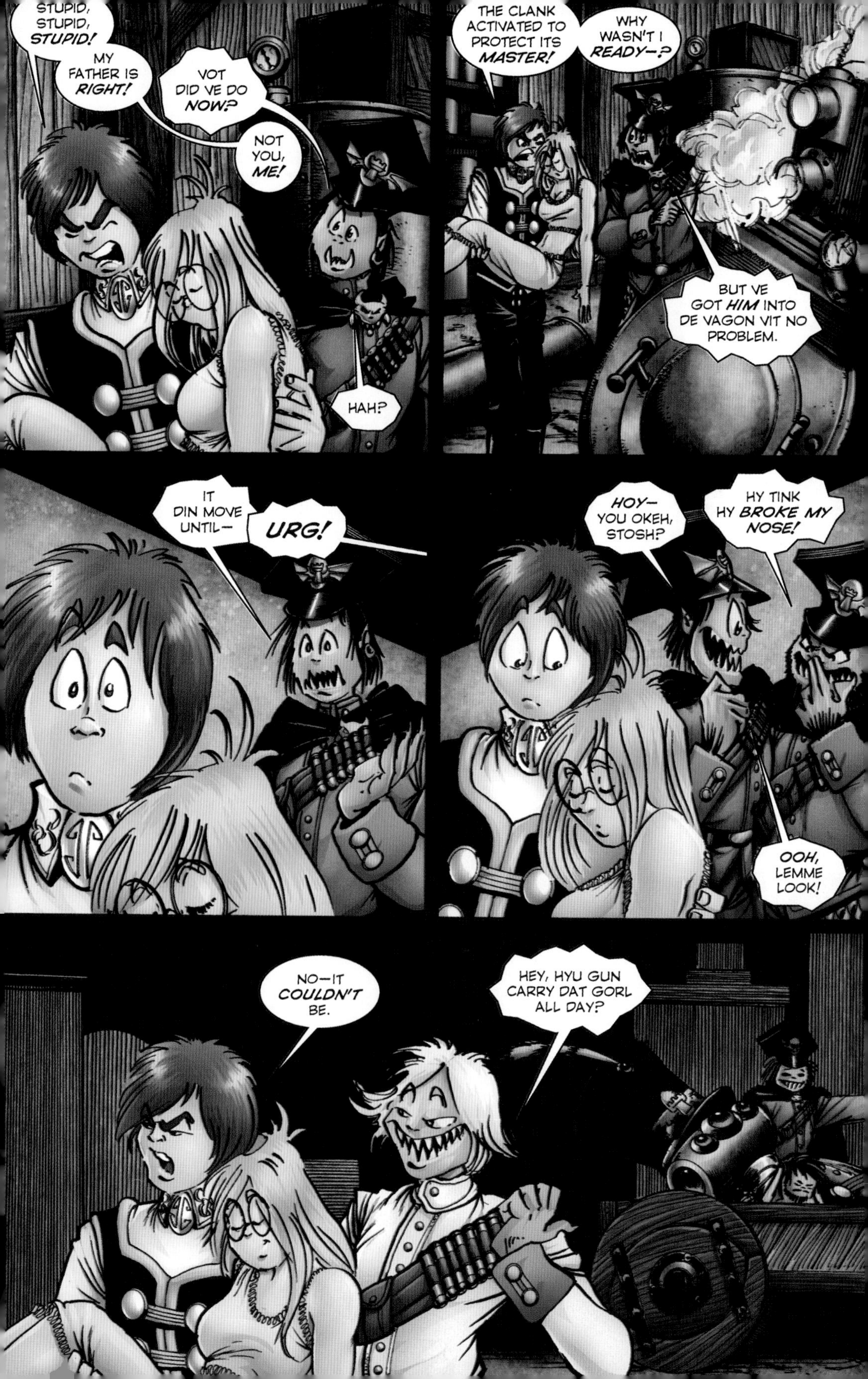
STUPID, STUPID, STUPID!
MY FATHER IS RIGHT!
VOT DID VE DO NOW?
NOT YOU, ME!
HAH?
THE CLANK ACTIVATED TO PROTECT ITS MASTER!
WHY WASN'T I READY—?
BUT VE GOT HIM INTO DE VAGON VIT NO PROBLEM.
IT DIN MOVE UNTIL—
URG!
HOY— YOU OKEH, STOSH?
HY TINK HY BROKE MY NOSE!
OOH, LEMME LOOK!
NO—IT COULDN'T BE.
HEY, HYU GUN CARRY DAT GORL ALL DAY?

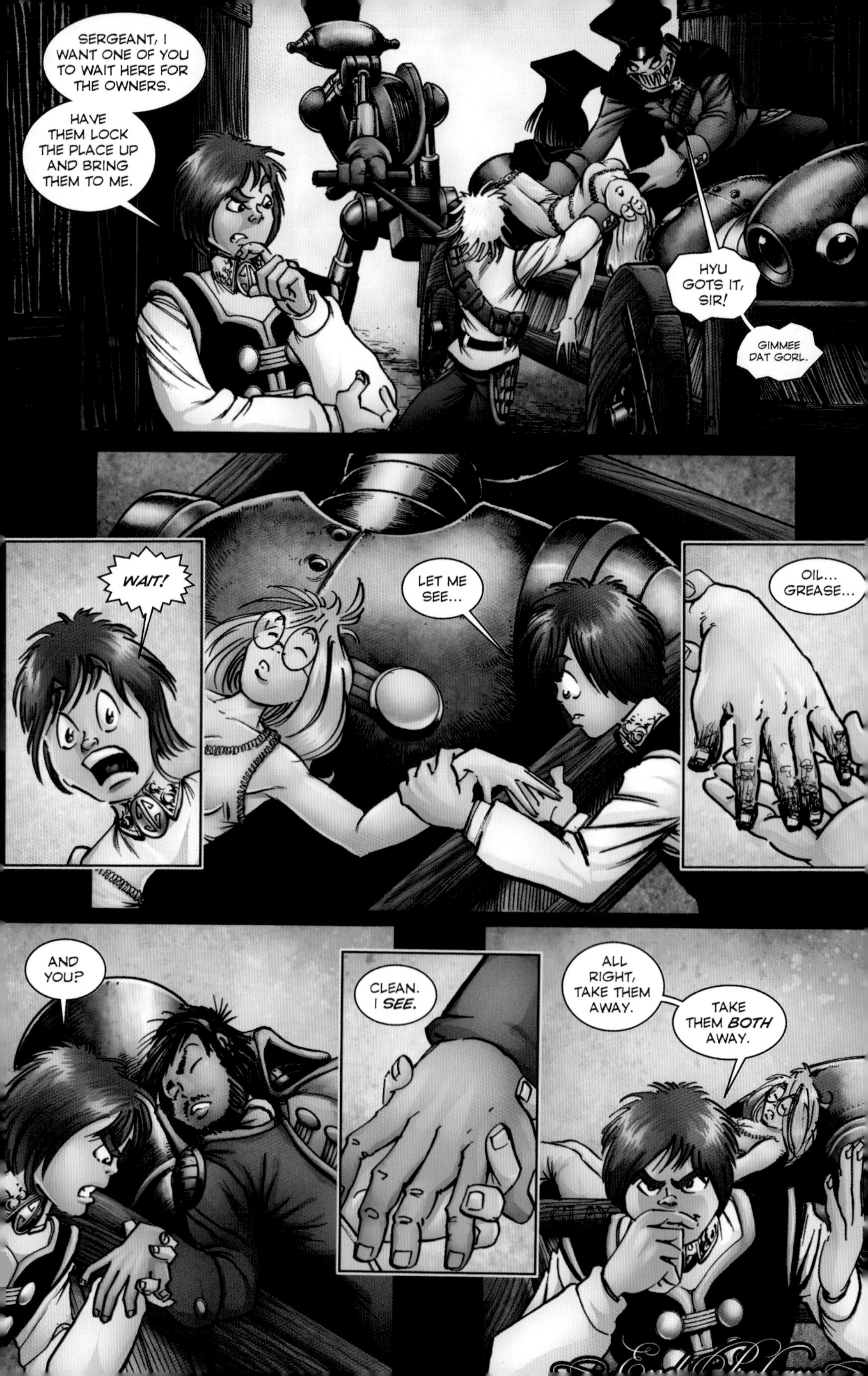
SERGEANT, I WANT ONE OF YOU TO WAIT HERE FOR THE OWNERS.
HAVE THEM LOCK THE PLACE UP AND BRING THEM TO ME.
HYU GOTS IT, SIR!
GIMMEE DAT GORL.
WAIT!
LET ME SEE...
OIL... GREASE...
AND YOU?
CLEAN. I SEE.
ALL RIGHT, TAKE THEM AWAY.
TAKE THEM BOTH AWAY.

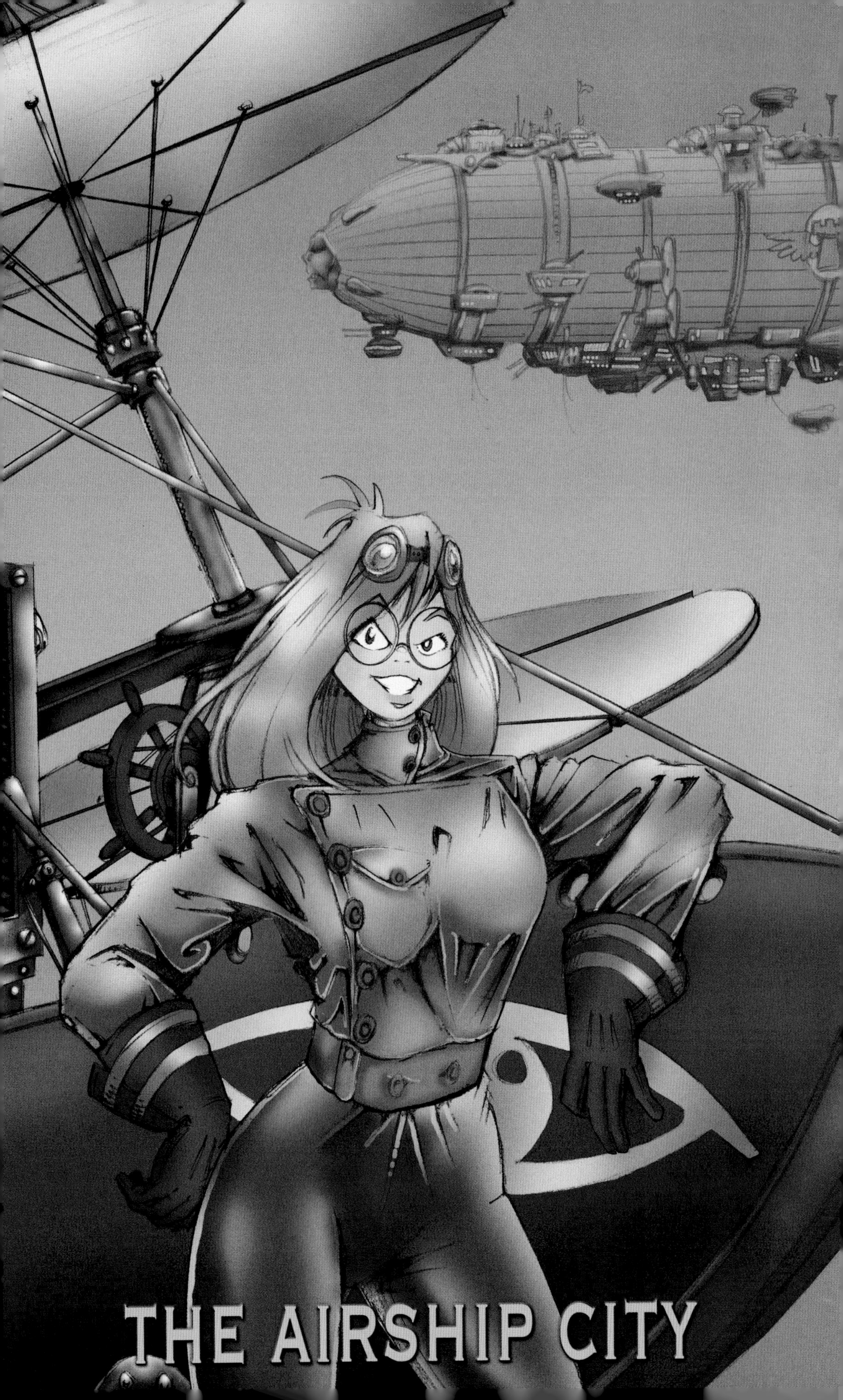

THE AIRSHIP CITY

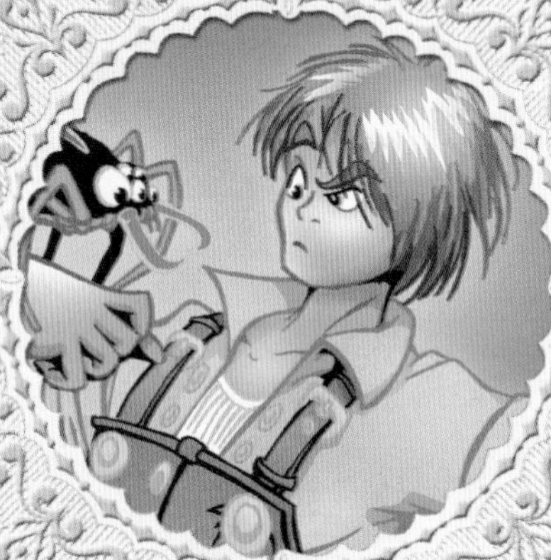

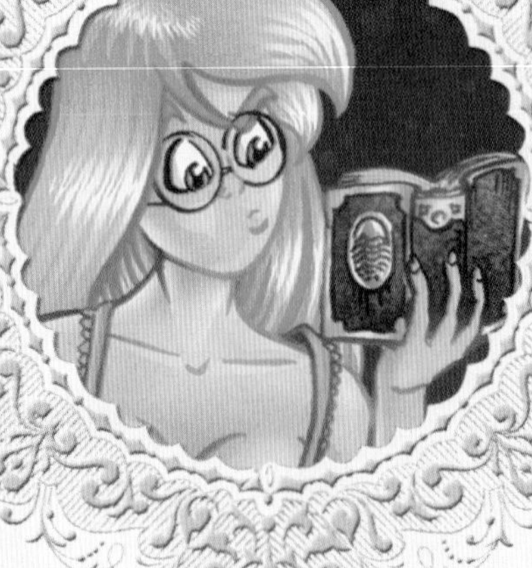

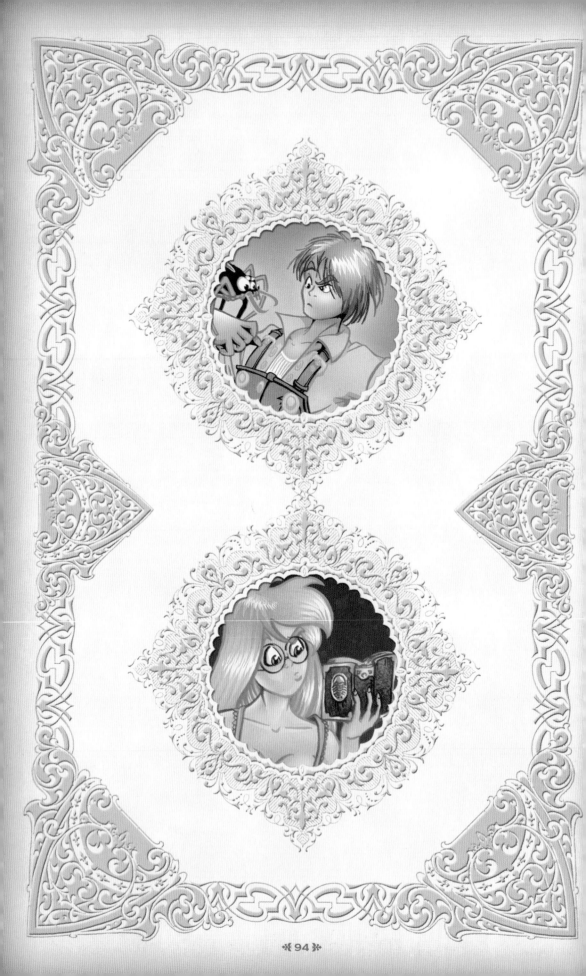

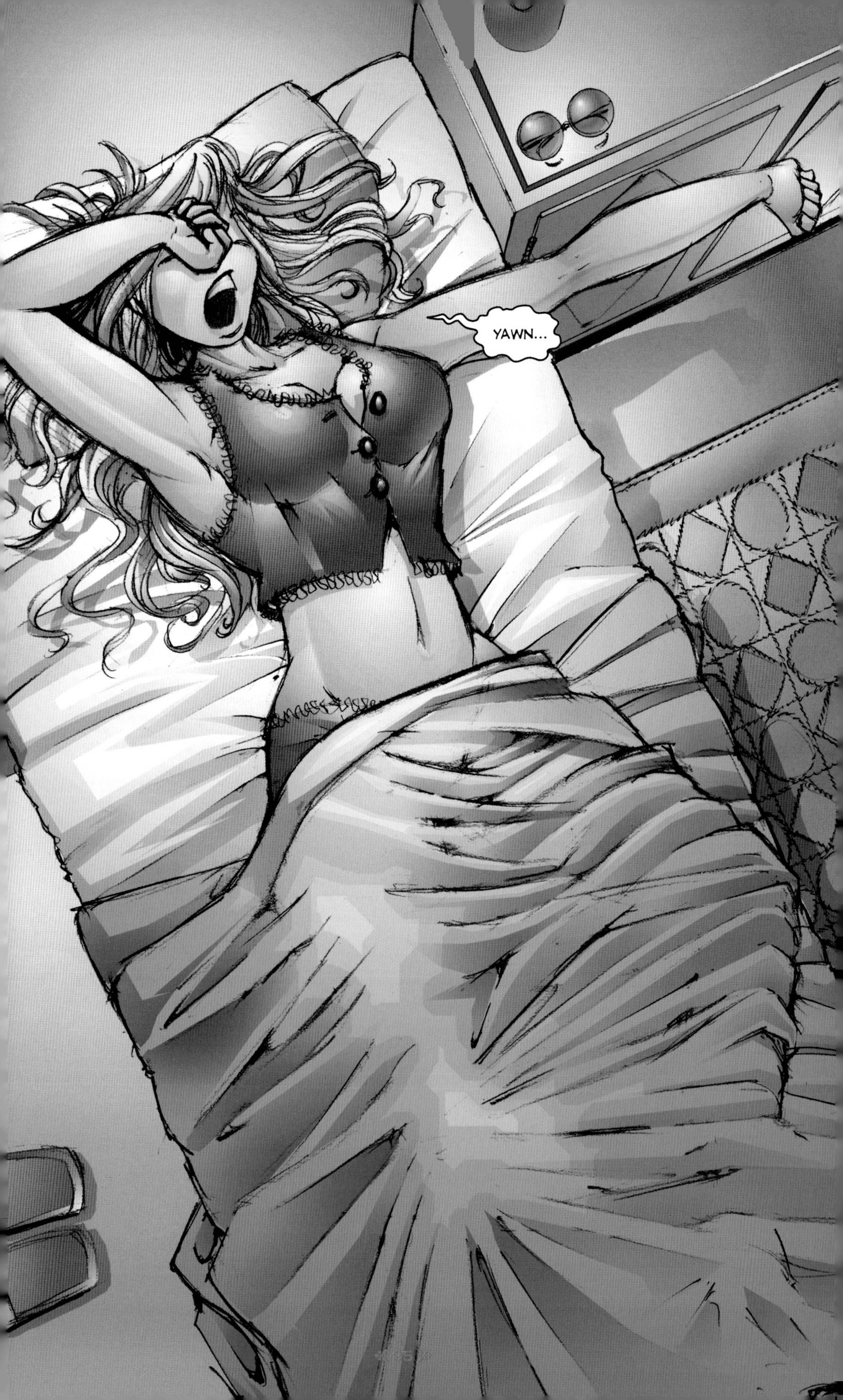
YAWN...

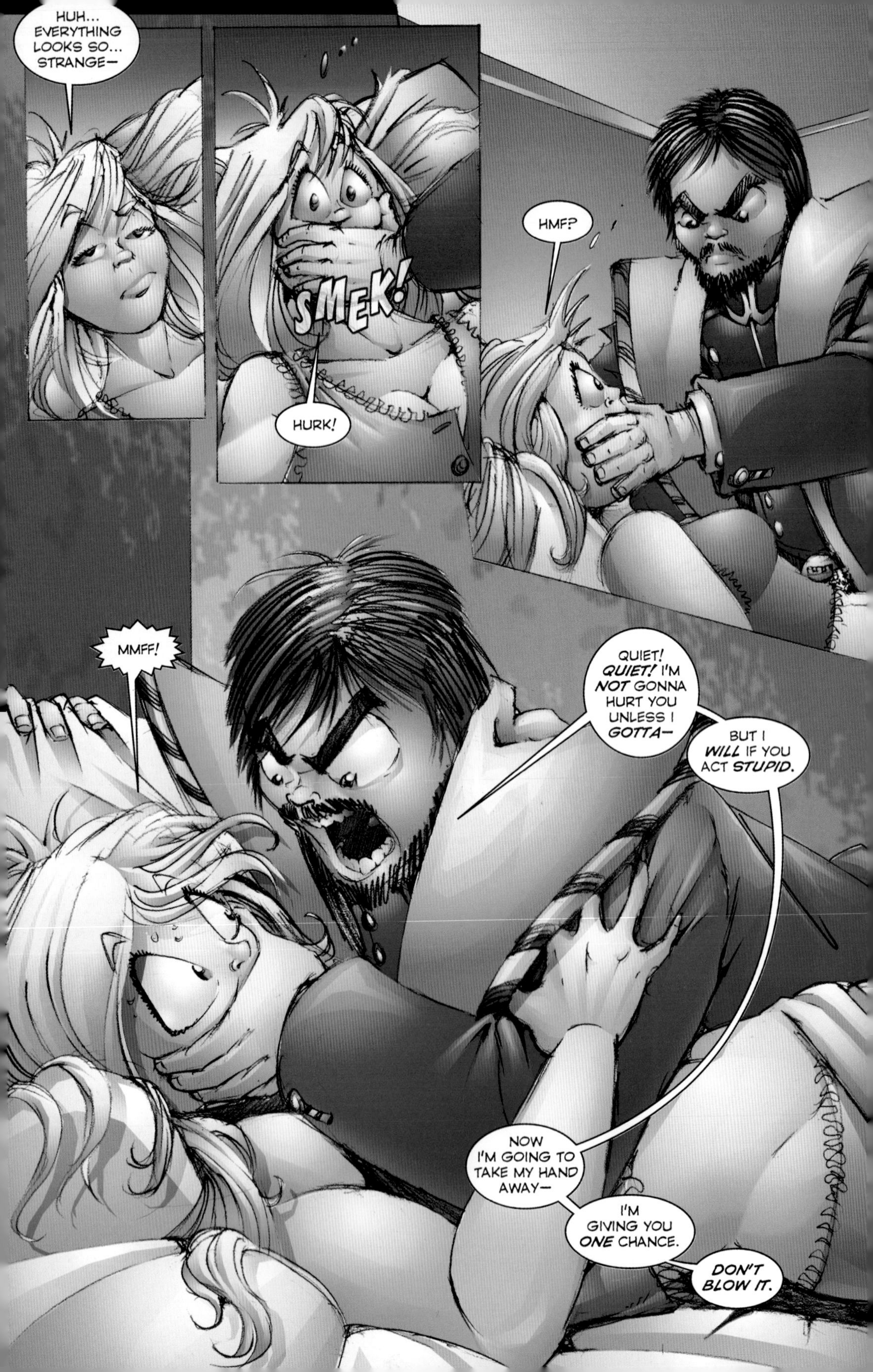
HUH... EVERYTHING LOOKS SO... STRANGE—
SMEK!
HURK!
HMF?
MMFF!
QUIET! QUIET! I'M NOT GONNA HURT YOU UNLESS I GOTTA—
BUT I WILL IF YOU ACT STUPID.
NOW I'M GOING TO TAKE MY HAND AWAY—
I'M GIVING YOU ONE CHANCE.
DON'T BLOW IT.

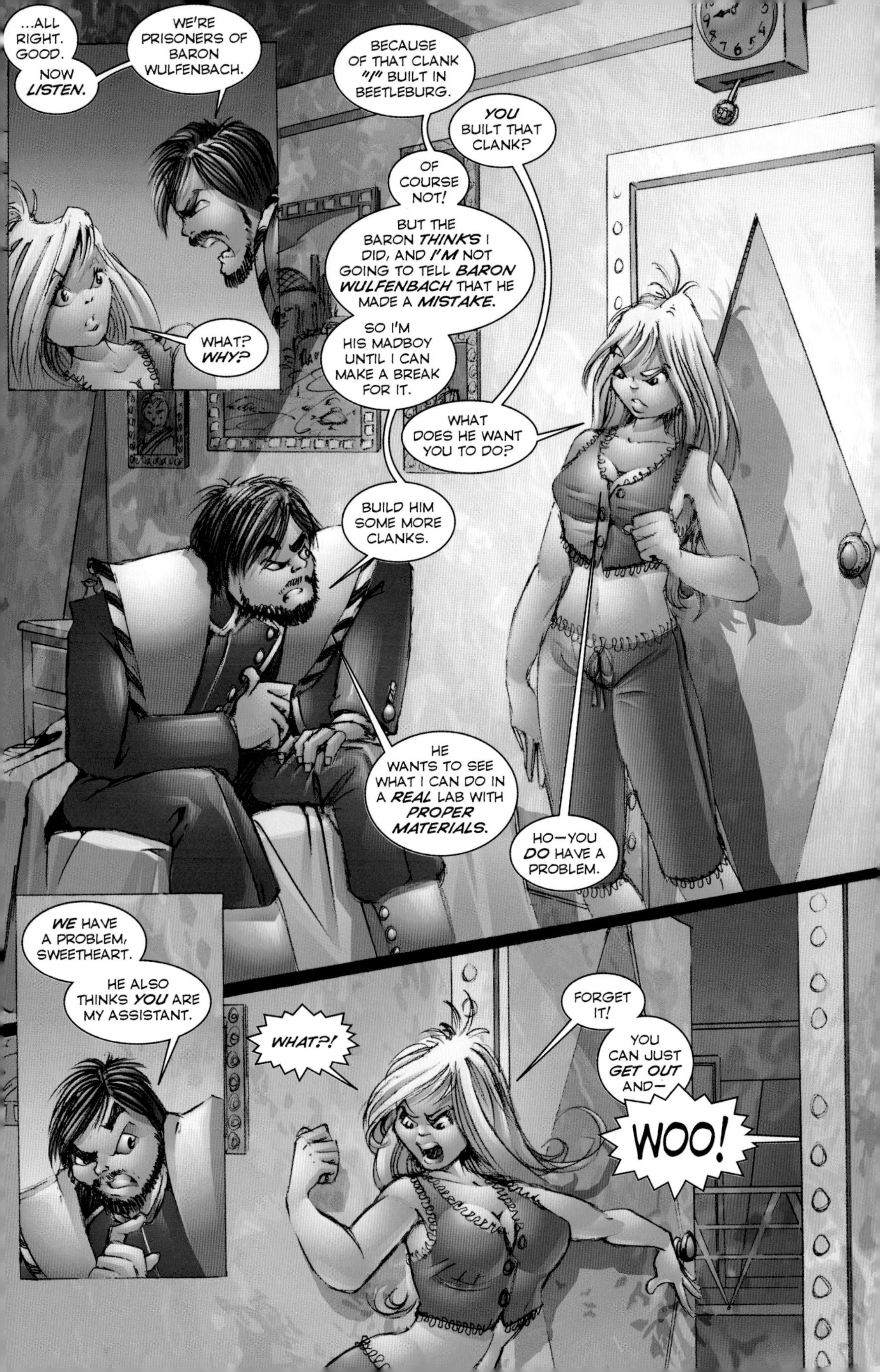
...ALL RIGHT. GOOD. NOW LISTEN.
WE'RE PRISONERS OF BARON WULFENBACH.
WHAT? WHY?
BECAUSE OF THAT CLANK "I" BUILT IN BEETLEBURG.
YOU BUILT THAT CLANK?
OF COURSE NOT!
BUT THE BARON THINKS I DID, AND I'M NOT GOING TO TELL BARON WULFENBACH THAT HE MADE A MISTAKE.
SO I'M HIS MADBOY UNTIL I CAN MAKE A BREAK FOR IT.
WHAT DOES HE WANT YOU TO DO?
BUILD HIM SOME MORE CLANKS.
HE WANTS TO SEE WHAT I CAN DO IN A REAL LAB WITH PROPER MATERIALS.
HO—YOU DO HAVE A PROBLEM.
WE HAVE A PROBLEM, SWEETHEART.
HE ALSO THINKS YOU ARE MY ASSISTANT.
WHAT?!
FORGET IT!
YOU CAN JUST GET OUT AND—
WOO!

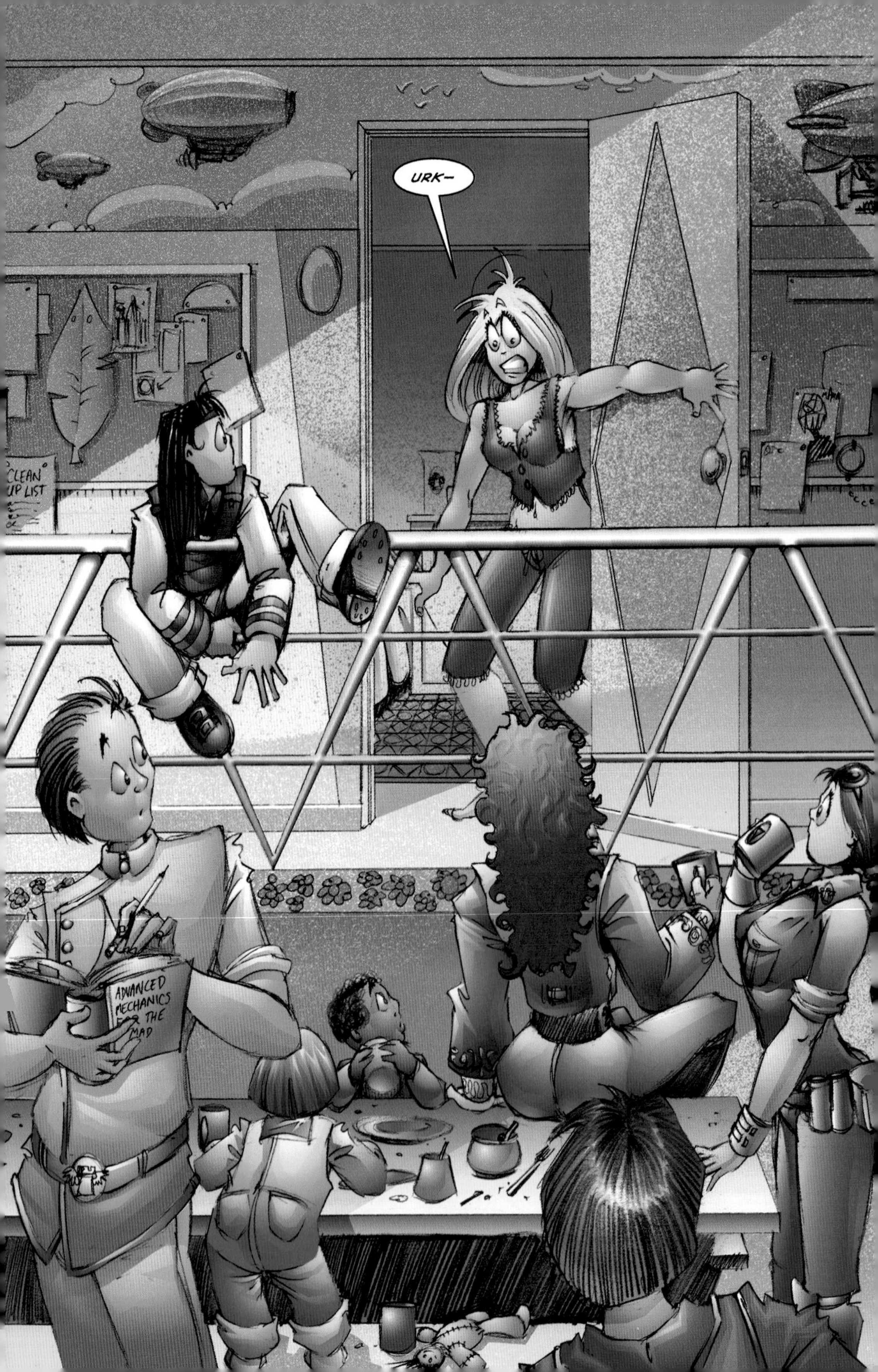
URK—
CLEAN UP LIST
ADVANCED MECHANICS FOR THE MAD

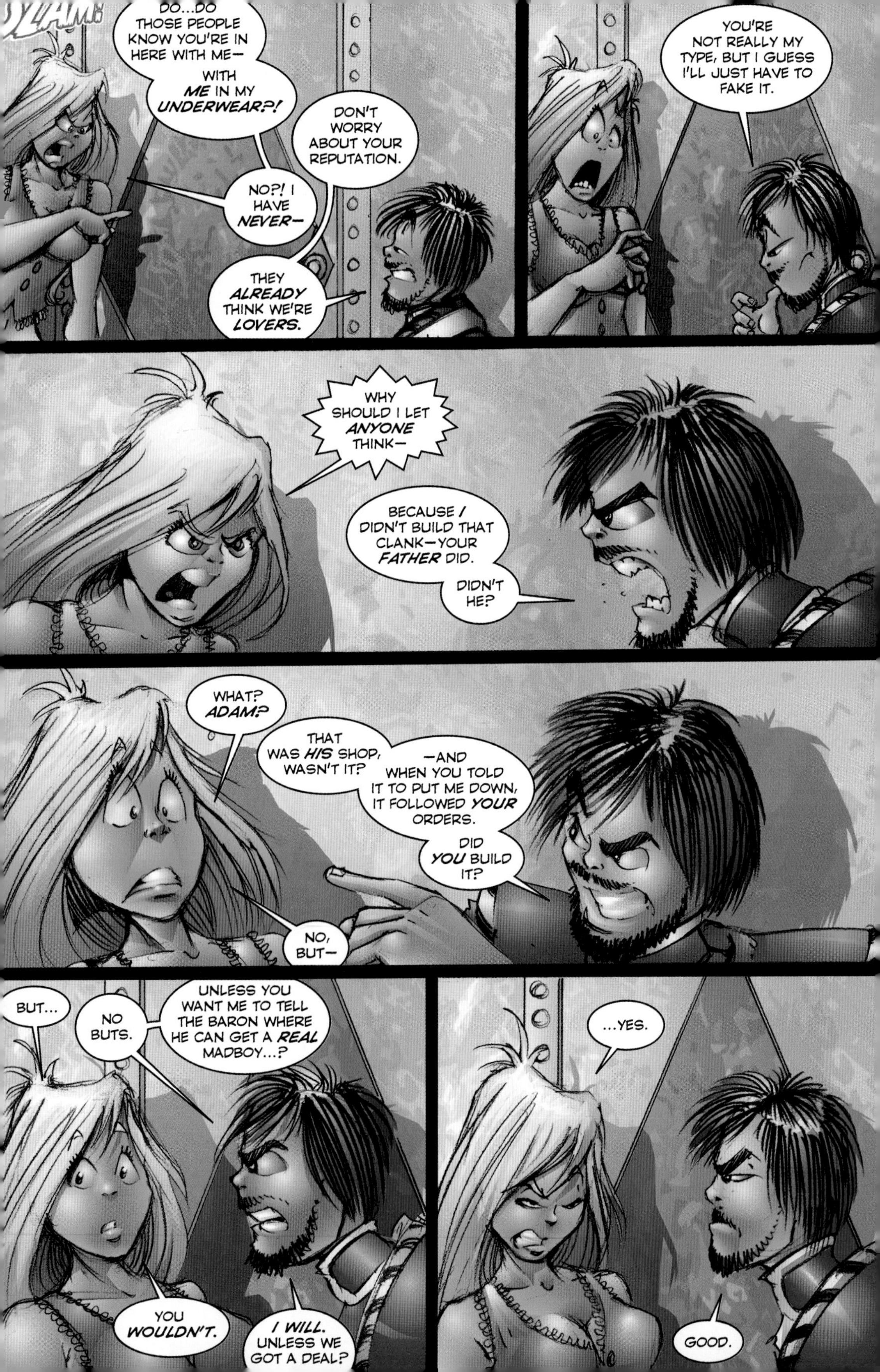
DO...DO THOSE PEOPLE KNOW YOU'RE IN HERE WITH ME—
WITH *ME* IN MY *UNDERWEAR?!*
DON'T WORRY ABOUT YOUR REPUTATION.
NO?! I HAVE *NEVER*—
THEY *ALREADY* THINK WE'RE *LOVERS.*
YOU'RE NOT REALLY MY TYPE, BUT I GUESS I'LL JUST HAVE TO FAKE IT.
WHY SHOULD I LET *ANYONE* THINK—
BECAUSE *I* DIDN'T BUILD THAT CLANK—YOUR *FATHER* DID.
DIDN'T HE?
WHAT? *ADAM?*
THAT WAS *HIS* SHOP, WASN'T IT?
—AND WHEN YOU TOLD IT TO PUT ME DOWN, IT FOLLOWED *YOUR* ORDERS.
DID *YOU* BUILD IT?
NO, BUT—
BUT...
NO BUTS.
UNLESS YOU WANT ME TO TELL THE BARON WHERE HE CAN GET A *REAL* MADBOY...?
YOU *WOULDN'T.*
I WILL. UNLESS WE GOT A DEAL?
...YES.
GOOD.

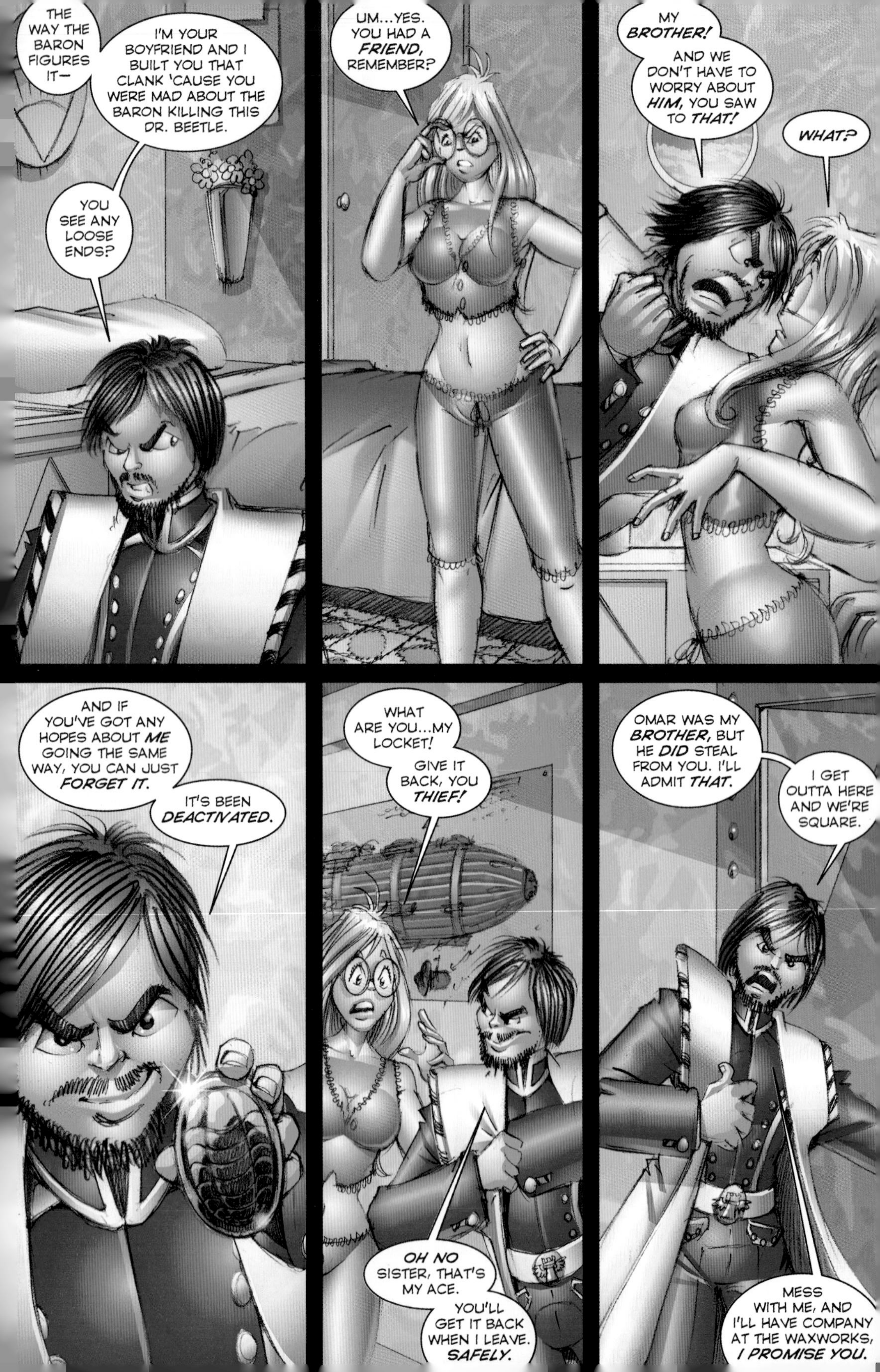
THE WAY THE BARON FIGURES IT—
I'M YOUR BOYFRIEND AND I BUILT YOU THAT CLANK 'CAUSE YOU WERE MAD ABOUT THE BARON KILLING THIS DR. BEETLE.
YOU SEE ANY LOOSE ENDS?
UM...YES. YOU HAD A FRIEND, REMEMBER?
MY BROTHER!
AND WE DON'T HAVE TO WORRY ABOUT HIM, YOU SAW TO THAT!
WHAT?
AND IF YOU'VE GOT ANY HOPES ABOUT ME GOING THE SAME WAY, YOU CAN JUST FORGET IT.
IT'S BEEN DEACTIVATED.
WHAT ARE YOU...MY LOCKET!
GIVE IT BACK, YOU THIEF!
OH NO SISTER, THAT'S MY ACE.
YOU'LL GET IT BACK WHEN I LEAVE. SAFELY.
OMAR WAS MY BROTHER, BUT HE DID STEAL FROM YOU. I'LL ADMIT THAT.
I GET OUTTA HERE AND WE'RE SQUARE.
MESS WITH ME, AND I'LL HAVE COMPANY AT THE WAXWORKS, I PROMISE YOU.

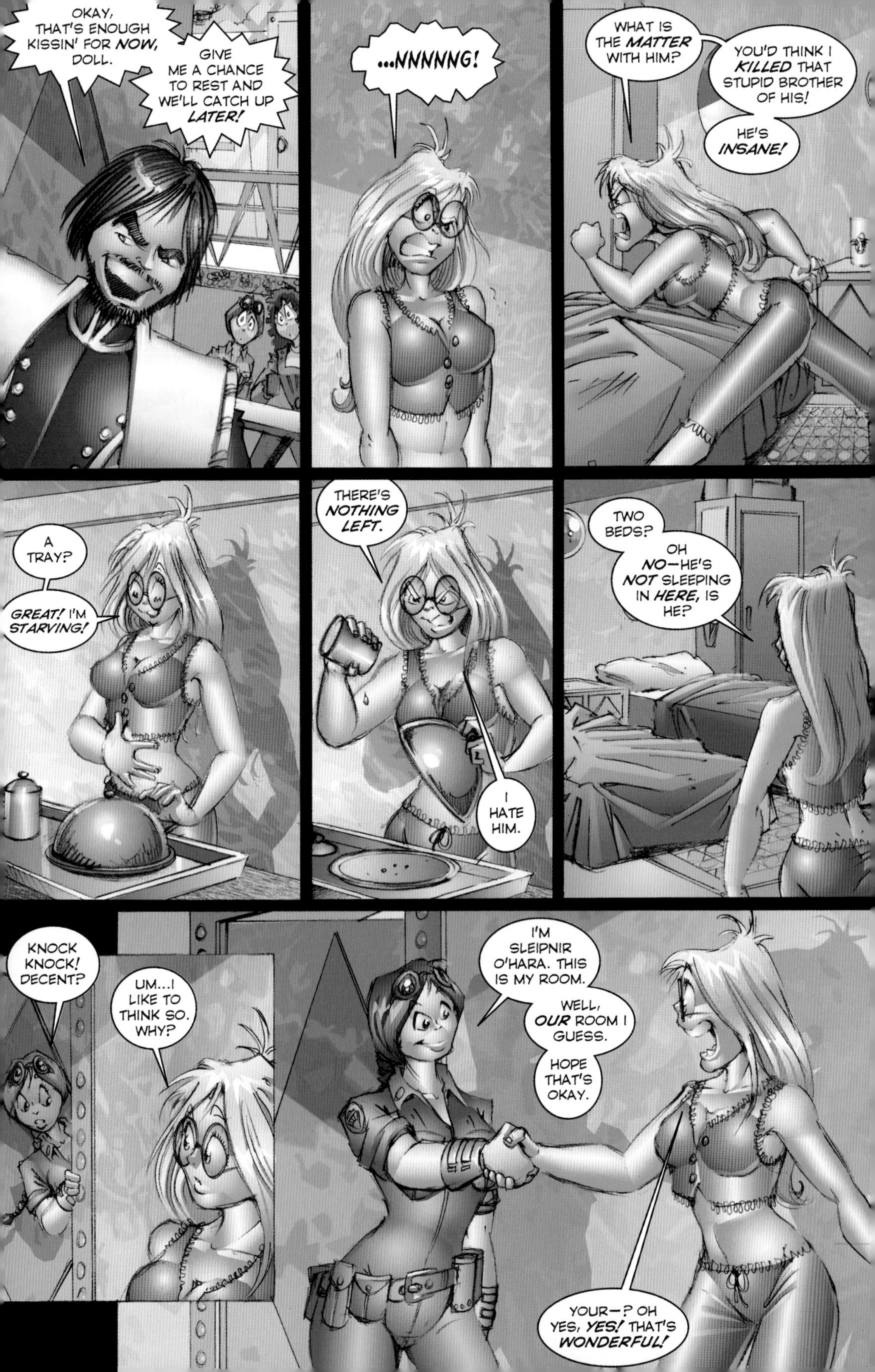
OKAY, THAT'S ENOUGH KISSIN' FOR NOW, DOLL.
GIVE ME A CHANCE TO REST AND WE'LL CATCH UP LATER!
...NNNNNG!
WHAT IS THE MATTER WITH HIM?
YOU'D THINK I KILLED THAT STUPID BROTHER OF HIS!
HE'S INSANE!
A TRAY?
GREAT! I'M STARVING!
THERE'S NOTHING LEFT.
I HATE HIM.
TWO BEDS?
OH NO—HE'S NOT SLEEPING IN HERE, IS HE?
KNOCK KNOCK! DECENT?
UM...I LIKE TO THINK SO. WHY?
I'M SLEIPNIR O'HARA. THIS IS MY ROOM.
WELL, OUR ROOM I GUESS.
HOPE THAT'S OKAY.
YOUR—? OH YES, YES! THAT'S WONDERFUL!

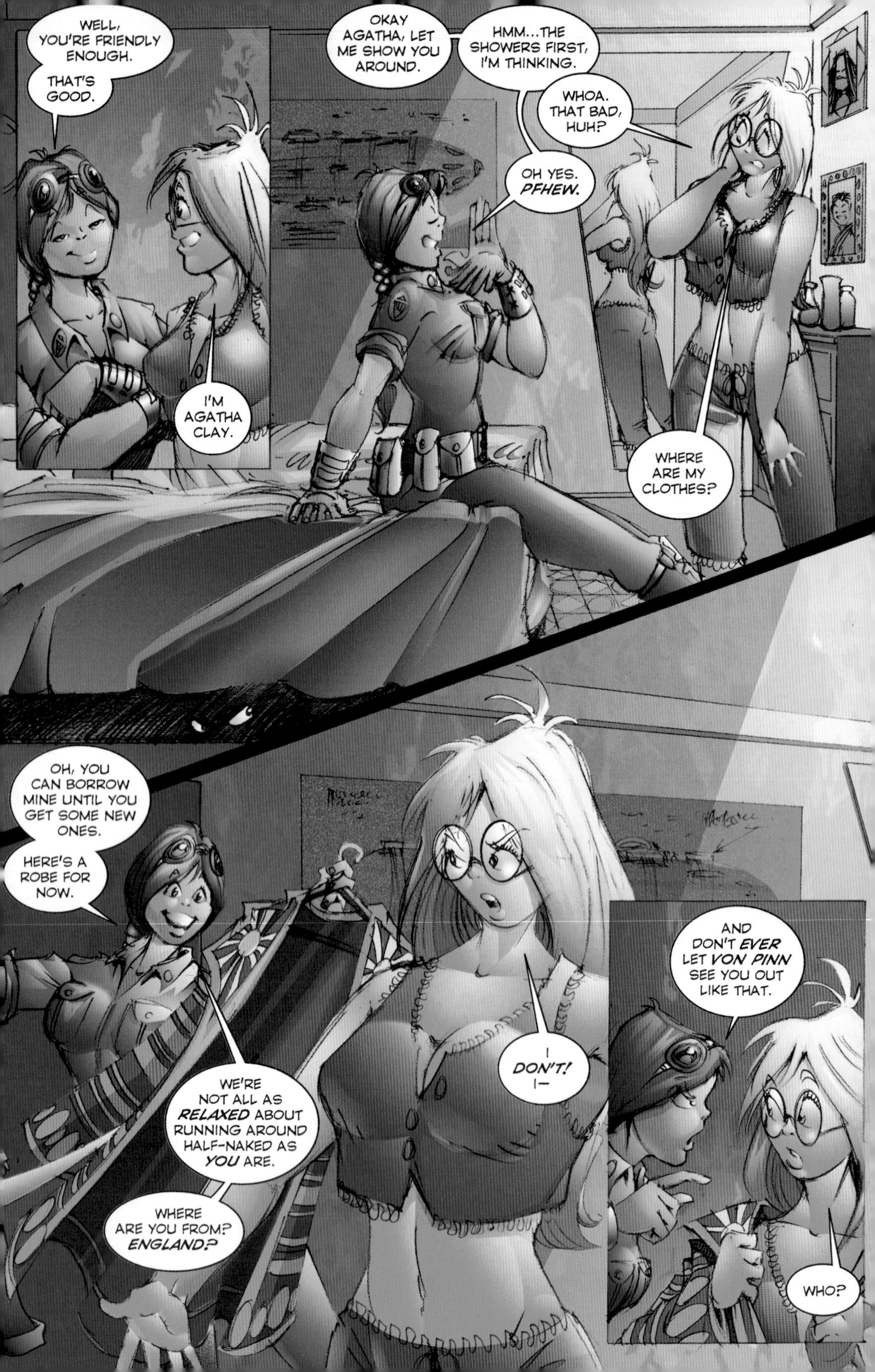
WELL, YOU'RE FRIENDLY ENOUGH.
THAT'S GOOD.
I'M AGATHA CLAY.
OKAY AGATHA, LET ME SHOW YOU AROUND.
HMM...THE SHOWERS FIRST, I'M THINKING.
WHOA. THAT BAD, HUH?
OH YES. PFHEW.
WHERE ARE MY CLOTHES?
OH, YOU CAN BORROW MINE UNTIL YOU GET SOME NEW ONES.
HERE'S A ROBE FOR NOW.
WE'RE NOT ALL AS RELAXED ABOUT RUNNING AROUND HALF-NAKED AS YOU ARE.
WHERE ARE YOU FROM? ENGLAND?
I DON'T! I—
AND DON'T EVER LET VON PINN SEE YOU OUT LIKE THAT.
WHO?

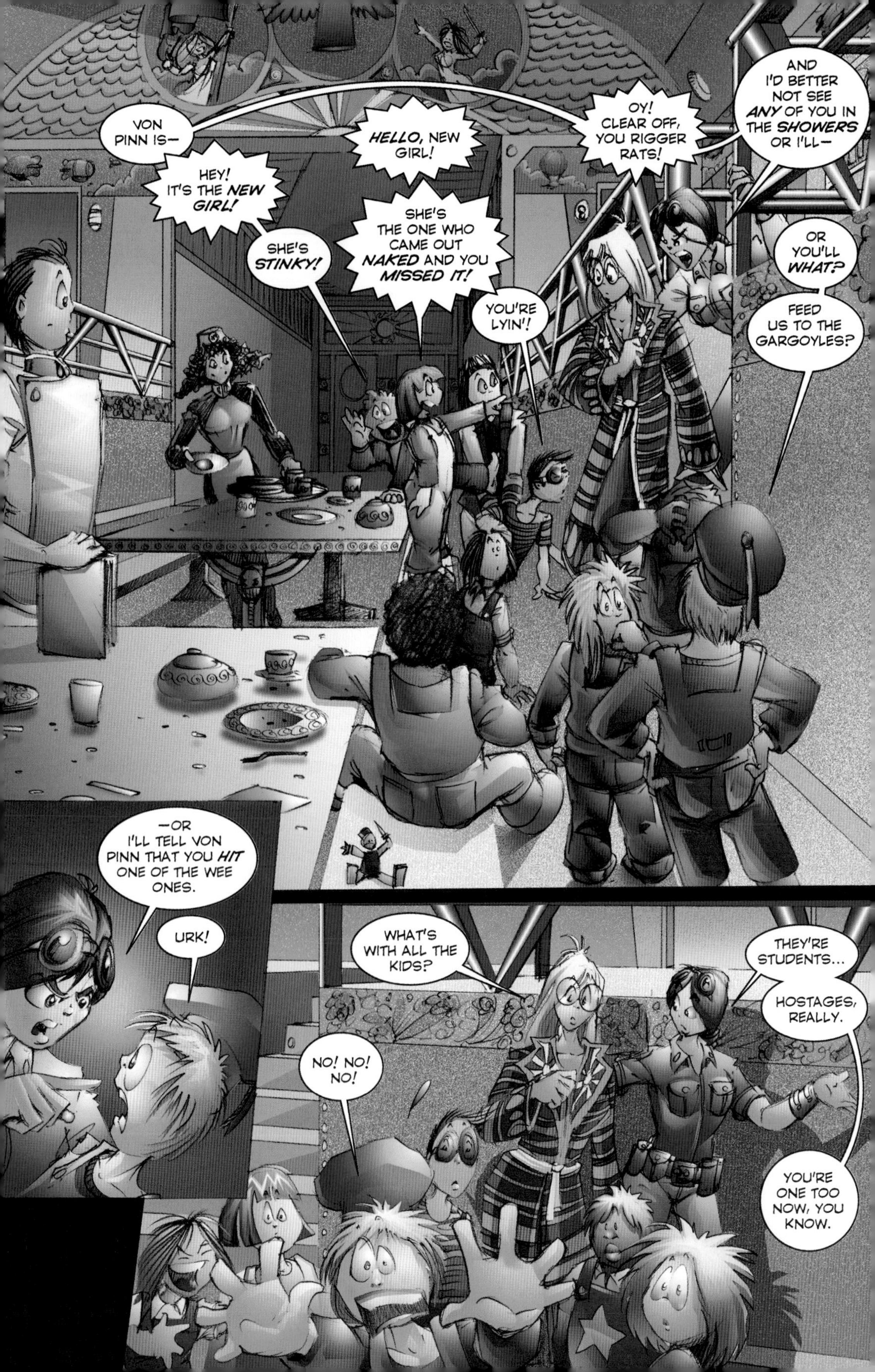
VON PINN IS—
HEY! IT'S THE NEW GIRL!
HELLO, NEW GIRL!
OY! CLEAR OFF, YOU RIGGER RATS!
AND I'D BETTER NOT SEE ANY OF YOU IN THE SHOWERS OR I'LL—
SHE'S STINKY!
SHE'S THE ONE WHO CAME OUT NAKED AND YOU MISSED IT!
YOU'RE LYIN'!
OR YOU'LL WHAT?
FEED US TO THE GARGOYLES?
—OR I'LL TELL VON PINN THAT YOU HIT ONE OF THE WEE ONES.
URK!
WHAT'S WITH ALL THE KIDS?
THEY'RE STUDENTS...
HOSTAGES, REALLY.
NO! NO! NO!
YOU'RE ONE TOO NOW, YOU KNOW.

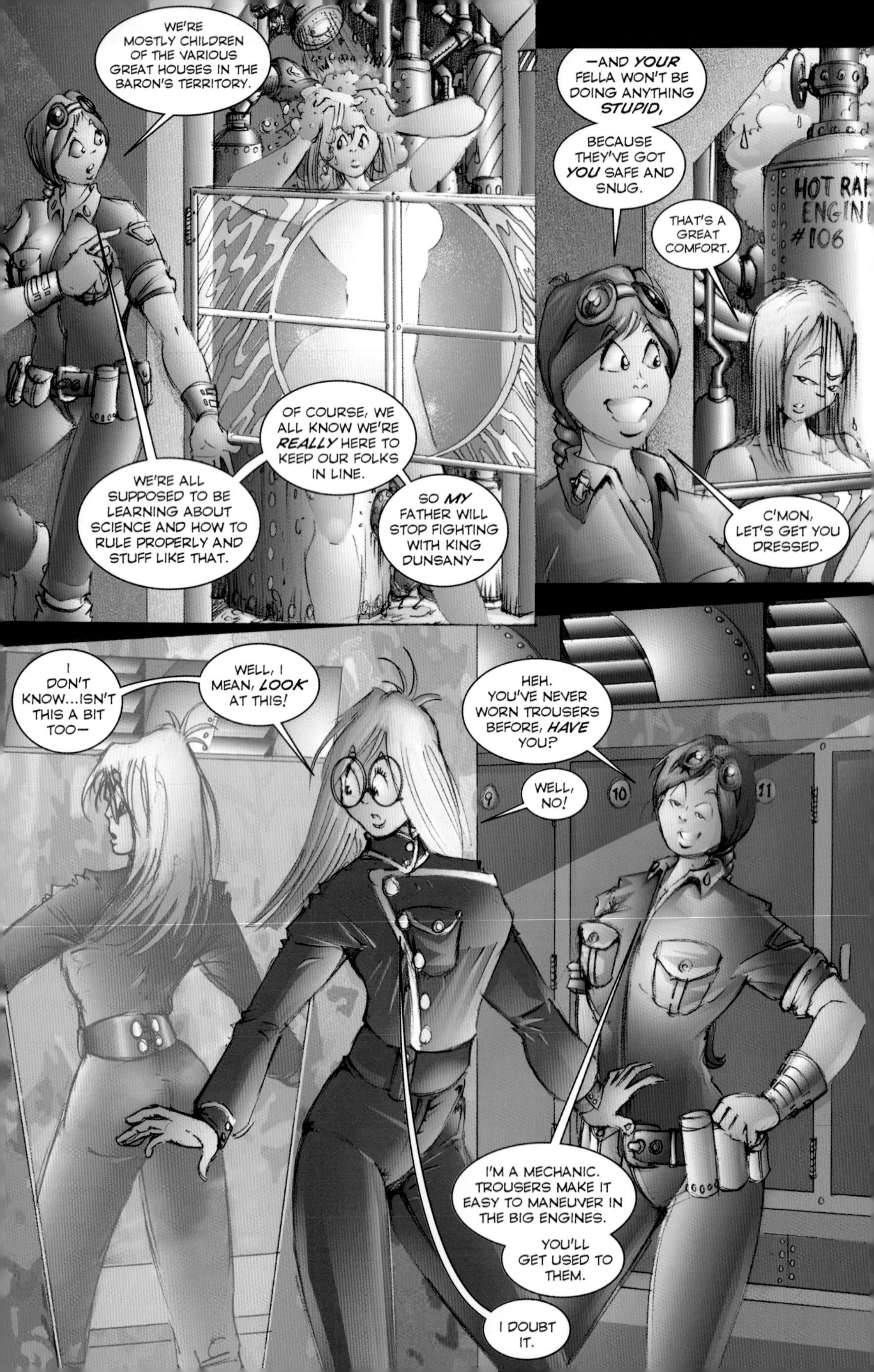
WE'RE MOSTLY CHILDREN OF THE VARIOUS GREAT HOUSES IN THE BARON'S TERRITORY.
WE'RE ALL SUPPOSED TO BE LEARNING ABOUT SCIENCE AND HOW TO RULE PROPERLY AND STUFF LIKE THAT.
OF COURSE, WE ALL KNOW WE'RE REALLY HERE TO KEEP OUR FOLKS IN LINE.
SO MY FATHER WILL STOP FIGHTING WITH KING DUNSANY—
—AND YOUR FELLA WON'T BE DOING ANYTHING STUPID,
BECAUSE THEY'VE GOT YOU SAFE AND SNUG.
HOT RA ENGIN #106
THAT'S A GREAT COMFORT.
C'MON, LET'S GET YOU DRESSED.
I DON'T KNOW...ISN'T THIS A BIT TOO—
WELL, I MEAN, LOOK AT THIS!
HEH. YOU'VE NEVER WORN TROUSERS BEFORE, HAVE YOU?
WELL, NO!
9
10
11
I'M A MECHANIC. TROUSERS MAKE IT EASY TO MANEUVER IN THE BIG ENGINES.
YOU'LL GET USED TO THEM.
I DOUBT IT.

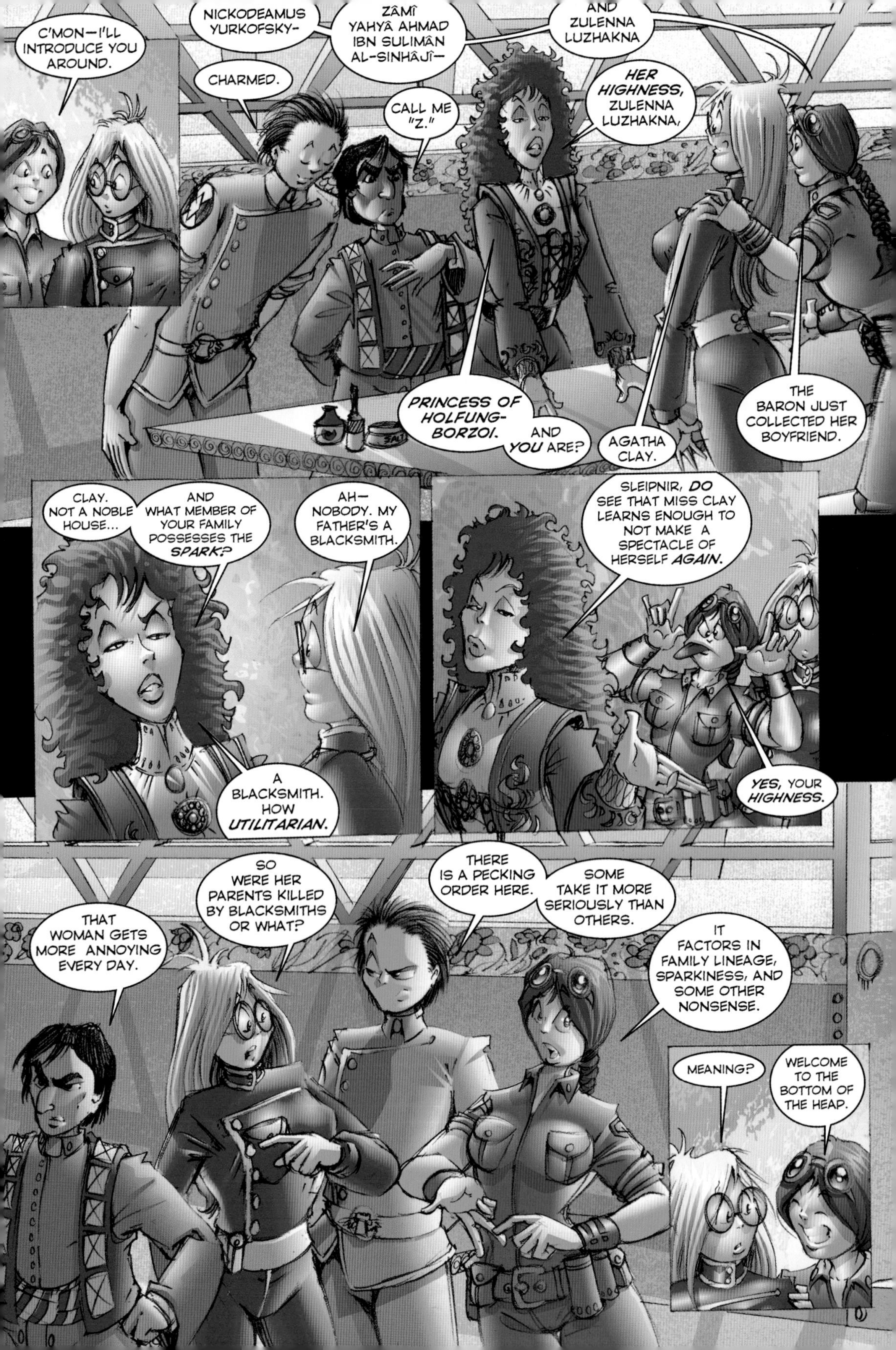
C'MON—I'LL INTRODUCE YOU AROUND.
NICKODEAMUS YURKOFSKY-
CHARMED.
ZÂMÎ YAHYÂ AHMAD IBN SULIMÂN AL-SINHÂJÎ—
CALL ME "Z."
AND ZULENNA LUZHAKNA
HER HIGHNESS, ZULENNA LUZHAKNA,
PRINCESS OF HOLFUNG-BORZOI.
AND YOU ARE?
AGATHA CLAY.
THE BARON JUST COLLECTED HER BOYFRIEND.
CLAY. NOT A NOBLE HOUSE...
AND WHAT MEMBER OF YOUR FAMILY POSSESSES THE SPARK?
AH—NOBODY. MY FATHER'S A BLACKSMITH.
A BLACKSMITH. HOW UTILITARIAN.
SLEIPNIR, DO SEE THAT MISS CLAY LEARNS ENOUGH TO NOT MAKE A SPECTACLE OF HERSELF AGAIN.
YES, YOUR HIGHNESS.
THAT WOMAN GETS MORE ANNOYING EVERY DAY.
SO WERE HER PARENTS KILLED BY BLACKSMITHS OR WHAT?
THERE IS A PECKING ORDER HERE.
SOME TAKE IT MORE SERIOUSLY THAN OTHERS.
IT FACTORS IN FAMILY LINEAGE, SPARKINESS, AND SOME OTHER NONSENSE.
MEANING?
WELCOME TO THE BOTTOM OF THE HEAP.

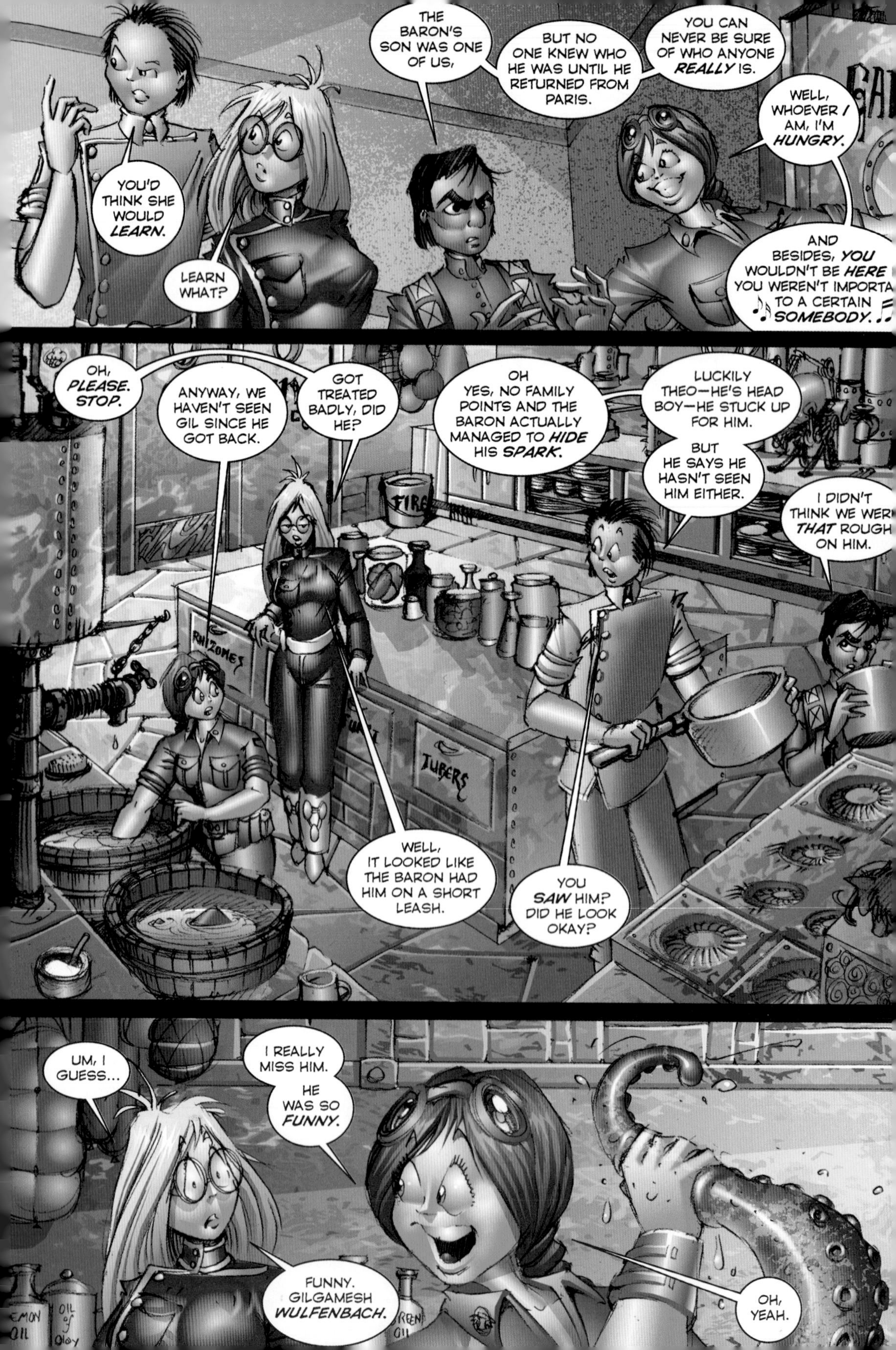
YOU'D THINK SHE WOULD LEARN.
LEARN WHAT?
THE BARON'S SON WAS ONE OF US,
BUT NO ONE KNEW WHO HE WAS UNTIL HE RETURNED FROM PARIS.
YOU CAN NEVER BE SURE OF WHO ANYONE REALLY IS.
WELL, WHOEVER I AM, I'M HUNGRY.
AND BESIDES, YOU WOULDN'T BE HERE YOU WEREN'T IMPORTA TO A CERTAIN SOMEBODY.
OH, PLEASE. STOP.
ANYWAY, WE HAVEN'T SEEN GIL SINCE HE GOT BACK.
GOT TREATED BADLY, DID HE?
OH YES, NO FAMILY POINTS AND THE BARON ACTUALLY MANAGED TO HIDE HIS SPARK.
LUCKILY THEO—HE'S HEAD BOY—HE STUCK UP FOR HIM.
BUT HE SAYS HE HASN'T SEEN HIM EITHER.
I DIDN'T THINK WE WER THAT ROUGH ON HIM.
RHIZOMES
TUBERS
WELL, IT LOOKED LIKE THE BARON HAD HIM ON A SHORT LEASH.
YOU SAW HIM? DID HE LOOK OKAY?
UM, I GUESS...
I REALLY MISS HIM.
HE WAS SO FUNNY.
FUNNY. GILGAMESH WULFENBACH.
OH, YEAH.

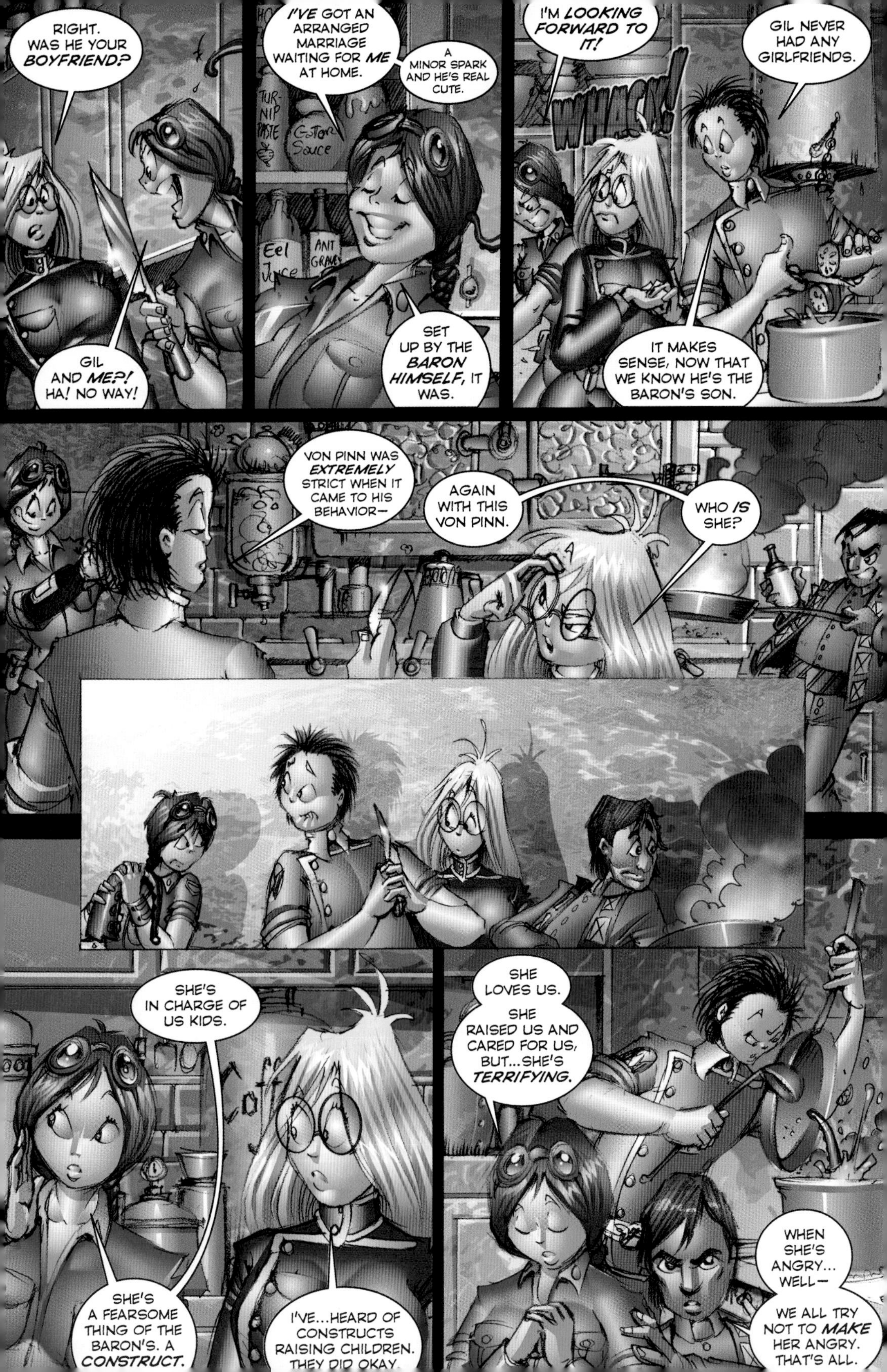
RIGHT. WAS HE YOUR BOYFRIEND?
GIL AND ME?! HA! NO WAY!
I'VE GOT AN ARRANGED MARRIAGE WAITING FOR ME AT HOME.
A MINOR SPARK AND HE'S REAL CUTE.
TURNIP PASTE
Gator Sauce
Eel Juice
ANT GRAVY
SET UP BY THE BARON HIMSELF, IT WAS.
I'M LOOKING FORWARD TO IT!
WHACK!
GIL NEVER HAD ANY GIRLFRIENDS.
IT MAKES SENSE, NOW THAT WE KNOW HE'S THE BARON'S SON.
VON PINN WAS EXTREMELY STRICT WHEN IT CAME TO HIS BEHAVIOR—
AGAIN WITH THIS VON PINN.
WHO IS SHE?
SHE'S IN CHARGE OF US KIDS.
SHE'S A FEARSOME THING OF THE BARON'S. A CONSTRUCT.
I'VE...HEARD OF CONSTRUCTS RAISING CHILDREN. THEY DID OKAY.
SHE LOVES US.
SHE RAISED US AND CARED FOR US, BUT...SHE'S TERRIFYING.
WHEN SHE'S ANGRY... WELL—
WE ALL TRY NOT TO MAKE HER ANGRY. THAT'S ALL.

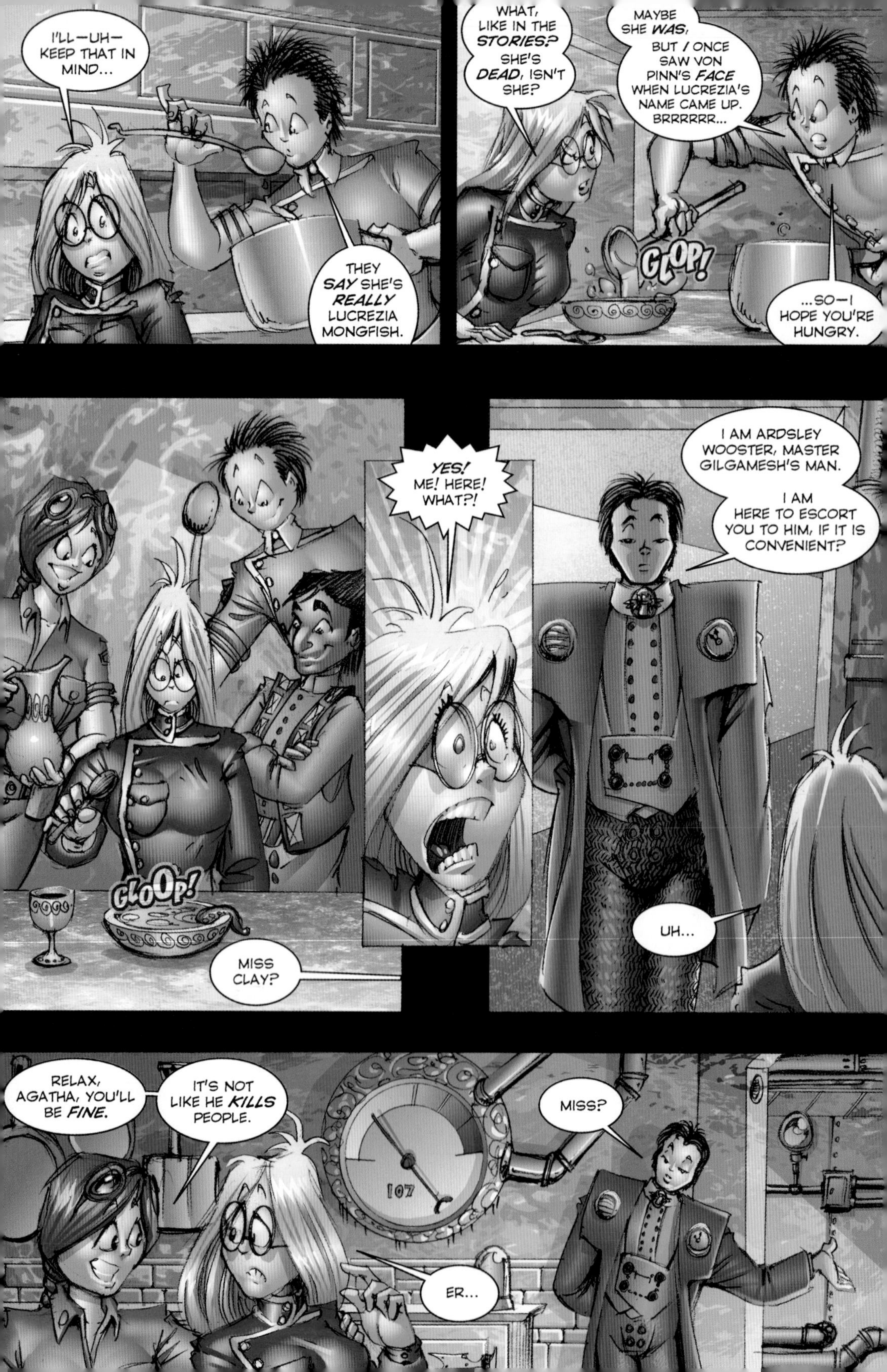
I'LL—UH—KEEP THAT IN MIND...
THEY *SAY* SHE'S *REALLY* LUCREZIA MONGFISH.
WHAT, LIKE IN THE *STORIES?* SHE'S *DEAD*, ISN'T SHE?
MAYBE SHE *WAS*, BUT *I* ONCE SAW VON PINN'S *FACE* WHEN LUCREZIA'S NAME CAME UP. BRRRRRR...
GLOP!
...SO—I HOPE YOU'RE HUNGRY.
GLOOP!
MISS CLAY?
YES! ME! HERE! WHAT?!
I AM ARDSLEY WOOSTER, MASTER GILGAMESH'S MAN.
I AM HERE TO ESCORT YOU TO HIM, IF IT IS CONVENIENT?
UH...
RELAX, AGATHA, YOU'LL BE *FINE*.
IT'S NOT LIKE HE *KILLS* PEOPLE.
107
MISS?
ER...

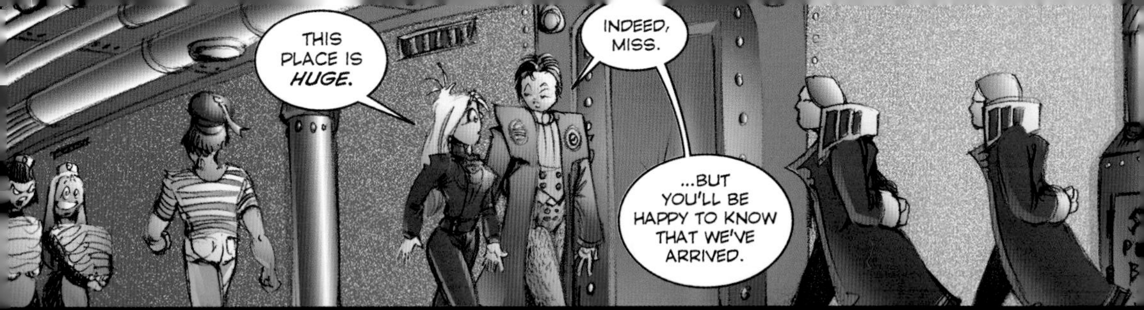
THIS PLACE IS *HUGE*.
INDEED, MISS.
...BUT YOU'LL BE HAPPY TO KNOW THAT WE'VE ARRIVED.

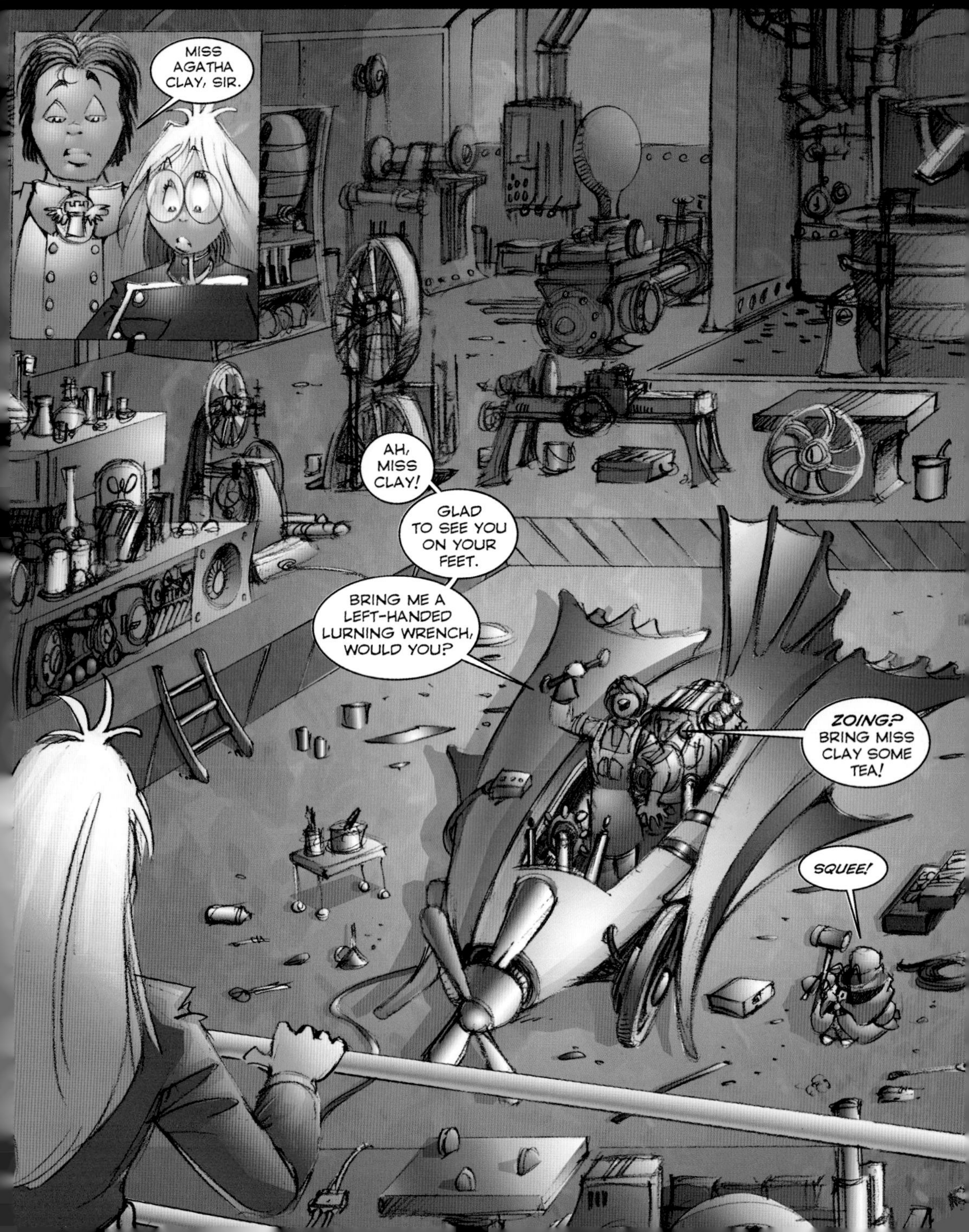
MISS AGATHA CLAY, SIR.
AH, MISS CLAY!
GLAD TO SEE YOU ON YOUR FEET.
BRING ME A LEFT-HANDED LURNING WRENCH, WOULD YOU?
ZOING? BRING MISS CLAY SOME TEA!
SQUEE!

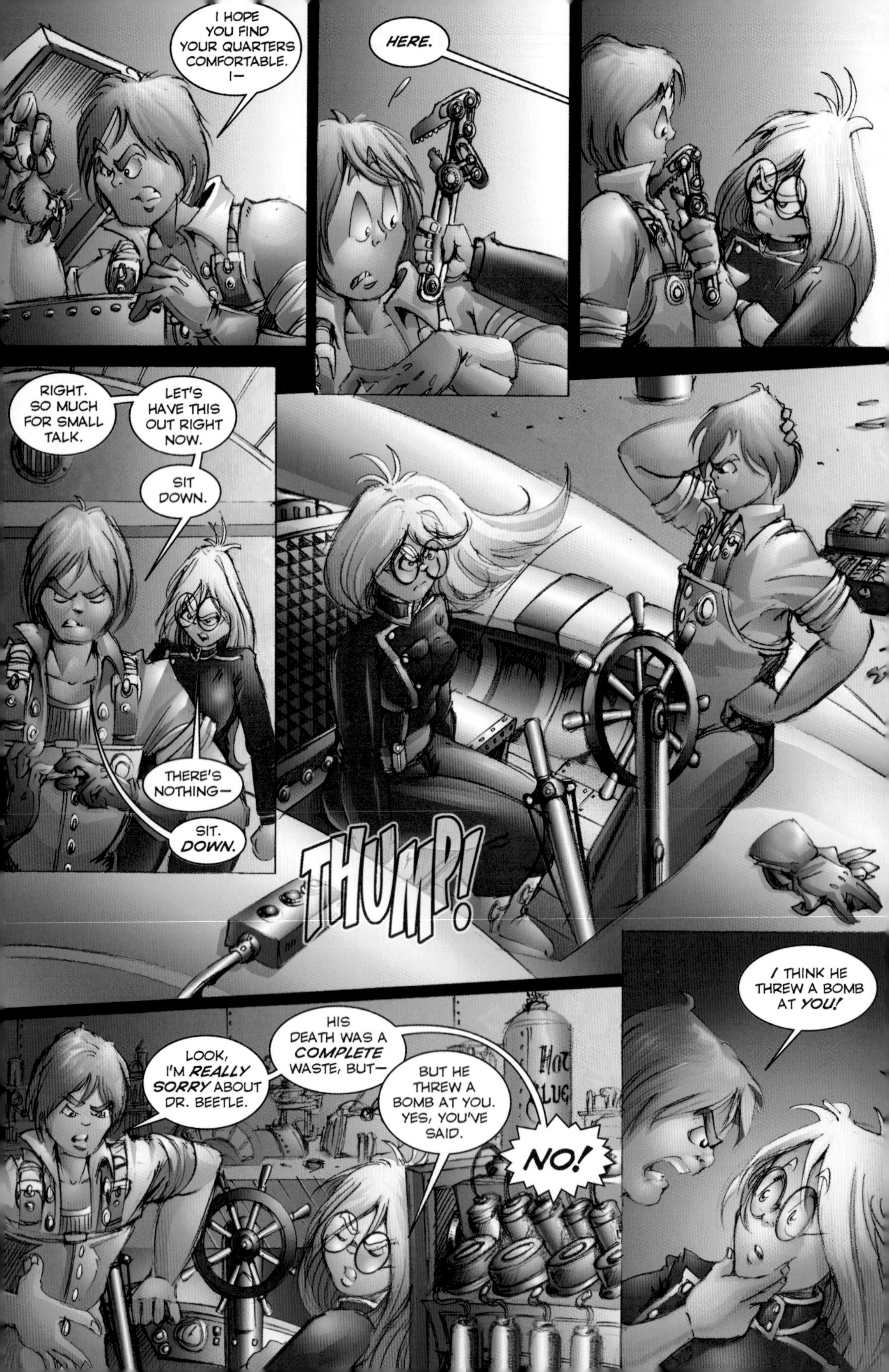
I HOPE YOU FIND YOUR QUARTERS COMFORTABLE. I—
HERE.
RIGHT. SO MUCH FOR SMALL TALK.
LET'S HAVE THIS OUT RIGHT NOW.
SIT DOWN.
THERE'S NOTHING—
SIT. DOWN.
THUMP!
LOOK, I'M REALLY SORRY ABOUT DR. BEETLE.
HIS DEATH WAS A COMPLETE WASTE, BUT—
BUT HE THREW A BOMB AT YOU. YES, YOU'VE SAID.
NO!
I THINK HE THREW A BOMB AT YOU!

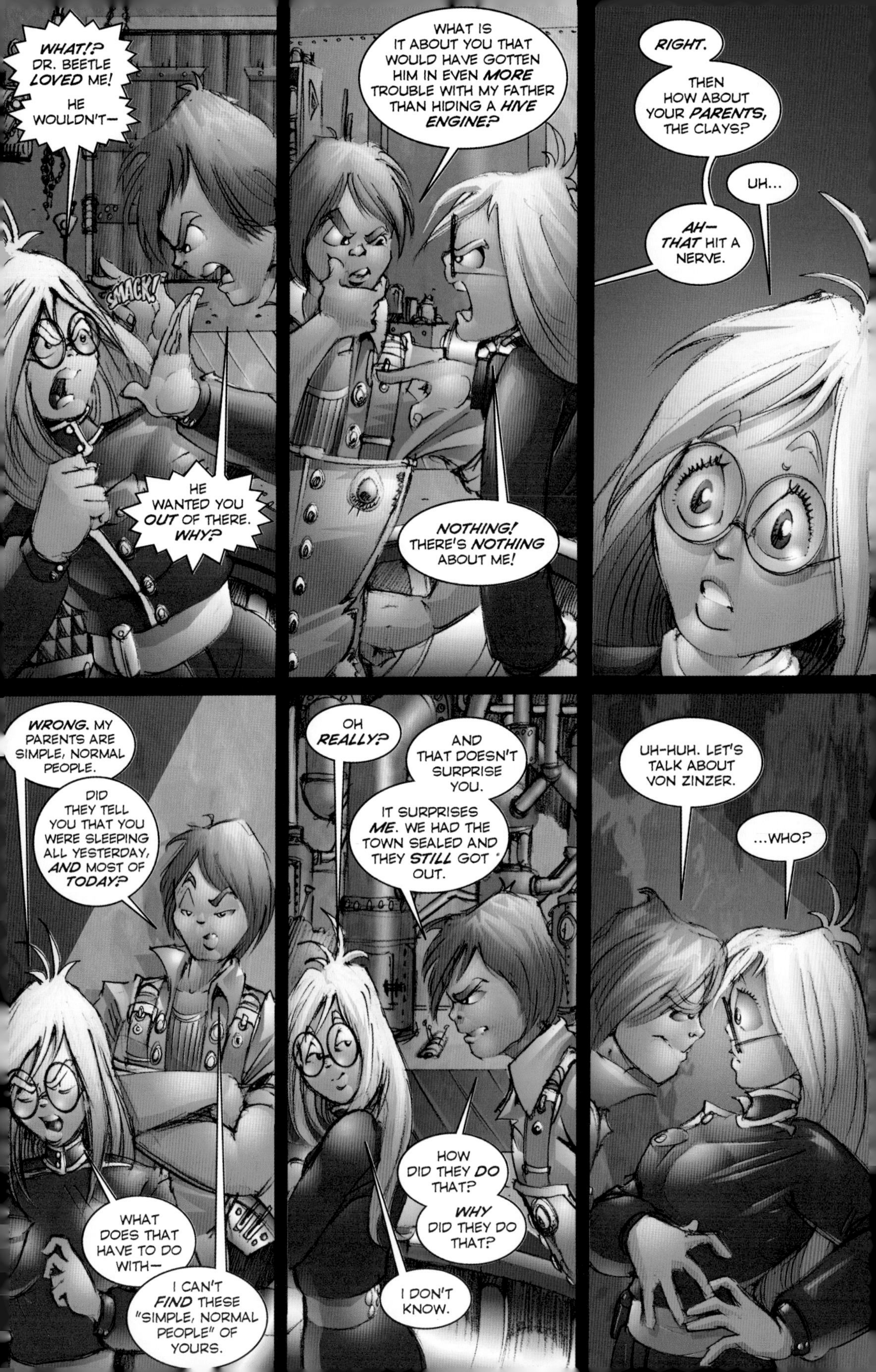
WHAT!? DR. BEETLE LOVED ME!
HE WOULDN'T—
SMACK!
HE WANTED YOU OUT OF THERE. WHY?
WHAT IS IT ABOUT YOU THAT WOULD HAVE GOTTEN HIM IN EVEN MORE TROUBLE WITH MY FATHER THAN HIDING A HIVE ENGINE?
NOTHING! THERE'S NOTHING ABOUT ME!
RIGHT.
THEN HOW ABOUT YOUR PARENTS, THE CLAYS?
UH...
AH— THAT HIT A NERVE.
WRONG. MY PARENTS ARE SIMPLE, NORMAL PEOPLE.
DID THEY TELL YOU THAT YOU WERE SLEEPING ALL YESTERDAY, AND MOST OF TODAY?
WHAT DOES THAT HAVE TO DO WITH—
I CAN'T FIND THESE "SIMPLE, NORMAL PEOPLE" OF YOURS.
OH REALLY?
AND THAT DOESN'T SURPRISE YOU.
IT SURPRISES ME. WE HAD THE TOWN SEALED AND THEY STILL GOT OUT.
HOW DID THEY DO THAT?
WHY DID THEY DO THAT?
I DON'T KNOW.
UH-HUH. LET'S TALK ABOUT VON ZINZER.
...WHO?

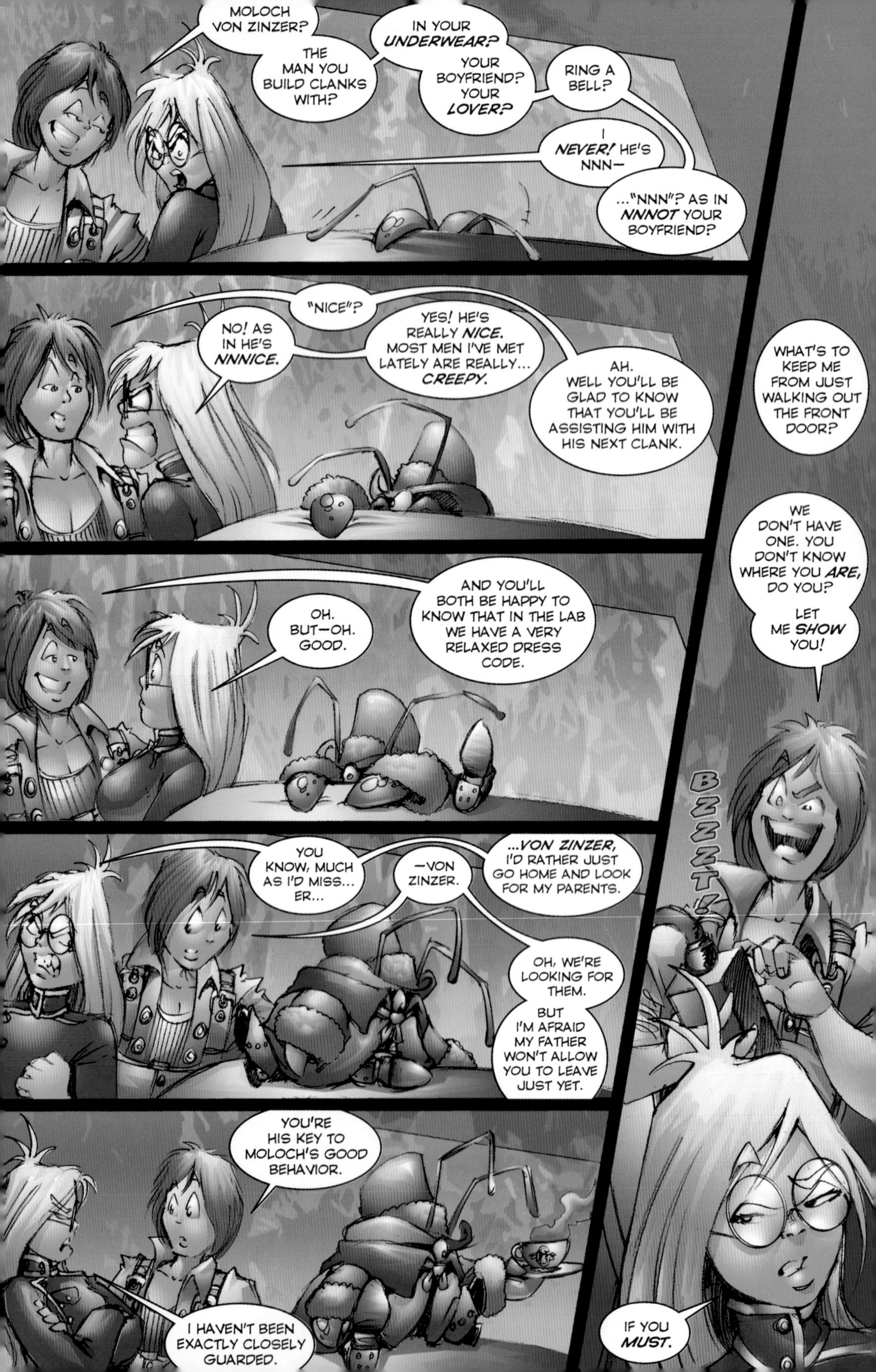
MOLOCH VON ZINZER?
THE MAN YOU BUILD CLANKS WITH?
IN YOUR UNDERWEAR?
YOUR BOYFRIEND? YOUR LOVER?
RING A BELL?
I NEVER! HE'S NNN—
..."NNN"? AS IN NNNOT YOUR BOYFRIEND?
NO! AS IN HE'S NNNICE.
"NICE"?
YES! HE'S REALLY NICE. MOST MEN I'VE MET LATELY ARE REALLY... CREEPY.
AH. WELL YOU'LL BE GLAD TO KNOW THAT YOU'LL BE ASSISTING HIM WITH HIS NEXT CLANK.
OH. BUT—OH. GOOD.
AND YOU'LL BOTH BE HAPPY TO KNOW THAT IN THE LAB WE HAVE A VERY RELAXED DRESS CODE.
YOU KNOW, MUCH AS I'D MISS... ER...
—VON ZINZER.
...VON ZINZER, I'D RATHER JUST GO HOME AND LOOK FOR MY PARENTS.
OH, WE'RE LOOKING FOR THEM.
BUT I'M AFRAID MY FATHER WON'T ALLOW YOU TO LEAVE JUST YET.
YOU'RE HIS KEY TO MOLOCH'S GOOD BEHAVIOR.
I HAVEN'T BEEN EXACTLY CLOSELY GUARDED.
WHAT'S TO KEEP ME FROM JUST WALKING OUT THE FRONT DOOR?
WE DON'T HAVE ONE. YOU DON'T KNOW WHERE YOU ARE, DO YOU?
LET ME SHOW YOU!
BZZZT!
IF YOU MUST.

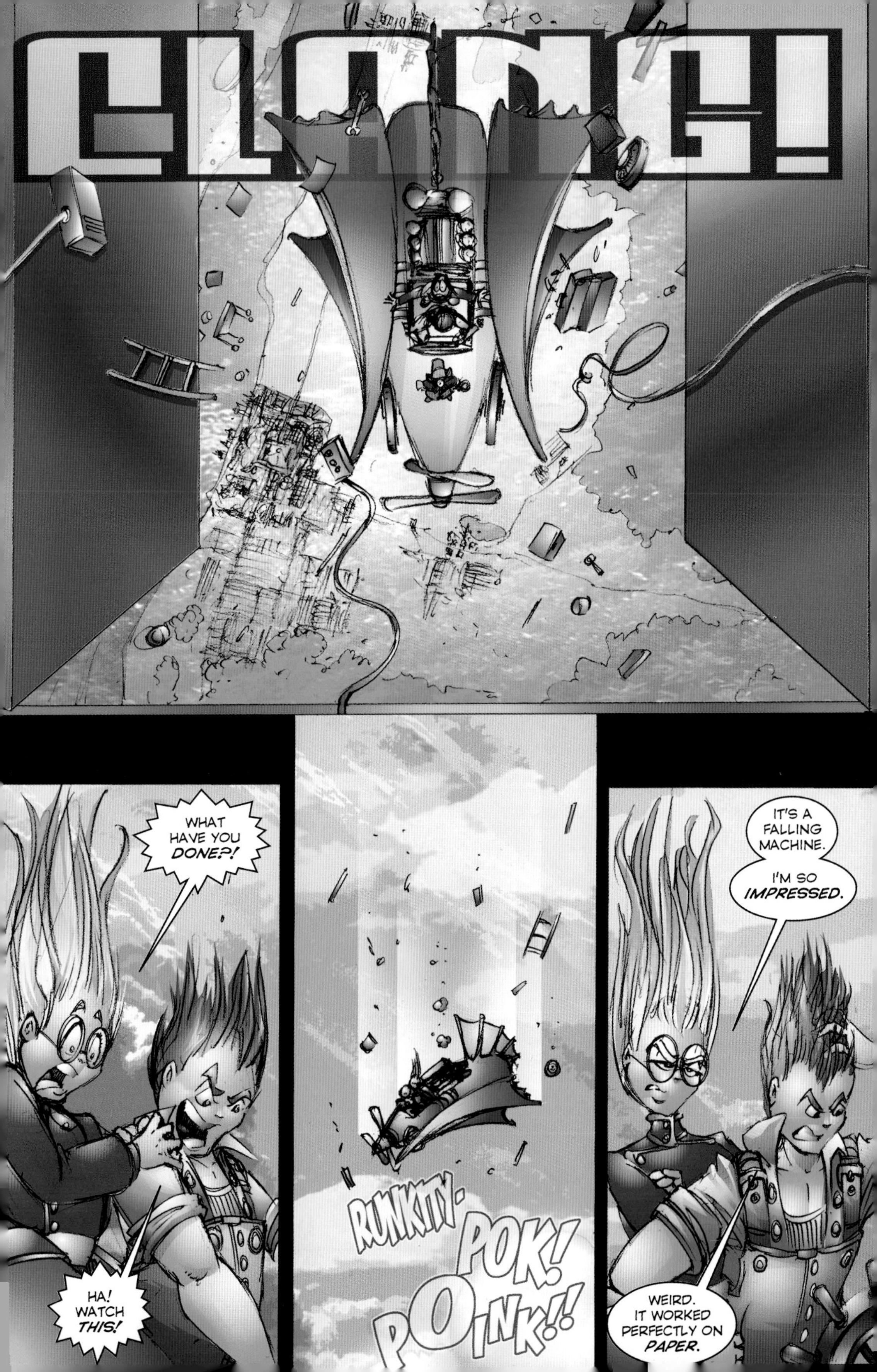
CLANG!
WHAT HAVE YOU DONE?!
HA! WATCH THIS!
RUNKITY-POK! POINK!!
IT'S A FALLING MACHINE.
I'M SO IMPRESSED.
WEIRD. IT WORKED PERFECTLY ON PAPER.

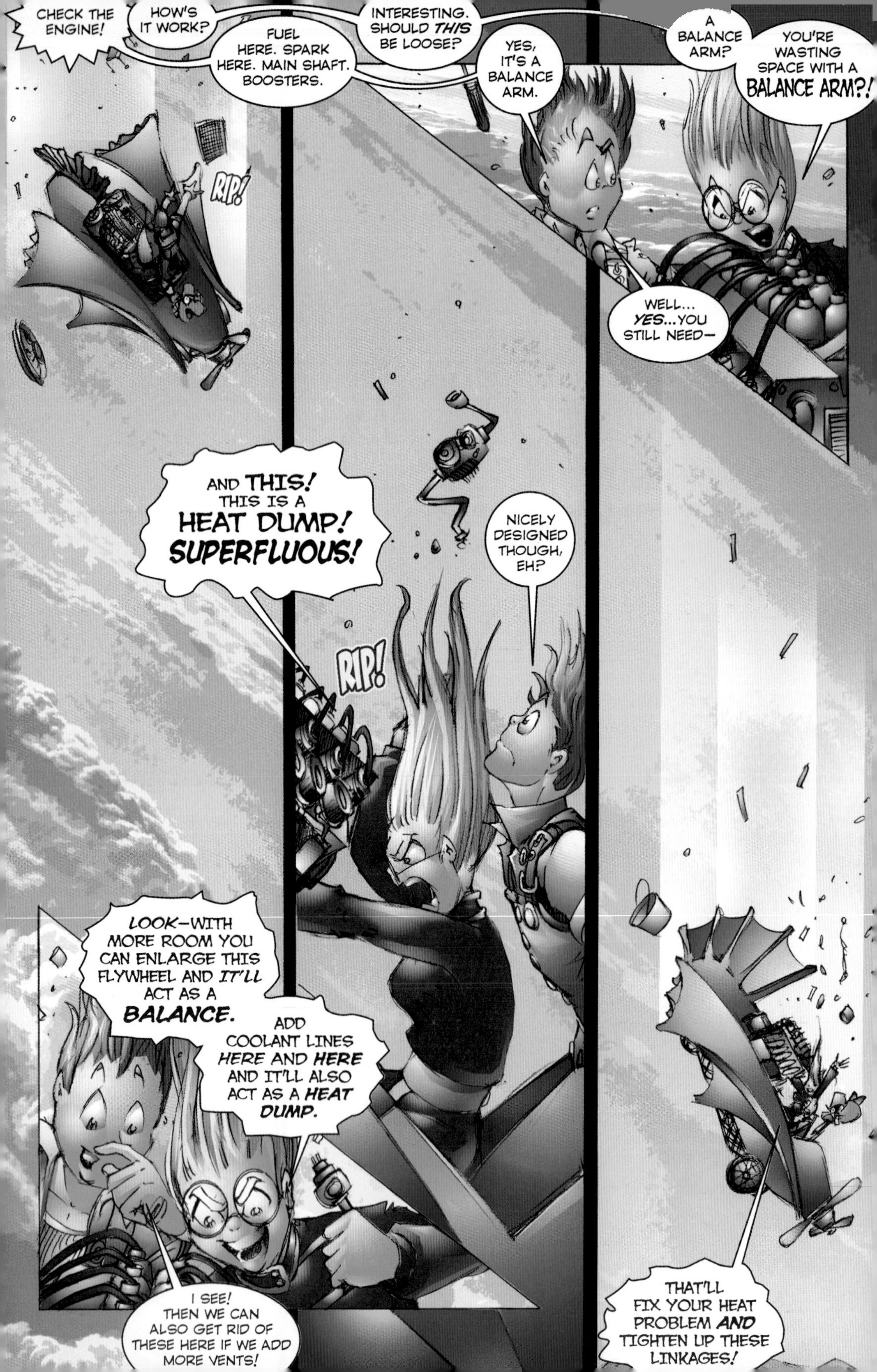
CHECK THE ENGINE!
HOW'S IT WORK?
FUEL HERE. SPARK HERE. MAIN SHAFT. BOOSTERS.
INTERESTING. SHOULD *THIS* BE LOOSE?
YES, IT'S A BALANCE ARM.
A BALANCE ARM?
YOU'RE WASTING SPACE WITH A BALANCE ARM?!
WELL... *YES*...YOU STILL NEED—
RIP!
AND **THIS!** THIS IS A **HEAT DUMP!** ***SUPERFLUOUS!***
NICELY DESIGNED THOUGH, EH?
RIP!
LOOK—WITH MORE ROOM YOU CAN ENLARGE THIS FLYWHEEL AND *IT'LL* ACT AS A ***BALANCE.***
ADD COOLANT LINES ***HERE*** AND ***HERE*** AND IT'LL ALSO ACT AS A ***HEAT DUMP.***
I SEE! THEN WE CAN ALSO GET RID OF THESE HERE IF WE ADD MORE VENTS!
THAT'LL FIX YOUR HEAT PROBLEM ***AND*** TIGHTEN UP THESE LINKAGES!

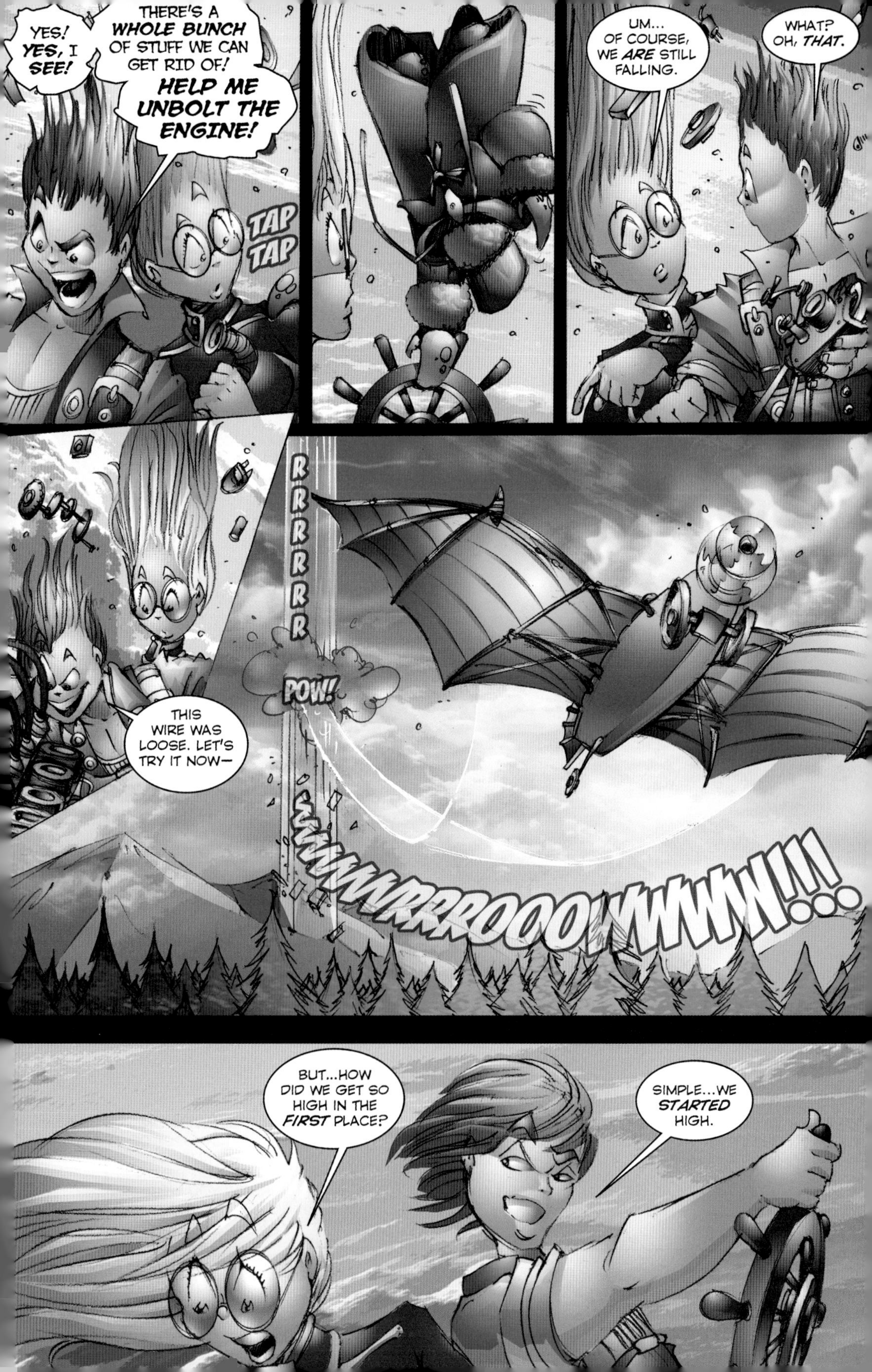
YES! YES, I SEE!
THERE'S A WHOLE BUNCH OF STUFF WE CAN GET RID OF! HELP ME UNBOLT THE ENGINE!
TAP TAP
UM... OF COURSE, WE ARE STILL FALLING.
WHAT? OH, THAT.
THIS WIRE WAS LOOSE. LET'S TRY IT NOW—
RRRRRRR
POW!
WWWWWRRROOOOWWWWN!!!...
BUT...HOW DID WE GET SO HIGH IN THE FIRST PLACE?
SIMPLE...WE STARTED HIGH.

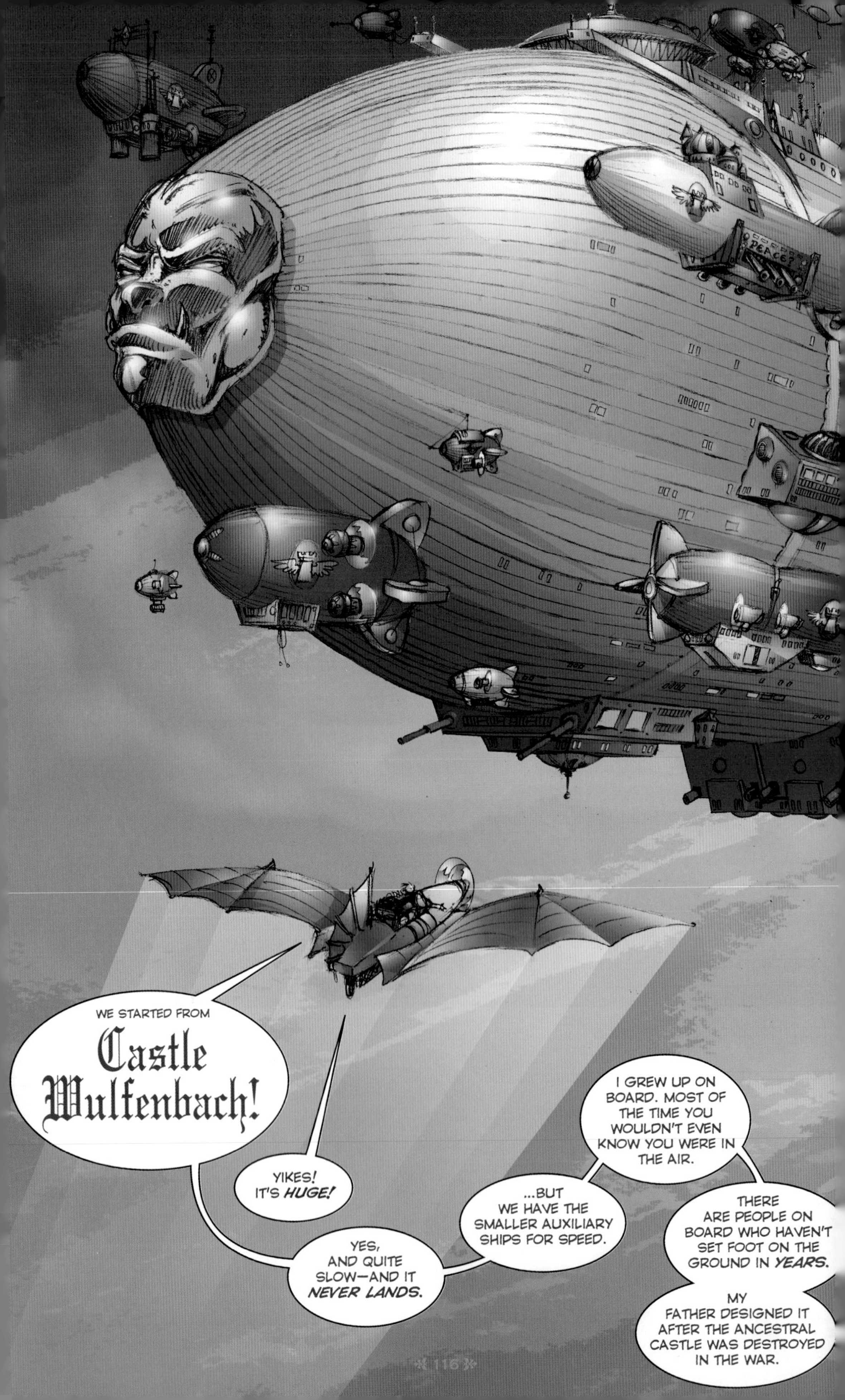
PEACE?
WE STARTED FROM Castle Wulfenbach!
YIKES! IT'S *HUGE!*
YES, AND QUITE SLOW—AND IT *NEVER LANDS*.
...BUT WE HAVE THE SMALLER AUXILIARY SHIPS FOR SPEED.
I GREW UP ON BOARD. MOST OF THE TIME YOU WOULDN'T EVEN KNOW YOU WERE IN THE AIR.
THERE ARE PEOPLE ON BOARD WHO HAVEN'T SET FOOT ON THE GROUND IN *YEARS*.
MY FATHER DESIGNED IT AFTER THE ANCESTRAL CASTLE WAS DESTROYED IN THE WAR.

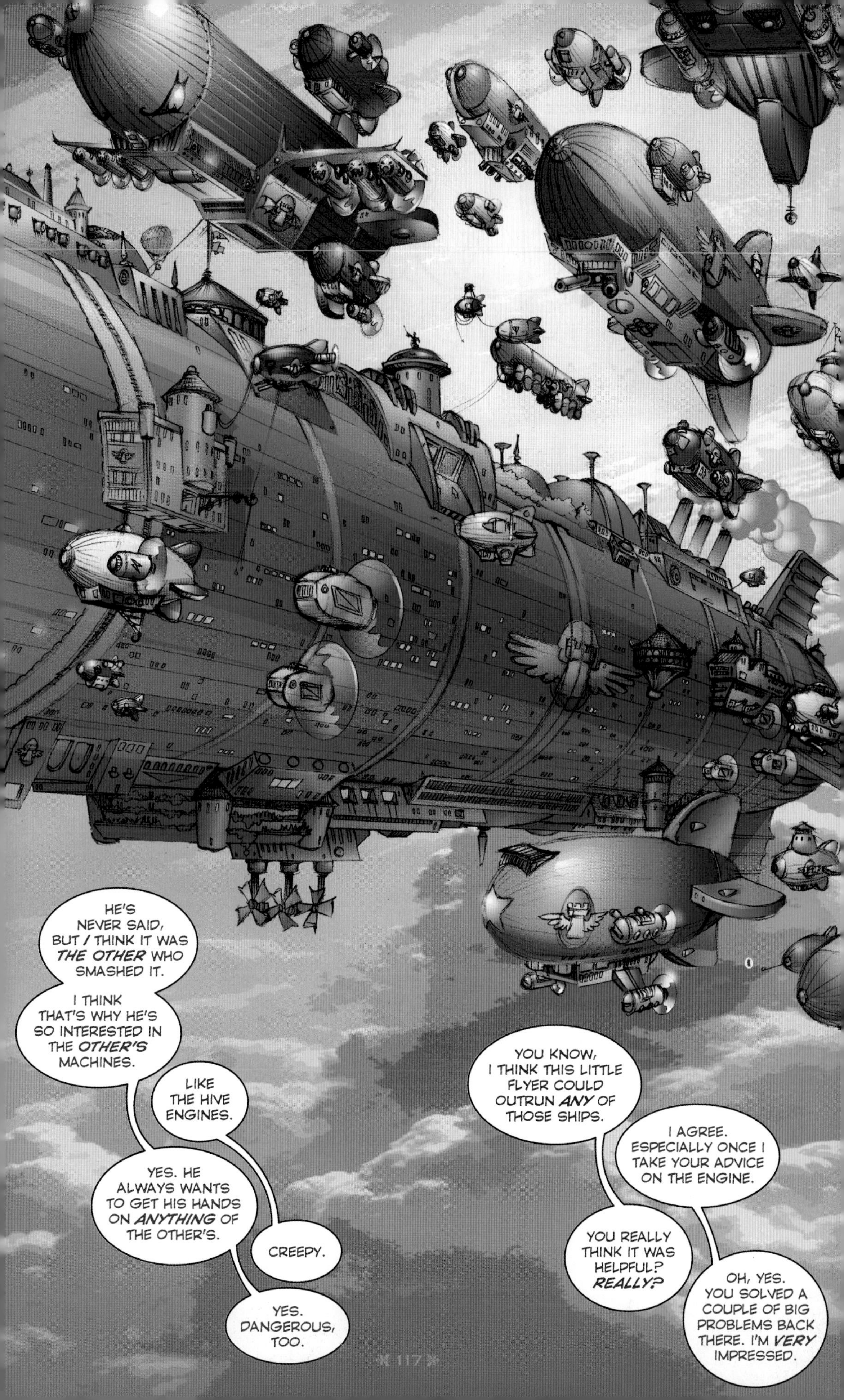
HE'S NEVER SAID, BUT *I* THINK IT WAS *THE OTHER* WHO SMASHED IT.
I THINK THAT'S WHY HE'S SO INTERESTED IN THE *OTHER'S* MACHINES.
LIKE THE HIVE ENGINES.
YES. HE ALWAYS WANTS TO GET HIS HANDS ON *ANYTHING* OF THE OTHER'S.
CREEPY.
YES. DANGEROUS, TOO.
YOU KNOW, I THINK THIS LITTLE FLYER COULD OUTRUN *ANY* OF THOSE SHIPS.
I AGREE. ESPECIALLY ONCE I TAKE YOUR ADVICE ON THE ENGINE.
YOU REALLY THINK IT WAS HELPFUL? *REALLY?*
OH, YES. YOU SOLVED A COUPLE OF BIG PROBLEMS BACK THERE. I'M *VERY* IMPRESSED.

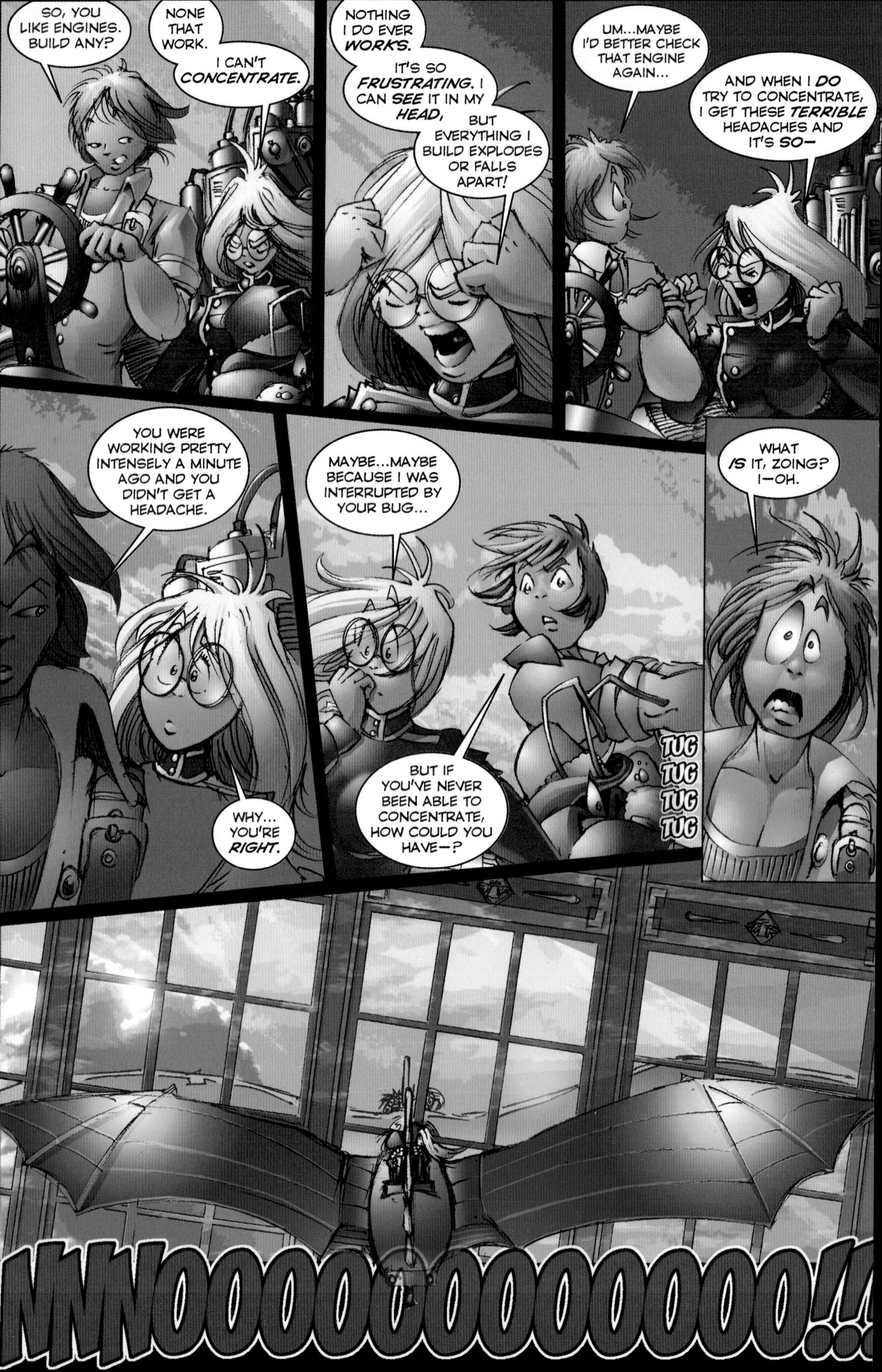
SO, YOU LIKE ENGINES. BUILD ANY?
NONE THAT WORK.
I CAN'T *CONCENTRATE.*
NOTHING I DO EVER *WORKS.*
IT'S SO *FRUSTRATING.* I CAN *SEE* IT IN MY *HEAD,*
BUT EVERYTHING I BUILD EXPLODES OR FALLS APART!
UM...MAYBE I'D BETTER CHECK THAT ENGINE AGAIN...
AND WHEN I *DO* TRY TO CONCENTRATE, I GET THESE *TERRIBLE* HEADACHES AND IT'S *SO—*
YOU WERE WORKING PRETTY INTENSELY A MINUTE AGO AND YOU DIDN'T GET A HEADACHE.
WHY... YOU'RE *RIGHT.*
MAYBE...MAYBE BECAUSE I WAS INTERRUPTED BY YOUR BUG...
BUT IF YOU'VE NEVER BEEN ABLE TO CONCENTRATE, HOW COULD YOU HAVE—?
TUG TUG TUG TUG
WHAT *IS* IT, ZOING? I—OH.
NNNOOOOOOOOOOOOOO!!

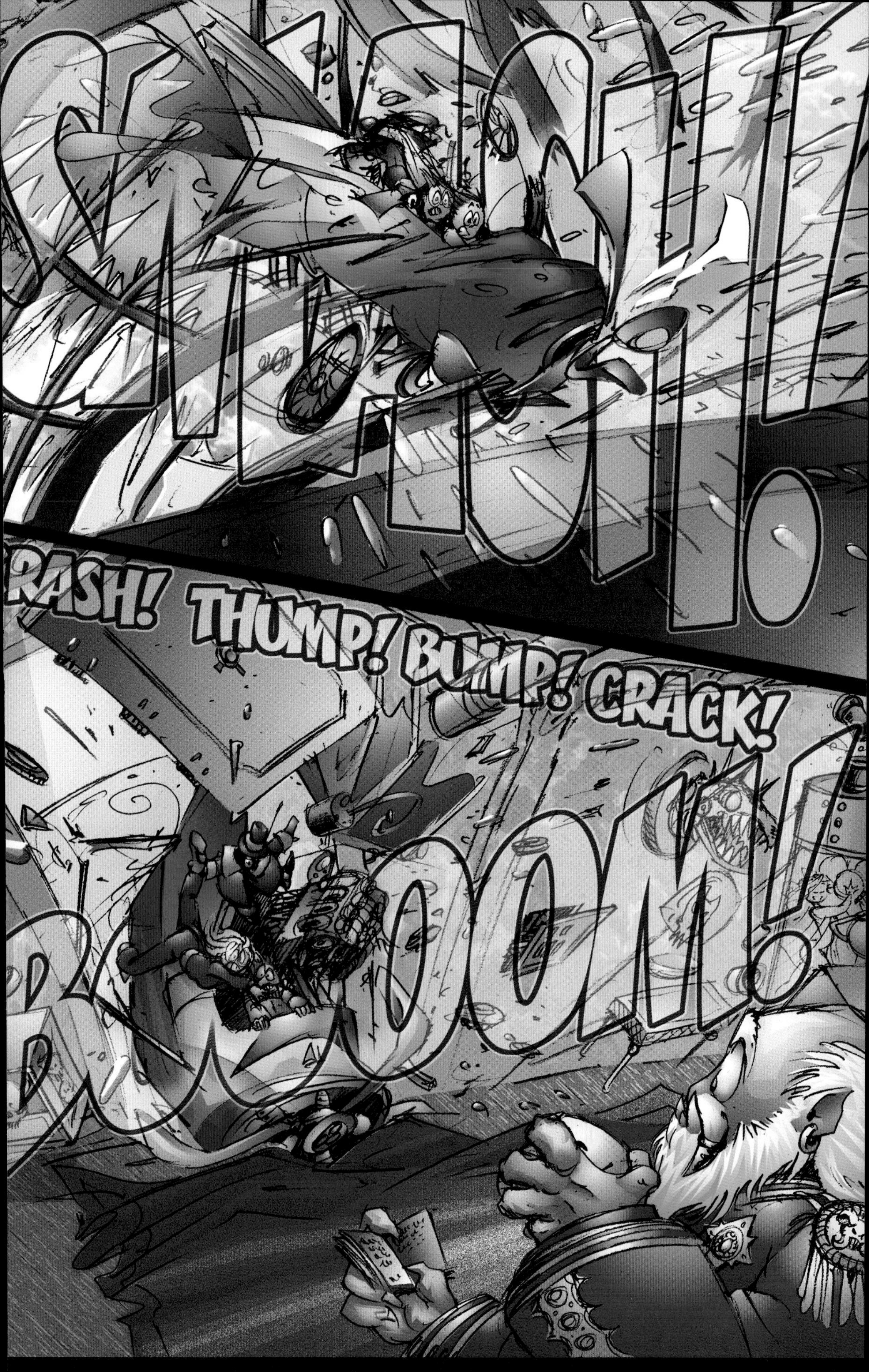
RASH! THUMP! BUMP! CRACK!

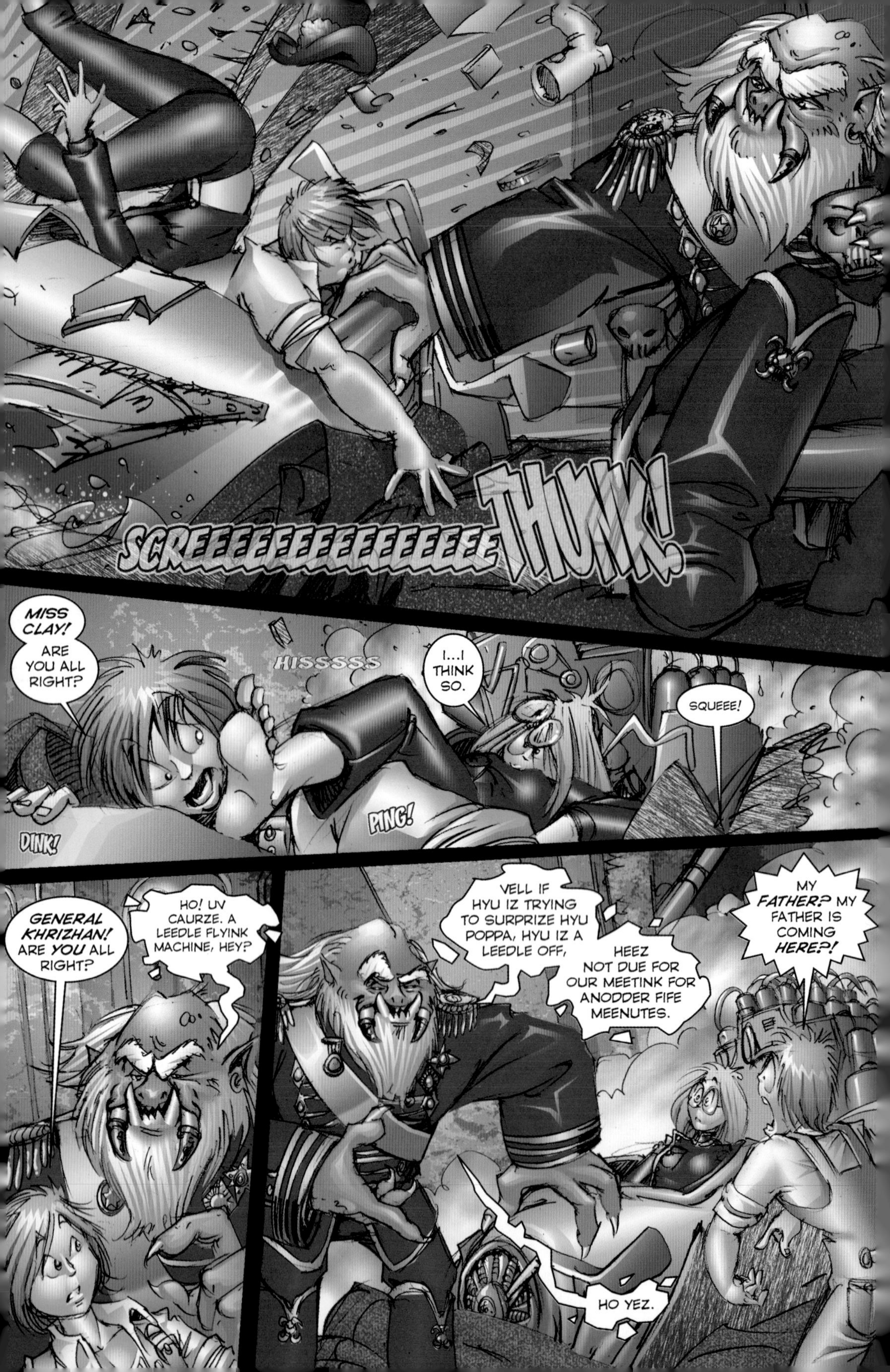
SCREEEEEEEEEEEEEEEE
THUNK!
MISS CLAY! ARE YOU ALL RIGHT?
HISSSSS
I...I THINK SO.
SQUEEE!
PING!
DINK!
GENERAL KHRIZHAN! ARE YOU ALL RIGHT?
HO! UV CAURZE. A LEEDLE FLYINK MACHINE, HEY?
VELL IF HYU IZ TRYING TO SURPRIZE HYU POPPA, HYU IZ A LEEDLE OFF,
HEEZ NOT DUE FOR OUR MEETINK FOR ANODDER FIFE MEENUTES.
MY FATHER? MY FATHER IS COMING HERE?!
HO YEZ.

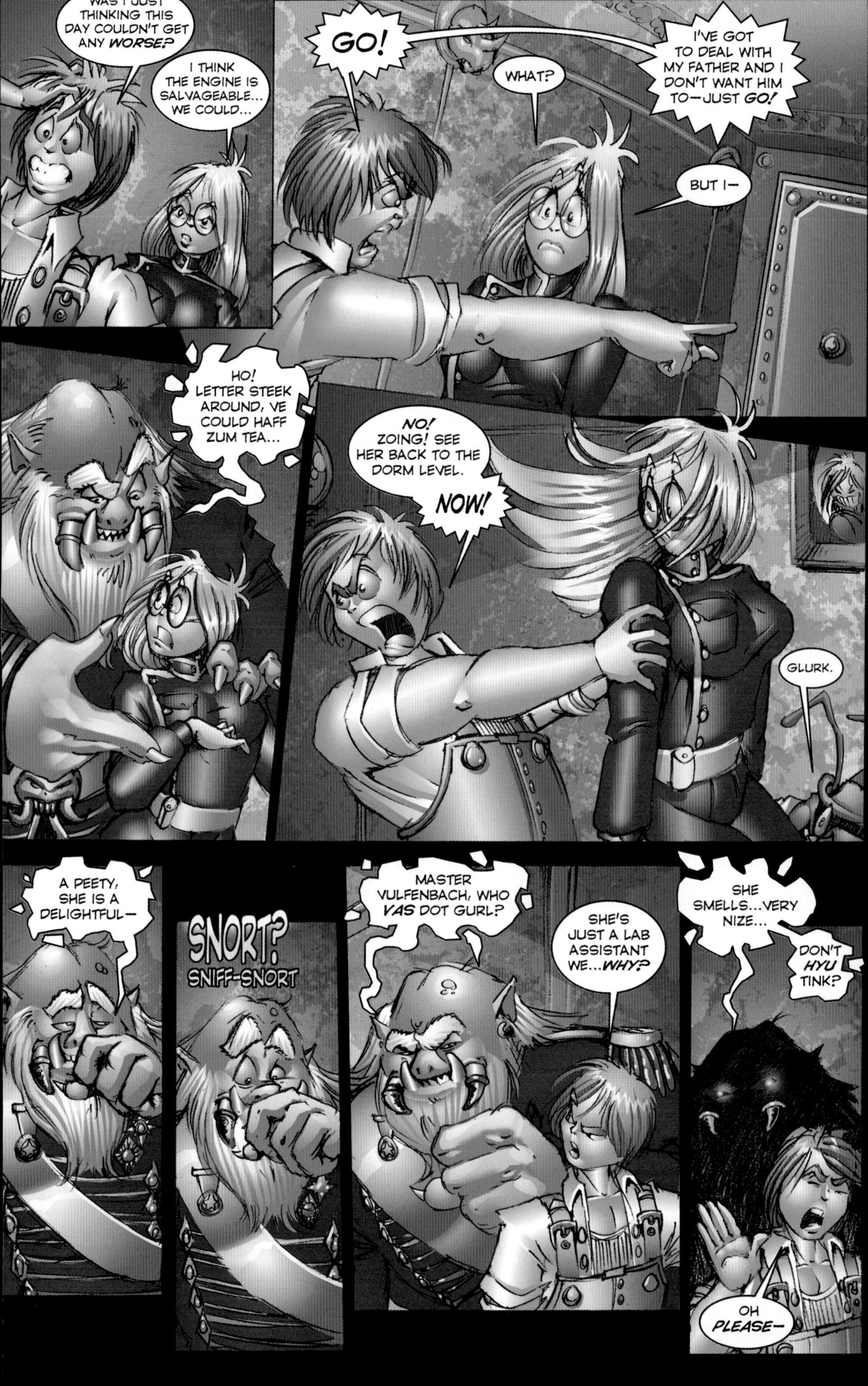
WAS I JUST THINKING THIS DAY COULDN'T GET ANY WORSE?
I THINK THE ENGINE IS SALVAGEABLE... WE COULD...
GO!
WHAT?
I'VE GOT TO DEAL WITH MY FATHER AND I DON'T WANT HIM TO—JUST GO!
BUT I—
HO! LETTER STEEK AROUND, VE COULD HAFF ZUM TEA...
NO! ZOING! SEE HER BACK TO THE DORM LEVEL.
NOW!
GLURK.
A PEETY, SHE IS A DELIGHTFUL—
SNORT?
SNIFF-SNORT
MASTER VULFENBACH, WHO VAS DOT GURL?
SHE'S JUST A LAB ASSISTANT WE...WHY?
SHE SMELLS...VERY NIZE...
DON'T HYU TINK?
OH PLEASE—

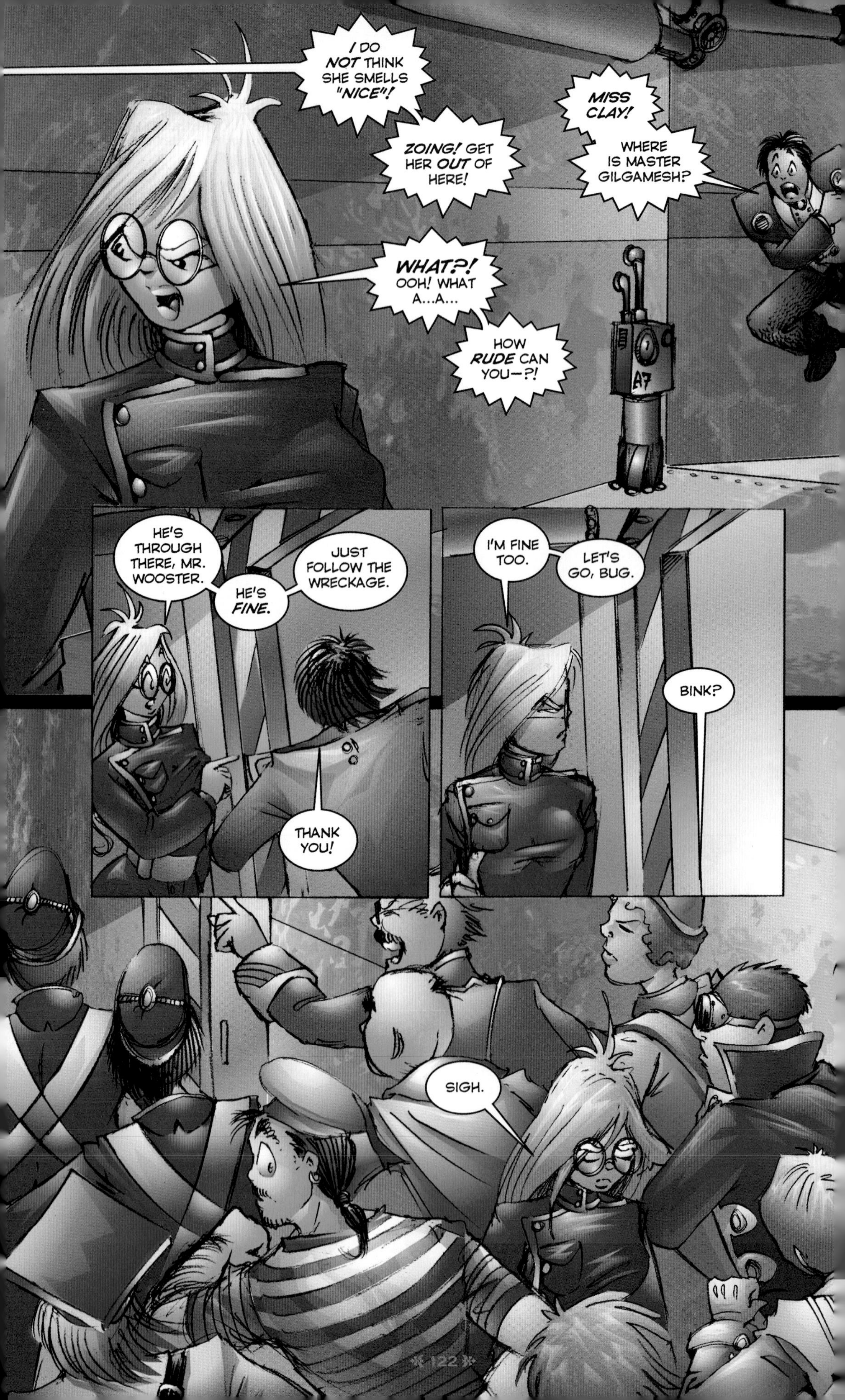
I DO NOT THINK SHE SMELLS "NICE"!
MISS CLAY!
WHERE IS MASTER GILGAMESH?
ZOING! GET HER OUT OF HERE!
WHAT?! OOH! WHAT A...A...
HOW RUDE CAN YOU—?!
A7
HE'S THROUGH THERE, MR. WOOSTER.
HE'S FINE.
JUST FOLLOW THE WRECKAGE.
THANK YOU!
I'M FINE TOO.
LET'S GO, BUG.
BINK?
SIGH.

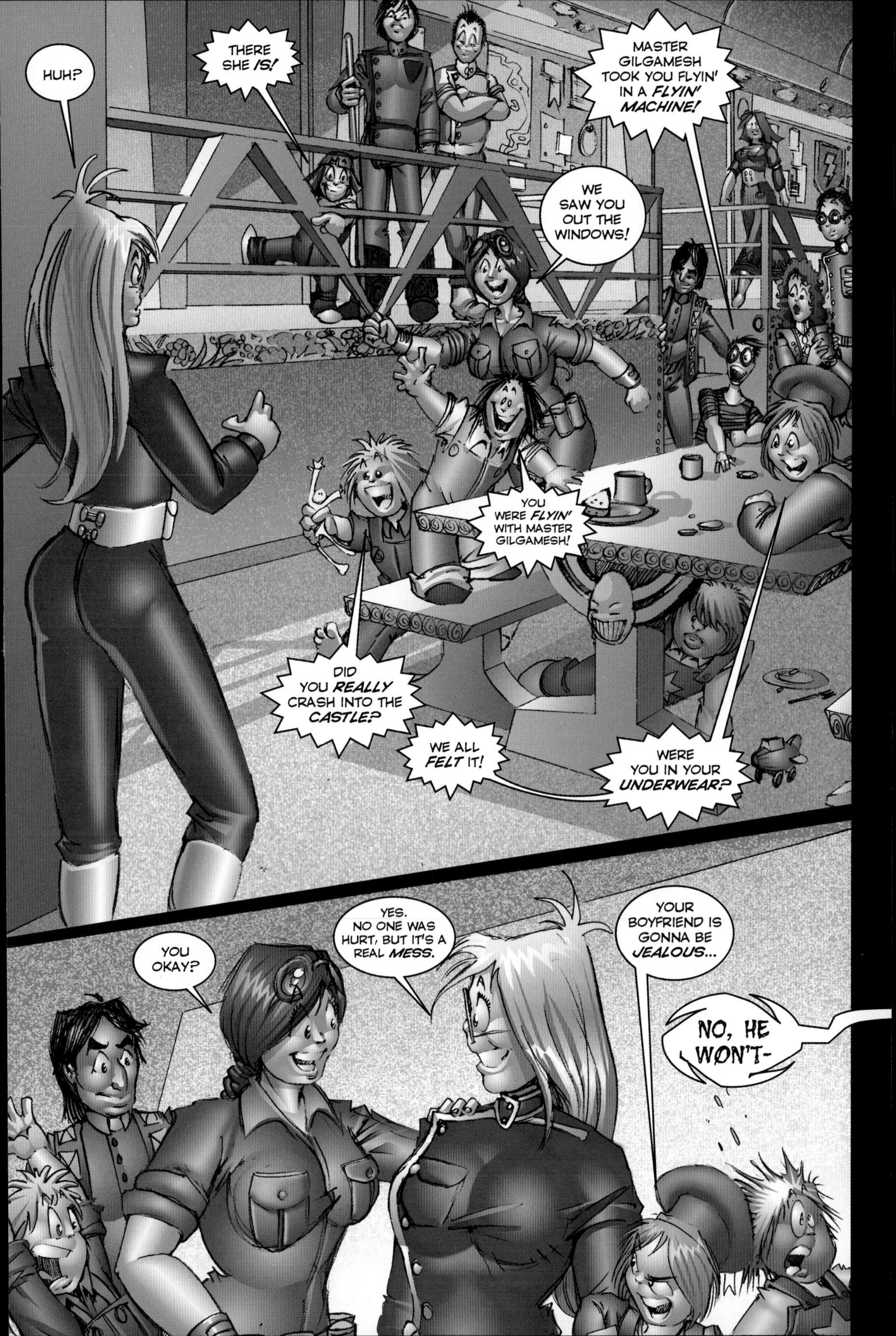
HUH?
THERE SHE IS!
MASTER GILGAMESH TOOK YOU FLYIN' IN A FLYIN' MACHINE!
WE SAW YOU OUT THE WINDOWS!
YOU WERE FLYIN' WITH MASTER GILGAMESH!
DID YOU REALLY CRASH INTO THE CASTLE?
WE ALL FELT IT!
WERE YOU IN YOUR UNDERWEAR?
YOU OKAY?
YES. NO ONE WAS HURT, BUT IT'S A REAL MESS.
YOUR BOYFRIEND IS GONNA BE JEALOUS...
NO, HE WON'T-

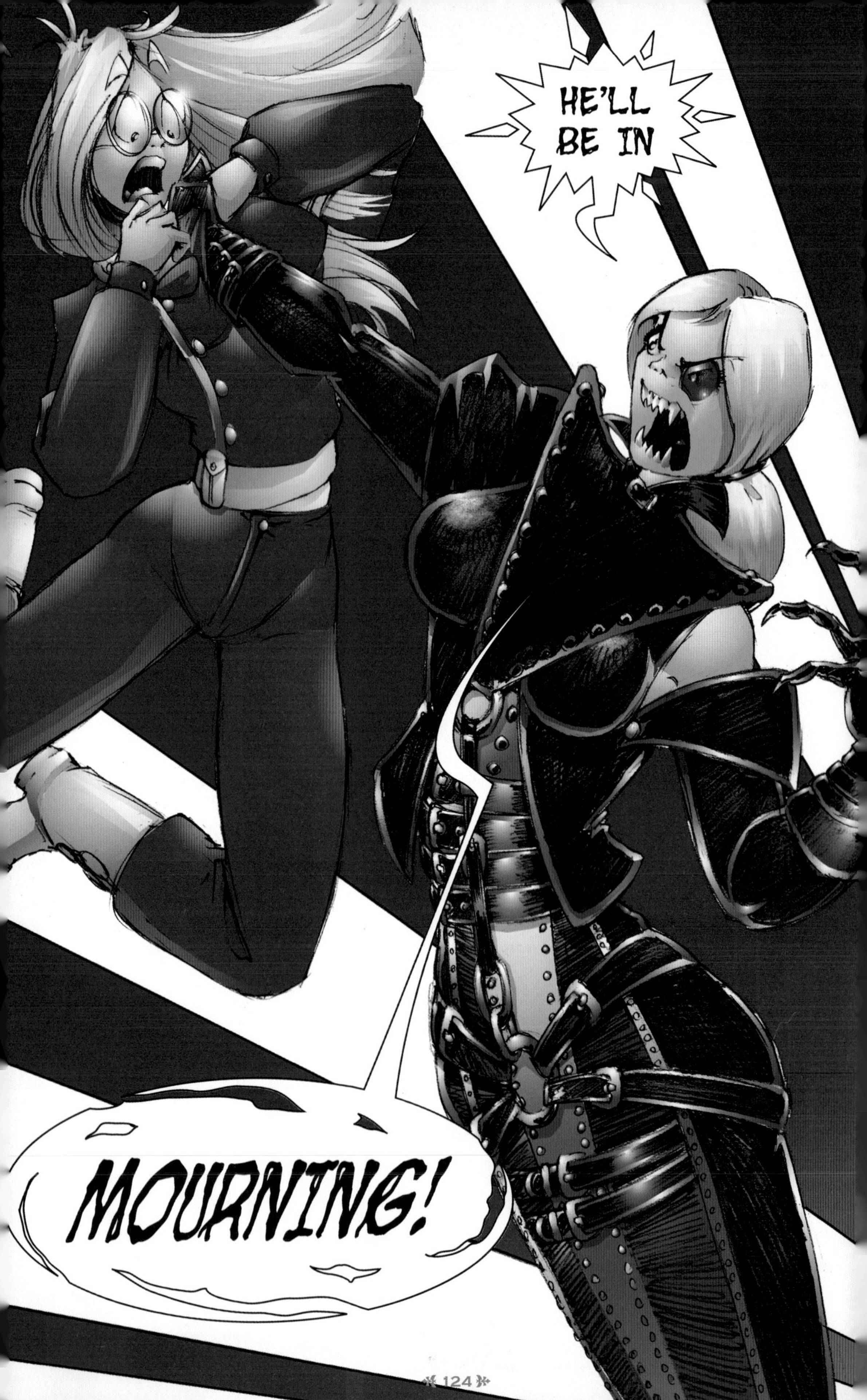
HE'LL BE IN
MOURNING!

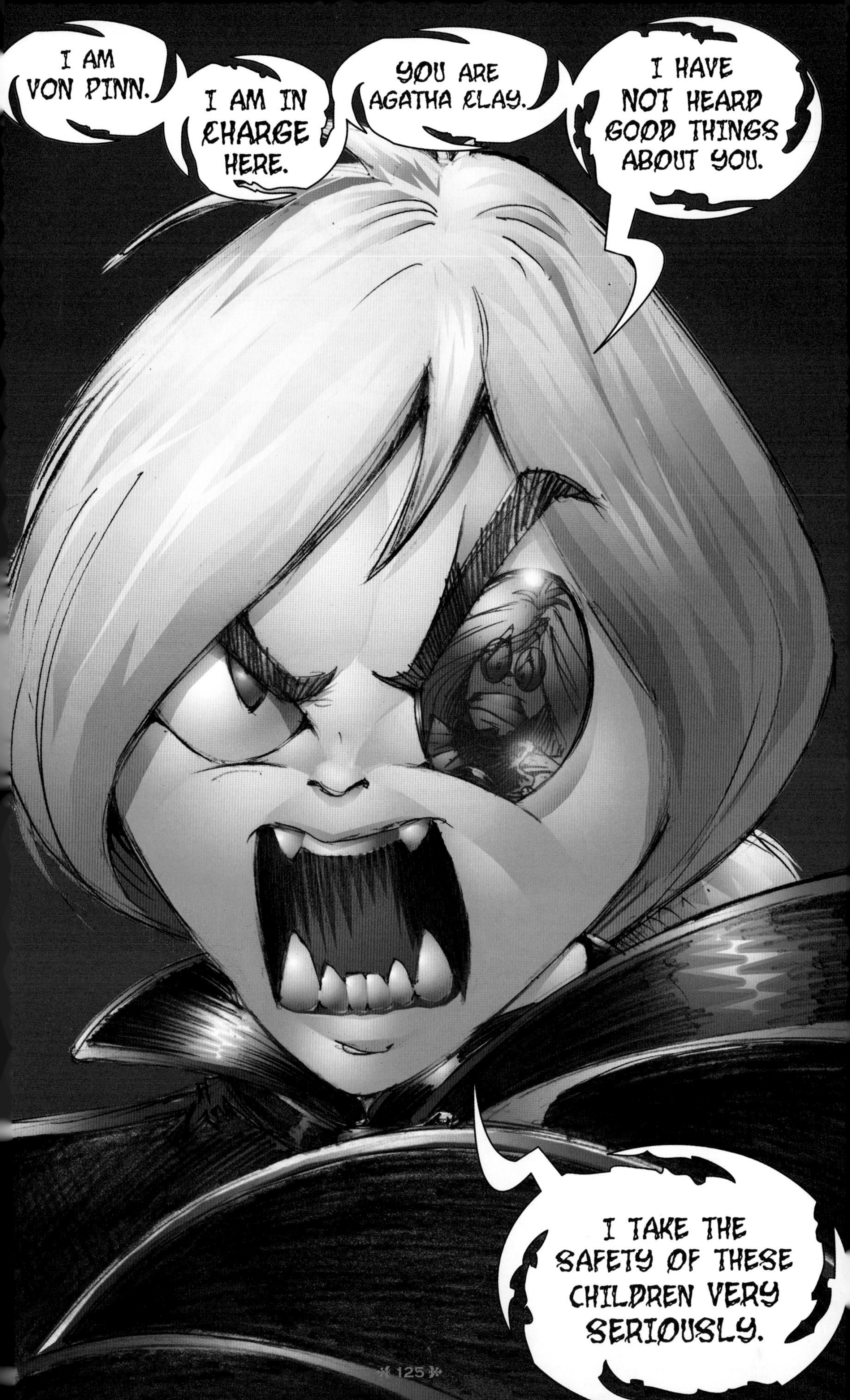
I AM VON PINN.
I AM IN CHARGE HERE.
YOU ARE AGATHA CLAY.
I HAVE NOT HEARD GOOD THINGS ABOUT YOU.
I TAKE THE SAFETY OF THESE CHILDREN VERY SERIOUSLY.

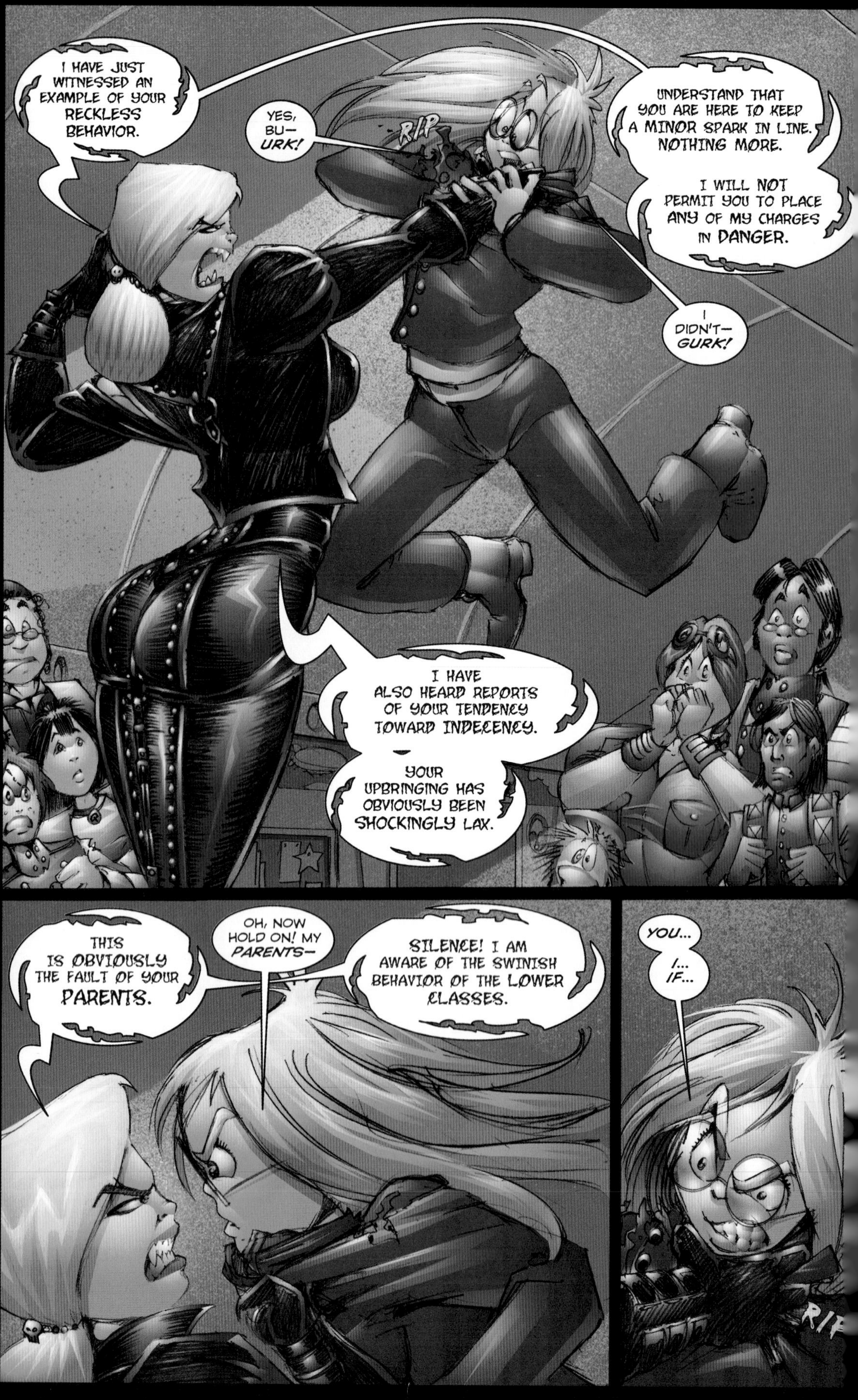
I HAVE JUST WITNESSED AN EXAMPLE OF YOUR RECKLESS BEHAVIOR.
YES, BU— URK!
RIP
UNDERSTAND THAT YOU ARE HERE TO KEEP A MINOR SPARK IN LINE. NOTHING MORE.
I WILL NOT PERMIT YOU TO PLACE ANY OF MY CHARGES IN DANGER.
I DIDN'T— GURK!
I HAVE ALSO HEARD REPORTS OF YOUR TENDENCY TOWARD INDECENCY.
YOUR UPBRINGING HAS OBVIOUSLY BEEN SHOCKINGLY LAX.
THIS IS OBVIOUSLY THE FAULT OF YOUR PARENTS.
OH, NOW HOLD ON! MY PARENTS—
SILENCE! I AM AWARE OF THE SWINISH BEHAVIOR OF THE LOWER CLASSES.
YOU...
I...
IF...
RIP

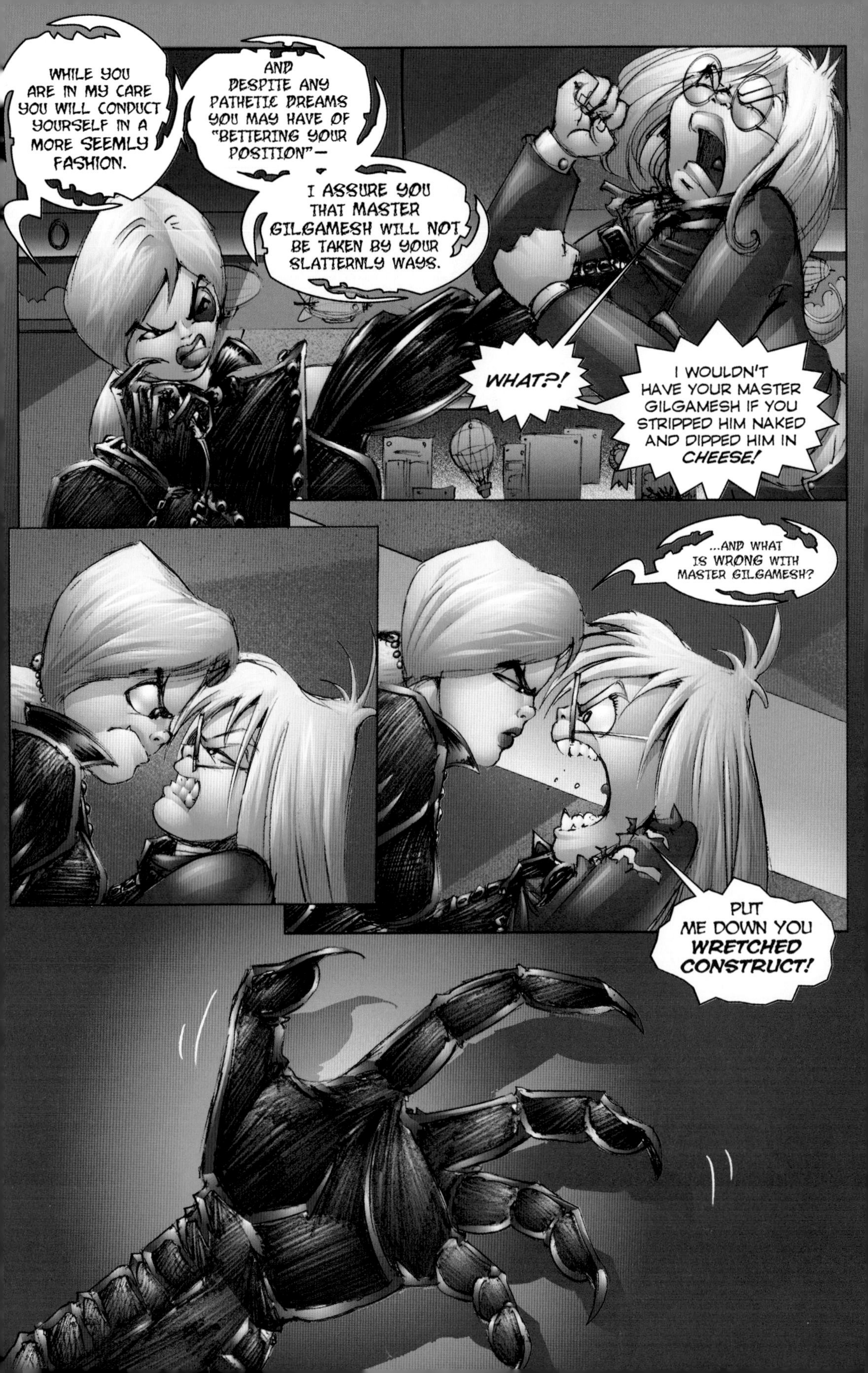
WHILE YOU ARE IN MY CARE YOU WILL CONDUCT YOURSELF IN A MORE SEEMLY FASHION.
AND DESPITE ANY PATHETIC DREAMS YOU MAY HAVE OF "BETTERING YOUR POSITION"—
I ASSURE YOU THAT MASTER GILGAMESH WILL NOT BE TAKEN BY YOUR SLATTERNLY WAYS.
WHAT?!
I WOULDN'T HAVE YOUR MASTER GILGAMESH IF YOU STRIPPED HIM NAKED AND DIPPED HIM IN CHEESE!
...AND WHAT IS WRONG WITH MASTER GILGAMESH?
PUT ME DOWN YOU WRETCHED CONSTRUCT!

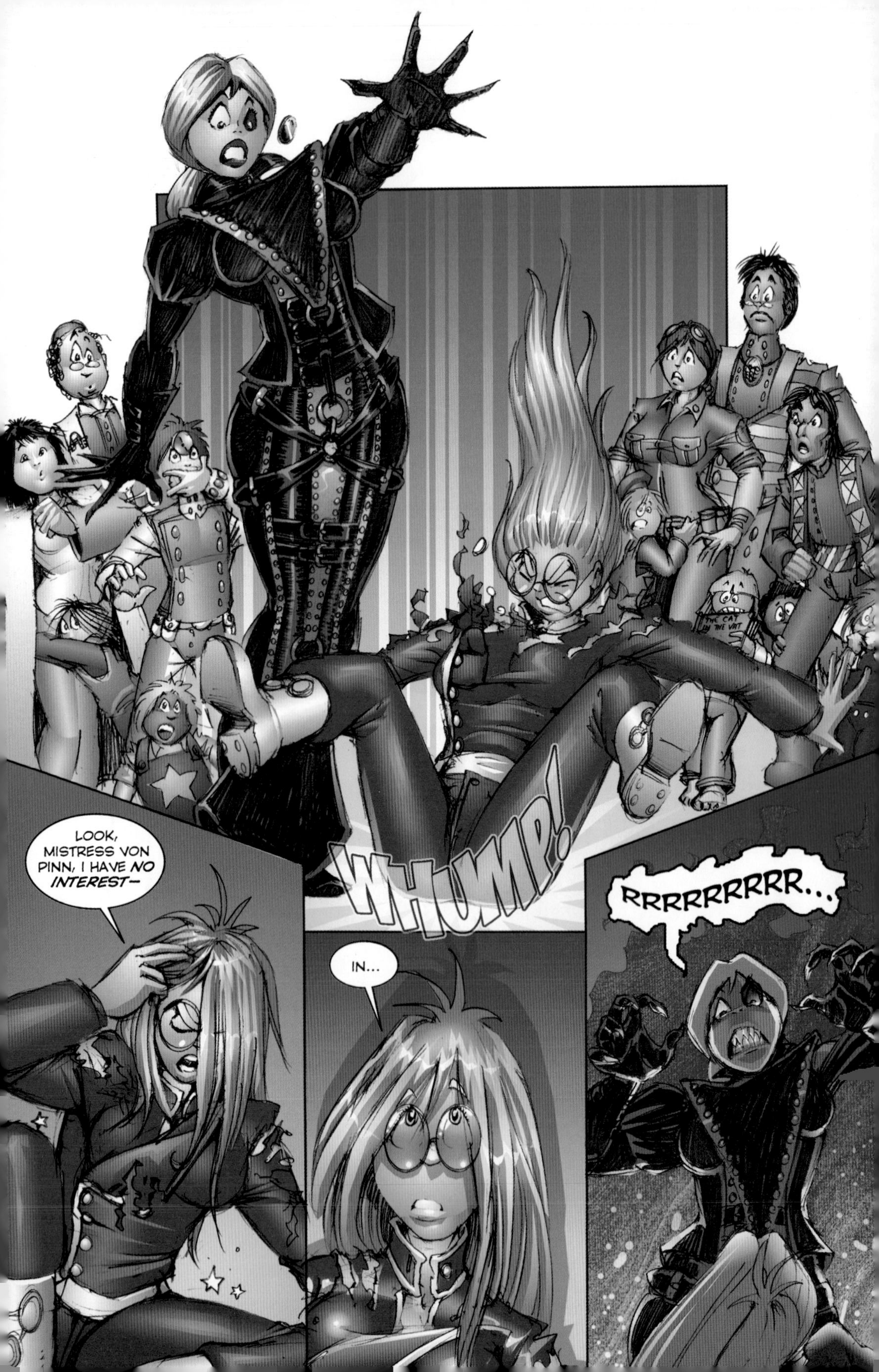
THE CAT IN THE VAT
WHUMP!
LOOK, MISTRESS VON PINN, I HAVE NO INTEREST—
IN...
RRRRRRRRR...

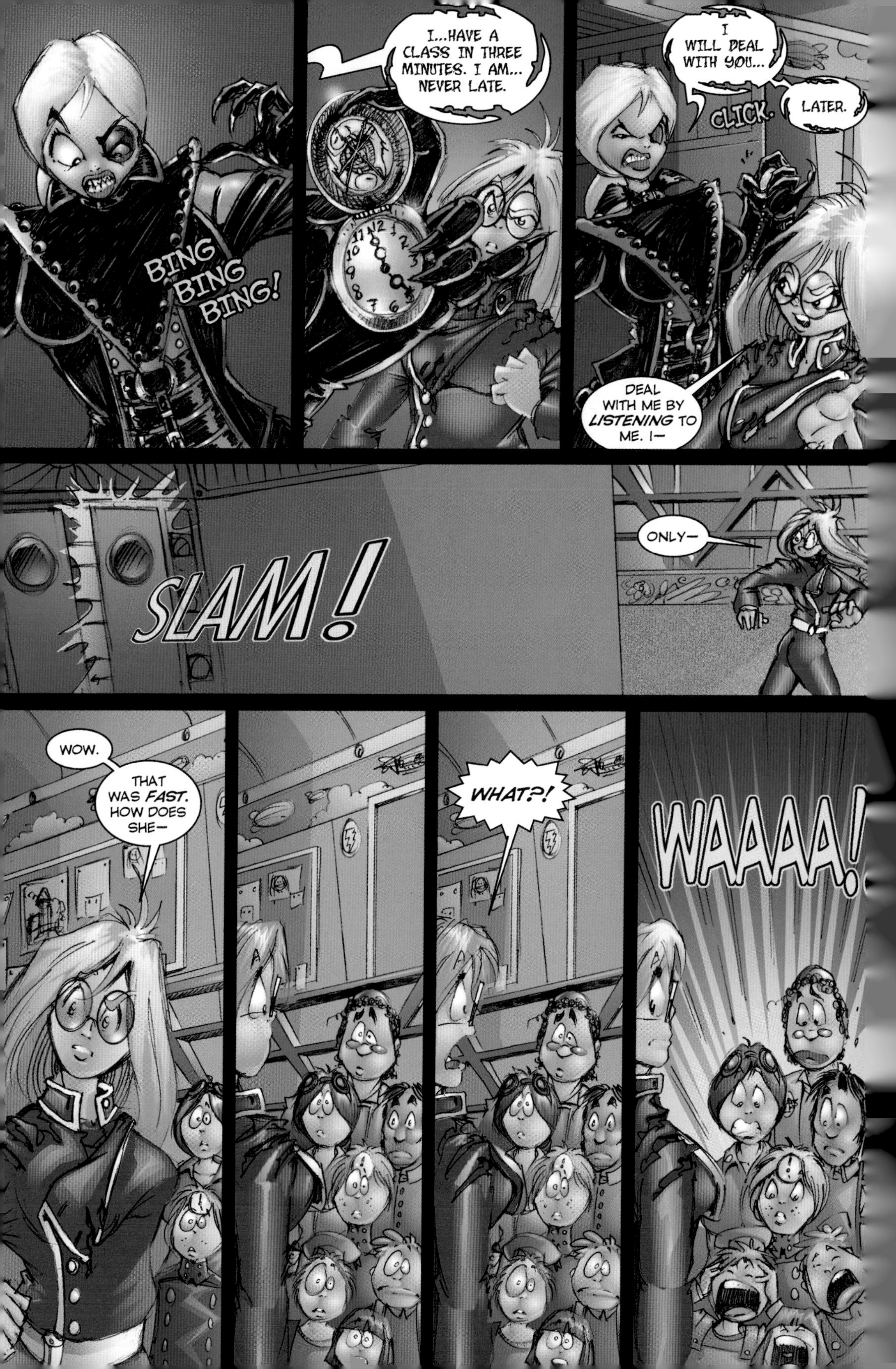
BING
BING
BING!
I...HAVE A CLASS IN THREE MINUTES. I AM... NEVER LATE.
I WILL DEAL WITH YOU...
CLICK.
LATER.
DEAL WITH ME BY LISTENING TO ME. I—
SLAM!
ONLY—
WOW.
THAT WAS FAST. HOW DOES SHE—
WHAT?!
WAAAA!

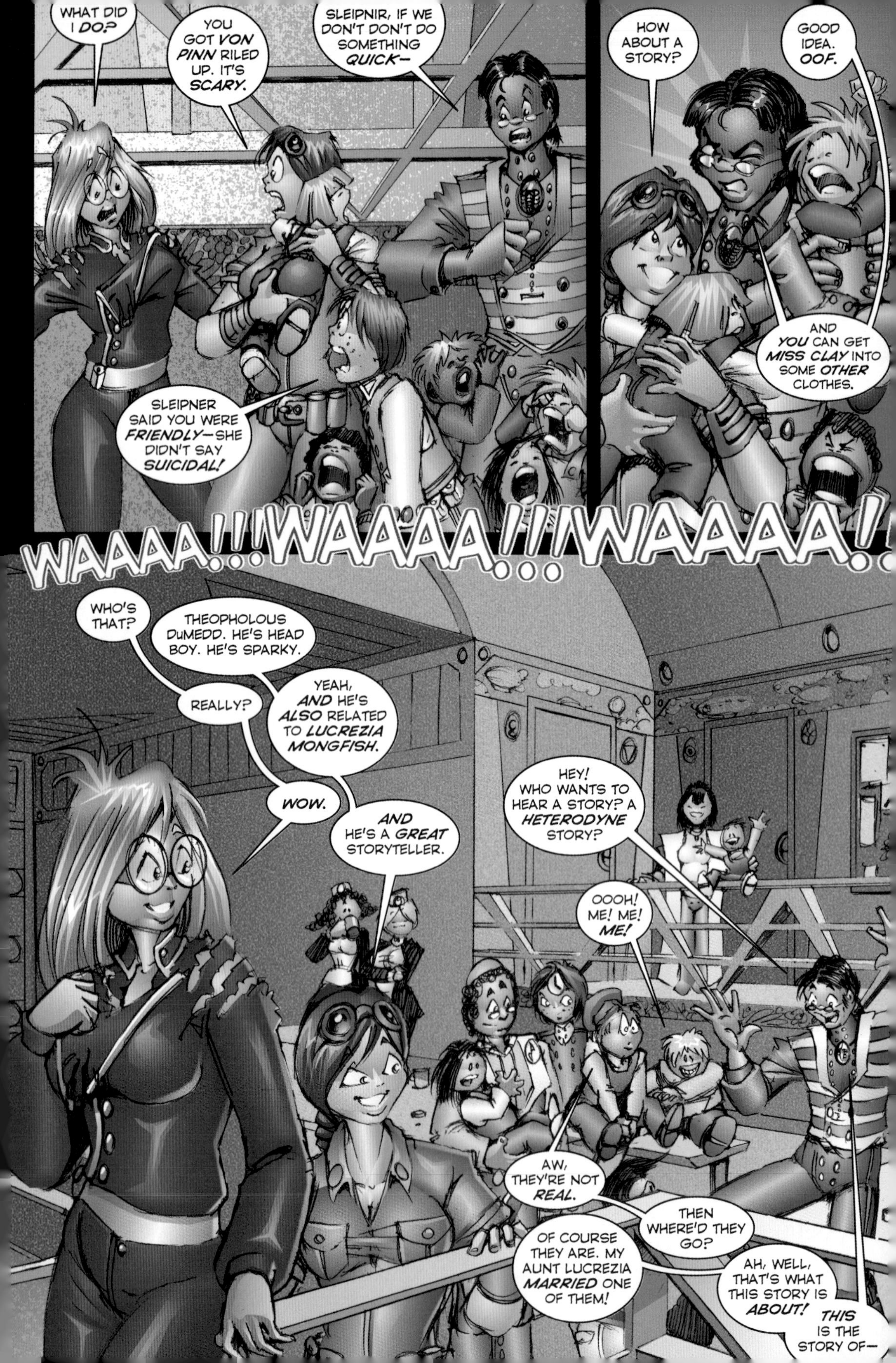
WHAT DID I DO?
YOU GOT VON PINN RILED UP. IT'S SCARY.
SLEIPNIR, IF WE DON'T DON'T DO SOMETHING QUICK—
SLEIPNER SAID YOU WERE FRIENDLY—SHE DIDN'T SAY SUICIDAL!
HOW ABOUT A STORY?
GOOD IDEA. OOF.
AND YOU CAN GET MISS CLAY INTO SOME OTHER CLOTHES.
WAAAA!!! WAAAAA!!! WAAAAA!!
WHO'S THAT?
THEOPHOLOUS DuMEDD. HE'S HEAD BOY. HE'S SPARKY.
REALLY?
YEAH, AND HE'S ALSO RELATED TO LUCREZIA MONGFISH.
WOW.
AND HE'S A GREAT STORYTELLER.
HEY! WHO WANTS TO HEAR A STORY? A HETERODYNE STORY?
OOOH! ME! ME! ME!
AW, THEY'RE NOT REAL.
OF COURSE THEY ARE. MY AUNT LUCREZIA MARRIED ONE OF THEM!
THEN WHERE'D THEY GO?
AH, WELL, THAT'S WHAT THIS STORY IS ABOUT!
THIS IS THE STORY OF—

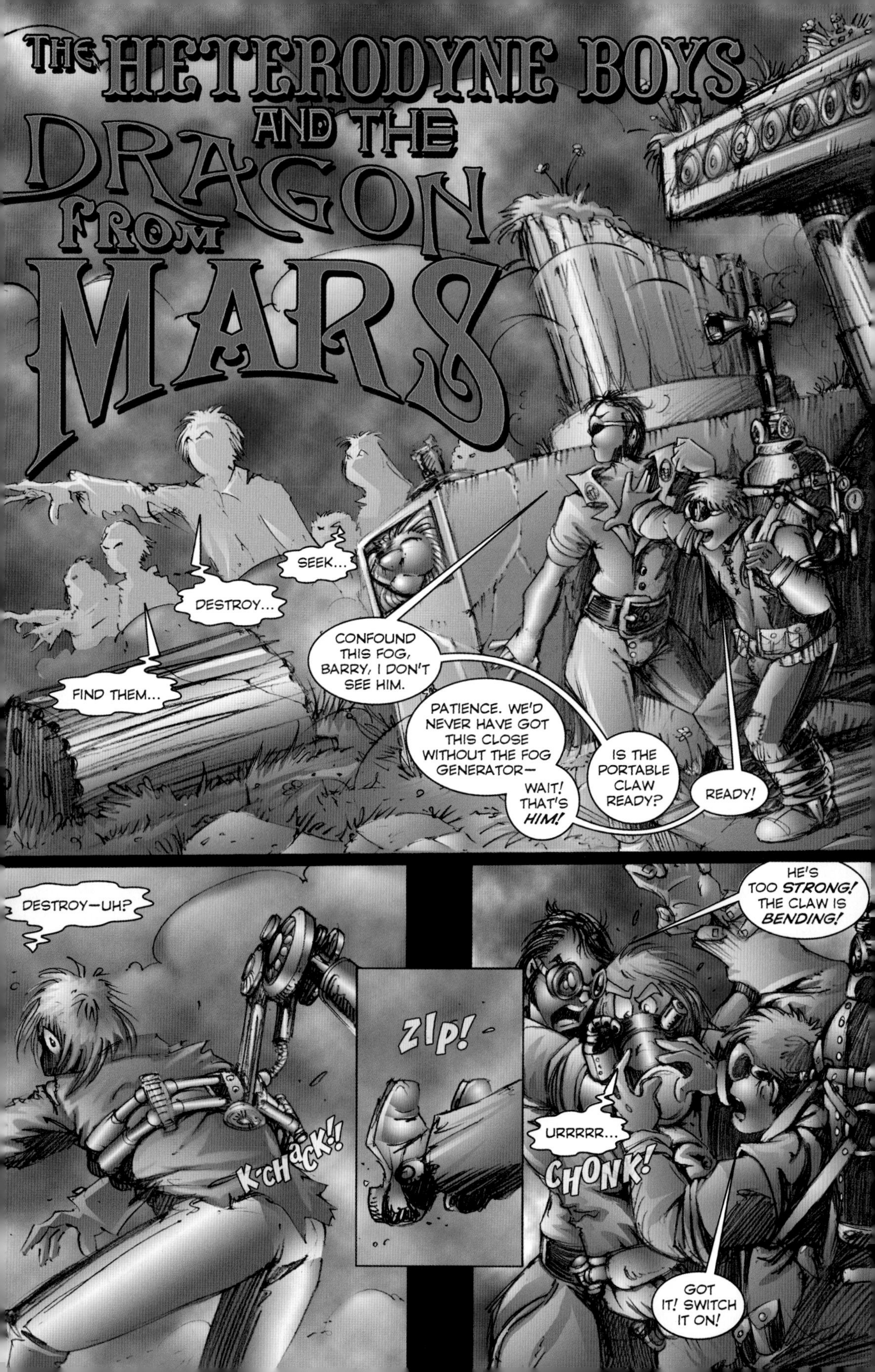
THE HETERODYNE BOYS AND THE DRAGON FROM MARS
SEEK...
DESTROY...
FIND THEM...
CONFOUND THIS FOG, BARRY, I DON'T SEE HIM.
PATIENCE. WE'D NEVER HAVE GOT THIS CLOSE WITHOUT THE FOG GENERATOR—
WAIT! THAT'S HIM!
IS THE PORTABLE CLAW READY?
READY!
DESTROY—UH?
K-CHACK!!
ZIP!
HE'S TOO STRONG! THE CLAW IS BENDING!
URRRRR...
CHONK!
GOT IT! SWITCH IT ON!

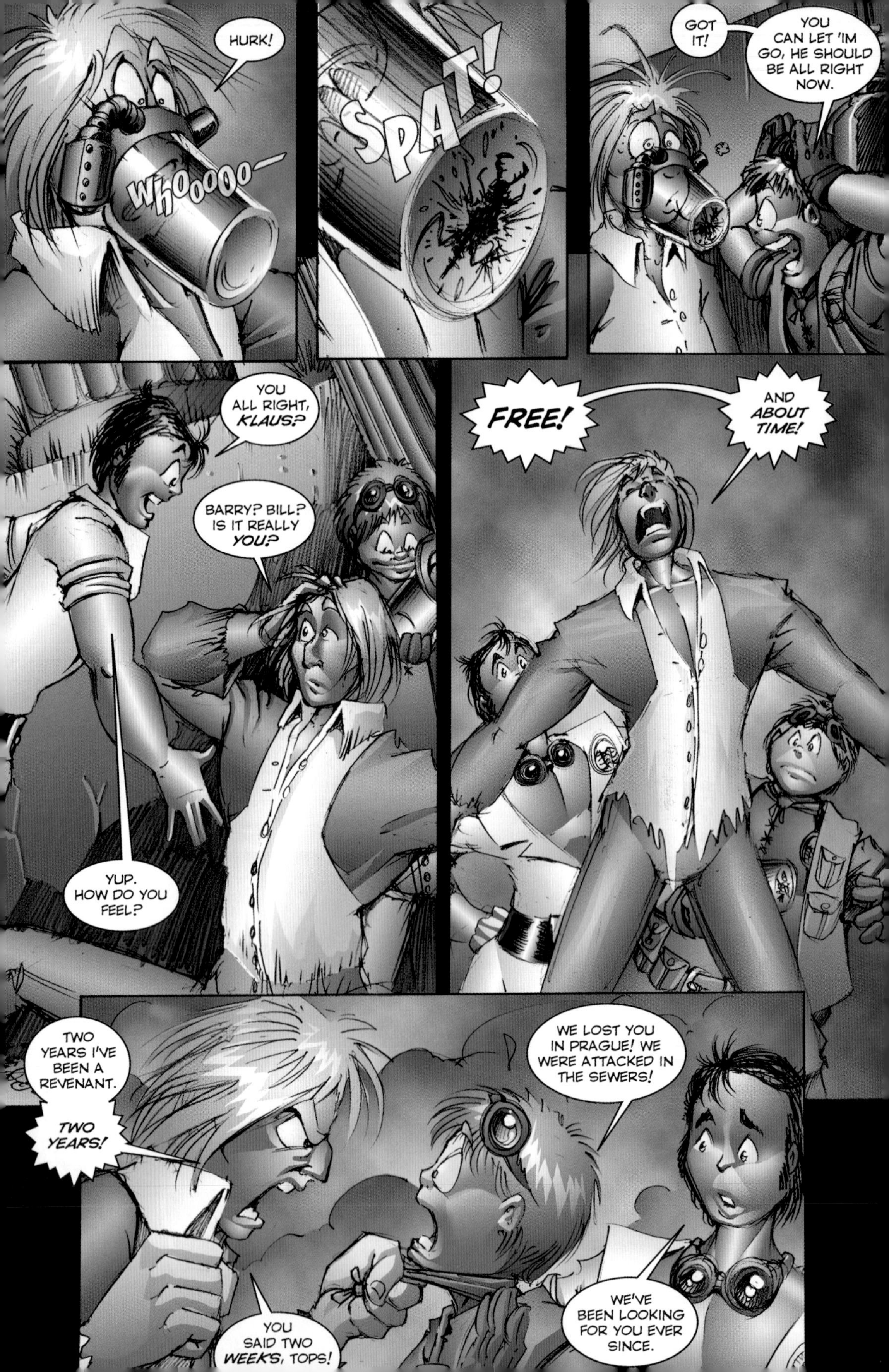
HURK!
WHOOOOO—
SPAT!
GOT IT!
YOU CAN LET 'IM GO, HE SHOULD BE ALL RIGHT NOW.
YOU ALL RIGHT, KLAUS?
BARRY? BILL? IS IT REALLY YOU?
YUP. HOW DO YOU FEEL?
FREE!
AND ABOUT TIME!
TWO YEARS I'VE BEEN A REVENANT.
TWO YEARS!
YOU SAID TWO WEEKS, TOPS!
WE LOST YOU IN PRAGUE! WE WERE ATTACKED IN THE SEWERS!
WE'VE BEEN LOOKING FOR YOU EVER SINCE.

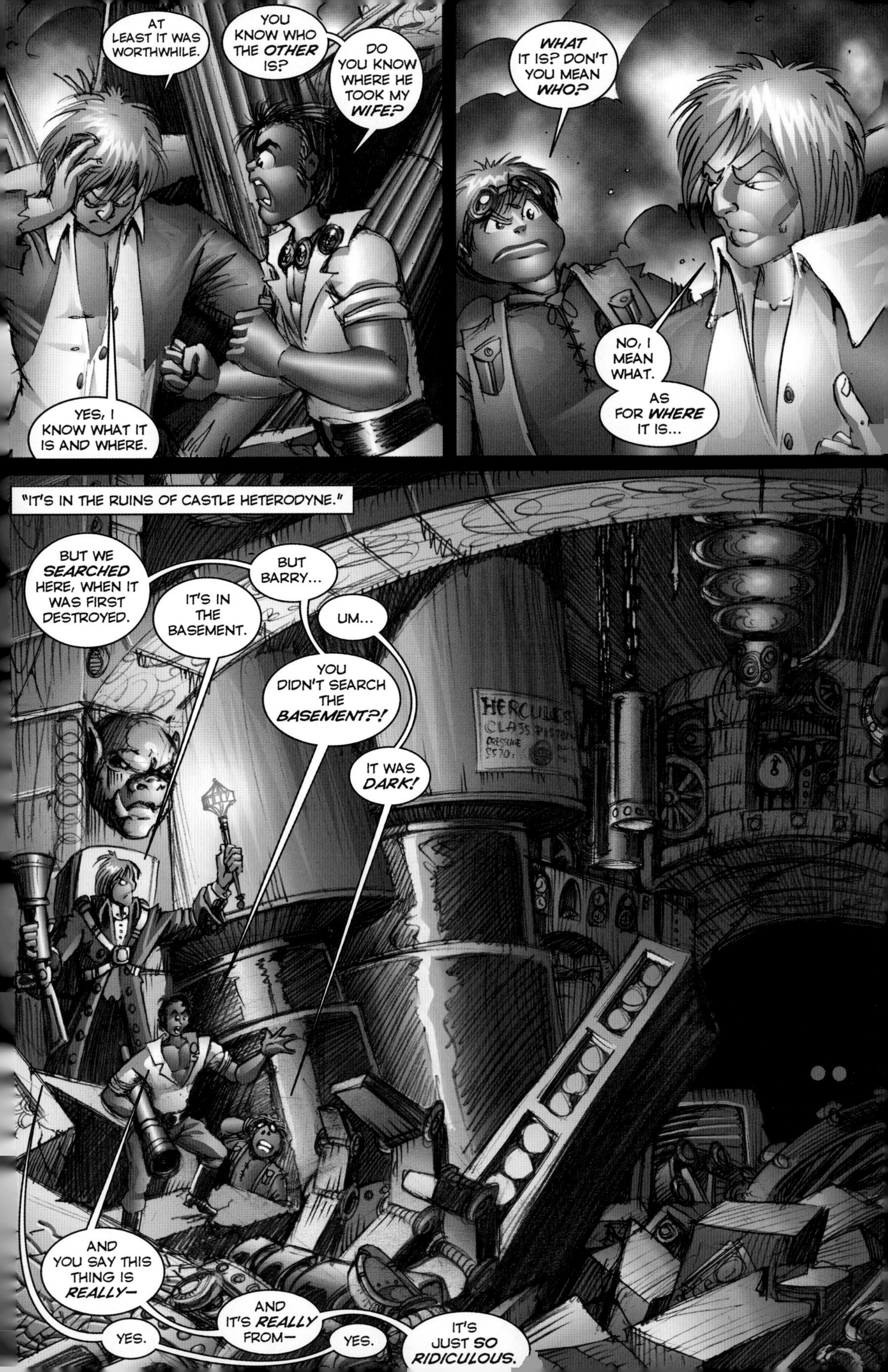
AT LEAST IT WAS WORTHWHILE.
YOU KNOW WHO THE *OTHER* IS?
DO YOU KNOW WHERE HE TOOK MY *WIFE?*
YES, I KNOW WHAT IT IS AND WHERE.
WHAT IT IS? DON'T YOU MEAN *WHO?*
NO, I MEAN WHAT.
AS FOR *WHERE* IT IS...
"IT'S IN THE RUINS OF CASTLE HETERODYNE."
BUT WE *SEARCHED* HERE, WHEN IT WAS FIRST DESTROYED.
BUT BARRY...
IT'S IN THE BASEMENT.
UM...
YOU DIDN'T SEARCH THE *BASEMENT?!*
IT WAS *DARK!*
HERCULES
AND YOU SAY THIS THING IS *REALLY*—
YES.
AND IT'S *REALLY* FROM—
YES.
IT'S JUST *SO RIDICULOUS.*

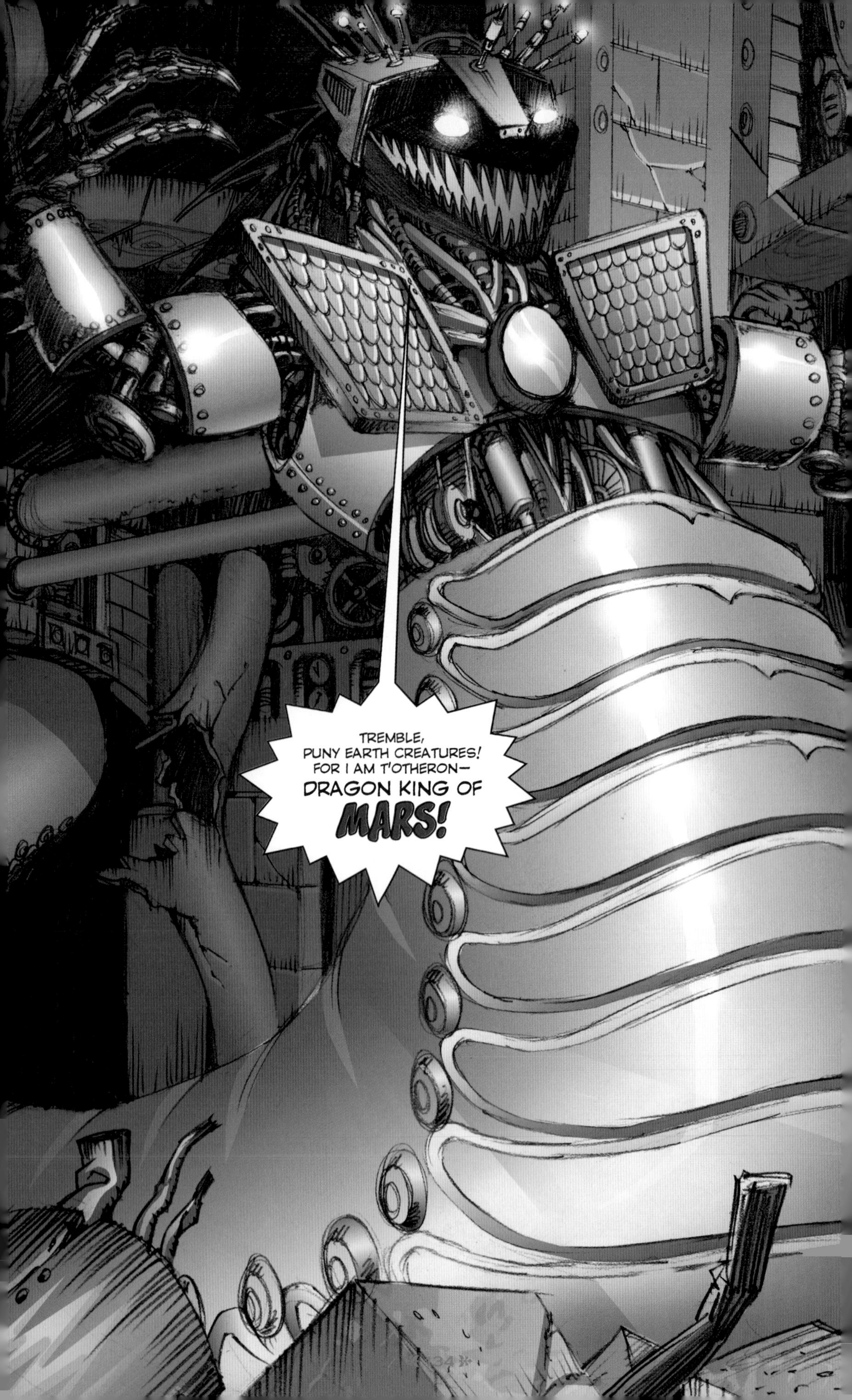
TREMBLE, PUNY EARTH CREATURES! FOR I AM T'OTHERON— DRAGON KING OF MARS!

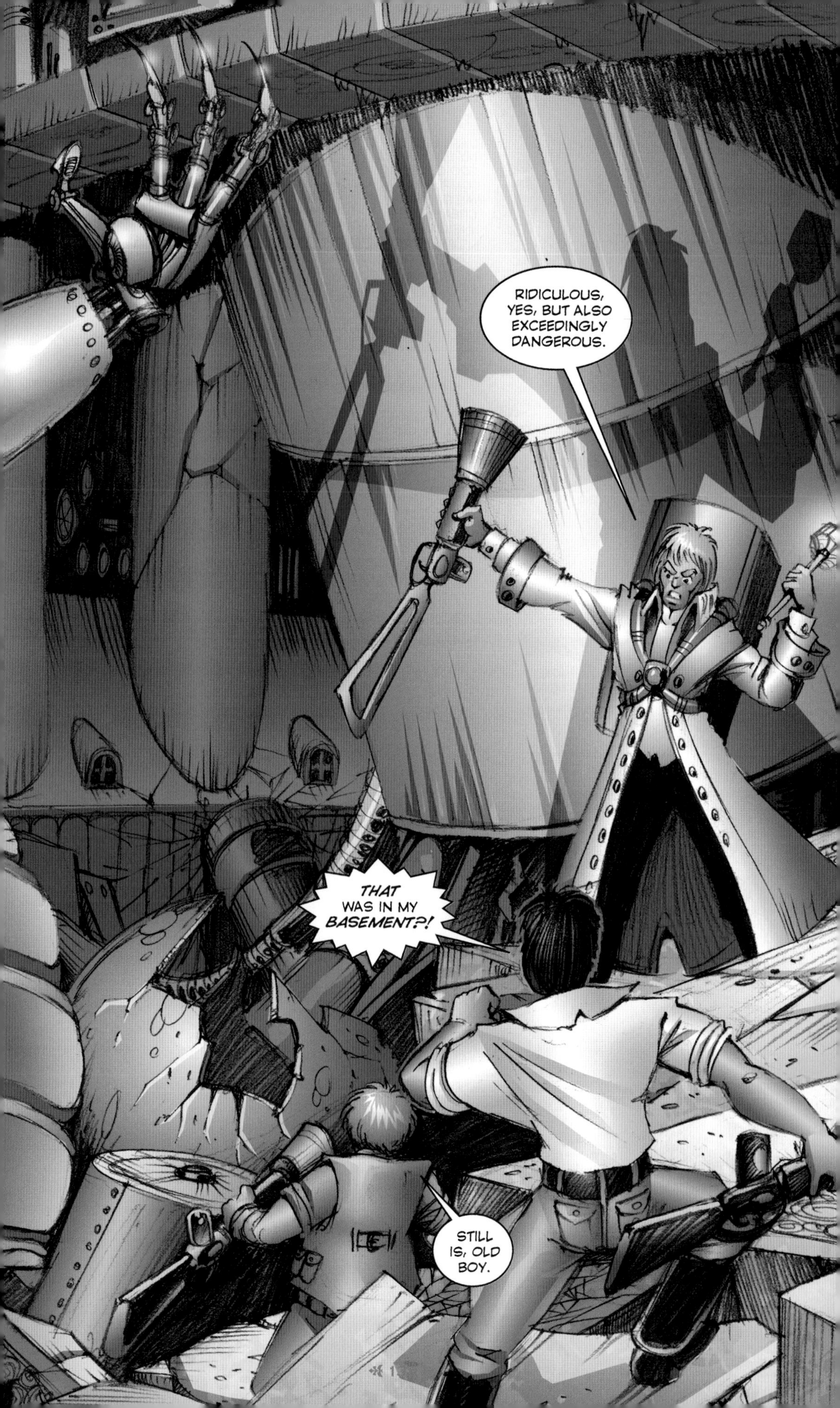
RIDICULOUS, YES, BUT ALSO EXCEEDINGLY DANGEROUS.
THAT WAS IN MY BASEMENT?!
STILL IS, OLD BOY.

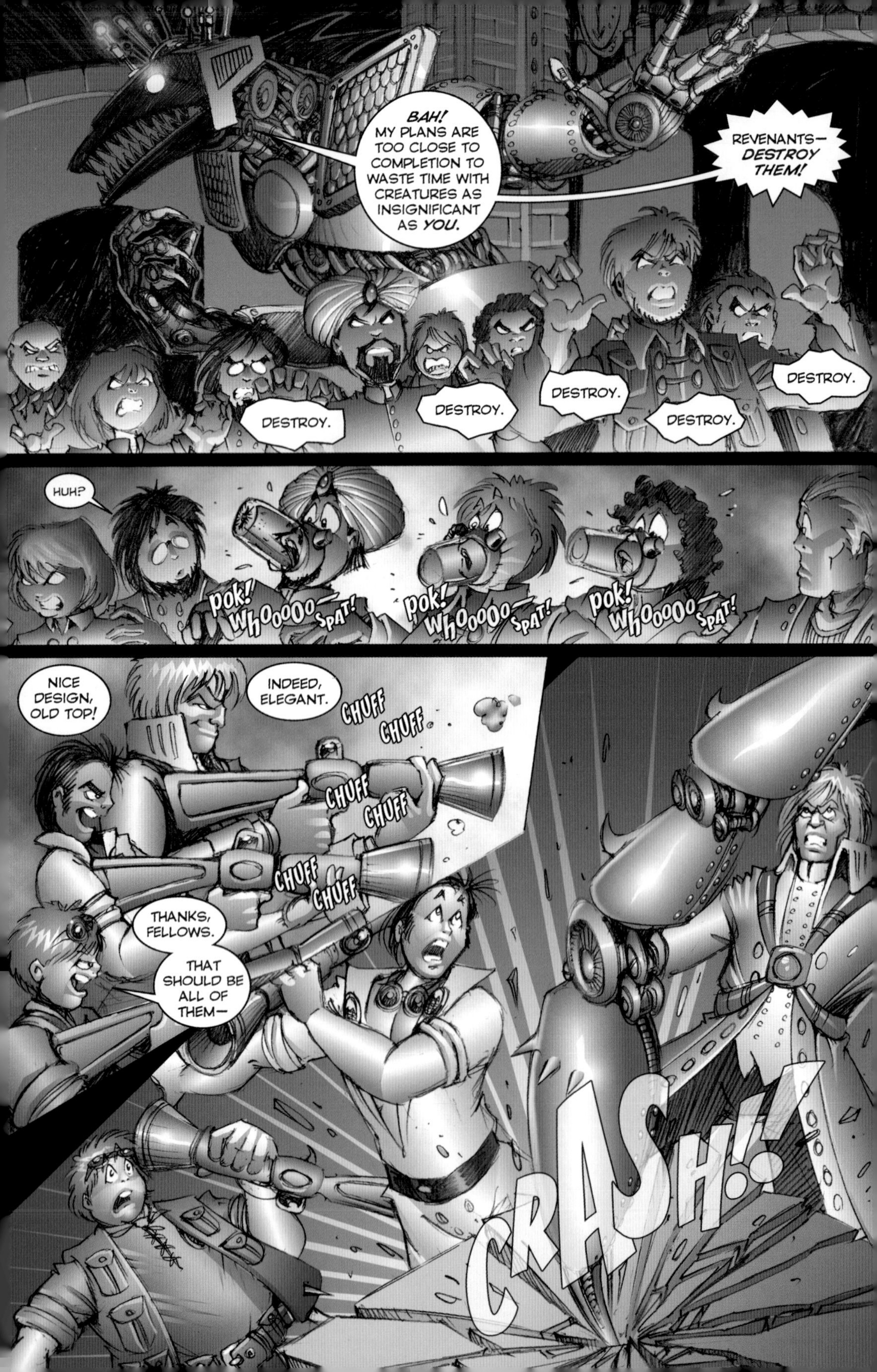
BAH! MY PLANS ARE TOO CLOSE TO COMPLETION TO WASTE TIME WITH CREATURES AS INSIGNIFICANT AS YOU.
REVENANTS— DESTROY THEM!
DESTROY.
DESTROY.
DESTROY.
DESTROY.
DESTROY.
HUH?
pok! WhOOOOO—SPAT!
pok! WhOOOOO—SPAT!
pok! WhOOOOO—SPAT!
NICE DESIGN, OLD TOP!
INDEED, ELEGANT.
CHUFF CHUFF
CHUFF CHUFF
CHUFF CHUFF
THANKS, FELLOWS.
THAT SHOULD BE ALL OF THEM—
CRASH!!

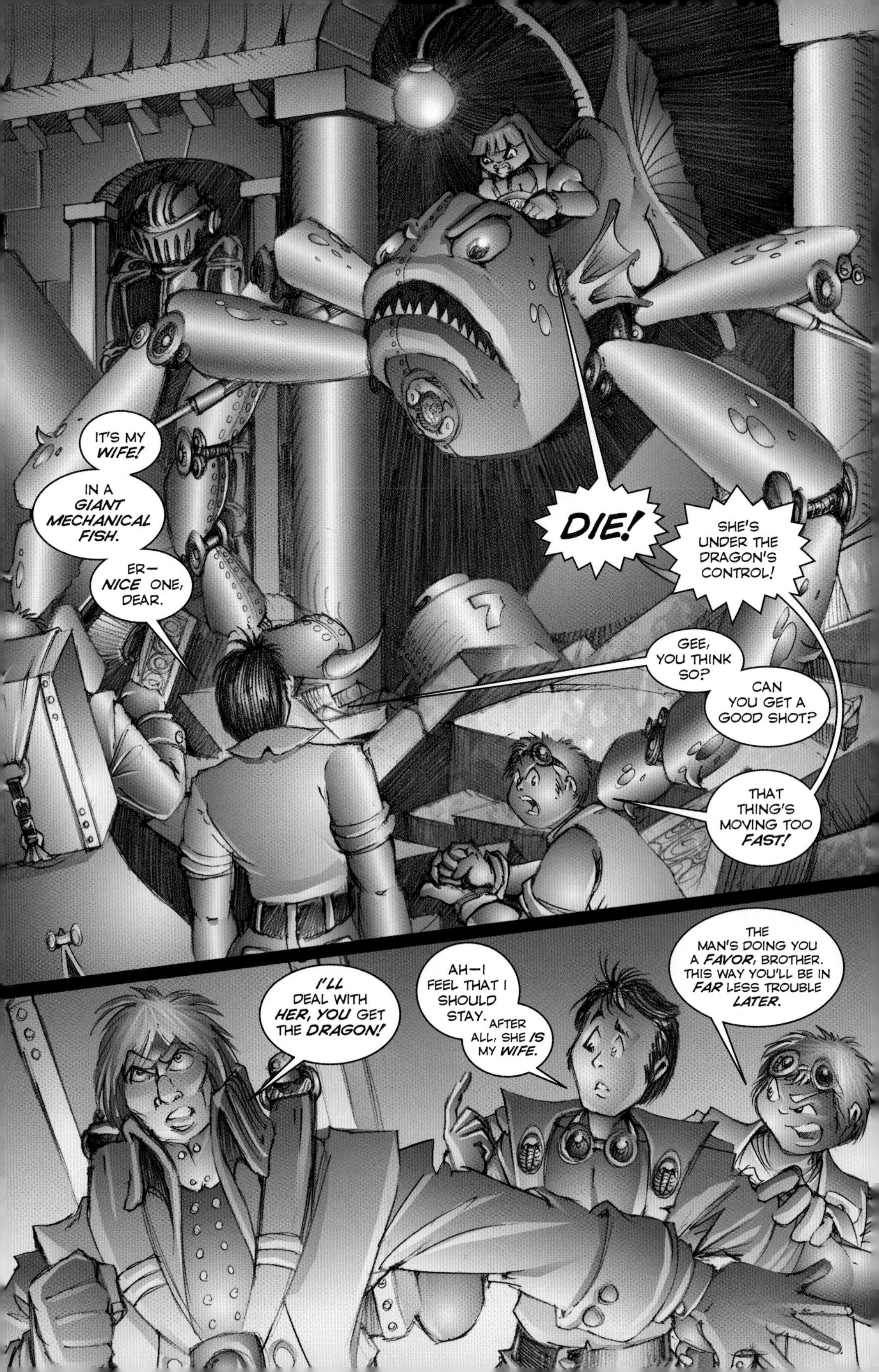
IT'S MY WIFE!
IN A GIANT MECHANICAL FISH.
ER— NICE ONE, DEAR.
DIE!
SHE'S UNDER THE DRAGON'S CONTROL!
GEE, YOU THINK SO?
CAN YOU GET A GOOD SHOT?
THAT THING'S MOVING TOO FAST!
I'LL DEAL WITH HER, YOU GET THE DRAGON!
AH—I FEEL THAT I SHOULD STAY. AFTER ALL, SHE IS MY WIFE.
THE MAN'S DOING YOU A FAVOR, BROTHER. THIS WAY YOU'LL BE IN FAR LESS TROUBLE LATER.

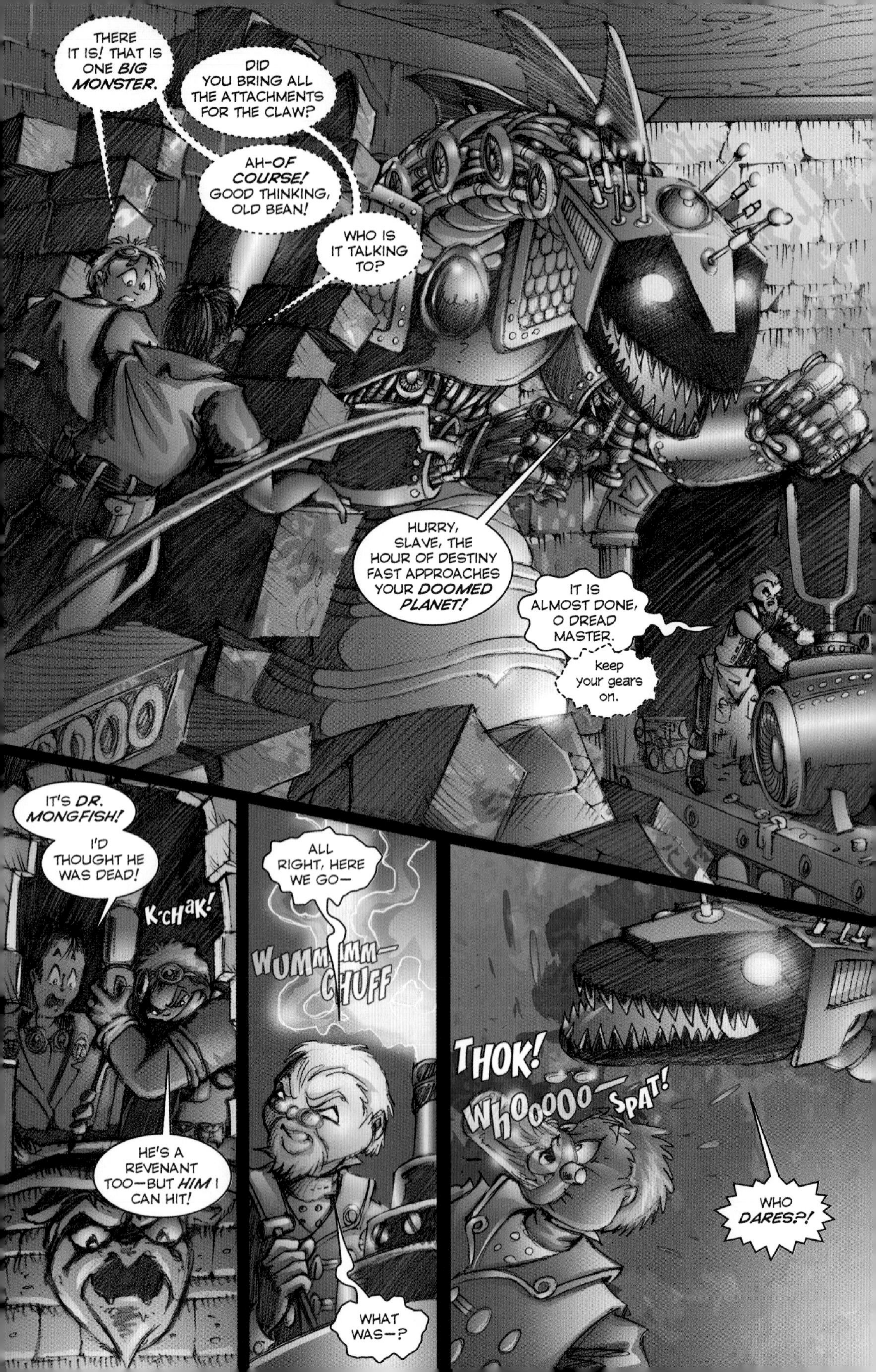
THERE IT IS! THAT IS ONE BIG MONSTER.
DID YOU BRING ALL THE ATTACHMENTS FOR THE CLAW?
AH-OF COURSE! GOOD THINKING, OLD BEAN!
WHO IS IT TALKING TO?
HURRY, SLAVE, THE HOUR OF DESTINY FAST APPROACHES YOUR DOOMED PLANET!
IT IS ALMOST DONE, O DREAD MASTER.
keep your gears on.
IT'S DR. MONGFISH!
I'D THOUGHT HE WAS DEAD!
K'CHAK!
HE'S A REVENANT TOO—BUT HIM I CAN HIT!
ALL RIGHT, HERE WE GO—
WUMMMMM-CHUFF
WHAT WAS—?
THOK!
WHOOOOO-SPAT!
WHO DARES?!

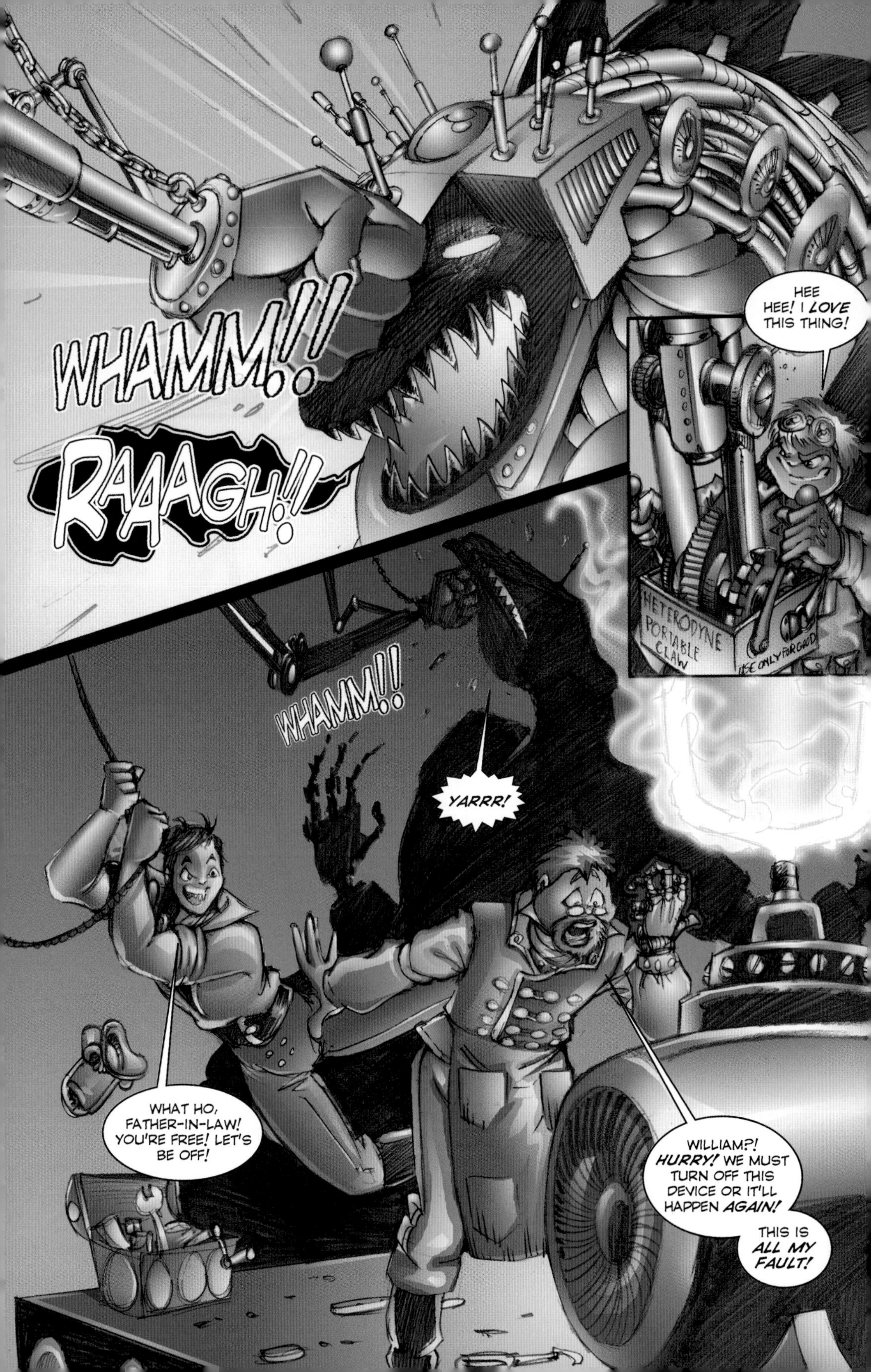
WHAMM!!
RAAAGH!!
HEE HEE! I LOVE THIS THING!
HETERODYNE PORTABLE CLAW
USE ONLY FOR GOOD
WHAMM!!
YARRR!
WHAT HO, FATHER-IN-LAW! YOU'RE FREE! LET'S BE OFF!
WILLIAM?! HURRY! WE MUST TURN OFF THIS DEVICE OR IT'LL HAPPEN AGAIN!
THIS IS ALL MY FAULT!

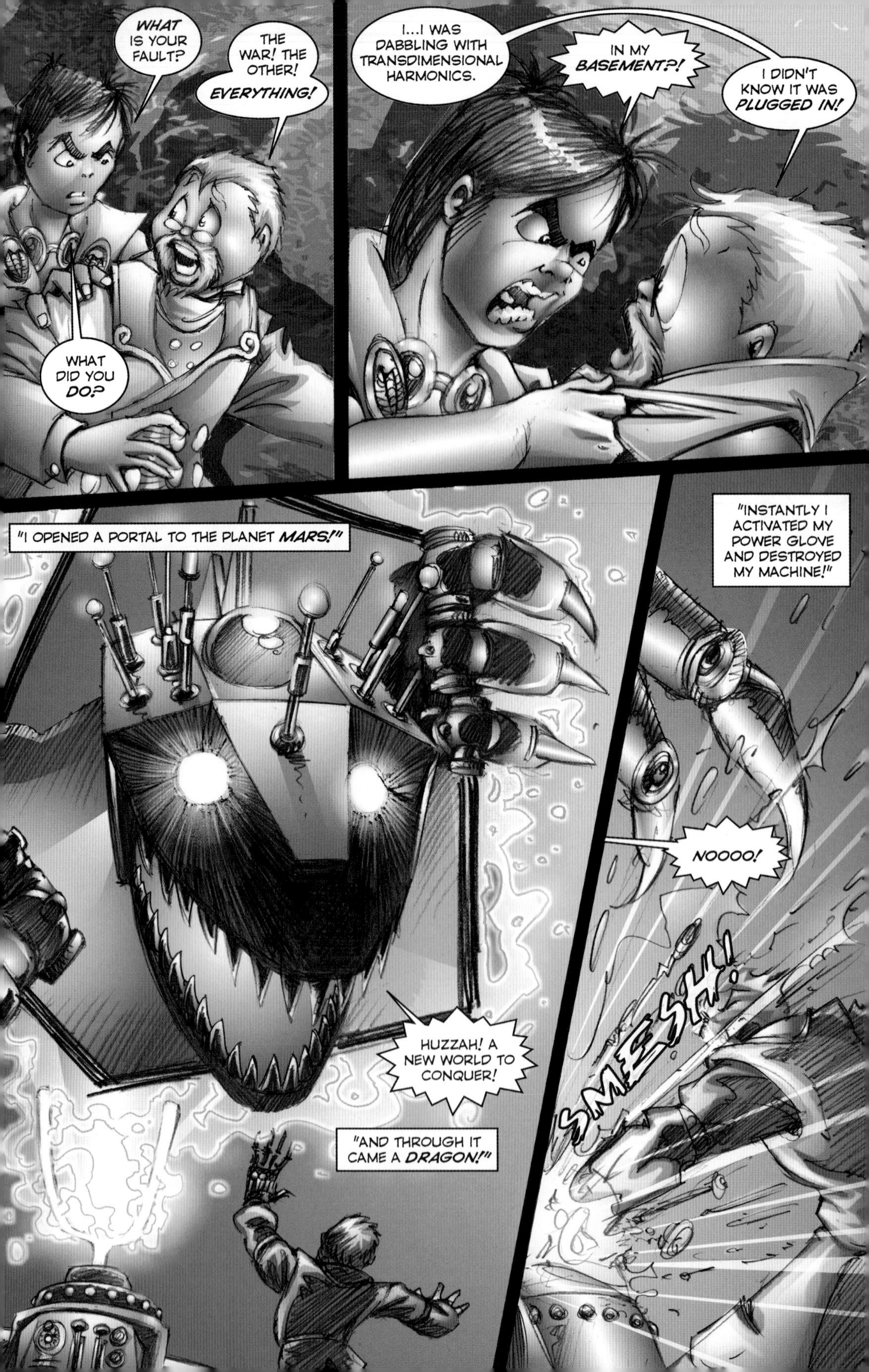
WHAT IS YOUR FAULT?
THE WAR! THE OTHER! EVERYTHING!
WHAT DID YOU DO?
I...I WAS DABBLING WITH TRANSDIMENSIONAL HARMONICS.
IN MY BASEMENT?!
I DIDN'T KNOW IT WAS PLUGGED IN!
"I OPENED A PORTAL TO THE PLANET MARS!"
HUZZAH! A NEW WORLD TO CONQUER!
"AND THROUGH IT CAME A DRAGON!"
"INSTANTLY I ACTIVATED MY POWER GLOVE AND DESTROYED MY MACHINE!"
NOOOO!
SMESH!

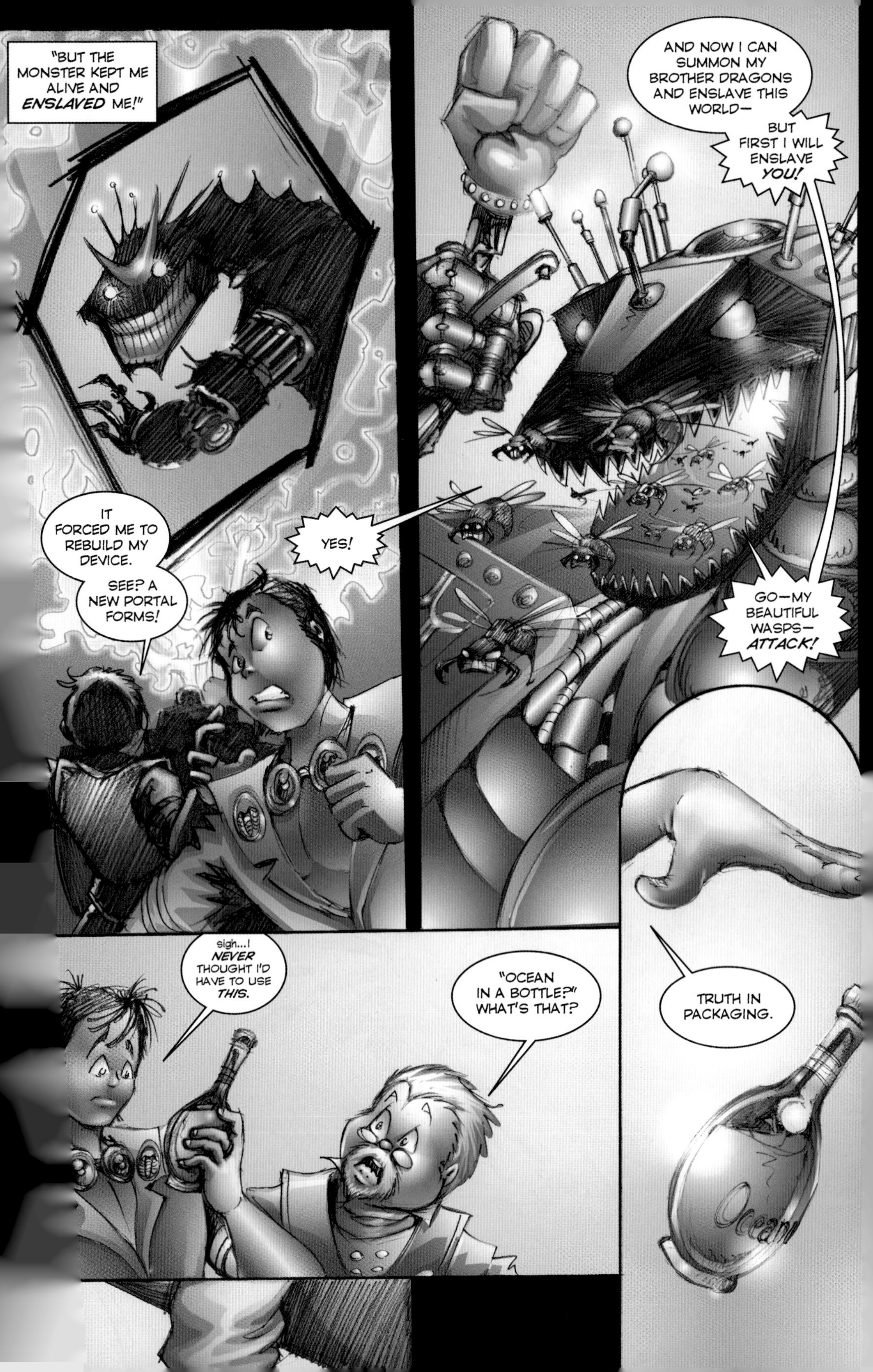
"BUT THE MONSTER KEPT ME ALIVE AND *ENSLAVED* ME!"
IT FORCED ME TO REBUILD MY DEVICE.
SEE? A NEW PORTAL FORMS!
YES!
AND NOW I CAN SUMMON MY BROTHER DRAGONS AND ENSLAVE THIS WORLD—
BUT FIRST I WILL ENSLAVE *YOU!*
GO—MY BEAUTIFUL WASPS— *ATTACK!*
sigh...I *NEVER* THOUGHT I'D HAVE TO USE *THIS*.
"OCEAN IN A BOTTLE?" WHAT'S THAT?
TRUTH IN PACKAGING.
Ocean

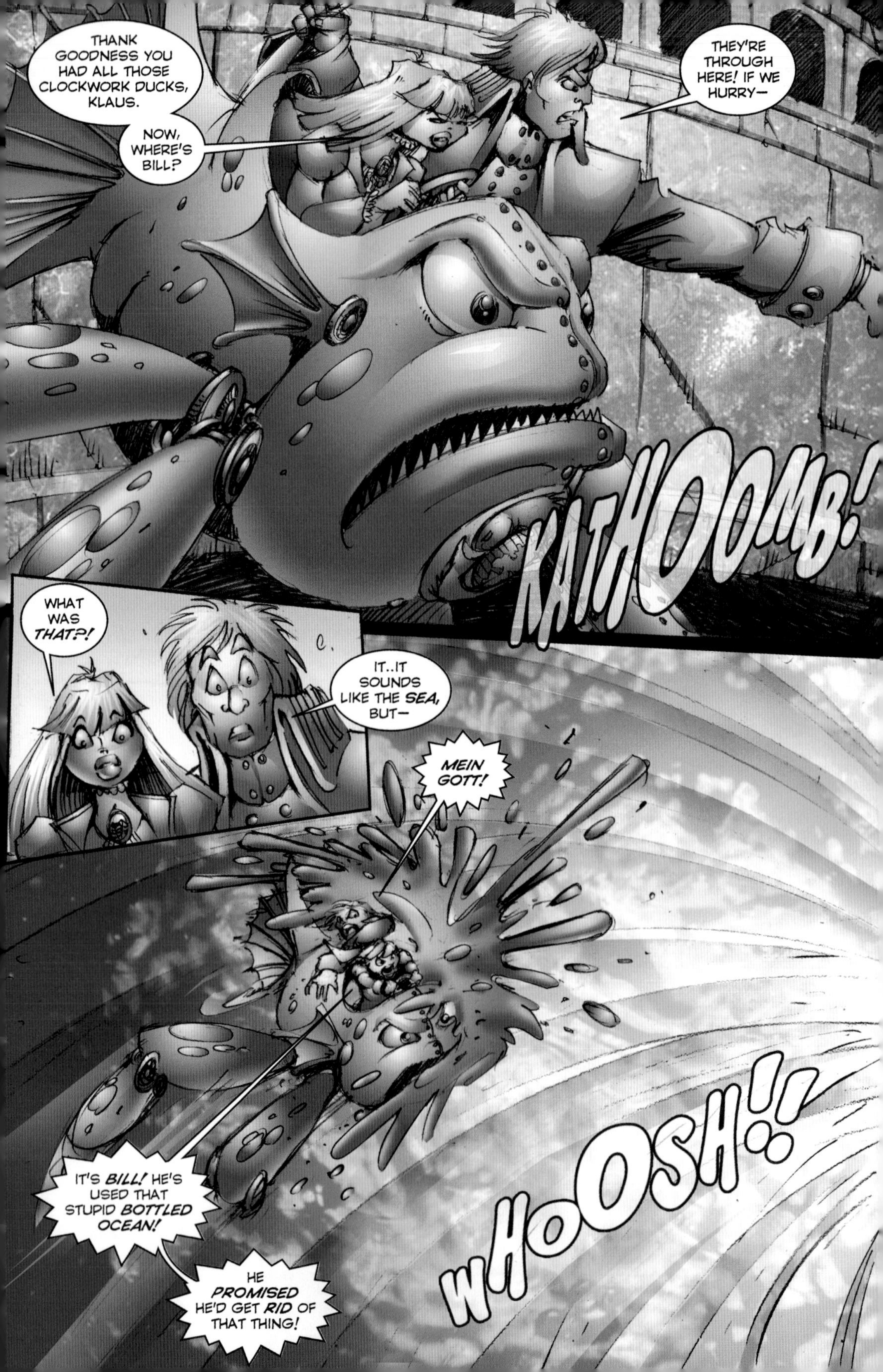
THANK GOODNESS YOU HAD ALL THOSE CLOCKWORK DUCKS, KLAUS.
NOW, WHERE'S BILL?
THEY'RE THROUGH HERE! IF WE HURRY—
KATHOOMB!
WHAT WAS THAT?!
IT..IT SOUNDS LIKE THE SEA, BUT—
MEIN GOTT!
IT'S BILL! HE'S USED THAT STUPID BOTTLED OCEAN!
HE PROMISED HE'D GET RID OF THAT THING!
WHOOSH!!!

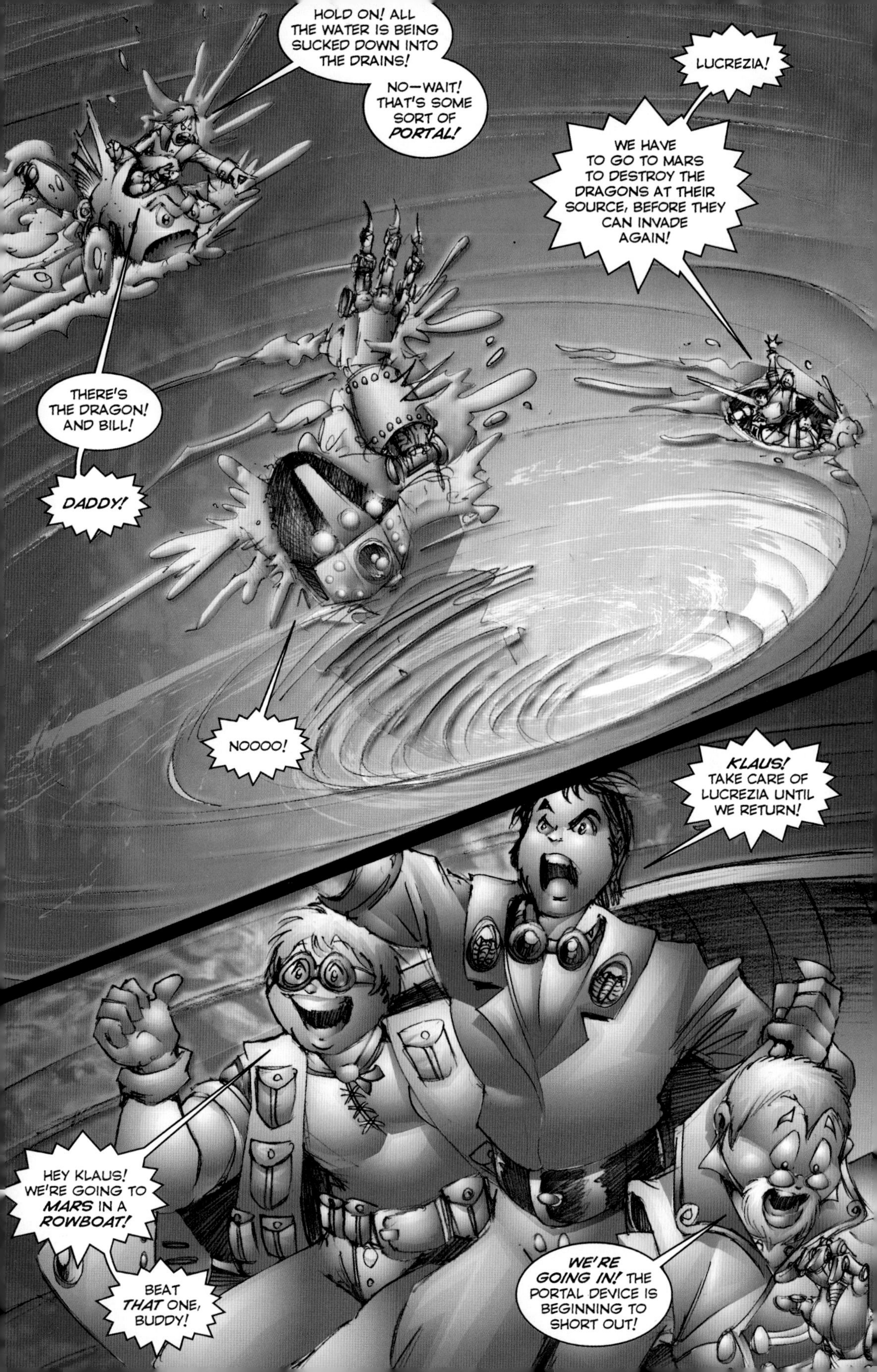
HOLD ON! ALL THE WATER IS BEING SUCKED DOWN INTO THE DRAINS!
NO—WAIT! THAT'S SOME SORT OF *PORTAL!*
LUCREZIA!
WE HAVE TO GO TO MARS TO DESTROY THE DRAGONS AT THEIR SOURCE, BEFORE THEY CAN INVADE AGAIN!
THERE'S THE DRAGON! AND BILL!
DADDY!
NOOOO!
KLAUS! TAKE CARE OF LUCREZIA UNTIL WE RETURN!
HEY KLAUS! WE'RE GOING TO *MARS* IN A *ROWBOAT!*
BEAT *THAT* ONE, BUDDY!
WE'RE GOING IN! THE PORTAL DEVICE IS BEGINNING TO SHORT OUT!

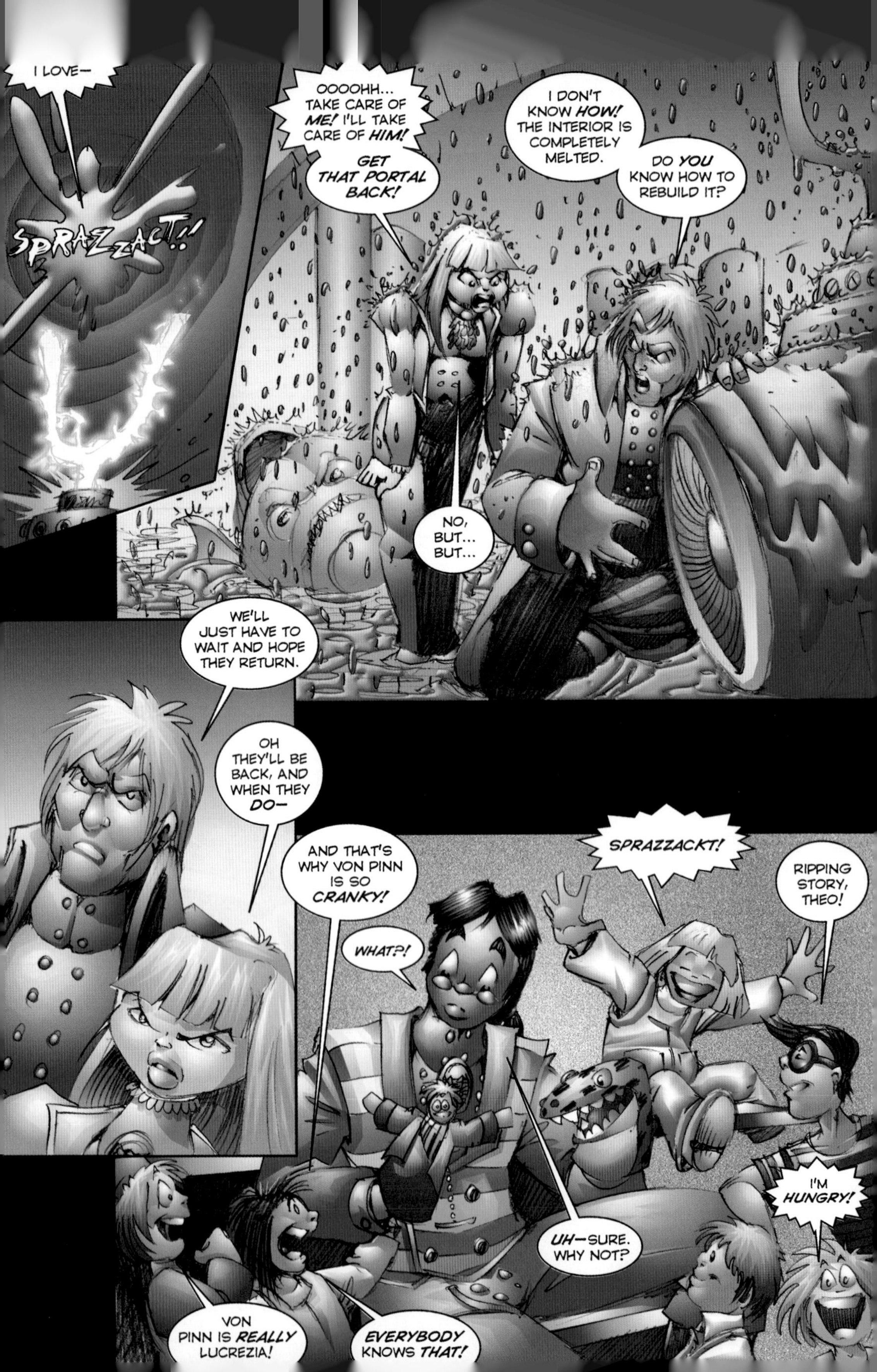
I LOVE—
SPRAZZACT!!
OOOOHH... TAKE CARE OF ME! I'LL TAKE CARE OF HIM!
GET THAT PORTAL BACK!
I DON'T KNOW HOW! THE INTERIOR IS COMPLETELY MELTED.
DO YOU KNOW HOW TO REBUILD IT?
NO, BUT... BUT...
WE'LL JUST HAVE TO WAIT AND HOPE THEY RETURN.
OH THEY'LL BE BACK, AND WHEN THEY DO—
AND THAT'S WHY VON PINN IS SO CRANKY!
WHAT?!
SPRAZZACKT!
RIPPING STORY, THEO!
I'M HUNGRY!
UH—SURE. WHY NOT?
VON PINN IS REALLY LUCREZIA!
EVERYBODY KNOWS THAT!

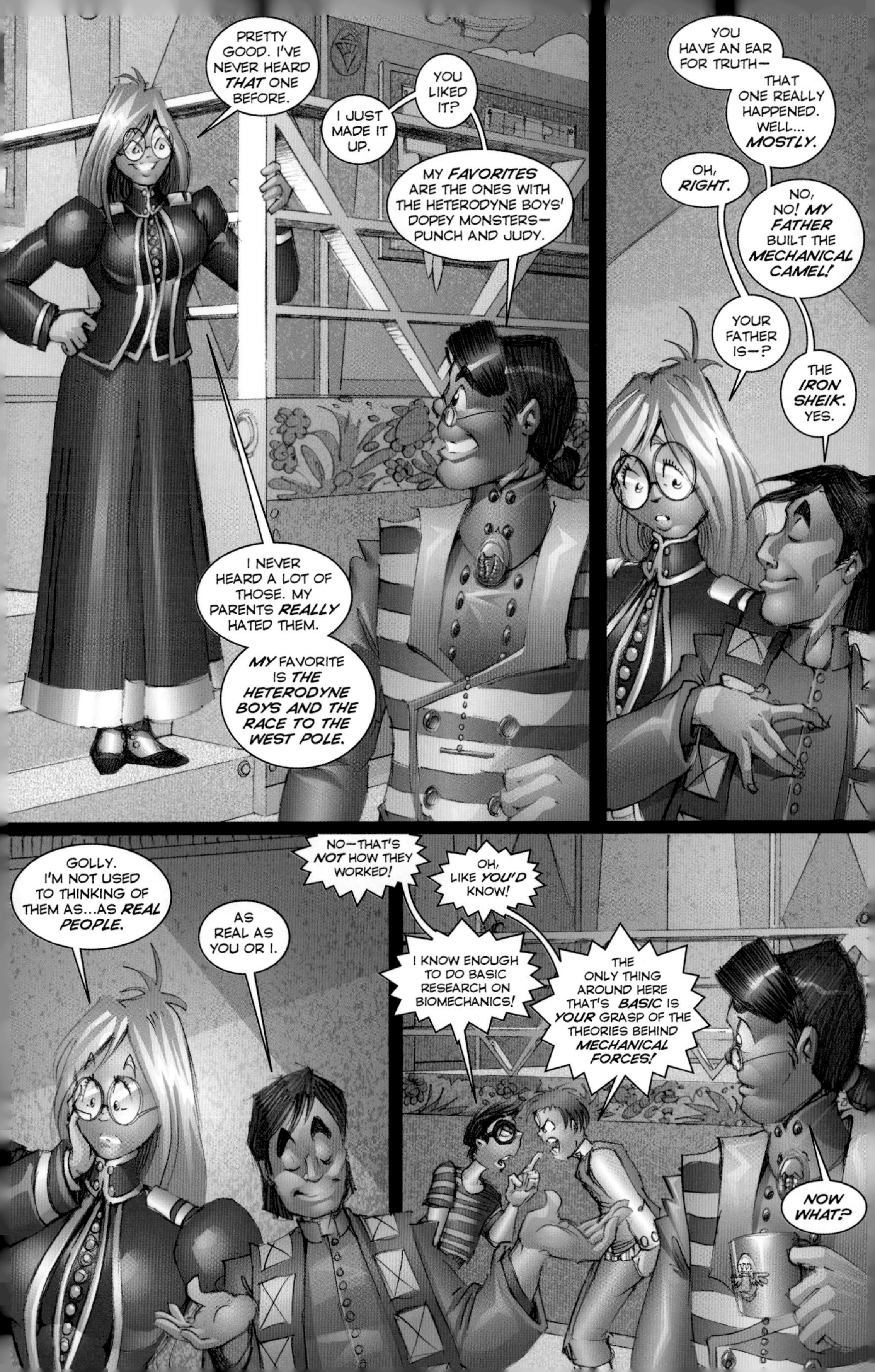
PRETTY GOOD. I'VE NEVER HEARD *THAT* ONE BEFORE.
I JUST MADE IT UP.
YOU LIKED IT?
MY *FAVORITES* ARE THE ONES WITH THE HETERODYNE BOYS' DOPEY MONSTERS— PUNCH AND JUDY.
I NEVER HEARD A LOT OF THOSE. MY PARENTS *REALLY* HATED THEM.
MY FAVORITE IS *THE HETERODYNE BOYS AND THE RACE TO THE WEST POLE.*
YOU HAVE AN EAR FOR TRUTH—
THAT ONE REALLY HAPPENED. WELL... *MOSTLY.*
OH, *RIGHT.*
NO, NO! *MY FATHER* BUILT THE *MECHANICAL CAMEL!*
YOUR FATHER IS—?
THE *IRON SHEIK.* YES.
GOLLY. I'M NOT USED TO THINKING OF THEM AS...AS *REAL PEOPLE.*
AS REAL AS YOU OR I.
NO—THAT'S *NOT* HOW THEY WORKED!
OH, LIKE *YOU'D* KNOW!
I KNOW ENOUGH TO DO BASIC RESEARCH ON BIOMECHANICS!
THE ONLY THING AROUND HERE THAT'S *BASIC* IS *YOUR* GRASP OF THE THEORIES BEHIND *MECHANICAL FORCES!*
NOW WHAT?

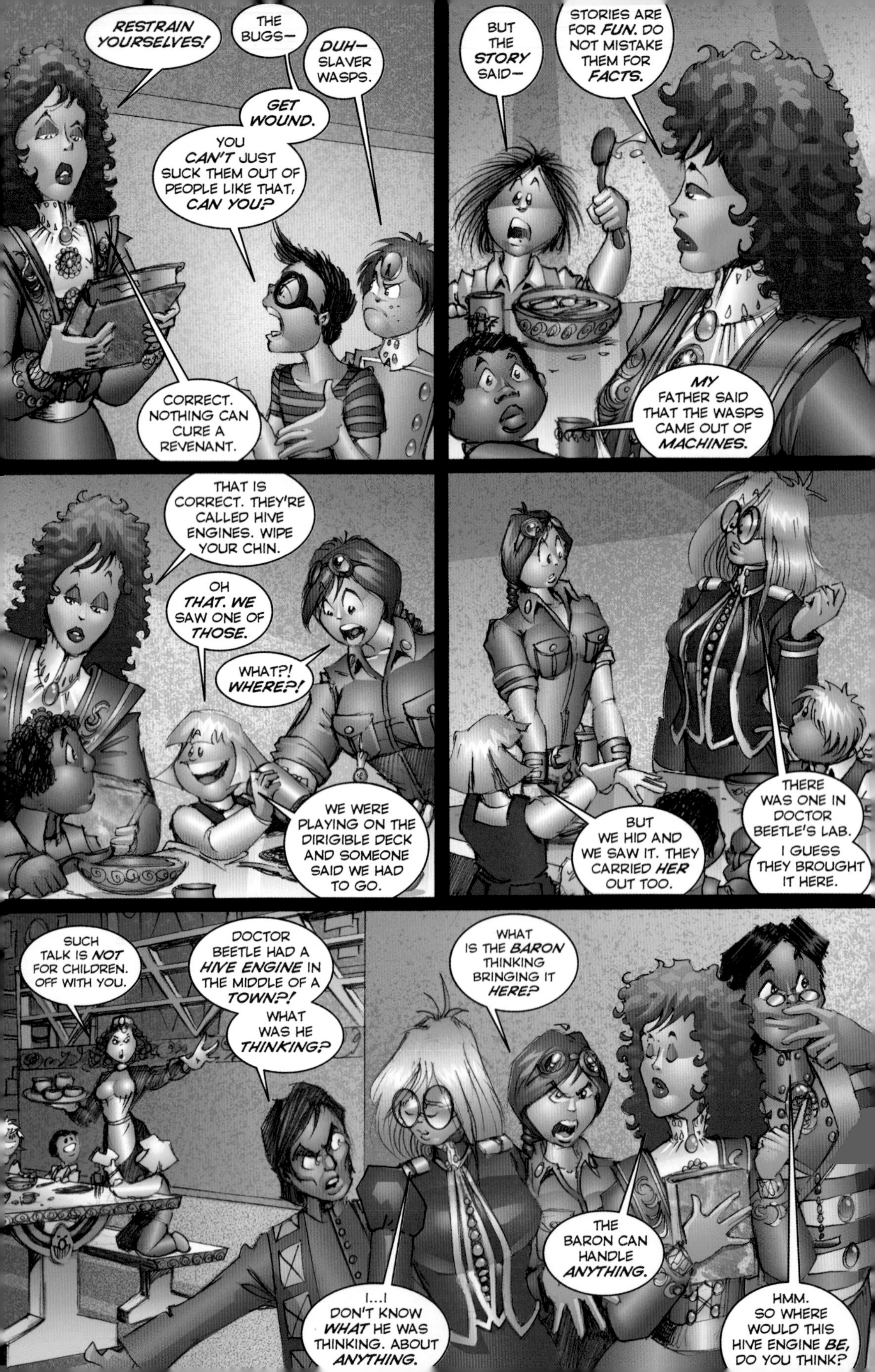
RESTRAIN YOURSELVES!
THE BUGS—
DUH—SLAVER WASPS.
GET WOUND.
YOU CAN'T JUST SUCK THEM OUT OF PEOPLE LIKE THAT, CAN YOU?
CORRECT. NOTHING CAN CURE A REVENANT.
BUT THE STORY SAID—
STORIES ARE FOR FUN. DO NOT MISTAKE THEM FOR FACTS.
MY FATHER SAID THAT THE WASPS CAME OUT OF MACHINES.
THAT IS CORRECT. THEY'RE CALLED HIVE ENGINES. WIPE YOUR CHIN.
OH THAT. WE SAW ONE OF THOSE.
WHAT?! WHERE?!
WE WERE PLAYING ON THE DIRIGIBLE DECK AND SOMEONE SAID WE HAD TO GO.
BUT WE HID AND WE SAW IT. THEY CARRIED HER OUT TOO.
THERE WAS ONE IN DOCTOR BEETLE'S LAB.
I GUESS THEY BROUGHT IT HERE.
SUCH TALK IS NOT FOR CHILDREN. OFF WITH YOU.
DOCTOR BEETLE HAD A HIVE ENGINE IN THE MIDDLE OF A TOWN?!
WHAT WAS HE THINKING?
WHAT IS THE BARON THINKING BRINGING IT HERE?
I...I DON'T KNOW WHAT HE WAS THINKING. ABOUT ANYTHING.
THE BARON CAN HANDLE ANYTHING.
HMM. SO WHERE WOULD THIS HIVE ENGINE BE, DO YOU THINK?

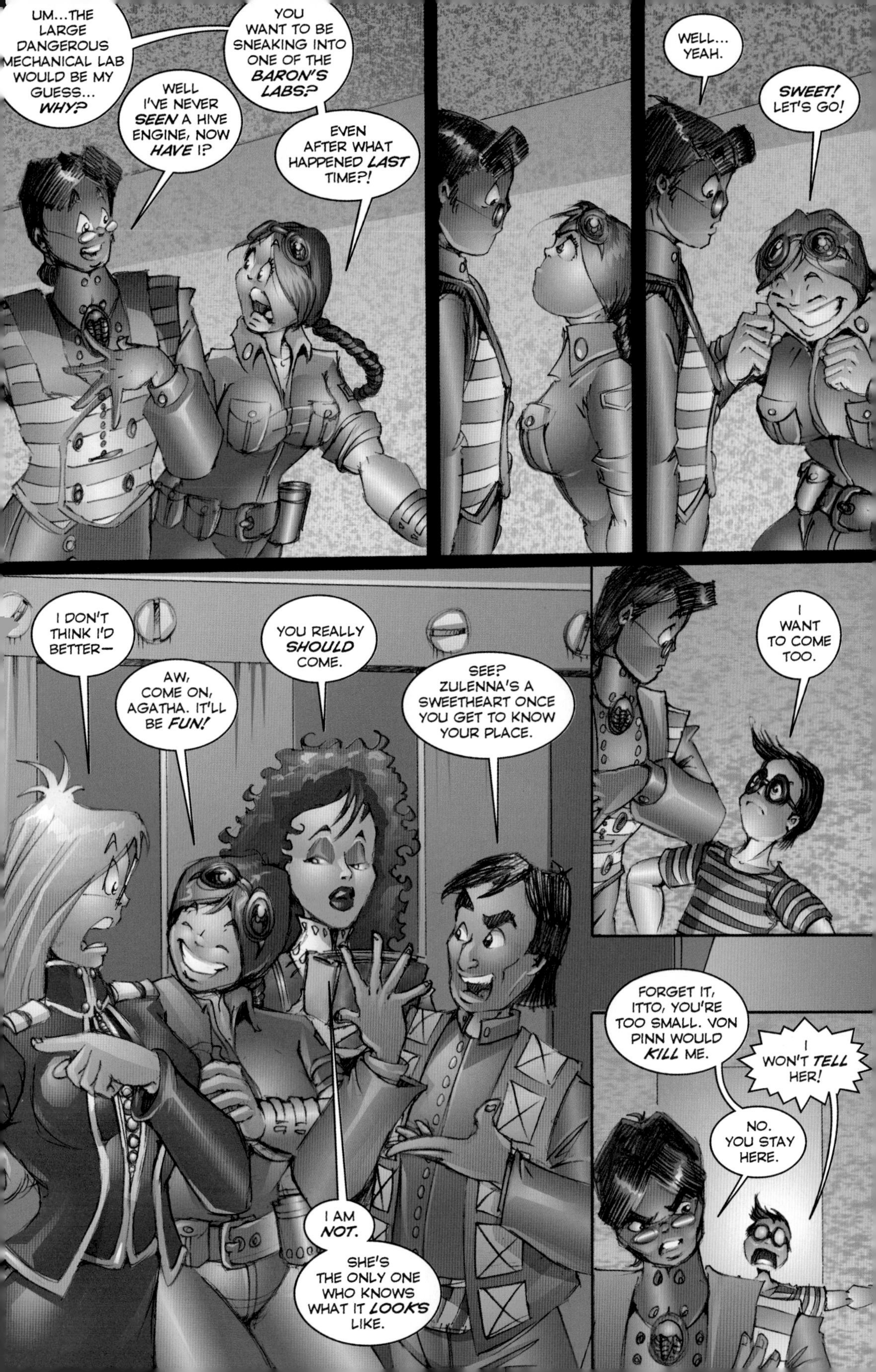
UM...THE LARGE DANGEROUS MECHANICAL LAB WOULD BE MY GUESS... *WHY?*
YOU WANT TO BE SNEAKING INTO ONE OF THE *BARON'S LABS?*
WELL I'VE NEVER *SEEN* A HIVE ENGINE, NOW *HAVE* I?
EVEN AFTER WHAT HAPPENED *LAST* TIME?!
WELL... YEAH.
SWEET! LET'S GO!
I DON'T THINK I'D BETTER—
AW, COME ON, AGATHA. IT'LL BE *FUN!*
YOU REALLY *SHOULD* COME.
SEE? ZULENNA'S A SWEETHEART ONCE YOU GET TO KNOW YOUR PLACE.
I AM *NOT.*
SHE'S THE ONLY ONE WHO KNOWS WHAT IT *LOOKS* LIKE.
I WANT TO COME TOO.
FORGET IT, ITTO, YOU'RE TOO SMALL. VON PINN WOULD *KILL* ME.
I WON'T *TELL* HER!
NO. YOU STAY HERE.

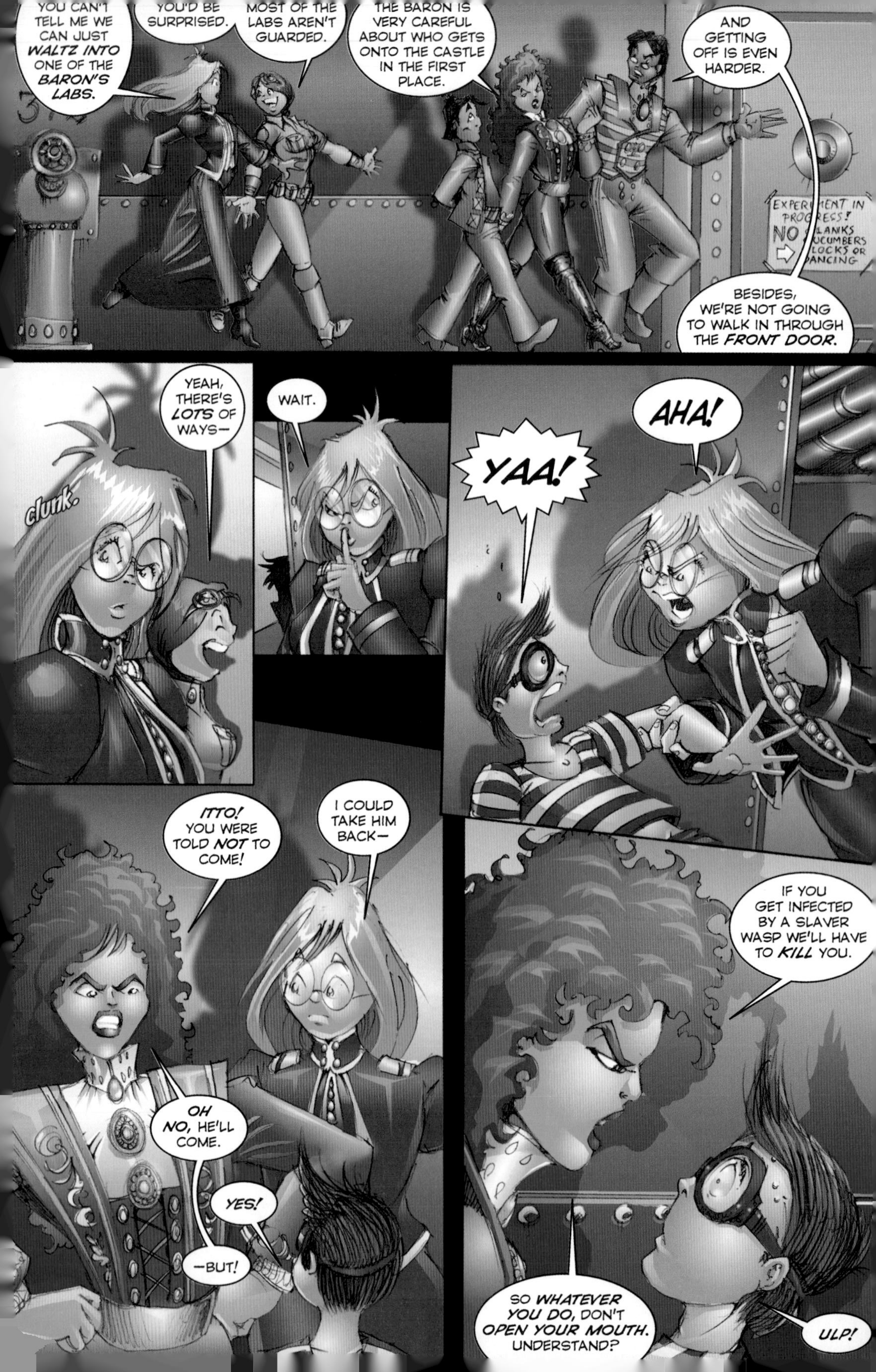

YOU CAN'T TELL ME WE CAN JUST *WALTZ INTO* ONE OF THE *BARON'S LABS.*
YOU'D BE SURPRISED.
MOST OF THE LABS AREN'T GUARDED.
THE BARON IS VERY CAREFUL ABOUT WHO GETS ONTO THE CASTLE IN THE FIRST PLACE.
AND GETTING OFF IS EVEN HARDER.
EXPERIMENT IN PROGRESS! NO CLANKS CUCUMBERS CLOCKS OR DANCING
BESIDES, WE'RE NOT GOING TO WALK IN THROUGH THE *FRONT DOOR.*
YEAH, THERE'S *LOTS* OF WAYS—
clunk.
WAIT.
AHA!
YAA!
ITTO! YOU WERE TOLD *NOT* TO COME!
I COULD TAKE HIM BACK—
OH NO, HE'LL COME.
YES!
—BUT!
IF YOU GET INFECTED BY A SLAVER WASP WE'LL HAVE TO *KILL* YOU.
SO *WHATEVER YOU DO,* DON'T *OPEN YOUR MOUTH.* UNDERSTAND?
ULP!

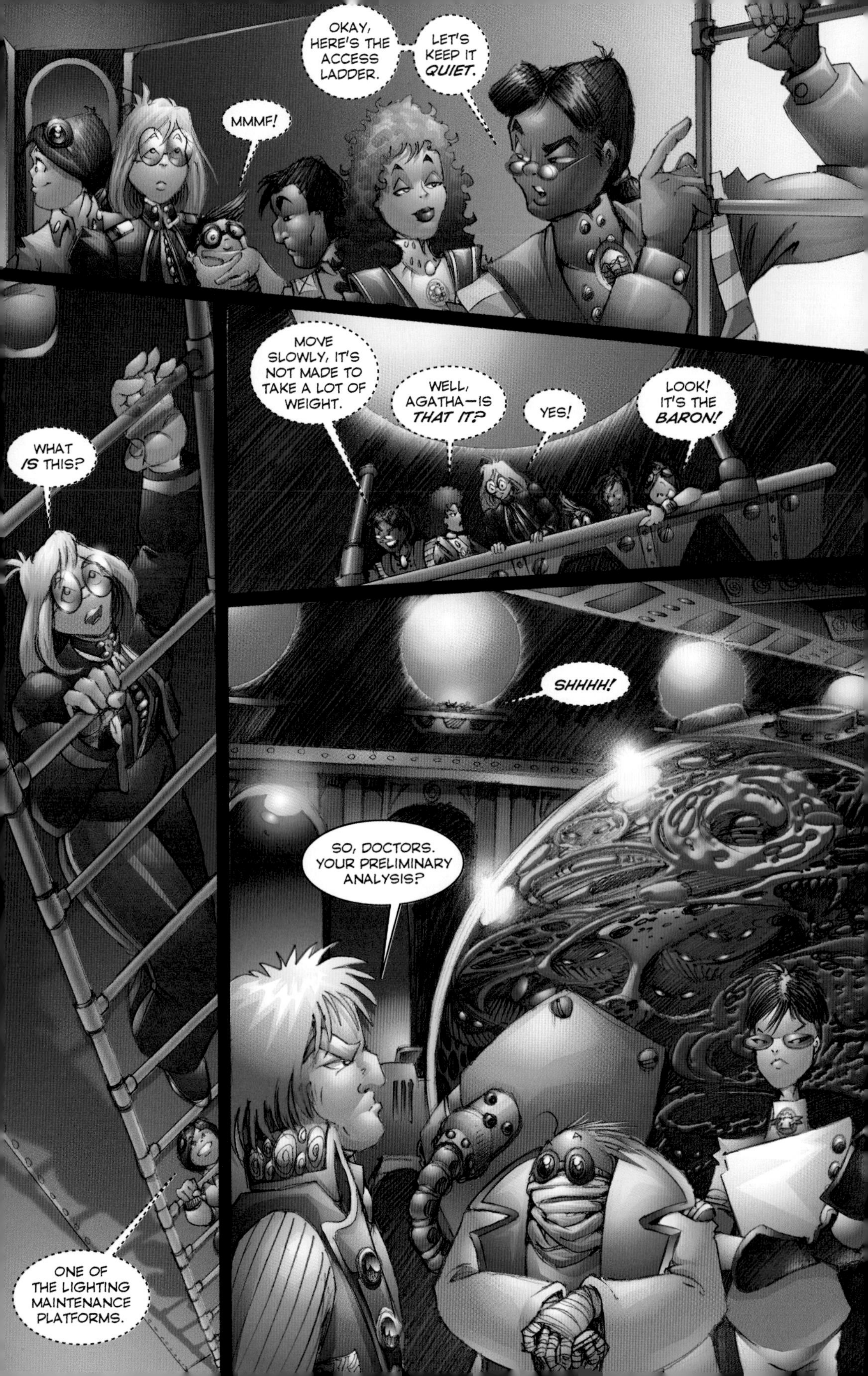

OKAY, HERE'S THE ACCESS LADDER.
LET'S KEEP IT QUIET.
MMMF!
WHAT IS THIS?
ONE OF THE LIGHTING MAINTENANCE PLATFORMS.
MOVE SLOWLY, IT'S NOT MADE TO TAKE A LOT OF WEIGHT.
WELL, AGATHA—IS THAT IT?
YES!
LOOK! IT'S THE BARON!
SHHHH!
SO, DOCTORS. YOUR PRELIMINARY ANALYSIS?

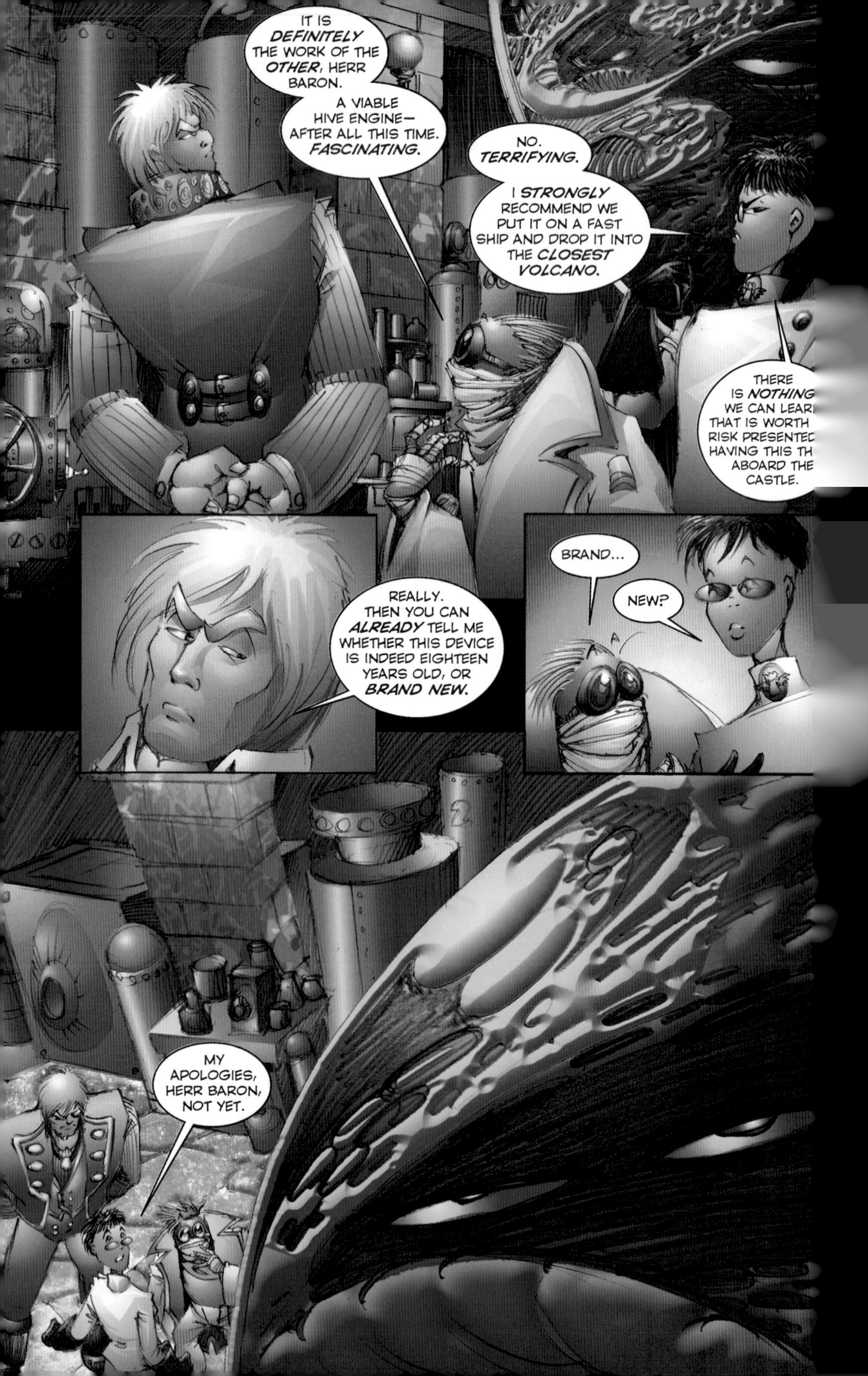
IT IS DEFINITELY THE WORK OF THE OTHER, HERR BARON.
A VIABLE HIVE ENGINE—AFTER ALL THIS TIME. FASCINATING.
NO. TERRIFYING.
I STRONGLY RECOMMEND WE PUT IT ON A FAST SHIP AND DROP IT INTO THE CLOSEST VOLCANO.
THERE IS NOTHING WE CAN LEAR THAT IS WORTH RISK PRESENTE HAVING THIS TH ABOARD THE CASTLE.
REALLY. THEN YOU CAN ALREADY TELL ME WHETHER THIS DEVICE IS INDEED EIGHTEEN YEARS OLD, OR BRAND NEW.
BRAND...
NEW?
MY APOLOGIES, HERR BARON, NOT YET.

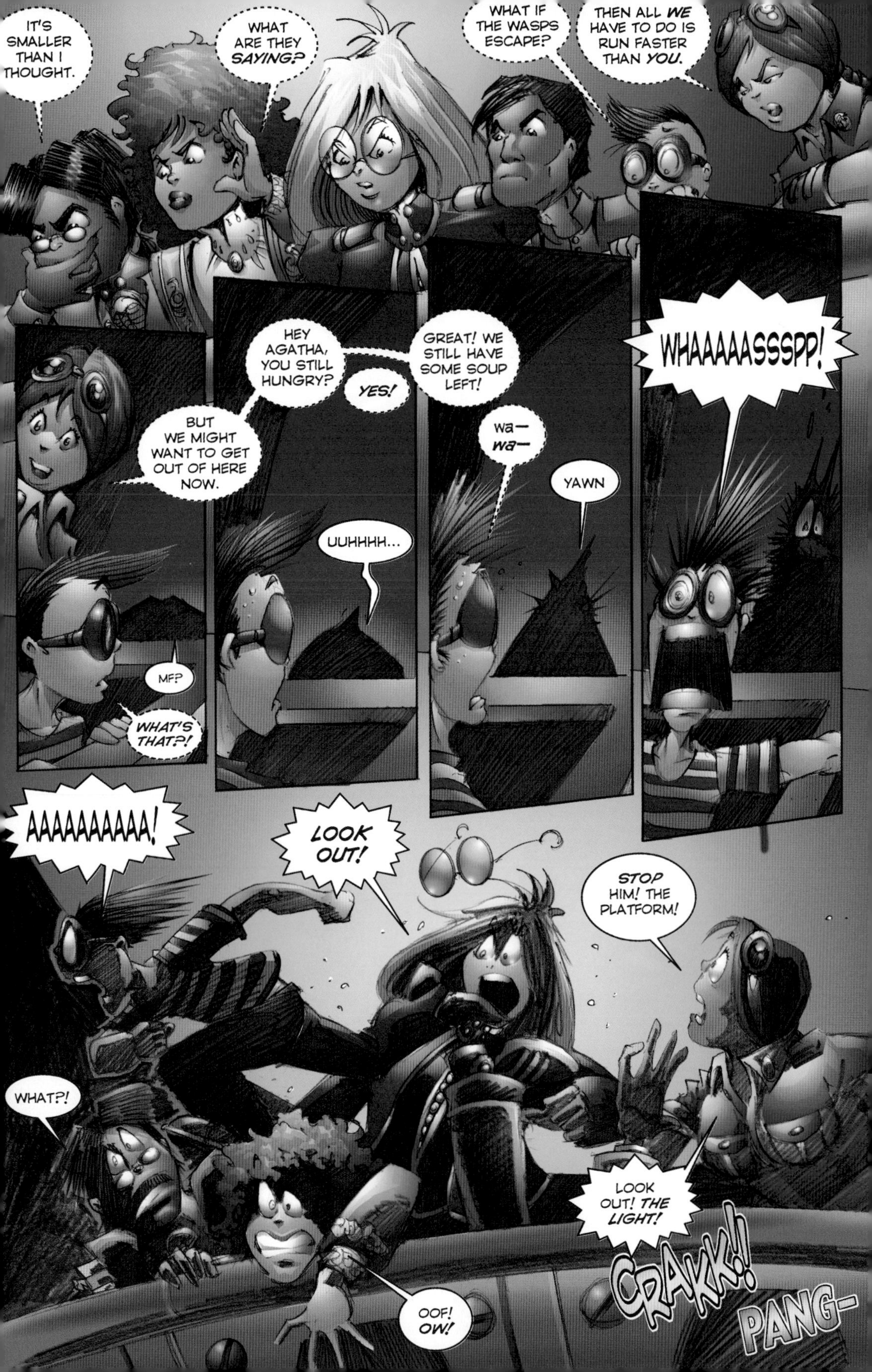
IT'S SMALLER THAN I THOUGHT.
WHAT ARE THEY *SAYING?*
WHAT IF THE WASPS ESCAPE?
THEN ALL *WE* HAVE TO DO IS RUN FASTER THAN *YOU.*
HEY AGATHA, YOU STILL HUNGRY?
YES!
GREAT! WE STILL HAVE SOME SOUP LEFT!
BUT WE MIGHT WANT TO GET OUT OF HERE NOW.
MF?
WHAT'S THAT?!
UUHHHH...
wa—
wa—
YAWN
WHAAAAASSSPP!
AAAAAAAAAA!
LOOK OUT!
STOP HIM! THE PLATFORM!
WHAT?!
LOOK OUT! *THE LIGHT!*
CRAKK!!
OOF! *OW!*
PANG-

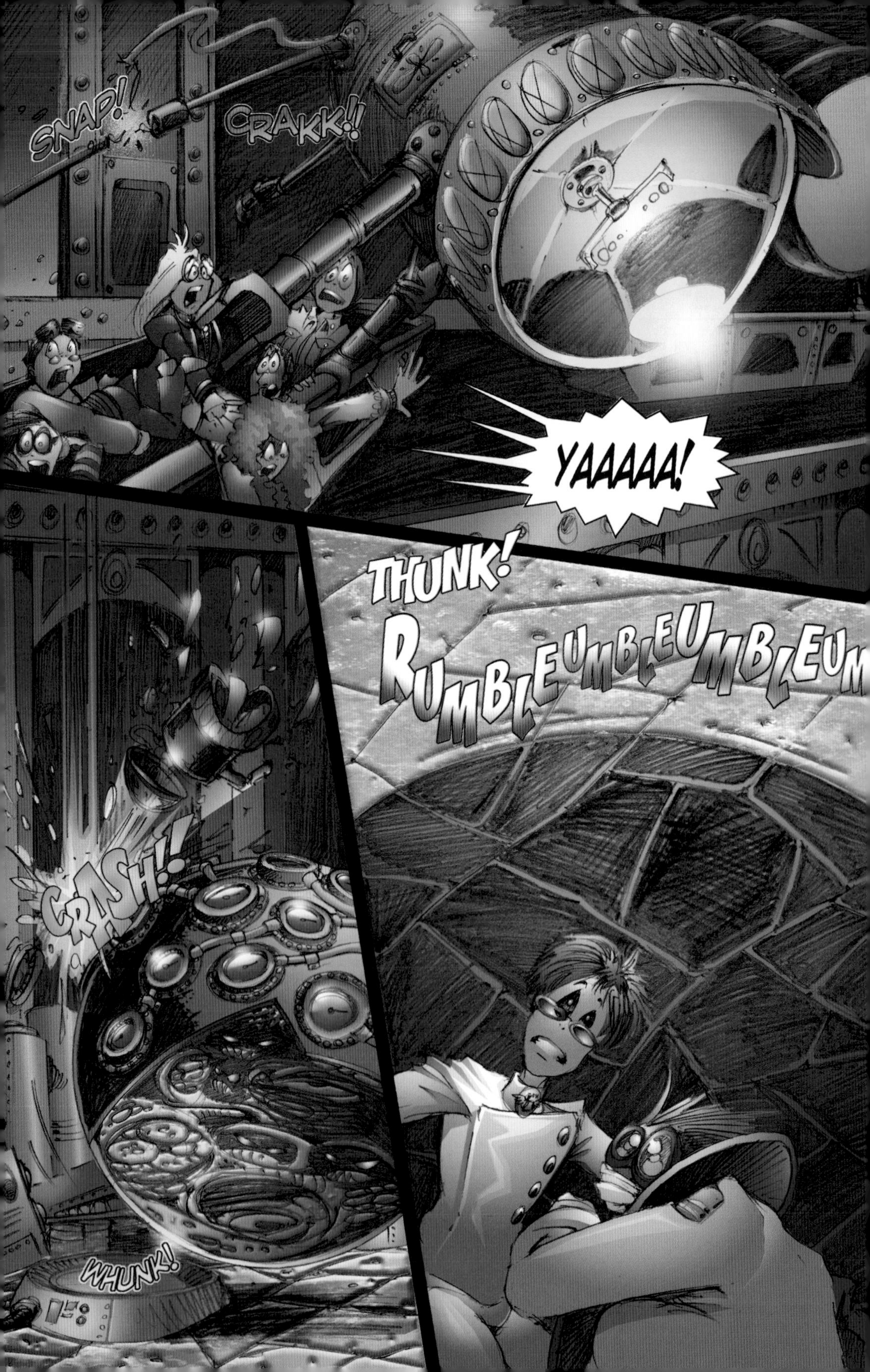
SNAP!!
CRAKK!!
YAAAAA!
CRASH!!
WHUNK!
THUNK!
RUMBLEUMBLEUMBLEUM

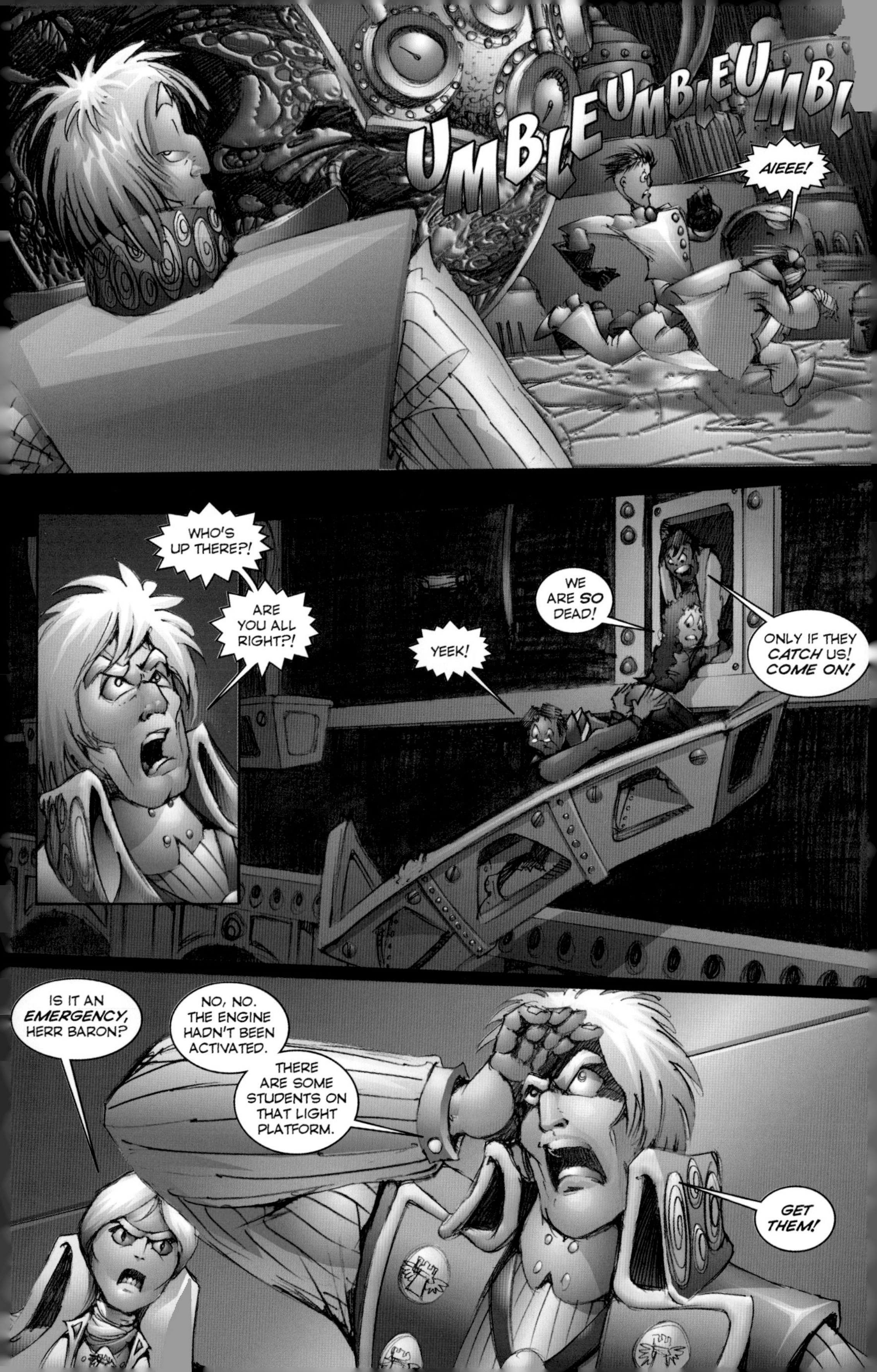
UMBLEUMBLEUMBL
AIEEE!
WHO'S UP THERE?!
ARE YOU ALL RIGHT?!
YEEK!
WE ARE SO DEAD!
ONLY IF THEY CATCH US! COME ON!
IS IT AN EMERGENCY, HERR BARON?
NO, NO. THE ENGINE HADN'T BEEN ACTIVATED.
THERE ARE SOME STUDENTS ON THAT LIGHT PLATFORM.
GET THEM!

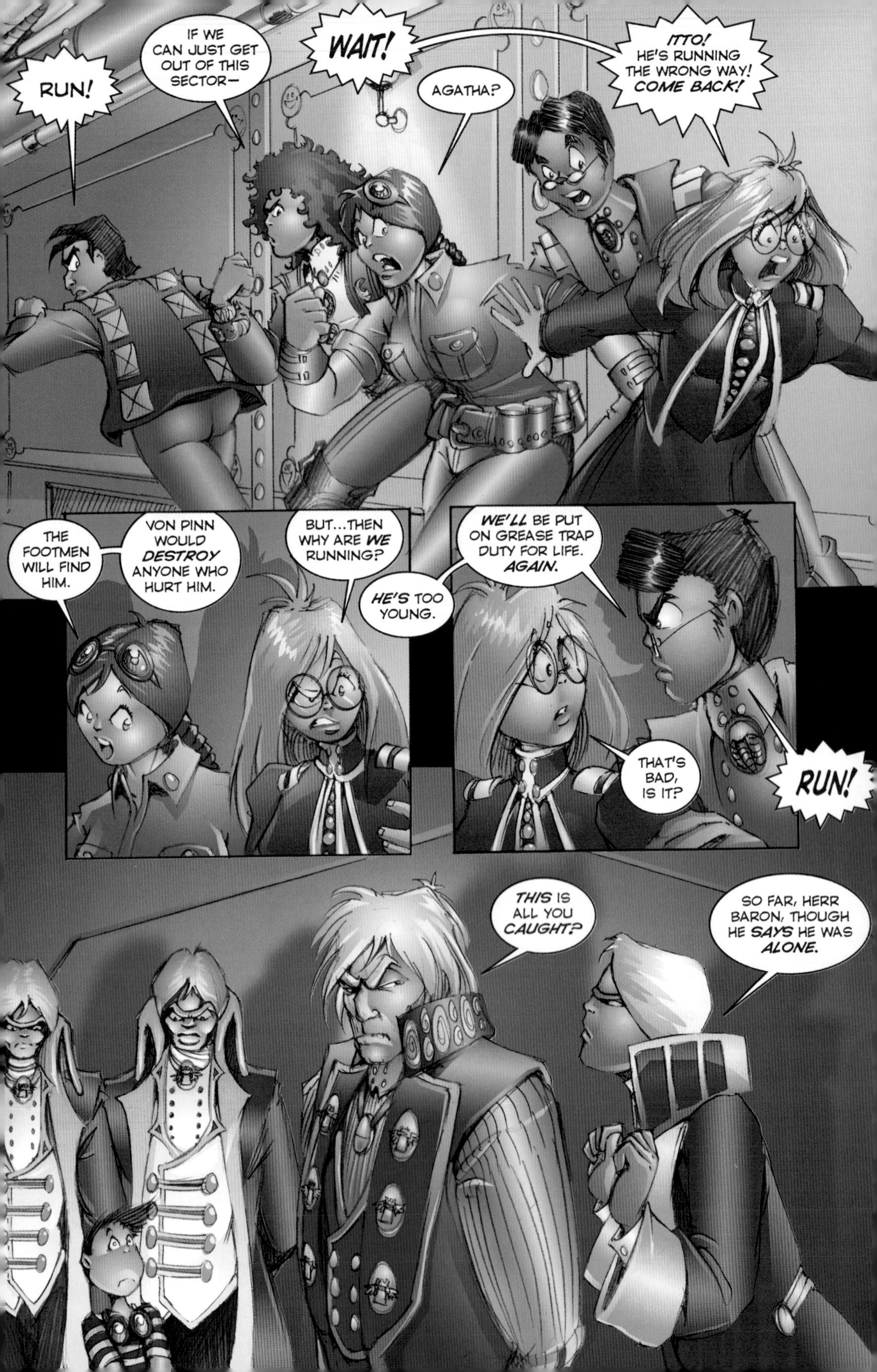
RUN!
IF WE CAN JUST GET OUT OF THIS SECTOR—
WAIT!
AGATHA?
ITTO! HE'S RUNNING THE WRONG WAY! COME BACK!
THE FOOTMEN WILL FIND HIM.
VON PINN WOULD DESTROY ANYONE WHO HURT HIM.
BUT...THEN WHY ARE WE RUNNING?
HE'S TOO YOUNG.
WE'LL BE PUT ON GREASE TRAP DUTY FOR LIFE. AGAIN.
THAT'S BAD, IS IT?
RUN!
THIS IS ALL YOU CAUGHT?
SO FAR, HERR BARON, THOUGH HE SAYS HE WAS ALONE.

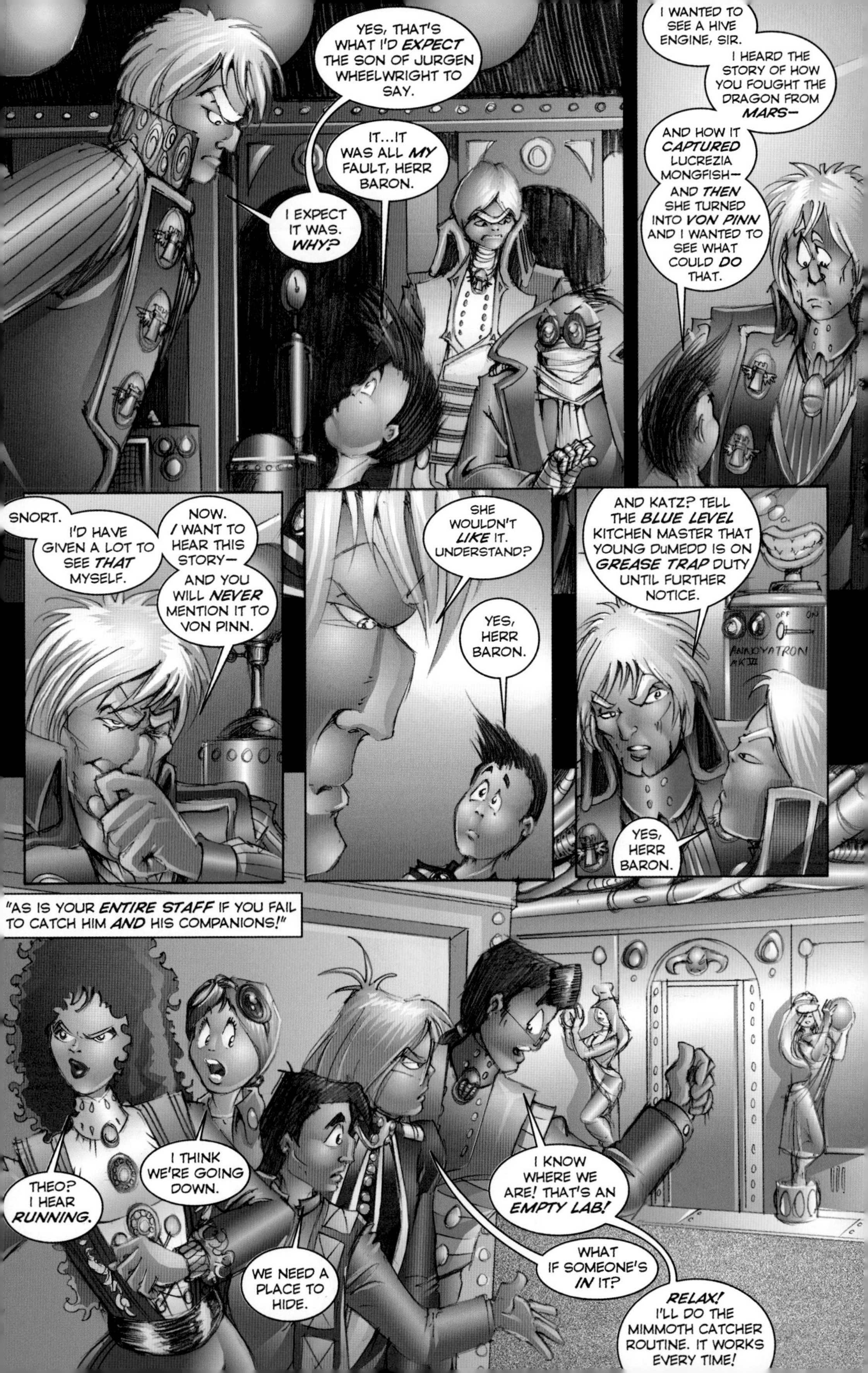

YES, THAT'S WHAT I'D EXPECT THE SON OF JURGEN WHEELWRIGHT TO SAY.
IT...IT WAS ALL MY FAULT, HERR BARON.
I EXPECT IT WAS. WHY?
I WANTED TO SEE A HIVE ENGINE, SIR.
I HEARD THE STORY OF HOW YOU FOUGHT THE DRAGON FROM MARS—
AND HOW IT CAPTURED LUCREZIA MONGFISH—
AND THEN SHE TURNED INTO VON PINN AND I WANTED TO SEE WHAT COULD DO THAT.
SNORT.
I'D HAVE GIVEN A LOT TO SEE THAT MYSELF.
NOW. I WANT TO HEAR THIS STORY—
AND YOU WILL NEVER MENTION IT TO VON PINN.
SHE WOULDN'T LIKE IT. UNDERSTAND?
YES, HERR BARON.
AND KATZ? TELL THE BLUE LEVEL KITCHEN MASTER THAT YOUNG DuMEDD IS ON GREASE TRAP DUTY UNTIL FURTHER NOTICE.
OFF ON
ANNOYATRON MK VI
YES, HERR BARON.
"AS IS YOUR ENTIRE STAFF IF YOU FAIL TO CATCH HIM AND HIS COMPANIONS!"
THEO? I HEAR RUNNING.
I THINK WE'RE GOING DOWN.
WE NEED A PLACE TO HIDE.
I KNOW WHERE WE ARE! THAT'S AN EMPTY LAB!
WHAT IF SOMEONE'S IN IT?
RELAX! I'LL DO THE MIMMOTH CATCHER ROUTINE. IT WORKS EVERY TIME!

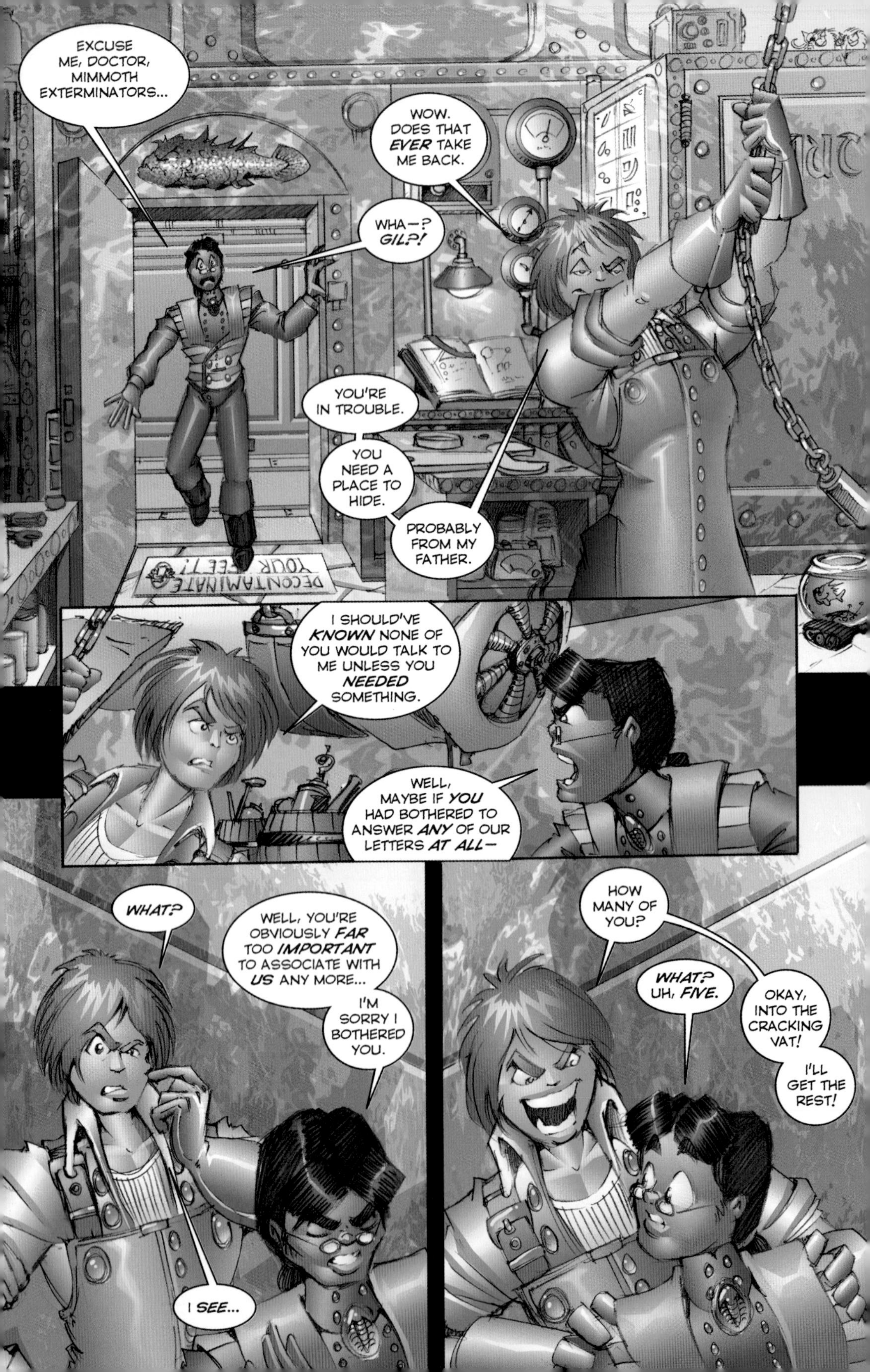

EXCUSE ME, DOCTOR, MIMMOTH EXTERMINATORS...
WOW. DOES THAT EVER TAKE ME BACK.
WHA—? GIL?!
YOU'RE IN TROUBLE.
YOU NEED A PLACE TO HIDE.
PROBABLY FROM MY FATHER.
DECONTAMINATE YOUR FEET!
I SHOULD'VE KNOWN NONE OF YOU WOULD TALK TO ME UNLESS YOU NEEDED SOMETHING.
WELL, MAYBE IF YOU HAD BOTHERED TO ANSWER ANY OF OUR LETTERS AT ALL—
WHAT?
WELL, YOU'RE OBVIOUSLY FAR TOO IMPORTANT TO ASSOCIATE WITH US ANY MORE...
I'M SORRY I BOTHERED YOU.
I SEE...
HOW MANY OF YOU?
WHAT? UH, FIVE.
OKAY, INTO THE CRACKING VAT!
I'LL GET THE REST!

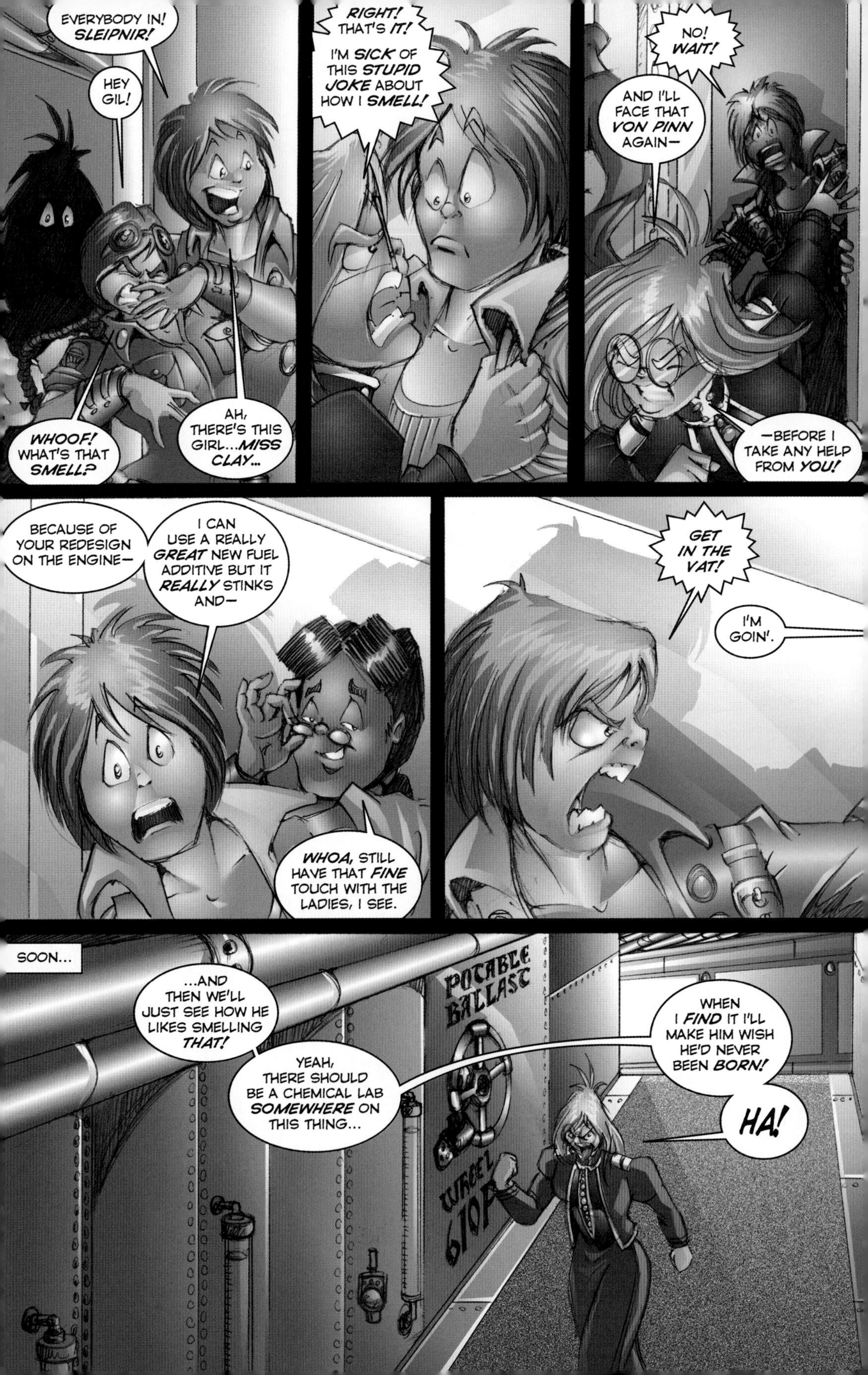
EVERYBODY IN! SLEIPNIR!
HEY GIL!
WHOOF! WHAT'S THAT SMELL?
AH, THERE'S THIS GIRL...MISS CLAY...
RIGHT! THAT'S IT!
I'M SICK OF THIS STUPID JOKE ABOUT HOW I SMELL!
AND I'LL FACE THAT VON PINN AGAIN—
NO! WAIT!
—BEFORE I TAKE ANY HELP FROM YOU!
BECAUSE OF YOUR REDESIGN ON THE ENGINE—
I CAN USE A REALLY GREAT NEW FUEL ADDITIVE BUT IT REALLY STINKS AND—
WHOA, STILL HAVE THAT FINE TOUCH WITH THE LADIES, I SEE.
GET IN THE VAT!
I'M GOIN'.
SOON...
...AND THEN WE'LL JUST SEE HOW HE LIKES SMELLING THAT!
YEAH, THERE SHOULD BE A CHEMICAL LAB SOMEWHERE ON THIS THING...
WHEN I FIND IT I'LL MAKE HIM WISH HE'D NEVER BEEN BORN!
HA!
POTABLE BALLAST

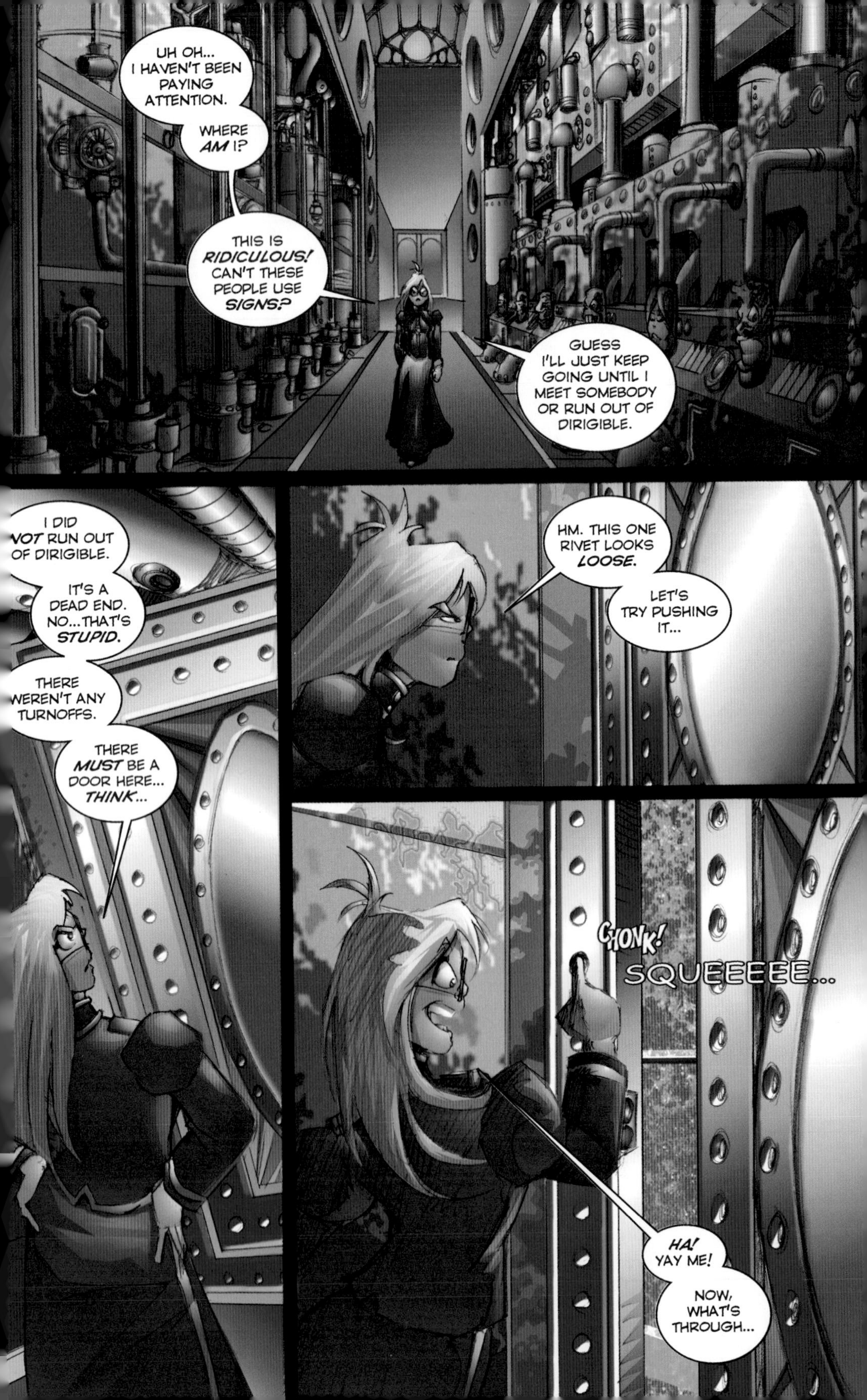
UH OH... I HAVEN'T BEEN PAYING ATTENTION.
WHERE AM I?
THIS IS RIDICULOUS! CAN'T THESE PEOPLE USE SIGNS?
GUESS I'LL JUST KEEP GOING UNTIL I MEET SOMEBODY OR RUN OUT OF DIRIGIBLE.
I DID NOT RUN OUT OF DIRIGIBLE.
IT'S A DEAD END. NO...THAT'S STUPID.
THERE WEREN'T ANY TURNOFFS.
THERE MUST BE A DOOR HERE... THINK...
HM. THIS ONE RIVET LOOKS LOOSE.
LET'S TRY PUSHING IT...
CHONK!
SQUEEEEEE...
HA! YAY ME!
NOW, WHAT'S THROUGH...

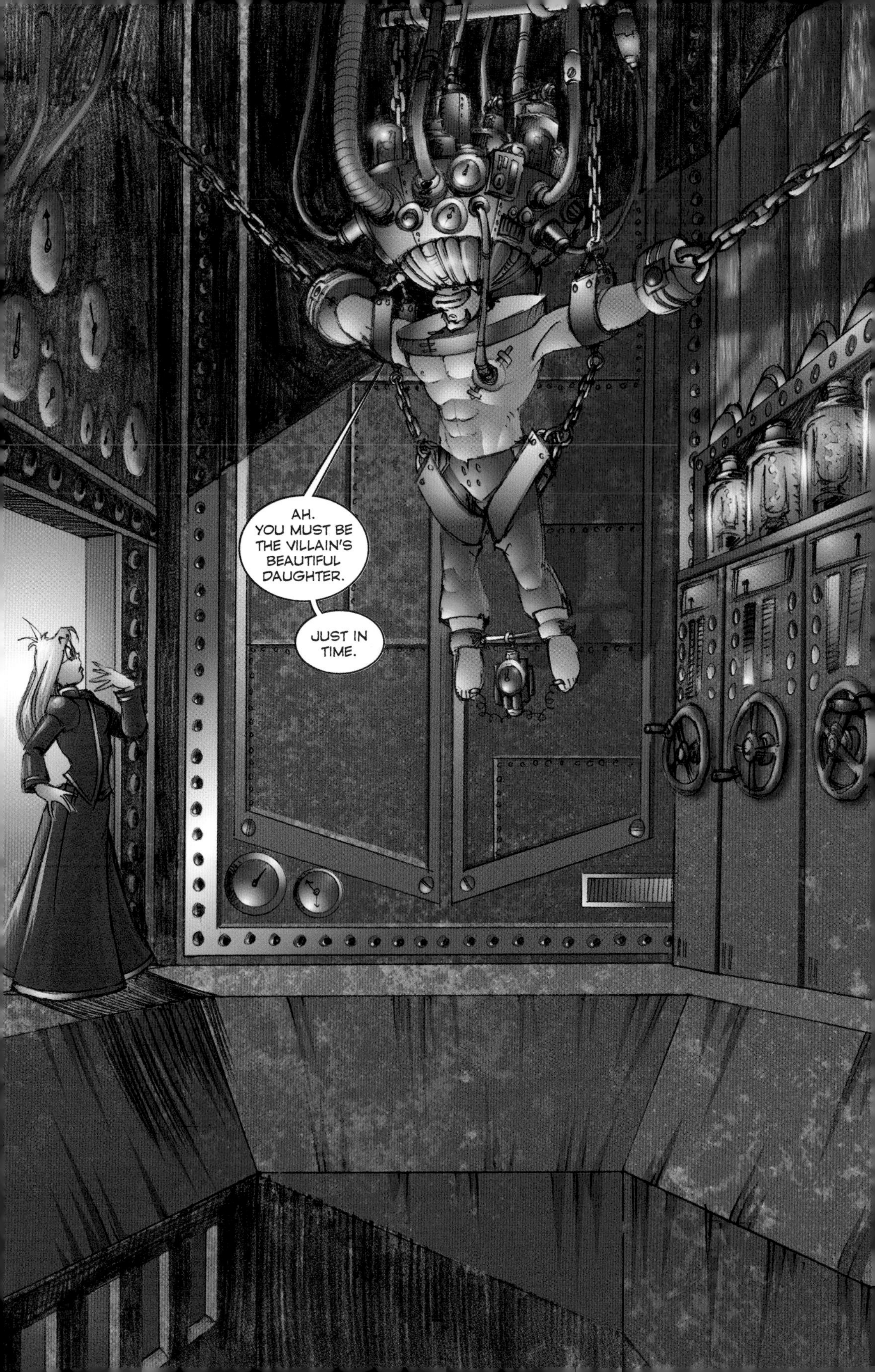
AH.
YOU MUST BE THE VILLAIN'S BEAUTIFUL DAUGHTER.
JUST IN TIME.

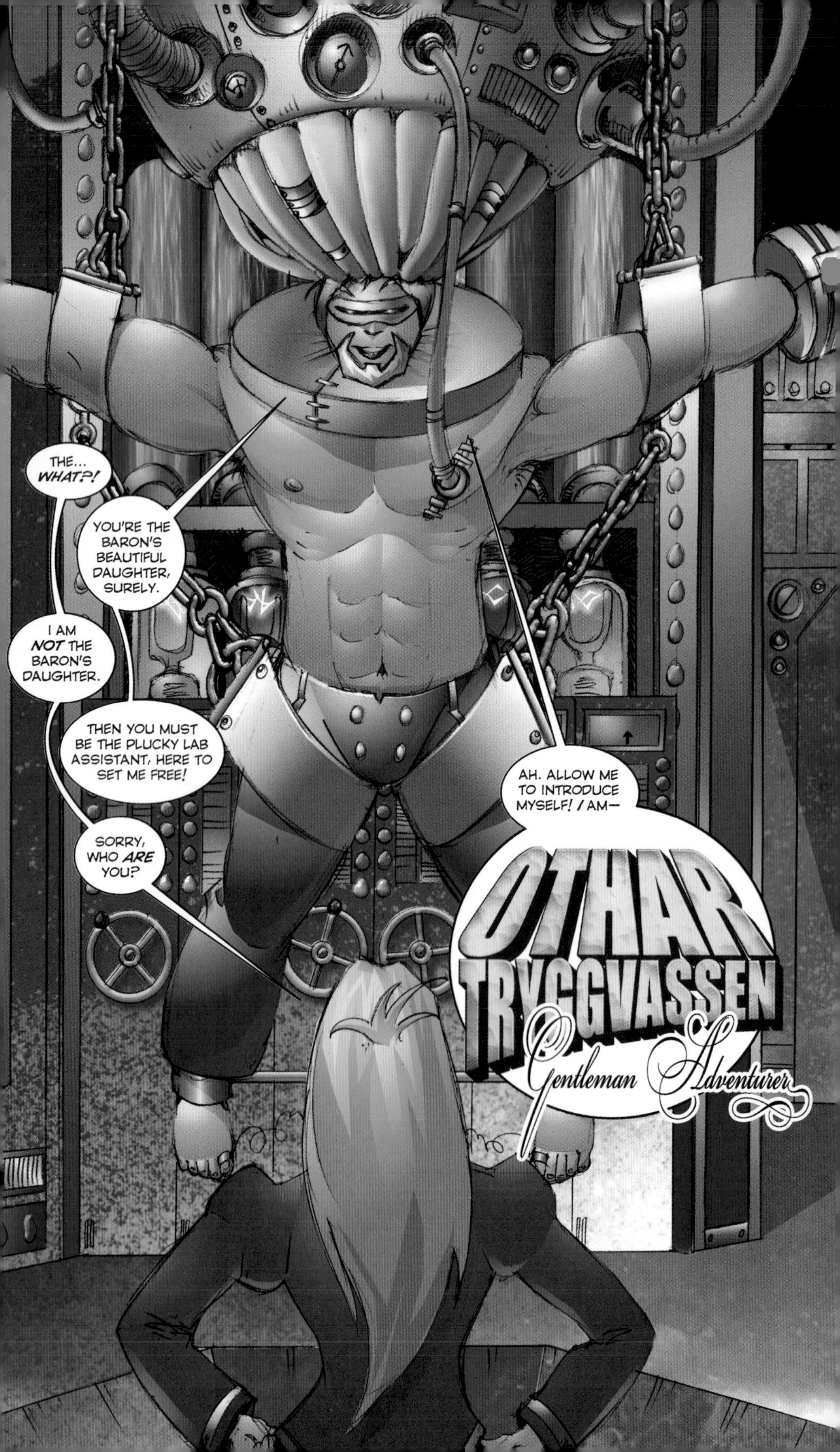
THE... WHAT?!
YOU'RE THE BARON'S BEAUTIFUL DAUGHTER, SURELY.
I AM NOT THE BARON'S DAUGHTER.
THEN YOU MUST BE THE PLUCKY LAB ASSISTANT, HERE TO SET ME FREE!
SORRY, WHO ARE YOU?
AH. ALLOW ME TO INTRODUCE MYSELF! I AM—
OTHAR TRYGGVASSEN
Gentleman Adventurer

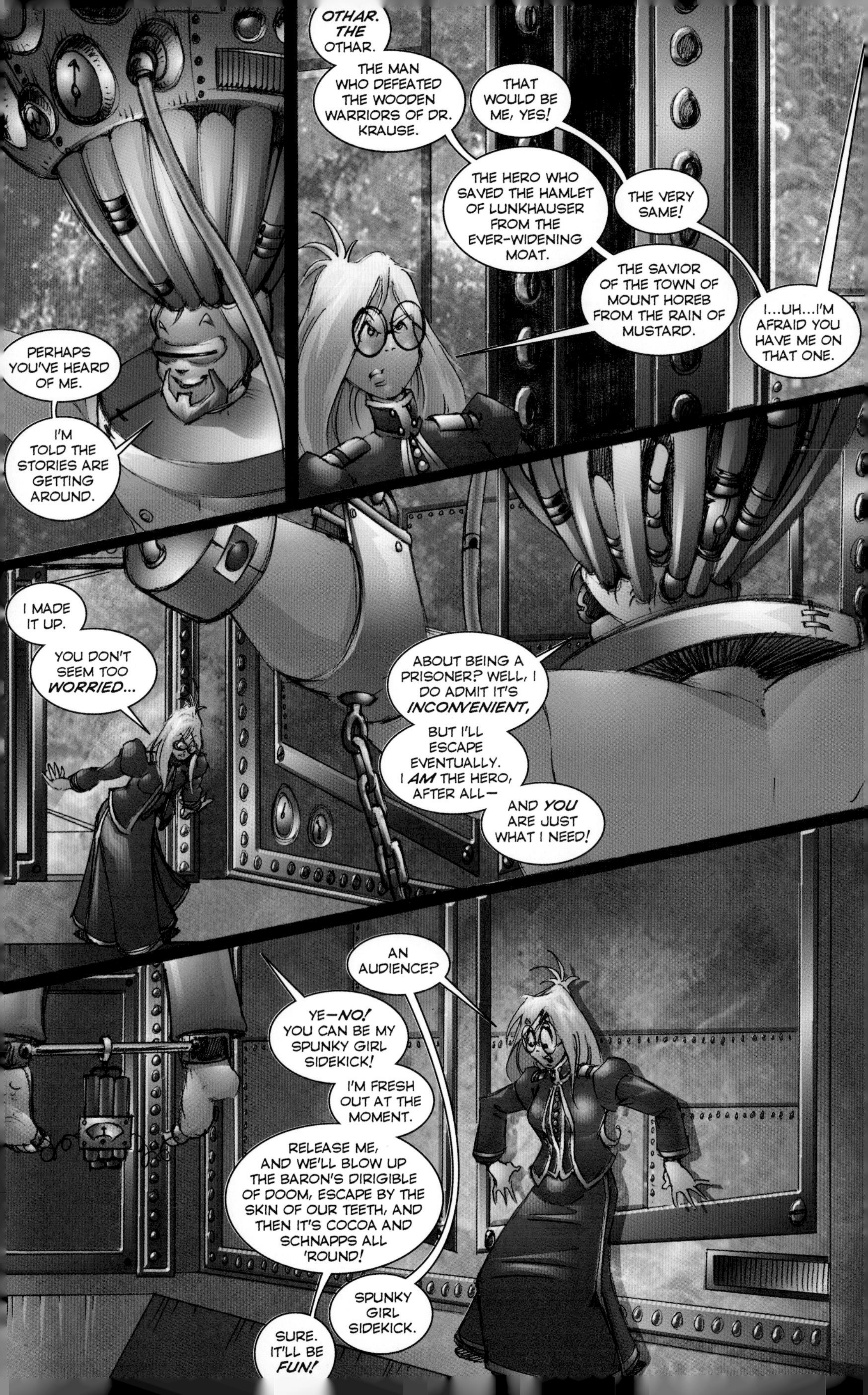
PERHAPS YOU'VE HEARD OF ME.
I'M TOLD THE STORIES ARE GETTING AROUND.
OTHAR. THE OTHAR.
THE MAN WHO DEFEATED THE WOODEN WARRIORS OF DR. KRAUSE.
THAT WOULD BE ME, YES!
THE HERO WHO SAVED THE HAMLET OF LUNKHAUSER FROM THE EVER-WIDENING MOAT.
THE VERY SAME!
THE SAVIOR OF THE TOWN OF MOUNT HOREB FROM THE RAIN OF MUSTARD.
I...UH...I'M AFRAID YOU HAVE ME ON THAT ONE.
I MADE IT UP.
YOU DON'T SEEM TOO WORRIED...
ABOUT BEING A PRISONER? WELL, I DO ADMIT IT'S INCONVENIENT,
BUT I'LL ESCAPE EVENTUALLY. I AM THE HERO, AFTER ALL—
AND YOU ARE JUST WHAT I NEED!
AN AUDIENCE?
YE—NO! YOU CAN BE MY SPUNKY GIRL SIDEKICK!
I'M FRESH OUT AT THE MOMENT.
RELEASE ME, AND WE'LL BLOW UP THE BARON'S DIRIGIBLE OF DOOM, ESCAPE BY THE SKIN OF OUR TEETH, AND THEN IT'S COCOA AND SCHNAPPS ALL 'ROUND!
SPUNKY GIRL SIDEKICK.
SURE. IT'LL BE FUN!

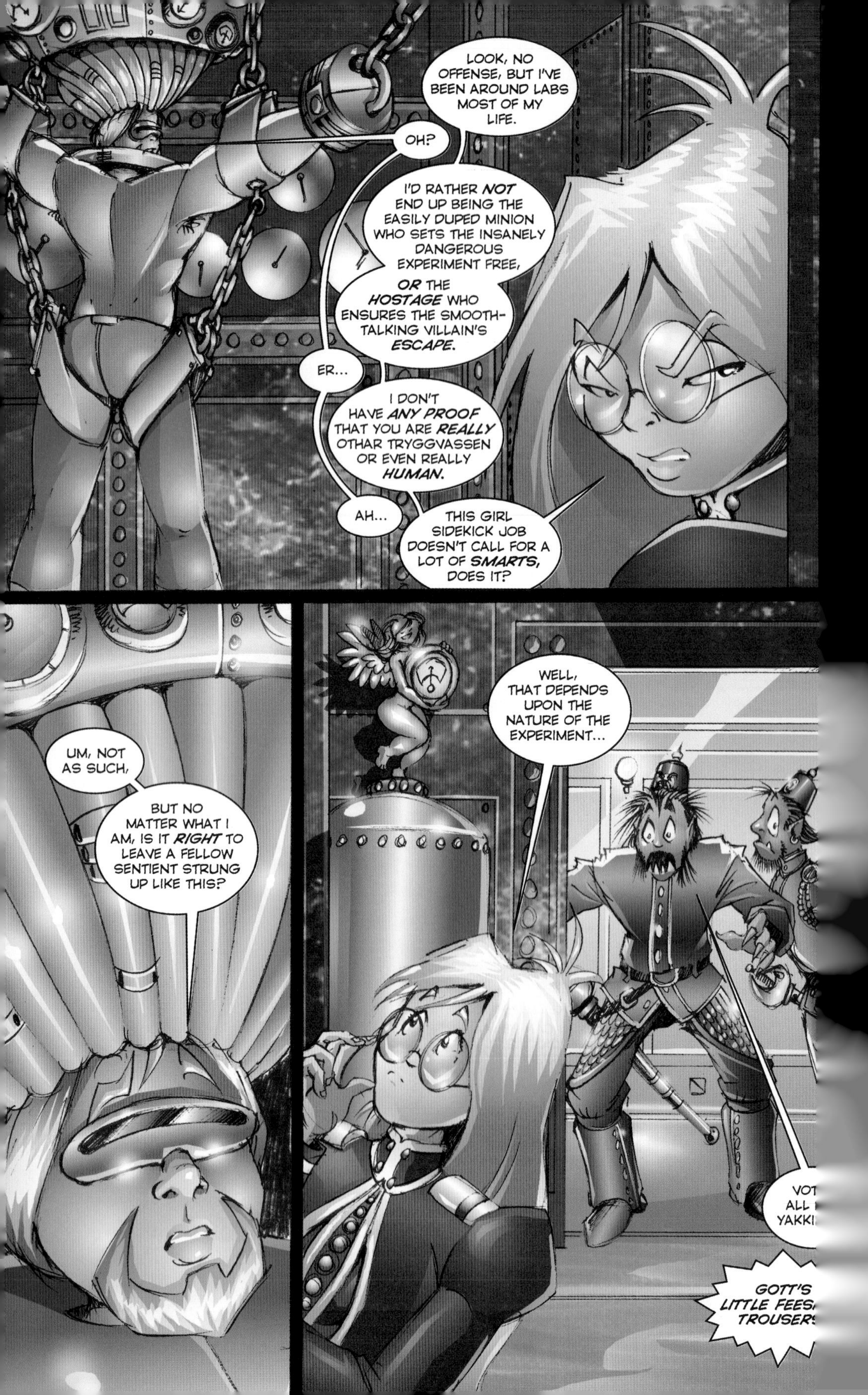
LOOK, NO OFFENSE, BUT I'VE BEEN AROUND LABS MOST OF MY LIFE.
OH?
I'D RATHER NOT END UP BEING THE EASILY DUPED MINION WHO SETS THE INSANELY DANGEROUS EXPERIMENT FREE,
OR THE HOSTAGE WHO ENSURES THE SMOOTH-TALKING VILLAIN'S ESCAPE.
ER...
I DON'T HAVE ANY PROOF THAT YOU ARE REALLY OTHAR TRYGGVASSEN OR EVEN REALLY HUMAN.
AH...
THIS GIRL SIDEKICK JOB DOESN'T CALL FOR A LOT OF SMARTS, DOES IT?
UM, NOT AS SUCH,
BUT NO MATTER WHAT I AM, IS IT RIGHT TO LEAVE A FELLOW SENTIENT STRUNG UP LIKE THIS?
WELL, THAT DEPENDS UPON THE NATURE OF THE EXPERIMENT...
GOTT'S LITTLE FEES TROUSERS

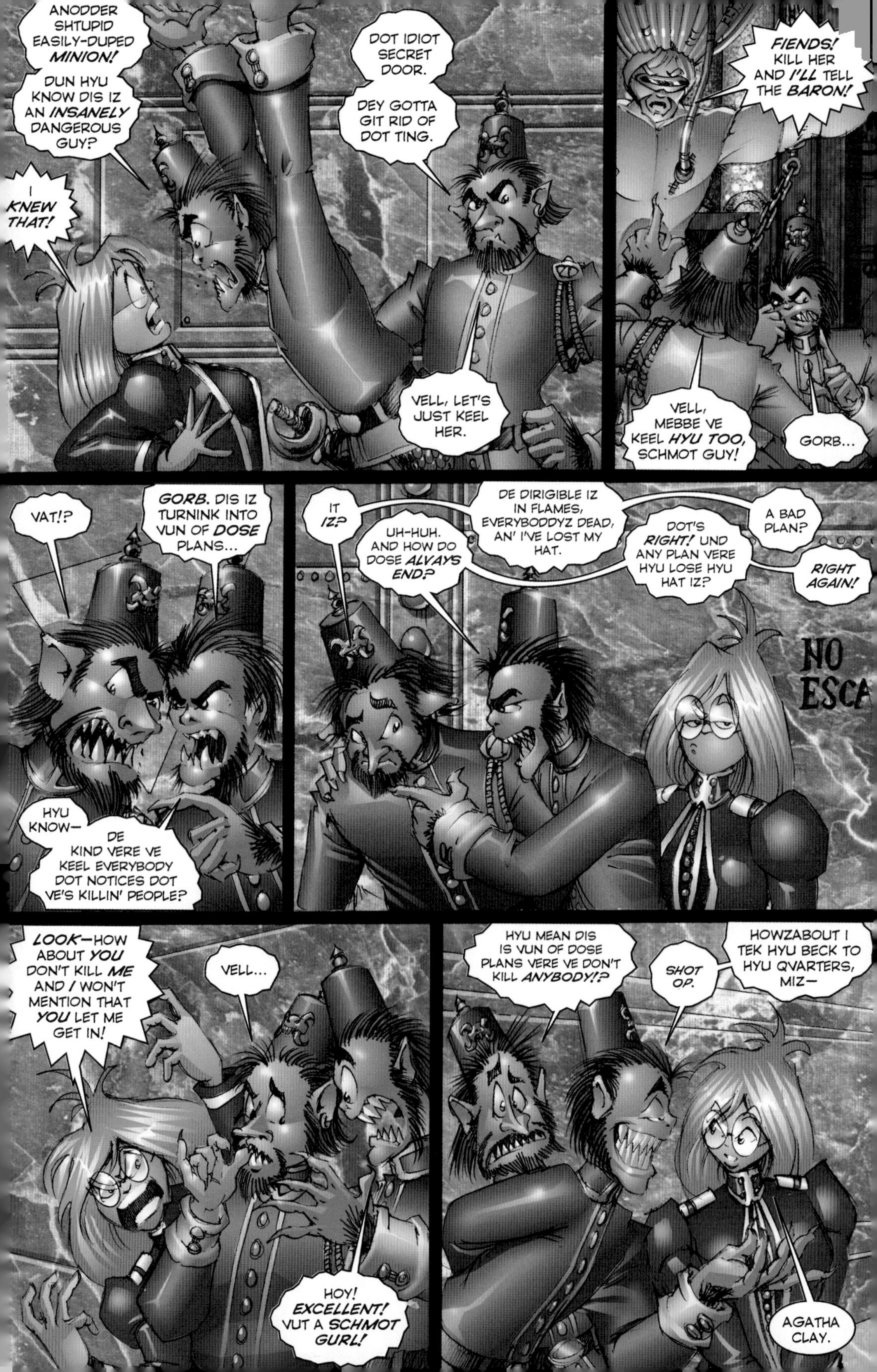
ANODDER SHTUPID EASILY-DUPED MINION!
DUN HYU KNOW DIS IZ AN INSANELY DANGEROUS GUY?
I KNEW THAT!
DOT IDIOT SECRET DOOR.
DEY GOTTA GIT RID OF DOT TING.
VELL, LET'S JUST KEEL HER.
FIENDS! KILL HER AND I'LL TELL THE BARON!
VELL, MEBBE VE KEEL HYU TOO, SCHMOT GUY!
GORB...
VAT!?
GORB. DIS IZ TURNINK INTO VUN OF DOSE PLANS...
HYU KNOW—
DE KIND VERE VE KEEL EVERYBODY DOT NOTICES DOT VE'S KILLIN' PEOPLE?
IT IZ?
UH-HUH. AND HOW DO DOSE ALVAYS END?
DE DIRIGIBLE IZ IN FLAMES, EVERYBODDYZ DEAD, AN' I'VE LOST MY HAT.
DOT'S RIGHT! UND ANY PLAN VERE HYU LOSE HYU HAT IZ?
A BAD PLAN?
RIGHT AGAIN!
NO ESCA
LOOK—HOW ABOUT YOU DON'T KILL ME AND I WON'T MENTION THAT YOU LET ME GET IN!
VELL...
HOY! EXCELLENT! VUT A SCHMOT GURL!
HYU MEAN DIS IS VUN OF DOSE PLANS VERE VE DON'T KILL ANYBODY!?
SHOT OP.
HOWZABOUT I TEK HYU BECK TO HYU QVARTERS, MIZ—
AGATHA CLAY.

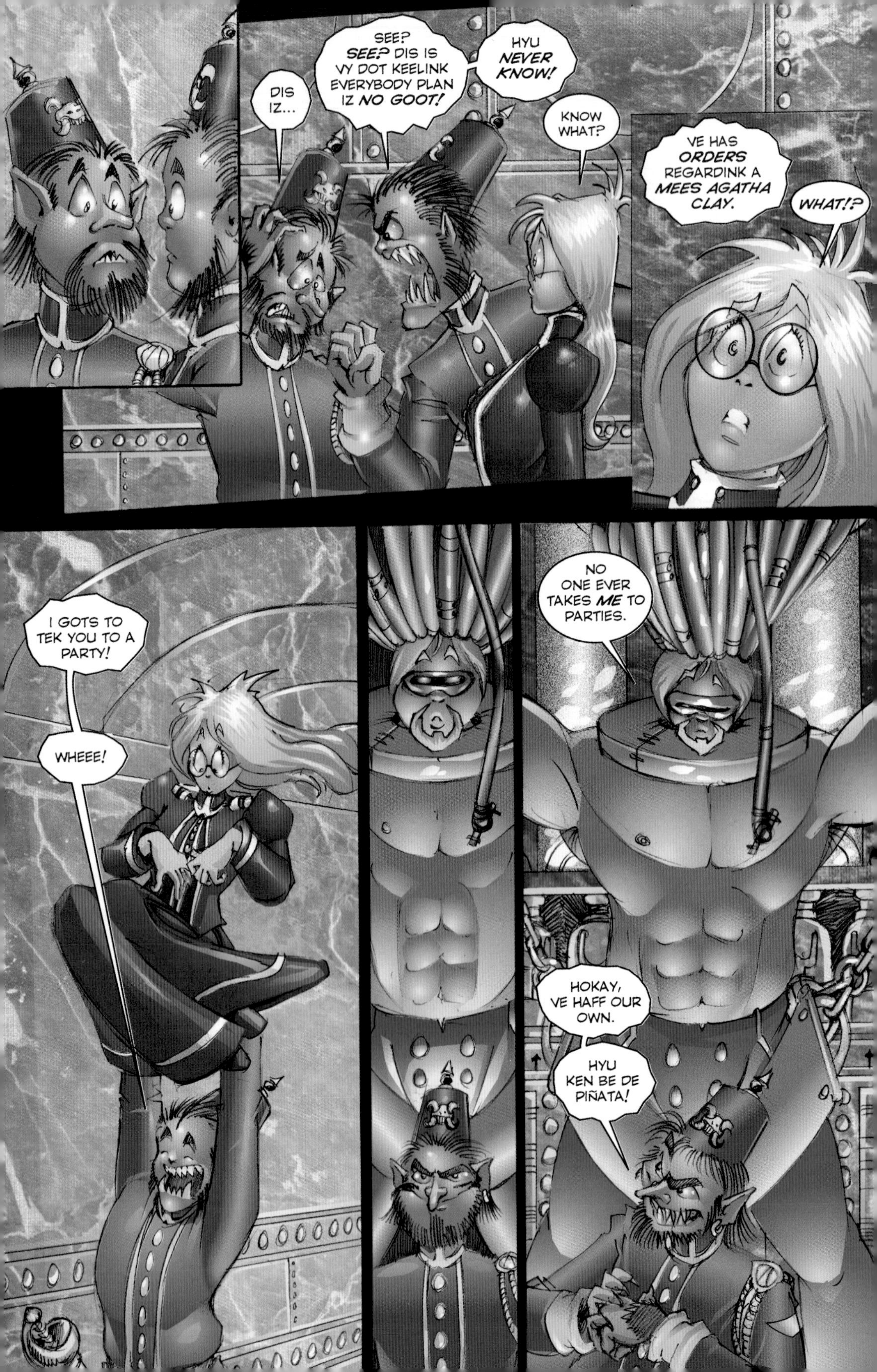
DIS IZ...
SEE? SEE? DIS IS VY DOT KEELINK EVERYBODY PLAN IZ NO GOOT!
HYU NEVER KNOW!
KNOW WHAT?
VE HAS ORDERS REGARDINK A MEES AGATHA CLAY.
WHAT!?
I GOTS TO TEK YOU TO A PARTY!
WHEEE!
NO ONE EVER TAKES ME TO PARTIES.
HOKAY, VE HAFF OUR OWN.
HYU KEN BE DE PIÑATA!

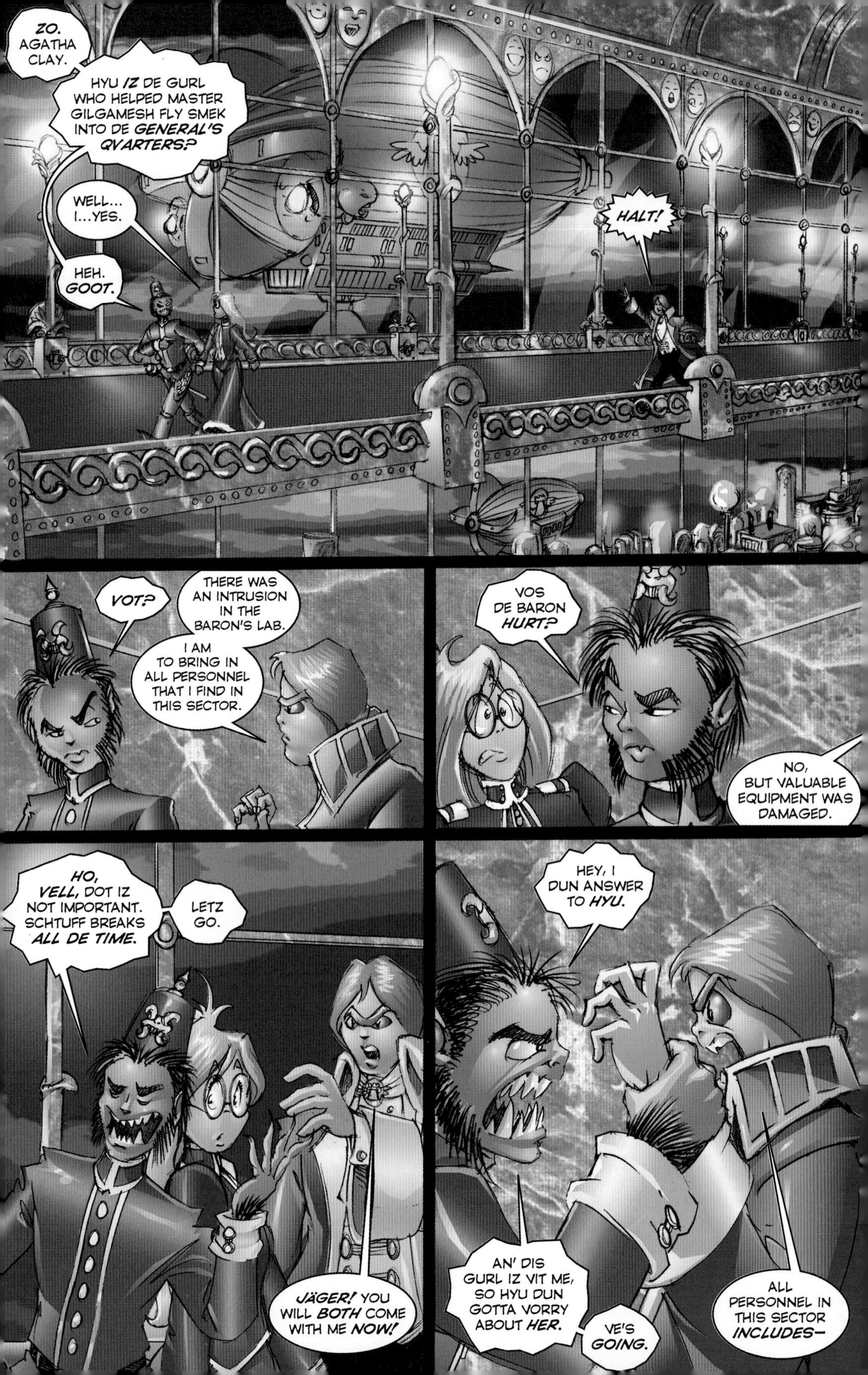
ZO. AGATHA CLAY.
HYU *IZ* DE GURL WHO HELPED MASTER GILGAMESH FLY SMEK INTO DE *GENERAL'S QVARTERS?*
WELL... I...YES.
HEH. *GOOT.*
HALT!
VOT?
THERE WAS AN INTRUSION IN THE BARON'S LAB.
I AM TO BRING IN ALL PERSONNEL THAT I FIND IN THIS SECTOR.
VOS DE BARON *HURT?*
NO, BUT VALUABLE EQUIPMENT WAS DAMAGED.
HO, VELL, DOT IZ NOT IMPORTANT. SCHTUFF BREAKS *ALL DE TIME.*
LETZ GO.
JÄGER! YOU WILL *BOTH* COME WITH ME *NOW!*
HEY, I DUN ANSWER TO *HYU.*
AN' DIS GURL IZ VIT ME, SO HYU DUN GOTTA VORRY ABOUT *HER.*
VE'S *GOING.*
ALL PERSONNEL IN THIS SECTOR *INCLUDES—*

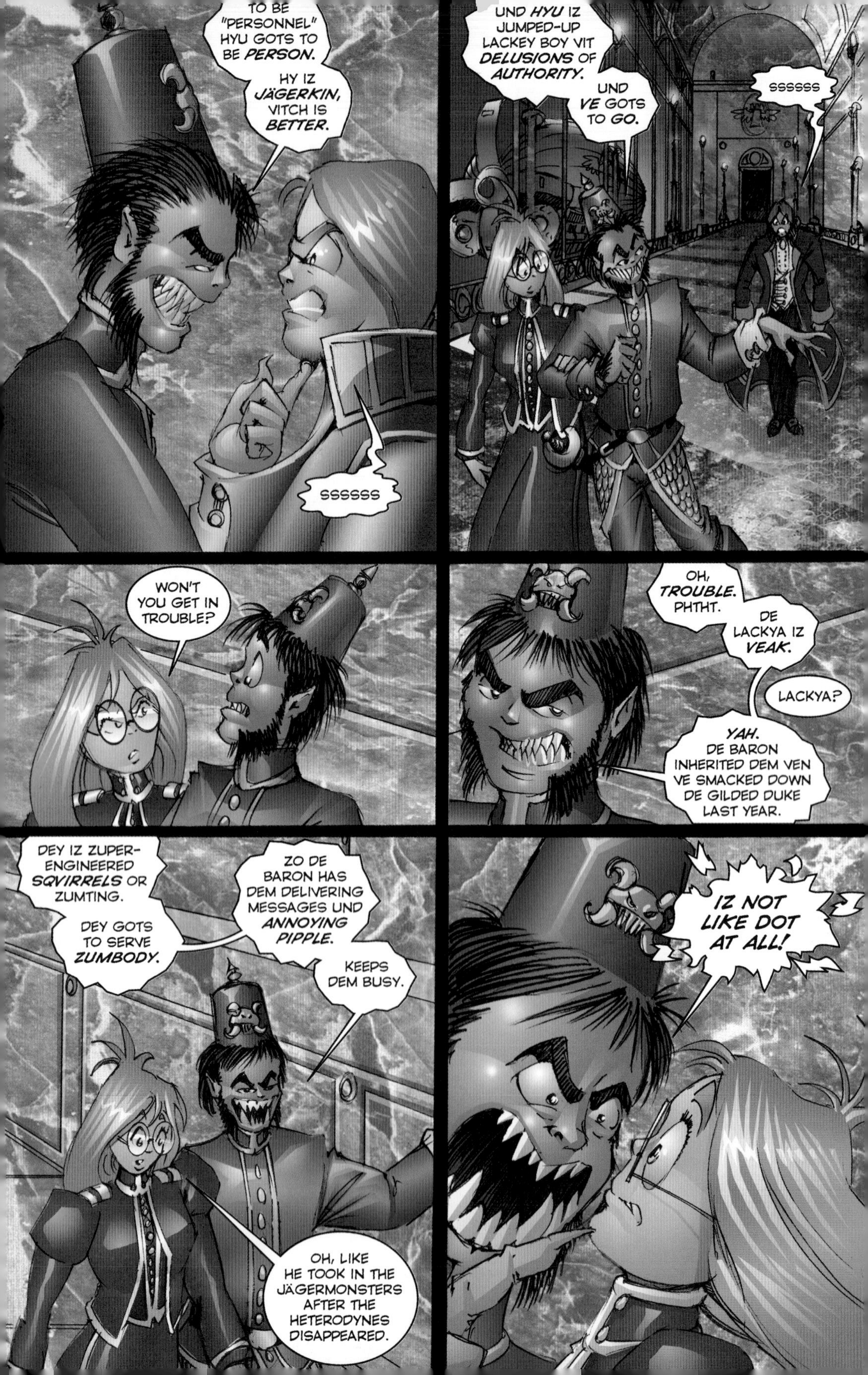
TO BE "PERSONNEL" HYU GOTS TO BE *PERSON*.
HY IZ *JÄGERKIN*, VITCH IS *BETTER*.
SSSSSS
UND *HYU* IZ JUMPED-UP LACKEY BOY VIT *DELUSIONS* OF *AUTHORITY*.
UND *VE* GOTS TO *GO*.
SSSSSS
WON'T YOU GET IN TROUBLE?
OH, *TROUBLE*. PHTHT.
DE LACKYA IZ *VEAK*.
LACKYA?
YAH. DE BARON INHERITED DEM VEN VE SMACKED DOWN DE GILDED DUKE LAST YEAR.
DEY IZ ZUPER-ENGINEERED *SQVIRRELS* OR ZUMTING.
DEY GOTS TO SERVE *ZUMBODY*.
ZO DE BARON HAS DEM DELIVERING MESSAGES UND *ANNOYING PIPPLE*.
KEEPS DEM BUSY.
OH, LIKE HE TOOK IN THE JÄGERMONSTERS AFTER THE HETERODYNES DISAPPEARED.
IZ NOT LIKE DOT AT ALL!

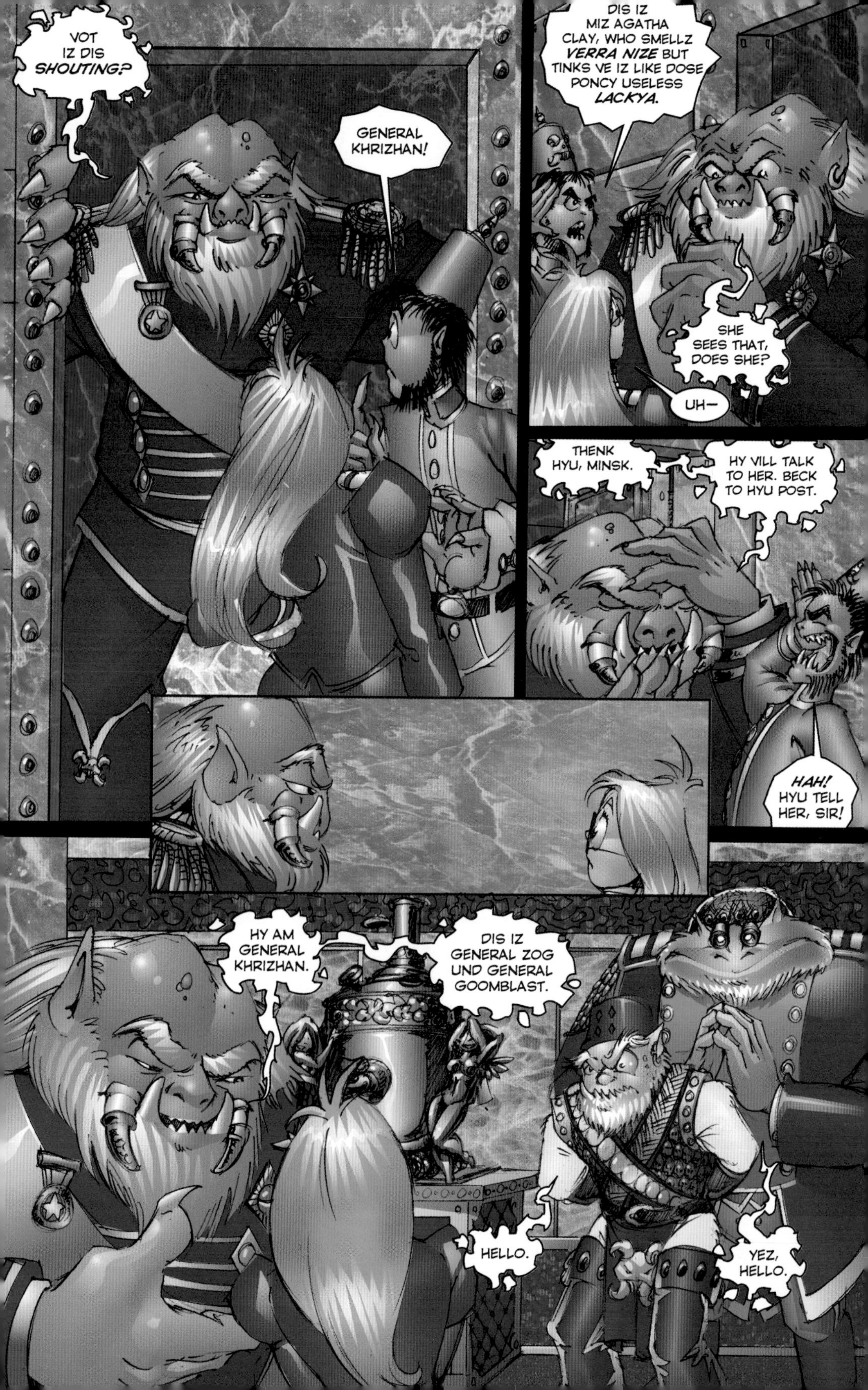
VOT IZ DIS SHOUTING?
GENERAL KHRIZHAN!
DIS IZ MIZ AGATHA CLAY, WHO SMELLZ VERRA NIZE BUT TINKS VE IZ LIKE DOSE PONCY USELESS LACKYA.
SHE SEES THAT, DOES SHE?
UH—
THENK HYU, MINSK.
HY VILL TALK TO HER. BECK TO HYU POST.
HAH! HYU TELL HER, SIR!
HY AM GENERAL KHRIZHAN.
DIS IZ GENERAL ZOG UND GENERAL GOOMBLAST.
HELLO.
YEZ, HELLO.

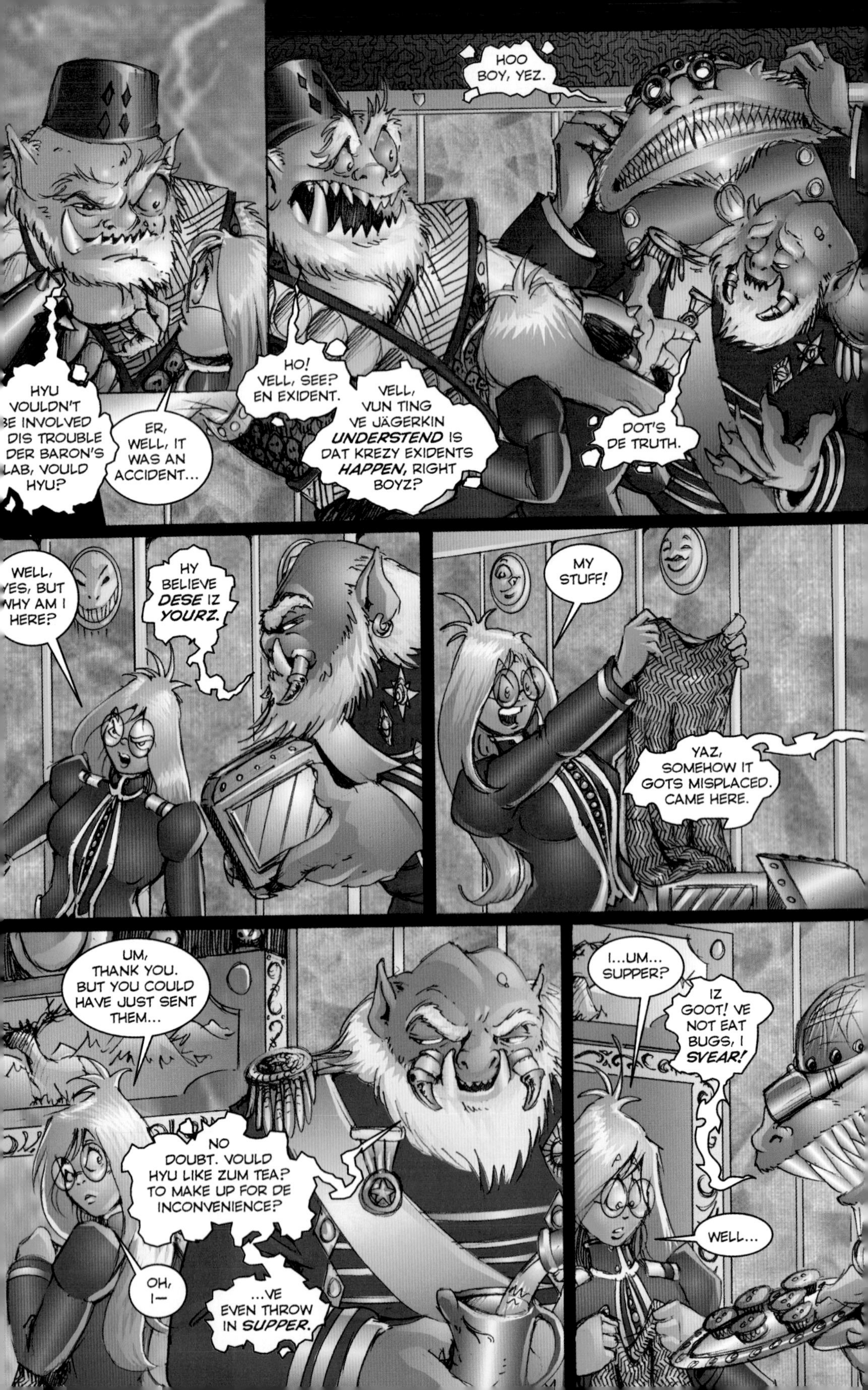
HOO BOY, YEZ.
HYU VOULDN'T BE INVOLVED DIS TROUBLE DER BARON'S LAB, VOULD HYU?
ER, WELL, IT WAS AN ACCIDENT...
HO! VELL, SEE? EN EXIDENT.
VELL, VUN TING VE JÄGERKIN UNDERSTEND IS DAT KREZY EXIDENTS HAPPEN, RIGHT BOYZ?
DOT'S DE TRUTH.
WELL, YES, BUT WHY AM I HERE?
HY BELIEVE DESE IZ YOURZ.
MY STUFF!
YAZ, SOMEHOW IT GOTS MISPLACED. CAME HERE.
UM, THANK YOU. BUT YOU COULD HAVE JUST SENT THEM...
NO DOUBT. VOULD HYU LIKE ZUM TEA? TO MAKE UP FOR DE INCONVENIENCE?
OH, I—
...VE EVEN THROW IN SUPPER.
I...UM... SUPPER?
IZ GOOT! VE NOT EAT BUGS, I SVEAR!
WELL...

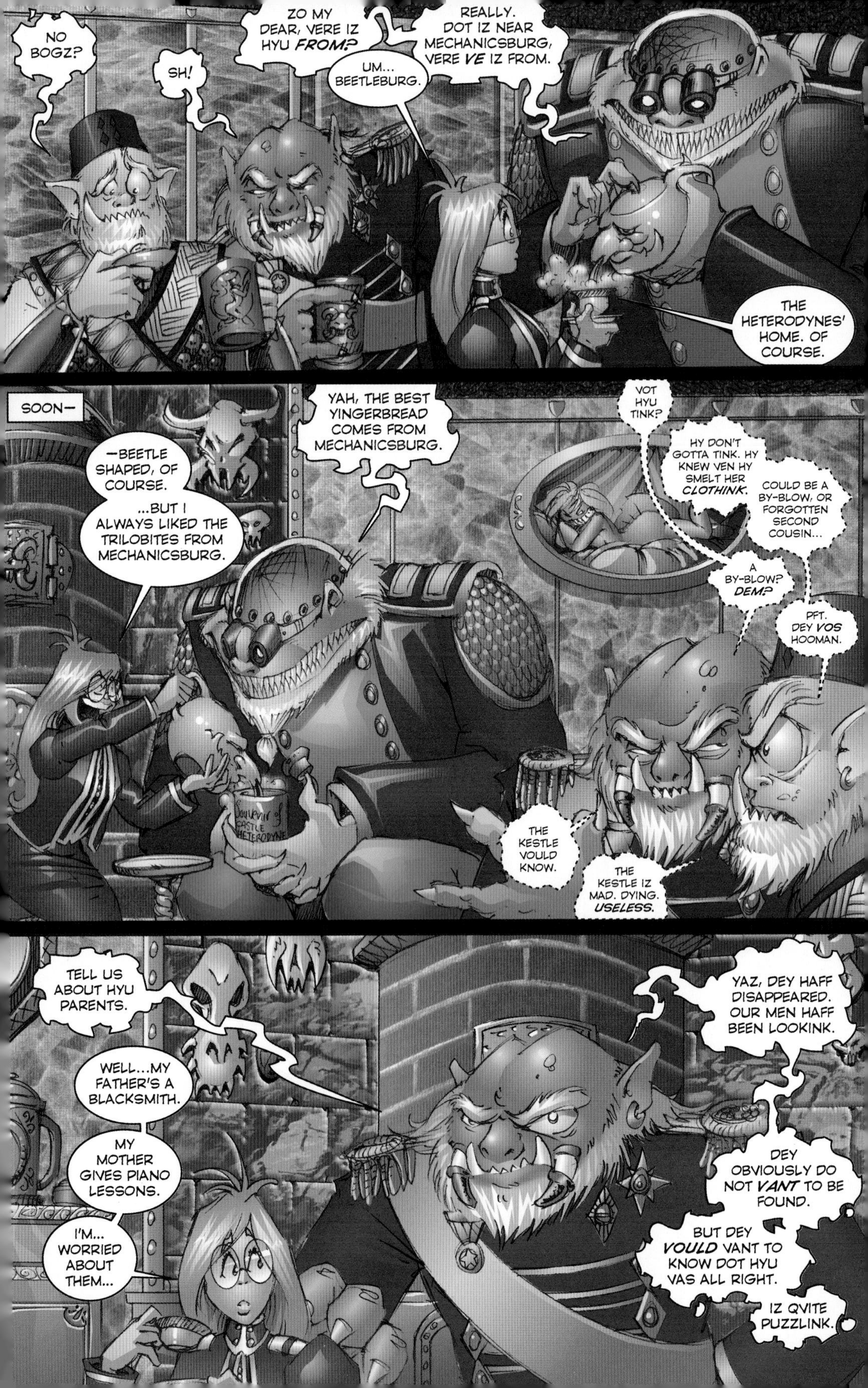
NO BOGZ?
SH!
ZO MY DEAR, VERE IZ HYU *FROM?*
UM... BEETLEBURG.
REALLY. DOT IZ NEAR MECHANICSBURG, VERE *VE* IZ FROM.
THE HETERODYNES' HOME. OF COURSE.
SOON—
—BEETLE SHAPED, OF COURSE.
...BUT I ALWAYS LIKED THE TRILOBITES FROM MECHANICSBURG.
YAH, THE BEST YINGERBREAD COMES FROM MECHANICSBURG.
VOT HYU TINK?
HY DON'T GOTTA TINK. HY KNEW VEN HY SMELT HER *CLOTHINK*.
COULD BE A BY-BLOW, OR FORGOTTEN SECOND COUSIN...
A BY-BLOW? *DEM?*
PFT. DEY *VOS* HOOMAN.
Souvenir of CASTLE HETERODYNE
THE KESTLE VOULD KNOW.
THE KESTLE IZ MAD. DYING. *USELESS*.
TELL US ABOUT HYU PARENTS.
WELL...MY FATHER'S A BLACKSMITH.
MY MOTHER GIVES PIANO LESSONS.
I'M... WORRIED ABOUT THEM...
YAZ, DEY HAFF DISAPPEARED. OUR MEN HAFF BEEN LOOKINK.
DEY OBVIOUSLY DO NOT *VANT* TO BE FOUND.
BUT DEY *VOULD* VANT TO KNOW DOT HYU VAS ALL RIGHT.
IZ QVITE PUZZLINK.

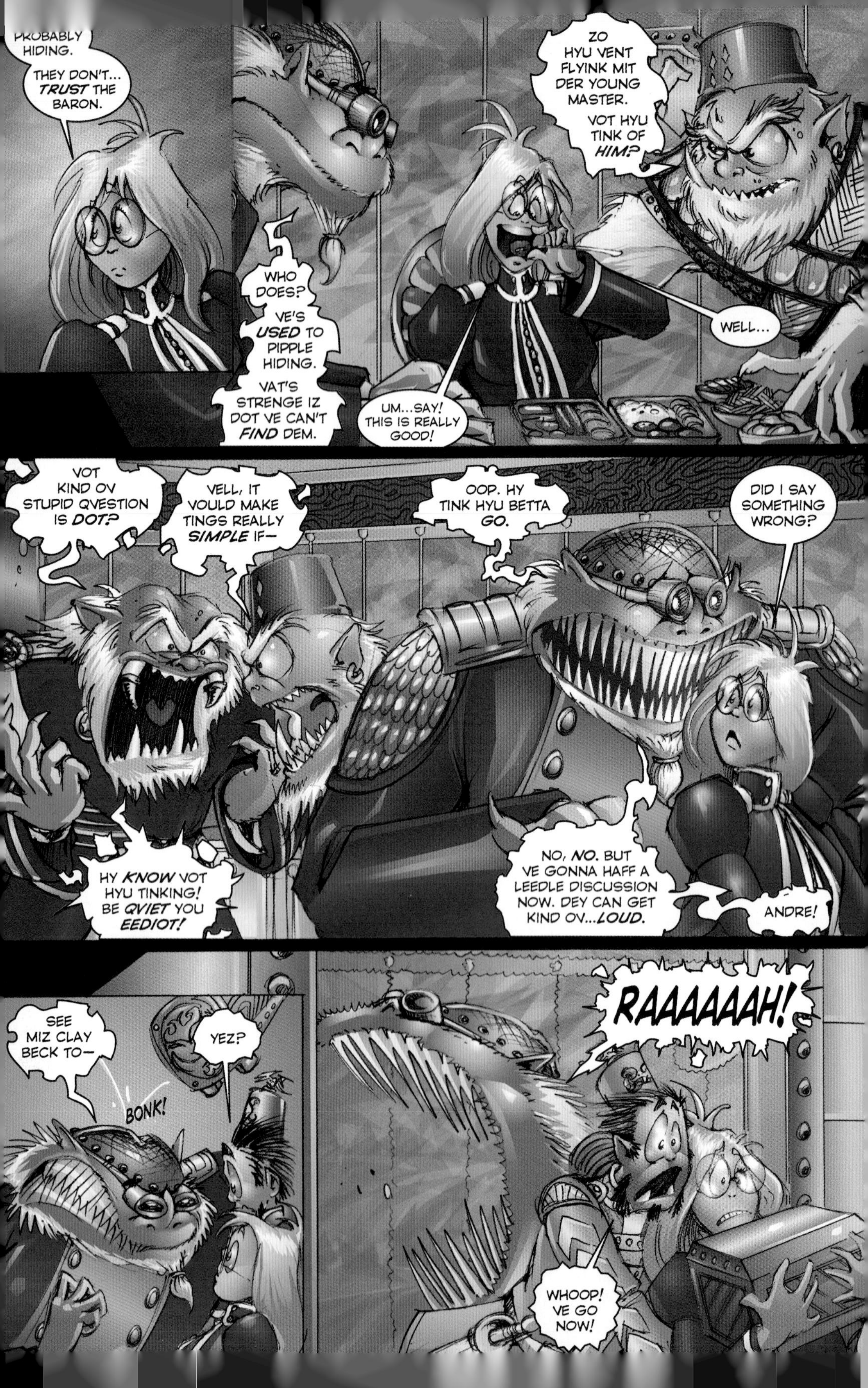
PROBABLY HIDING.
THEY DON'T... TRUST THE BARON.
WHO DOES? VE'S USED TO PIPPLE HIDING.
VAT'S STRENGE IZ DOT VE CAN'T FIND DEM.
ZO HYU VENT FLYINK MIT DER YOUNG MASTER.
VOT HYU TINK OF HIM?
WELL...
UM...SAY! THIS IS REALLY GOOD!
VOT KIND OV STUPID QVESTION IS DOT?
VELL, IT VOULD MAKE TINGS REALLY SIMPLE IF—
HY KNOW VOT HYU TINKING! BE QVIET YOU EEDIOT!
OOP. HY TINK HYU BETTA GO.
DID I SAY SOMETHING WRONG?
NO, NO. BUT VE GONNA HAFF A LEEDLE DISCUSSION NOW. DEY CAN GET KIND OV...LOUD.
ANDRE!
SEE MIZ CLAY BECK TO—
YEZ?
BONK!
RAAAAAAH!
WHOOP! VE GO NOW!

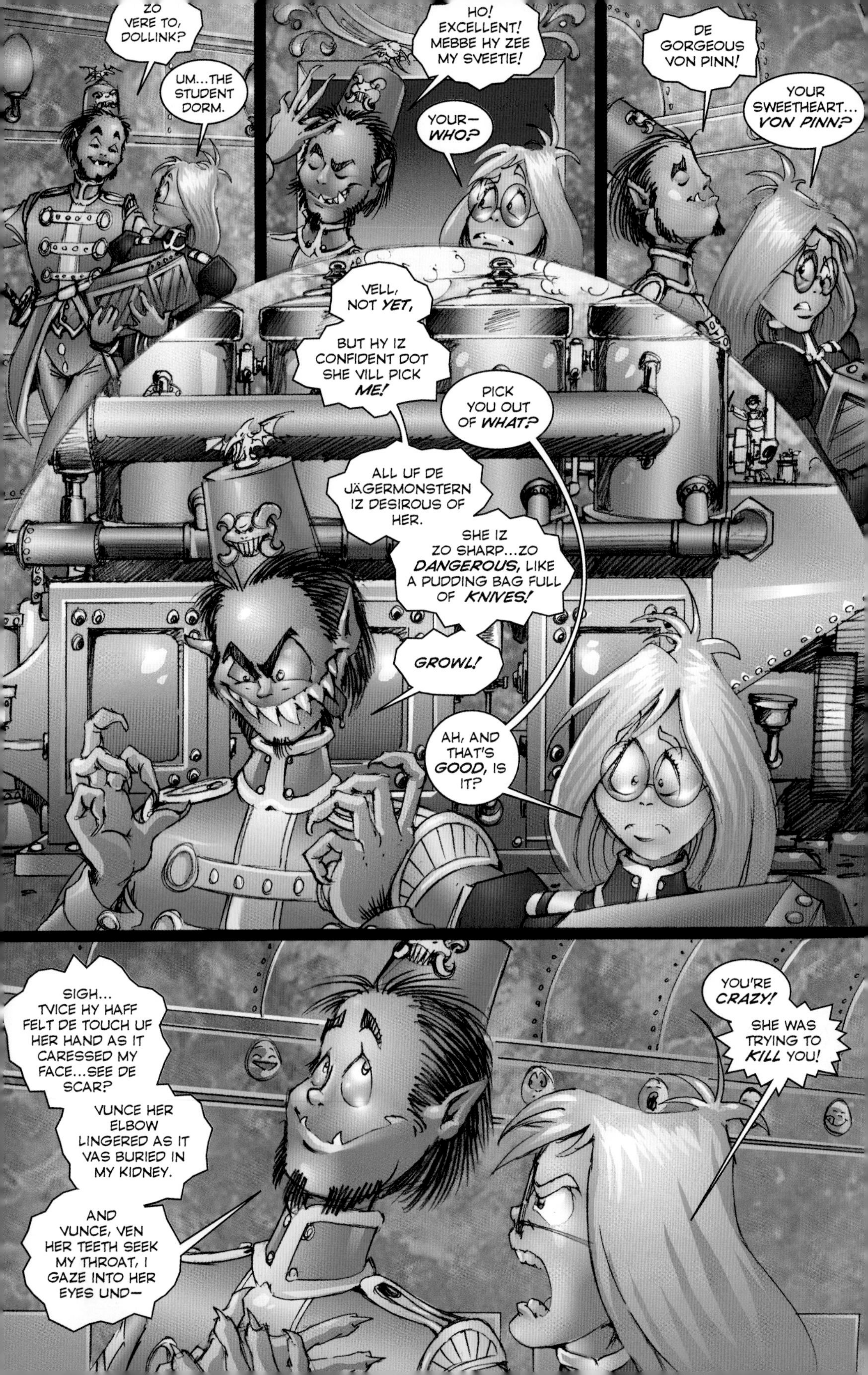
ZO VERE TO, DOLLINK?
UM...THE STUDENT DORM.
HO! EXCELLENT! MEBBE HY ZEE MY SVEETIE!
YOUR— WHO?
DE GORGEOUS VON PINN!
YOUR SWEETHEART... VON PINN?
VELL, NOT YET,
BUT HY IZ CONFIDENT DOT SHE VILL PICK ME!
PICK YOU OUT OF WHAT?
ALL UF DE JÄGERMONSTERN IZ DESIROUS OF HER.
SHE IZ ZO SHARP...ZO DANGEROUS, LIKE A PUDDING BAG FULL OF KNIVES!
GROWL!
AH, AND THAT'S GOOD, IS IT?
SIGH... TVICE HY HAFF FELT DE TOUCH UF HER HAND AS IT CARESSED MY FACE...SEE DE SCAR?
VUNCE HER ELBOW LINGERED AS IT VAS BURIED IN MY KIDNEY.
AND VUNCE, VEN HER TEETH SEEK MY THROAT, I GAZE INTO HER EYES UND—
YOU'RE CRAZY!
SHE WAS TRYING TO KILL YOU!

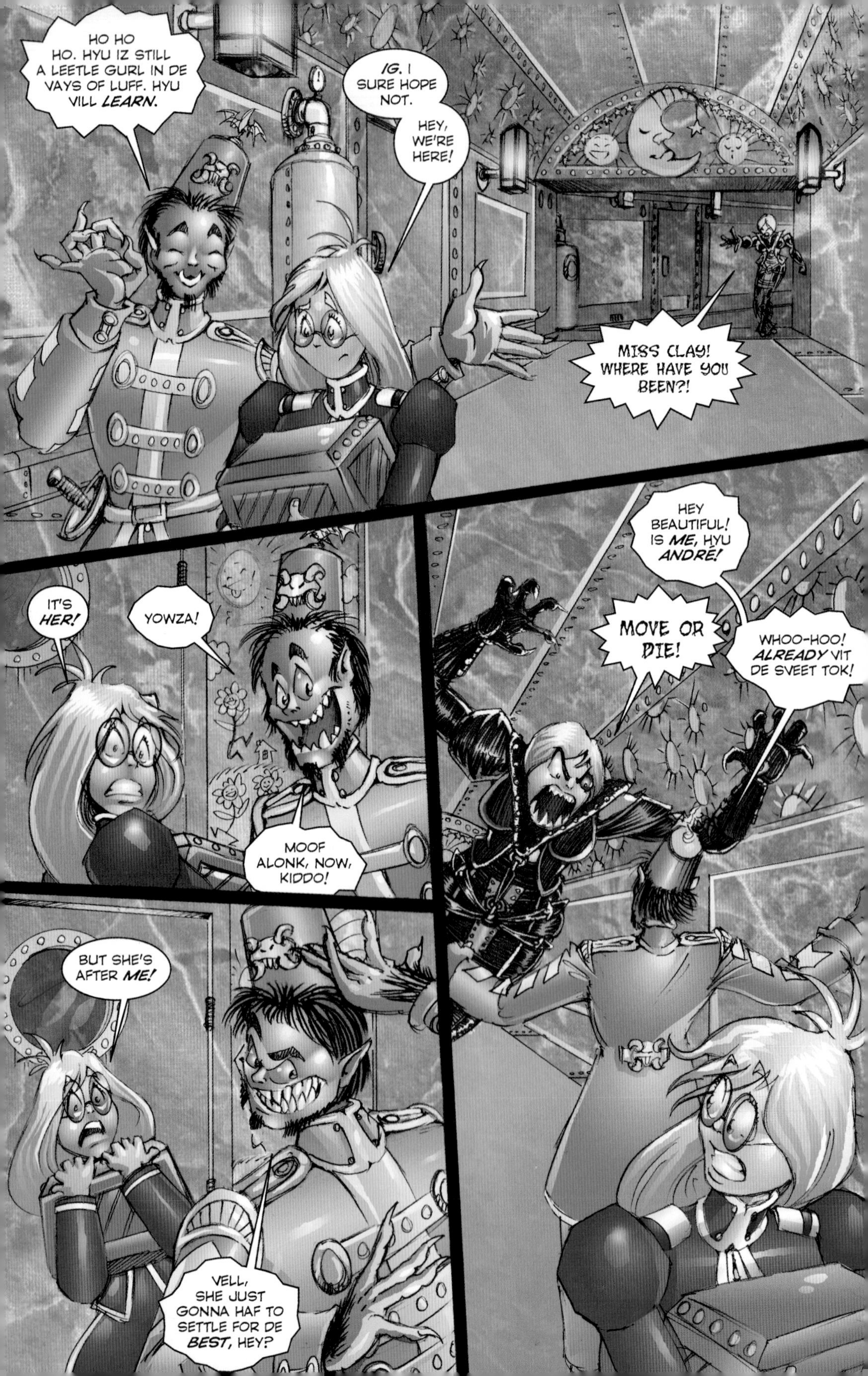
HO HO HO. HYU IZ STILL A LEETLE GURL IN DE VAYS OF LUFF. HYU VILL LEARN.
IG. I SURE HOPE NOT.
HEY, WE'RE HERE!
MISS CLAY! WHERE HAVE YOU BEEN?!
IT'S HER!
YOWZA!
MOOF ALONK, NOW, KIDDO!
HEY BEAUTIFUL! IS ME, HYU ANDRÉ!
MOVE OR DIE!
WHOO-HOO! ALREADY VIT DE SVEET TOK!
BUT SHE'S AFTER ME!
VELL, SHE JUST GONNA HAF TO SETTLE FOR DE BEST, HEY?

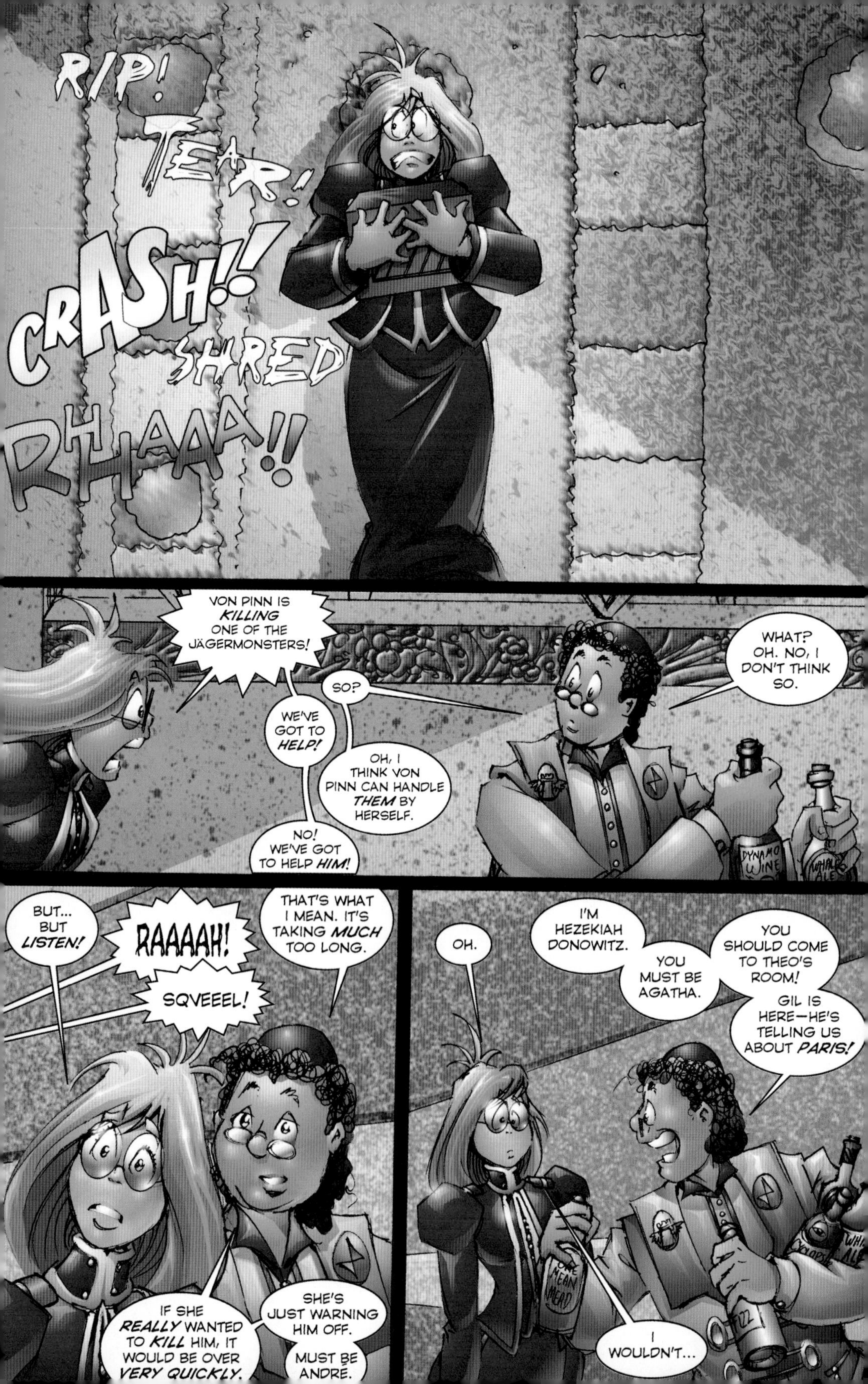
RIP!
TEAR!
CRASH!!
SHRED
RHAAA!!
VON PINN IS KILLING ONE OF THE JÄGERMONSTERS!
SO?
WE'VE GOT TO HELP!
OH, I THINK VON PINN CAN HANDLE THEM BY HERSELF.
NO! WE'VE GOT TO HELP HIM!
WHAT? OH. NO, I DON'T THINK SO.
DYNAMO WINE
WHALE ALE
BUT... BUT LISTEN!
RAAAAH!
SQVEEEL!
THAT'S WHAT I MEAN. IT'S TAKING MUCH TOO LONG.
IF SHE REALLY WANTED TO KILL HIM, IT WOULD BE OVER VERY QUICKLY.
SHE'S JUST WARNING HIM OFF.
MUST BE ANDRÉ.
OH.
I'M HEZEKIAH DONOWITZ.
YOU MUST BE AGATHA.
YOU SHOULD COME TO THEO'S ROOM!
GIL IS HERE—HE'S TELLING US ABOUT PARIS!
I WOULDN'T...
ONE MEAN MEAD

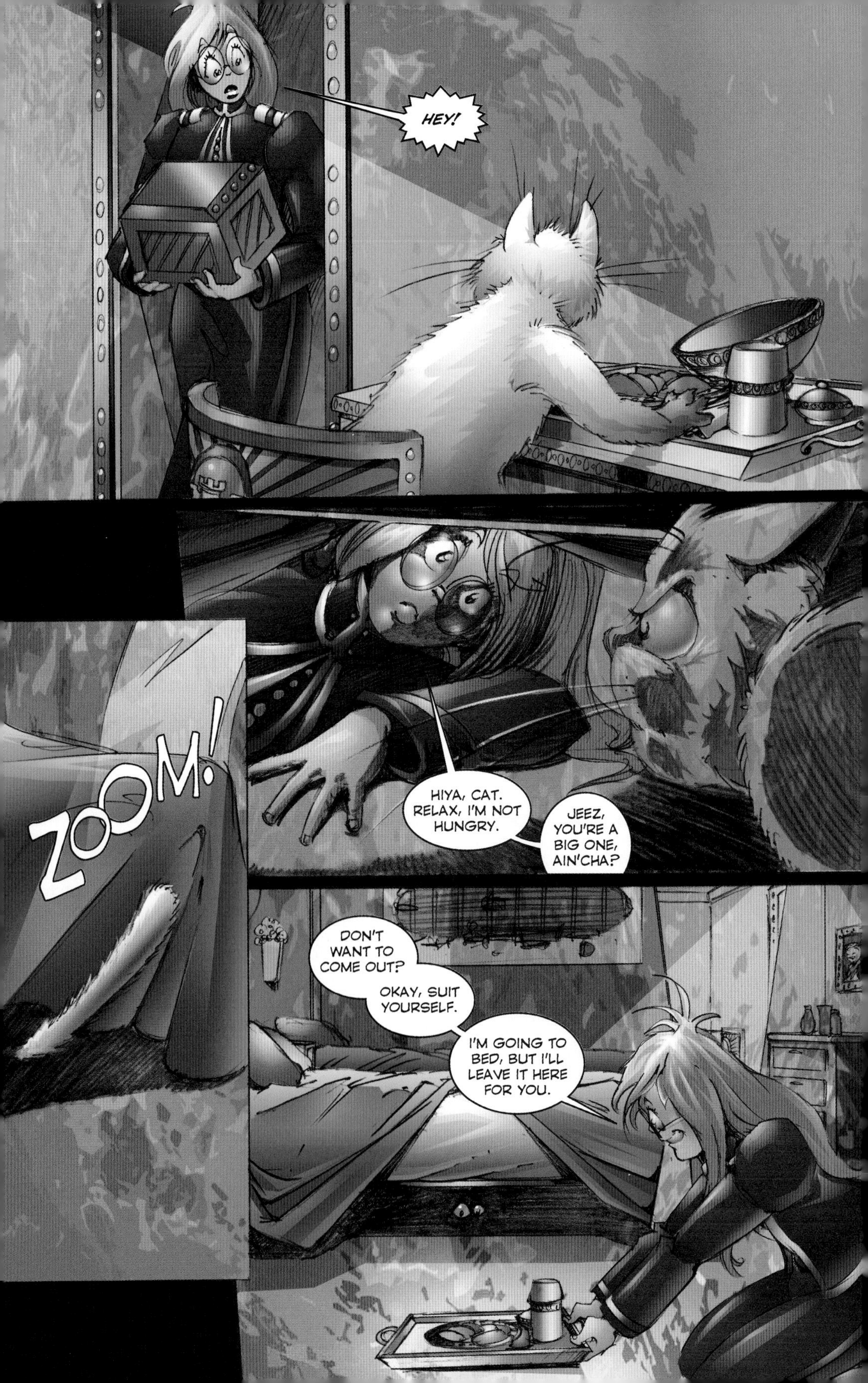
HEY!
ZOOM!
HIYA, CAT. RELAX, I'M NOT HUNGRY.
JEEZ, YOU'RE A BIG ONE, AIN'CHA?
DON'T WANT TO COME OUT?
OKAY, SUIT YOURSELF.
I'M GOING TO BED, BUT I'LL LEAVE IT HERE FOR YOU.

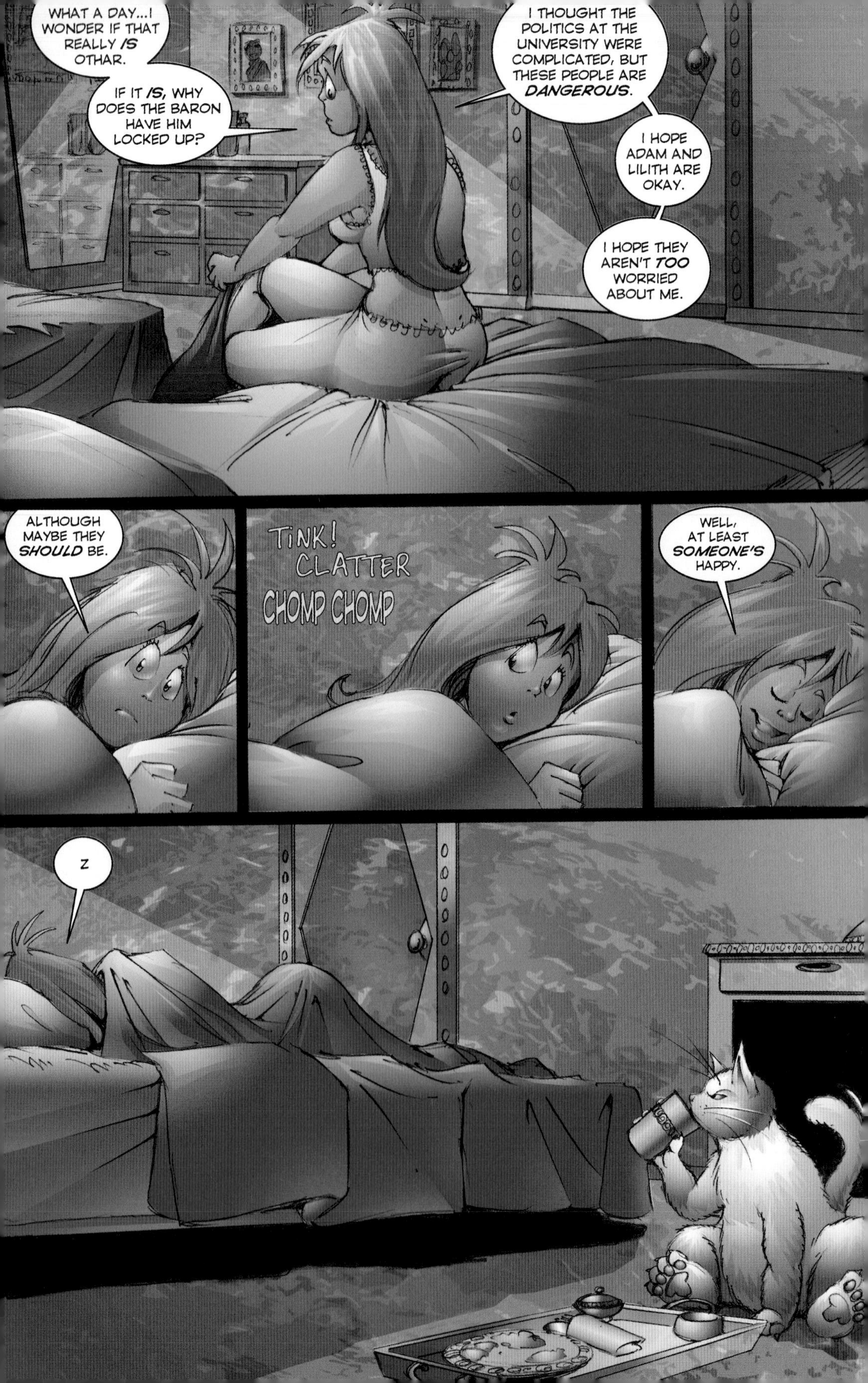
WHAT A DAY...I WONDER IF THAT REALLY IS OTHAR.
IF IT IS, WHY DOES THE BARON HAVE HIM LOCKED UP?
I THOUGHT THE POLITICS AT THE UNIVERSITY WERE COMPLICATED, BUT THESE PEOPLE ARE DANGEROUS.
I HOPE ADAM AND LILITH ARE OKAY.
I HOPE THEY AREN'T TOO WORRIED ABOUT ME.
ALTHOUGH MAYBE THEY SHOULD BE.
TINK! CLATTER
CHOMP CHOMP
WELL, AT LEAST SOMEONE'S HAPPY.
Z

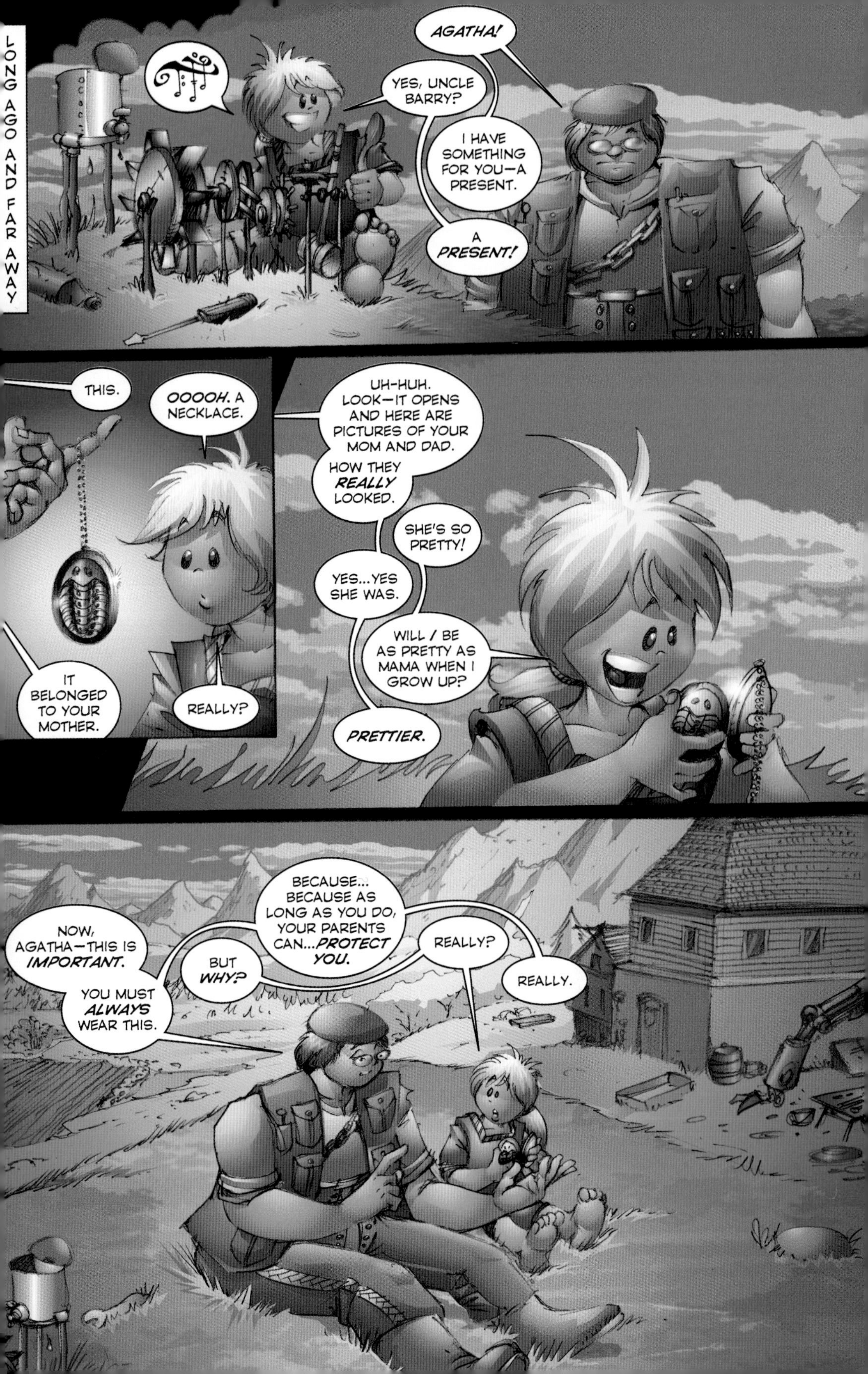
LONG AGO AND FAR AWAY
AGATHA!
YES, UNCLE BARRY?
I HAVE SOMETHING FOR YOU—A PRESENT.
A PRESENT!
THIS.
OOOOH. A NECKLACE.
IT BELONGED TO YOUR MOTHER.
REALLY?
UH-HUH. LOOK—IT OPENS AND HERE ARE PICTURES OF YOUR MOM AND DAD.
HOW THEY REALLY LOOKED.
SHE'S SO PRETTY!
YES...YES SHE WAS.
WILL I BE AS PRETTY AS MAMA WHEN I GROW UP?
PRETTIER.
NOW, AGATHA—THIS IS IMPORTANT.
YOU MUST ALWAYS WEAR THIS.
BUT WHY?
BECAUSE... BECAUSE AS LONG AS YOU DO, YOUR PARENTS CAN...PROTECT YOU.
REALLY?
REALLY.

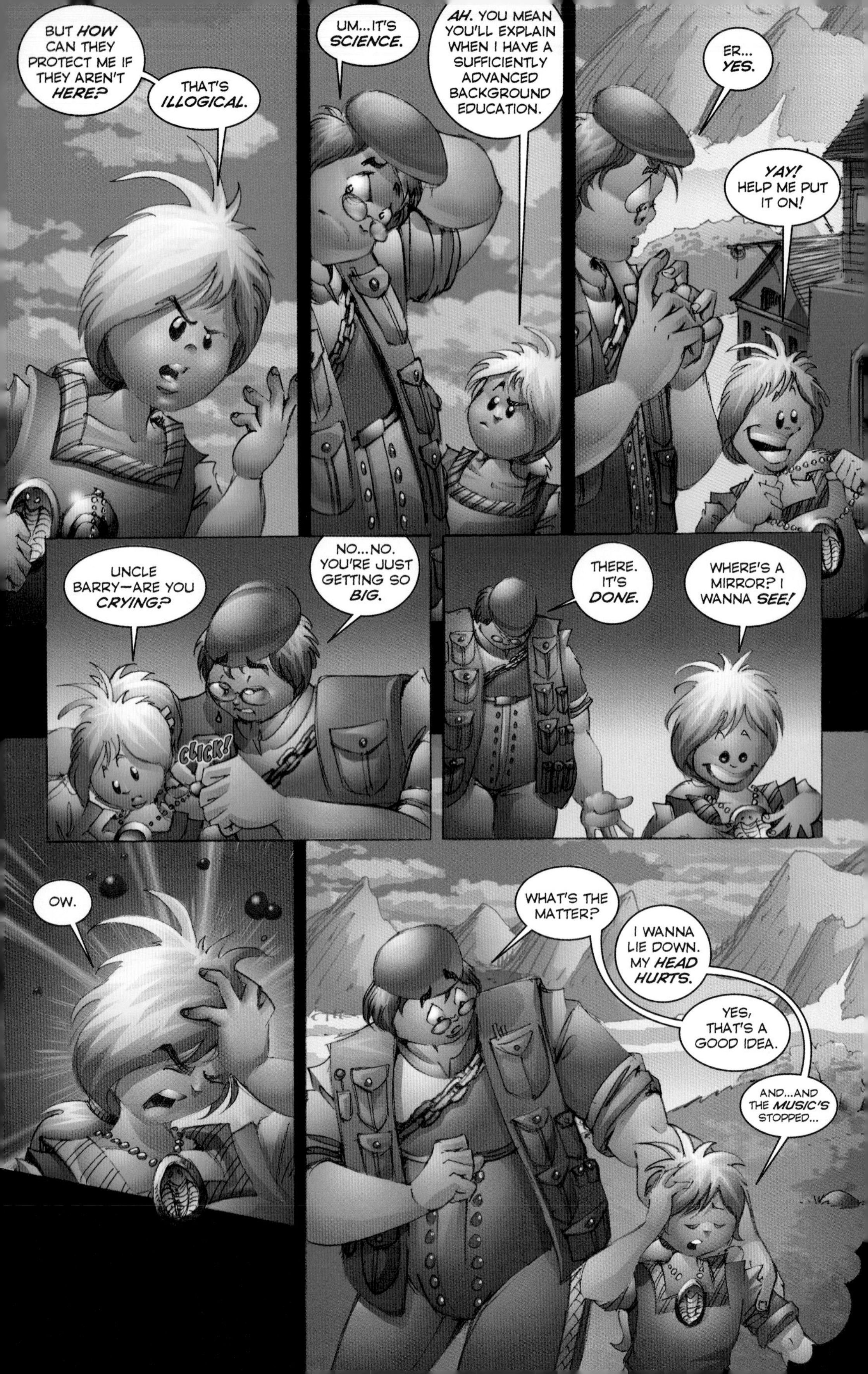
BUT *HOW* CAN THEY PROTECT ME IF THEY AREN'T *HERE?*
THAT'S *ILLOGICAL*.
UM...IT'S *SCIENCE*.
AH. YOU MEAN YOU'LL EXPLAIN WHEN I HAVE A SUFFICIENTLY ADVANCED BACKGROUND EDUCATION.
ER... *YES*.
YAY! HELP ME PUT IT ON!
UNCLE BARRY—ARE YOU *CRYING?*
NO...NO. YOU'RE JUST GETTING SO *BIG*.
CLICK!
THERE. IT'S *DONE*.
WHERE'S A MIRROR? I WANNA *SEE!*
OW.
WHAT'S THE MATTER?
I WANNA LIE DOWN. MY *HEAD HURTS*.
YES, THAT'S A GOOD IDEA.
AND...AND THE *MUSIC'S* STOPPED...

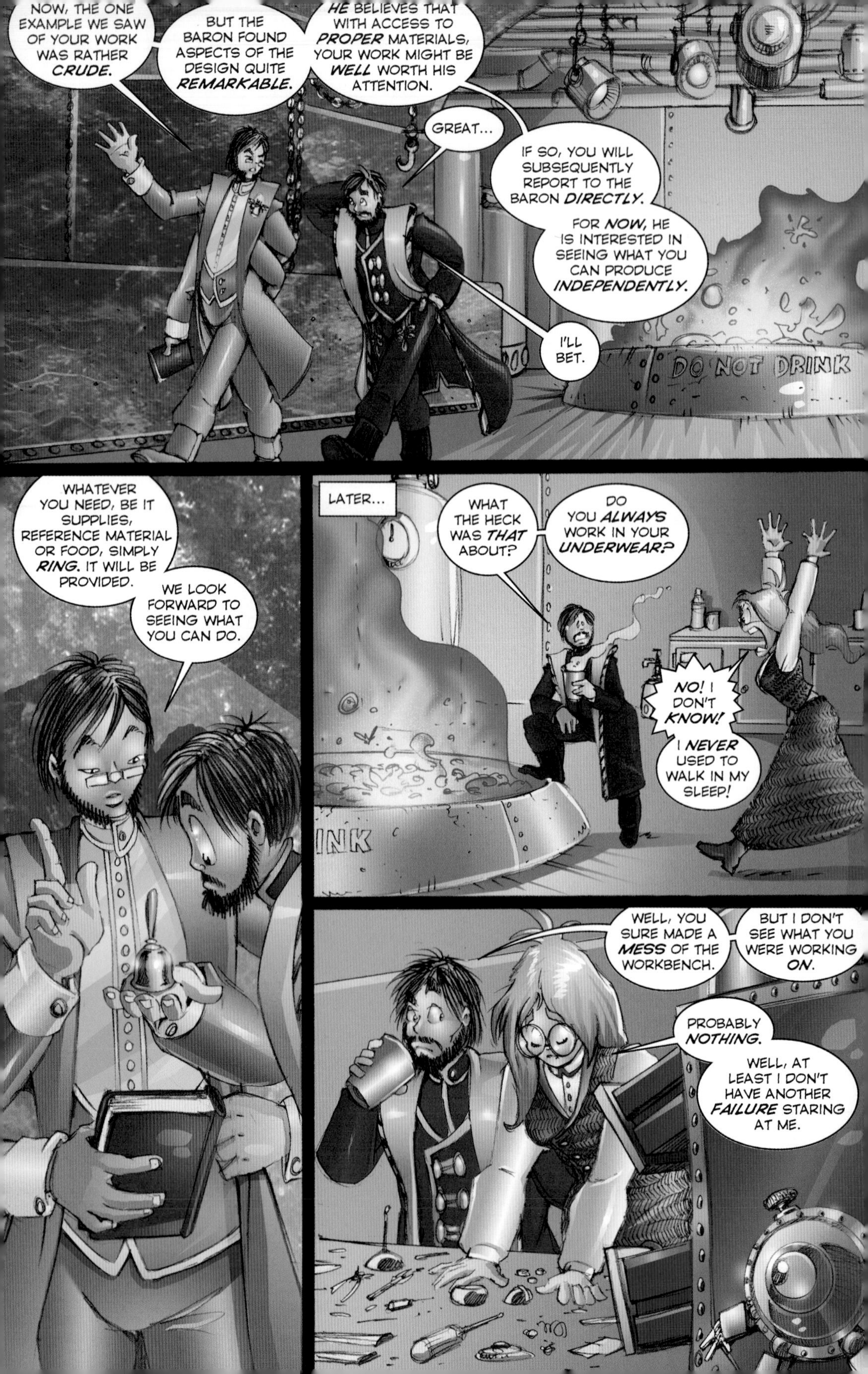
NOW, THE ONE EXAMPLE WE SAW OF YOUR WORK WAS RATHER *CRUDE.*
BUT THE BARON FOUND ASPECTS OF THE DESIGN QUITE *REMARKABLE.*
HE BELIEVES THAT WITH ACCESS TO *PROPER* MATERIALS, YOUR WORK MIGHT BE *WELL* WORTH HIS ATTENTION.
GREAT...
IF SO, YOU WILL SUBSEQUENTLY REPORT TO THE BARON *DIRECTLY.*
FOR *NOW,* HE IS INTERESTED IN SEEING WHAT YOU CAN PRODUCE *INDEPENDENTLY.*
I'LL BET.
DO NOT DRINK
WHATEVER YOU NEED, BE IT SUPPLIES, REFERENCE MATERIAL OR FOOD, SIMPLY *RING.* IT WILL BE PROVIDED.
WE LOOK FORWARD TO SEEING WHAT YOU CAN DO.
LATER...
WHAT THE HECK WAS *THAT* ABOUT?
DO YOU *ALWAYS* WORK IN YOUR *UNDERWEAR?*
NO! I DON'T *KNOW!*
I *NEVER* USED TO WALK IN MY SLEEP!
INK
WELL, YOU SURE MADE A *MESS* OF THE WORKBENCH.
BUT I DON'T SEE WHAT YOU WERE WORKING *ON.*
PROBABLY *NOTHING.*
WELL, AT LEAST I DON'T HAVE ANOTHER *FAILURE* STARING AT ME.

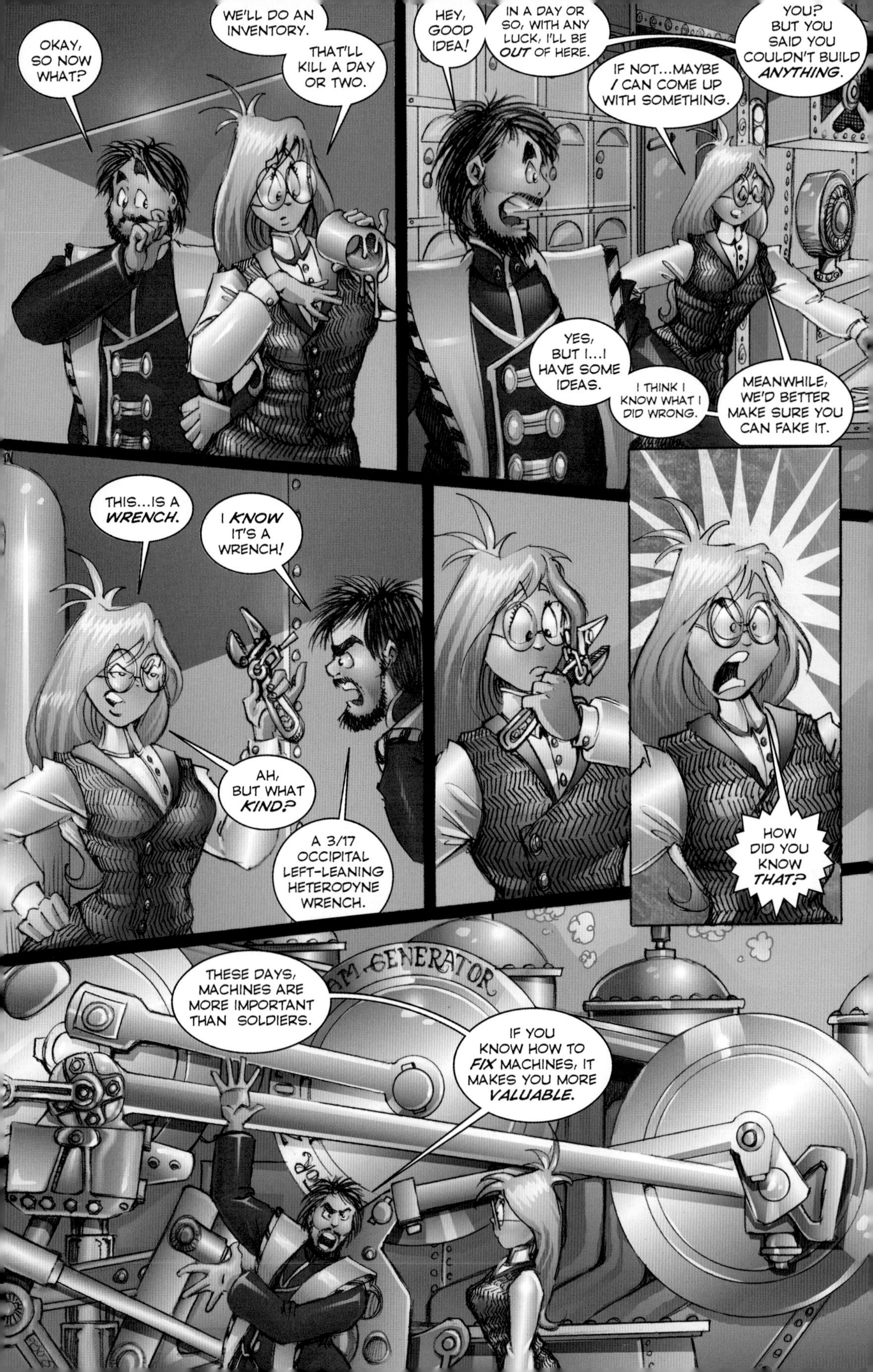
OKAY, SO NOW WHAT?
WE'LL DO AN INVENTORY.
THAT'LL KILL A DAY OR TWO.
HEY, GOOD IDEA!
IN A DAY OR SO, WITH ANY LUCK, I'LL BE OUT OF HERE.
IF NOT...MAYBE I CAN COME UP WITH SOMETHING.
YOU? BUT YOU SAID YOU COULDN'T BUILD ANYTHING.
YES, BUT I...I HAVE SOME IDEAS.
I THINK I KNOW WHAT I DID WRONG.
MEANWHILE, WE'D BETTER MAKE SURE YOU CAN FAKE IT.
THIS...IS A WRENCH.
I KNOW IT'S A WRENCH!
AH, BUT WHAT KIND?
A 3/17 OCCIPITAL LEFT-LEANING HETERODYNE WRENCH.
HOW DID YOU KNOW THAT?
GENERATOR
THESE DAYS, MACHINES ARE MORE IMPORTANT THAN SOLDIERS.
IF YOU KNOW HOW TO FIX MACHINES, IT MAKES YOU MORE VALUABLE.

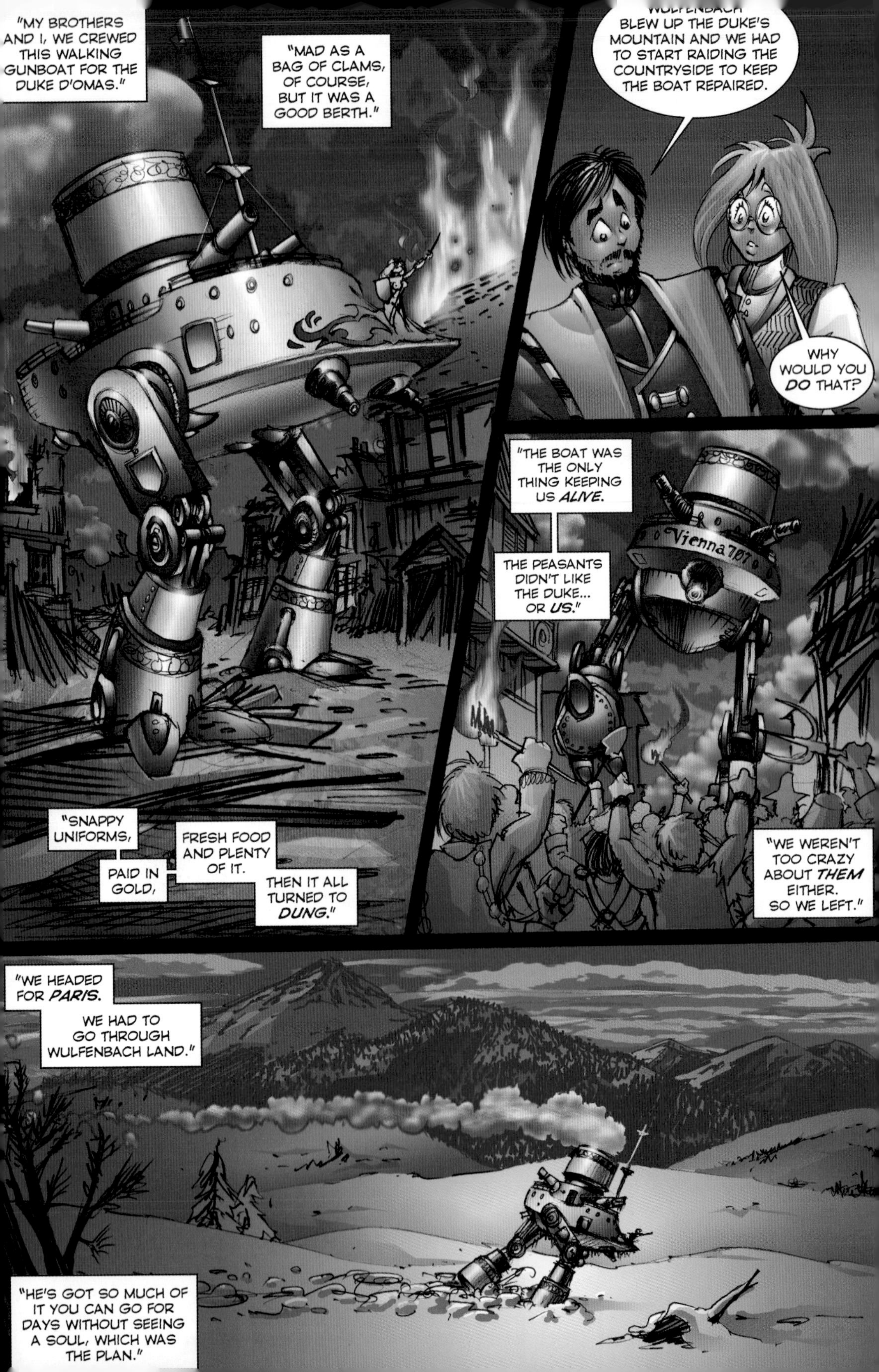
"MY BROTHERS AND I, WE CREWED THIS WALKING GUNBOAT FOR THE DUKE D'OMAS."
"MAD AS A BAG OF CLAMS, OF COURSE, BUT IT WAS A GOOD BERTH."
"SNAPPY UNIFORMS,
PAID IN GOLD,
FRESH FOOD AND PLENTY OF IT.
THEN IT ALL TURNED TO *DUNG*."
BLEW UP THE DUKE'S MOUNTAIN AND WE HAD TO START RAIDING THE COUNTRYSIDE TO KEEP THE BOAT REPAIRED.
WHY WOULD YOU *DO* THAT?
"THE BOAT WAS THE ONLY THING KEEPING US *ALIVE*.
THE PEASANTS DIDN'T LIKE THE DUKE... OR *US*."
Vienna707
"WE WEREN'T TOO CRAZY ABOUT *THEM* EITHER. SO WE LEFT."
"WE HEADED FOR *PARIS*.
WE HAD TO GO THROUGH WULFENBACH LAND."
"HE'S GOT SO MUCH OF IT YOU CAN GO FOR DAYS WITHOUT SEEING A SOUL, WHICH WAS THE PLAN."

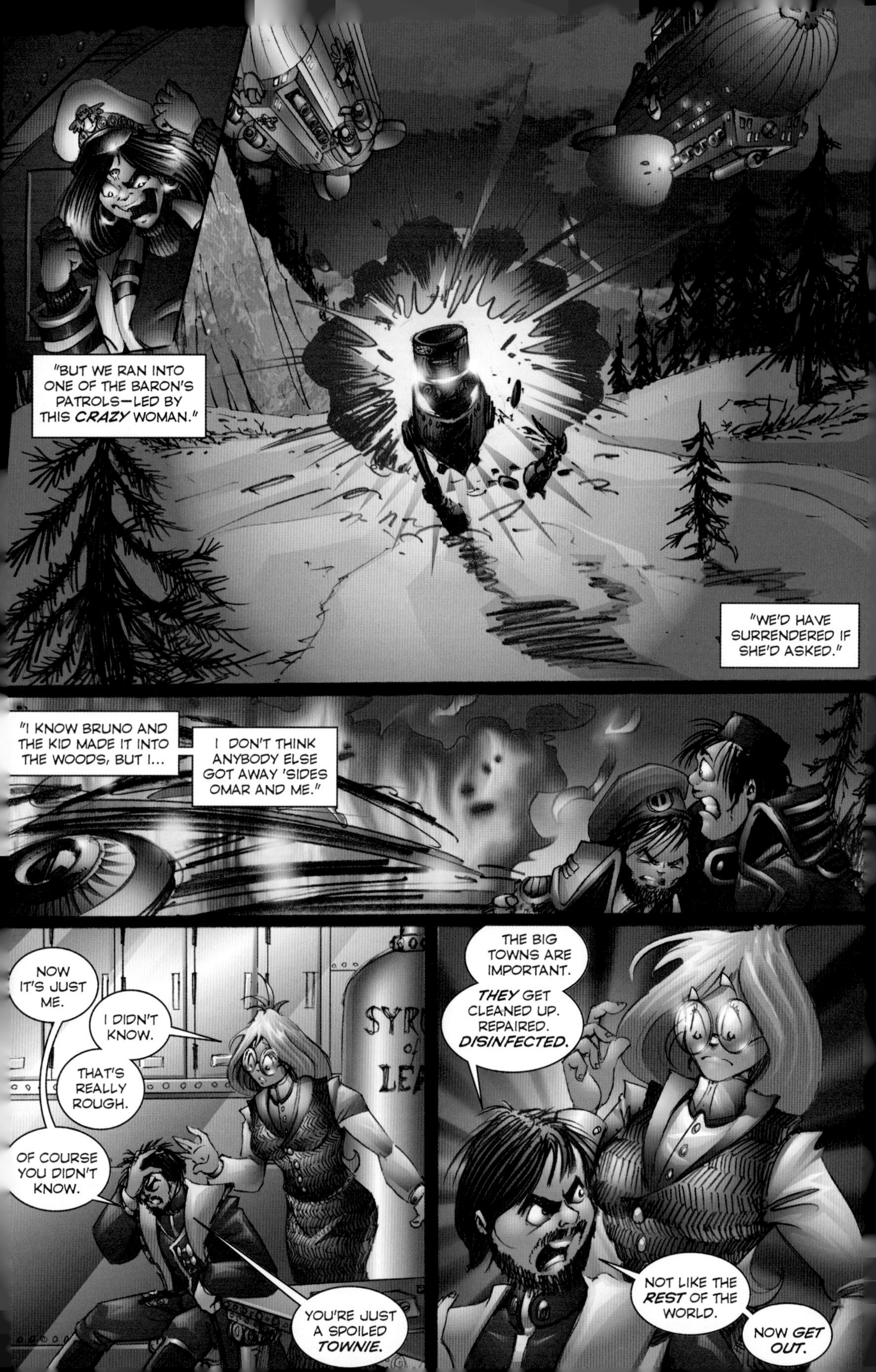
"BUT WE RAN INTO ONE OF THE BARON'S PATROLS—LED BY THIS *CRAZY* WOMAN."
"WE'D HAVE SURRENDERED IF SHE'D ASKED."
"I KNOW BRUNO AND THE KID MADE IT INTO THE WOODS, BUT I...
I DON'T THINK ANYBODY ELSE GOT AWAY 'SIDES OMAR AND ME."
NOW IT'S JUST ME.
I DIDN'T KNOW.
THAT'S REALLY ROUGH.
OF COURSE YOU DIDN'T KNOW.
YOU'RE JUST A SPOILED *TOWNIE.*
THE BIG TOWNS ARE IMPORTANT.
THEY GET CLEANED UP. REPAIRED. ***DISINFECTED.***
NOT LIKE THE *REST* OF THE WORLD.
NOW *GET OUT.*

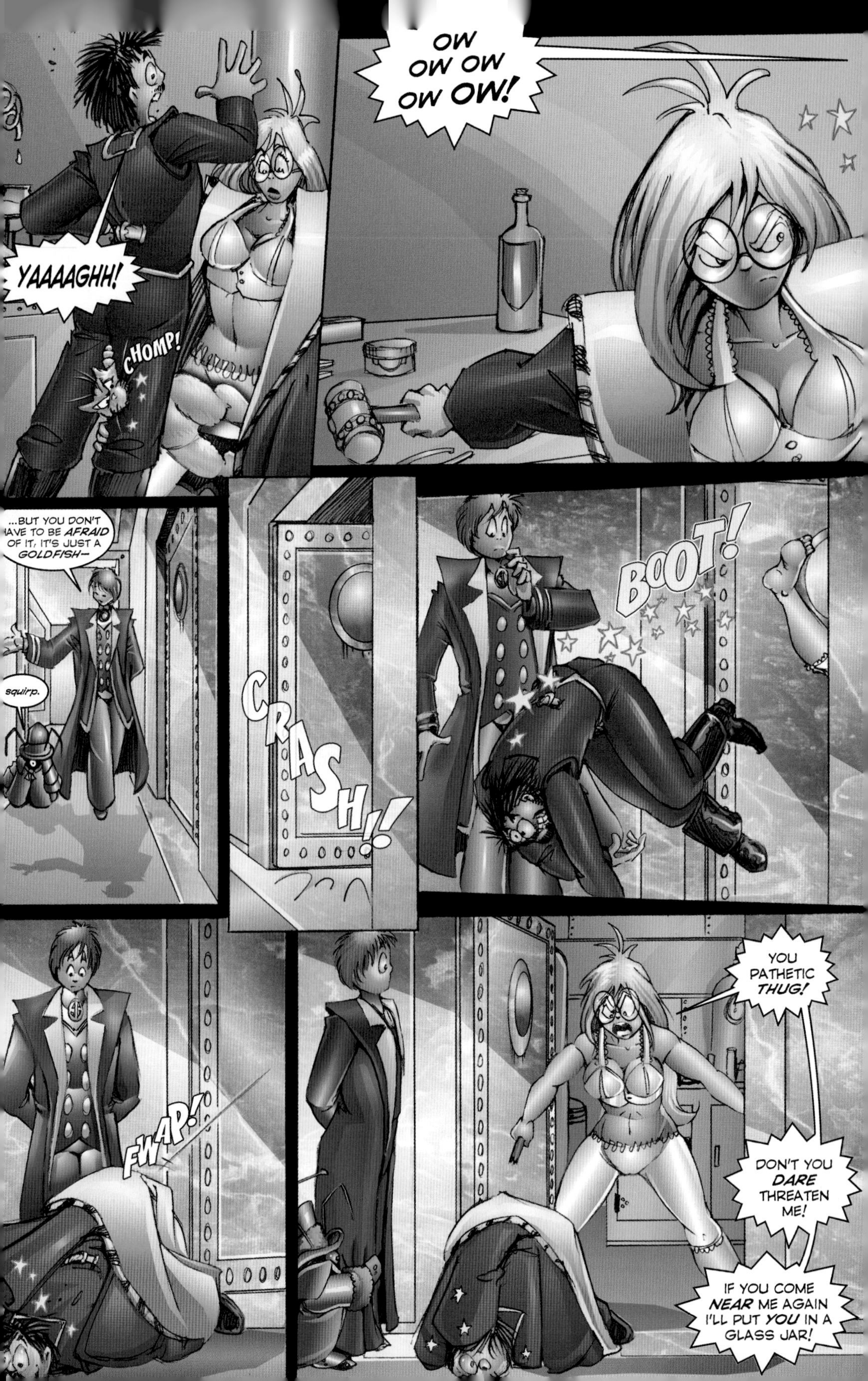
YAAAAGHH!
CHOMP!
OW OW OW OW OW!
...BUT YOU DON'T HAVE TO BE AFRAID OF IT, IT'S JUST A GOLDFISH—
squirp.
CRASH!!
BOOT!
FWAP!
YOU PATHETIC THUG!
DON'T YOU DARE THREATEN ME!
IF YOU COME NEAR ME AGAIN I'LL PUT YOU IN A GLASS JAR!

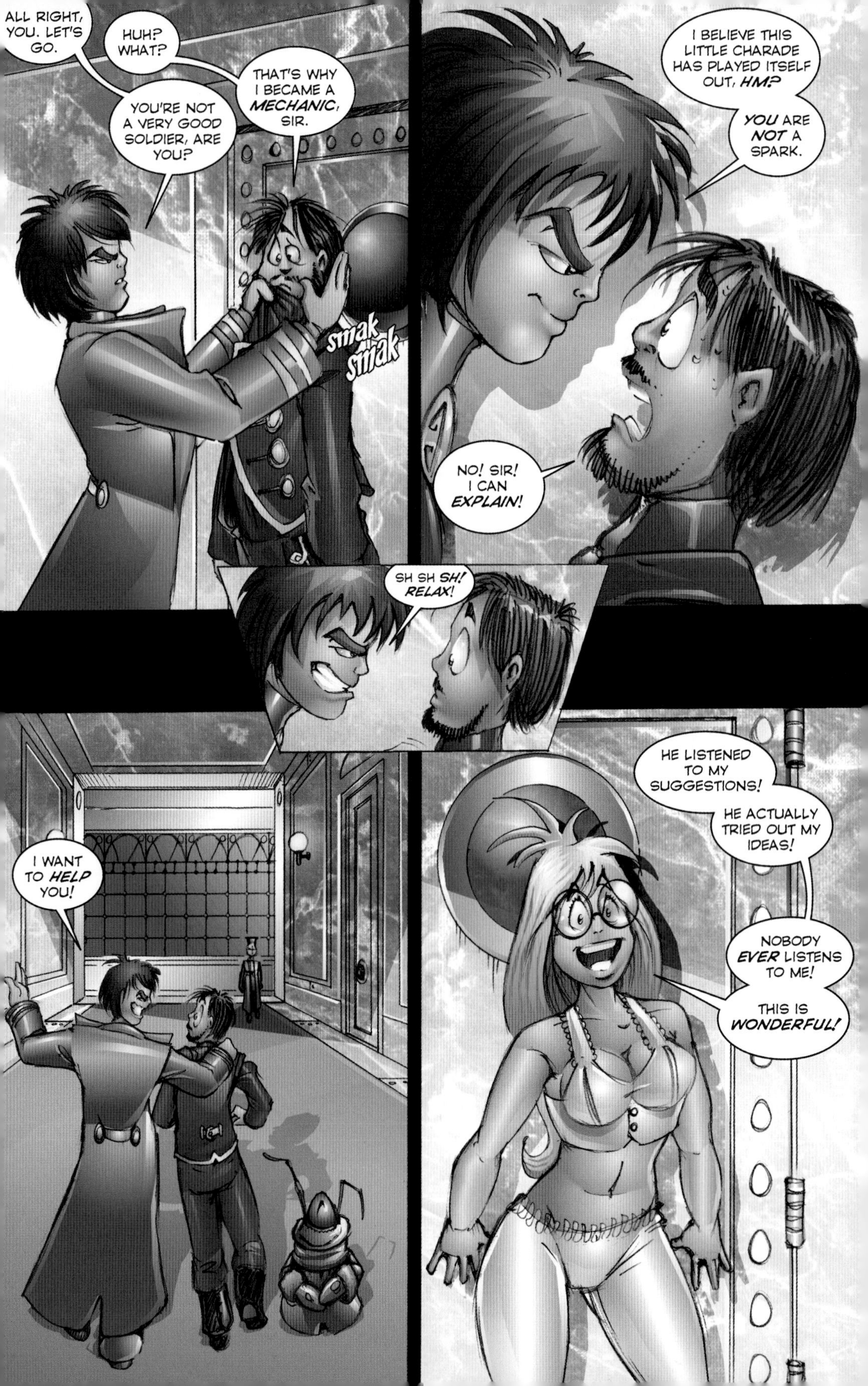
ALL RIGHT, YOU. LET'S GO.
HUH? WHAT?
YOU'RE NOT A VERY GOOD SOLDIER, ARE YOU?
THAT'S WHY I BECAME A *MECHANIC*, SIR.
smak smak
I BELIEVE THIS LITTLE CHARADE HAS PLAYED ITSELF OUT, *HM?*
YOU ARE *NOT* A SPARK.
NO! SIR! I CAN *EXPLAIN*!
SH SH *SH! RELAX*!
I WANT TO *HELP* YOU!
HE LISTENED TO MY SUGGESTIONS!
HE ACTUALLY TRIED OUT MY IDEAS!
NOBODY *EVER* LISTENS TO ME!
THIS IS *WONDERFUL!*

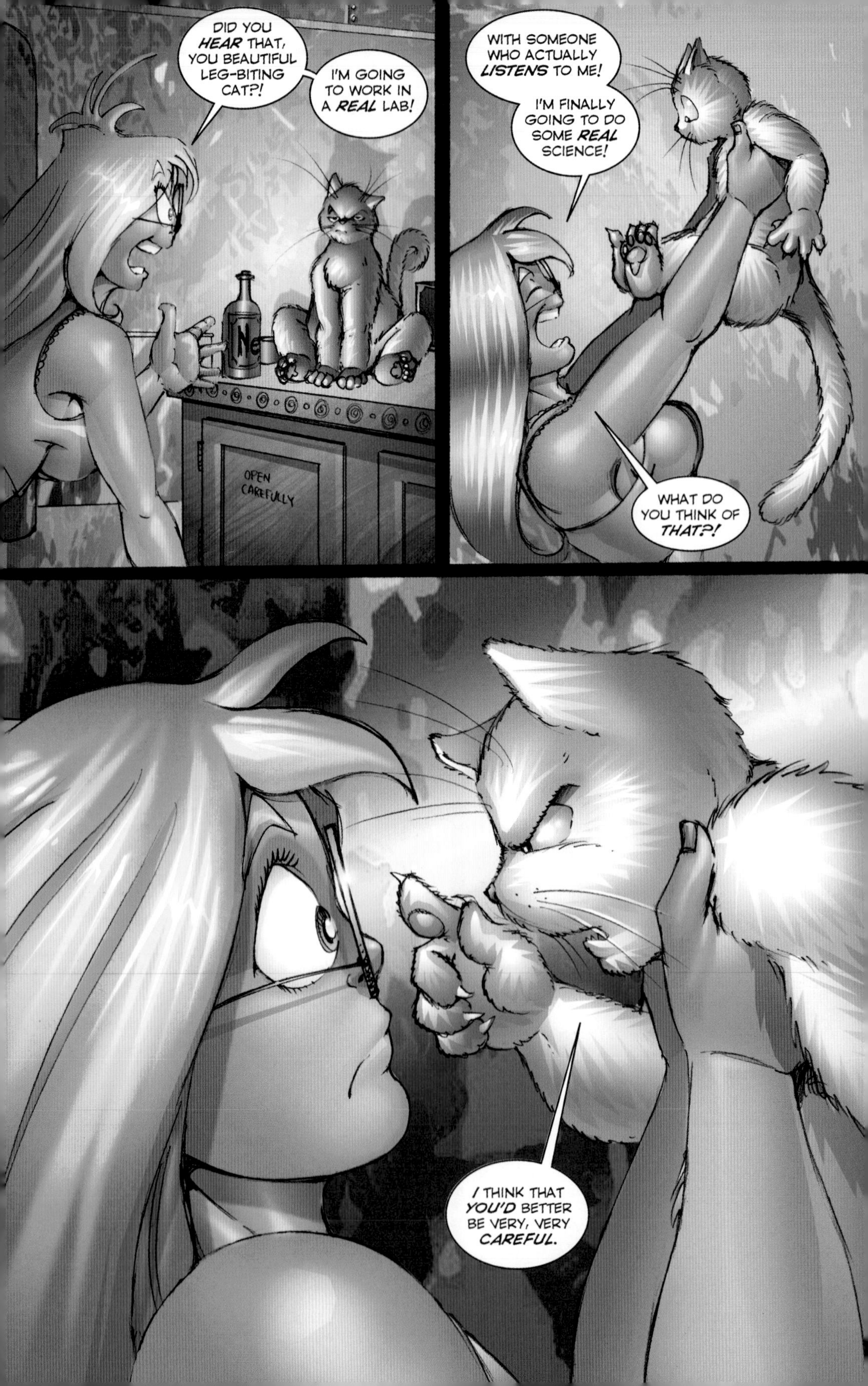
DID YOU HEAR THAT, YOU BEAUTIFUL LEG-BITING CAT?!
I'M GOING TO WORK IN A REAL LAB!
Ne
OPEN CAREFULLY
WITH SOMEONE WHO ACTUALLY LISTENS TO ME!
I'M FINALLY GOING TO DO SOME REAL SCIENCE!
WHAT DO YOU THINK OF THAT?!
I THINK THAT YOU'D BETTER BE VERY, VERY CAREFUL.

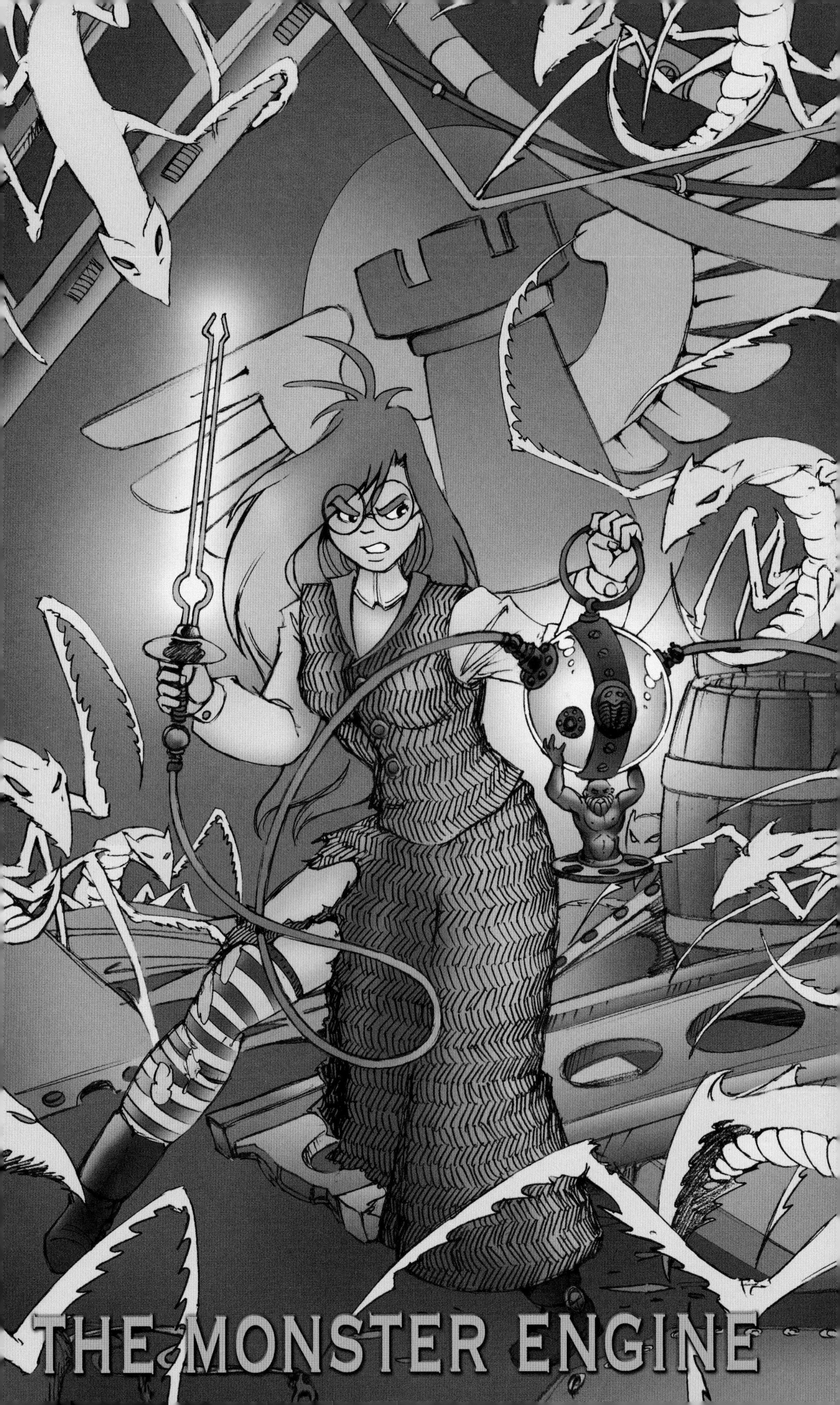
THE MONSTER ENGINE

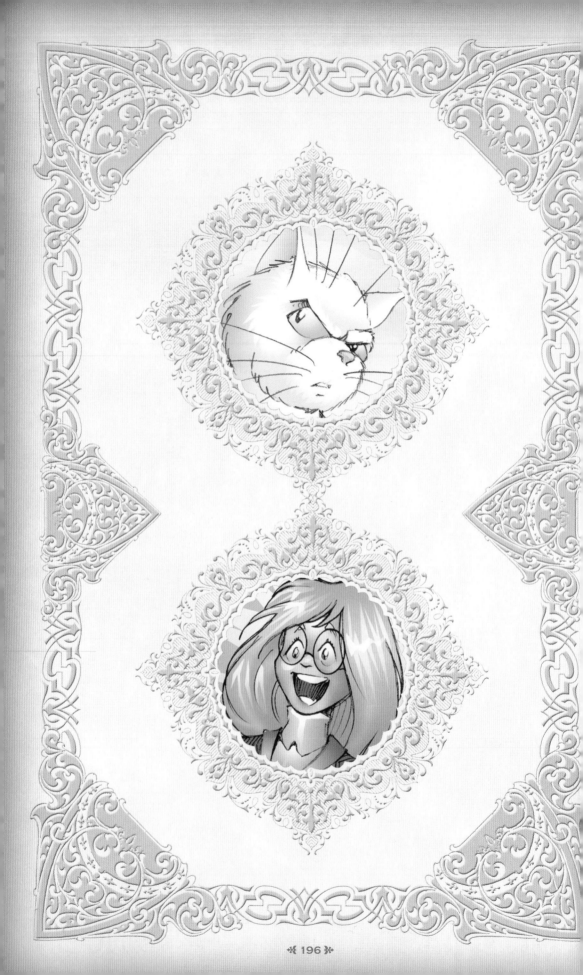

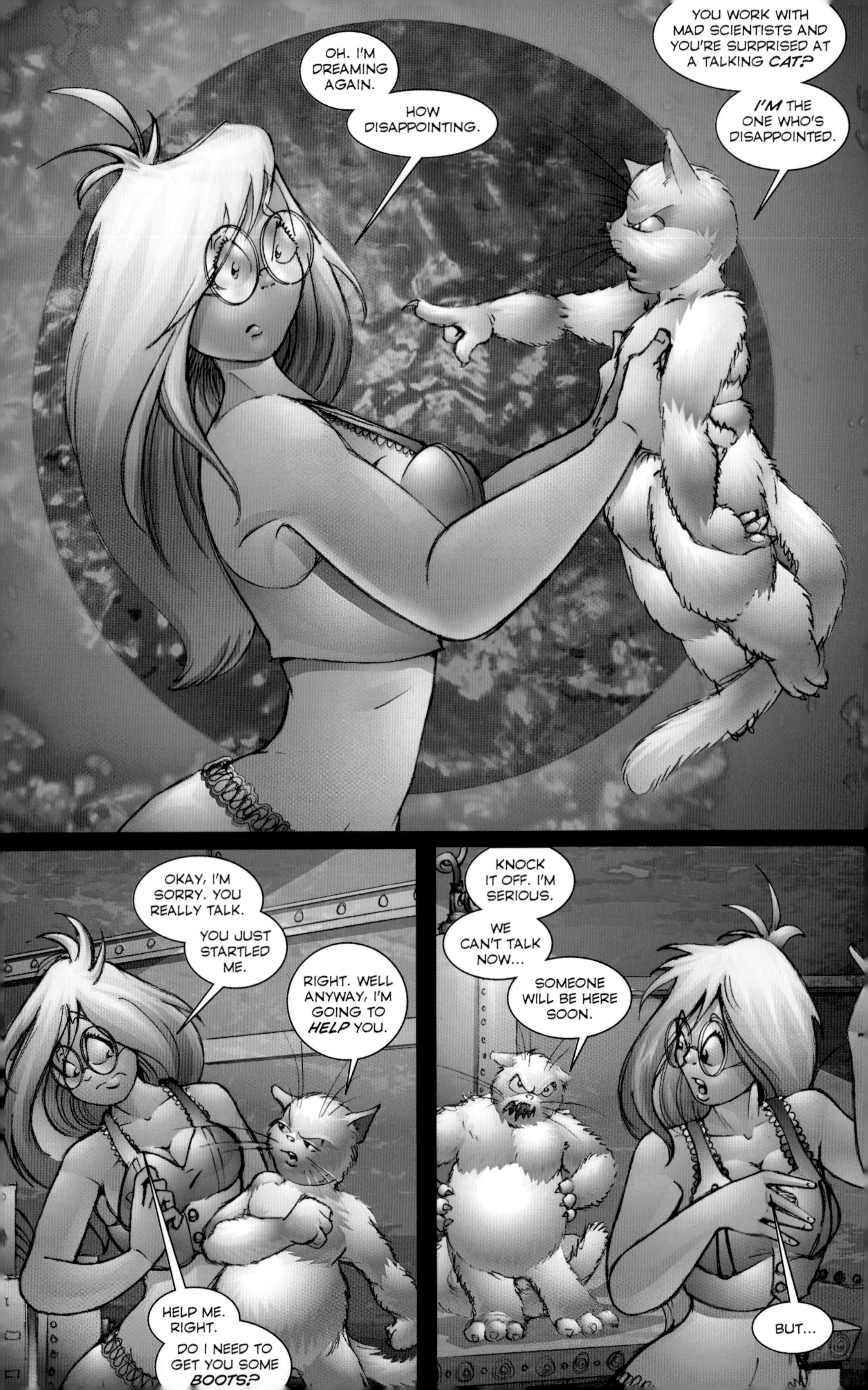
OH. I'M DREAMING AGAIN.
HOW DISAPPOINTING.
YOU WORK WITH MAD SCIENTISTS AND YOU'RE SURPRISED AT A TALKING *CAT?*
I'M THE ONE WHO'S DISAPPOINTED.
OKAY, I'M SORRY. YOU REALLY TALK.
YOU JUST STARTLED ME.
RIGHT. WELL ANYWAY, I'M GOING TO *HELP* YOU.
HELP ME. RIGHT.
DO I NEED TO GET YOU SOME *BOOTS?*
KNOCK IT OFF. I'M SERIOUS.
WE CAN'T TALK NOW...
SOMEONE WILL BE HERE SOON.
BUT...

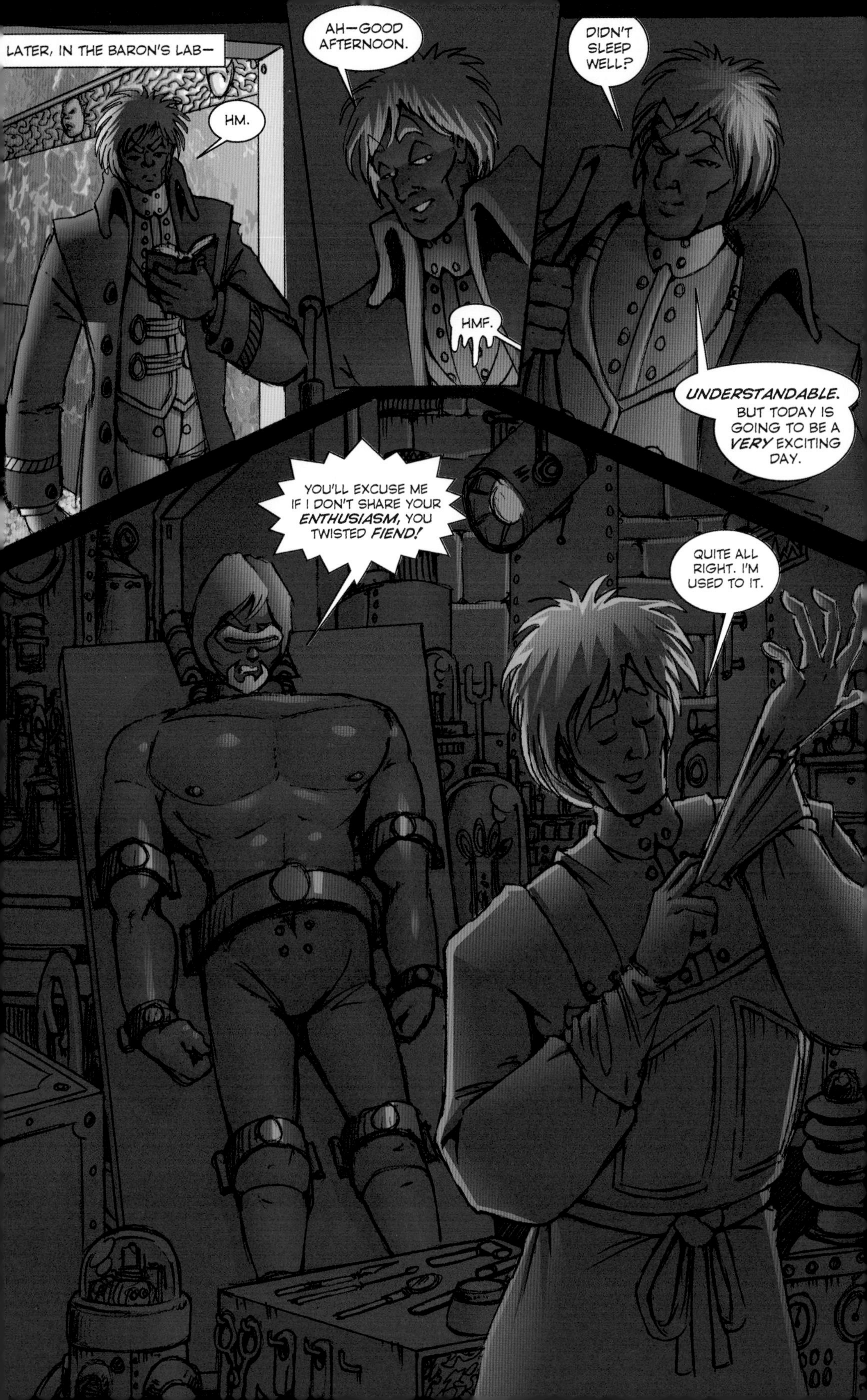
LATER, IN THE BARON'S LAB—
HM.
AH—GOOD AFTERNOON.
DIDN'T SLEEP WELL?
HMF.
UNDERSTANDABLE. BUT TODAY IS GOING TO BE A *VERY* EXCITING DAY.
YOU'LL EXCUSE ME IF I DON'T SHARE YOUR *ENTHUSIASM,* YOU TWISTED *FIEND!*
QUITE ALL RIGHT. I'M USED TO IT.

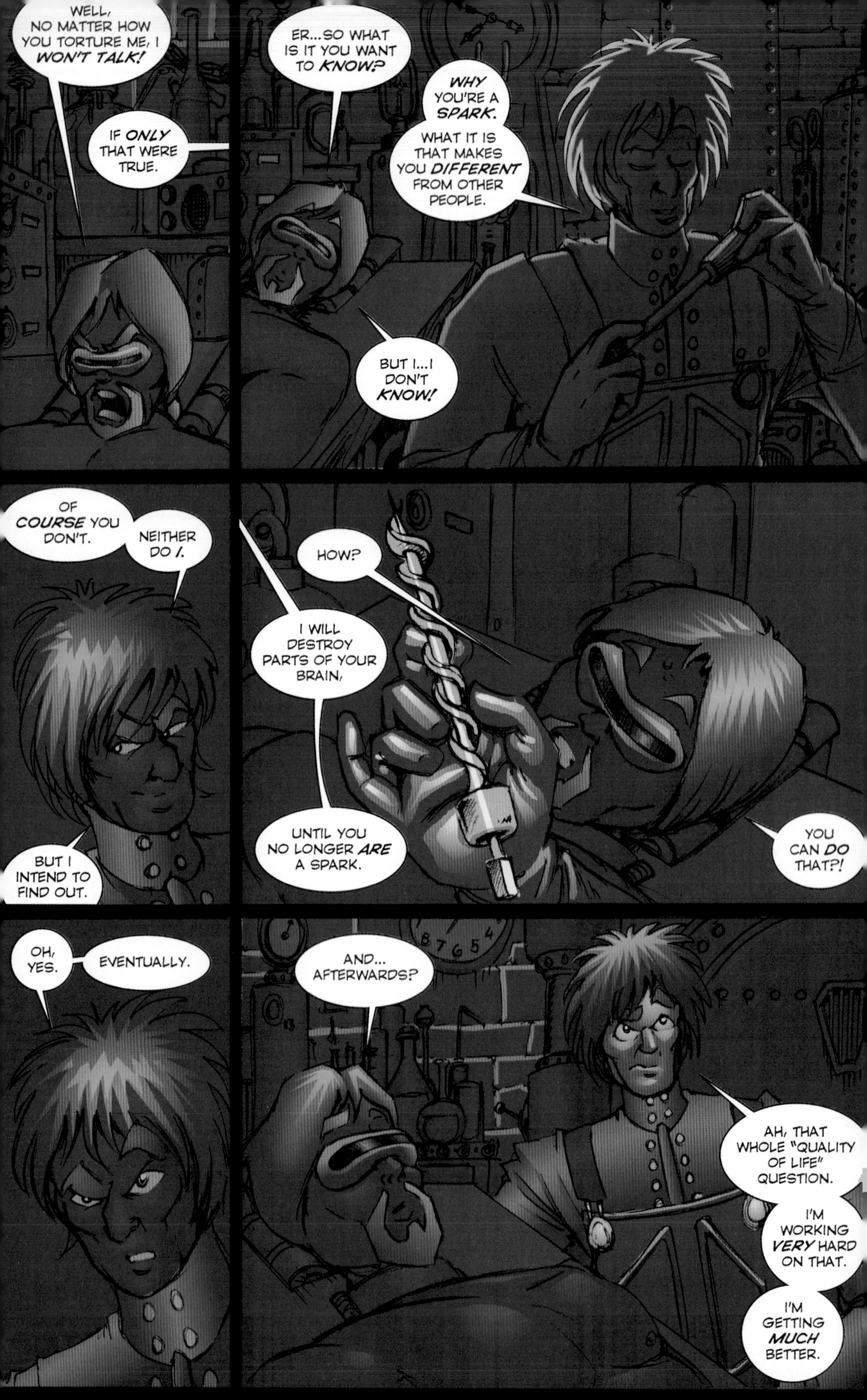
WELL, NO MATTER HOW YOU TORTURE ME, I WON'T TALK!
IF ONLY THAT WERE TRUE.
ER...SO WHAT IS IT YOU WANT TO KNOW?
WHY YOU'RE A SPARK.
WHAT IT IS THAT MAKES YOU DIFFERENT FROM OTHER PEOPLE.
BUT I...I DON'T KNOW!
OF COURSE YOU DON'T.
NEITHER DO I.
BUT I INTEND TO FIND OUT.
HOW?
I WILL DESTROY PARTS OF YOUR BRAIN,
UNTIL YOU NO LONGER ARE A SPARK.
YOU CAN DO THAT?!
OH, YES.
EVENTUALLY.
AND... AFTERWARDS?
AH, THAT WHOLE "QUALITY OF LIFE" QUESTION.
I'M WORKING VERY HARD ON THAT.
I'M GETTING MUCH BETTER.

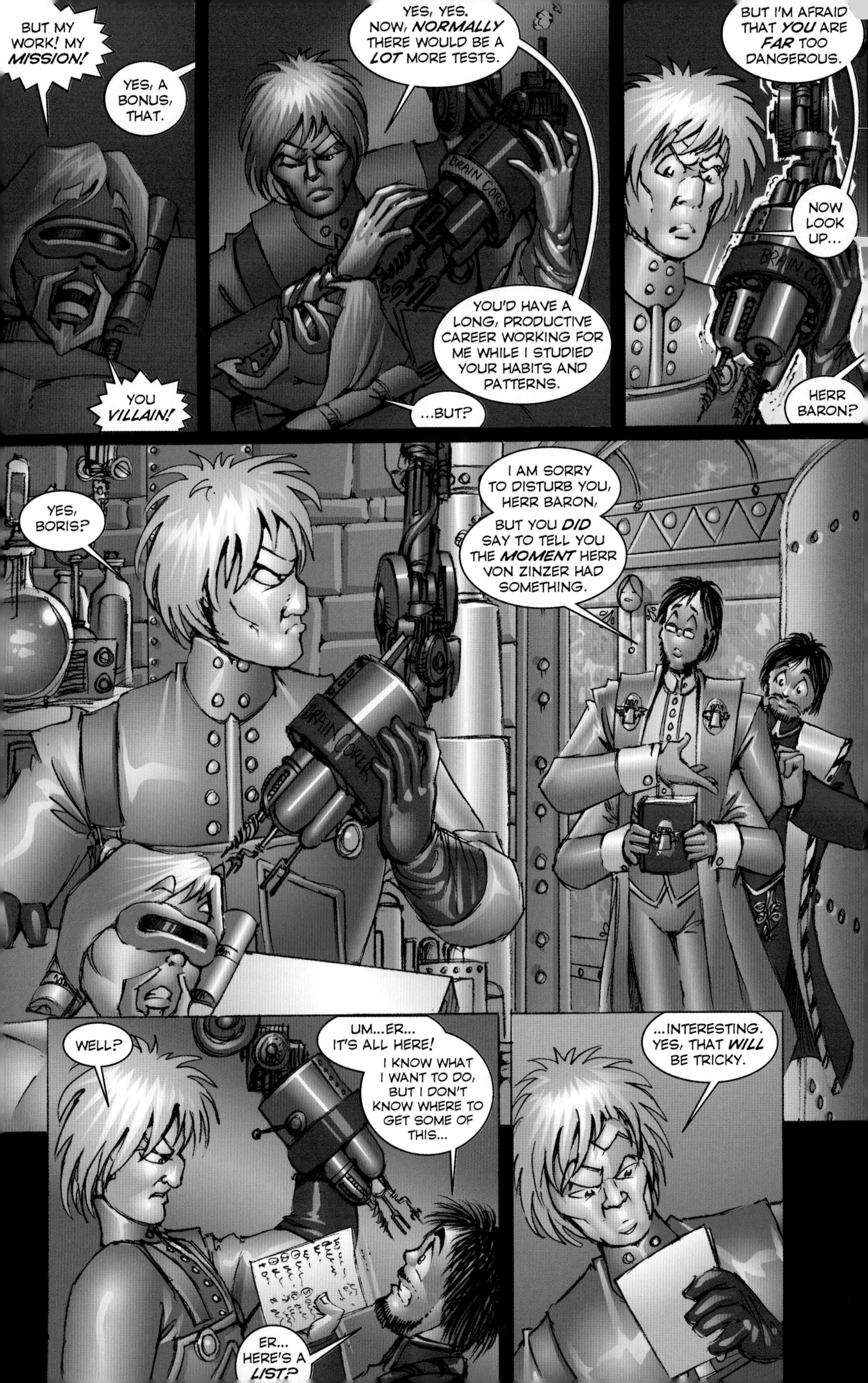
BUT MY WORK! MY MISSION!
YES, A BONUS, THAT.
YOU VILLAIN!
YES, YES. NOW, NORMALLY THERE WOULD BE A LOT MORE TESTS.
BRAIN CORER
YOU'D HAVE A LONG, PRODUCTIVE CAREER WORKING FOR ME WHILE I STUDIED YOUR HABITS AND PATTERNS.
...BUT?
BUT I'M AFRAID THAT YOU ARE FAR TOO DANGEROUS.
NOW LOOK UP...
HERR BARON?
YES, BORIS?
I AM SORRY TO DISTURB YOU, HERR BARON,
BUT YOU DID SAY TO TELL YOU THE MOMENT HERR VON ZINZER HAD SOMETHING.
BRAIN CORER
WELL?
UM...ER... IT'S ALL HERE!
I KNOW WHAT I WANT TO DO, BUT I DON'T KNOW WHERE TO GET SOME OF THIS...
ER... HERE'S A LIST?
...INTERESTING. YES, THAT WILL BE TRICKY.

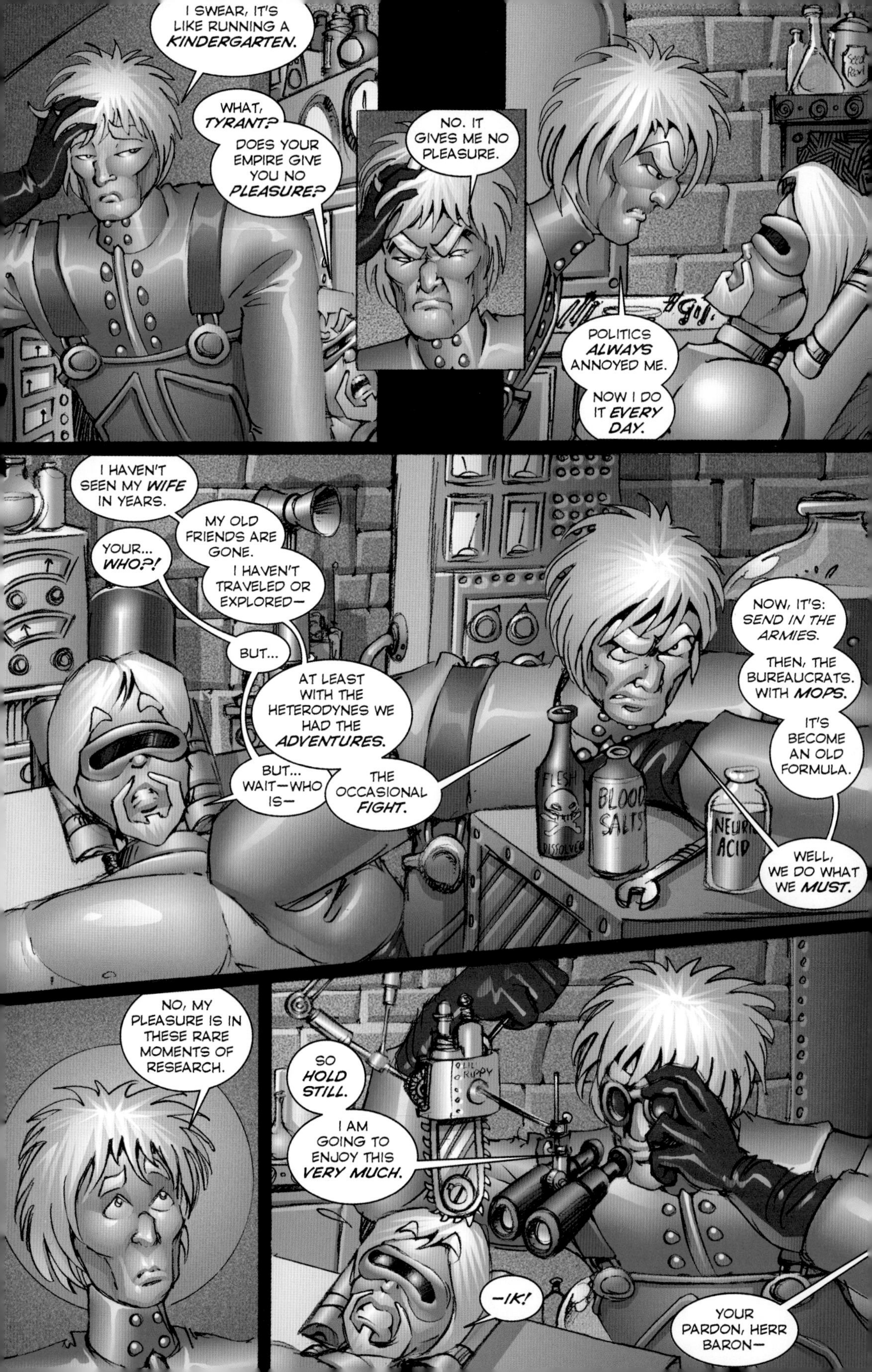
I SWEAR, IT'S LIKE RUNNING A *KINDERGARTEN.*
WHAT, *TYRANT?*
DOES YOUR EMPIRE GIVE YOU NO *PLEASURE?*
NO. IT GIVES ME NO PLEASURE.
POLITICS *ALWAYS* ANNOYED ME.
NOW I DO IT *EVERY DAY.*
I HAVEN'T SEEN MY *WIFE* IN YEARS.
MY OLD FRIENDS ARE GONE.
YOUR... *WHO?!*
I HAVEN'T TRAVELED OR EXPLORED—
BUT...
AT LEAST WITH THE HETERODYNES WE HAD THE *ADVENTURES.*
BUT... WAIT—WHO IS—
THE OCCASIONAL *FIGHT.*
FLESH DISSOLVER
BLOOD SALTS
NEURIC ACID
NOW, IT'S: *SEND IN THE ARMIES.*
THEN, THE BUREAUCRATS. WITH *MOPS.*
IT'S BECOME AN OLD FORMULA.
WELL, WE DO WHAT WE *MUST.*
NO, MY PLEASURE IS IN THESE RARE MOMENTS OF RESEARCH.
SO *HOLD STILL.*
I AM GOING TO ENJOY THIS *VERY MUCH.*
LIL RIPPY
—*IK!*
YOUR PARDON, HERR BARON—

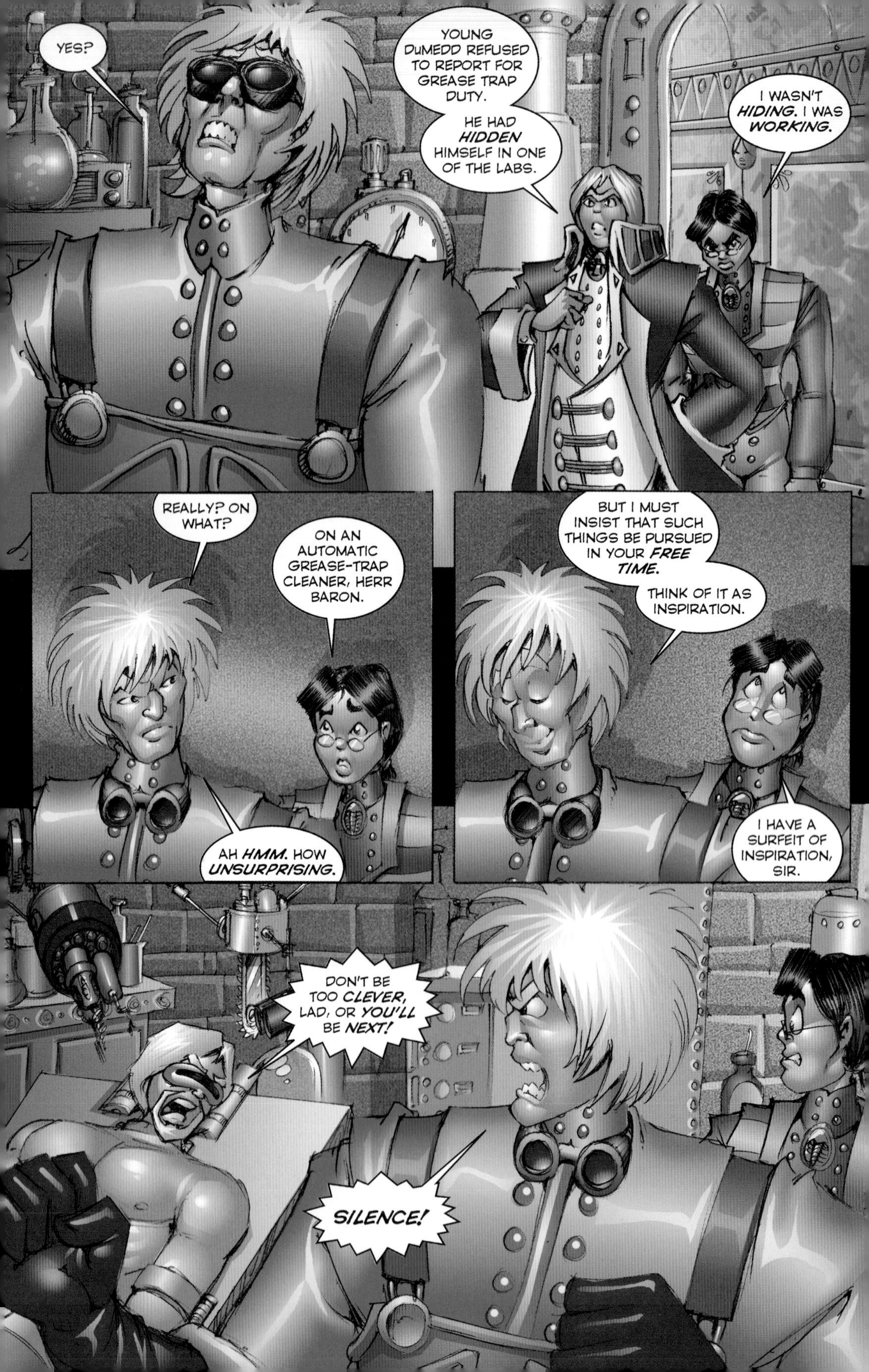

YES?
YOUNG DuMEDD REFUSED TO REPORT FOR GREASE TRAP DUTY.
HE HAD *HIDDEN* HIMSELF IN ONE OF THE LABS.
I WASN'T *HIDING*. I WAS *WORKING*.
REALLY? ON WHAT?
ON AN AUTOMATIC GREASE-TRAP CLEANER, HERR BARON.
AH *HMM*. HOW *UNSURPRISING*.
BUT I MUST INSIST THAT SUCH THINGS BE PURSUED IN YOUR *FREE TIME*.
THINK OF IT AS INSPIRATION.
I HAVE A SURFEIT OF INSPIRATION, SIR.
DON'T BE TOO *CLEVER*, LAD, OR *YOU'LL* BE *NEXT!*
SILENCE!

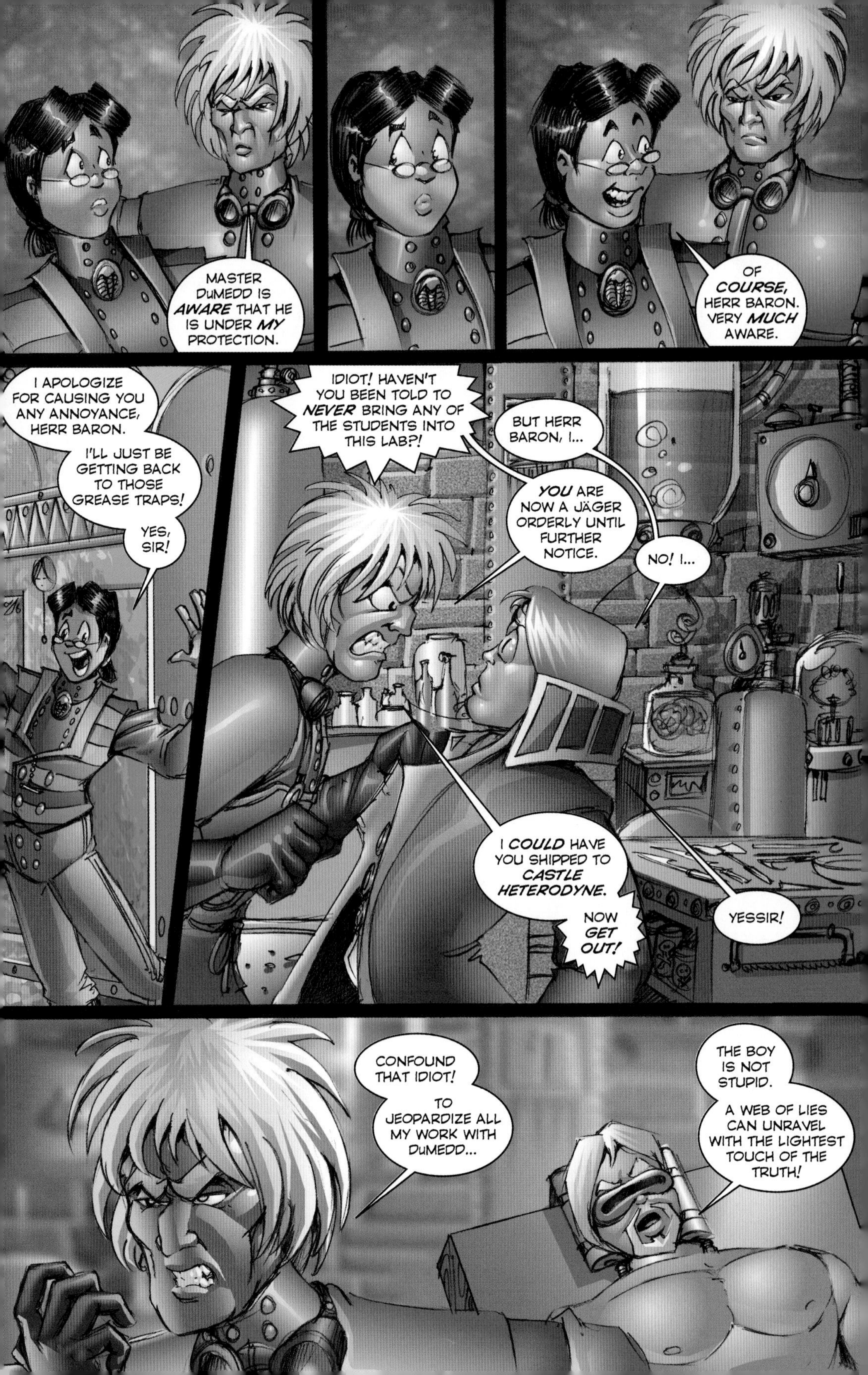
MASTER DuMEDD IS *AWARE* THAT HE IS UNDER *MY* PROTECTION.
OF *COURSE,* HERR BARON. VERY *MUCH* AWARE.
I APOLOGIZE FOR CAUSING YOU ANY ANNOYANCE, HERR BARON.
I'LL JUST BE GETTING BACK TO THOSE GREASE TRAPS!
YES, SIR!
IDIOT! HAVEN'T YOU BEEN TOLD TO *NEVER* BRING ANY OF THE STUDENTS INTO THIS LAB?!
BUT HERR BARON, I...
YOU ARE NOW A JÄGER ORDERLY UNTIL FURTHER NOTICE.
NO! I...
I *COULD* HAVE YOU SHIPPED TO *CASTLE HETERODYNE.*
NOW *GET OUT!*
YESSIR!
CONFOUND THAT IDIOT!
TO JEOPARDIZE ALL MY WORK WITH DuMEDD...
THE BOY IS NOT STUPID.
A WEB OF LIES CAN UNRAVEL WITH THE LIGHTEST TOUCH OF THE TRUTH!

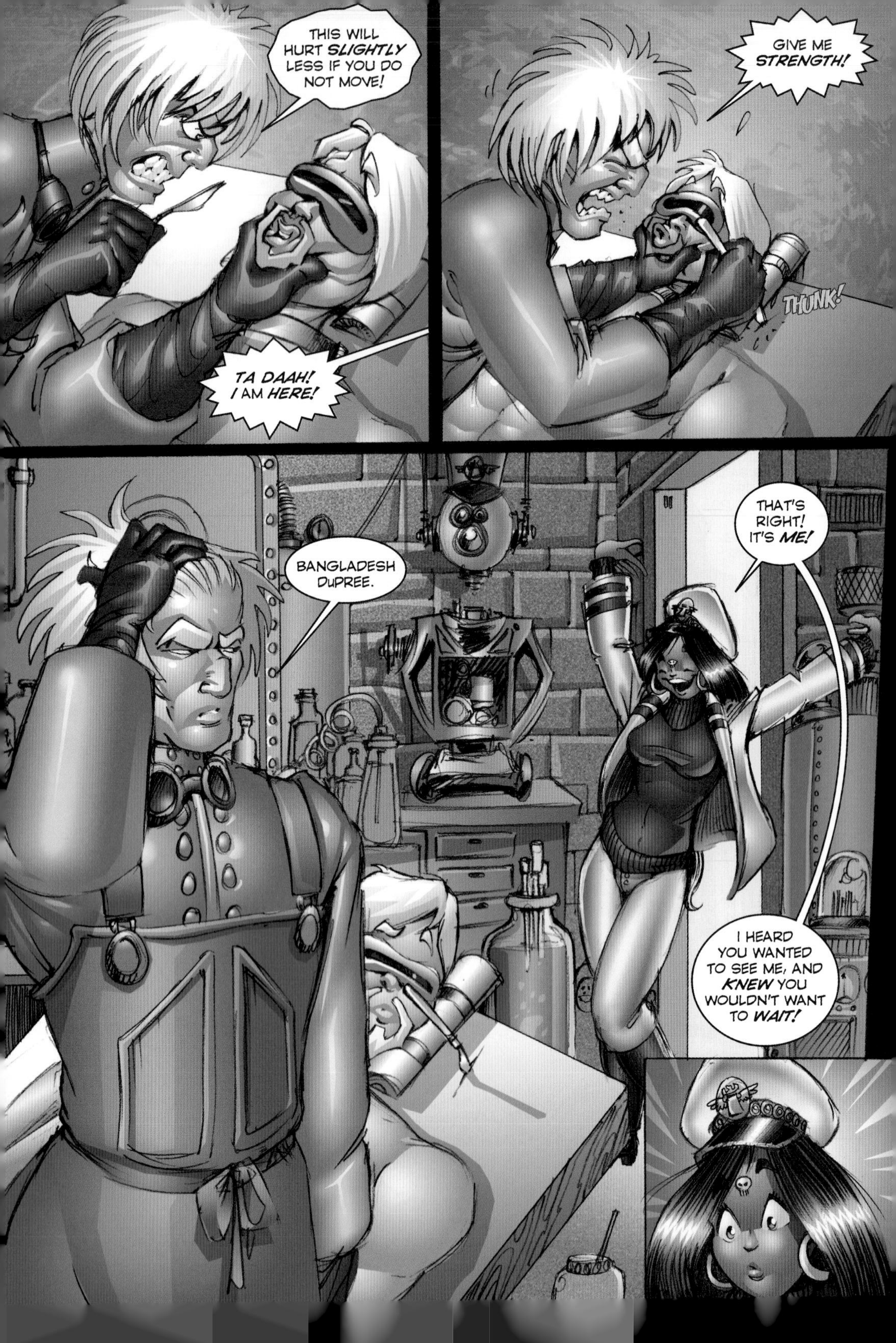

THIS WILL HURT *SLIGHTLY* LESS IF YOU DO NOT MOVE!
TA DAAH! I AM HERE!
GIVE ME *STRENGTH!*
THUNK!
BANGLADESH DuPREE.
THAT'S RIGHT! IT'S *ME!*
I HEARD YOU WANTED TO SEE ME, AND *KNEW* YOU WOULDN'T WANT TO *WAIT!*

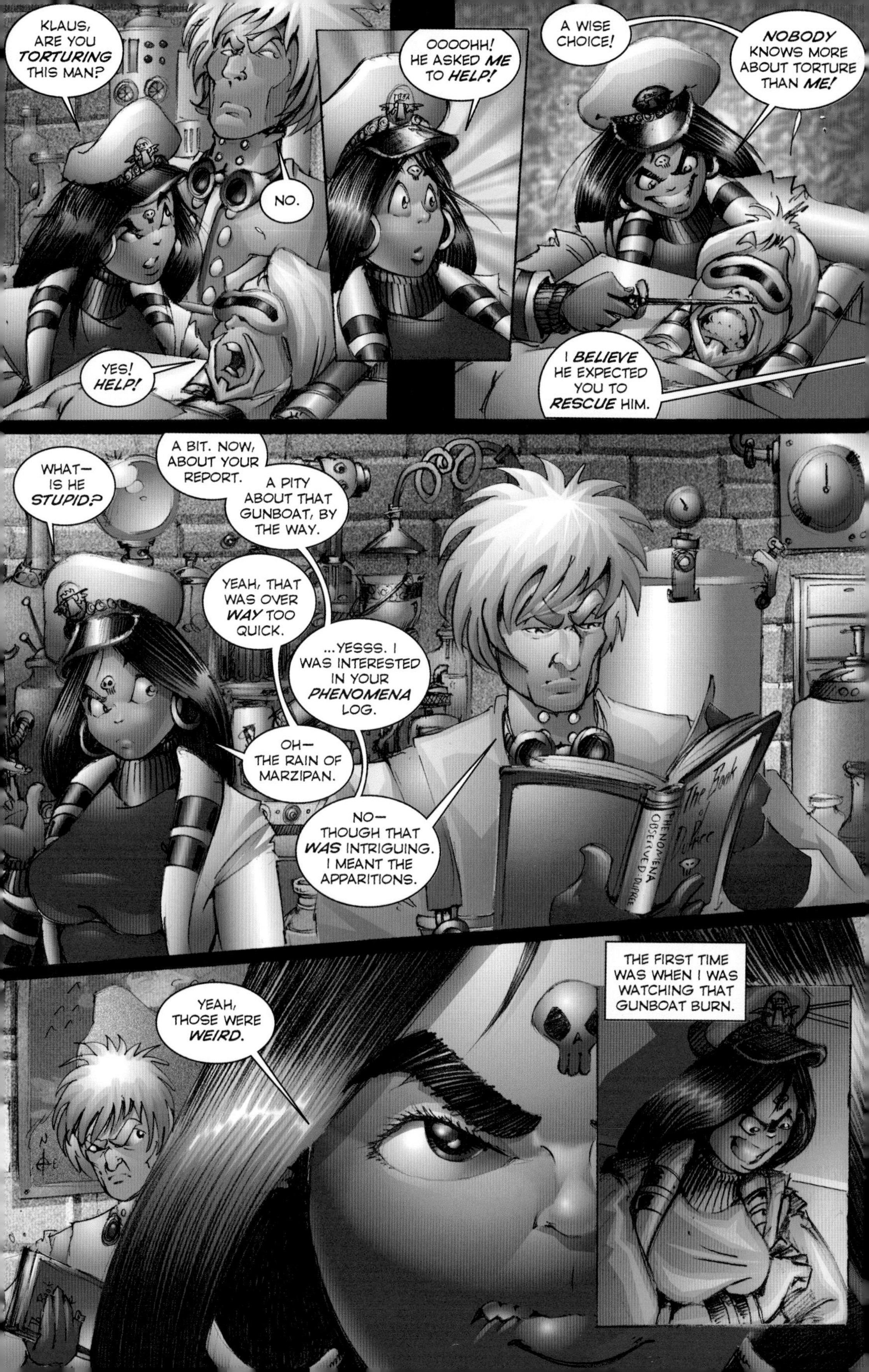

KLAUS, ARE YOU TORTURING THIS MAN?
NO.
YES! HELP!
OOOOHH! HE ASKED ME TO HELP!
A WISE CHOICE!
NOBODY KNOWS MORE ABOUT TORTURE THAN ME!
I BELIEVE HE EXPECTED YOU TO RESCUE HIM.
WHAT— IS HE STUPID?
A BIT. NOW, ABOUT YOUR REPORT.
A PITY ABOUT THAT GUNBOAT, BY THE WAY.
YEAH, THAT WAS OVER WAY TOO QUICK.
...YESSS. I WAS INTERESTED IN YOUR PHENOMENA LOG.
OH— THE RAIN OF MARZIPAN.
NO— THOUGH THAT WAS INTRIGUING. I MEANT THE APPARITIONS.
The Book of DuPree
PHENOMENA OBSERVED: DUPREE
YEAH, THOSE WERE WEIRD.
THE FIRST TIME WAS WHEN I WAS WATCHING THAT GUNBOAT BURN.

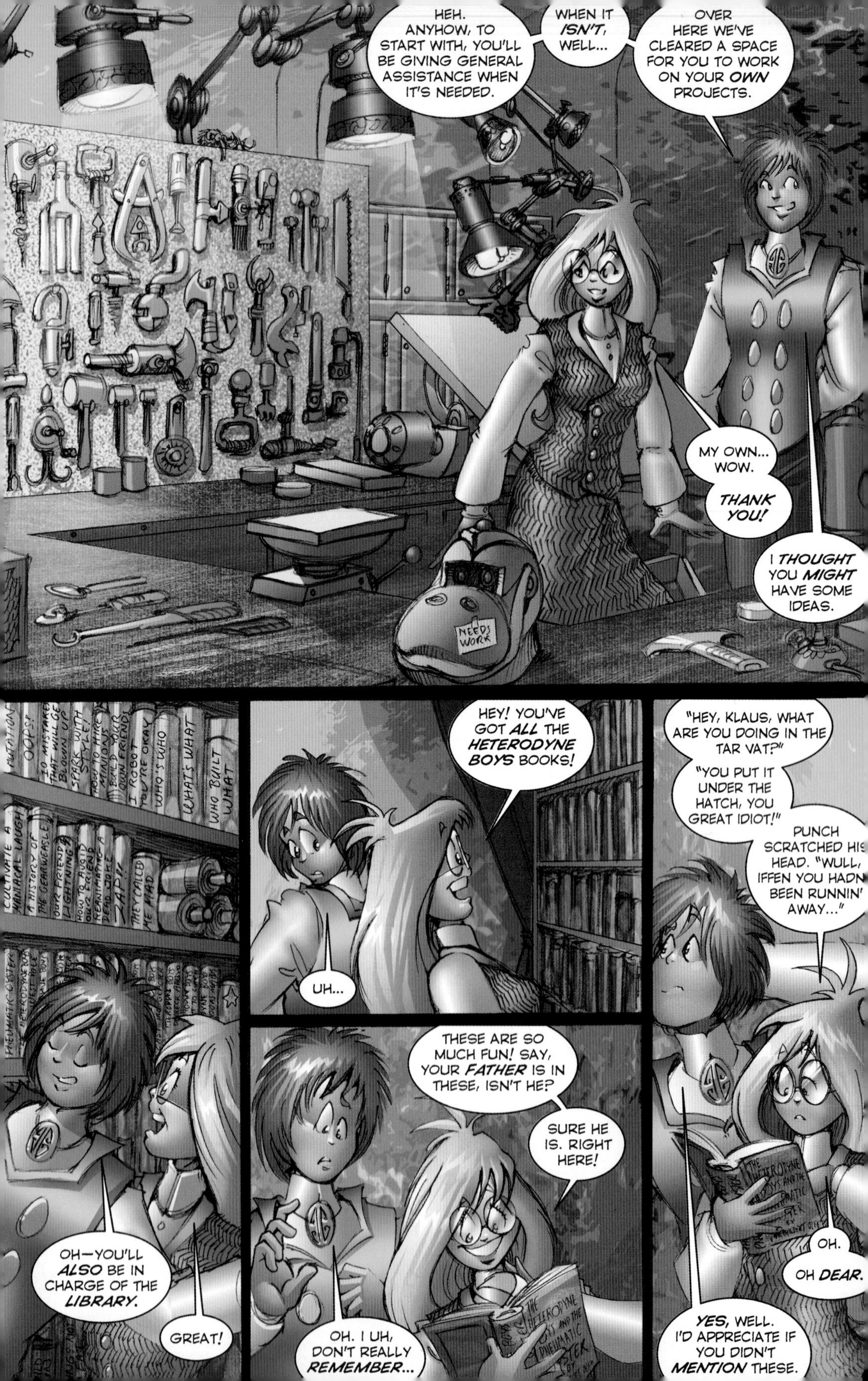
HEH. ANYHOW, TO START WITH, YOU'LL BE GIVING GENERAL ASSISTANCE WHEN IT'S NEEDED.
WHEN IT *ISN'T*, WELL...
OVER HERE WE'VE CLEARED A SPACE FOR YOU TO WORK ON YOUR *OWN* PROJECTS.
MY OWN... WOW.
THANK YOU!
I ***THOUGHT*** YOU ***MIGHT*** HAVE SOME IDEAS.
NEEDS WORK
OOPS!
WHO'S WHO
WHAT'S WHAT
WHO BUILT WHAT
ZAP!!
THEY CALLED ME MAD
OH—YOU'LL ***ALSO*** BE IN CHARGE OF THE ***LIBRARY***.
GREAT!
HEY! YOU'VE GOT ***ALL*** THE ***HETERODYNE BOYS*** BOOKS!
UH...
THESE ARE SO MUCH FUN! SAY, YOUR ***FATHER*** IS IN THESE, ISN'T HE?
SURE HE IS. RIGHT HERE!
OH. I UH, DON'T REALLY ***REMEMBER***...
"HEY, KLAUS, WHAT ARE YOU DOING IN THE TAR VAT?"
"YOU PUT IT UNDER THE HATCH, YOU GREAT IDIOT!"
PUNCH SCRATCHED HIS HEAD. "WULL, IFFEN YOU HADN' BEEN RUNNIN' AWAY..."
OH.
OH ***DEAR***.
YES, WELL. I'D APPRECIATE IF YOU DIDN'T ***MENTION*** THESE.

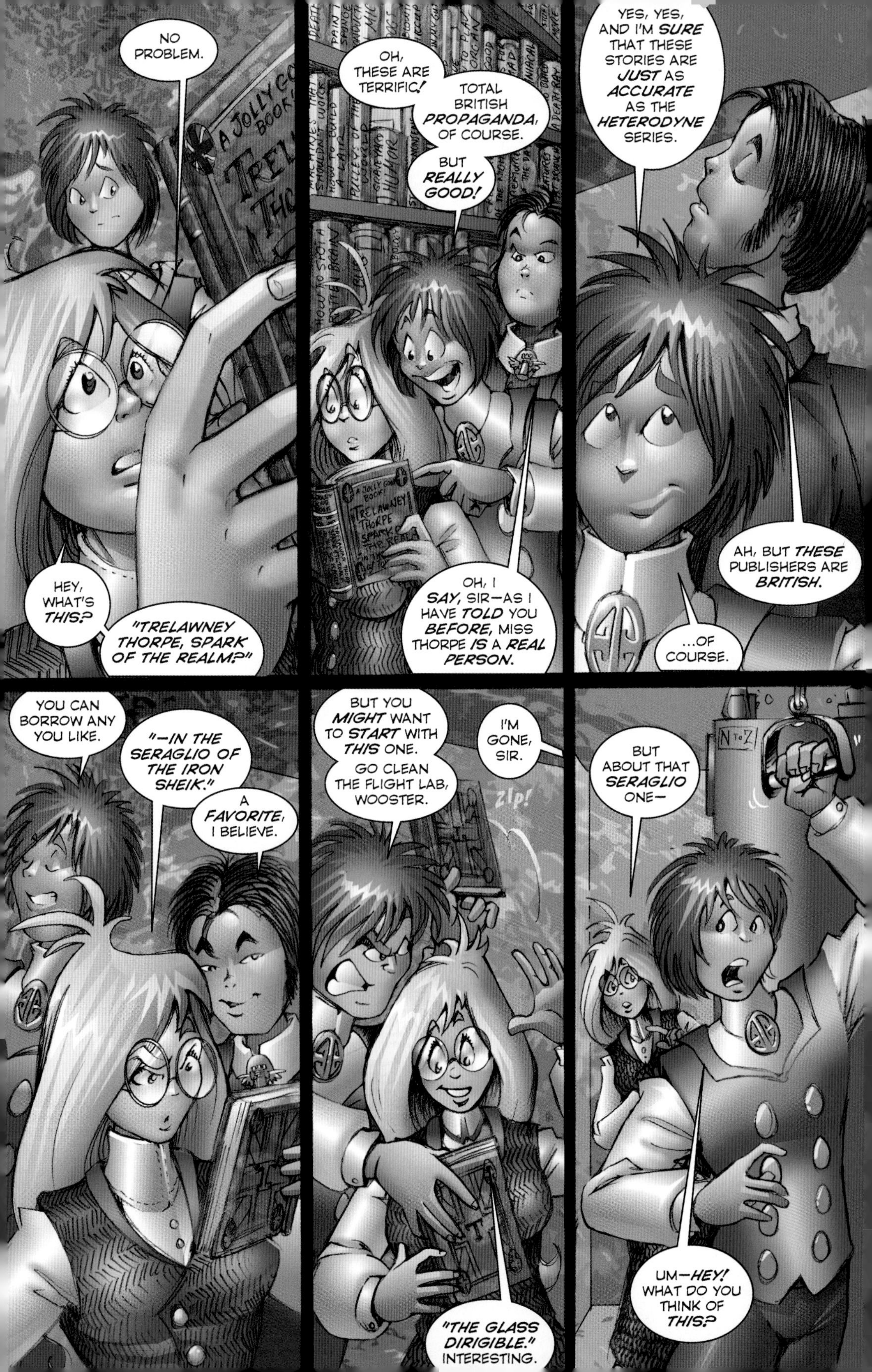

NO PROBLEM.
HEY, WHAT'S *THIS?*
"TRELAWNEY THORPE, SPARK OF THE REALM?"
OH, THESE ARE TERRIFIC!
TOTAL BRITISH *PROPAGANDA*, OF COURSE.
BUT *REALLY GOOD!*
OH, I *SAY,* SIR—AS I HAVE *TOLD* YOU *BEFORE,* MISS THORPE *IS* A *REAL PERSON.*
YES, YES, AND I'M *SURE* THAT THESE STORIES ARE *JUST* AS *ACCURATE* AS THE *HETERODYNE* SERIES.
AH, BUT *THESE* PUBLISHERS ARE *BRITISH.*
...OF COURSE.
YOU CAN BORROW ANY YOU LIKE.
"—IN THE SERAGLIO OF THE IRON SHEIK."
A *FAVORITE,* I BELIEVE.
BUT YOU *MIGHT* WANT TO *START* WITH *THIS* ONE.
GO CLEAN THE FLIGHT LAB, WOOSTER.
I'M GONE, SIR.
ZIP!
"THE GLASS DIRIGIBLE." INTERESTING.
BUT ABOUT THAT *SERAGLIO* ONE—
UM—*HEY!* WHAT DO YOU THINK OF *THIS?*

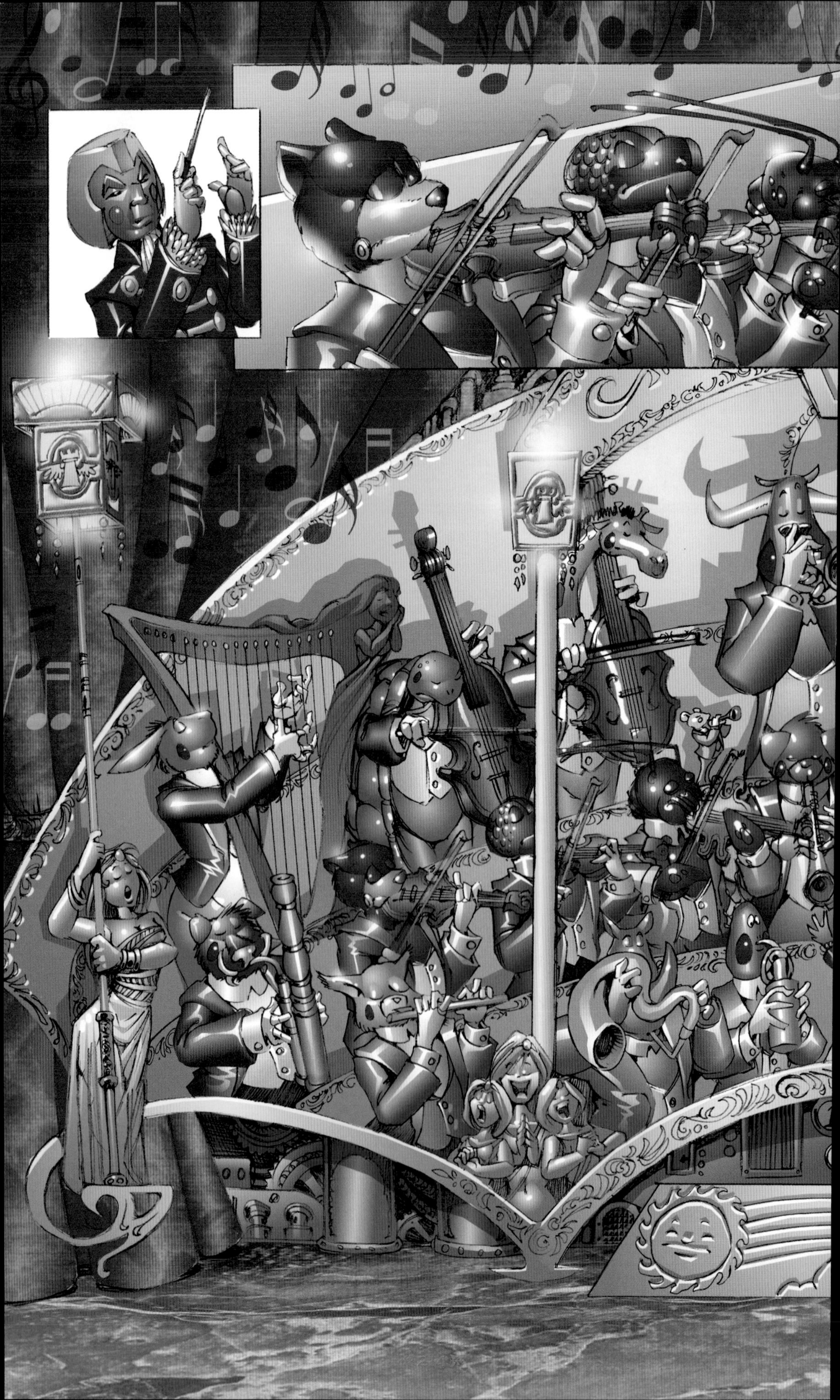

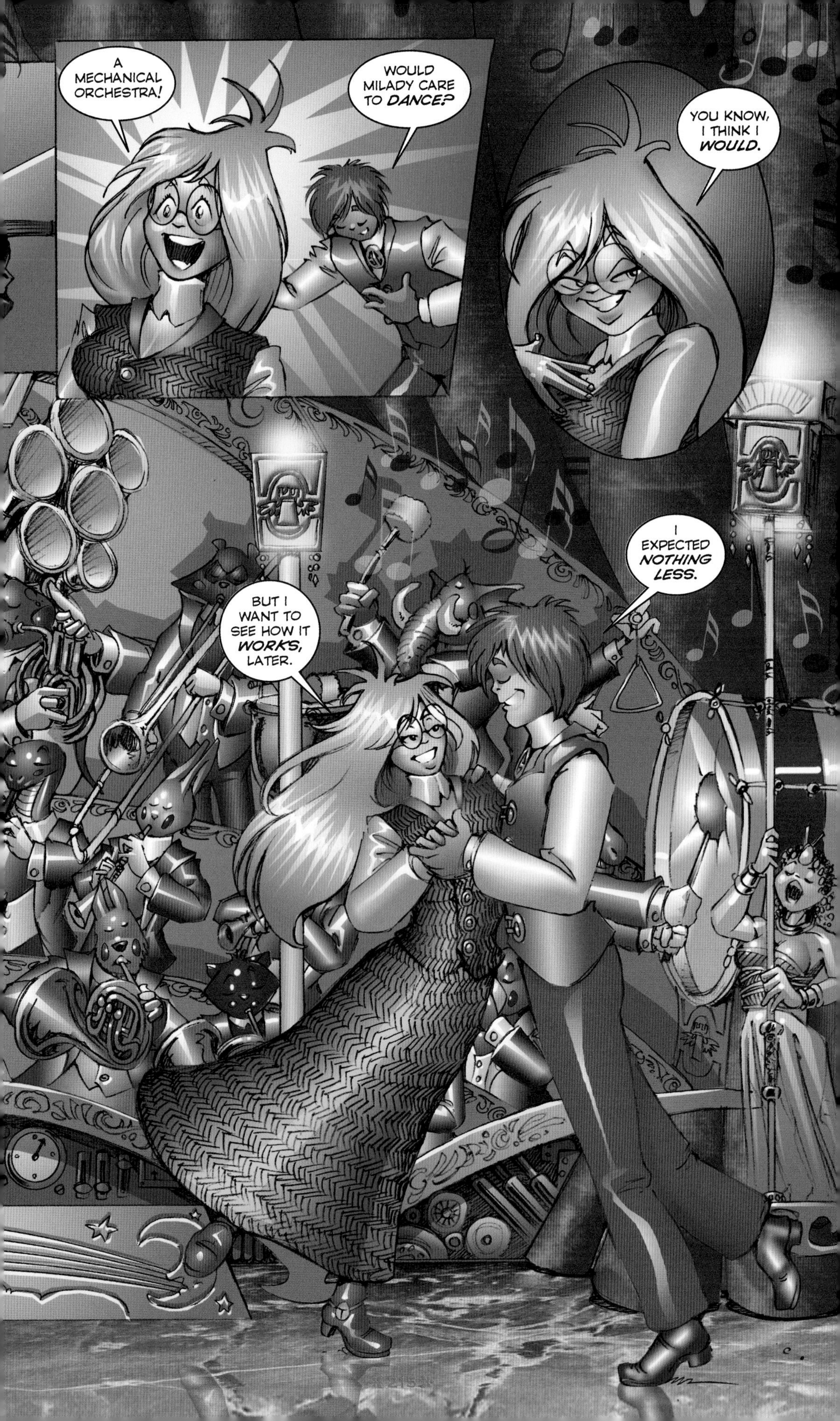
A MECHANICAL ORCHESTRA!
WOULD MILADY CARE TO *DANCE?*
YOU KNOW, I THINK I *WOULD.*
BUT I WANT TO SEE HOW IT *WORKS,* LATER.
I EXPECTED *NOTHING LESS.*

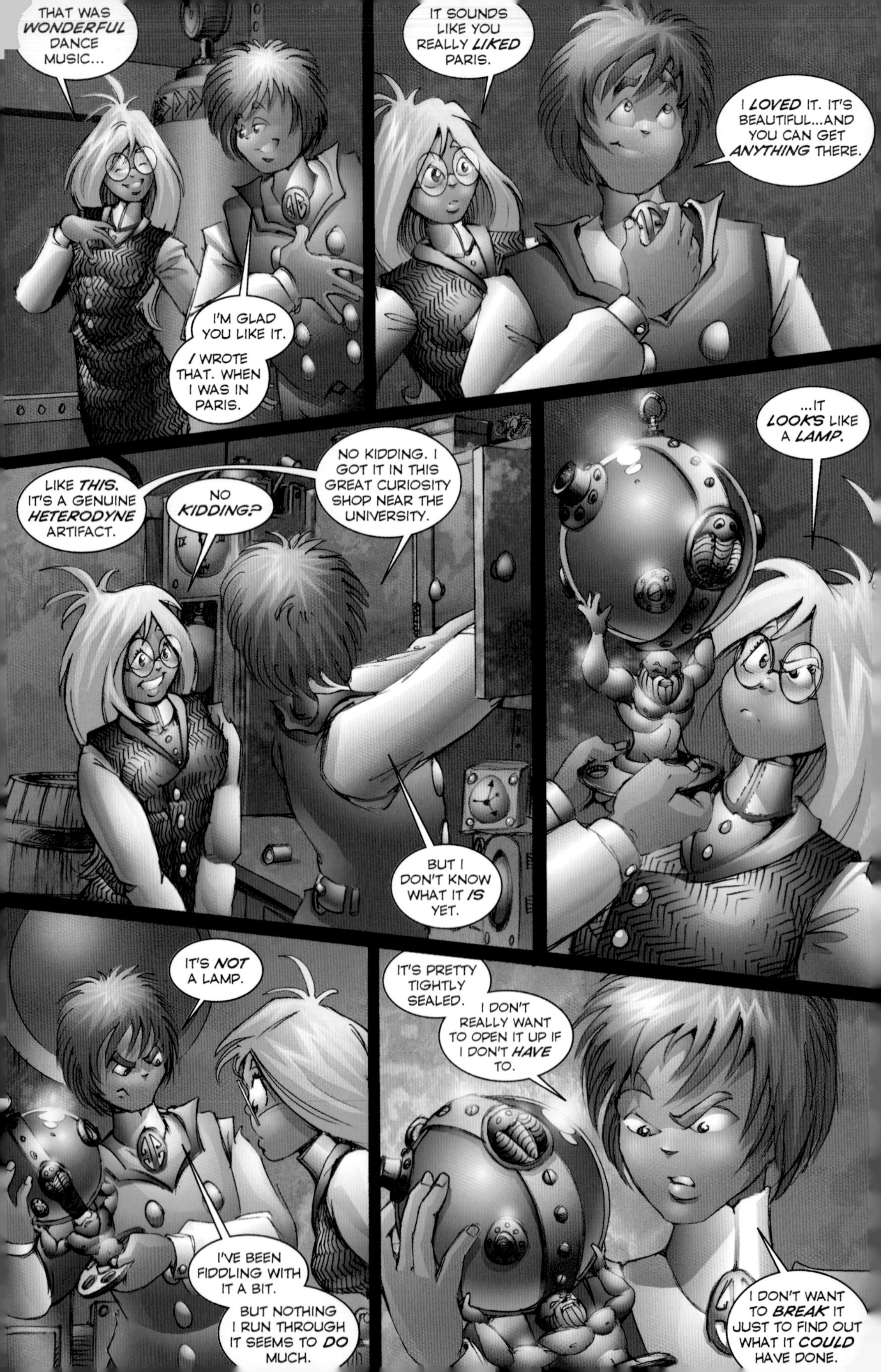
THAT WAS WONDERFUL DANCE MUSIC...
I'M GLAD YOU LIKE IT.
I WROTE THAT. WHEN I WAS IN PARIS.
IT SOUNDS LIKE YOU REALLY LIKED PARIS.
I LOVED IT. IT'S BEAUTIFUL...AND YOU CAN GET ANYTHING THERE.
LIKE THIS. IT'S A GENUINE HETERODYNE ARTIFACT.
NO KIDDING?
NO KIDDING. I GOT IT IN THIS GREAT CURIOSITY SHOP NEAR THE UNIVERSITY.
BUT I DON'T KNOW WHAT IT IS YET.
...IT LOOKS LIKE A LAMP.
IT'S NOT A LAMP.
I'VE BEEN FIDDLING WITH IT A BIT.
BUT NOTHING I RUN THROUGH IT SEEMS TO DO MUCH.
IT'S PRETTY TIGHTLY SEALED.
I DON'T REALLY WANT TO OPEN IT UP IF I DON'T HAVE TO.
I DON'T WANT TO BREAK IT JUST TO FIND OUT WHAT IT COULD HAVE DONE.

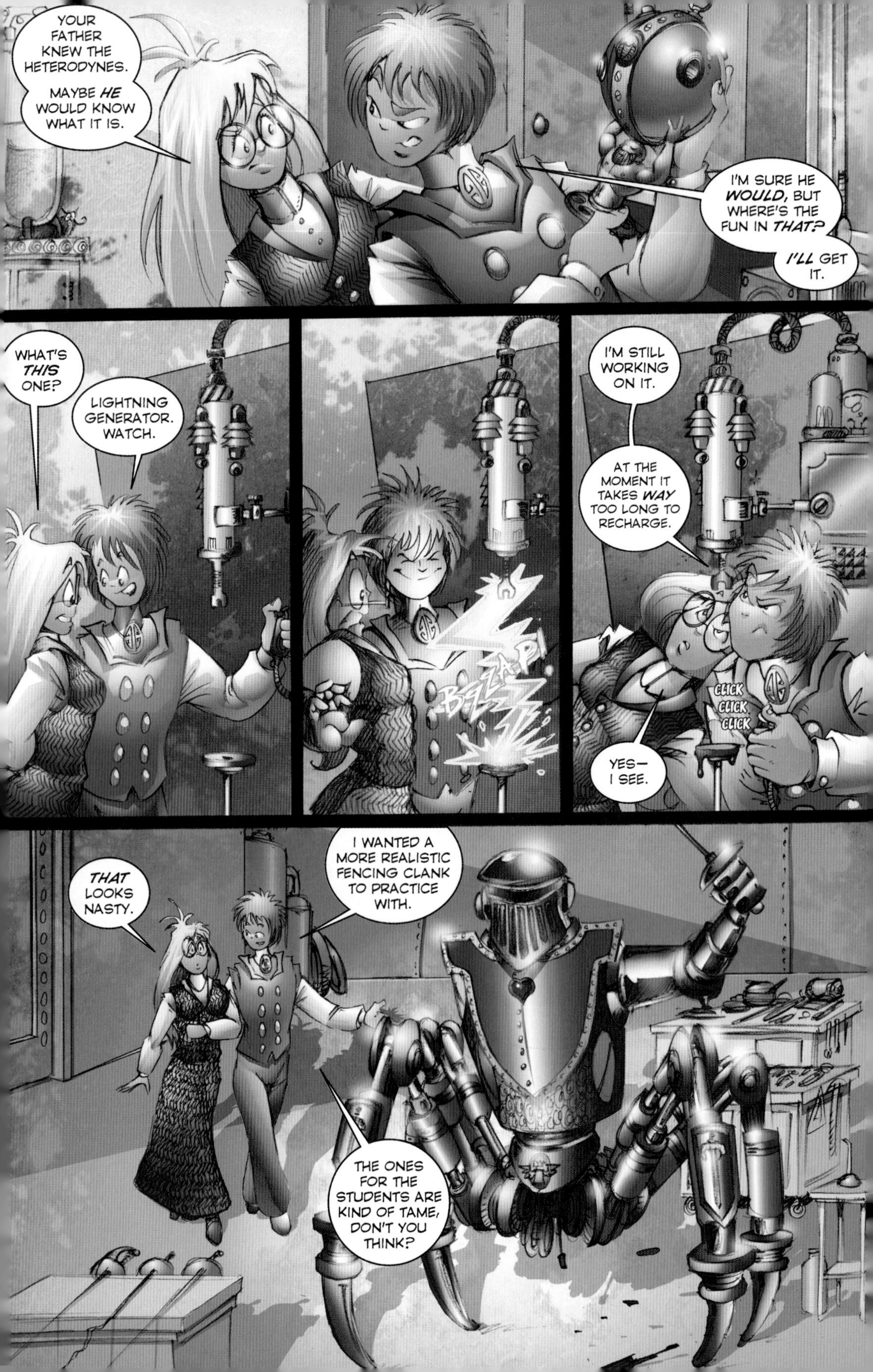

YOUR FATHER KNEW THE HETERODYNES.
MAYBE *HE* WOULD KNOW WHAT IT IS.
I'M SURE HE *WOULD,* BUT WHERE'S THE FUN IN *THAT?*
I'LL GET IT.
WHAT'S *THIS* ONE?
LIGHTNING GENERATOR. WATCH.
BZZAP!
I'M STILL WORKING ON IT.
AT THE MOMENT IT TAKES *WAY* TOO LONG TO RECHARGE.
CLICK CLICK CLICK
YES— I SEE.
THAT LOOKS NASTY.
I WANTED A MORE REALISTIC FENCING CLANK TO PRACTICE WITH.
THE ONES FOR THE STUDENTS ARE KIND OF TAME, DON'T YOU THINK?

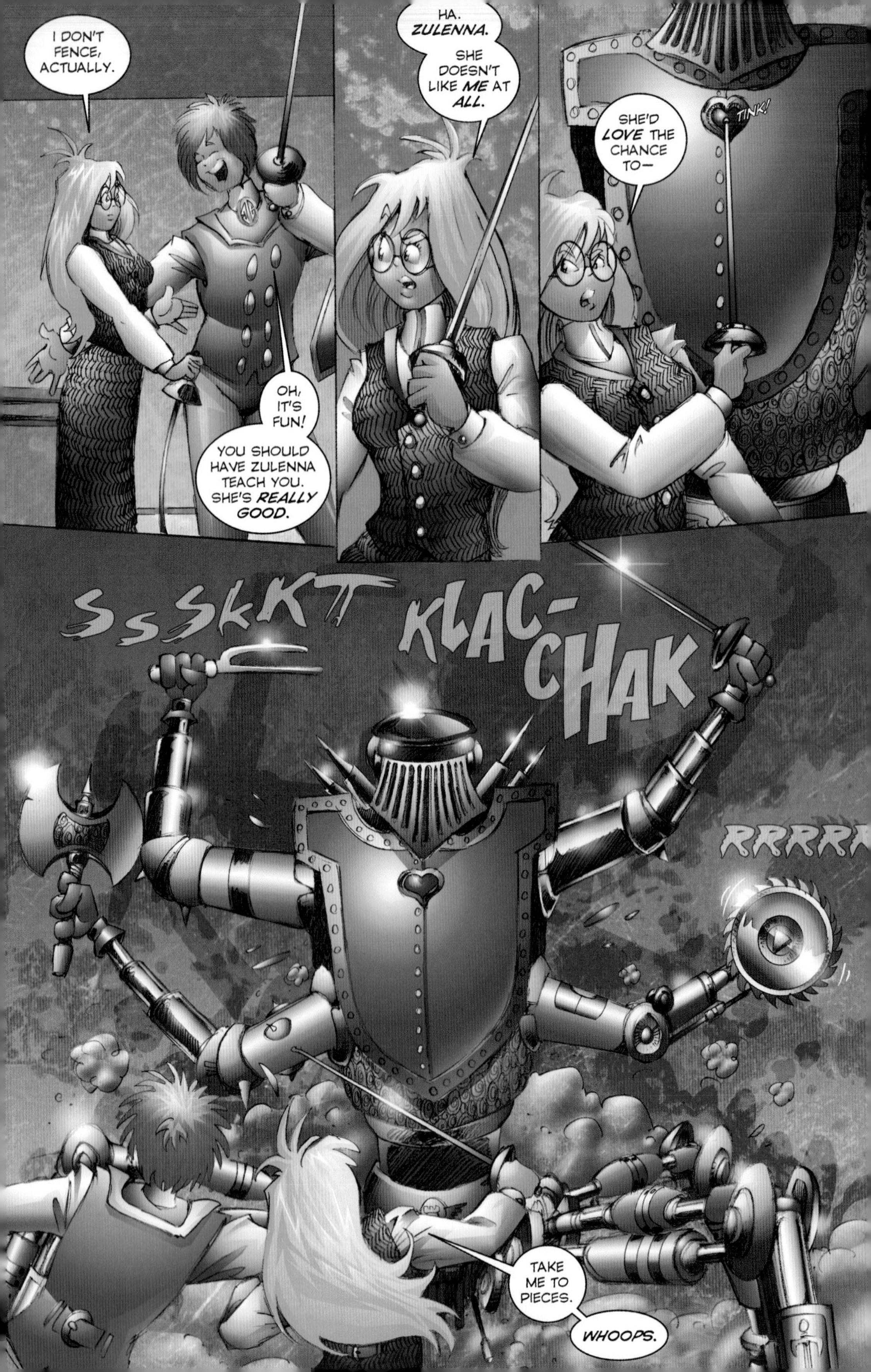
I DON'T FENCE, ACTUALLY.
OH, IT'S FUN!
YOU SHOULD HAVE ZULENNA TEACH YOU. SHE'S *REALLY GOOD*.
HA. *ZULENNA*.
SHE DOESN'T LIKE *ME* AT *ALL*.
SHE'D *LOVE* THE CHANCE TO—
TINK!
SSSKKT
KLAC-CHAK
RRRRR
TAKE ME TO PIECES.
WHOOPS.

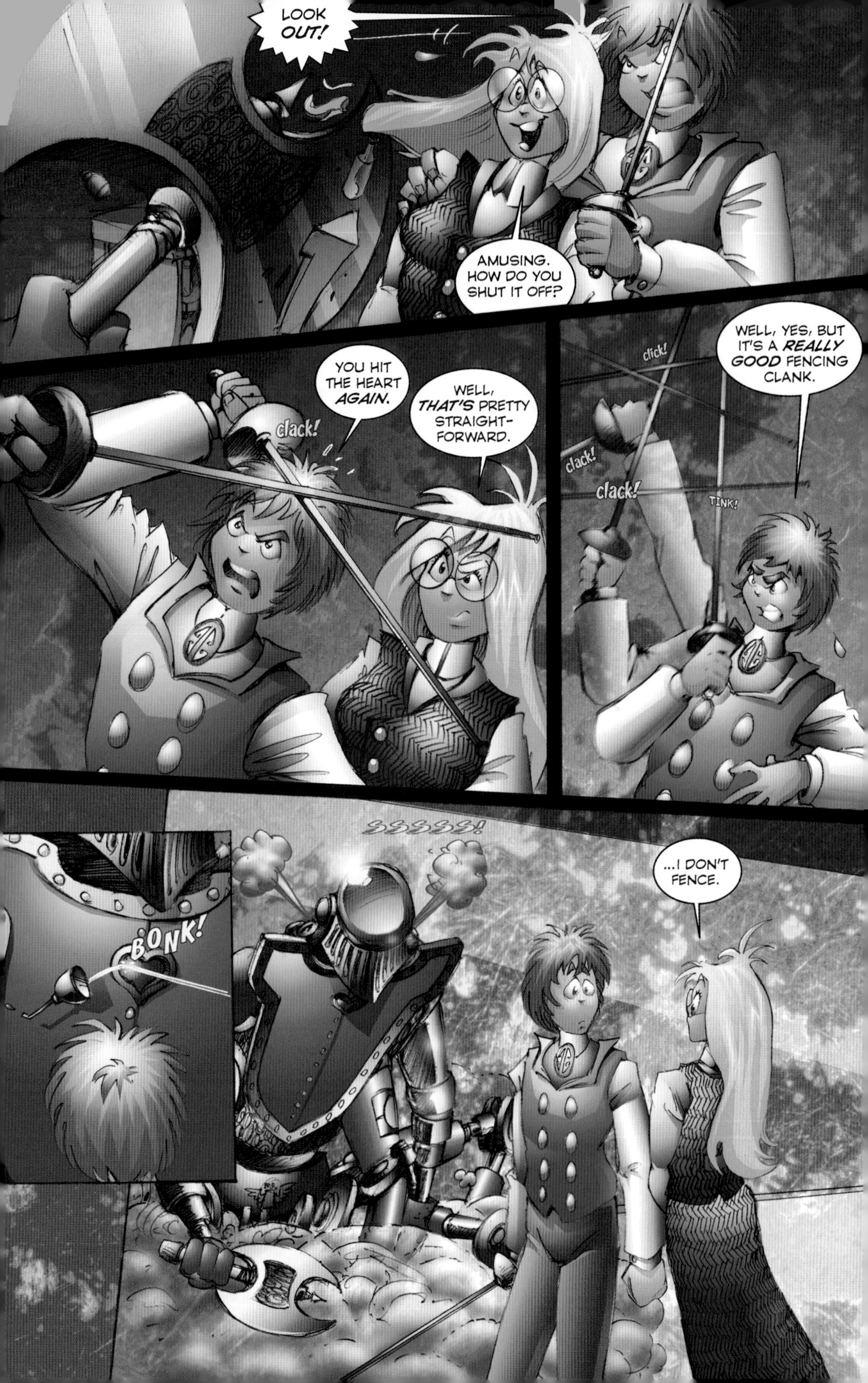
LOOK OUT!
AMUSING. HOW DO YOU SHUT IT OFF?
clack!
YOU HIT THE HEART AGAIN.
WELL, THAT'S PRETTY STRAIGHT-FORWARD.
click!
clack!
clack!
TINK!
WELL, YES, BUT IT'S A REALLY GOOD FENCING CLANK.
SSSSSS!
BONK!
...I DON'T FENCE.

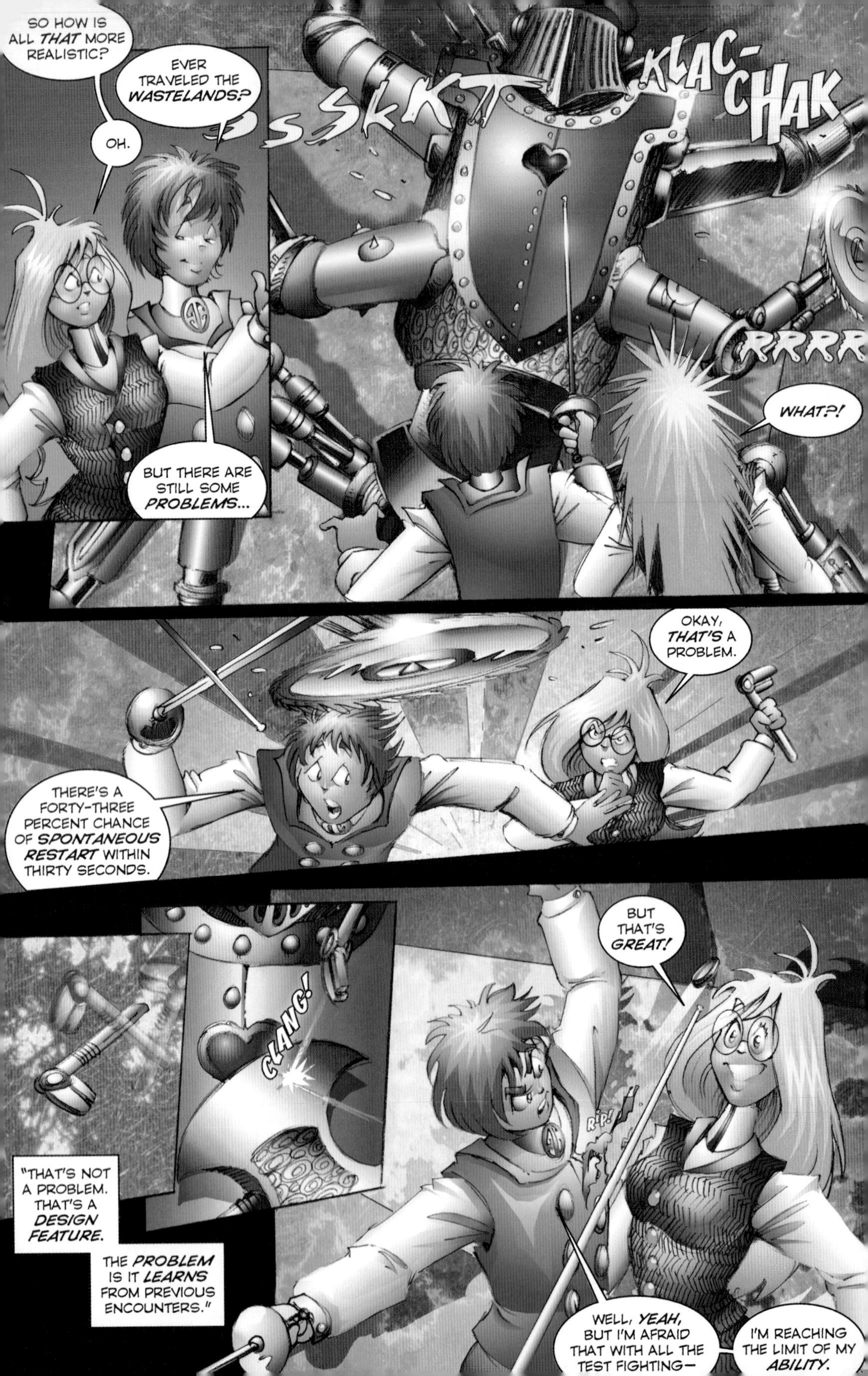
SO HOW IS ALL THAT MORE REALISTIC?
EVER TRAVELED THE WASTELANDS?
OH.
SSSKKT
KLAC-CHAK
RRRR
BUT THERE ARE STILL SOME PROBLEMS...
WHAT?!
OKAY, THAT'S A PROBLEM.
THERE'S A FORTY-THREE PERCENT CHANCE OF SPONTANEOUS RESTART WITHIN THIRTY SECONDS.
BUT THAT'S GREAT!
CLANG!
RIP!
"THAT'S NOT A PROBLEM. THAT'S A DESIGN FEATURE.
THE PROBLEM IS IT LEARNS FROM PREVIOUS ENCOUNTERS."
WELL, YEAH, BUT I'M AFRAID THAT WITH ALL THE TEST FIGHTING—
I'M REACHING THE LIMIT OF MY ABILITY.

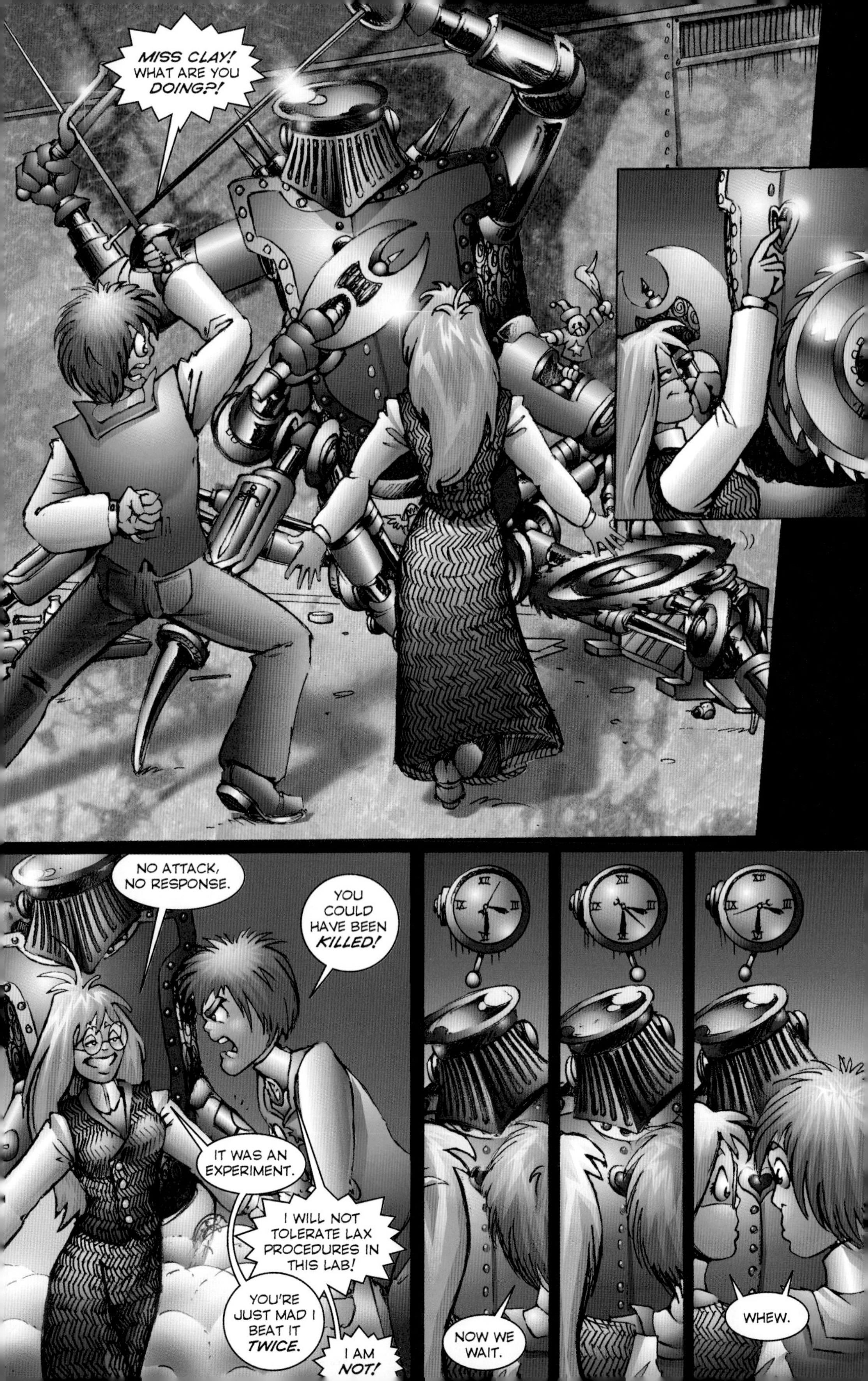
MISS CLAY! WHAT ARE YOU DOING?!
NO ATTACK, NO RESPONSE.
YOU COULD HAVE BEEN KILLED!
IT WAS AN EXPERIMENT.
I WILL NOT TOLERATE LAX PROCEDURES IN THIS LAB!
YOU'RE JUST MAD I BEAT IT TWICE.
I AM NOT!
NOW WE WAIT.
WHEW.

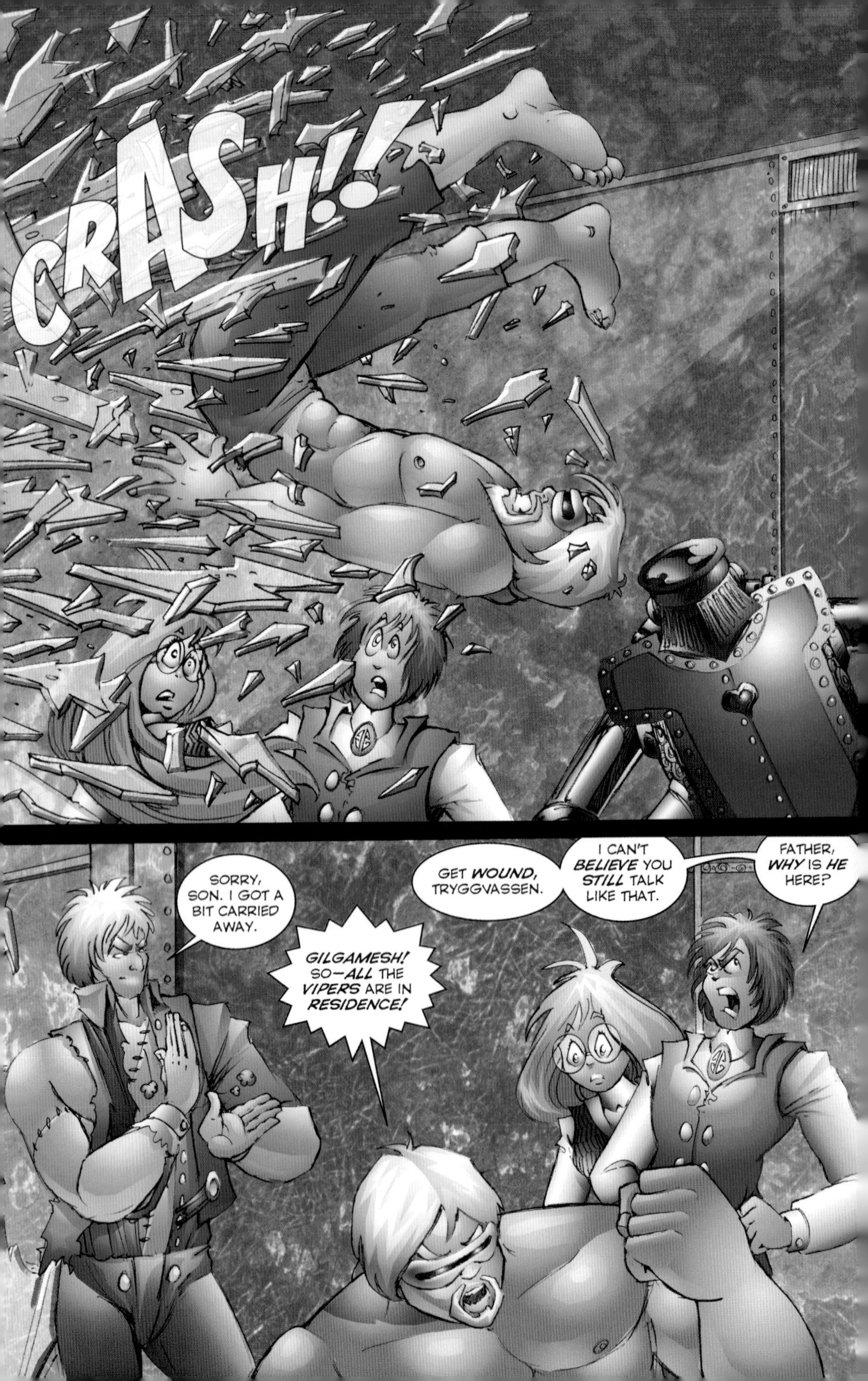
CRASH!!
SORRY, SON. I GOT A BIT CARRIED AWAY.
GILGAMESH! SO—ALL THE VIPERS ARE IN RESIDENCE!
GET WOUND, TRYGGVASSEN.
I CAN'T BELIEVE YOU STILL TALK LIKE THAT.
FATHER, WHY IS HE HERE?

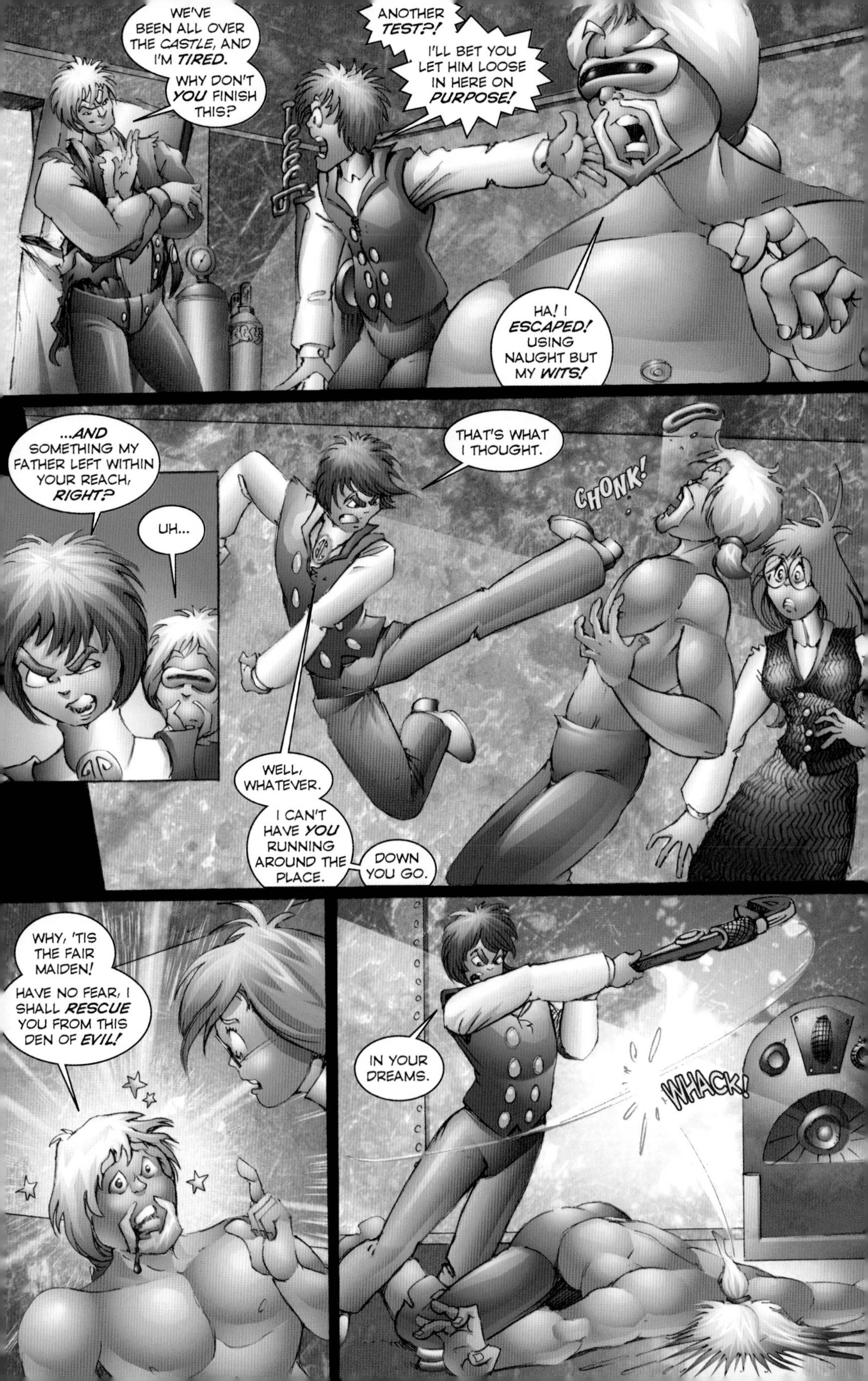

WE'VE BEEN ALL OVER THE CASTLE, AND I'M TIRED.
WHY DON'T YOU FINISH THIS?
ANOTHER TEST?!
I'LL BET YOU LET HIM LOOSE IN HERE ON PURPOSE!
HA! I ESCAPED! USING NAUGHT BUT MY WITS!
...AND SOMETHING MY FATHER LEFT WITHIN YOUR REACH, RIGHT?
UH...
THAT'S WHAT I THOUGHT.
CHONK!
WELL, WHATEVER.
I CAN'T HAVE YOU RUNNING AROUND THE PLACE.
DOWN YOU GO.
WHY, 'TIS THE FAIR MAIDEN!
HAVE NO FEAR, I SHALL RESCUE YOU FROM THIS DEN OF EVIL!
IN YOUR DREAMS.
WHACK!

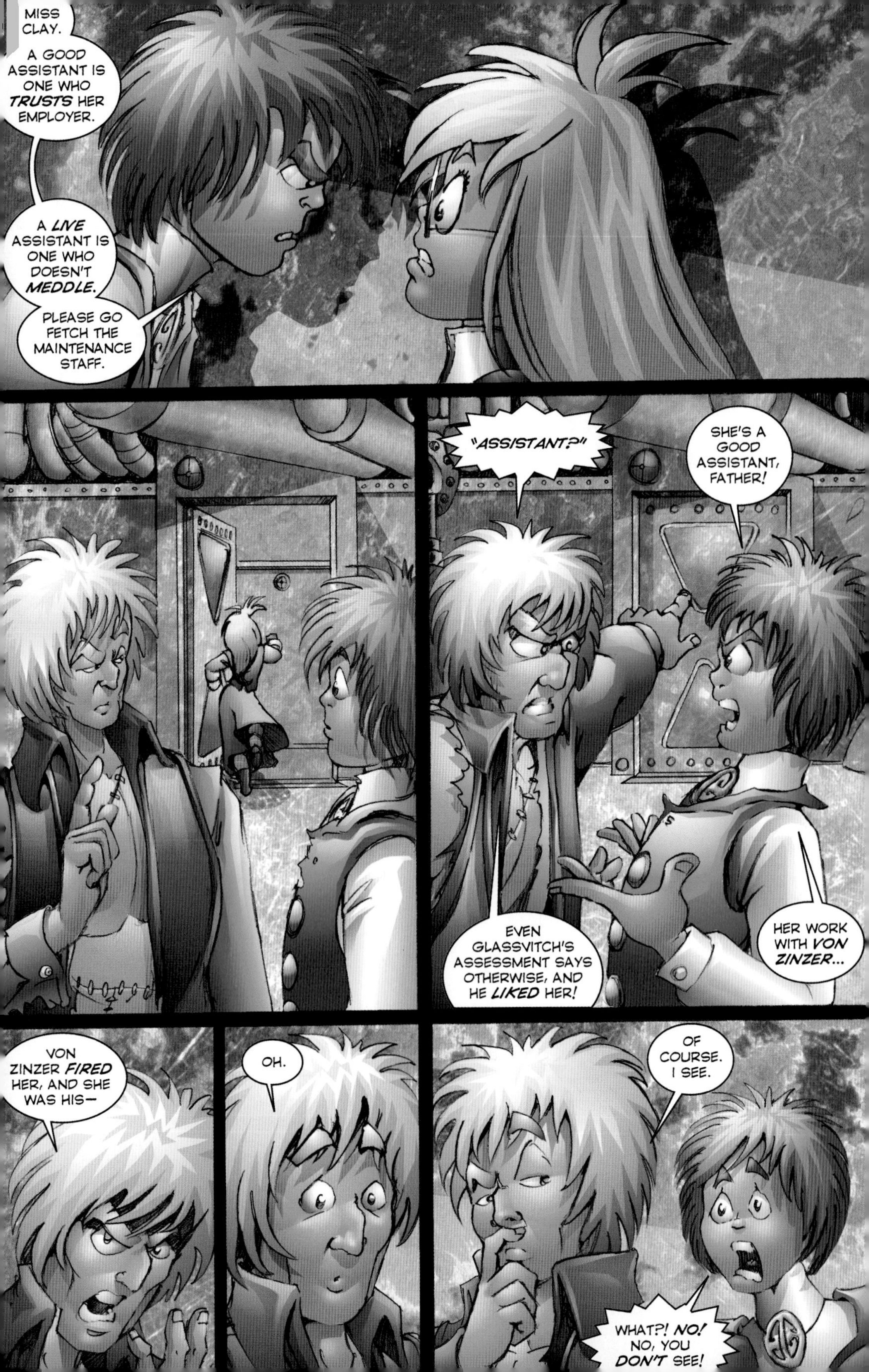
MISS CLAY.
A GOOD ASSISTANT IS ONE WHO *TRUSTS* HER EMPLOYER.
A *LIVE* ASSISTANT IS ONE WHO DOESN'T *MEDDLE*.
PLEASE GO FETCH THE MAINTENANCE STAFF.
"ASSISTANT?"
SHE'S A GOOD ASSISTANT, FATHER!
EVEN GLASSVITCH'S ASSESSMENT SAYS OTHERWISE, AND HE *LIKED* HER!
HER WORK WITH *VON ZINZER*...
VON ZINZER *FIRED* HER, AND SHE WAS HIS—
OH.
OF COURSE. I SEE.
WHAT?! *NO!* NO, YOU *DON'T* SEE!

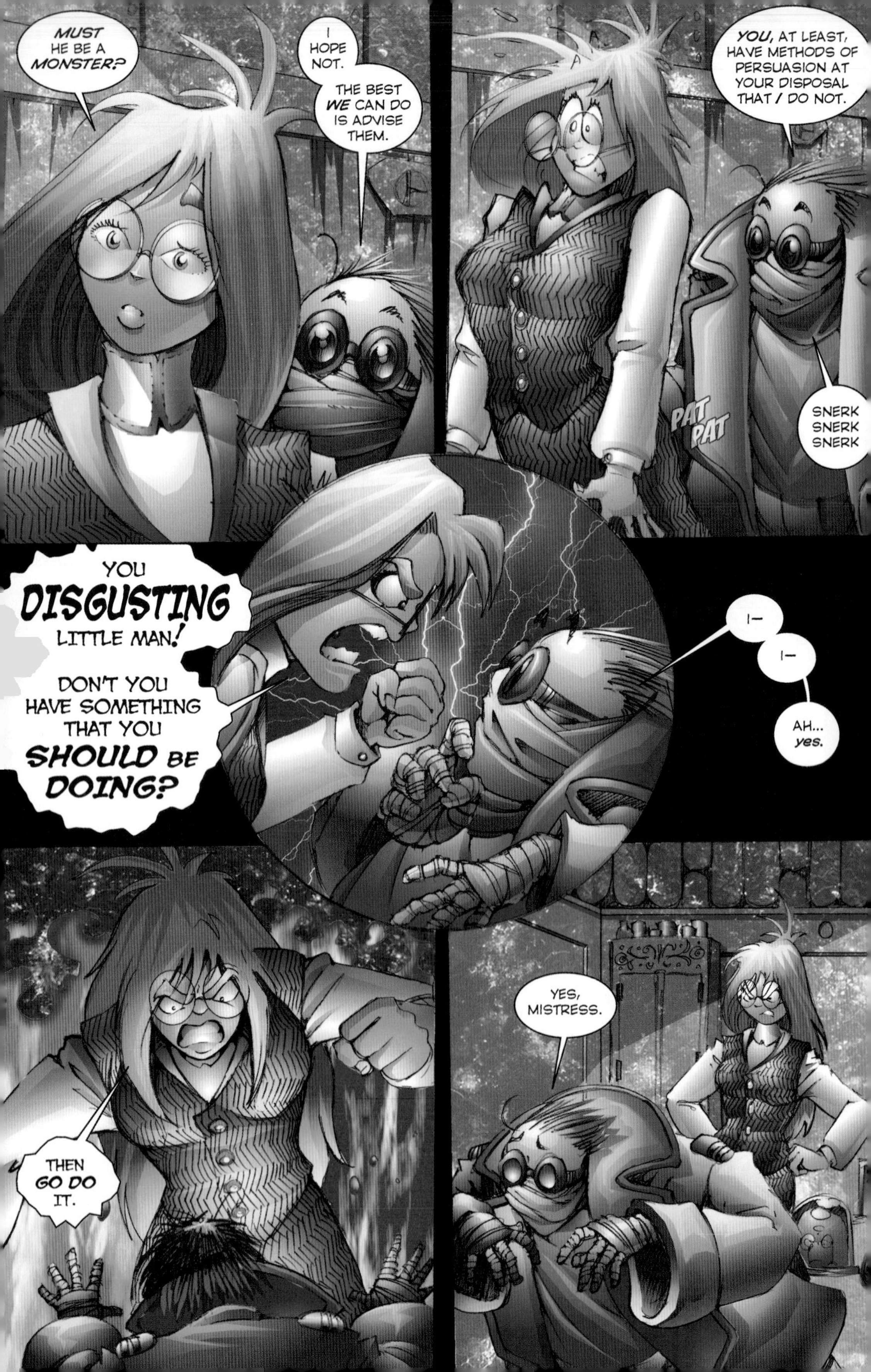

MUST HE BE A MONSTER?
I HOPE NOT.
THE BEST WE CAN DO IS ADVISE THEM.
YOU, AT LEAST, HAVE METHODS OF PERSUASION AT YOUR DISPOSAL THAT I DO NOT.
PAT PAT
SNERK SNERK SNERK
YOU DISGUSTING LITTLE MAN!
DON'T YOU HAVE SOMETHING THAT YOU SHOULD BE DOING?
I—
I—
AH... yes.
THEN GO DO IT.
YES, MISTRESS.

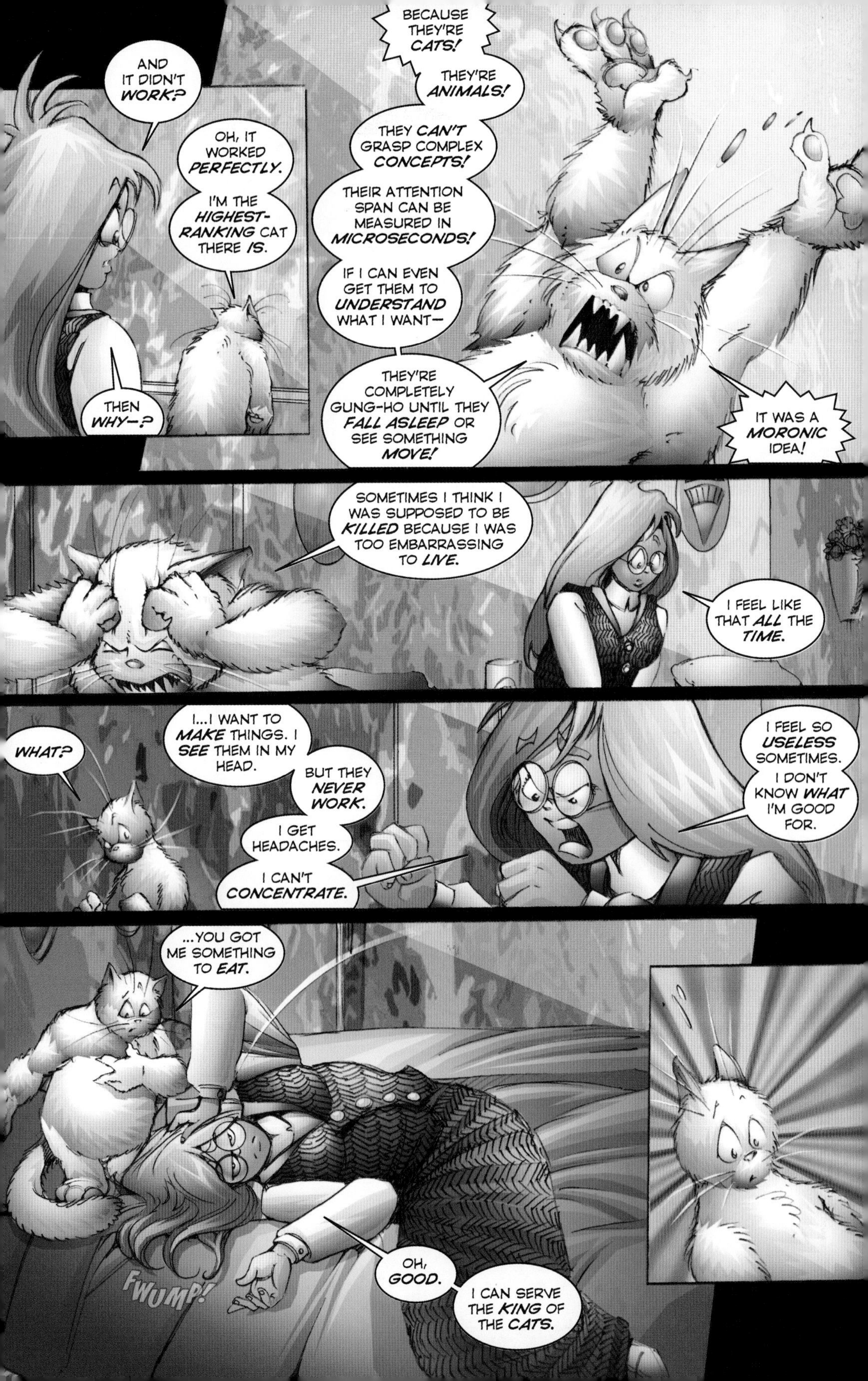
AND IT DIDN'T WORK?
OH, IT WORKED PERFECTLY.
I'M THE HIGHEST-RANKING CAT THERE IS.
THEN WHY—?
BECAUSE THEY'RE CATS!
THEY'RE ANIMALS!
THEY CAN'T GRASP COMPLEX CONCEPTS!
THEIR ATTENTION SPAN CAN BE MEASURED IN MICROSECONDS!
IF I CAN EVEN GET THEM TO UNDERSTAND WHAT I WANT—
THEY'RE COMPLETELY GUNG-HO UNTIL THEY FALL ASLEEP OR SEE SOMETHING MOVE!
IT WAS A MORONIC IDEA!
SOMETIMES I THINK I WAS SUPPOSED TO BE KILLED BECAUSE I WAS TOO EMBARRASSING TO LIVE.
I FEEL LIKE THAT ALL THE TIME.
WHAT?
I...I WANT TO MAKE THINGS. I SEE THEM IN MY HEAD.
BUT THEY NEVER WORK.
I GET HEADACHES.
I CAN'T CONCENTRATE.
I FEEL SO USELESS SOMETIMES.
I DON'T KNOW WHAT I'M GOOD FOR.
...YOU GOT ME SOMETHING TO EAT.
FWUMP!
OH, GOOD.
I CAN SERVE THE KING OF THE CATS.

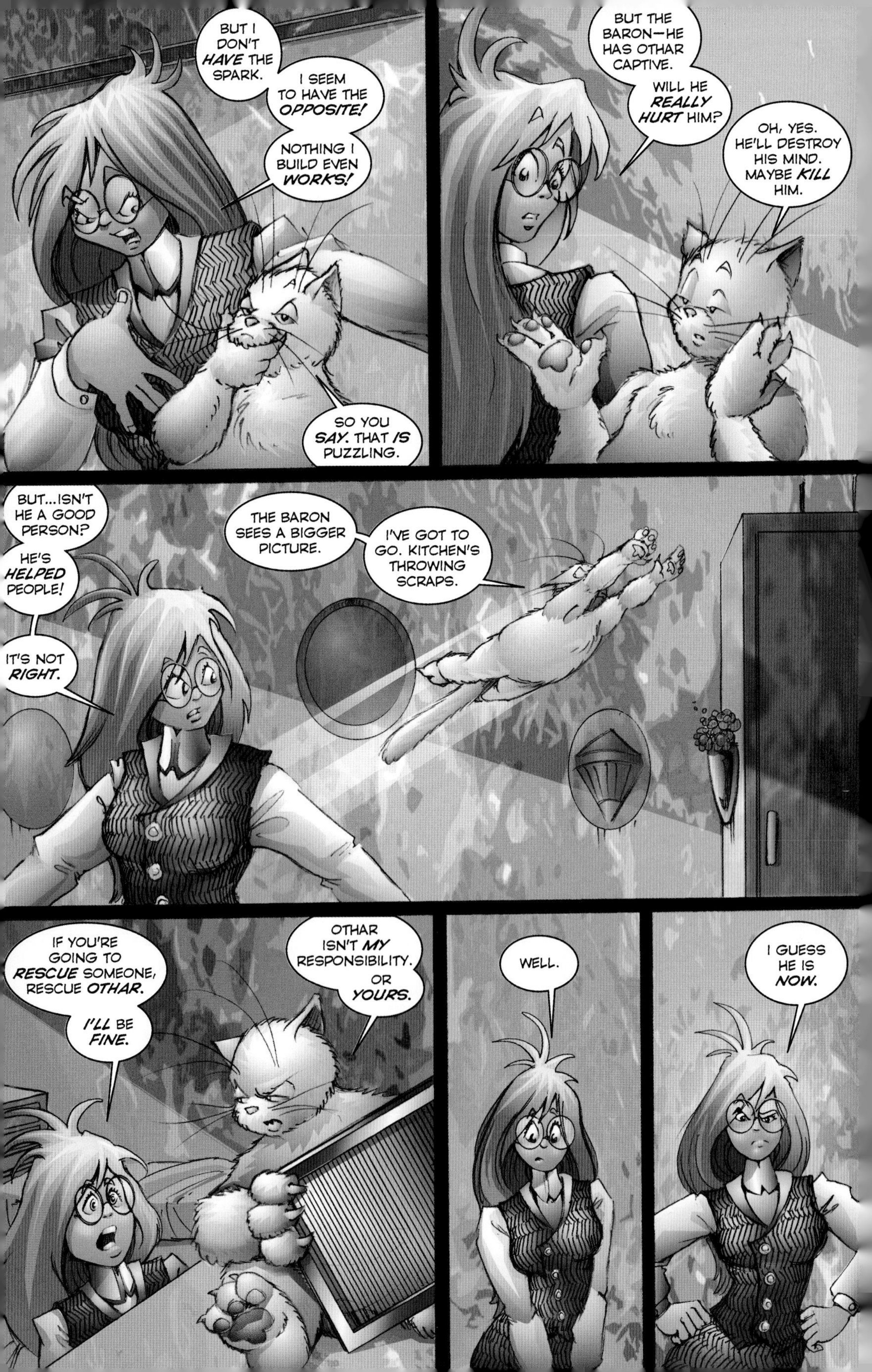

BUT I DON'T *HAVE* THE SPARK.
I SEEM TO HAVE THE *OPPOSITE!*
NOTHING I BUILD EVEN *WORKS!*
SO YOU *SAY.* THAT *IS* PUZZLING.
BUT THE BARON—HE HAS OTHAR CAPTIVE.
WILL HE *REALLY HURT* HIM?
OH, YES. HE'LL DESTROY HIS MIND. MAYBE *KILL* HIM.
BUT...ISN'T HE A GOOD PERSON?
HE'S *HELPED* PEOPLE!
IT'S NOT *RIGHT.*
THE BARON SEES A BIGGER PICTURE.
I'VE GOT TO GO. KITCHEN'S THROWING SCRAPS.
IF YOU'RE GOING TO *RESCUE* SOMEONE, RESCUE *OTHAR.*
I'LL BE *FINE.*
OTHAR ISN'T *MY* RESPONSIBILITY.
OR *YOURS.*
WELL.
I GUESS HE IS *NOW.*

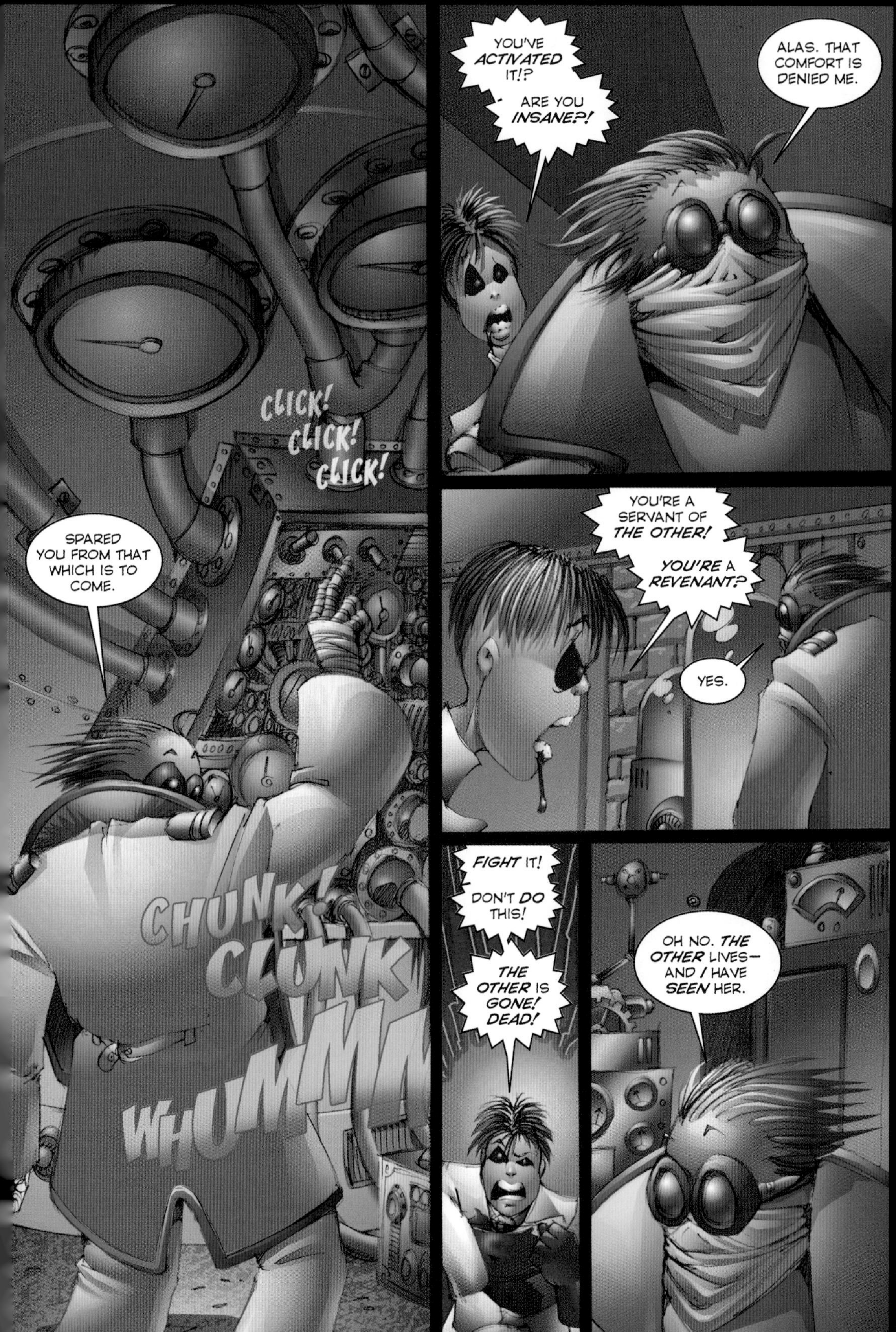

CLICK! CLICK! CLICK!
SPARED YOU FROM THAT WHICH IS TO COME.
CHUNK! CLUNK! WHUMM
YOU'VE *ACTIVATED* IT!?
ARE YOU *INSANE?!*
ALAS. THAT COMFORT IS DENIED ME.
YOU'RE A SERVANT OF *THE OTHER!*
YOU'RE A *REVENANT?*
YES.
FIGHT IT!
DON'T *DO* THIS!
THE OTHER IS *GONE! DEAD!*
OH NO. *THE OTHER* LIVES— AND *I* HAVE *SEEN* HER.

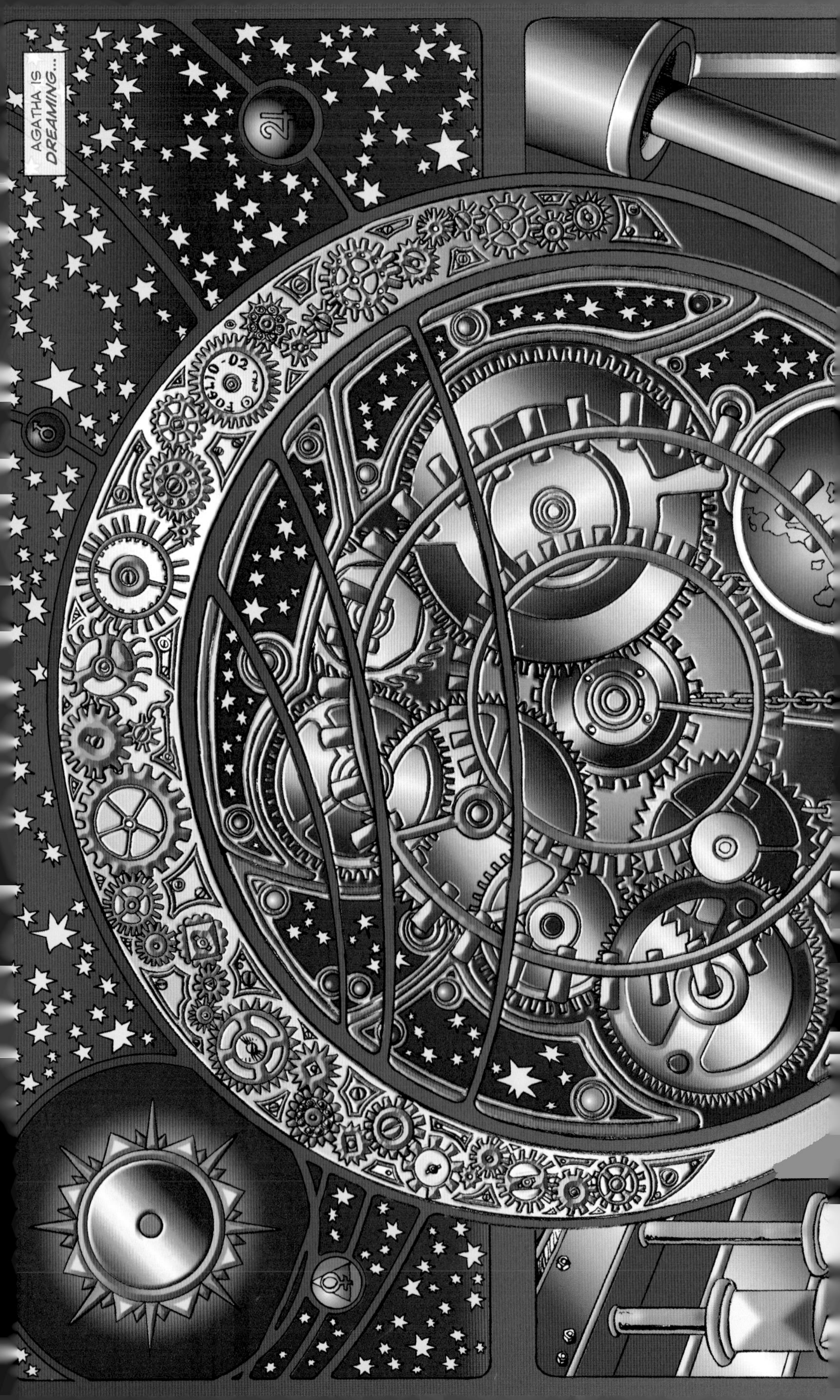
AGATHA IS DREAMING...

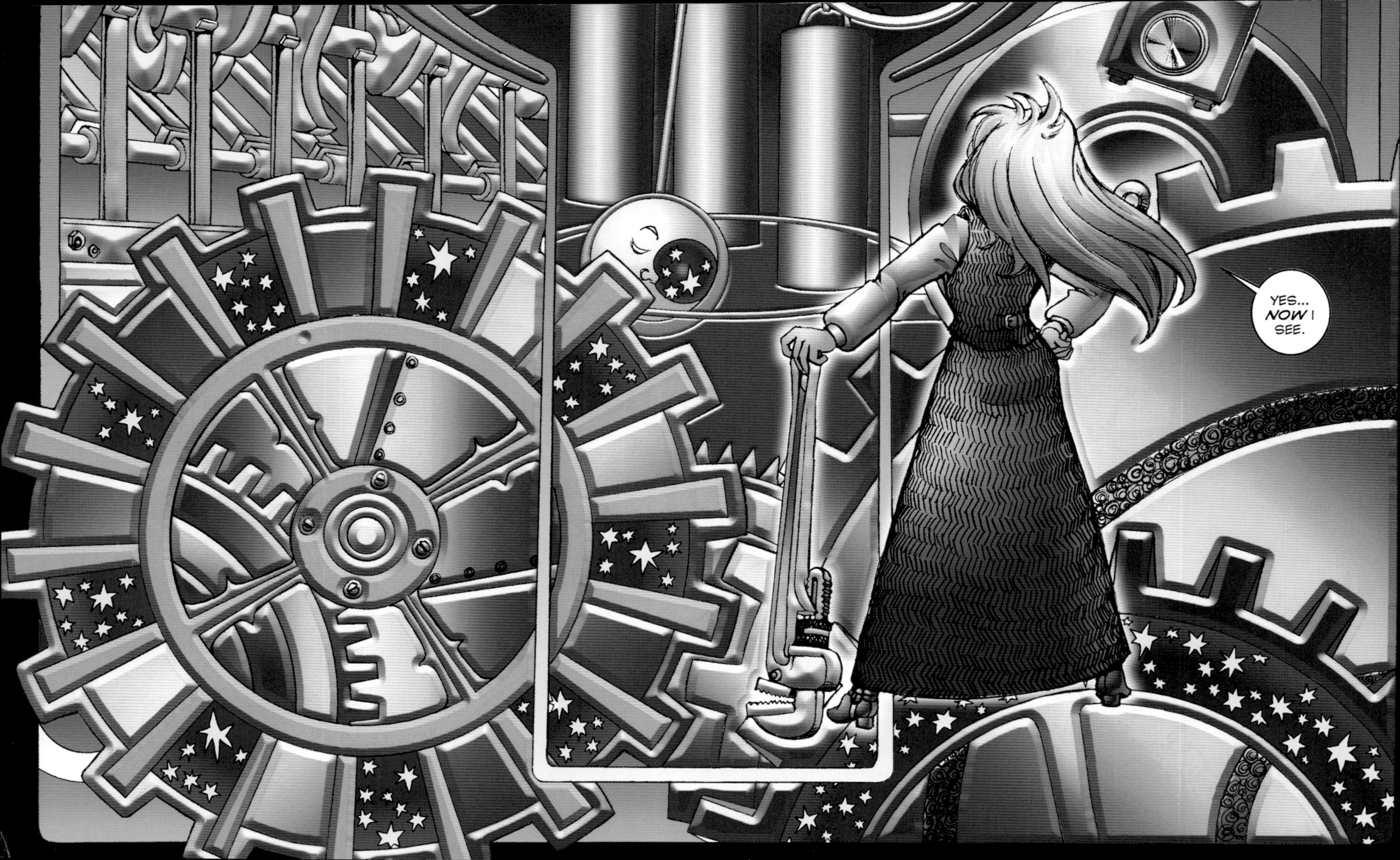
YES... NOW I SEE.

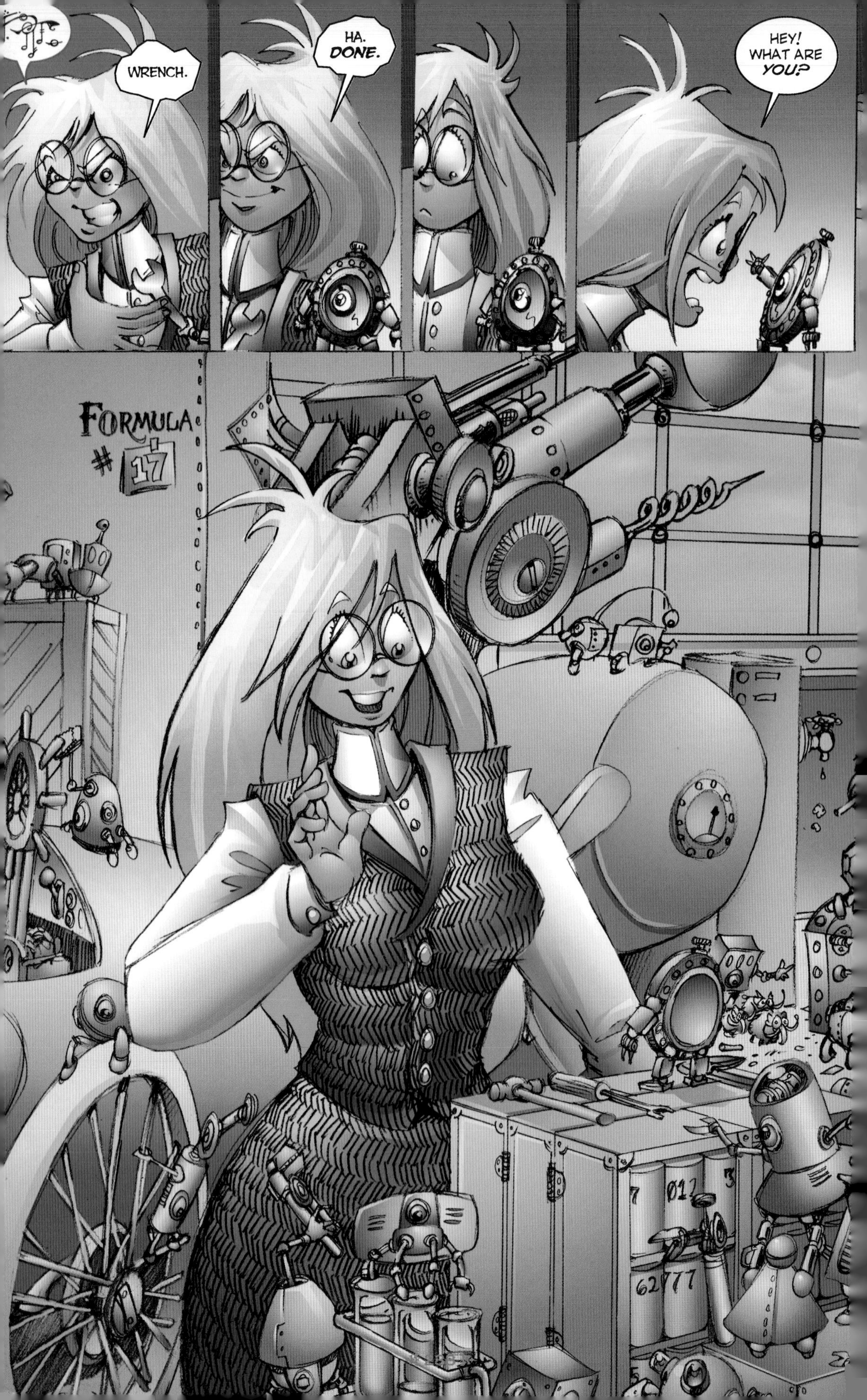
WRENCH.
HA. DONE.
HEY! WHAT ARE YOU?
FORMULA # 17

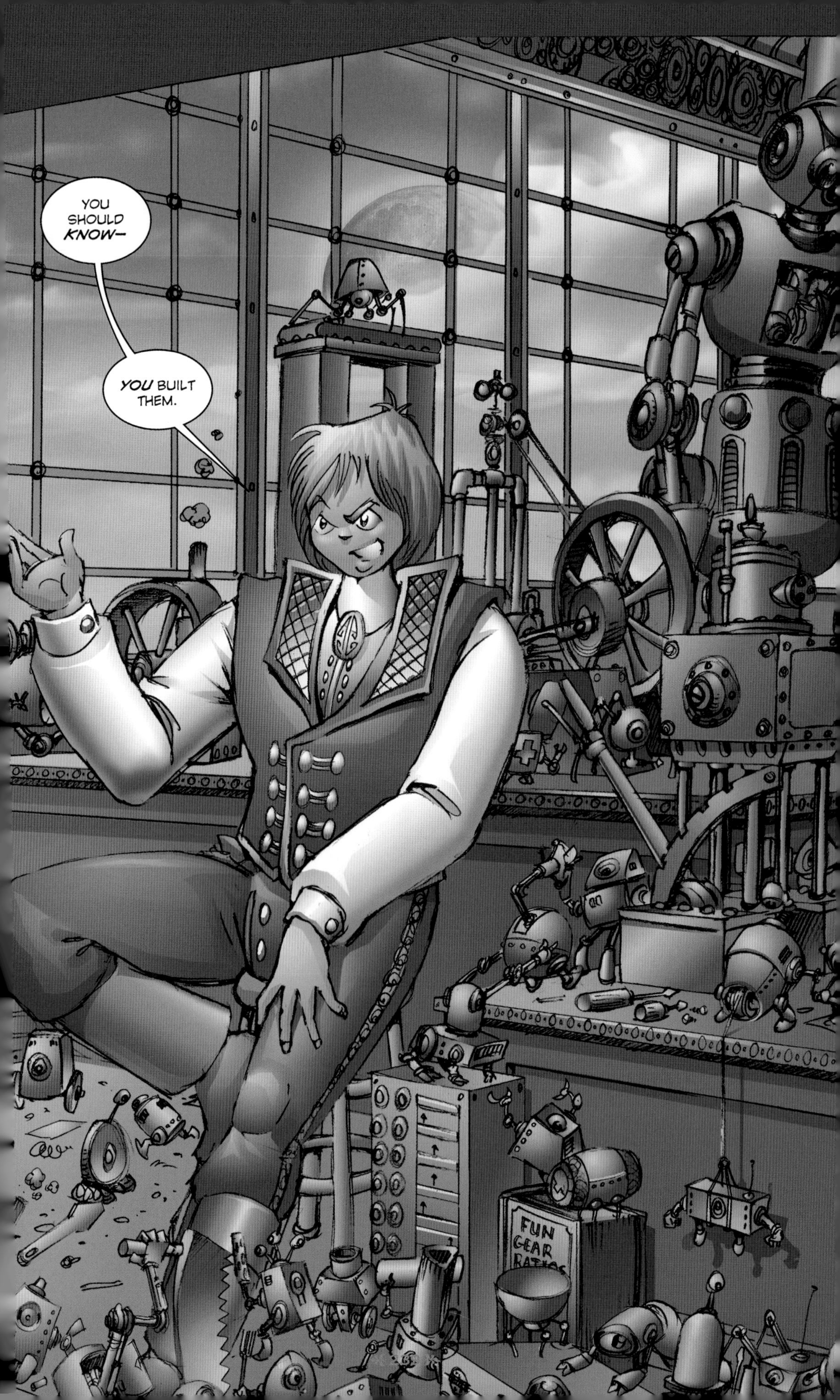

YOU SHOULD *KNOW*—
YOU BUILT THEM.
FUN GEAR

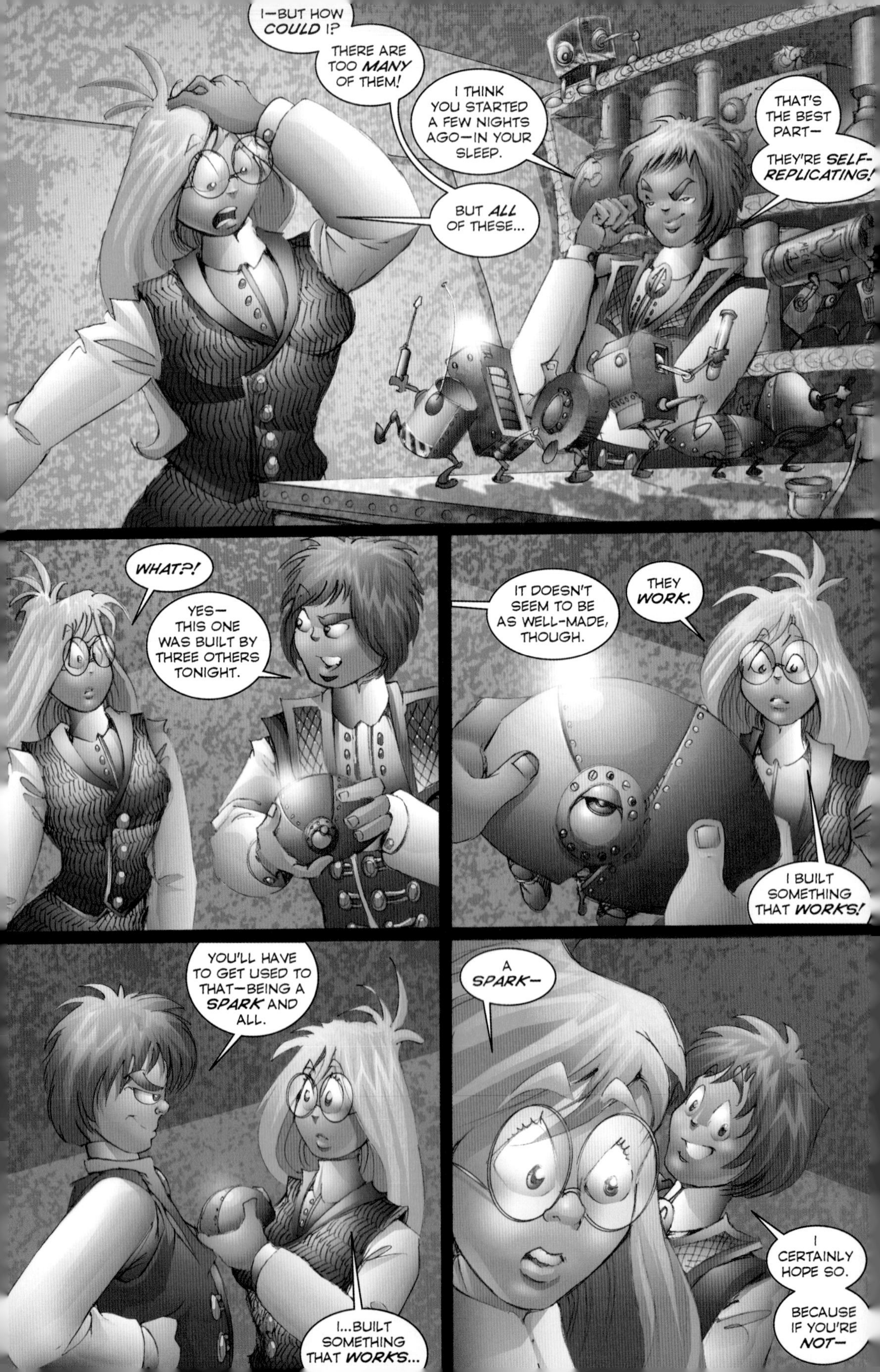
I—BUT HOW COULD I?
THERE ARE TOO MANY OF THEM!
I THINK YOU STARTED A FEW NIGHTS AGO—IN YOUR SLEEP.
BUT ALL OF THESE...
THAT'S THE BEST PART—
THEY'RE SELF-REPLICATING!
WHAT?!
YES— THIS ONE WAS BUILT BY THREE OTHERS TONIGHT.
IT DOESN'T SEEM TO BE AS WELL-MADE, THOUGH.
THEY WORK.
I BUILT SOMETHING THAT WORKS!
YOU'LL HAVE TO GET USED TO THAT—BEING A SPARK AND ALL.
I...BUILT SOMETHING THAT WORKS...
A SPARK—
I CERTAINLY HOPE SO.
BECAUSE IF YOU'RE NOT—

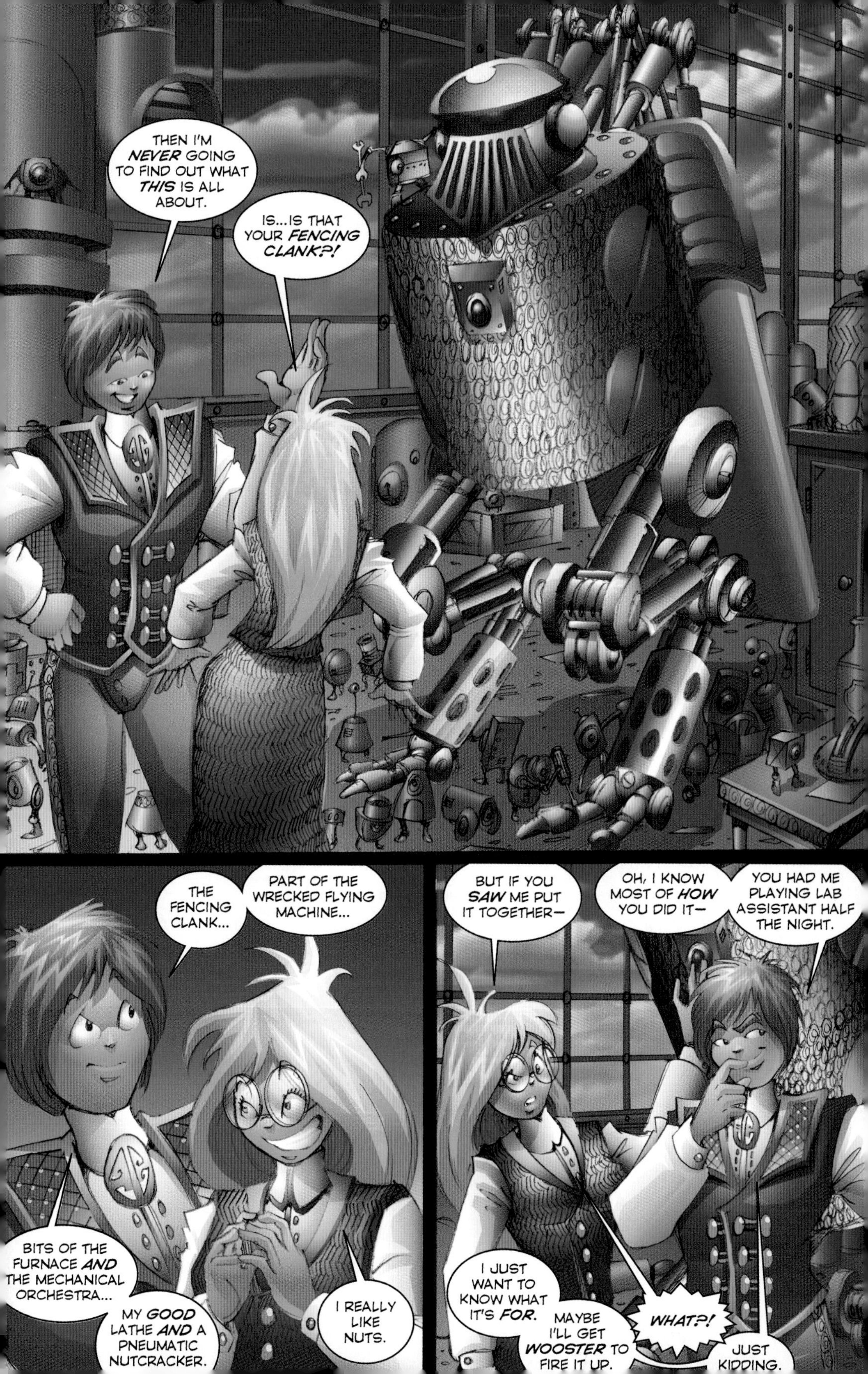
THEN I'M *NEVER* GOING TO FIND OUT WHAT *THIS* IS ALL ABOUT.
IS...IS THAT YOUR *FENCING CLANK?!*
THE FENCING CLANK...
PART OF THE WRECKED FLYING MACHINE...
BITS OF THE FURNACE *AND* THE MECHANICAL ORCHESTRA...
MY *GOOD* LATHE *AND* A PNEUMATIC NUTCRACKER.
I REALLY LIKE NUTS.
BUT IF YOU *SAW* ME PUT IT TOGETHER—
OH, I KNOW MOST OF *HOW* YOU DID IT—
YOU HAD ME PLAYING LAB ASSISTANT HALF THE NIGHT.
I JUST WANT TO KNOW WHAT IT'S *FOR*.
MAYBE I'LL GET *WOOSTER* TO FIRE IT UP.
WHAT?!
JUST KIDDING.

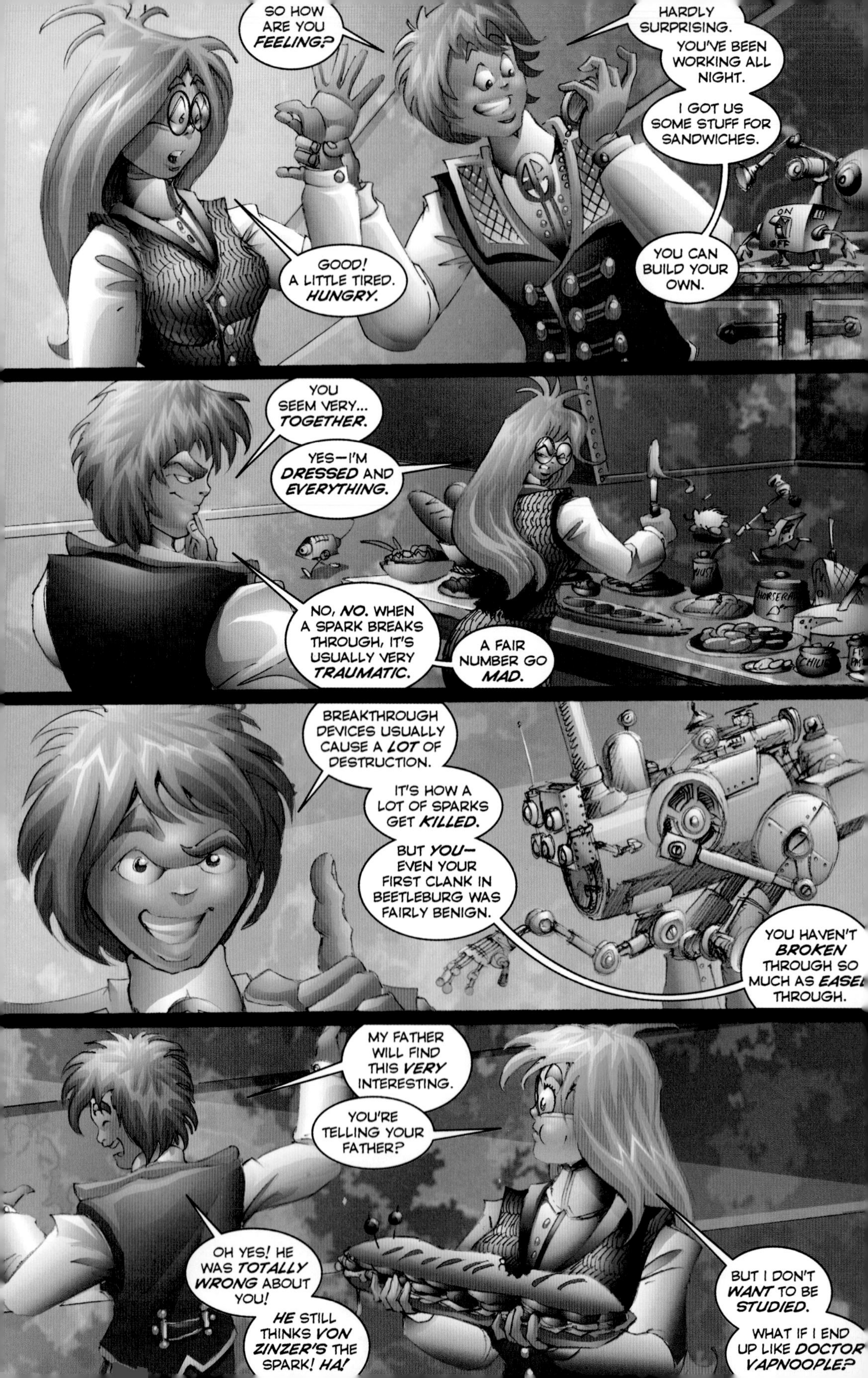
SO HOW ARE YOU *FEELING?*
HARDLY SURPRISING.
YOU'VE BEEN WORKING ALL NIGHT.
I GOT US SOME STUFF FOR SANDWICHES.
YOU CAN BUILD YOUR OWN.
GOOD! A LITTLE TIRED. *HUNGRY.*
ON
OFF
YOU SEEM VERY... *TOGETHER.*
YES—I'M *DRESSED* AND *EVERYTHING.*
NO, *NO.* WHEN A SPARK BREAKS THROUGH, IT'S USUALLY VERY *TRAUMATIC.*
A FAIR NUMBER GO *MAD.*
HORSERADISH
CHILI
BREAKTHROUGH DEVICES USUALLY CAUSE A *LOT* OF DESTRUCTION.
IT'S HOW A LOT OF SPARKS GET *KILLED.*
BUT *YOU*— EVEN YOUR FIRST CLANK IN BEETLEBURG WAS FAIRLY BENIGN.
YOU HAVEN'T *BROKEN* THROUGH SO MUCH AS *EASED* THROUGH.
MY FATHER WILL FIND THIS *VERY* INTERESTING.
YOU'RE TELLING YOUR FATHER?
OH YES! HE WAS *TOTALLY WRONG* ABOUT YOU!
HE STILL THINKS *VON ZINZER'S* THE SPARK! *HA!*
BUT I DON'T *WANT* TO BE *STUDIED.*
WHAT IF I END UP LIKE *DOCTOR VAPNOOPLE?*

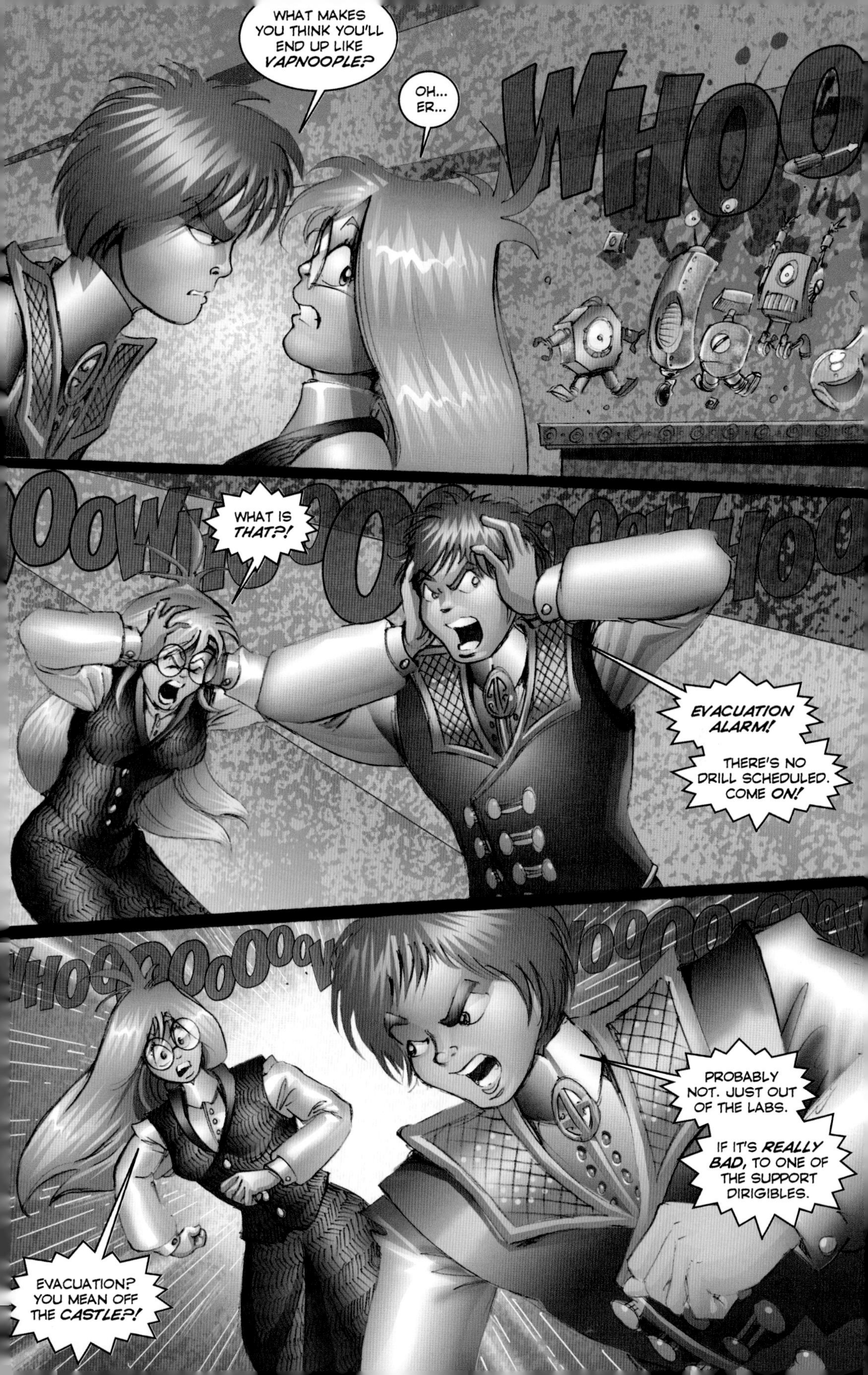
WHAT MAKES YOU THINK YOU'LL END UP LIKE *VAPNOOPLE?*
OH... ER...
WHOO
OOWHOOOOOOOWHOO
WHAT IS *THAT?!*
EVACUATION ALARM!
THERE'S NO DRILL SCHEDULED. COME *ON!*
WHOOOOOoOOOOW
PROBABLY NOT. JUST OUT OF THE LABS.
IF IT'S *REALLY BAD,* TO ONE OF THE SUPPORT DIRIGIBLES.
EVACUATION? YOU MEAN OFF THE *CASTLE?!*

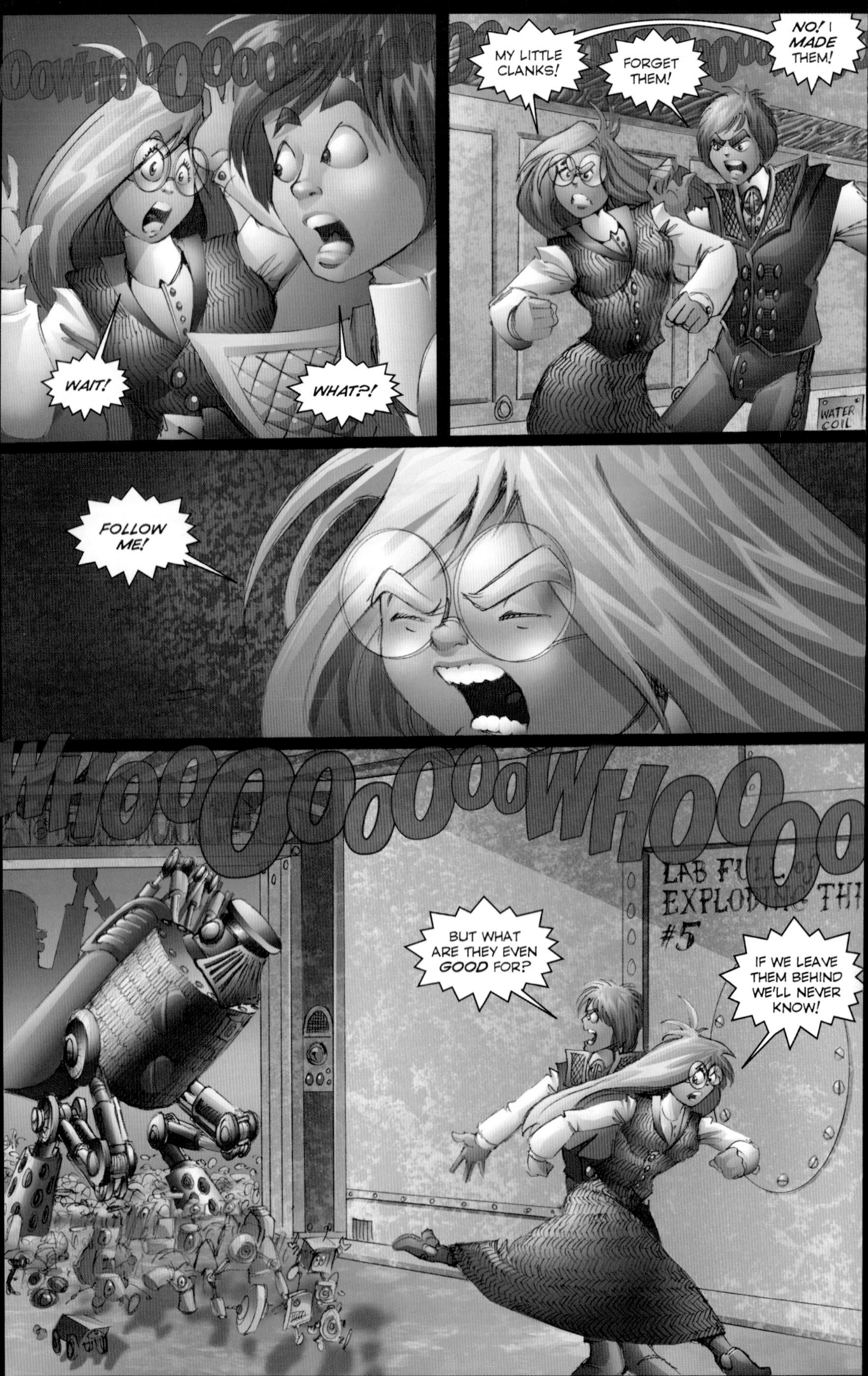
OOWHOOOOOOOWHOOO
WAIT!
WHAT?!
MY LITTLE CLANKS!
FORGET THEM!
NO! I MADE THEM!
WATER COIL
FOLLOW ME!
WHOOOOOOOOWHOOOO
BUT WHAT ARE THEY EVEN GOOD FOR?
IF WE LEAVE THEM BEHIND WE'LL NEVER KNOW!
#5

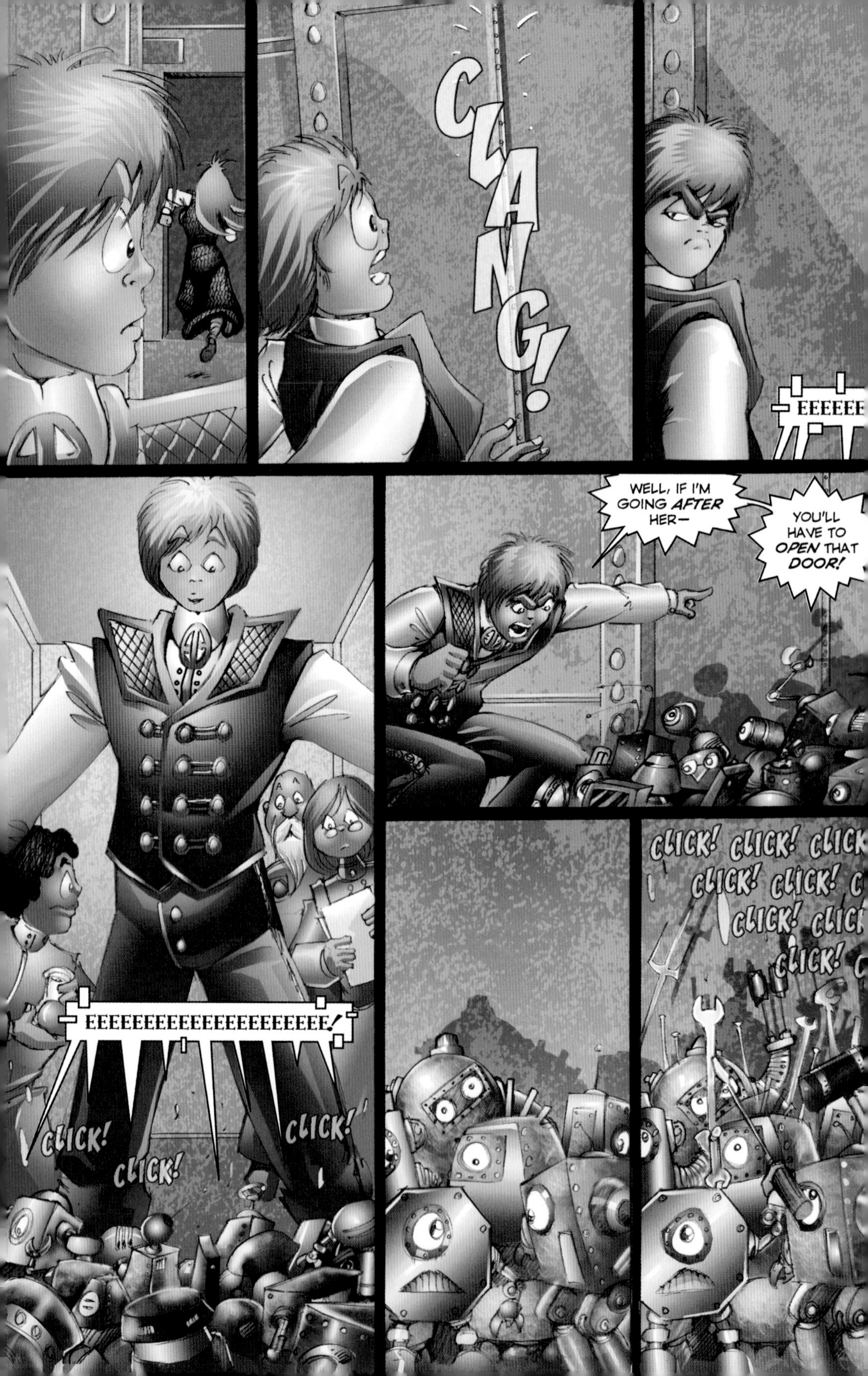
CLANG!
EEEEEE
EEEEEEEEEEEEEEEEEEEEE!
CLICK!
CLICK!
CLICK!
WELL, IF I'M GOING AFTER HER—
YOU'LL HAVE TO OPEN THAT DOOR!
CLICK! CLICK! CLICK!
CLICK! CLICK!
CLICK! CLICK!
CLICK!

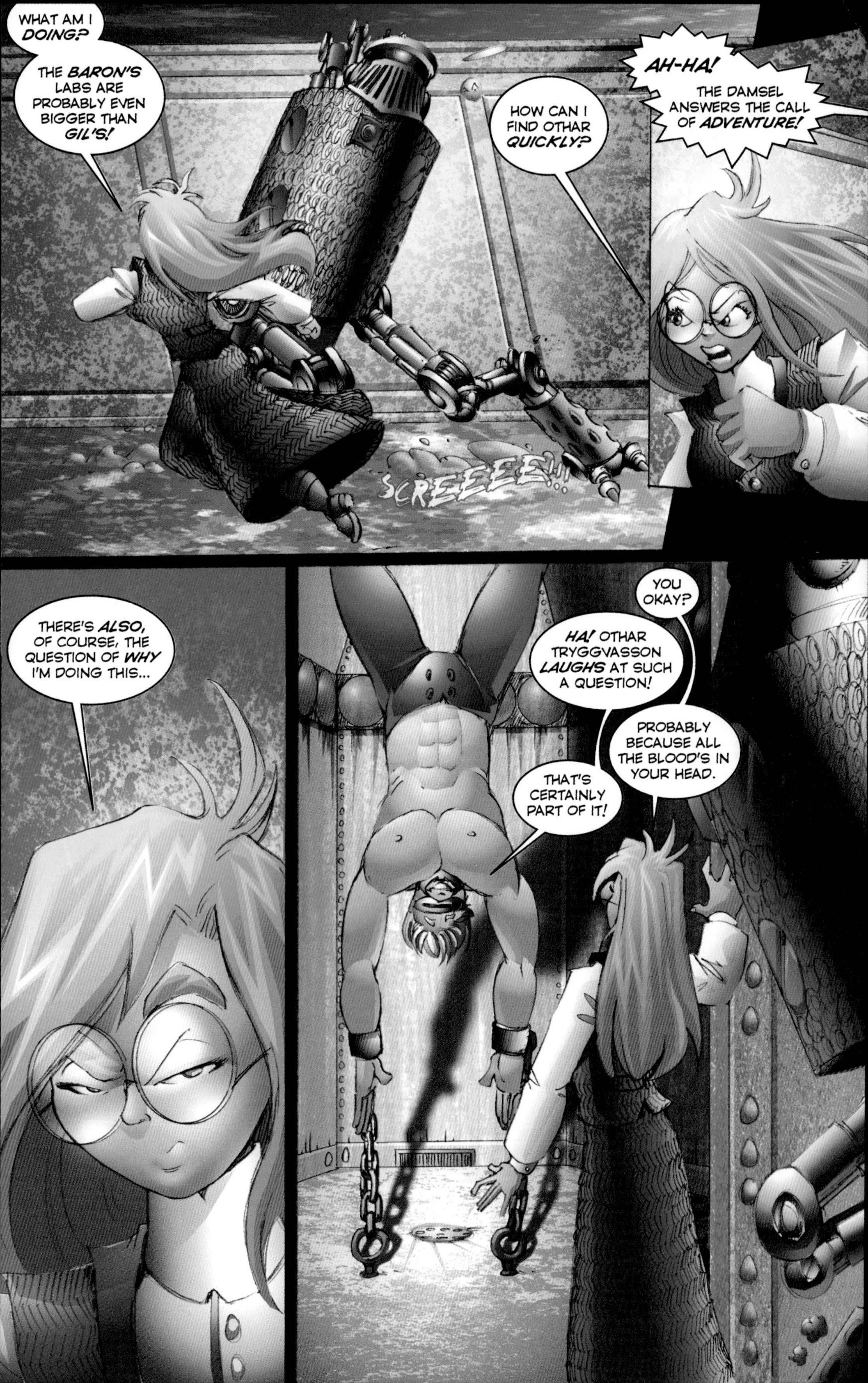
WHAT AM I DOING?
THE BARON'S LABS ARE PROBABLY EVEN BIGGER THAN GIL'S!
HOW CAN I FIND OTHAR QUICKLY?
AH-HA!
THE DAMSEL ANSWERS THE CALL OF ADVENTURE!
SCREEEEE!!!
THERE'S ALSO, OF COURSE, THE QUESTION OF WHY I'M DOING THIS...
YOU OKAY?
HA! OTHAR TRYGGVASSON LAUGHS AT SUCH A QUESTION!
PROBABLY BECAUSE ALL THE BLOOD'S IN YOUR HEAD.
THAT'S CERTAINLY PART OF IT!

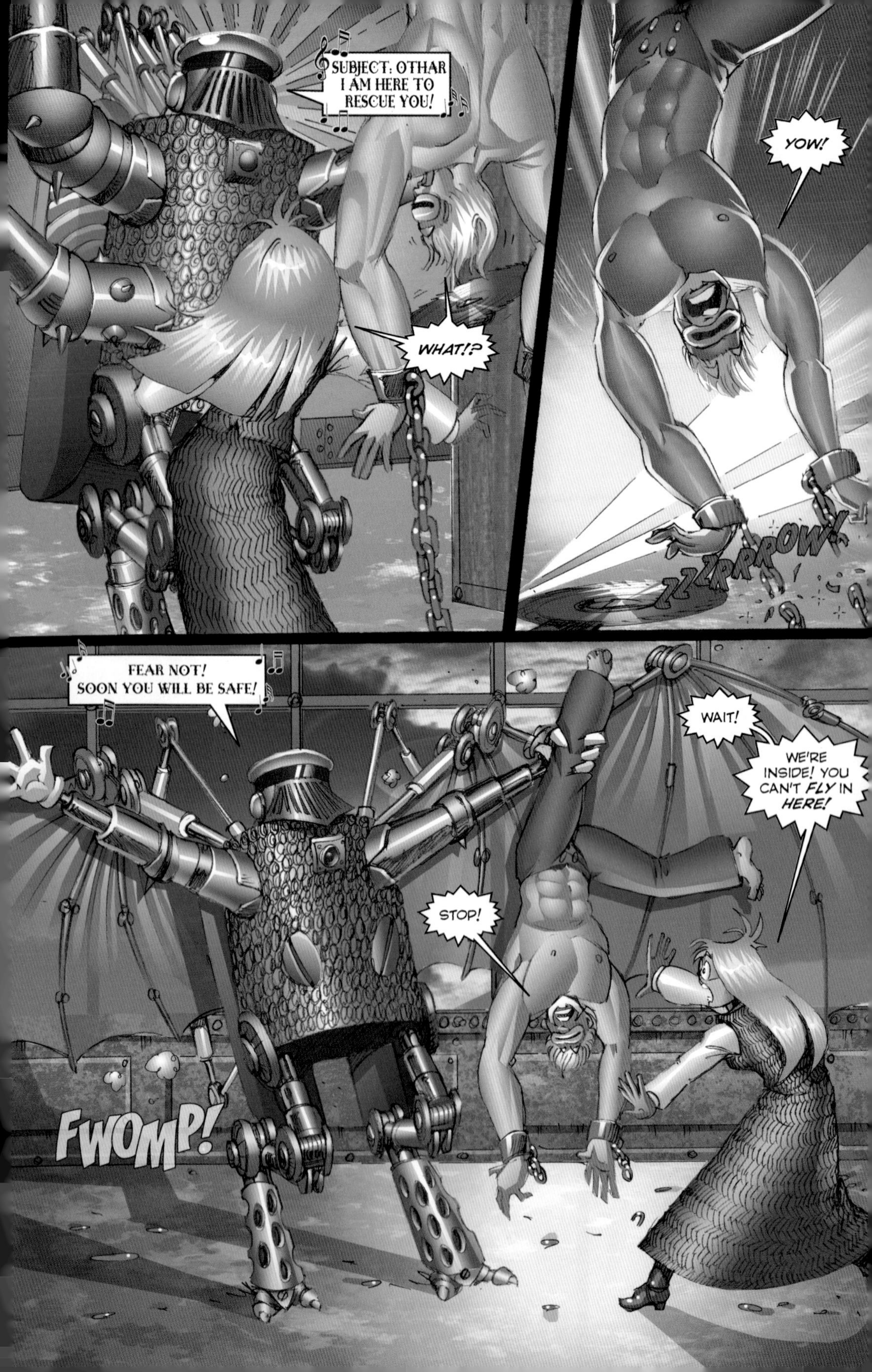
SUBJECT: OTHAR I AM HERE TO RESCUE YOU!
WHAT!?
YOW!
ZZZRRROW!
FEAR NOT! SOON YOU WILL BE SAFE!
WAIT!
WE'RE INSIDE! YOU CAN'T FLY IN HERE!
STOP!
FWOMP!

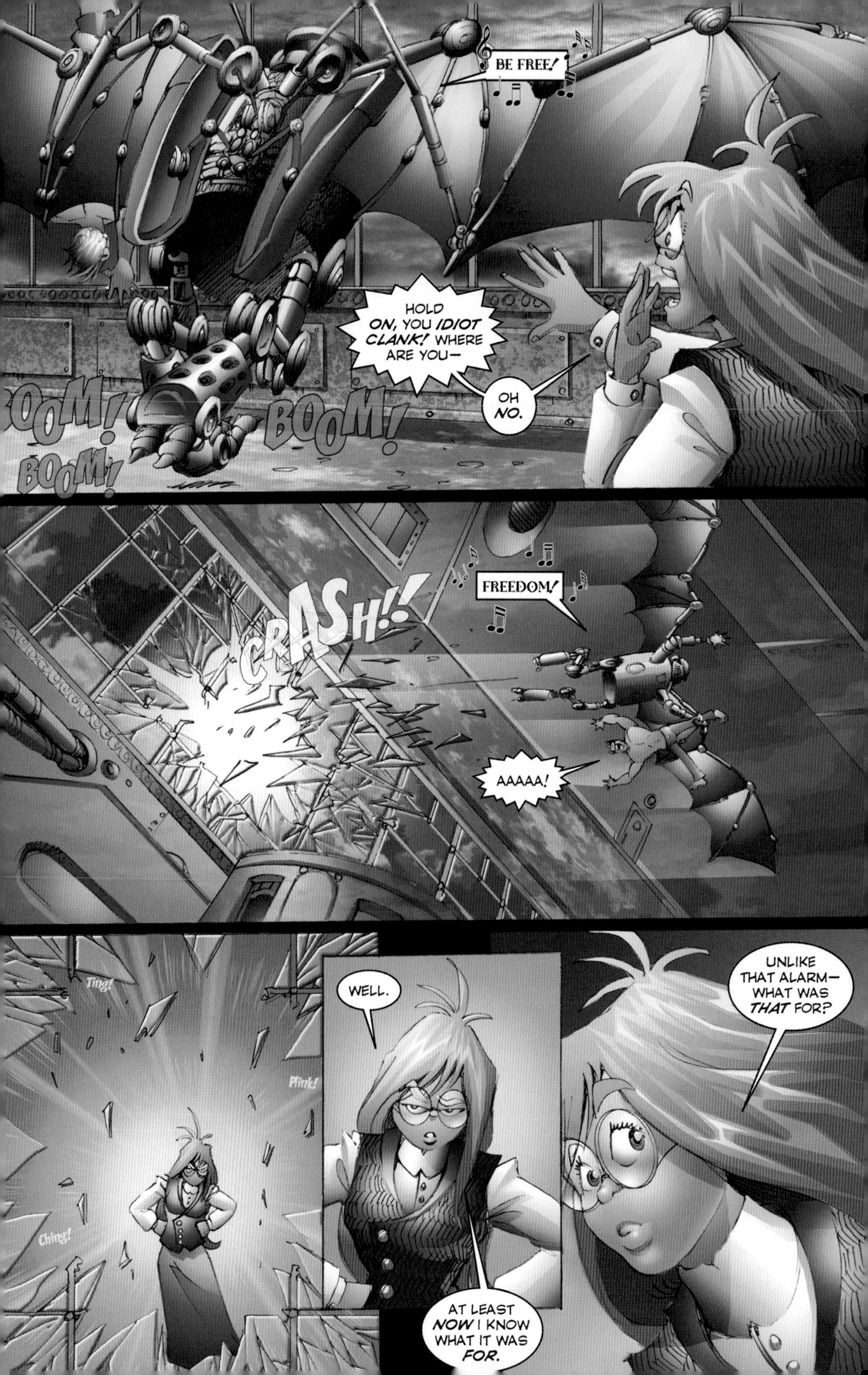
BE FREE!
HOLD ON, YOU IDIOT CLANK! WHERE ARE YOU—
OH NO.
BOOM!
BOOM!
BOOM!
FREEDOM!
CRASH!!
AAAAA!
Ting!
Plink!
Ching!
WELL.
AT LEAST NOW I KNOW WHAT IT WAS FOR.
UNLIKE THAT ALARM— WHAT WAS THAT FOR?

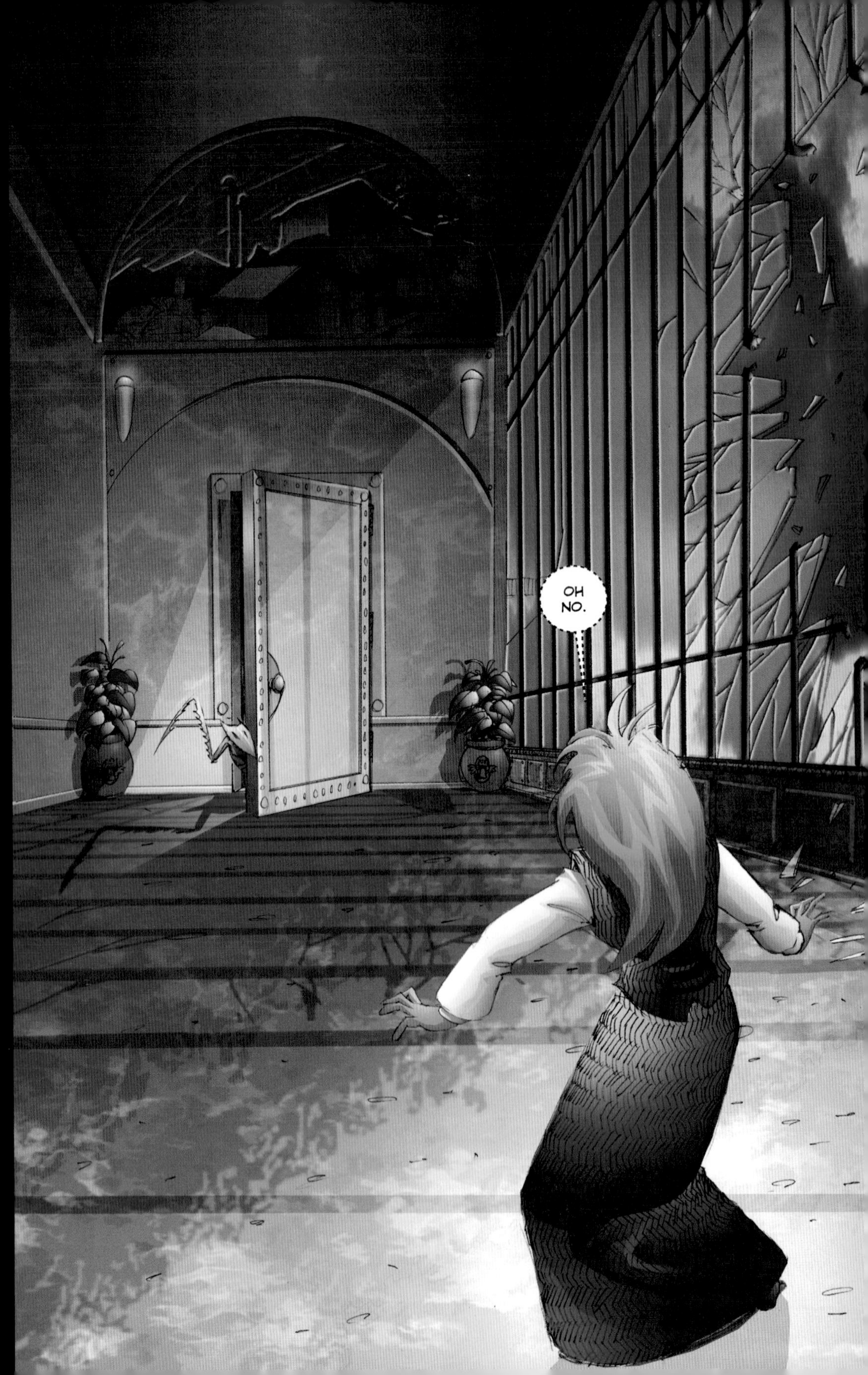
OH NO.

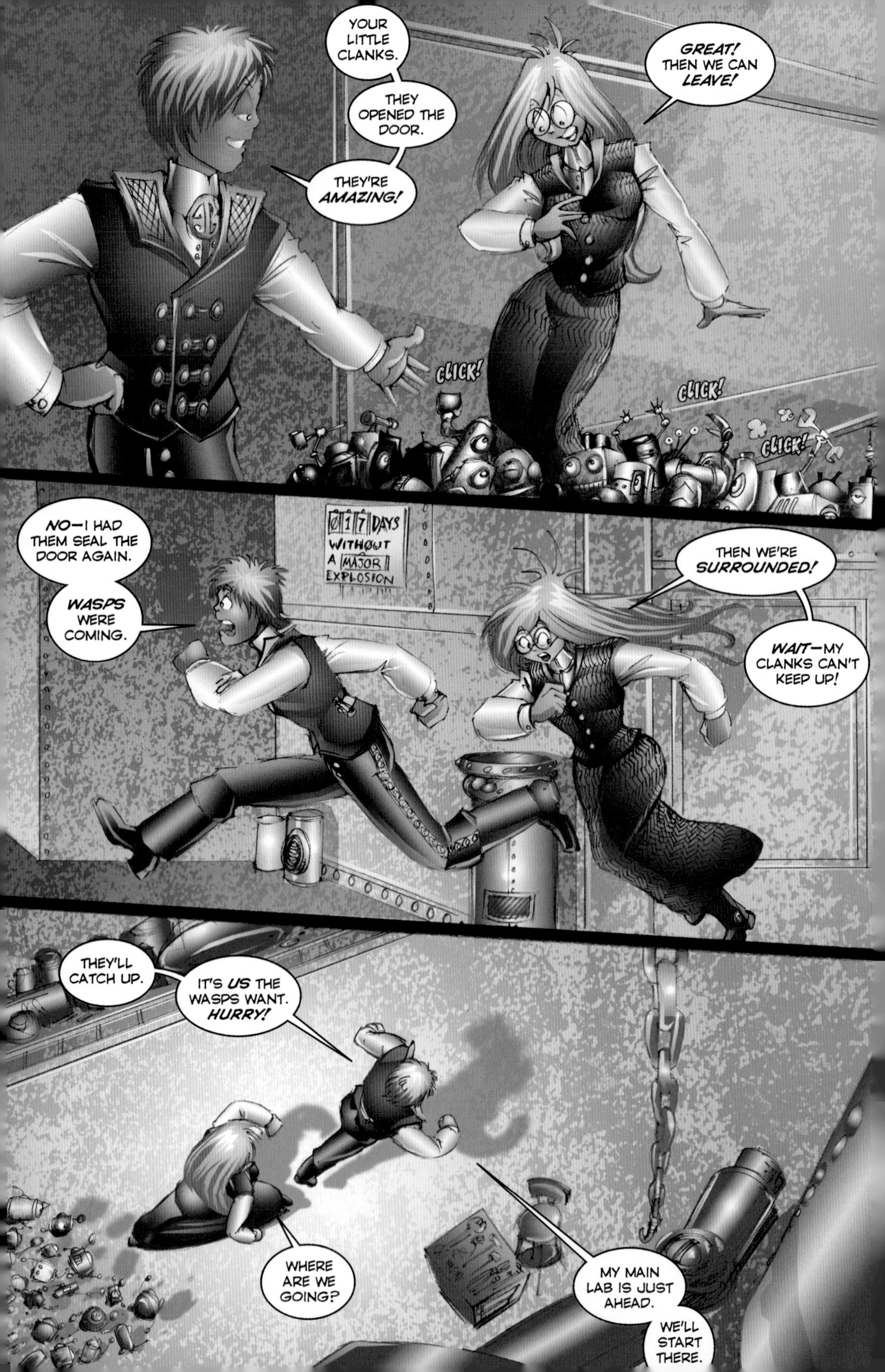
YOUR LITTLE CLANKS.
THEY OPENED THE DOOR.
THEY'RE *AMAZING!*
GREAT! THEN WE CAN *LEAVE!*
CLICK!
CLICK!
CLICK!
NO—I HAD THEM SEAL THE DOOR AGAIN.
WASPS WERE COMING.
017 DAYS WITHOUT A MAJOR EXPLOSION
THEN WE'RE *SURROUNDED!*
WAIT—MY CLANKS CAN'T KEEP UP!
THEY'LL CATCH UP.
IT'S *US* THE WASPS WANT. *HURRY!*
WHERE ARE WE GOING?
MY MAIN LAB IS JUST AHEAD.
WE'LL START THERE.

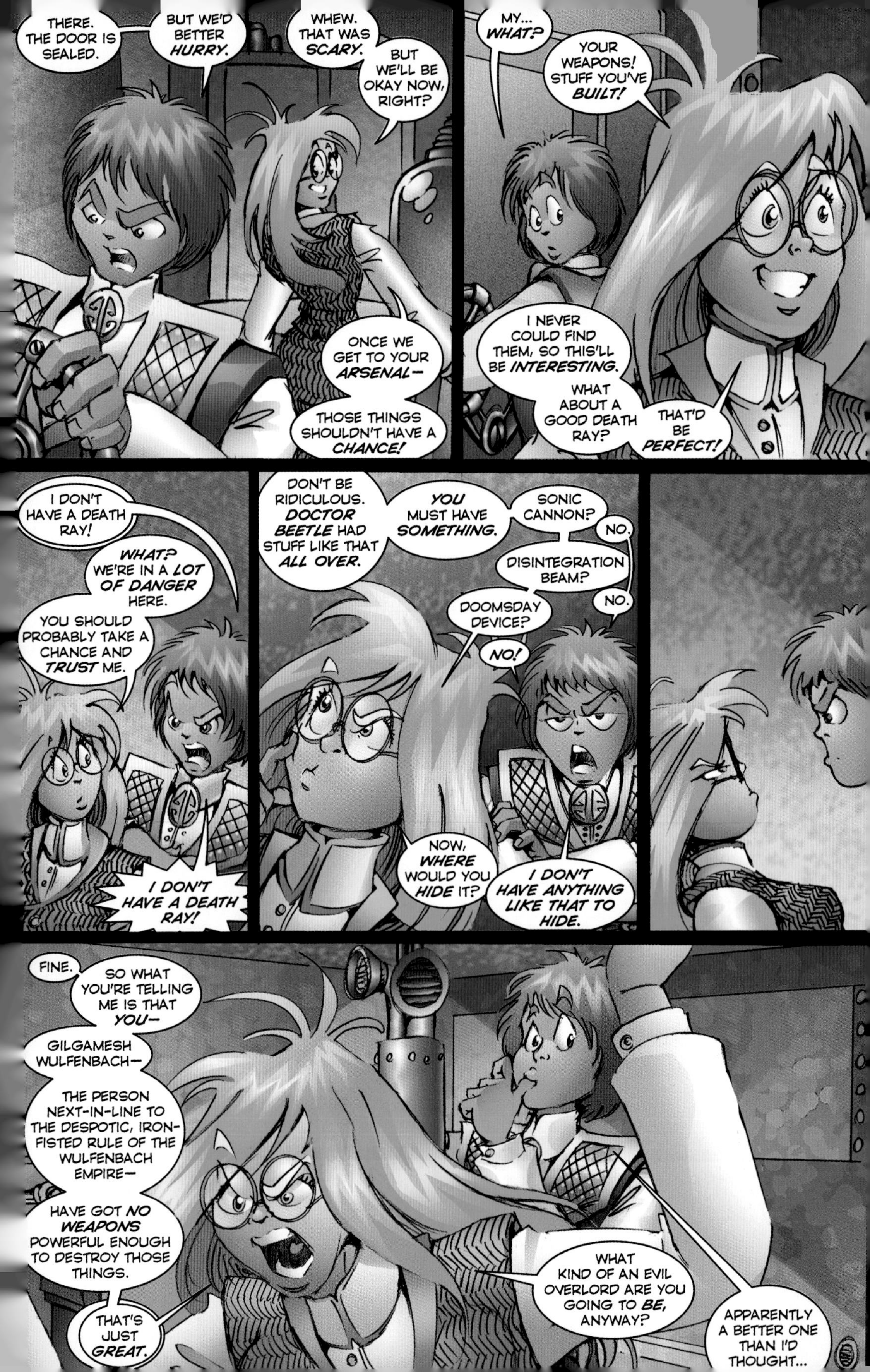
THERE. THE DOOR IS SEALED.
BUT WE'D BETTER *HURRY.*
WHEW. THAT WAS *SCARY.*
BUT WE'LL BE OKAY NOW, RIGHT?
ONCE WE GET TO YOUR *ARSENAL—*
THOSE THINGS SHOULDN'T HAVE A *CHANCE!*
MY... *WHAT?*
YOUR WEAPONS! STUFF YOU'VE *BUILT!*
I NEVER COULD FIND THEM, SO THIS'LL BE *INTERESTING.*
WHAT ABOUT A GOOD DEATH RAY?
THAT'D BE *PERFECT!*
I DON'T HAVE A DEATH RAY!
WHAT? WE'RE IN A *LOT OF DANGER* HERE.
YOU SHOULD PROBABLY TAKE A CHANCE AND *TRUST* ME.
I DON'T HAVE A DEATH RAY!
DON'T BE RIDICULOUS. *DOCTOR BEETLE* HAD STUFF LIKE THAT *ALL OVER.*
YOU MUST HAVE *SOMETHING.*
SONIC CANNON?
NO.
DISINTEGRATION BEAM?
NO.
DOOMSDAY DEVICE?
NO!
NOW, *WHERE* WOULD YOU *HIDE* IT?
I DON'T HAVE ANYTHING LIKE THAT TO HIDE.
FINE.
SO WHAT YOU'RE TELLING ME IS THAT *YOU—*
GILGAMESH WULFENBACH—
THE PERSON NEXT-IN-LINE TO THE DESPOTIC, IRON-FISTED RULE OF THE WULFENBACH EMPIRE—
HAVE GOT *NO WEAPONS* POWERFUL ENOUGH TO DESTROY THOSE THINGS.
THAT'S JUST *GREAT.*
WHAT KIND OF AN EVIL OVERLORD ARE YOU GOING TO *BE,* ANYWAY?
APPARENTLY A BETTER ONE THAN I'D THOUGHT...

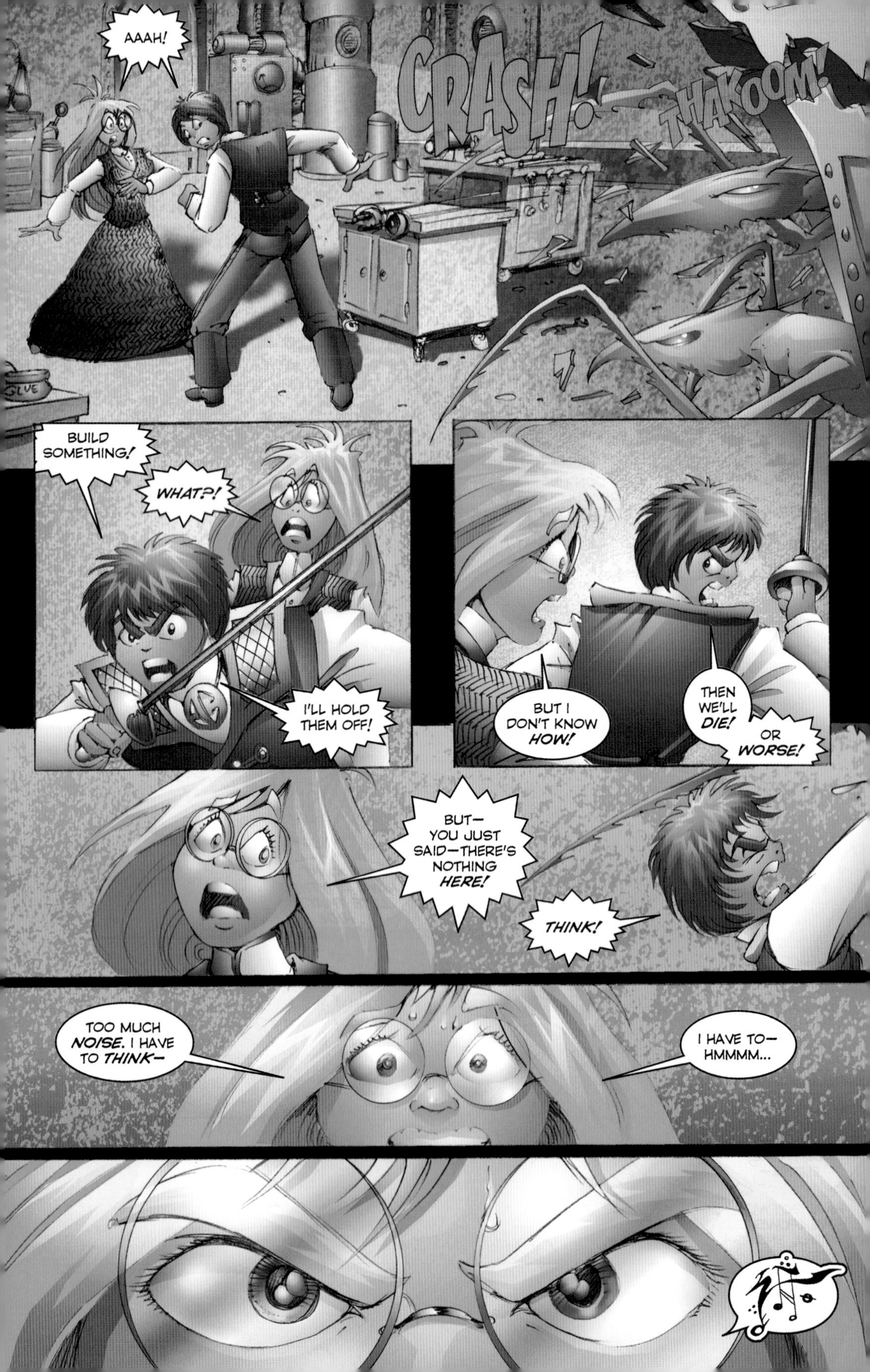
AAAH!
CRASH!
THAKOOM!
GLUE
BUILD SOMETHING!
WHAT?!
I'LL HOLD THEM OFF!
BUT I DON'T KNOW HOW!
THEN WE'LL DIE!
OR WORSE!
BUT— YOU JUST SAID—THERE'S NOTHING HERE!
THINK!
TOO MUCH NOISE. I HAVE TO THINK—
I HAVE TO— HMMMM...

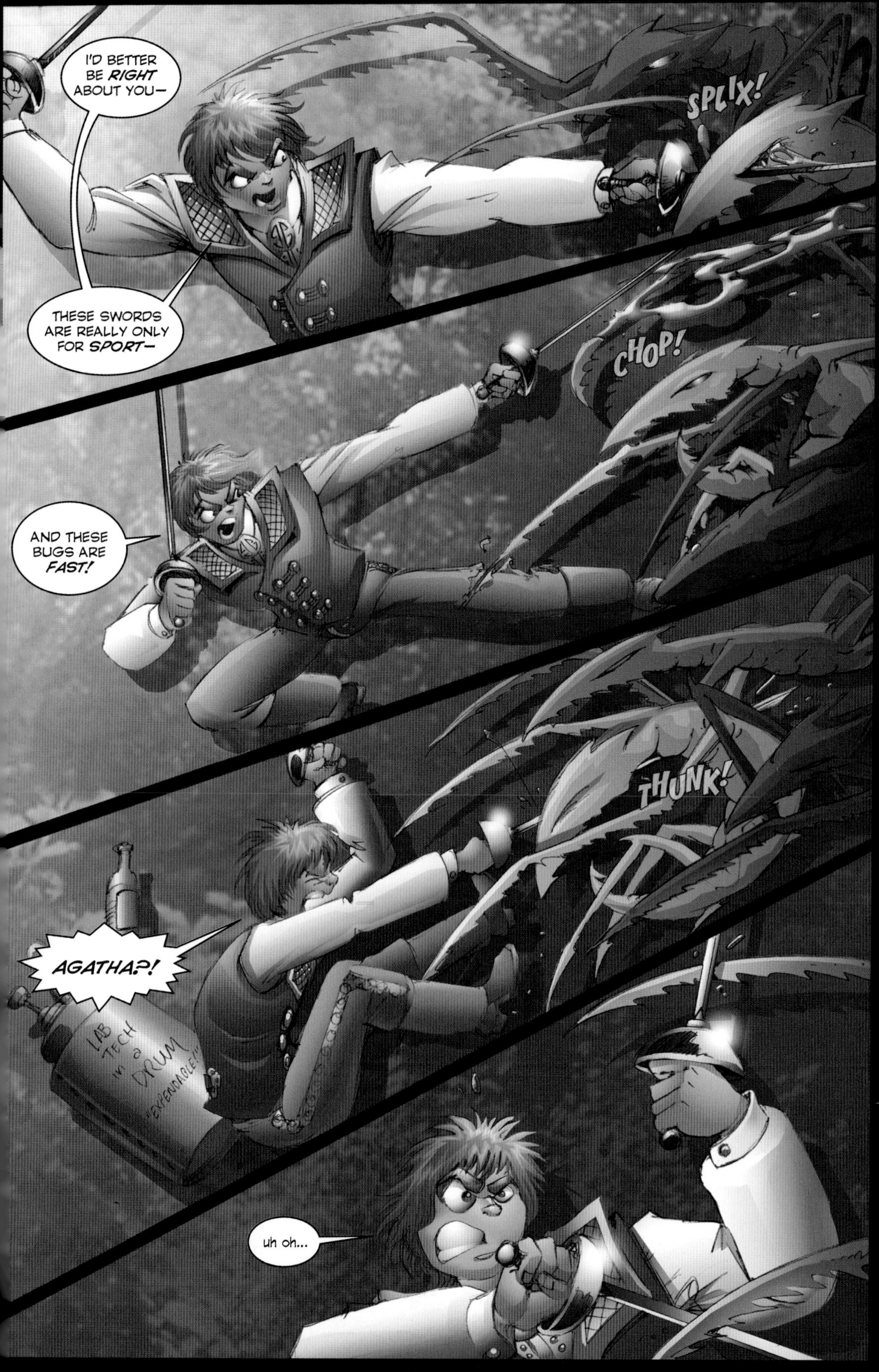
I'D BETTER BE RIGHT ABOUT YOU—
SPLIX!
THESE SWORDS ARE REALLY ONLY FOR SPORT—
CHOP!
AND THESE BUGS ARE FAST!
THUNK!
AGATHA?!
LAB TECH in a DRUM "EXPENDABLE!"
uh oh...

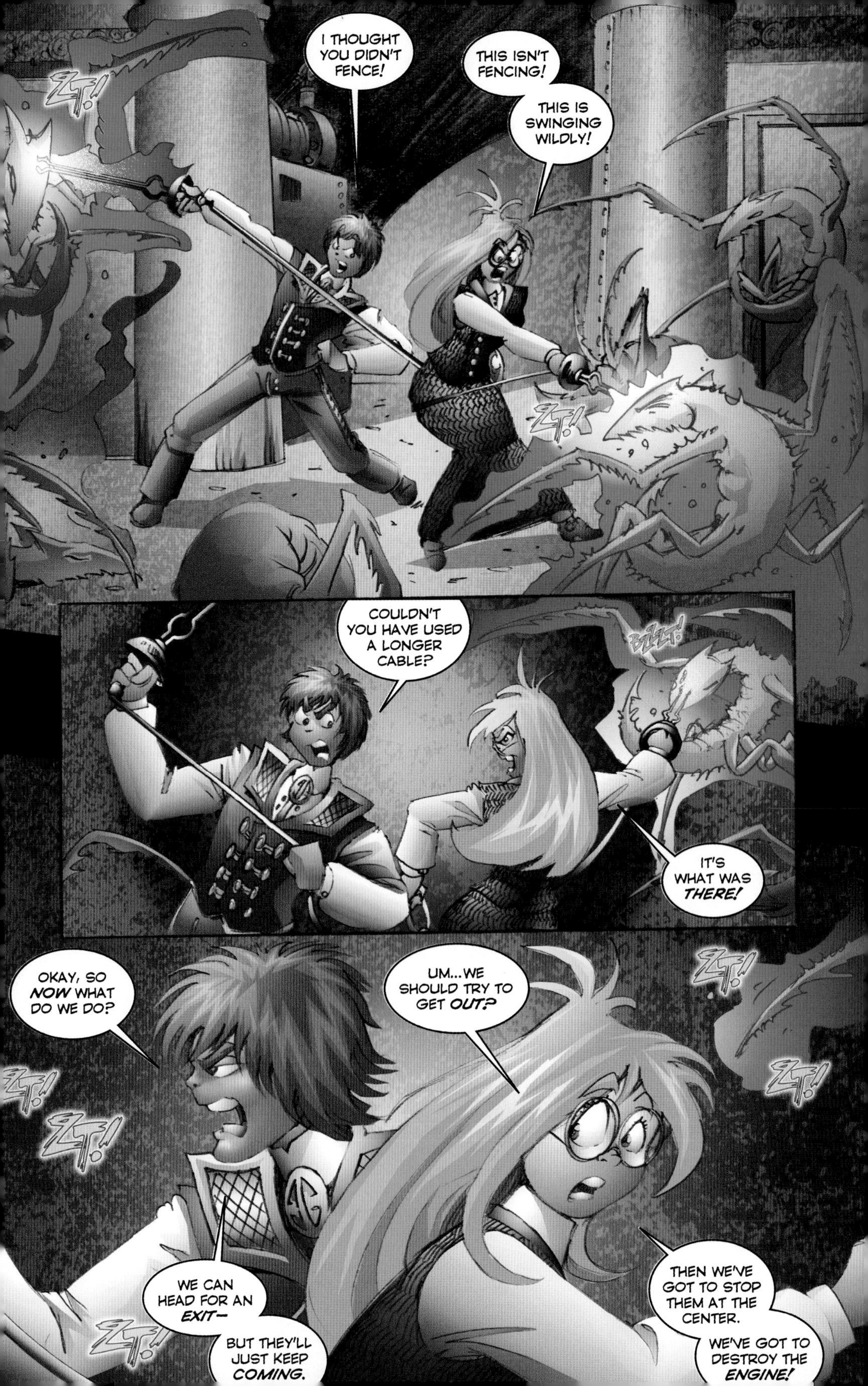

ZT!
I THOUGHT YOU DIDN'T FENCE!
THIS ISN'T FENCING!
THIS IS SWINGING WILDLY!
ZT!
COULDN'T YOU HAVE USED A LONGER CABLE?
BZZT!
IT'S WHAT WAS *THERE!*
OKAY, SO *NOW* WHAT DO WE DO?
UM...WE SHOULD TRY TO GET *OUT?*
ZT!
ZT!
ZT!
ZT!
WE CAN HEAD FOR AN *EXIT—*
BUT THEY'LL JUST KEEP *COMING.*
ZT!
THEN WE'VE GOT TO STOP THEM AT THE CENTER.
WE'VE GOT TO DESTROY THE *ENGINE!*

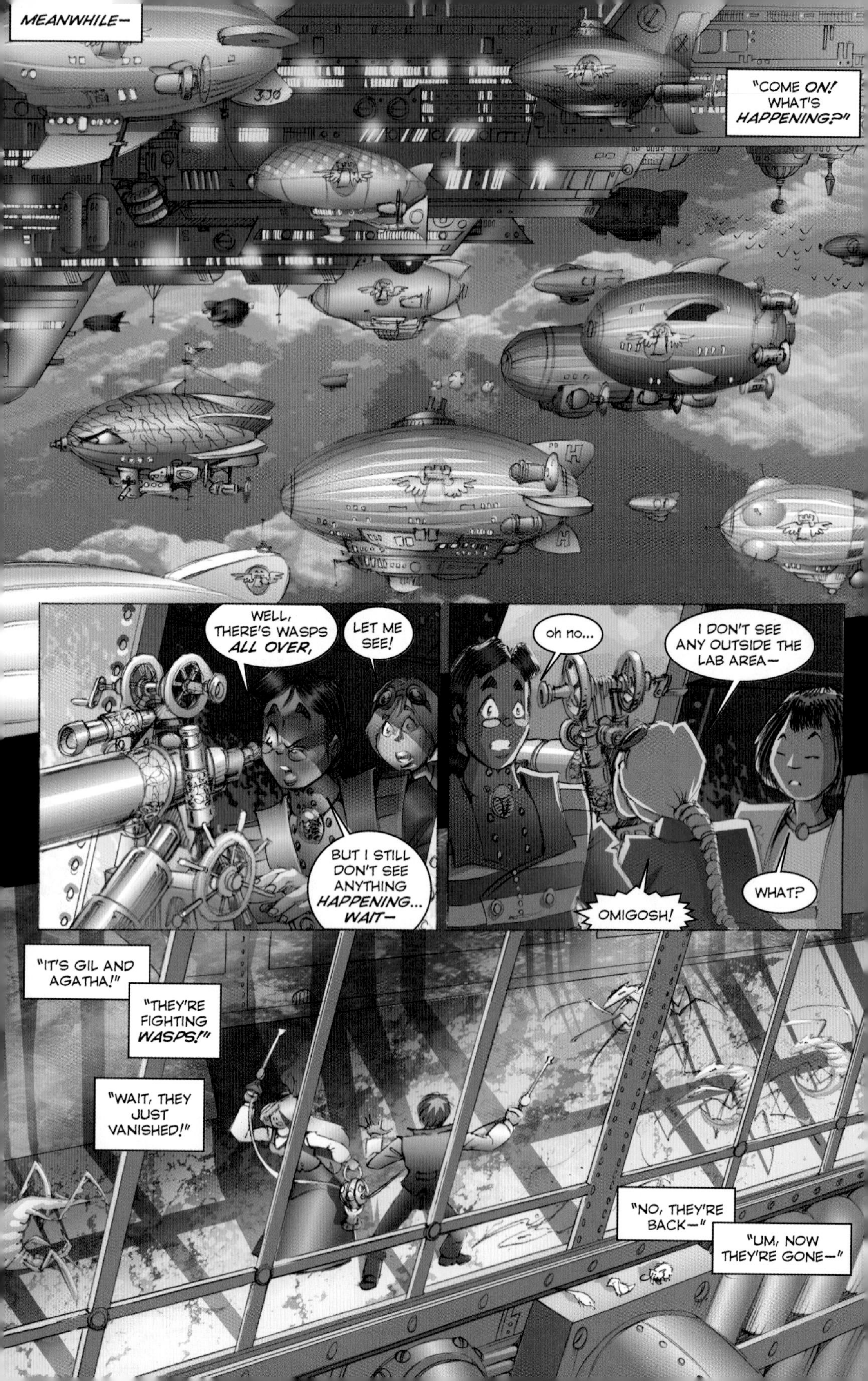
MEANWHILE—
"COME ON! WHAT'S HAPPENING?"
WELL, THERE'S WASPS ALL OVER,
LET ME SEE!
BUT I STILL DON'T SEE ANYTHING HAPPENING... WAIT—
oh no...
I DON'T SEE ANY OUTSIDE THE LAB AREA—
OMIGOSH!
WHAT?
"IT'S GIL AND AGATHA!"
"THEY'RE FIGHTING WASPS!"
"WAIT, THEY JUST VANISHED!"
"NO, THEY'RE BACK—"
"UM, NOW THEY'RE GONE—"

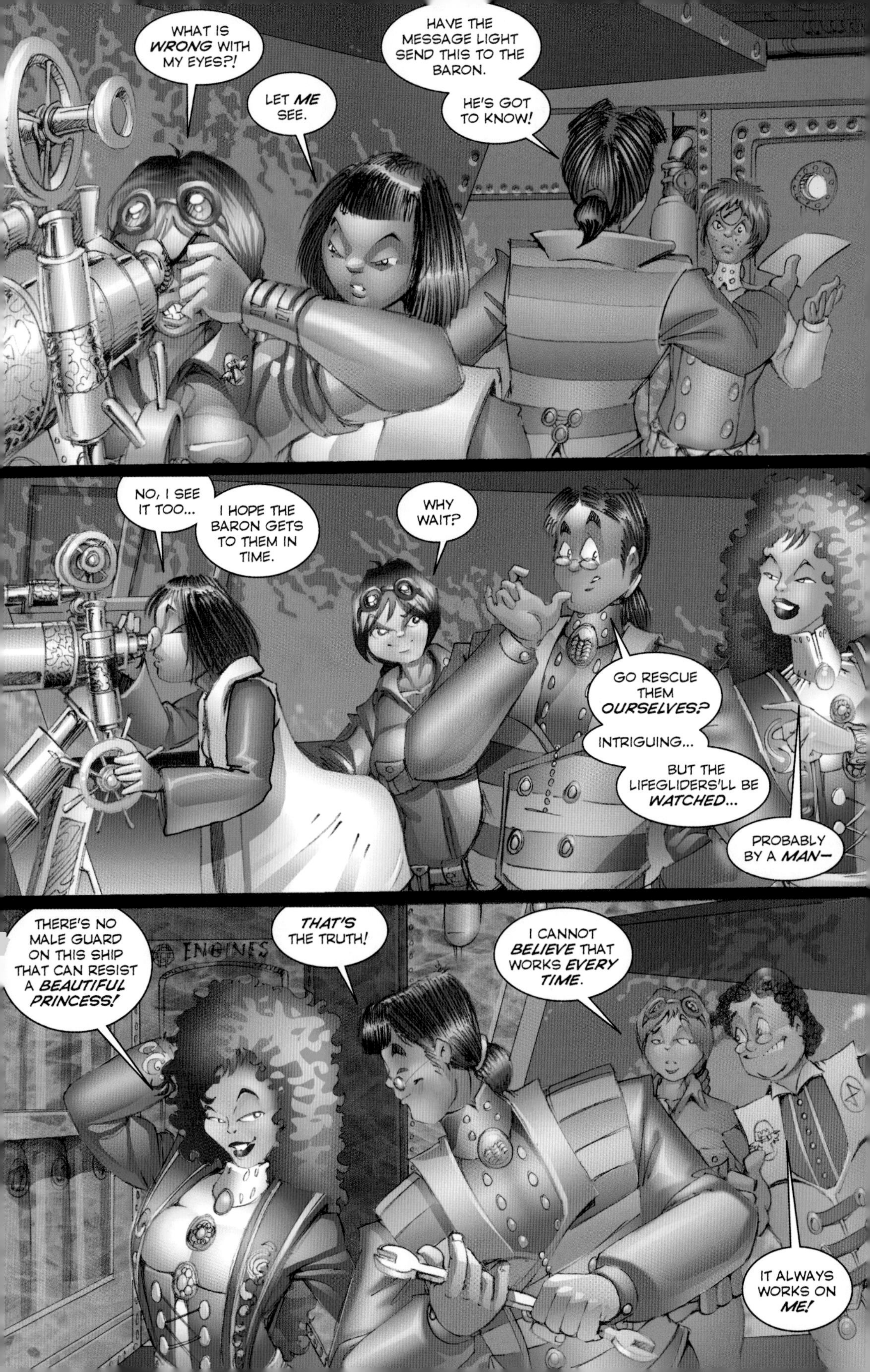

WHAT IS *WRONG* WITH MY EYES?!
LET *ME* SEE.
HAVE THE MESSAGE LIGHT SEND THIS TO THE BARON.
HE'S GOT TO KNOW!
NO, I SEE IT TOO...
I HOPE THE BARON GETS TO THEM IN TIME.
WHY WAIT?
GO RESCUE THEM *OURSELVES?*
INTRIGUING...
BUT THE LIFEGLIDERS'LL BE *WATCHED*...
PROBABLY BY A *MAN*—
THERE'S NO MALE GUARD ON THIS SHIP THAT CAN RESIST A *BEAUTIFUL PRINCESS!*
THAT'S THE TRUTH!
ENGINES
I CANNOT *BELIEVE* THAT WORKS *EVERY TIME*.
IT ALWAYS WORKS ON *ME!*

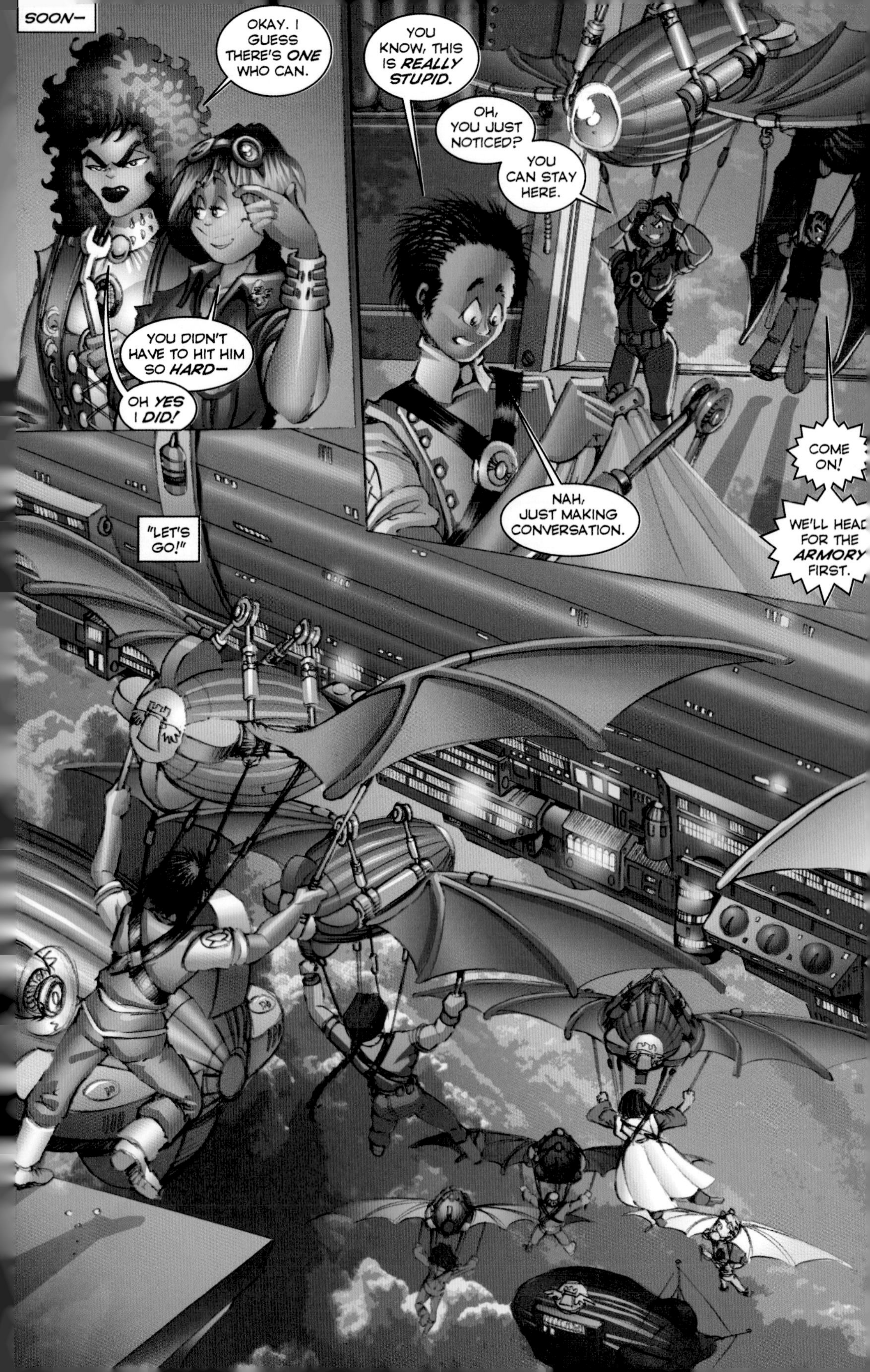
SOON—
OKAY. I GUESS THERE'S ONE WHO CAN.
YOU DIDN'T HAVE TO HIT HIM SO HARD—
OH YES I DID!
YOU KNOW, THIS IS REALLY STUPID.
OH, YOU JUST NOTICED?
YOU CAN STAY HERE.
NAH, JUST MAKING CONVERSATION.
COME ON!
WE'LL HEAD FOR THE ARMORY FIRST.
"LET'S GO!"

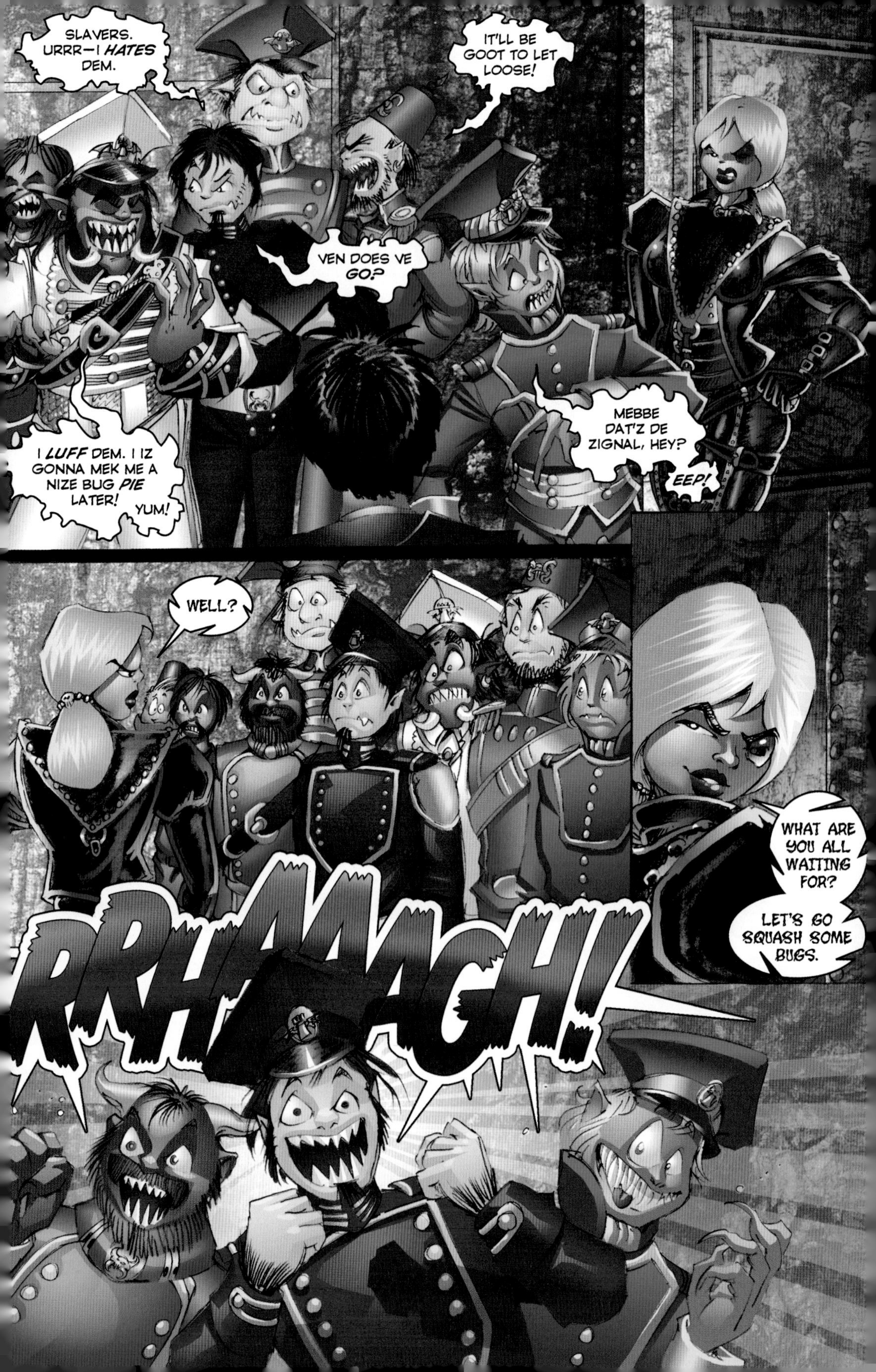
SLAVERS. URRR—I *HATES* DEM.
IT'LL BE GOOT TO LET LOOSE!
VEN DOES VE *GO?*
I *LUFF* DEM. I IZ GONNA MEK ME A NIZE BUG *PIE* LATER!
YUM!
MEBBE DAT'Z DE ZIGNAL, HEY?
EEP!
WELL?
WHAT ARE YOU ALL WAITING FOR?
LET'S GO SQUASH SOME BUGS.
RRHAAAAGH!

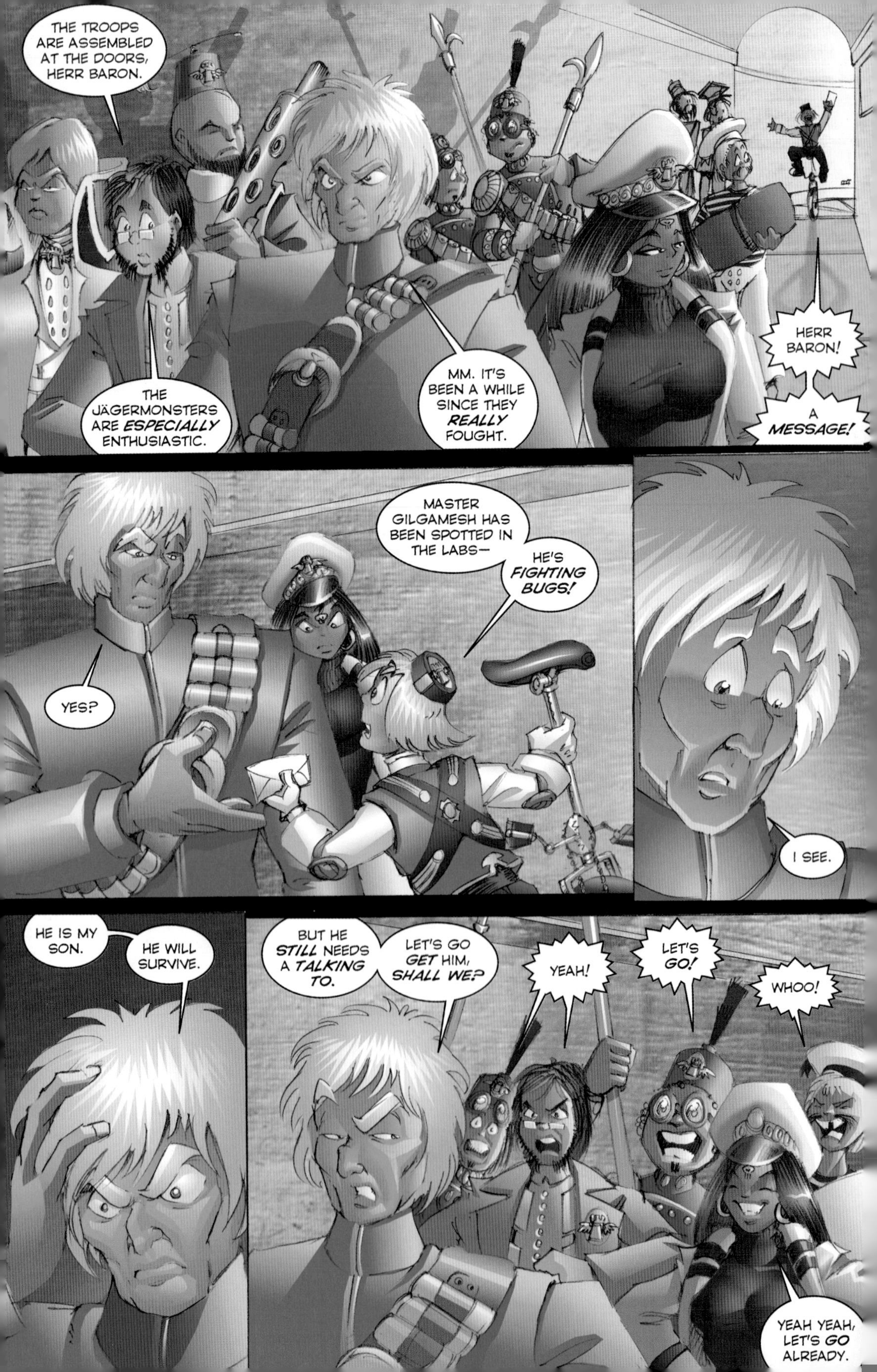
THE TROOPS ARE ASSEMBLED AT THE DOORS, HERR BARON.
THE JÄGERMONSTERS ARE *ESPECIALLY* ENTHUSIASTIC.
MM. IT'S BEEN A WHILE SINCE THEY *REALLY* FOUGHT.
HERR BARON!
A *MESSAGE!*
YES?
MASTER GILGAMESH HAS BEEN SPOTTED IN THE LABS—
HE'S *FIGHTING BUGS!*
I SEE.
HE IS MY SON.
HE WILL SURVIVE.
BUT HE *STILL* NEEDS A *TALKING TO.*
LET'S GO *GET* HIM, *SHALL WE?*
YEAH!
LET'S *GO!*
WHOO!
YEAH YEAH, LET'S *GO* ALREADY.

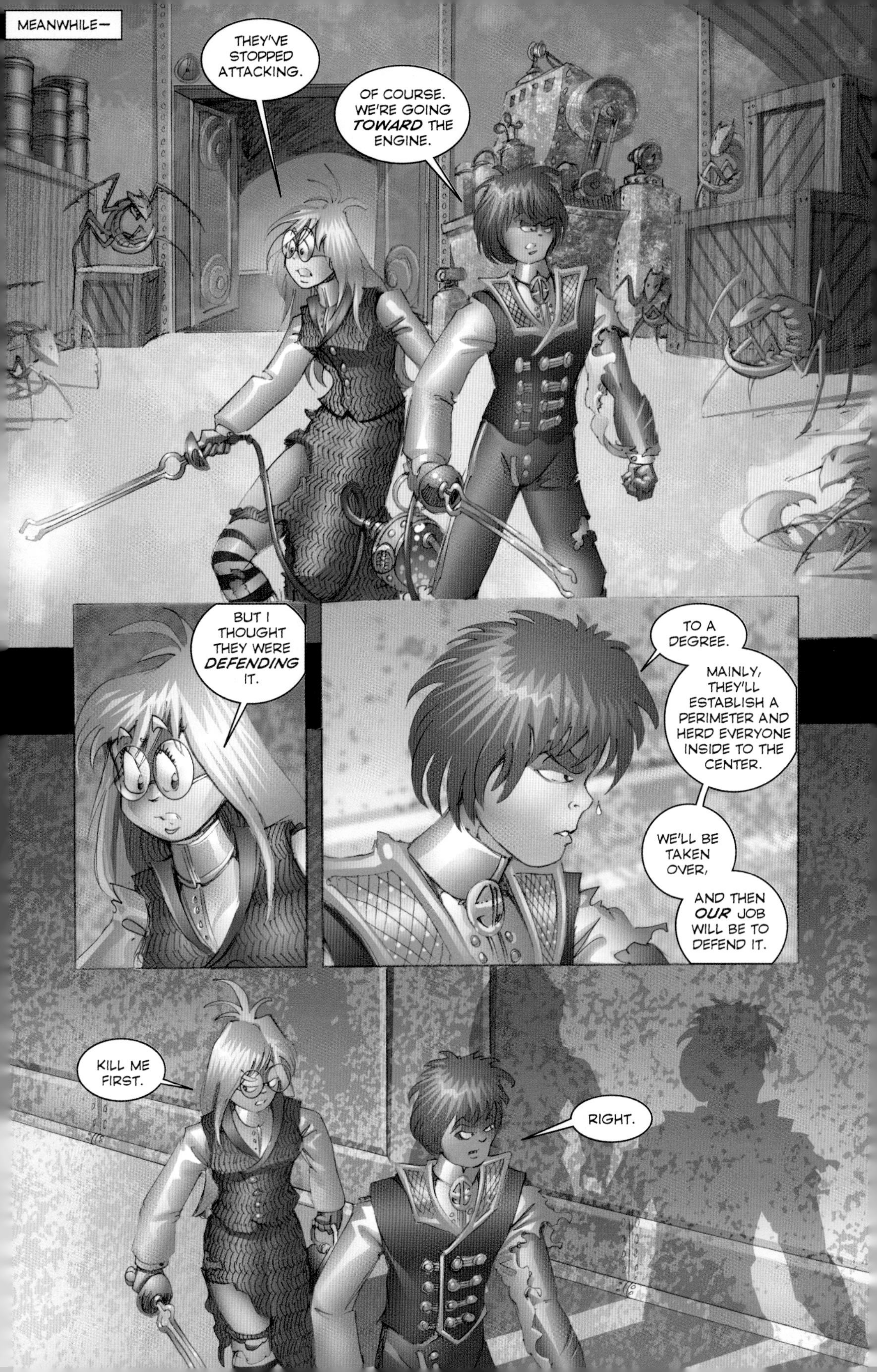
MEANWHILE—
THEY'VE STOPPED ATTACKING.
OF COURSE. WE'RE GOING *TOWARD* THE ENGINE.
BUT I THOUGHT THEY WERE *DEFENDING* IT.
TO A DEGREE.
MAINLY, THEY'LL ESTABLISH A PERIMETER AND HERD EVERYONE INSIDE TO THE CENTER.
WE'LL BE TAKEN OVER,
AND THEN *OUR* JOB WILL BE TO DEFEND IT.
KILL ME FIRST.
RIGHT.

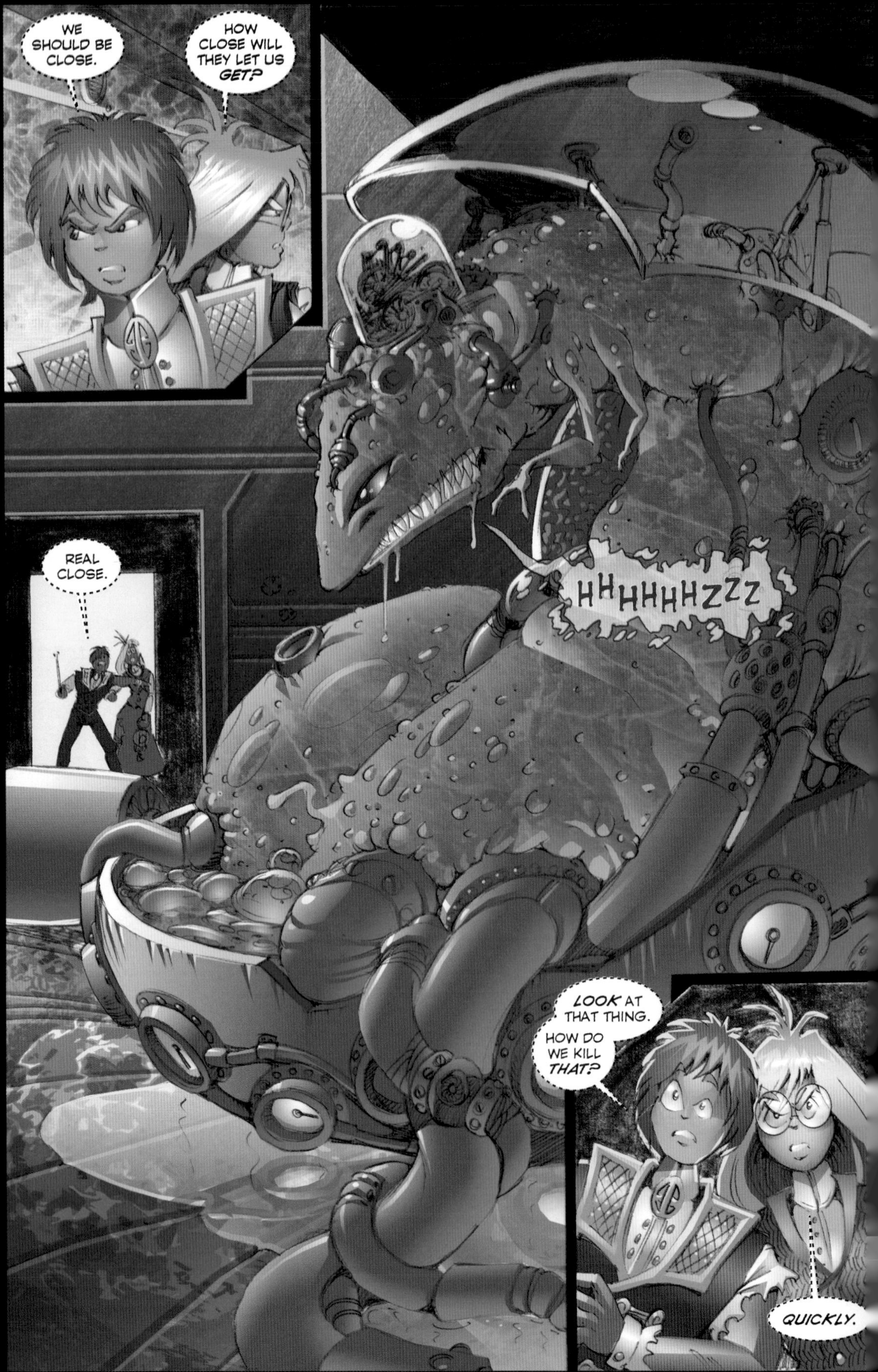
WE SHOULD BE CLOSE.
HOW CLOSE WILL THEY LET US *GET?*
REAL CLOSE.
HHHHHHZZZ
LOOK AT THAT THING.
HOW DO WE KILL *THAT?*
QUICKLY.

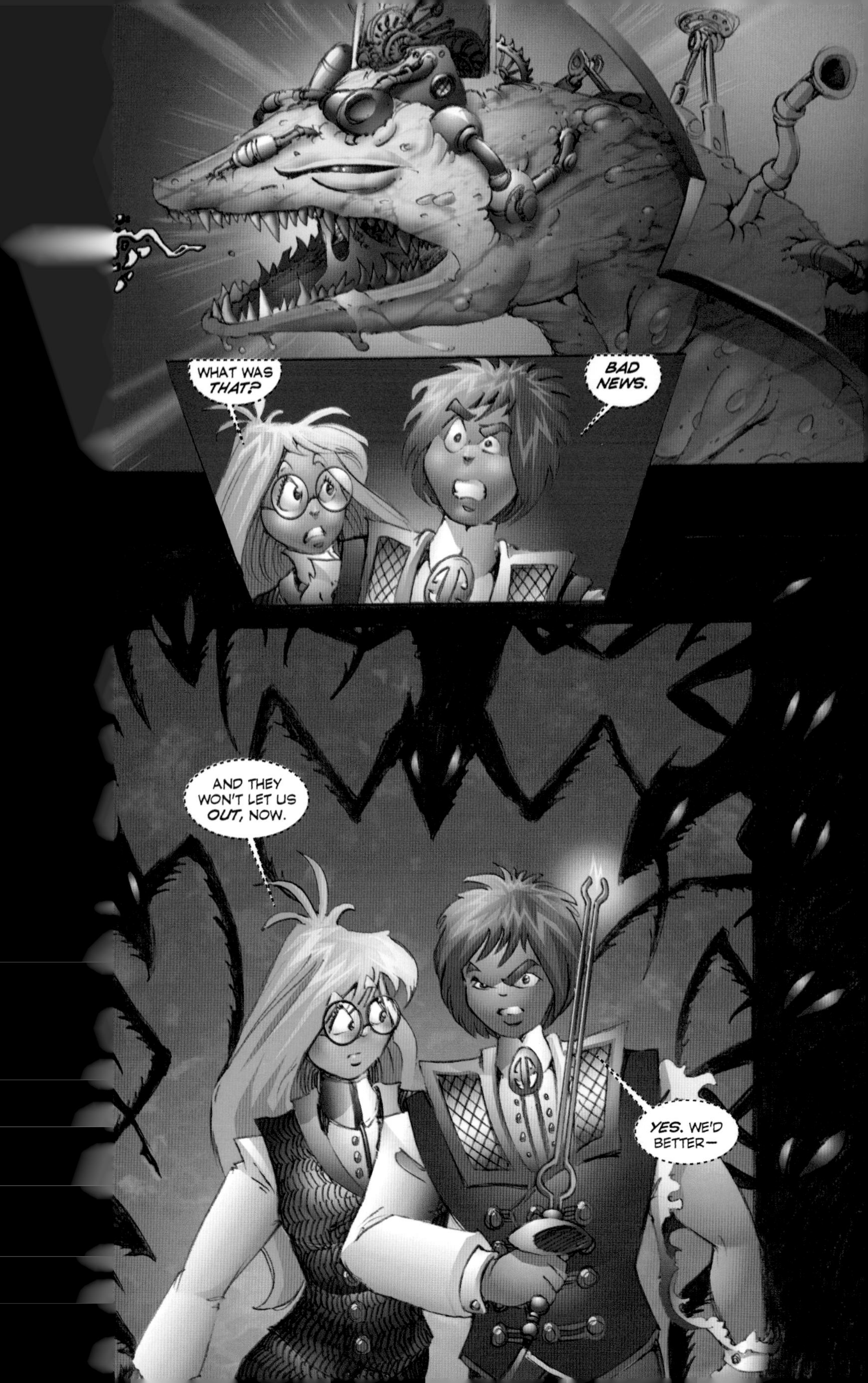
WHAT WAS THAT?
BAD NEWS.
AND THEY WON'T LET US OUT, NOW.
YES. WE'D BETTER—

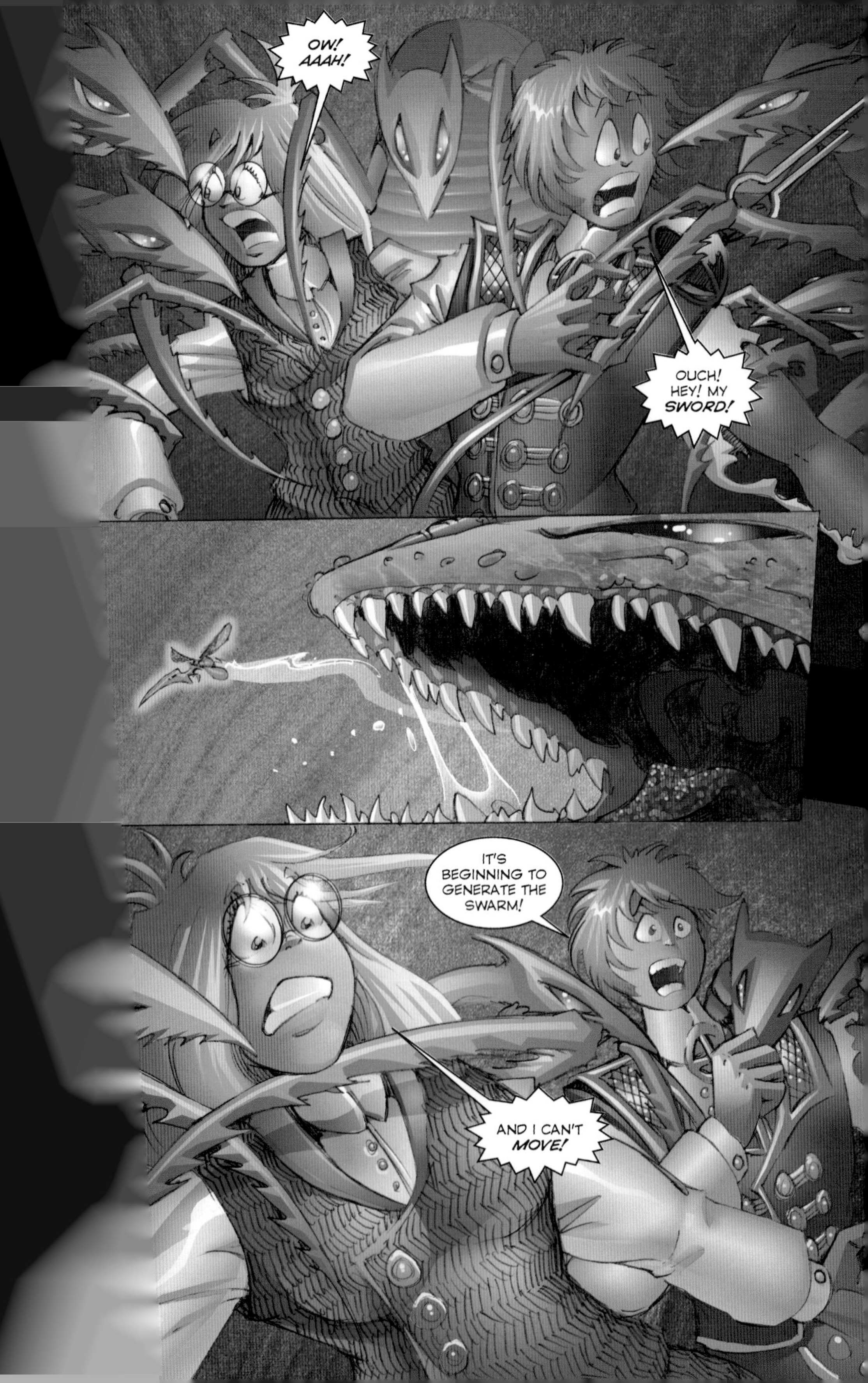
OW! AAAH!
OUCH! HEY! MY SWORD!
IT'S BEGINNING TO GENERATE THE SWARM!
AND I CAN'T MOVE!

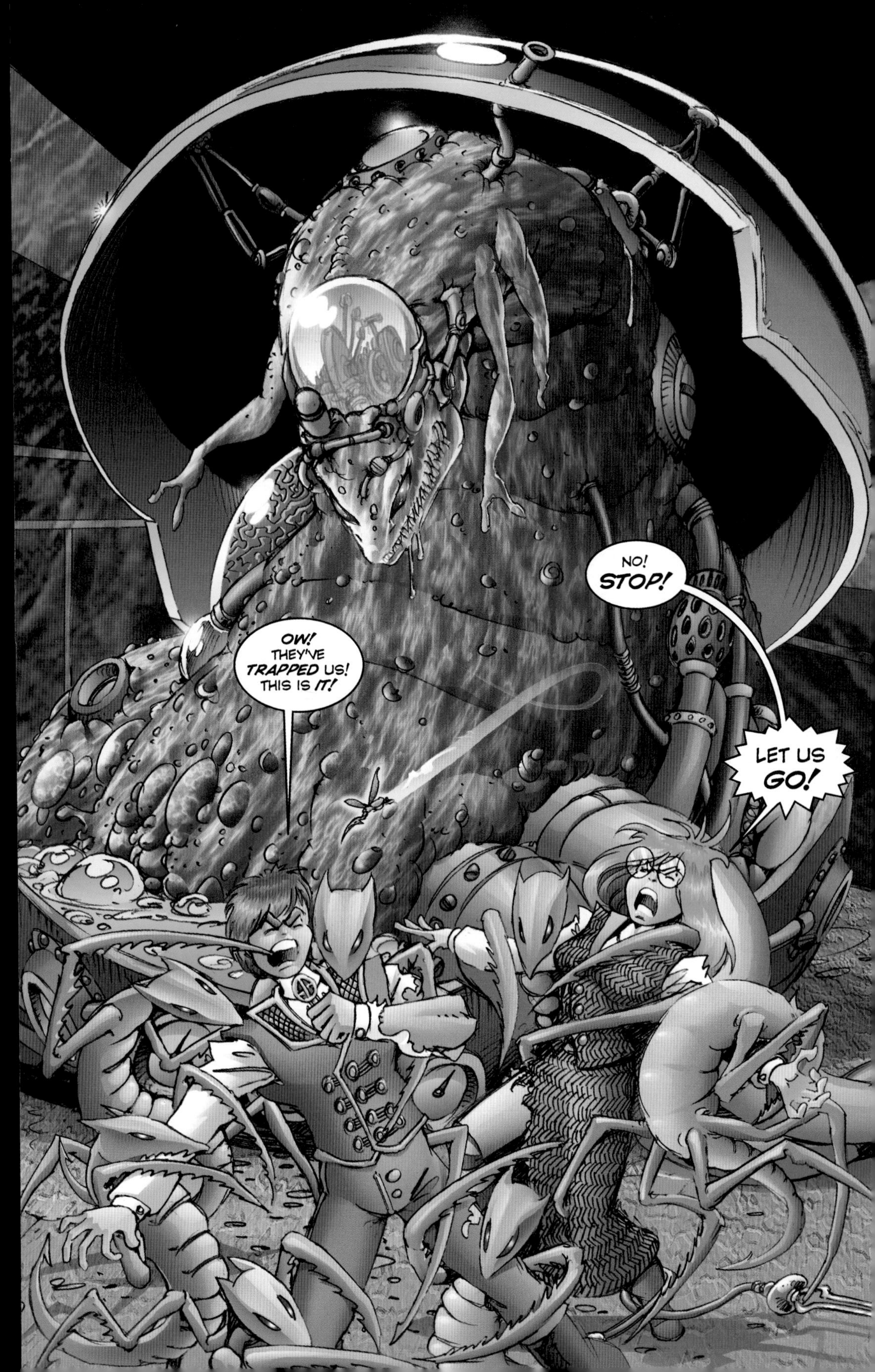
OW! THEY'VE TRAPPED US! THIS IS IT!
NO! STOP!
LET US GO!

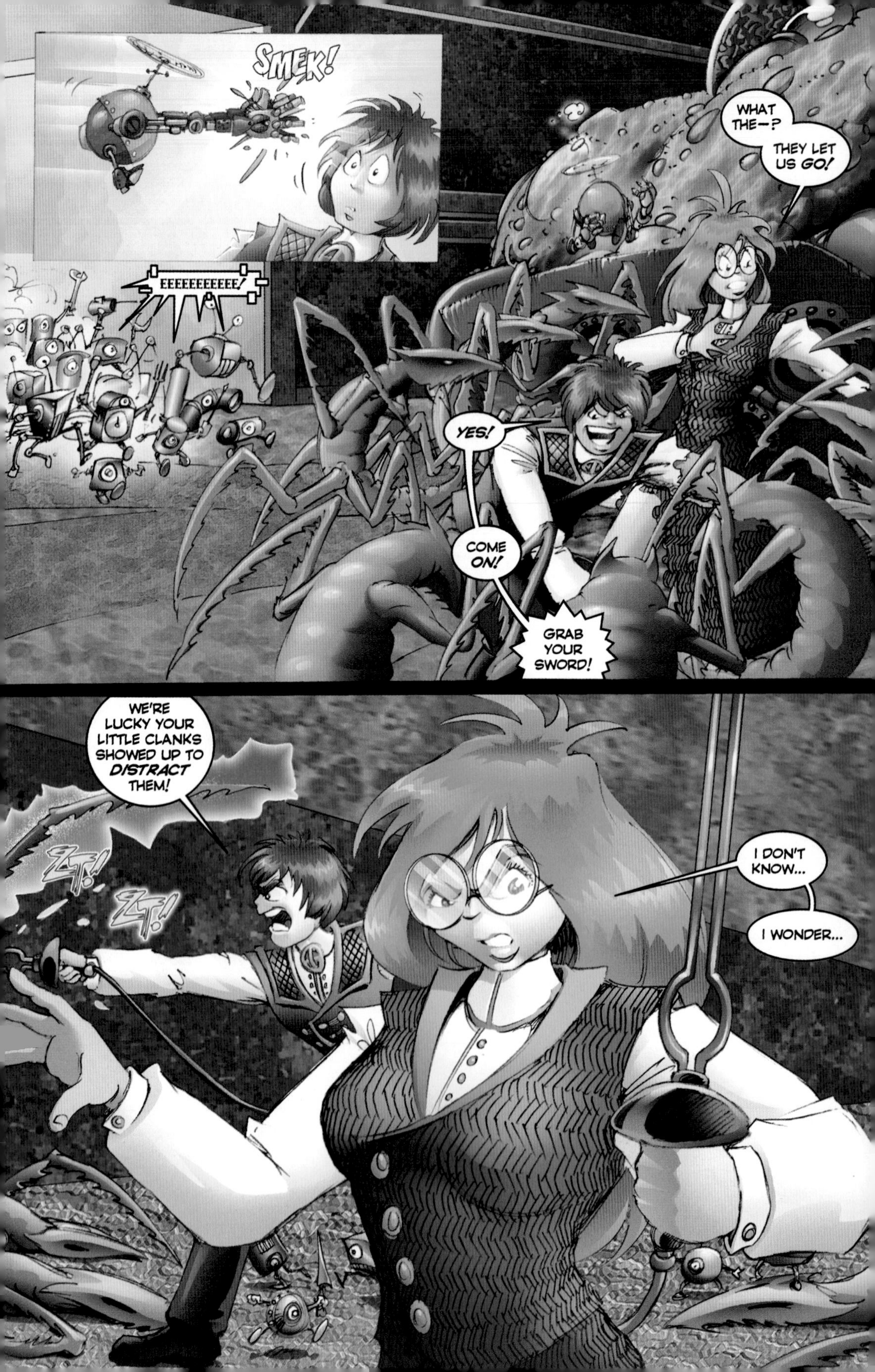
SMEK!
WHAT THE—?
THEY LET US GO!
EEEEEEEEEEE!
YES!
COME ON!
GRAB YOUR SWORD!
WE'RE LUCKY YOUR LITTLE CLANKS SHOWED UP TO DISTRACT THEM!
I DON'T KNOW...
I WONDER...

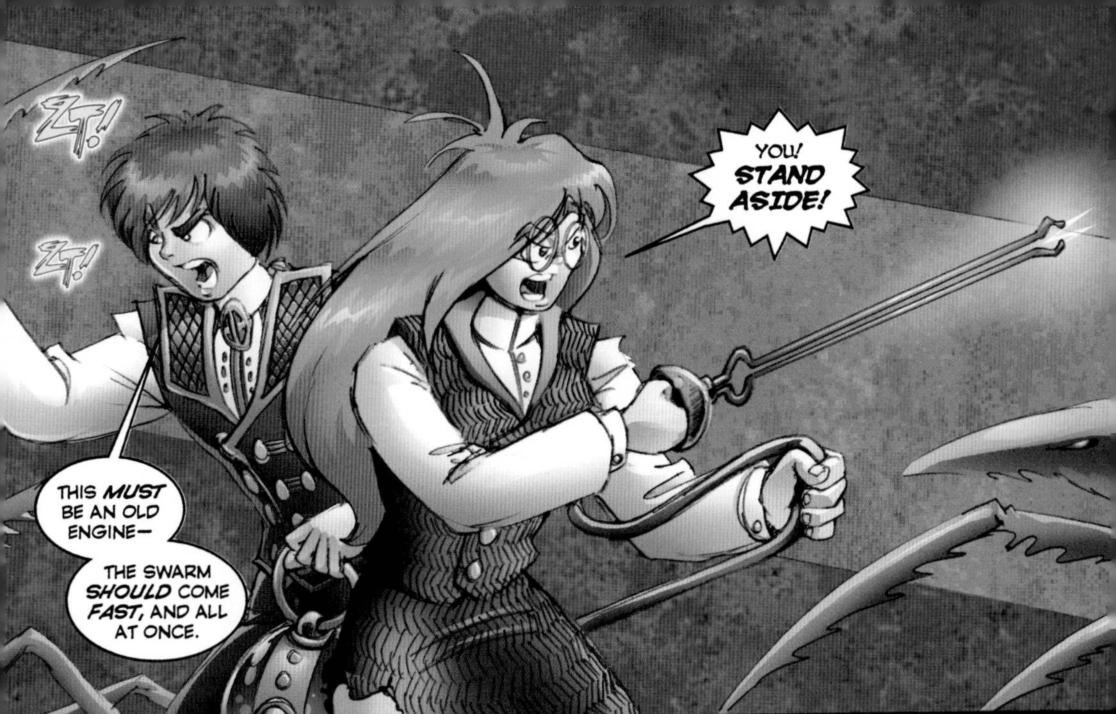
ZZT!
ZZT!
YOU! STAND ASIDE!
THIS MUST BE AN OLD ENGINE—
THE SWARM SHOULD COME FAST, AND ALL AT ONCE.

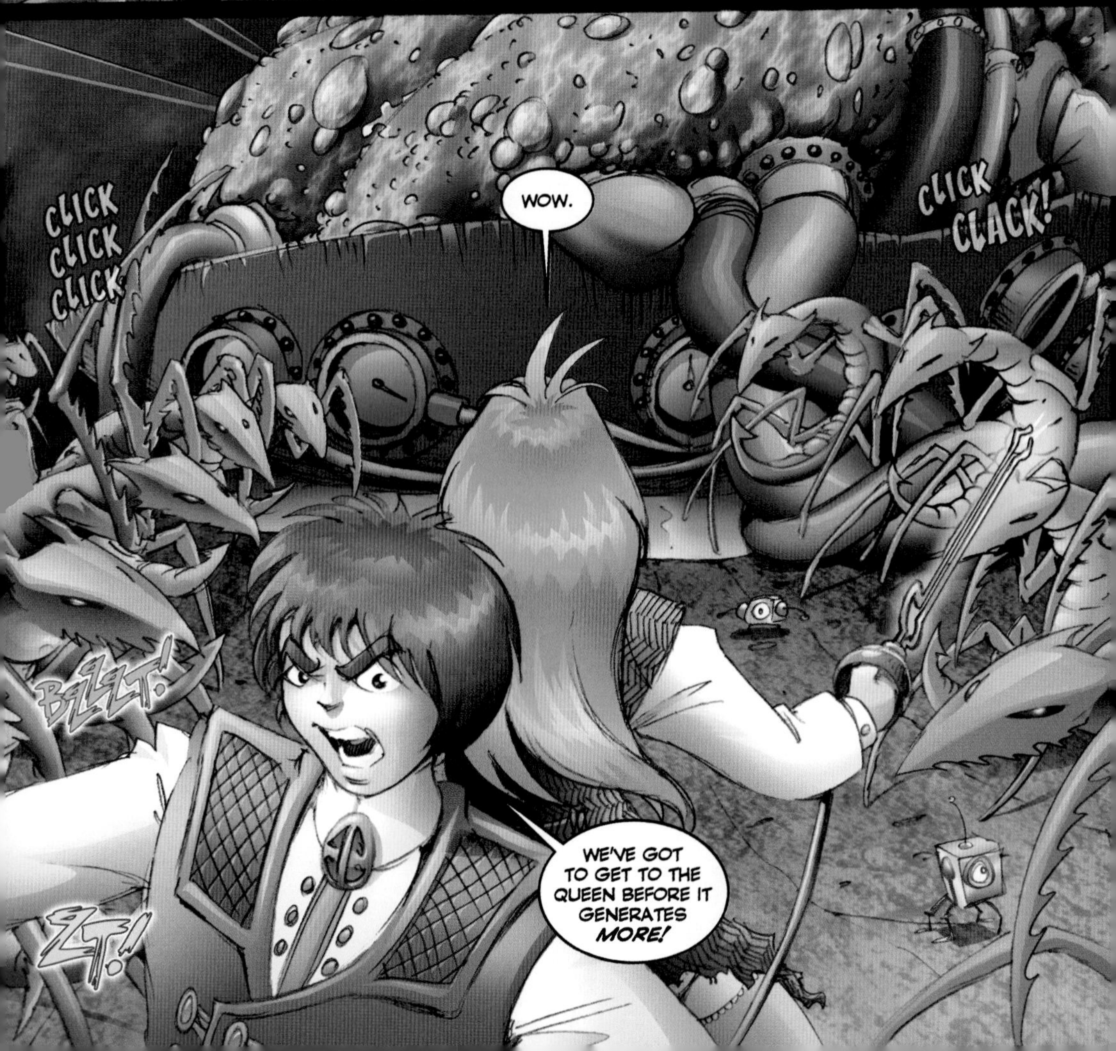
CLICK CLICK CLICK
WOW.
CLICK CLACK!
BZZT!
ZZT!
WE'VE GOT TO GET TO THE QUEEN BEFORE IT GENERATES MORE!

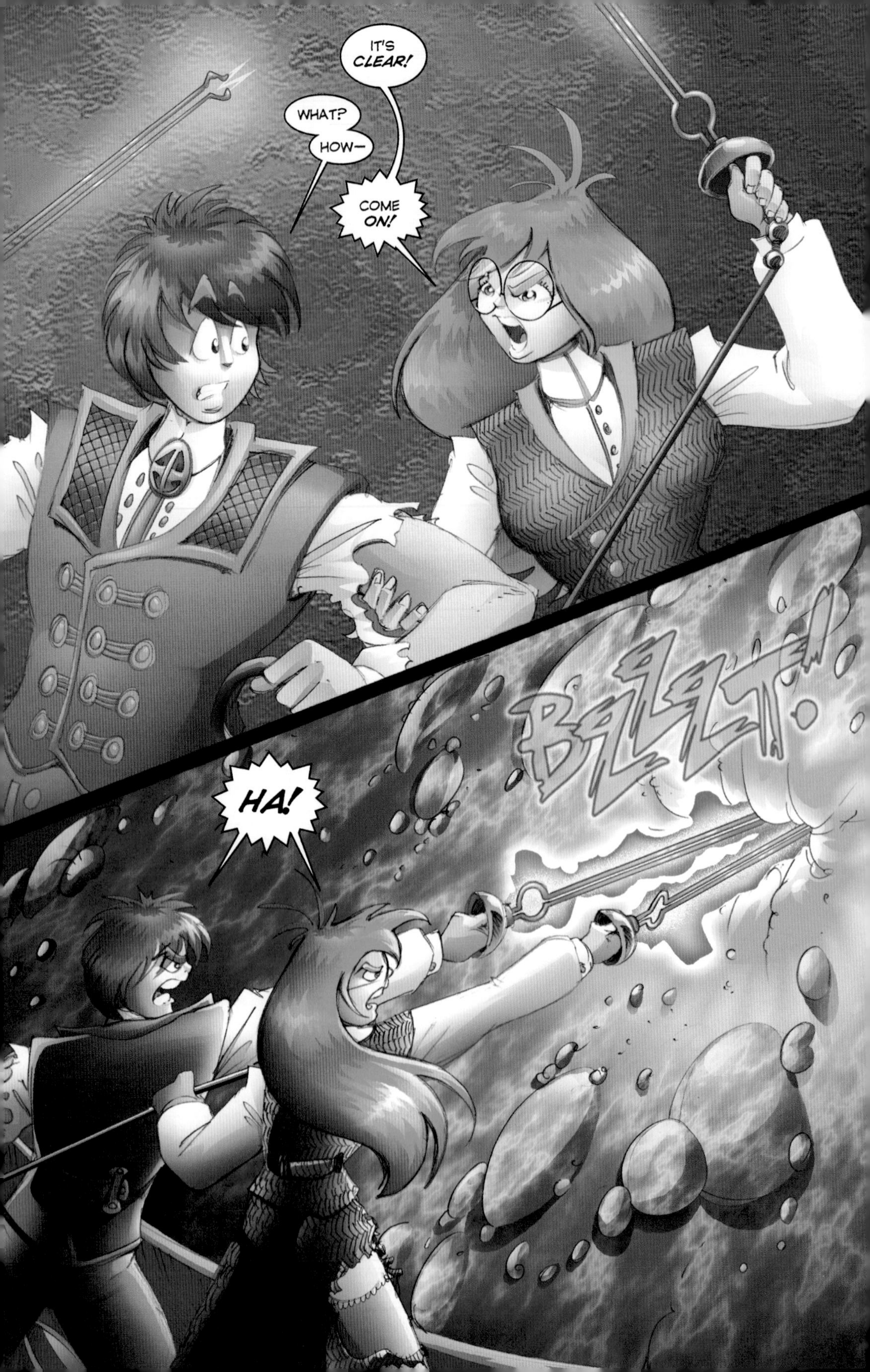
IT'S CLEAR!
WHAT?
HOW—
COME ON!
HA!
BZZZT!

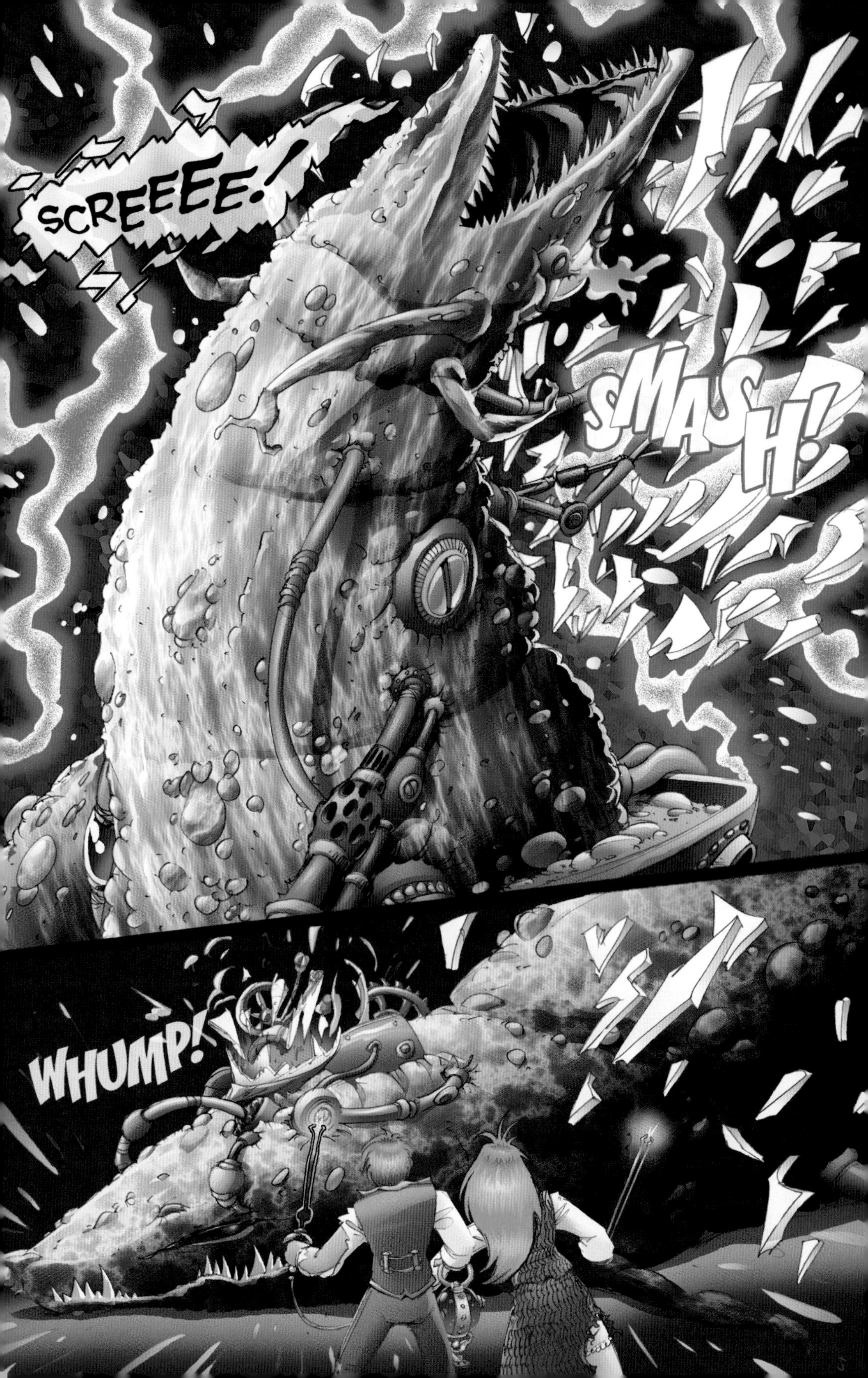
SCREEEEE!
SMASH!
WHUMP!

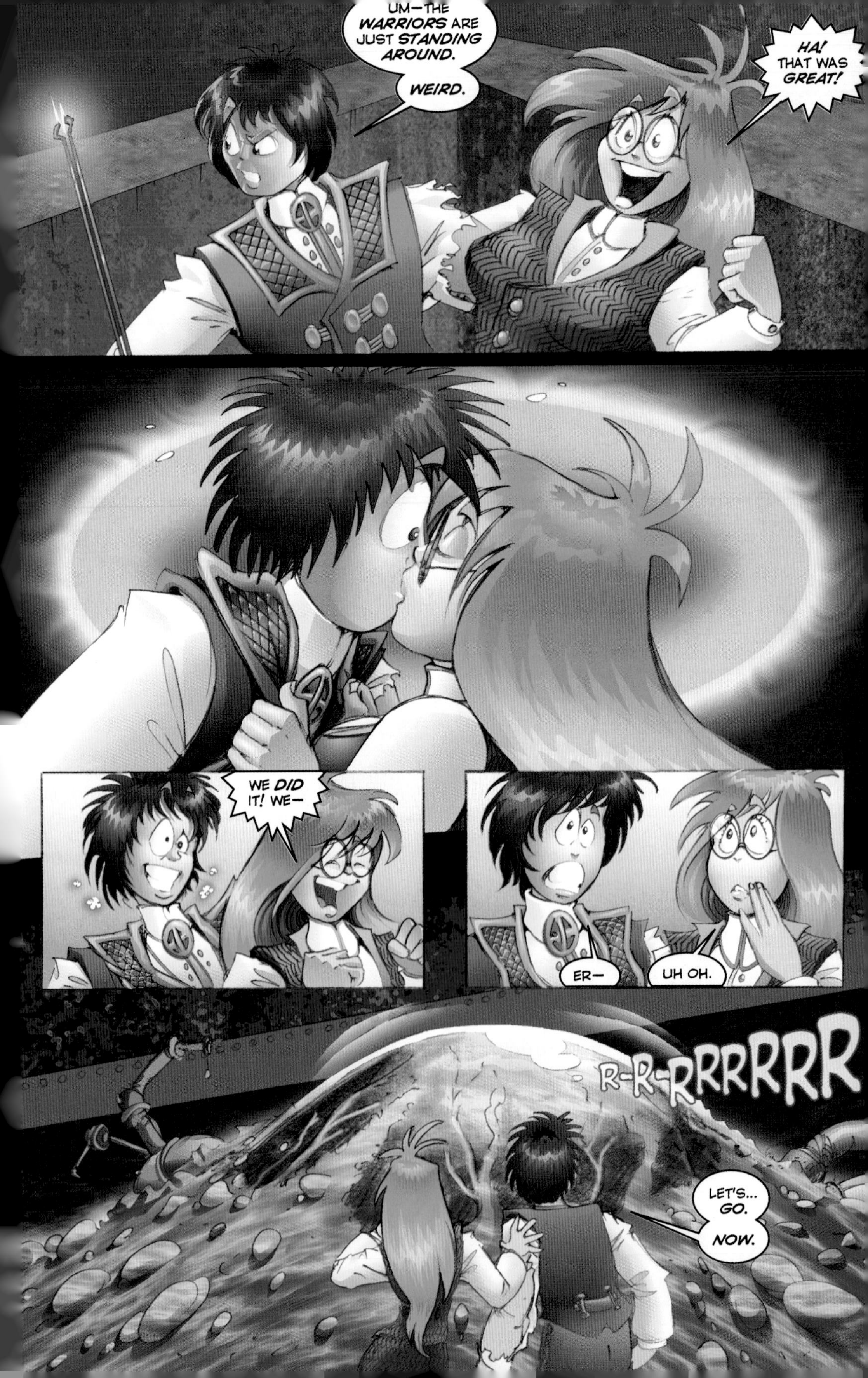
UM—THE WARRIORS ARE JUST STANDING AROUND.
WEIRD.
HA! THAT WAS GREAT!
WE DID IT! WE—
ER—
UH OH.
R-R-RRRRRR
LET'S... GO.
NOW.

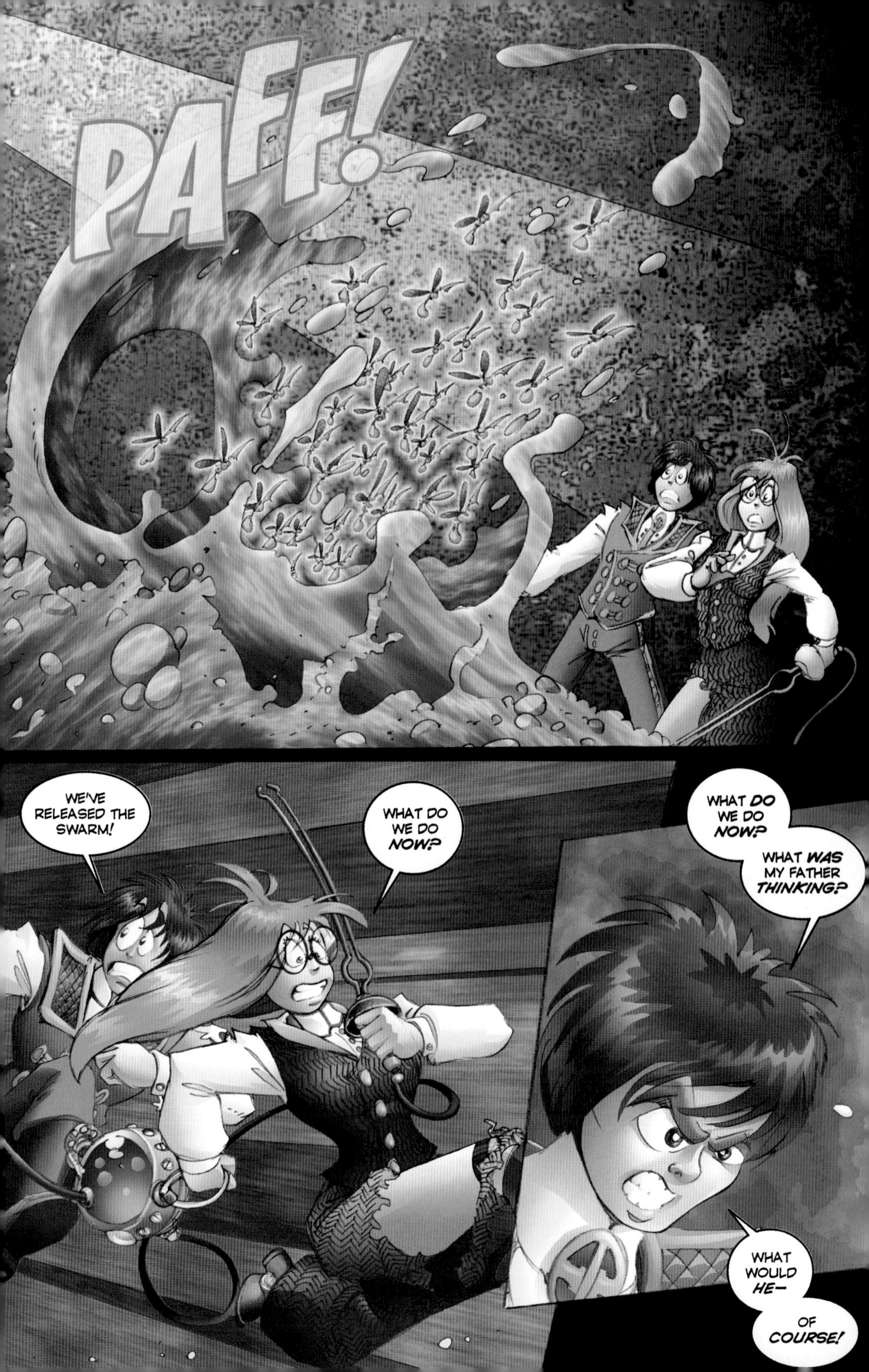
PAFF!
WE'VE RELEASED THE SWARM!
WHAT DO WE DO NOW?
WHAT DO WE DO NOW?
WHAT WAS MY FATHER THINKING?
WHAT WOULD HE—
OF COURSE!

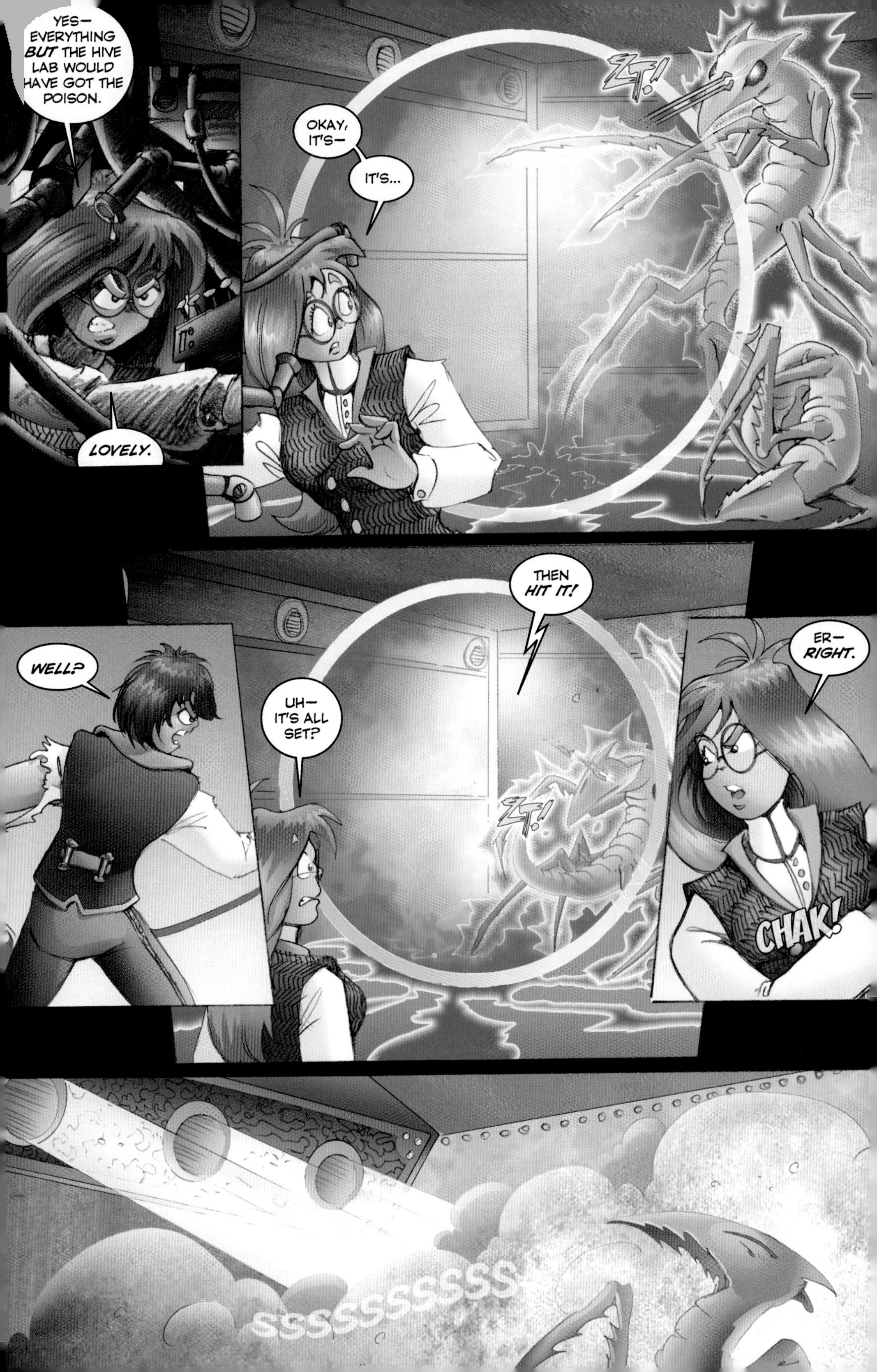
YES—EVERYTHING *BUT* THE HIVE LAB WOULD HAVE GOT THE POISON.
LOVELY.
OKAY, IT'S—
IT'S...
ZZT!
WELL?
UH—IT'S ALL SET?
THEN *HIT IT!*
ZZT!
ER—*RIGHT.*
CHAK!
SSSSSSSSSSSSSS

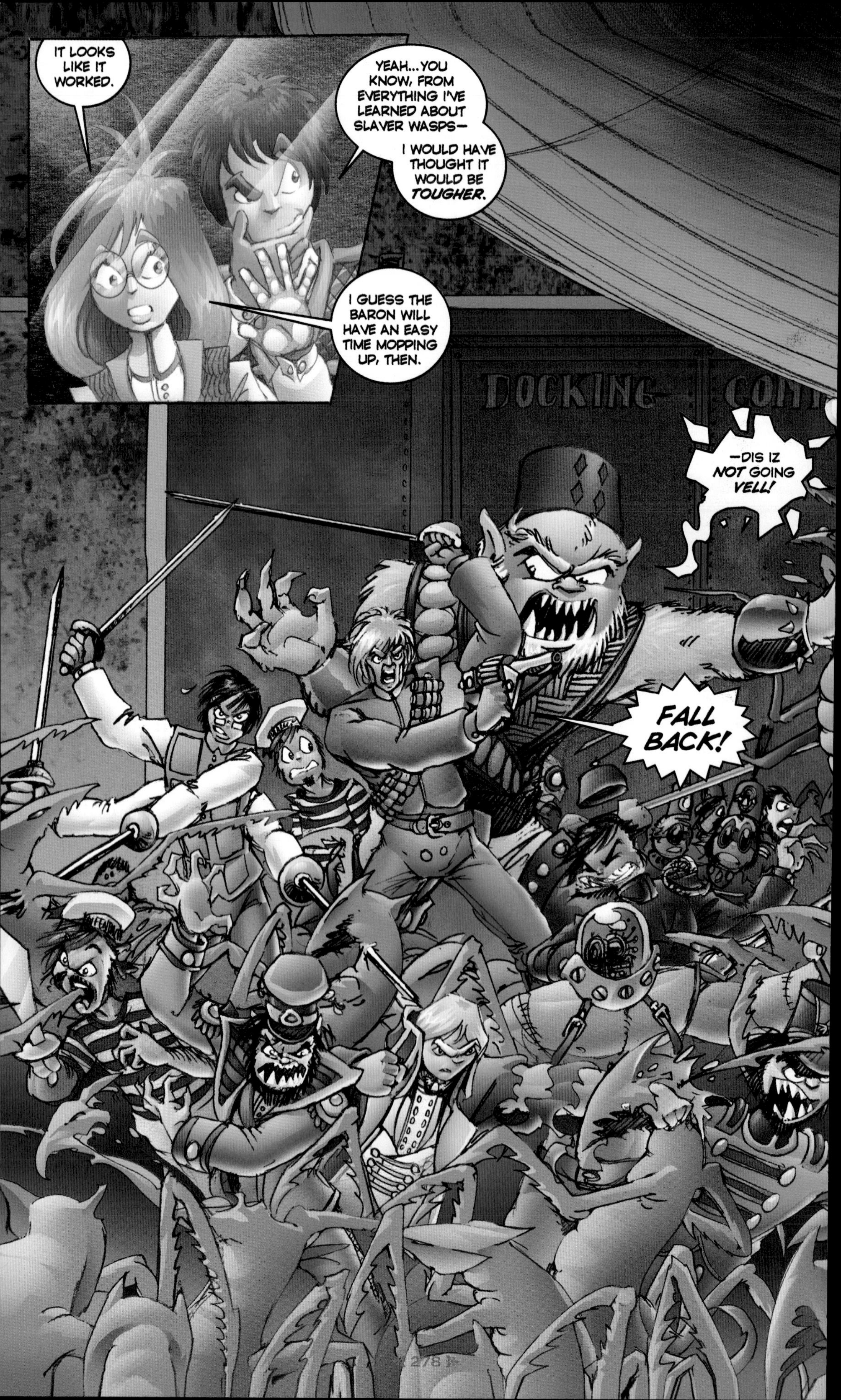

IT LOOKS LIKE IT WORKED.
YEAH...YOU KNOW, FROM EVERYTHING I'VE LEARNED ABOUT SLAVER WASPS—
I WOULD HAVE THOUGHT IT WOULD BE *TOUGHER*.
I GUESS THE BARON WILL HAVE AN EASY TIME MOPPING UP, THEN.
DOCKING
—DIS IZ *NOT* GOING *VELL!*
FALL BACK!

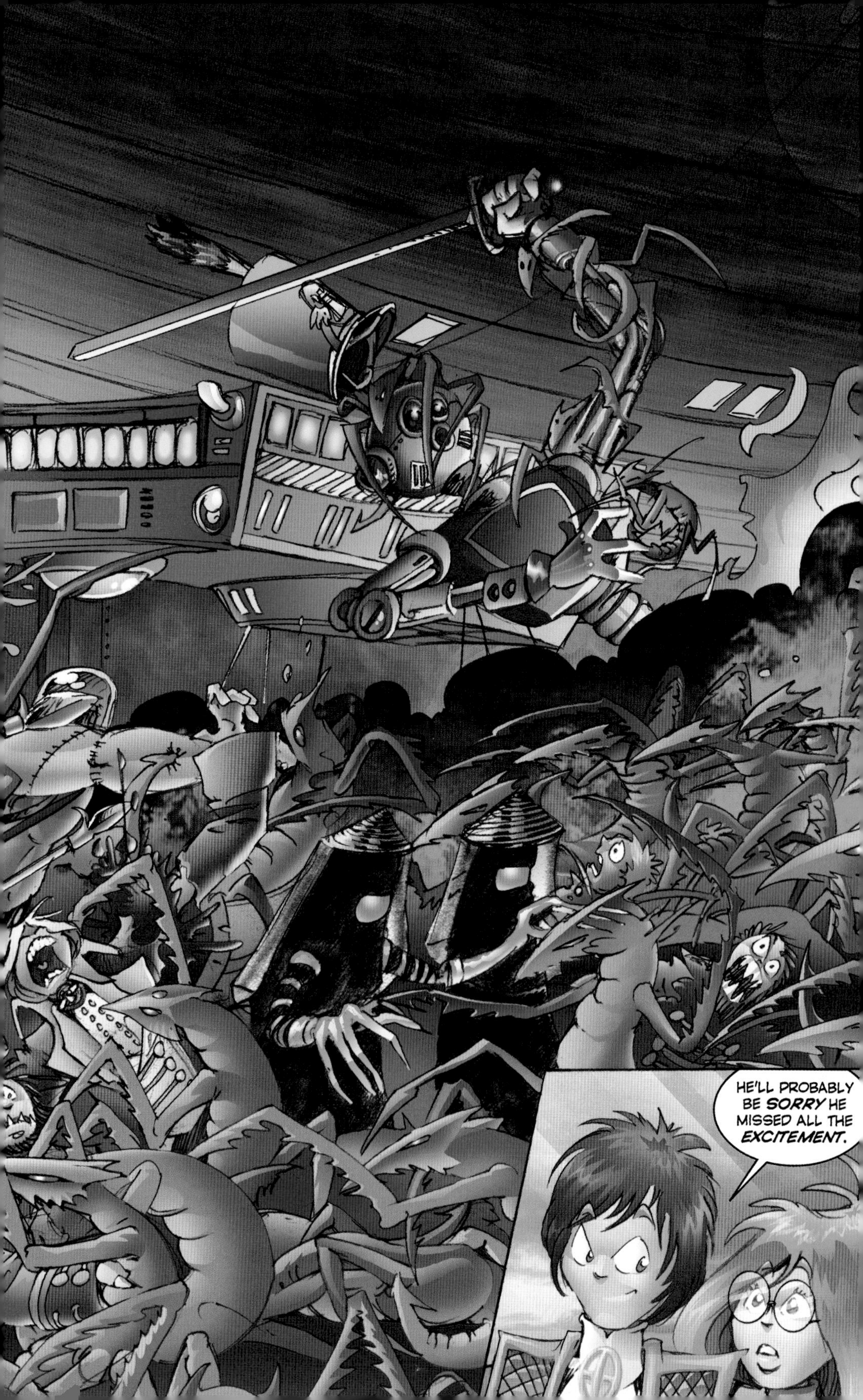
HE'LL PROBABLY BE SORRY HE MISSED ALL THE EXCITEMENT.

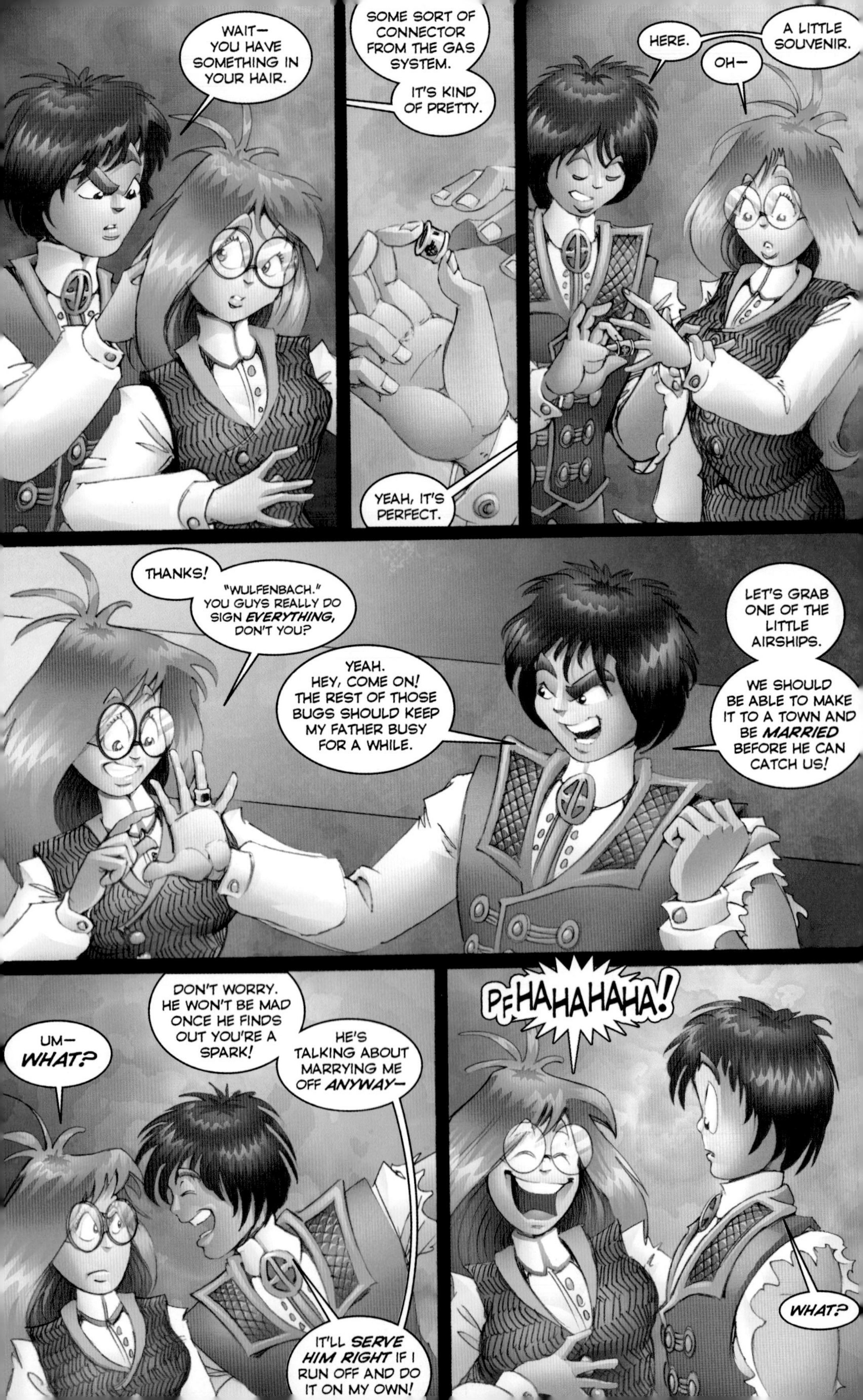
WAIT— YOU HAVE SOMETHING IN YOUR HAIR.
SOME SORT OF CONNECTOR FROM THE GAS SYSTEM.
IT'S KIND OF PRETTY.
YEAH, IT'S PERFECT.
HERE.
A LITTLE SOUVENIR.
OH—
THANKS!
"WULFENBACH." YOU GUYS REALLY DO SIGN *EVERYTHING*, DON'T YOU?
YEAH. HEY, COME ON! THE REST OF THOSE BUGS SHOULD KEEP MY FATHER BUSY FOR A WHILE.
LET'S GRAB ONE OF THE LITTLE AIRSHIPS.
WE SHOULD BE ABLE TO MAKE IT TO A TOWN AND BE *MARRIED* BEFORE HE CAN CATCH US!
UM— *WHAT?*
DON'T WORRY. HE WON'T BE MAD ONCE HE FINDS OUT YOU'RE A SPARK!
HE'S TALKING ABOUT MARRYING ME OFF *ANYWAY*—
IT'LL *SERVE HIM RIGHT* IF I RUN OFF AND DO IT ON MY OWN!
PFHAHAHAHAHA!
WHAT?

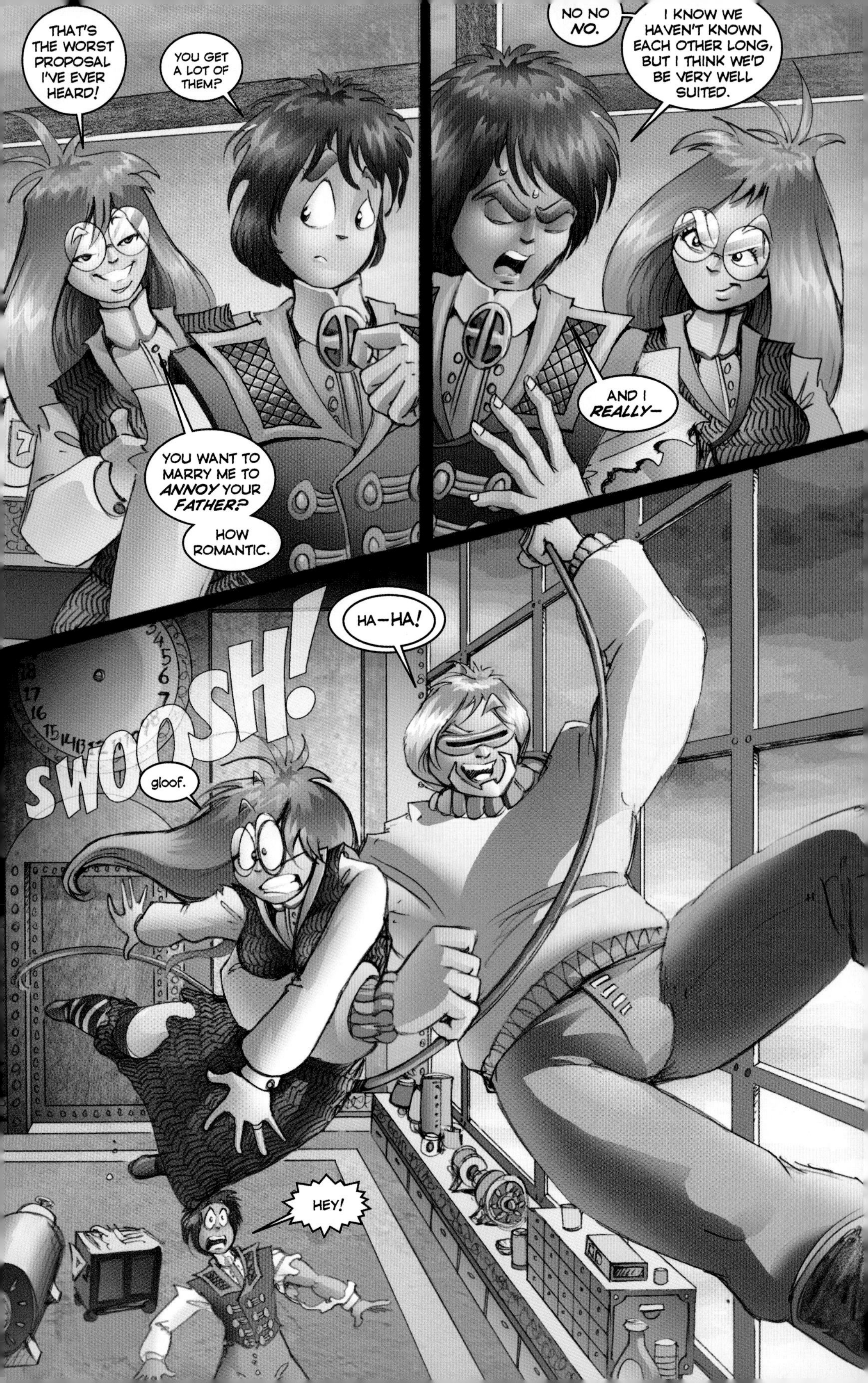
THAT'S THE WORST PROPOSAL I'VE EVER HEARD!
YOU GET A LOT OF THEM?
YOU WANT TO MARRY ME TO *ANNOY* YOUR *FATHER?*
HOW ROMANTIC.
NO NO *NO.*
I KNOW WE HAVEN'T KNOWN EACH OTHER LONG, BUT I THINK WE'D BE VERY WELL SUITED.
AND I *REALLY—*
HA—*HA!*
SWOOSH!
gloof.
HEY!

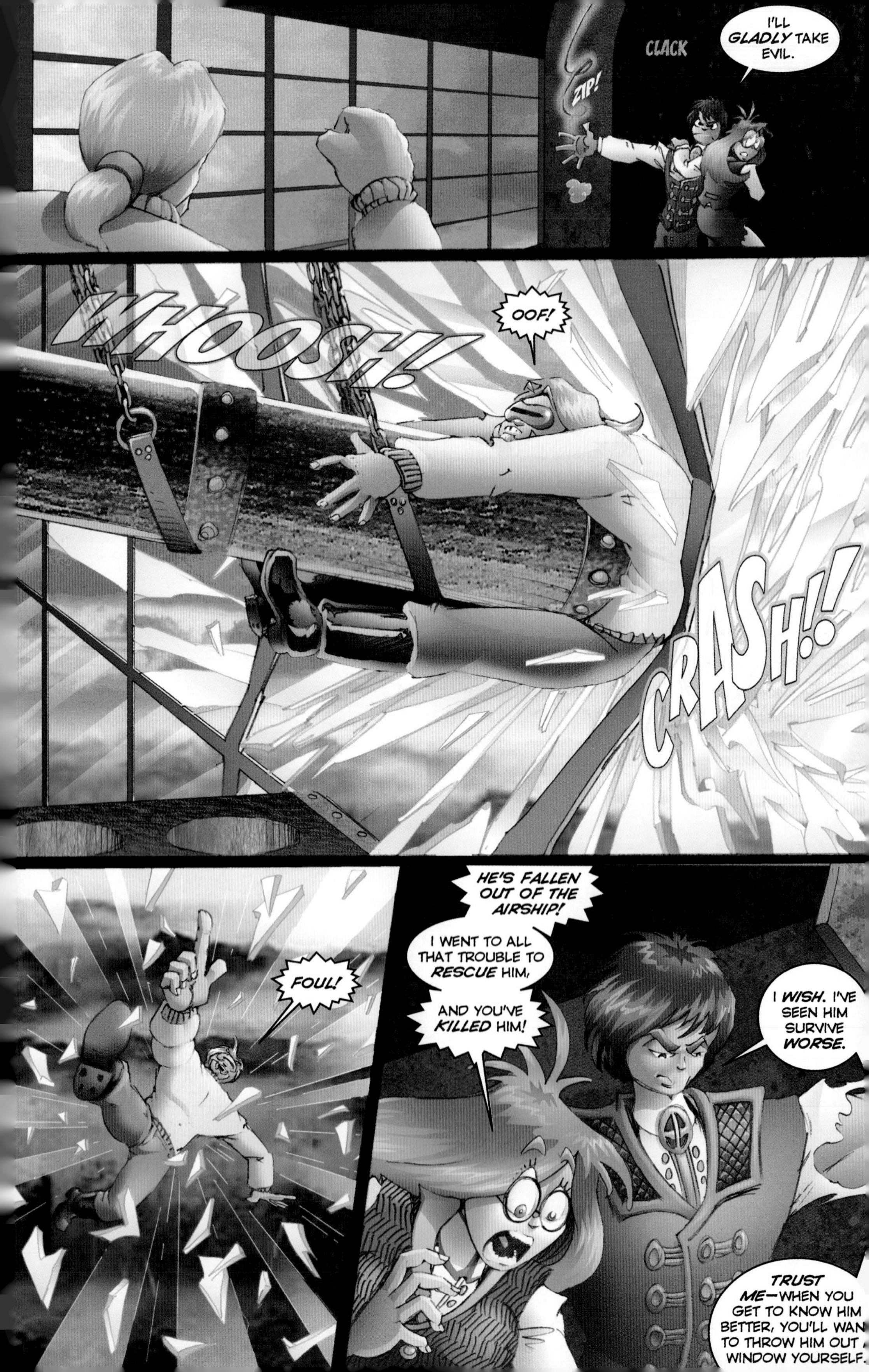
ZIP!
CLACK
I'LL GLADLY TAKE EVIL.
WHOOSH!!
OOF!
CRASH!!!
FOUL!
HE'S FALLEN OUT OF THE AIRSHIP!
I WENT TO ALL THAT TROUBLE TO RESCUE HIM,
AND YOU'VE KILLED HIM!
I WISH. I'VE SEEN HIM SURVIVE WORSE.
TRUST ME—WHEN YOU GET TO KNOW HIM BETTER, YOU'LL WAN TO THROW HIM OUT WINDOW YOURSELF.

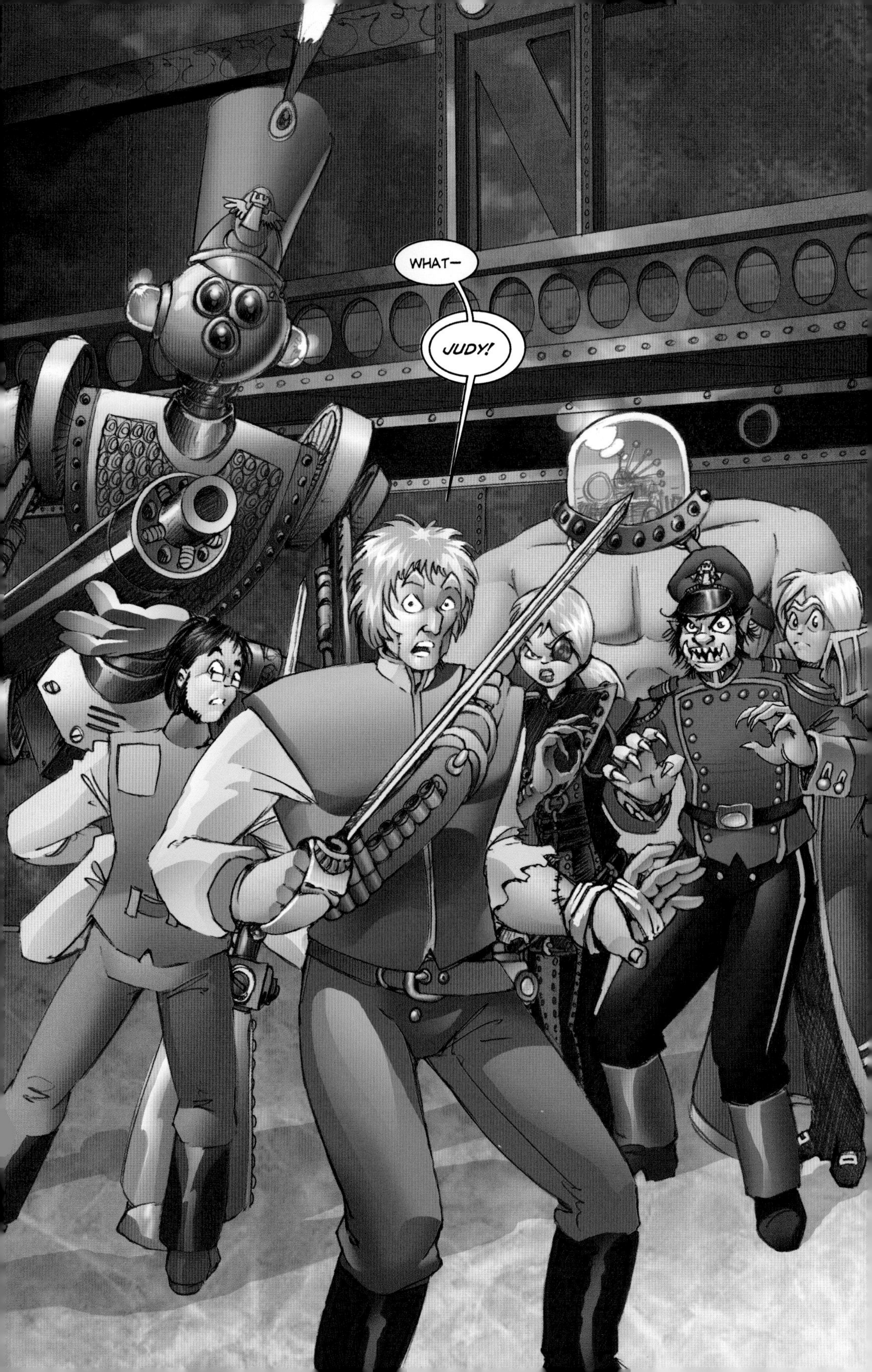
WHAT—
JUDY!

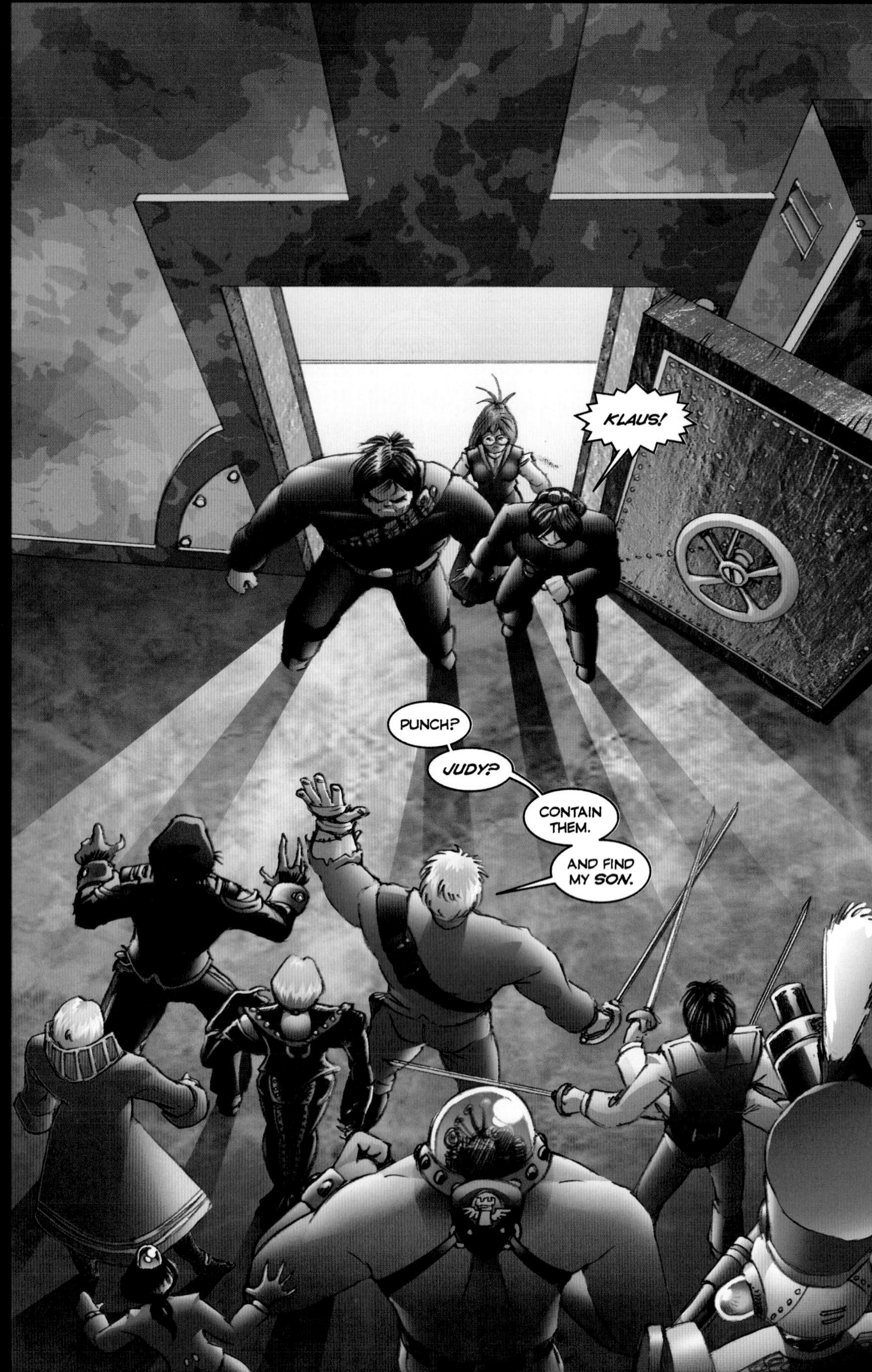
KLAUS!
PUNCH?
JUDY?
CONTAIN THEM.
AND FIND MY SON.

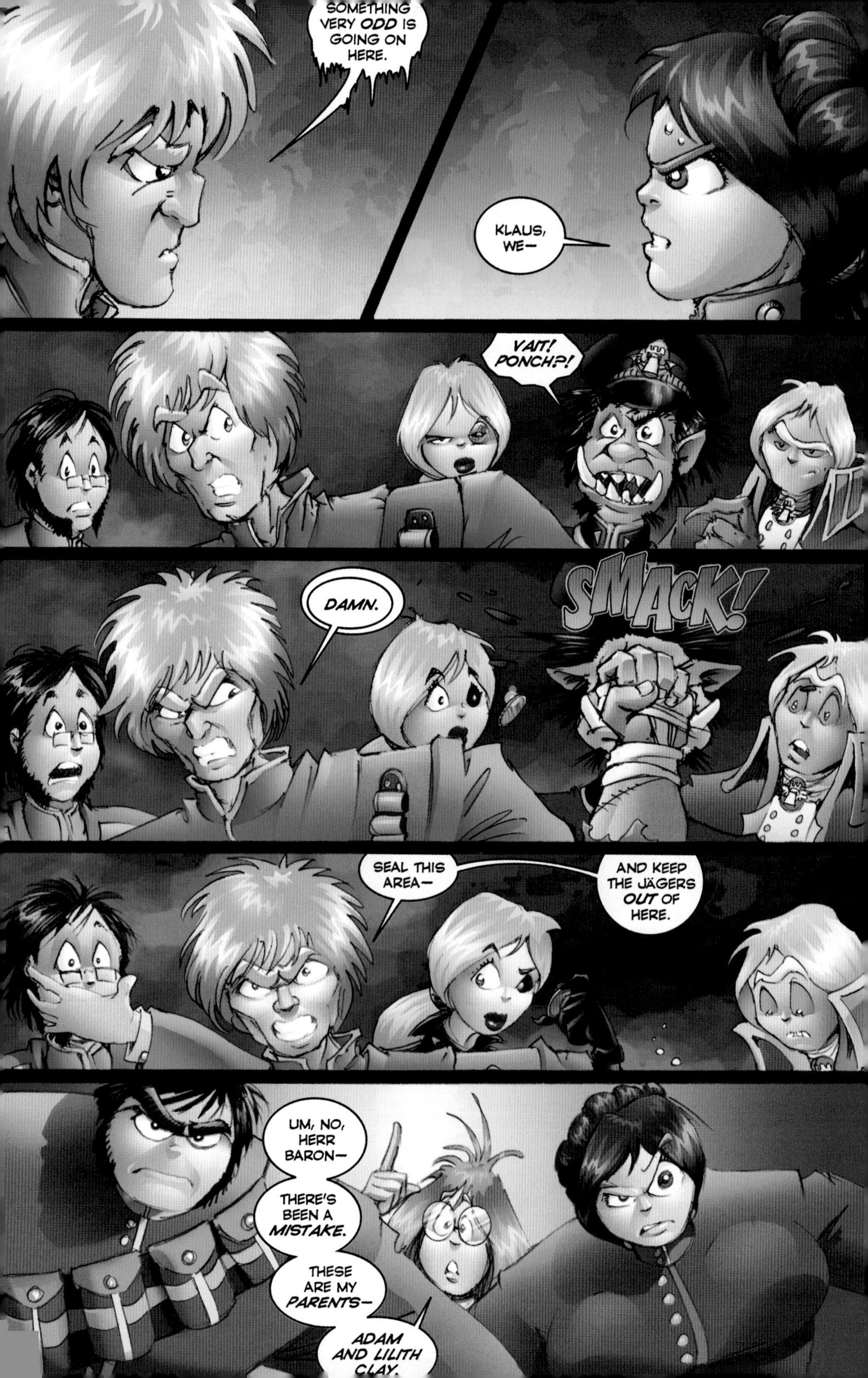
SOMETHING VERY ODD IS GOING ON HERE.
KLAUS, WE—
VAIT! PONCH?!
DAMN.
SMACK!
SEAL THIS AREA—
AND KEEP THE JÄGERS OUT OF HERE.
UM, NO, HERR BARON—
THERE'S BEEN A MISTAKE.
THESE ARE MY PARENTS—
ADAM AND LILITH CLAY.

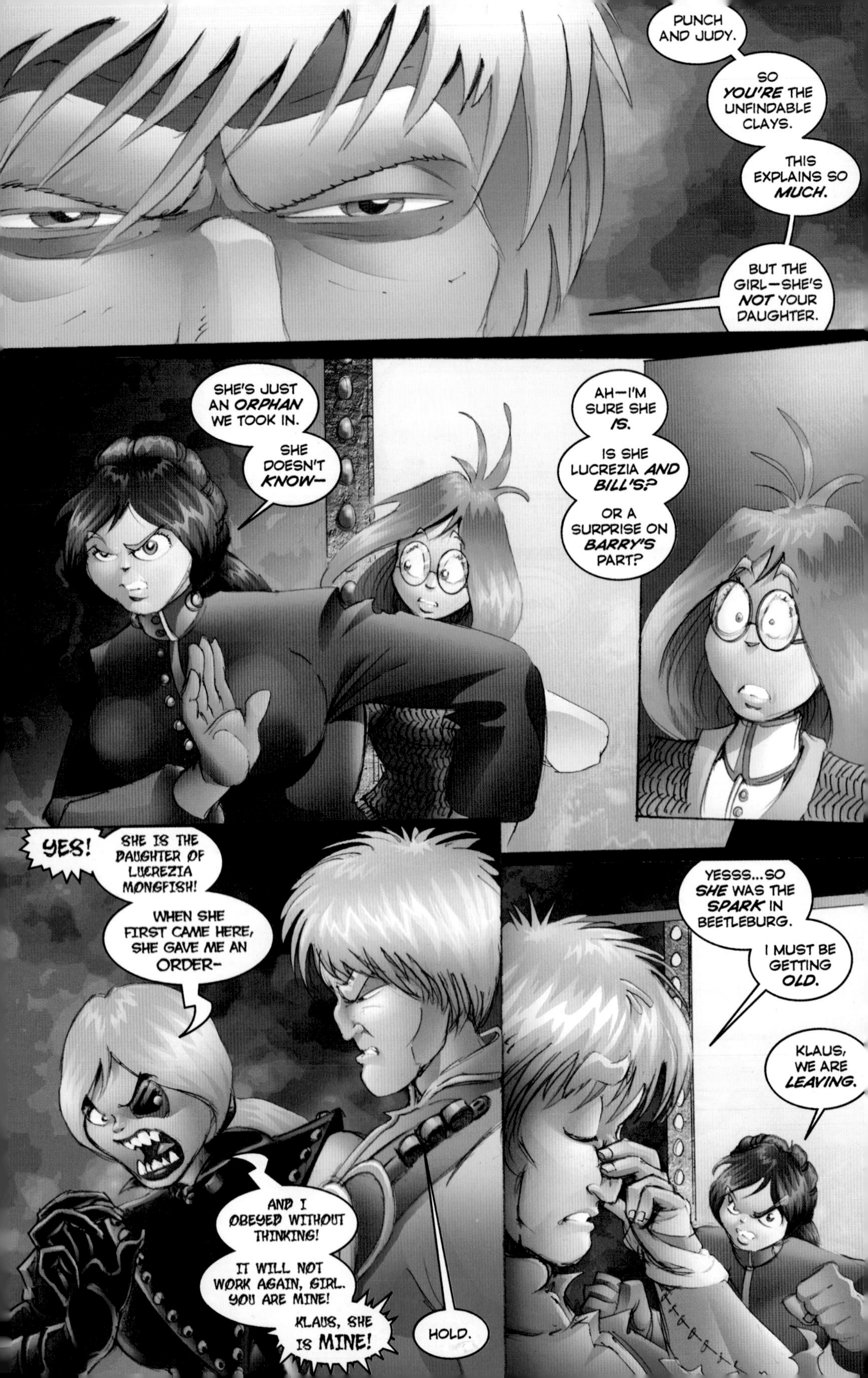
PUNCH AND JUDY.
SO *YOU'RE* THE UNFINDABLE CLAYS.
THIS EXPLAINS SO *MUCH*.
BUT THE GIRL—SHE'S *NOT* YOUR DAUGHTER.
SHE'S JUST AN *ORPHAN* WE TOOK IN.
SHE DOESN'T *KNOW*-
AH—I'M SURE SHE *IS*.
IS SHE LUCREZIA *AND BILL'S?*
OR A SURPRISE ON *BARRY'S* PART?
YES!
SHE IS THE DAUGHTER OF LUCREZIA MONGFISH!
WHEN SHE FIRST CAME HERE, SHE GAVE ME AN ORDER-
AND I OBEYED WITHOUT THINKING!
IT WILL NOT WORK AGAIN, GIRL. YOU ARE MINE!
KLAUS, SHE IS MINE!
HOLD.
YESSS...SO *SHE* WAS THE *SPARK* IN BEETLEBURG.
I MUST BE GETTING *OLD*.
KLAUS, WE ARE *LEAVING*.

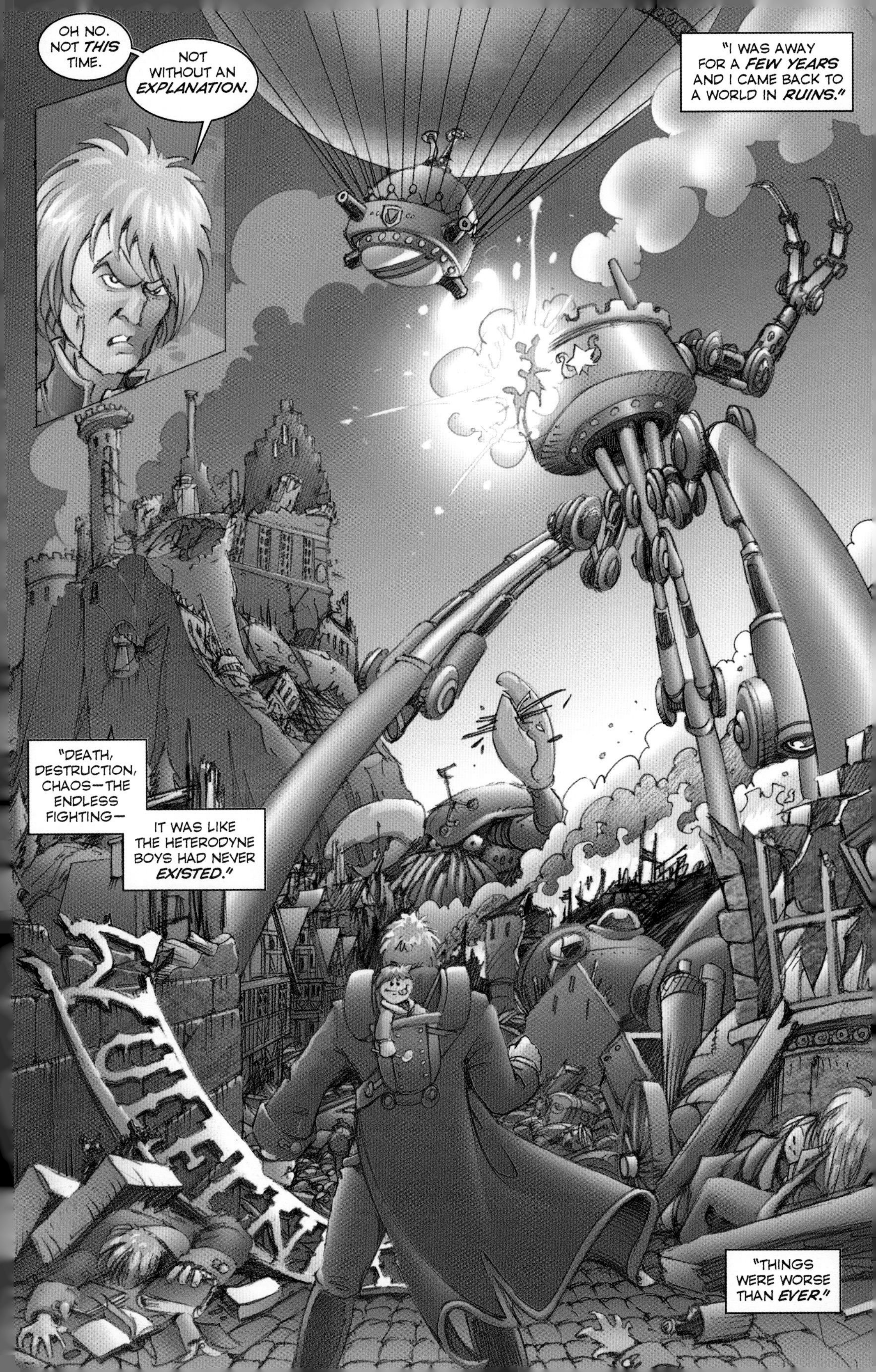
OH NO. NOT *THIS* TIME.
NOT WITHOUT AN *EXPLANATION*.
"I WAS AWAY FOR A *FEW YEARS* AND I CAME BACK TO A WORLD IN *RUINS*."
"DEATH, DESTRUCTION, CHAOS—THE ENDLESS FIGHTING—
IT WAS LIKE THE HETERODYNE BOYS HAD NEVER *EXISTED*."
"THINGS WERE WORSE THAN *EVER*."

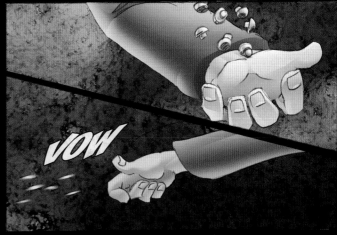

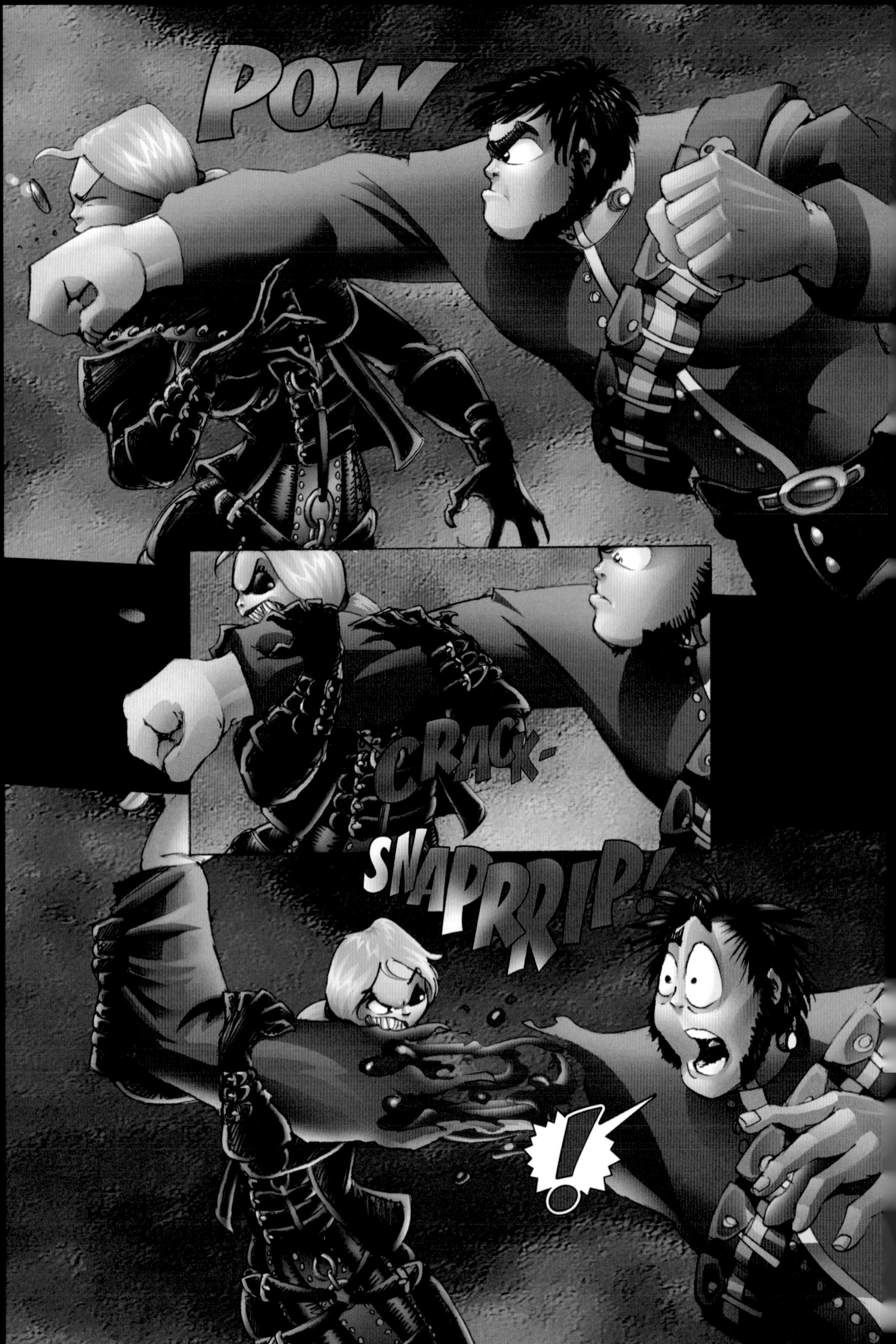
POW
CRACK-
SNAPRRRIP!
!

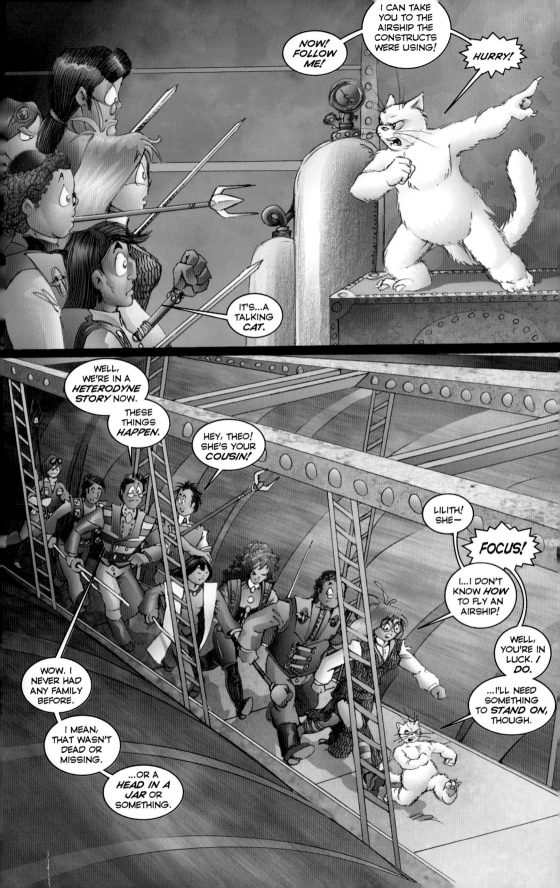

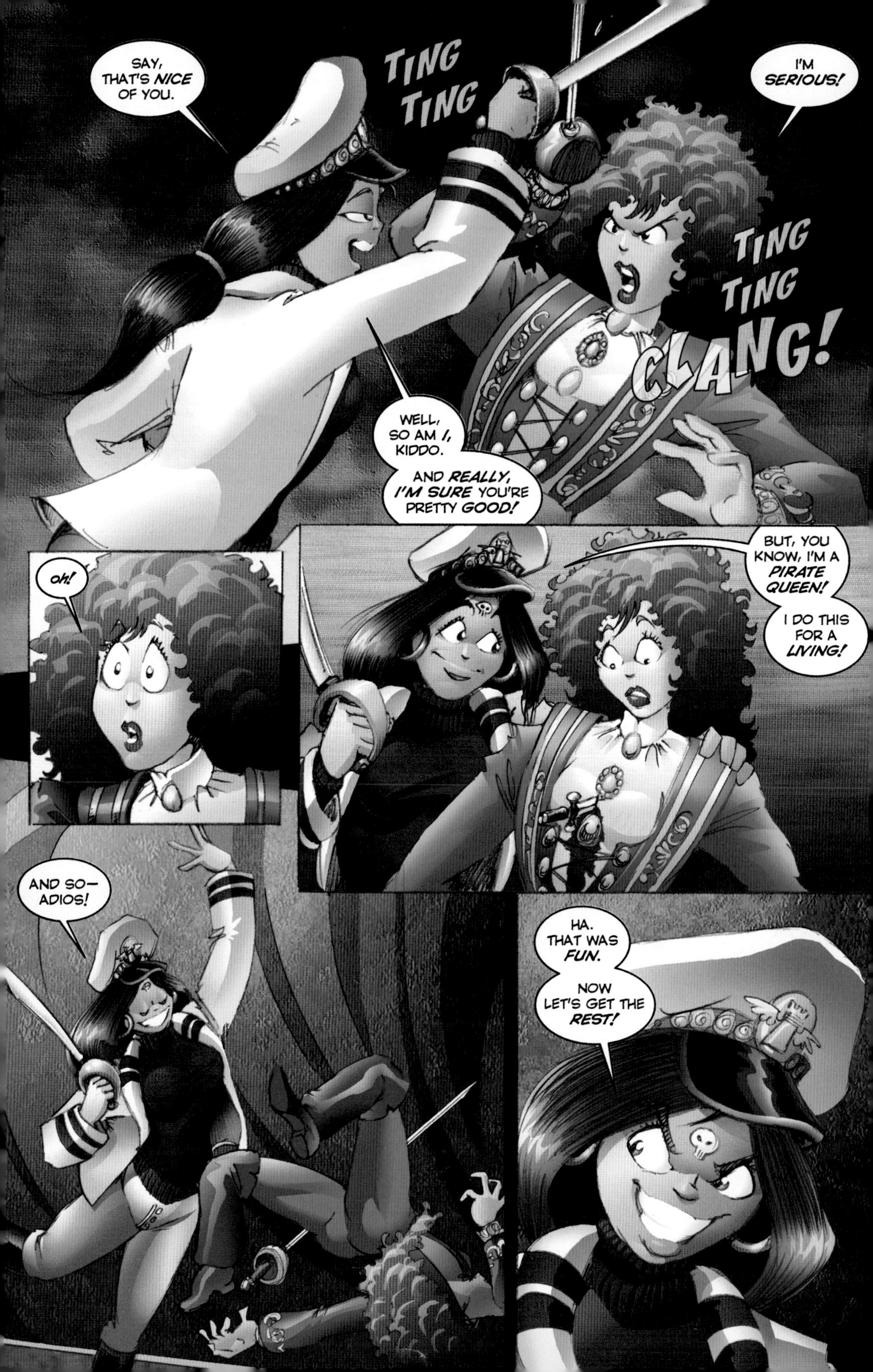
SAY, THAT'S NICE OF YOU.
TING TING
I'M SERIOUS!
TING TING CLANG!
WELL, SO AM I, KIDDO.
AND REALLY, I'M SURE YOU'RE PRETTY GOOD!
oh!
BUT, YOU KNOW, I'M A PIRATE QUEEN!
I DO THIS FOR A LIVING!
AND SO— ADIOS!
HA. THAT WAS FUN.
NOW LET'S GET THE REST!

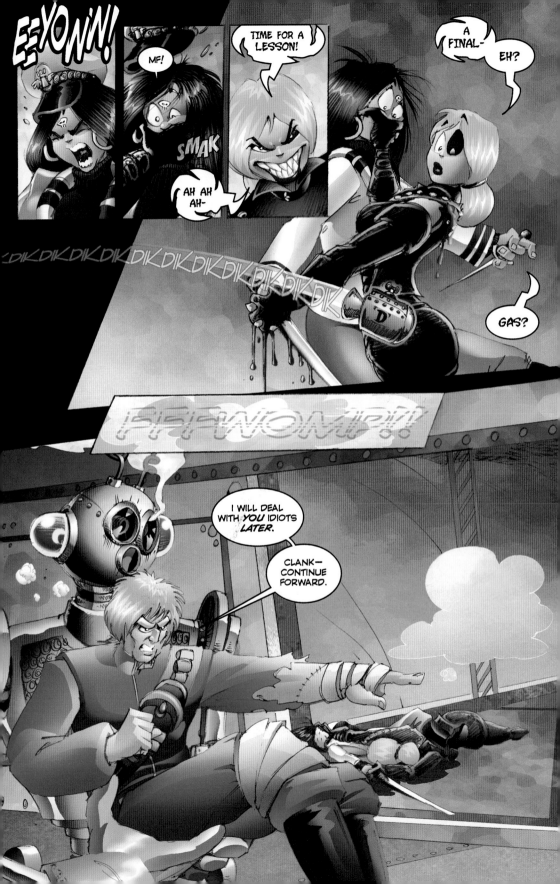

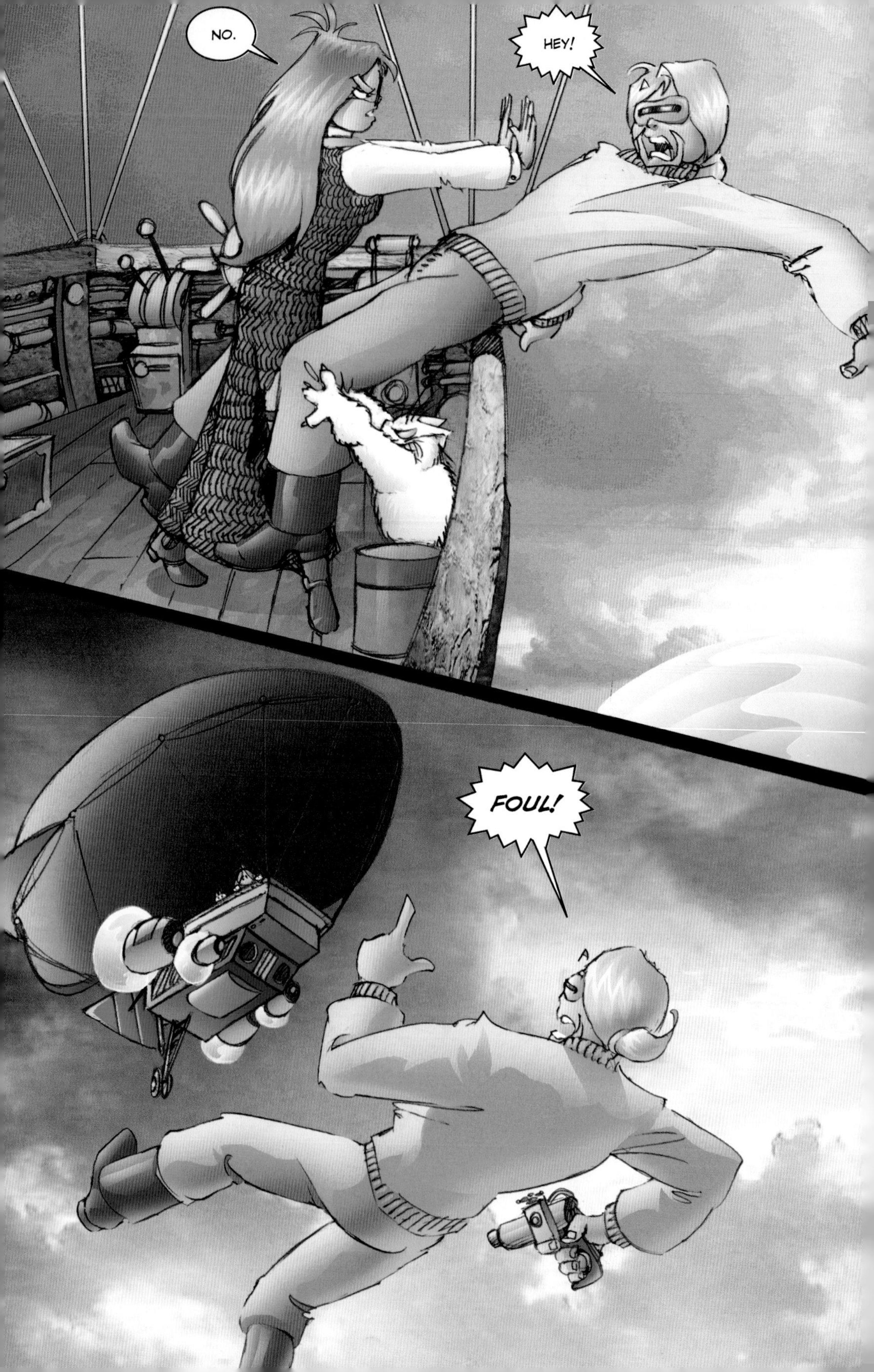
NO.
HEY!
FOUL!